W9-CEI-899

The Ultimate SEWING BOOK

The Ultimate SEWING BOOK

Maggi McCormick Gordon

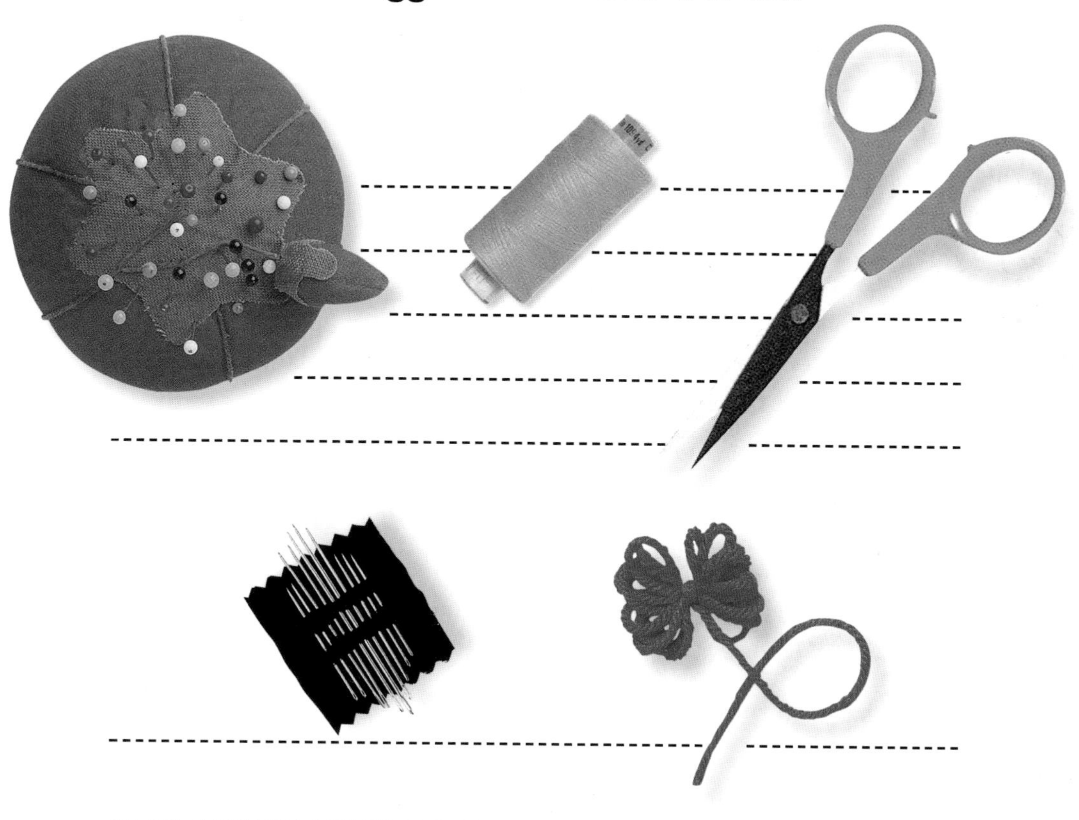

COLLINS & BROWN

First published in Great Britain in 2002 by
Collins & Brown Limited
64 Brewery Road
London N7 9NT

9 8 7 6 5 4 3 2 1

British Library Cataloguing-in-Publication Data:
A catalogue record for
this book is available from the British Library.

ISBN 1 84340 050 2

Designed and project-managed by Axis Design Editions Ltd
Copy-edited by Charlotte Stock
Indexed by Sue Bosanko

Color reproduction by Classicscan, Singapore
Printed In USA

Contents

Home Furnishings 130

Care and Repair 306

About this book

THE ULTIMATE SEWING BOOK is a step-by-step guide to successful sewing for beginners and for those who wish to improve their skills or try a new technique. Beginning with the basics, the book looks at the component parts of a garment and illustrates the process involved in making each one. In the same way, the chapter on home furnishings shows you how to make curtains, drapes, and blinds; bed linen; table linen; and cushion and seat covers.

Each section contains projects that allow you to practice the techniques learned and to give you ideas for creating your own items of clothing and textiles for the home.

The final chapter looks at care and repair, including mending, stain removal, and laundry and cleaning symbols.

Note that both standard and metric measurements have been used throughout the book. Conversions are not precise, so it is important to use one system consistently.

Introduction
Each section begins with a heading, an explanation of the technique and when it is used.

Cross references
Pages often contain cross-references to related techniques and other useful information throughout the book.

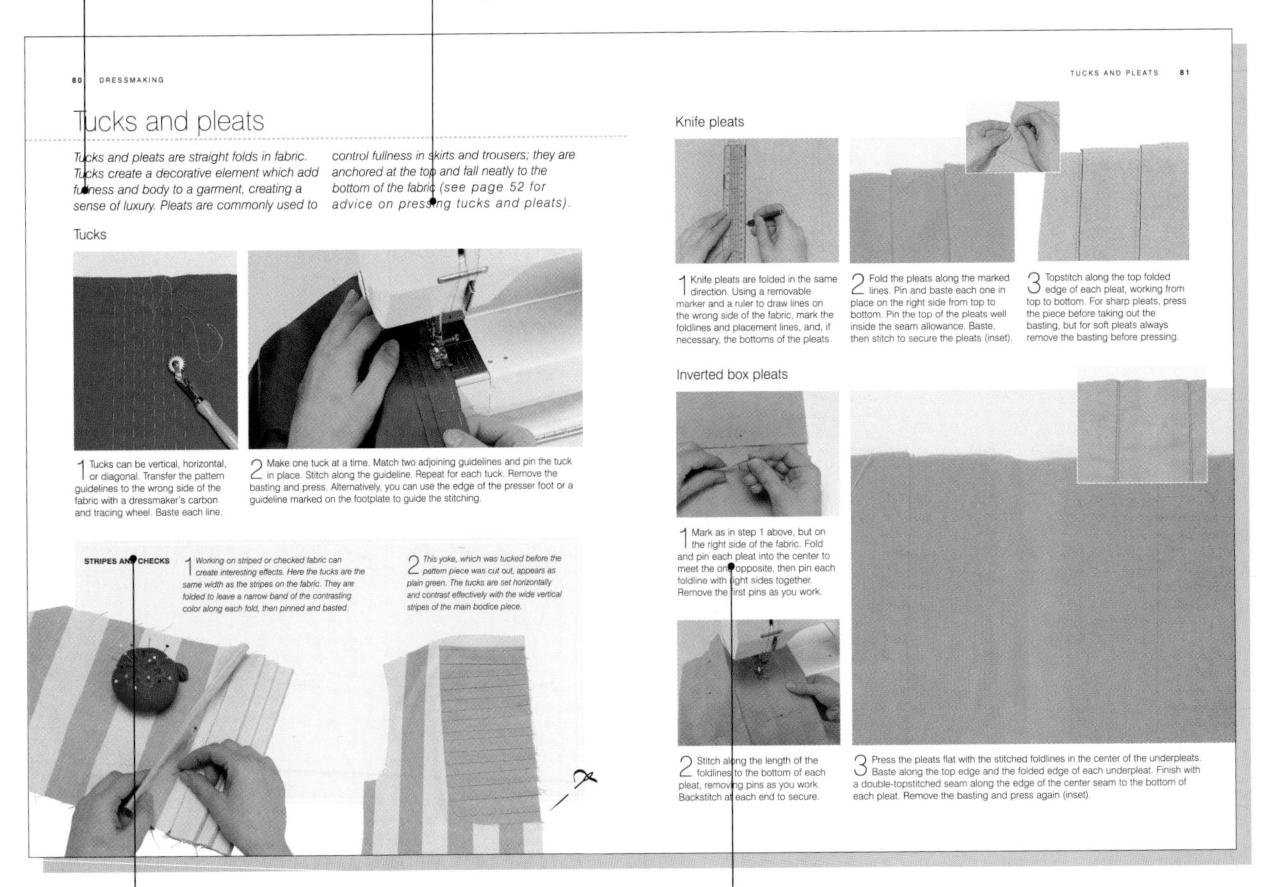

80 DRESSMAKING

Tucks and pleats

Tucks and pleats are straight folds in fabric. Tucks create a decorative element which add fullness and body to a garment, creating a sense of luxury. Pleats are commonly used to control fullness in skirts and trousers; they are anchored at the top and fall neatly to the bottom of the fabric (see page 52 for advice on pressing tucks and pleats).

Tucks

1 Tucks can be vertical, horizontal, or diagonal. Transfer the pattern guidelines to the wrong side of the fabric with a dressmaker's carbon and tracing wheel. Baste each line.

2 Make one tuck at a time. Match two adjoining guidelines and pin the tuck in place. Stitch along the guideline. Repeat for each tuck. Remove the basting and press. Alternatively, you can use the edge of the presser foot or a guideline marked on the footplate to guide the stitching.

STRIPES AND CHECKS

1 Working on striped or checked fabric can create interesting effects. Here the tucks are the same width as the stripes on the fabric. They are folded to leave a narrow band of the contrasting color along each fold, then pinned and basted.

2 This yoke, which was tucked before the pattern piece was cut out, appears as plain green. The tucks are set horizontally and contrast effectively with the wide vertical stripes of the main bodice piece.

TUCKS AND PLEATS 81

Knife pleats

1 Knife pleats are folded in the same direction. Using a removable marker and a ruler to draw lines on the wrong side of the fabric, mark the foldlines and placement lines, and, if necessary, the bottoms of the pleats.

2 Fold the pleats along the marked lines. Pin and baste each one in place on the right side from top to bottom. Pin the top of the pleats well inside the seam allowance. Baste, then stitch to secure the pleats (inset).

3 Topstitch along the top folded edge of each pleat, working from top to bottom. For sharp pleats, press the piece before taking out the basting, but for soft pleats always remove the basting before pressing.

Inverted box pleats

1 Mark as in step 1 above, but on the right side of the fabric. Fold and pin each pleat into the center to meet the one opposite, then pin each foldline with right sides together. Remove the first pins as you work.

2 Stitch along the length of the foldlines to the bottom of each pleat, removing pins as you work. Backstitch at each end to secure.

3 Press the pleats flat with the stitched foldlines in the center of the underpleats. Baste along the top edge and the folded edge of each underpleat. Finish with a double-topstitched seam along the edge of the center seam to the bottom of each pleat. Remove the basting and press again (inset).

Useful tips
Where relevant, additional hints and tips, as well as professional tricks of the trade, are shown as photographs or diagrams.

Step-by-step
Each technique is shown in clear, full-color step-by-step photographs accompanied by easy-to-follow text. The stitching is often shown in a contrasting color for clarity.

Materials list
Each project contains a list of all the materials you will need to complete the item.

Photo-finish
Each project has a large, full-color picture of the finished item.

126 DRESSMAKING

Project: Beach bag

This roomy canvas bag is handy for carrying all the gear you need for a trip to the beach or swimming pool, and the rope adds a suitably nautical touch. It is also sturdy and attractive enough to carry shopping or in-flight necessities.

There are borders along the top and bottom which are actually exterior facings that reinforce the bag. The templates are on pages 128–129. Enlarge them according to the instructions and transfer them onto pattern paper.

YOU WILL NEED
- *1¾ yd (1.5 m) canvas, 36 in (90 cm) wide*
- *Pattern paper and pencil*
- *Scissors*
- *Thread*
- *Heavy-duty machine needle*
- *½ in (12 mm) eyelet kit*
- *1¼ yd (1.1 m) rope, ⅜ in (9 mm) thick*

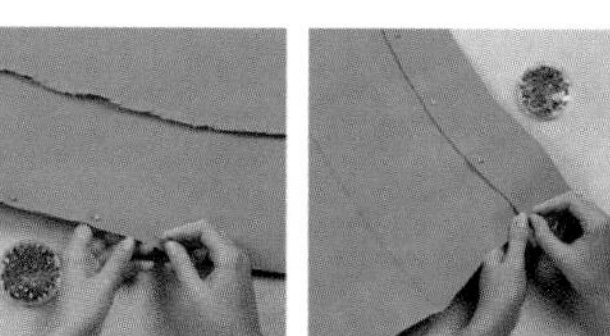

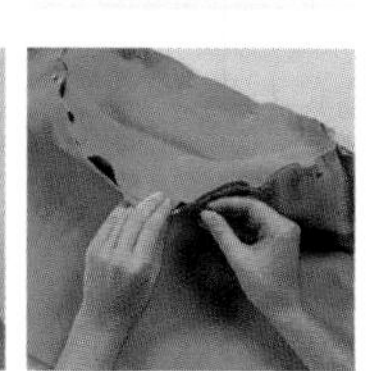

1 Cut out the canvas pieces using the enlarged templates. Fold under the seam allowance along the bottom edges of both top borders, clip the curves, and press. With the right side of the top border to the wrong side of the side piece, pin in place, matching the side edges. Stitch along top edges. Trim and clip the seams, then turn borders to the right side. Press the seam and pin bottom edge of the border piece in place on the side piece along folded edge. Topstitch close to the fold.

2 Fold under the seam allowances on the top edges of both bottom borders, clip the curves, and press. With the wrong side of the bottom borders facing the right side of the side pieces, pin in position, matching both bottom and side edges. Topstitch close to the border fold, then baste along the other three sides to hold the layers together.

3 With right sides together, pin and stitch both side seams. With right sides together, pin and stitch the base into the bag, matching the notches to the side seams. Bind all the raw seam allowances with bias binding to prevent them from fraying. Turn the bag right side out.

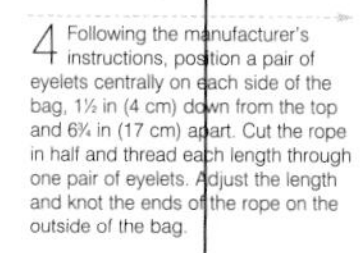

4 Following the manufacturer's instructions, position a pair of eyelets centrally on each side of the bag, 1½ in (4 cm) down from the top and 6¾ in (17 cm) apart. Cut the rope in half and thread each length through one pair of eyelets. Adjust the length and knot the ends of the rope on the outside of the bag.

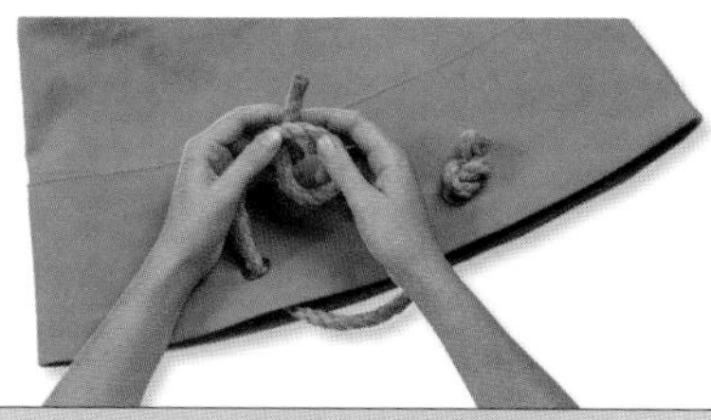

Step-by-steps
The method for making the project is shown in clear, easy-to-follow steps with full-color photographs.

312 HOME FURNISHINGS

STAIN REMOVAL CHART
These treatments apply to washable fabrics. Stains on non-washable and delicate fabrics should be handled by a professional drycleaner. Find the stain to be treated in the left-hand column. Follow the numbers in sequence. Where the numbers are repeated, use the most convenient method. Repeat the treatment if necessary. Set the temperature and washing cycle specified on the garment label.

Key: Cold water; Warm water; Hot water

STAIN	PROCEDURE											
	Soak	Rinse	Wash	Blot	Harden by rubbing with an ice cube	Scrape	Petreat with appropriate chemical	Bleach (whites only)	Lemon	Salt	Press	Remarks
Adhesive and glue	4		4		1	2	3					
Alcohol			1									1 part white wine vinegar to 3 parts water if stain persists
Blood	1						2					
Chewing gum			4		1	2	3					
Chocolate		1					2					
Cosmetics							1					
Eggs							1					Treat basically as grease
Grass							1	2				Use enzyme (biological) washing powder
Grease and oil			2				1					
Ink			2				1					Washing may set the stain
Mildew			2					1	1	1		Mix lemon juice with salt and sun-dry
Milk			1									
Paint: water-based		1	2									
Paint: oil-based			3	1			2					
Perspiration	1		2									Soak affected area in water with a spoonful of borax added
Rust			3						1	2		Mix lemon juice and salt and hold over steaming water
Scorch marks			1						2	2		
Shoe polish						1	2					
Tea and coffee	1						2					
Wax			3		1						2	
Wine and fruit juice	1		4	2			3			1		

NB: If no temperature symbol is given, follow the washing instructions for the garment.

Charts and diagrams
Diagrams or charts have been used in cases where the information can be shown more clearly or concisely than in photographs.

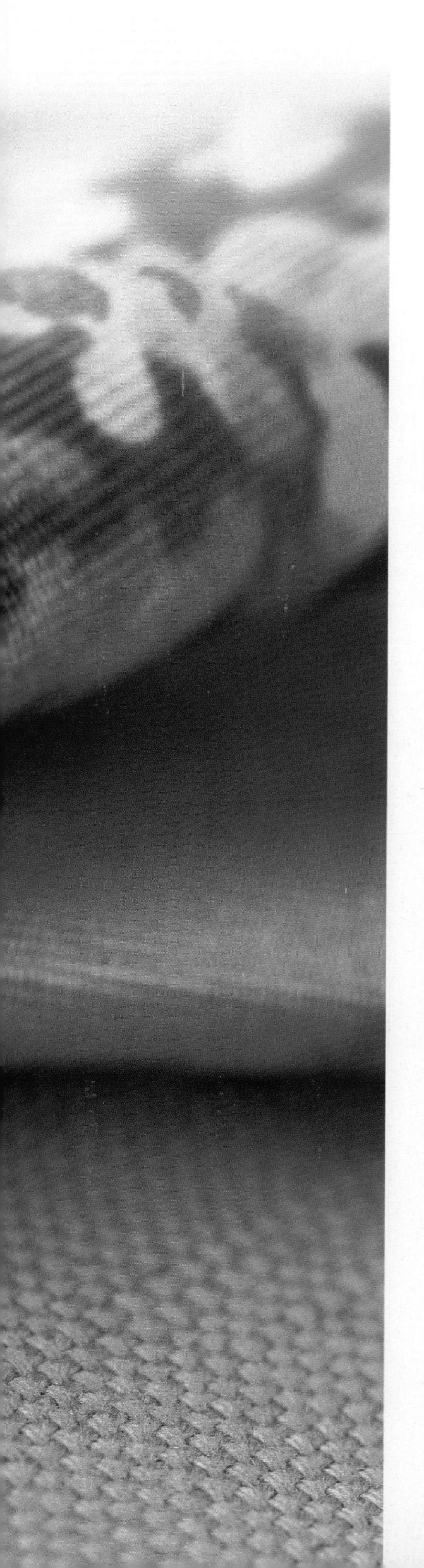

Getting Started

To learn a new skill, it is best to start at the beginning. In this chapter you will find valuable information about tools and equipment, including sewing machines, and about identifying and handling a variety of natural and synthetic fabrics. In addition, there are hints for setting up a convenient working area to organize your sewing for maximum efficiency and enjoyment.

Tools and equipment

For basic projects, you may not need all the tools and equipment shown here. You may also decide to use some other tools that are available. The key items that you need on hand are needles, pins, a tape measure and ruler, some marking implements, dressmaker's shears, and small sewing scissors. The choice of marker depends on personal preference and the type of fabric you are using (see also page 59).

Tools such as a flexible curve and an adjustable seam gauge will be useful for any specific measuring tasks that you have to carry out. A flexible tape measure is recommended for accurate body measurements or when measuring pieces of furniture. Use a ruler for measuring on a hard surface. You will also need an iron and ironing board for pressing the piece or garment (see also page 52).

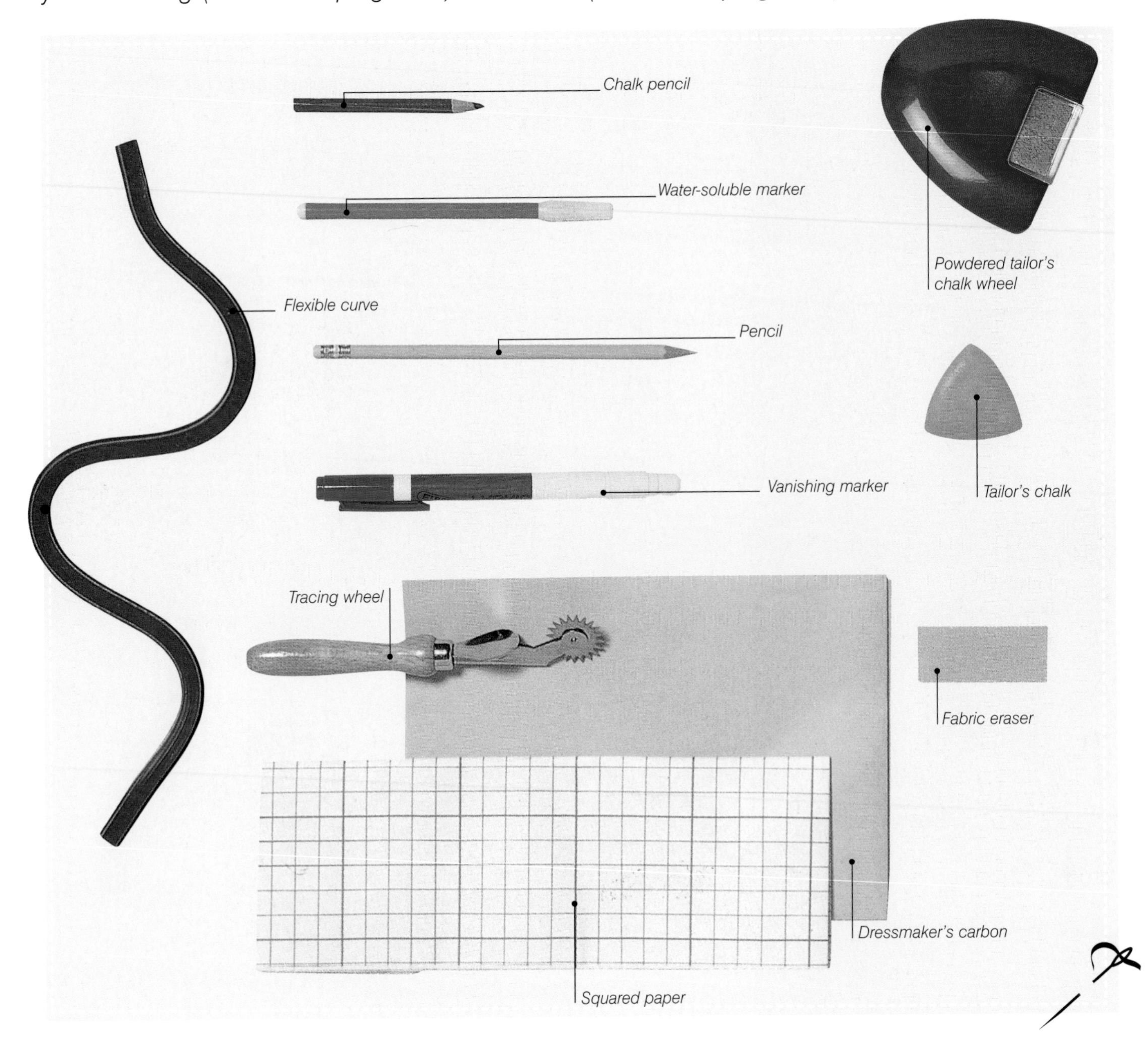

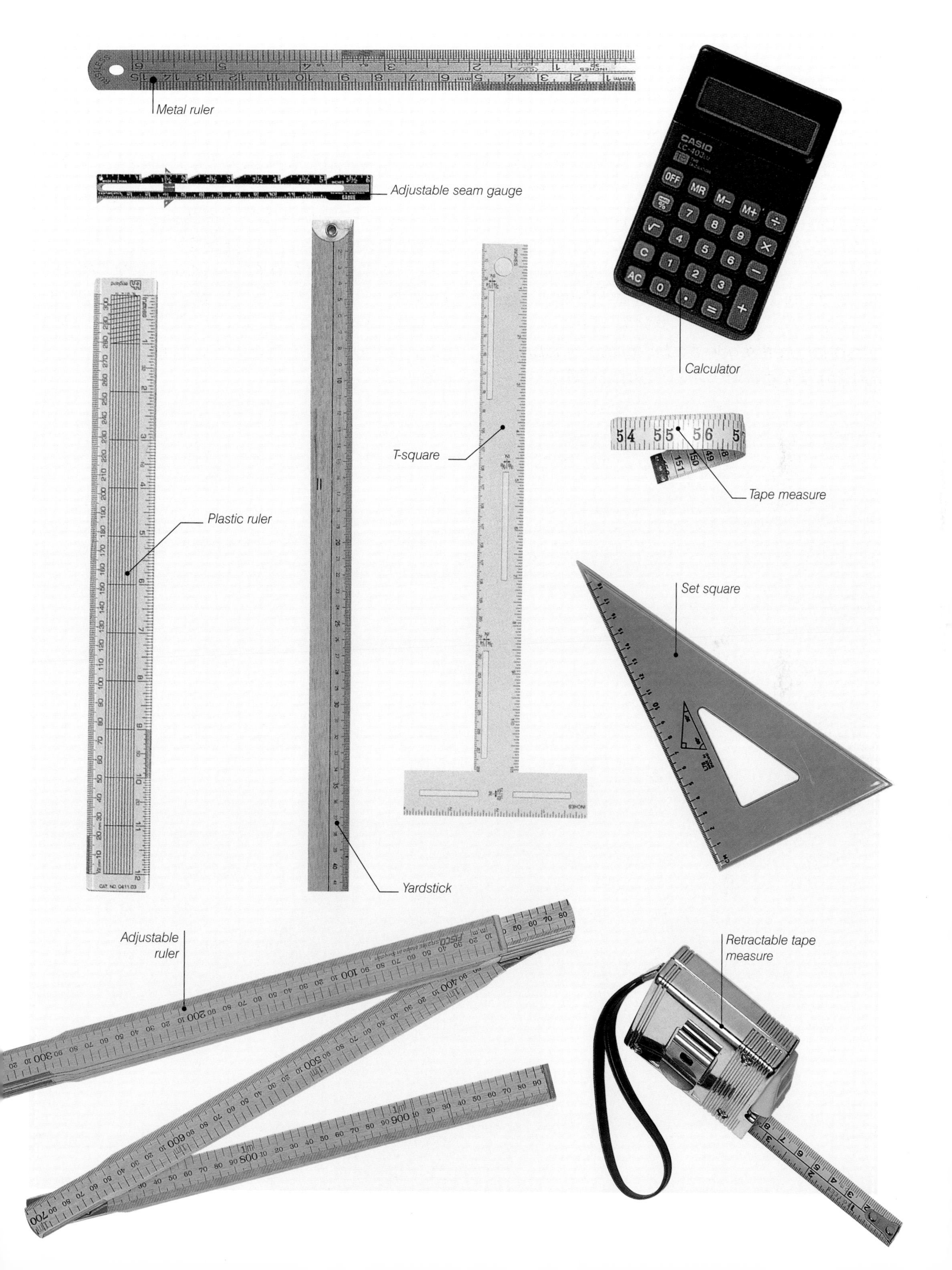
Metal ruler
Adjustable seam gauge
Calculator
T-square
Tape measure
Plastic ruler
Set square
Yardstick
Adjustable ruler
Retractable tape measure

CUTTING

Cutting tools can be basic, but you should never use fabric scissors on paper or batting (wadding), because the blades will become blunt and eventually ruin the shears. Small sewing scissors are essential for detailed tasks like clipping and trimming seams. If possible, try to use a second pair to cut thread, because, again, the blades will become dull over time.

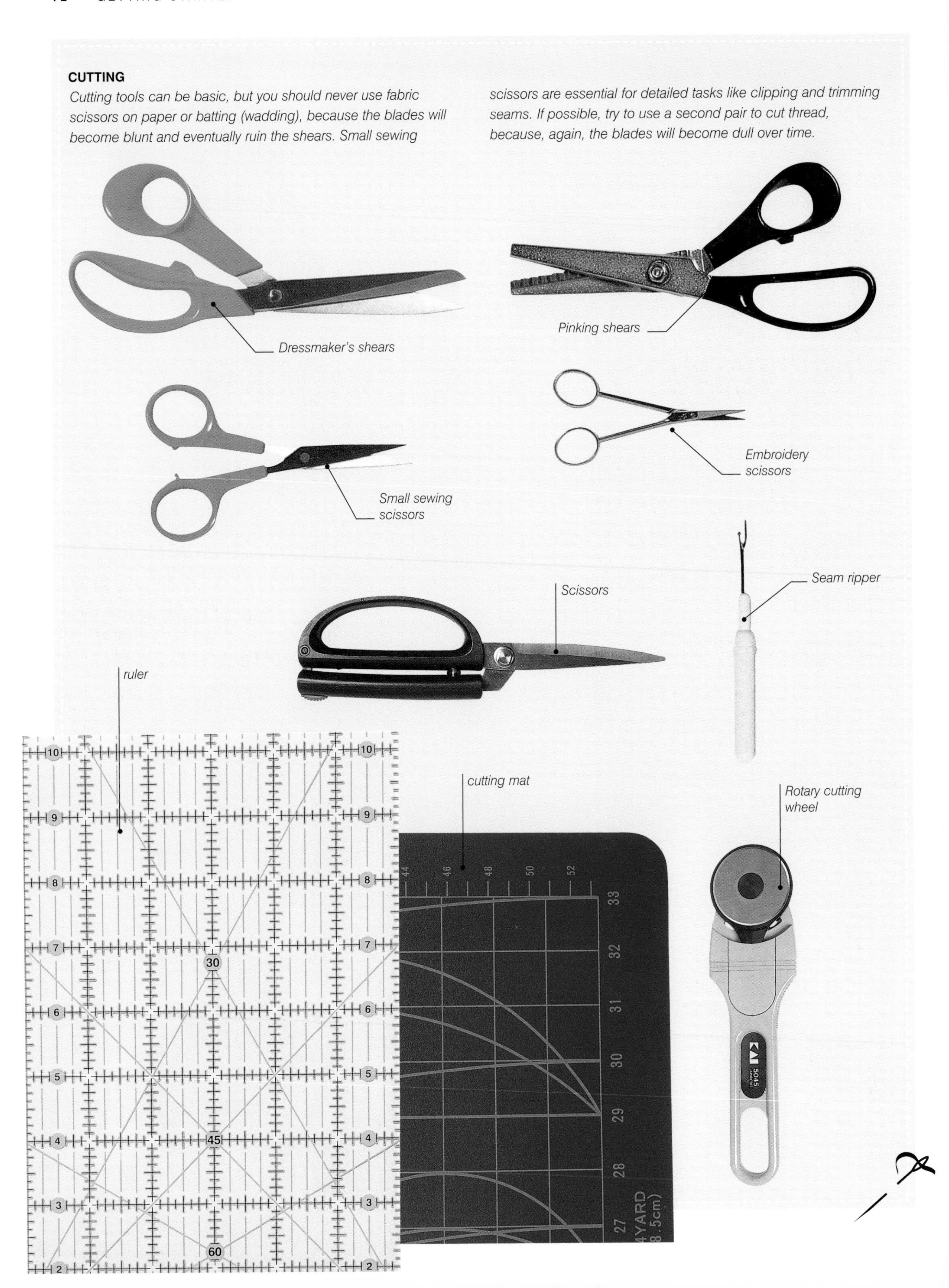

STITCHING

Pins, needles, and thread are all essential stitching tools. Useful items include pincushions, needle threaders, and thimbles, all of which help to make sewing by hand or machine easier.

A bodkin is a blunt needle with an eye at one end. It has several specialized uses, including teasing out sharp points and corners, and threading elastic through casings.

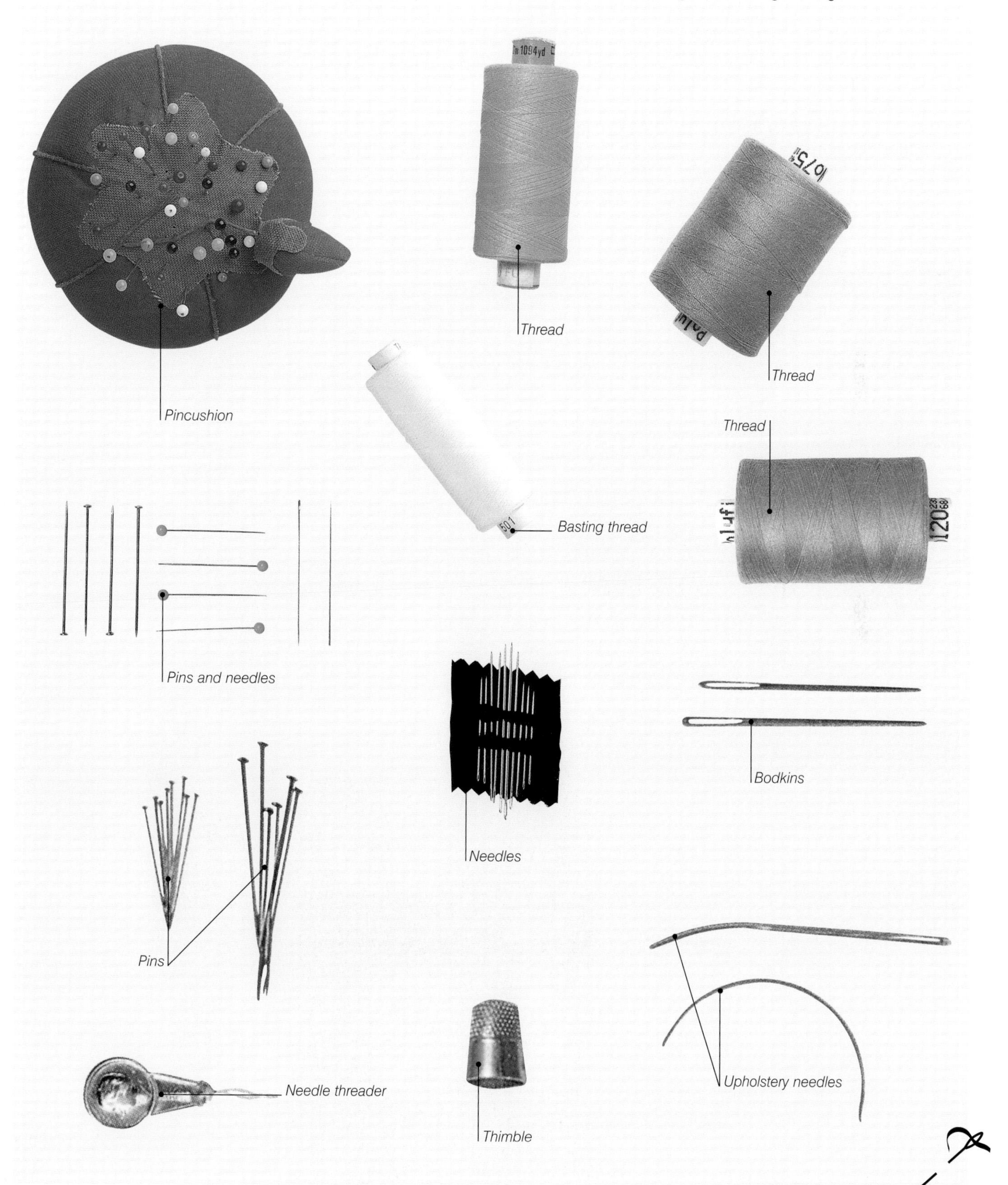

Special equipment for curtain making and home furnishings

Many lengths of fabric are needed to make certain items for the home, such as blinds, curtains, and covers for tables, beds, sofas, and chairs. To make handling the fabric more manageable, equip yourself with a large work surface. Devices to hold the fabric flat are among the most useful tools when making large items.

Trimmed raw edges
A long table, such as this folding paper-hanger's table, is an ideal working surface for measuring, cutting, and trimming the large area of fabric used in many home-furnishing projects.

HOLDING FABRICS

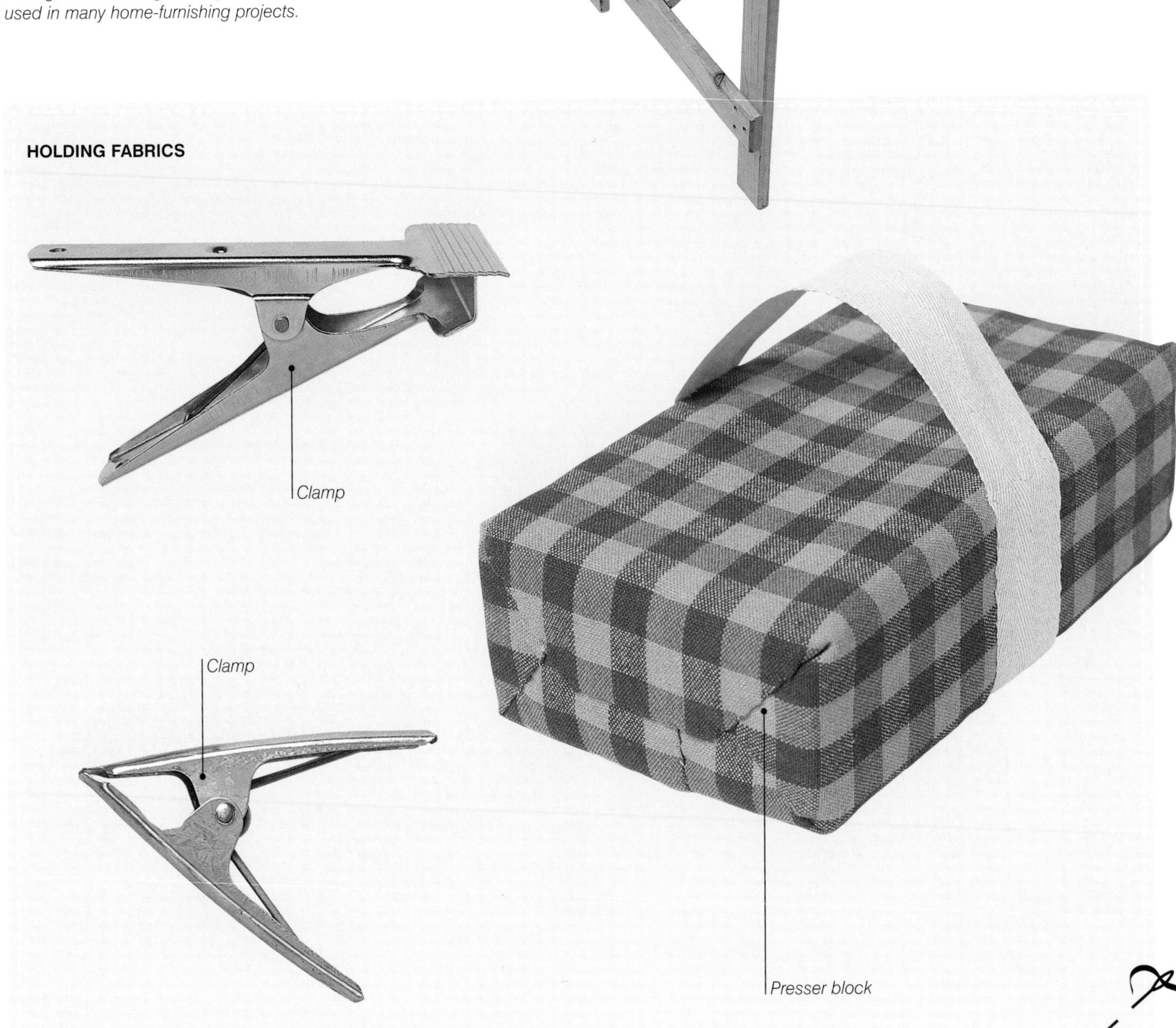

PRESSING

A steam iron and an ironing surface are essential pieces of sewing equipment. In addition, a tailor's ham for pressing awkward areas like darts and curved seams, and a sleeveboard are also useful, particularly in dressmaking.

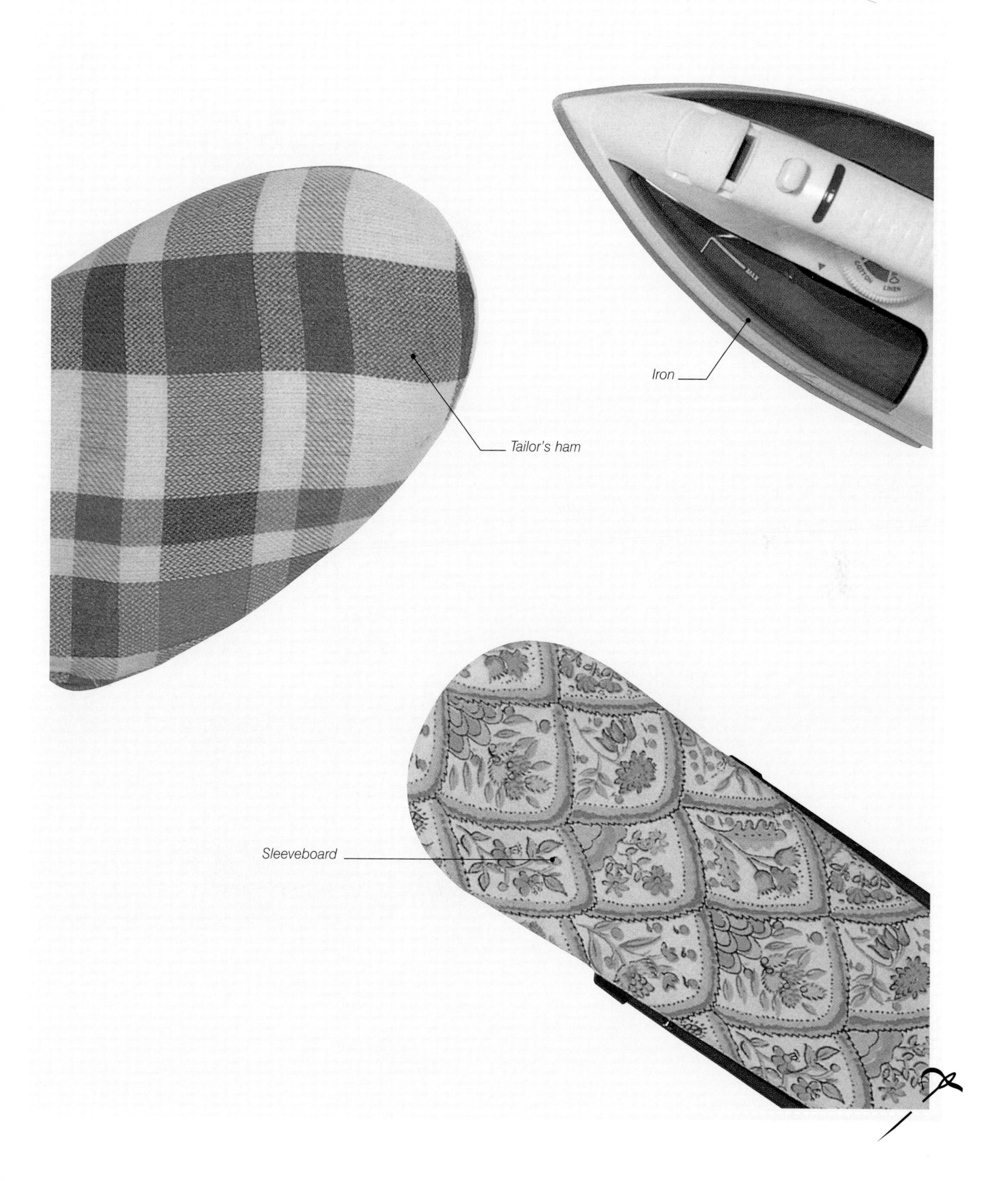

Sewing machine

The sewing machine is one of the most important pieces of equipment that anyone who sews will use, and it is probably the most expensive. Every model has its own characteristics, even within the range offered by a single manufacturer. The best way to become familiar with your machine is to use it.

All sewing machines have certain common features. The diagram below will help you to understand the basic parts shared by all models, but the instruction manual will give you specific information about how to operate your machine. *(see also page 33).*

BUYING A MACHINE

When buying a machine, consider not just the price, but the immediate tasks you expect to use it for, your long-term aspirations, and whether you can cope with its complexities. Always try out a machine before you buy. If possible, see a demonstration by someone who knows the machine and its capabilities, and take advantage of any instruction offered by the manufacturer.

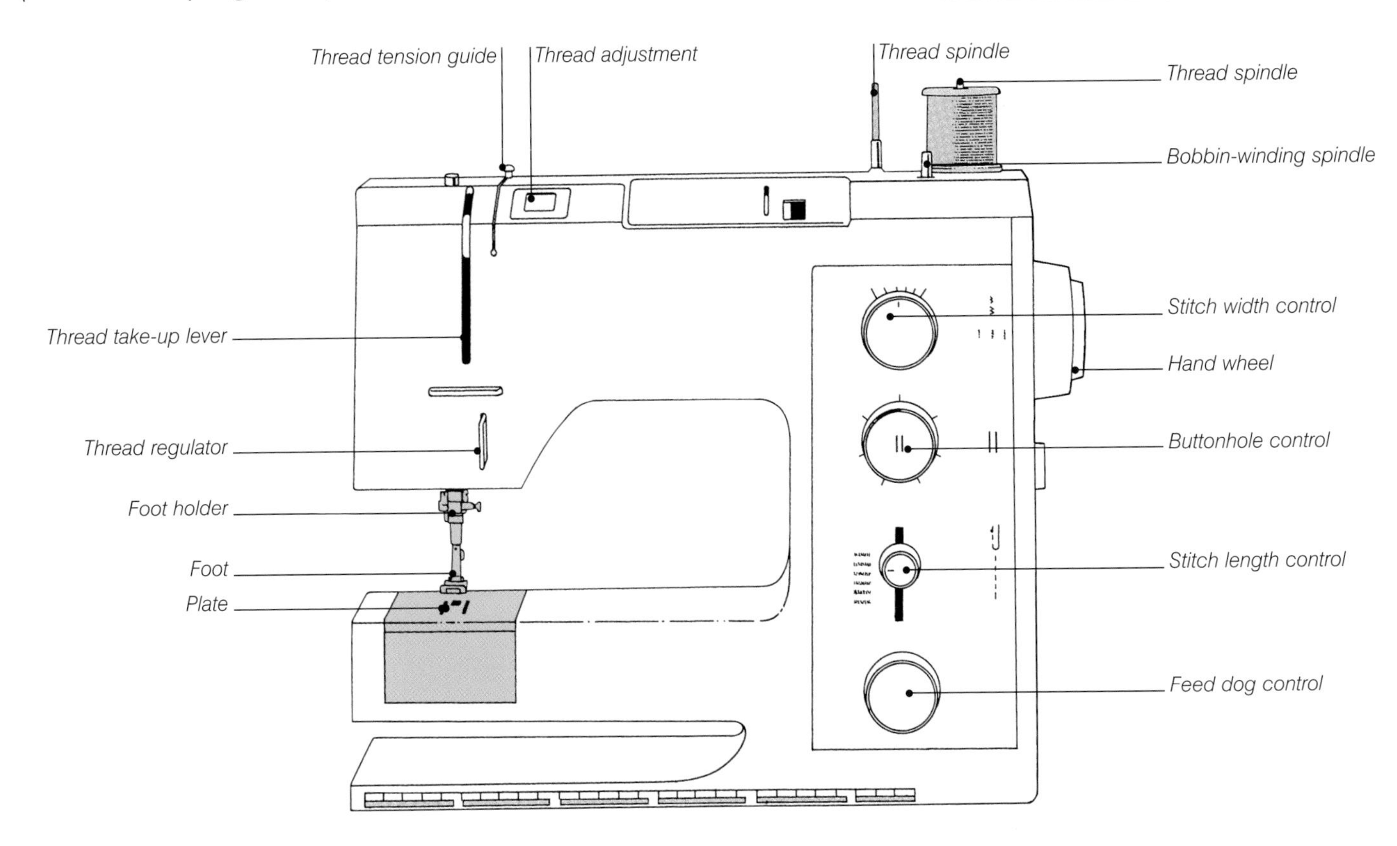

THREADING THE MACHINE

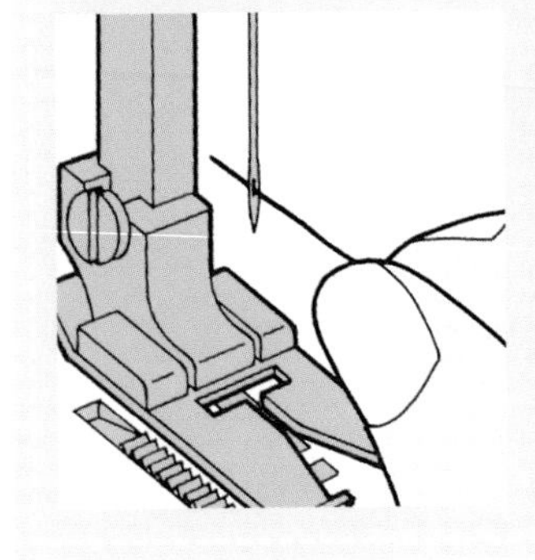

Make sure the needle is positioned properly and that it is sharp and appropriate to the fabric. Insert the thread through the eye of the needle in the direction stated in the instruction manual. Pull it through gently from the other side and leave it long enough to give a smooth start to stitching.

PULLING UP THE BOBBIN THREAD

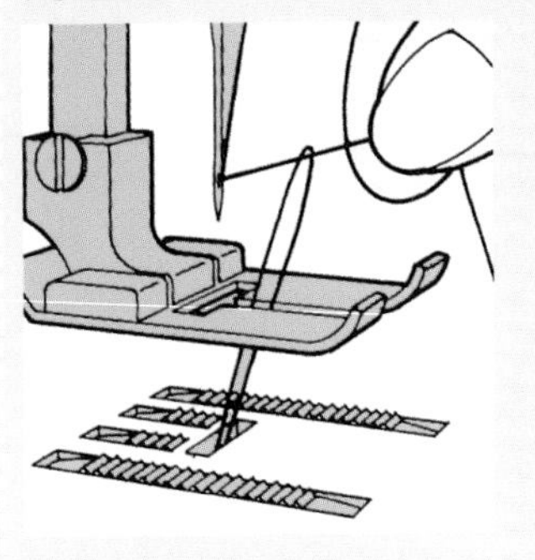

Once the needle is threaded, put the bobbin in its case as shown in the manual. Leave a long end trailing below the machine plate. Turn the wheel once by hand. The top thread should catch the bobbin thread and pull it to the top as a loop. Use your fingers or a pin to pull the end through to the top.

Thread tension

Thread tension must be balanced top and bottom to achieve a perfect stitch. Most new machines can adjust tension internally, but older models may need to be adjusted by hand when, for example, you switch from heavy to lightweight fabric or drop the feed dog to work machine embroidery.

Balanced stitch The two threads join in the middle of the layers of fabric and look the same on both sides. To check the tension is correct, test a row of stitching on a scrap of the fabric you are using before starting to work.

Bottom thread is too tight If the bottom thread lies in a line and the top one shows through onto the back of the seam, loosen the bobbin thread carefully, as recommended by the instruction manual. Usually a screw in the bobbin case needs adjustment.

Top thread is too tight If the top thread lies in a line and the bobbin thread is visible on the top of the seam, loosen the needle thread using the thread adjustment control, following instructions in the manual.

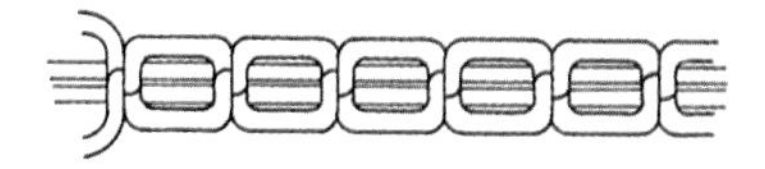

Balanced stitch

Bottom thread is too tight

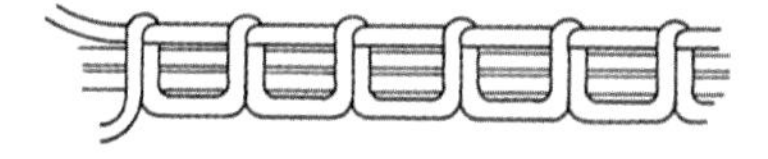

Top thread is too tight

FEET

A variety of different feet are available for sewing machines, and most new models come with at least two or three extra feet. Changing the foot allows you to create a range of special sewing effects, but many of them tend to be highly specialized and may be expensive. Try to experiment with any optional foot before investing in it to make sure that it suits your purpose.

A zipper foot *is essential for putting in zippers neatly and makes it easier to insert piping into seams.*

A buttonhole foot *is designed specifically to make buttonholes, but some machines already have a built-in function that enables you to make buttonholes in a garment using a standard presser foot.*

A hemming foot *has a "curl" at the leading edge that turns medium and lightweight fabric into a double fold and so eliminates the need to pin and baste.*

A pintuck foot *features a series of ridges along its underside that draw the fabric into neat, small tucks so that it can be stitched in even rows.*

A darning/quilting/embroidery/appliqué foot *has a distinctive open-ring or "c" shape and is generally used with the feed dog in the down position.*

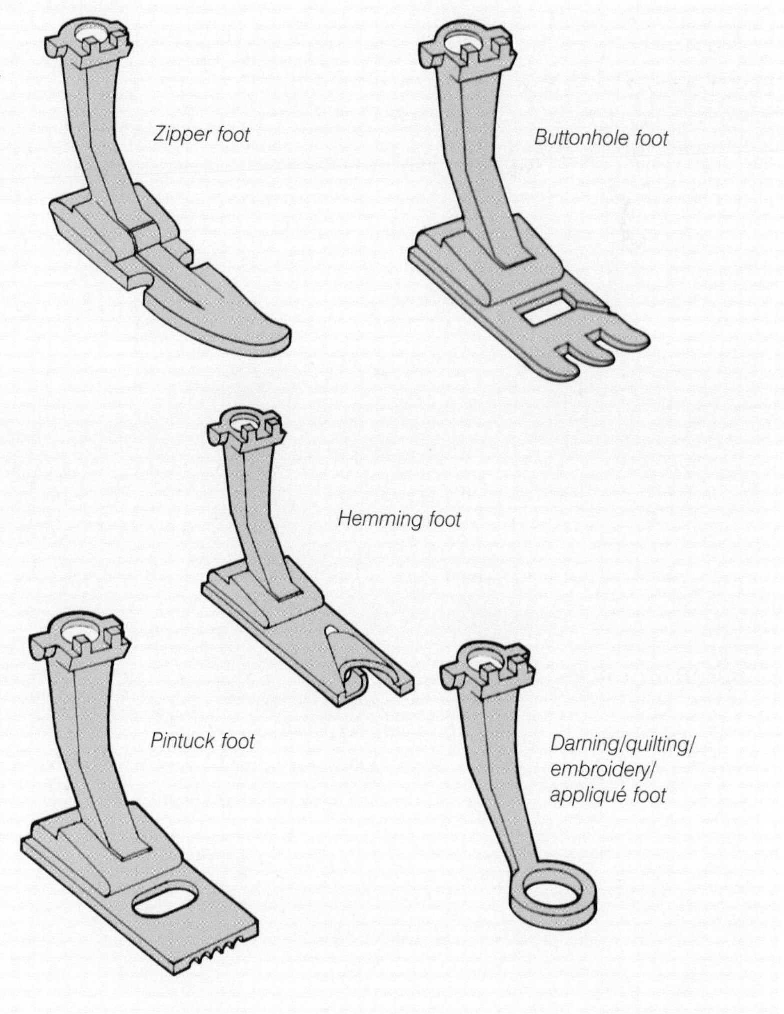

Creating a workspace

An organized workspace can make the difference between enjoying the time spent sewing and finding sewing a chore. Everyday objects like empty boxes with lids, pretty glass jars, or mugs without handles can be recycled to make excellent storage containers. The addition of a couple of shelves for books and some storage boxes will help to create an orderly working environment.

Use ready-made toolboxes or hardware units, especially those with clear plastic drawer fronts, for storing small items like needles and bobbins as well as thread, which can be organized by color or type. A carpenter's toolbox with a carrying handle is ideal for storing rulers, scissors, and pens while shoeboxes are just the right size for filing patterns.

WORKING PRACTICE

Wherever you work, make sure your chair and table are at a comfortable height. Keep all electrical wires safely out of the way and turn off the sewing machine if you stop work for any length of time. (Be sure to make a note of any special settings you may be using before you turn it off.)

Keep all frequently used tools and equipment close by so you don't have to get up every time you need them, but remember that sewing for long stretches is tiring, so take regular breaks and stand up and move around from time to time.

Organizing a workroom

If you are lucky enough to have an extra room that you can devote to sewing, take the opportunity to exploit it to its full potential. Otherwise, a spare bedroom or home office can easily do double duty, by using the desk as a sewing-machine table.

If you don't have a room available, perhaps you could convert a small unused space such as an area under the stairs or in the eaves of an attic. To use all the available space, set up a sewing table at the high end of the area and build shelves above the table and in the low end. Dividing the high and low areas with a partition wall and door makes it easier to keep the storage space clean and provides an extra place to hang equipment like an ironing board or pinboard.

There are several essential requirements for any sewing area. Adequate electrical outlets are a necessity and, unless you have sufficient daylight, you will need a table or floor lamp to light the area. You will also need a table for the sewing machine, deep cupboards or drawers for storing fabrics and tools, and shelf space for books and boxes.

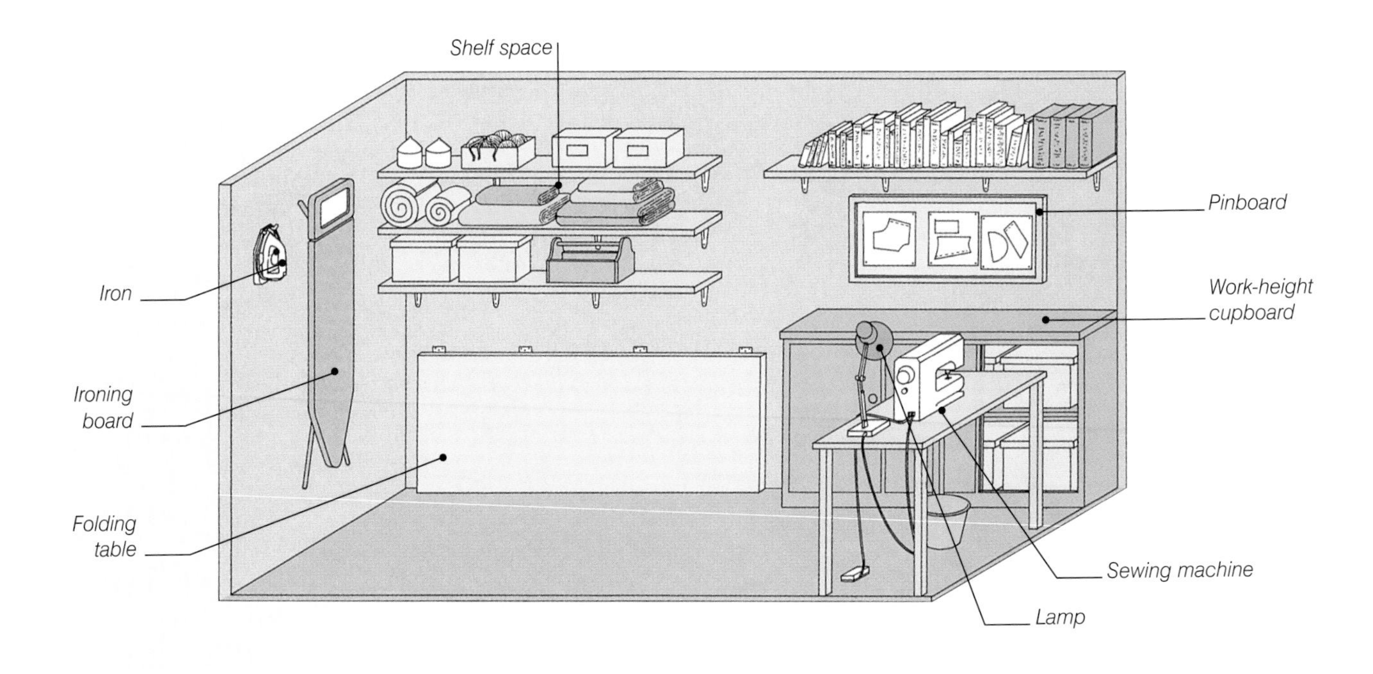

LIGHTING

Good lighting is an important aspect of safe sewing. It reduces the risk of an accident and of eyestrain. All sewing machines have a built-in light that shines directly on the plate. If the bulb burns out, replace it immediately.

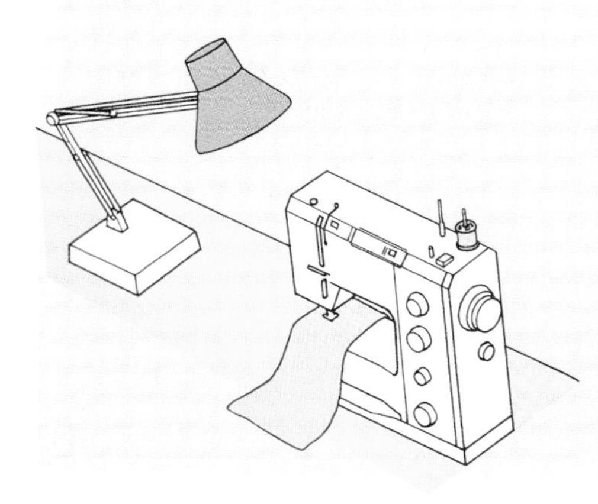

SEATING

The rules for working at a computer apply equally to sewing. Make sure the sewing-machine table and chair are at the correct height. A chair with a straight back and no arms is generally the most comfortable option. You should be able to reach the piece being stitched without stretching or straining—wrists should fall level between the waist and the chest, and the foot pedal should be placed slightly forward but within easy reach of your right foot to prevent ankle strain. Sitting up straight will reduce the possibility of backache or neck strain, and getting up from the chair and moving around at regular intervals alleviates the tension that builds up when you concentrate in one position for long periods.

A large table is required for cutting fabric. Use a house-decorator's folding table if you have the storage space; otherwise, you can use a dining table. An iron and ironing board must be easily accessible. It is handy to have a pinboard for notes and sketches, and a full-length mirror and dressmaker's dummy if you are dressmaking.

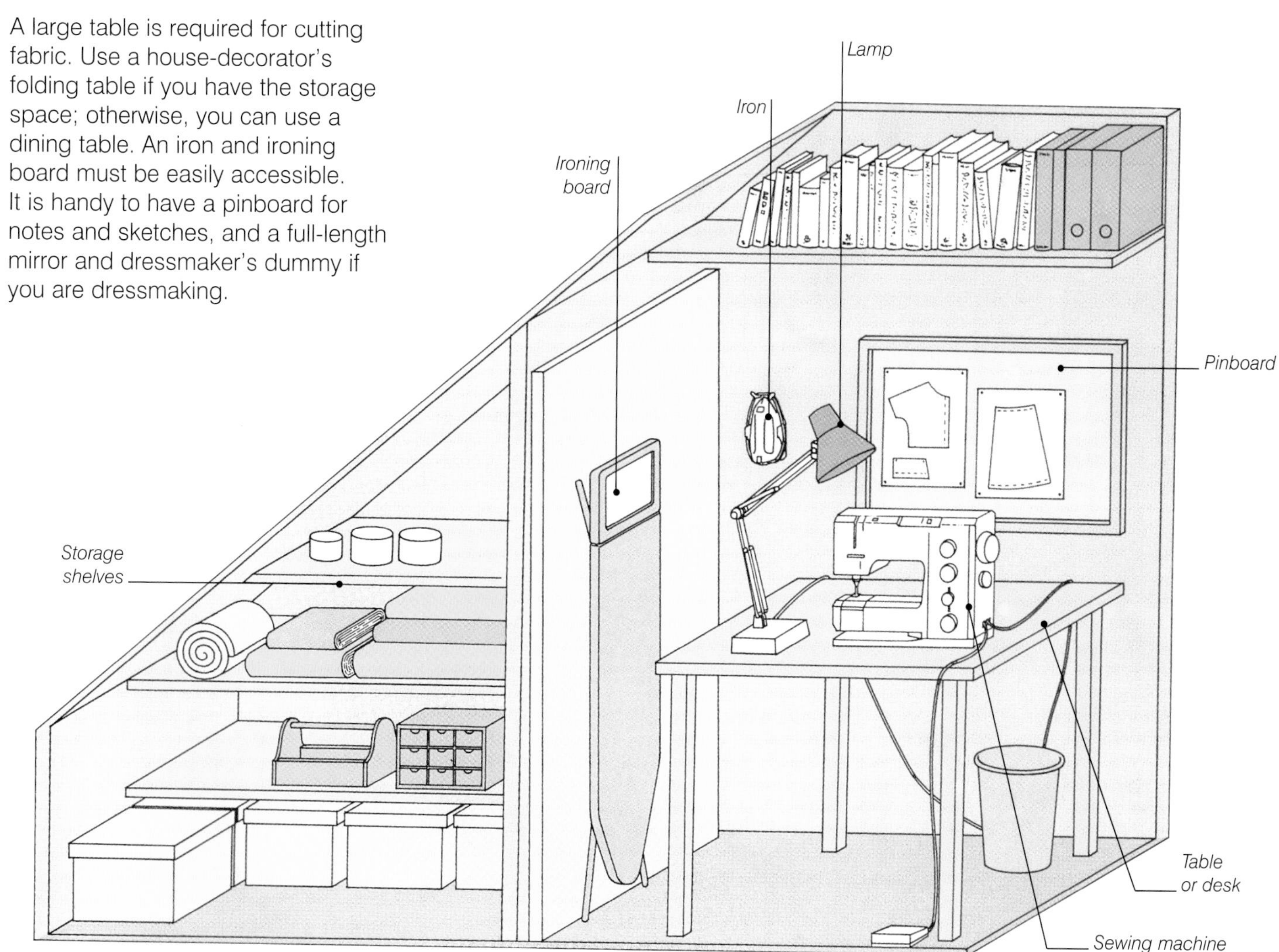

Understanding fabrics

There are so many different fabrics available today that it would be impossible to list them all, but most fabrics have certain common characteristics. Woven fabrics, such as the ones shown in this section, are by far the most numerous, but there are also non-woven fabrics, mainly felt and interfacing; knits; and lace and net, which are composed of threads knotted into highly intricate patterns.

USING FABRIC

Most items made for the home, and many garments, are made from woven fabrics. The weight of the fabric, from light to heavy, will be one of the main characteristics that determine its use. Heavyweight materials are more likely to be used for upholstery, while gossamer silk is most likely to be found in a special-occasion dress, although lightweight silk and voile are widely used for curtains. Because knitted fabrics tend to stretch, they are less likely to be found in furnishings.

The fine diagonal ridge that runs through every piece of twill is very distinctive and occurs whichever type of thread is used to make the fabric. Its interesting texture makes twill a popular choice for suits and coats.

Warp and weft

All woven fabrics have a warp (the threads that run lengthwise in the loom) and a weft (threads woven in and out of the warp threads at a right angle to create the widthwise grain). The weft is also called the woof. The selvage is the non-fray, tightly woven border that forms the lengthwise fabric edge. The lengthwise and widthwise grains are firm, without much give. However, when fabric is folded or cut at a 45-degree angle to the selvage, the fabric becomes easy to stretch and has more "give." This crosswise grain is called the bias.

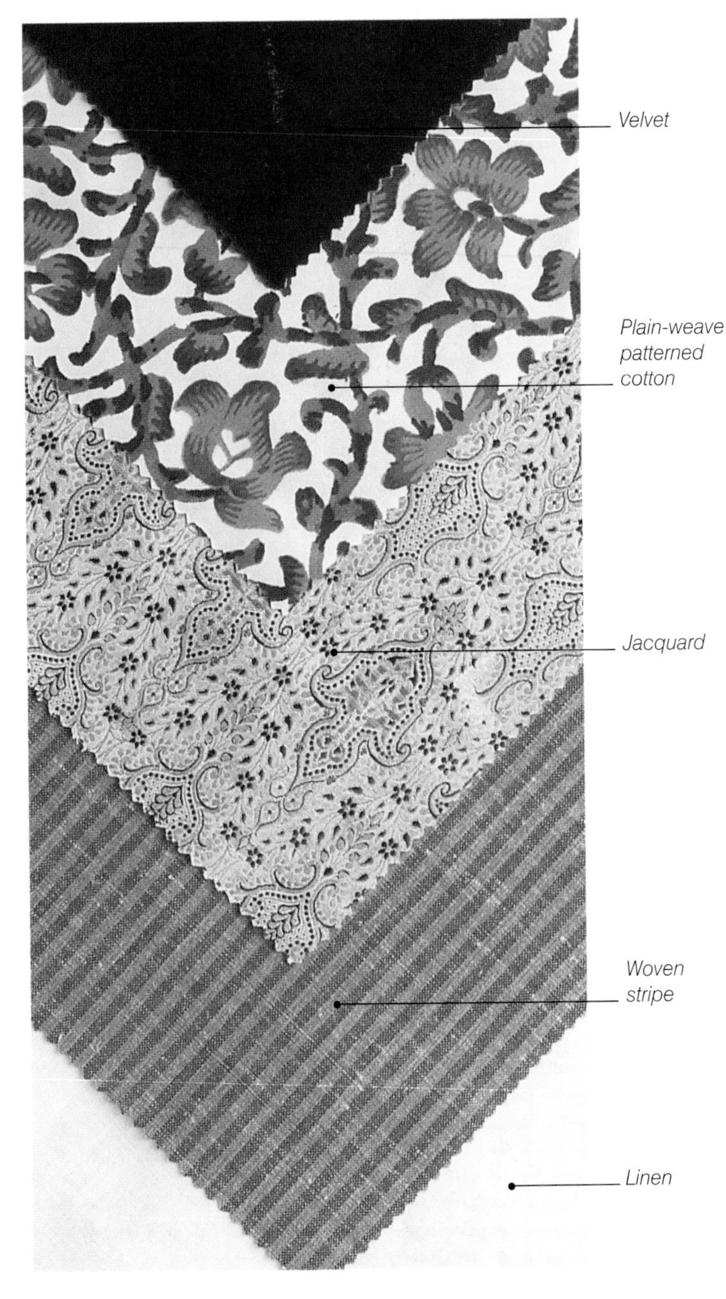

Printed chintz

Printed striped knit

Woven stripe

Woven printed stripe

Woven wool bouclé

Woven wool plaid

Woven gingham check

Printed plaid

Weaves

In addition to plain-weave fabrics, in which a weft thread goes over and under one warp thread at a time, there are two other basic weaves. Twill creates a diagonal finish by taking the weft under a certain number of threads and then over a different number, staggering the position from row to row. Satin weave crosses unequal numbers of threads in an alternating fashion to make a regular gridlike pattern. All thread combinations cross each other at right angles.

Pile and napped weaves have a raised surface. Pile is a velvety surface created by weaving in extra threads that rise above the woven surface of the fabric. Nap is a wooly surface made by drawing out the short fibers and brushing them in one direction on the right side of the fabric.

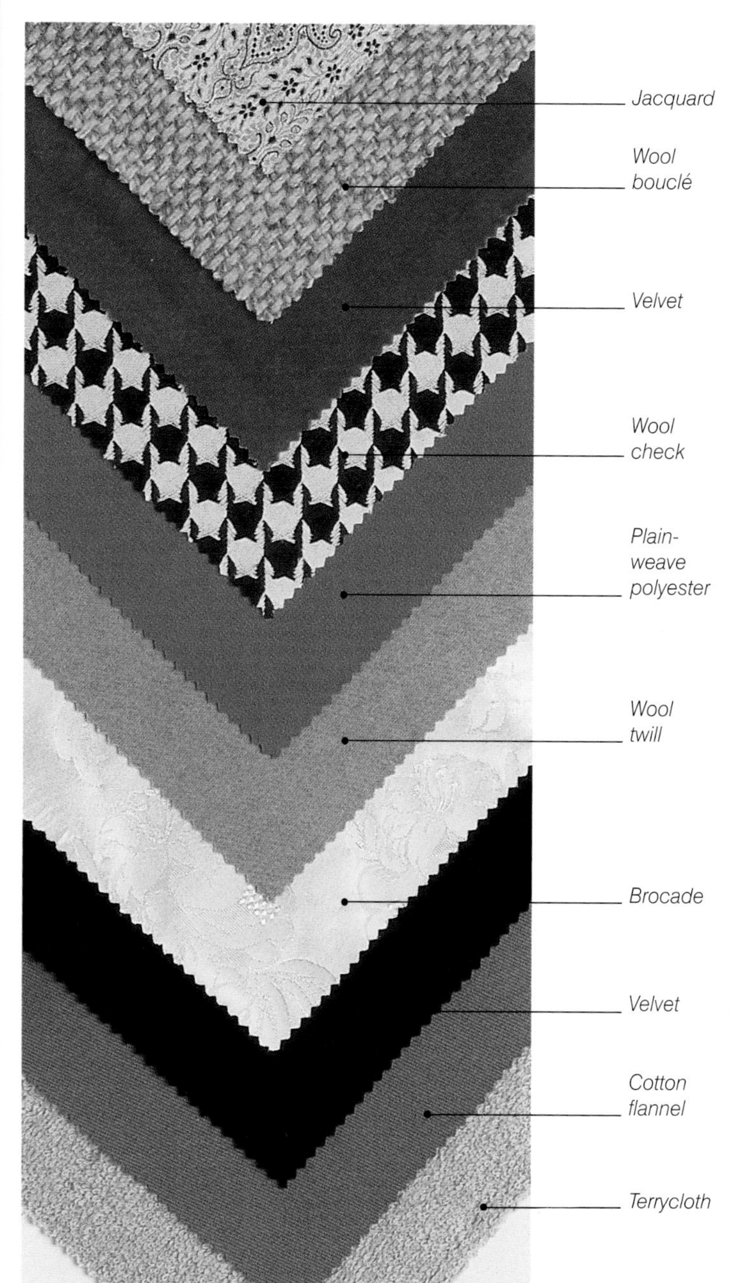

Patterns

Patterns can be woven into the fabric, as is usually the case with plaids, checks, and stripes, or printed on the right-side surface after the material has been woven. Most chintzes and calico prints fall into this second group. Regular patterns must be matched in all sewing projects, both dressmaking and home furnishings, to achieve a professional-looking finish.

There is a huge variety of medium and lightweight fabrics suitable for dressmaking, and an equally vast choice of types and fibers for use in home furnishings. Curtains can range from gossamer sheers to heavy lined and interlined velvets, and covers for sofas, chairs, tables, cushions, and beds vary almost as widely.

Silks

Silk ranges from fine and light to heavy raw silk, and is a favorite for elegant curtains and, in its sturdier versions, for chair and sofa covers. It must be dry-cleaned, and upholstery should be treated with a stain guard. The color choices include every hue in the rainbow, plus neutrals, and patterns abound.

Moiré and ottoman

Moiré describes a wavy, watermarked fabric with a silky finish, and works well for home furnishings. Ottoman is a heavy upholstery fabric that also works well for Roman blinds.

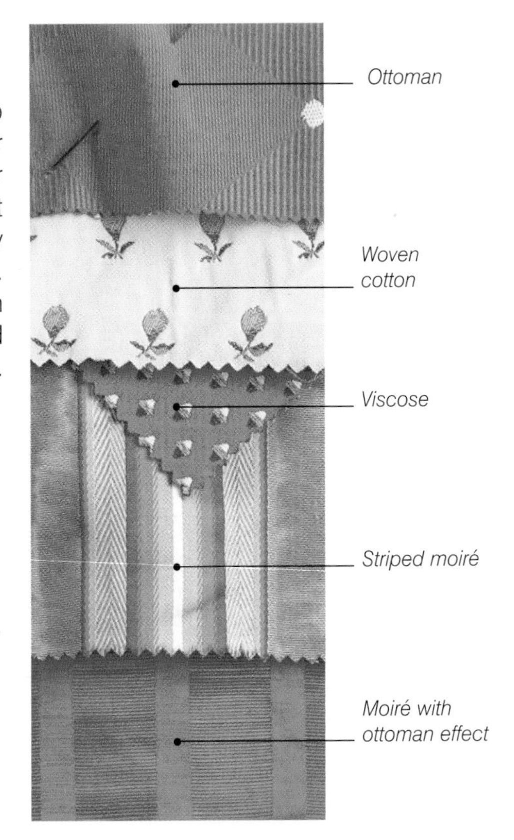

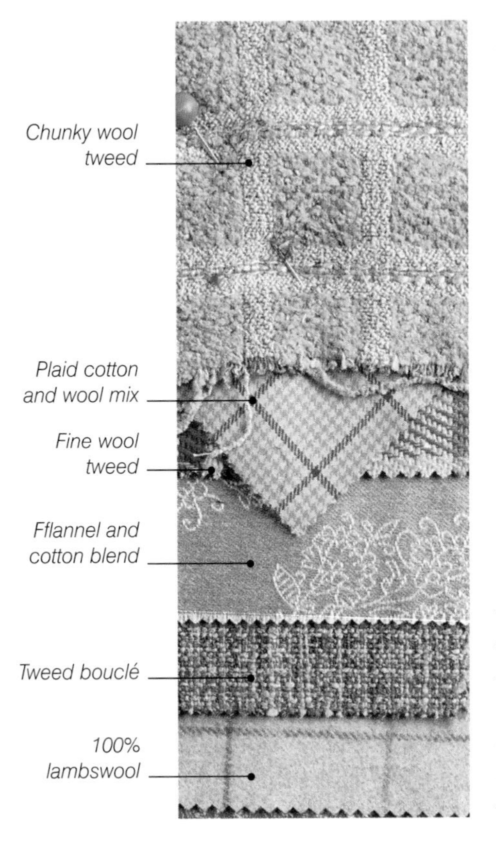

Wool

This natural fiber is easy to handle; comes in an astonishing choice of weights, weaves, and colors; and makes a statement when it is used for home furnishings. Wool curtains should be simple, with a traditional heading and pole and a lack of fullness—even lightweight wool fabric has a great deal of body and can look too heavy. Its warmth and elasticity are especially suited for making cushion and seat covers.

Velvet and chenille

Both velvet and chenille are pile fabrics that can be woven from a variety of fibers. Chenille has a sheen, while velvet is matte, and both are luxurious and synonymous with elegance. The color choice is large, and both are available in patterns as well as plain solid colors.

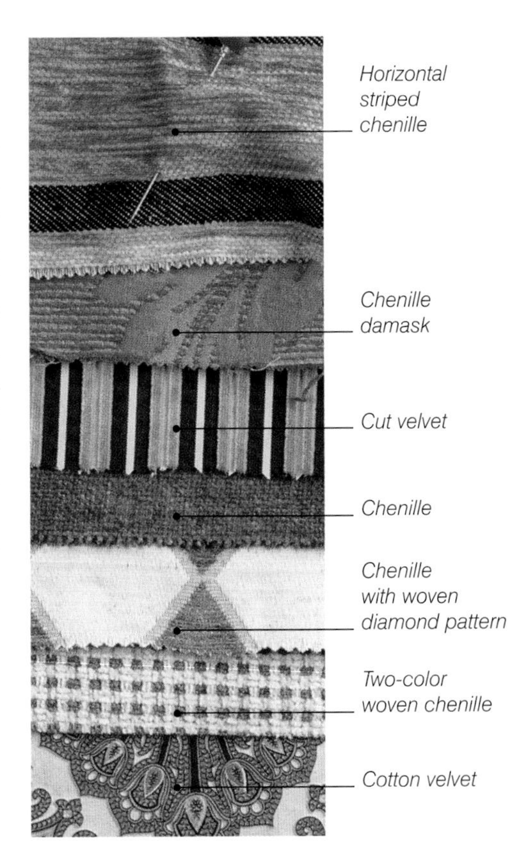

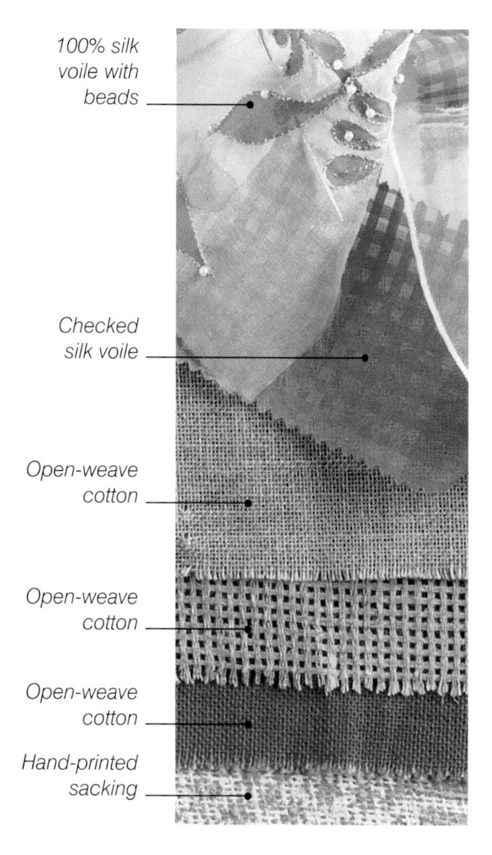

Voiles and open weaves

Voile is a thin sheer fabric that can be woven from silk, cotton, or synthetic fibers. It drapes well and tends to cling to the body. Open-weave fabrics like net and sacking are also made from a variety of fibers. They are all effective for dressing windows, particularly if the look is full and generous.

Rough weaves (raffia, jute, and horsehair)

Roughly woven fabrics such as jute and raffia are particularly good for home furnishings like blinds and table mats, and woven horsehair has been used for centuries to make hard-wearing and long-lasting upholstery. Jute is used to make burlap (hessian), which can be effectively used as a wall-covering fabric.

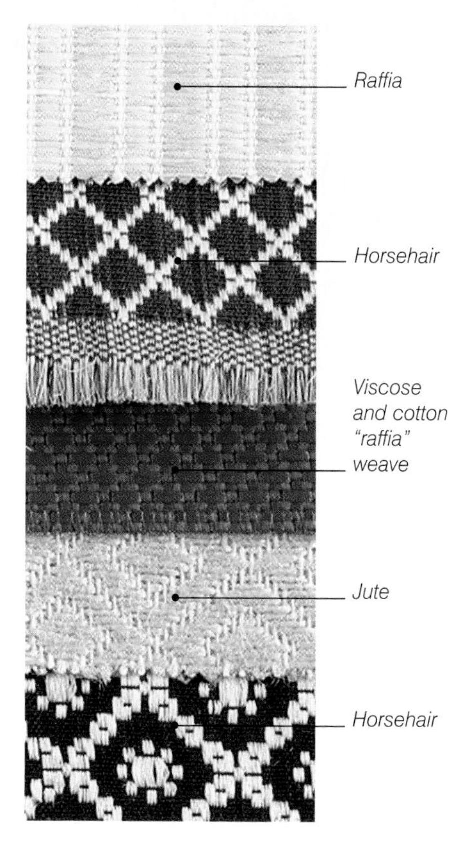

Silk damask

Silk and cotton damask

Grosgrain weave

Grosgrain weave

Spotted weave

Flower and stripe jacquard

Damask

Damask is a firm jacquard fabric that comes in a variety of weights and a wide choice of colors. It has a sheen that makes it an elegant choice for curtains and covers in formal rooms. It needs to be used generously, and works best if it is lined.

Linen and cotton

Linen and cotton are widely used as dressmaking fabrics, but they are also popular choices for a wide range of home furnishings. In particular, they work especially well in relaxed, casual settings. In lighter weights, linen and cotton are ideal for curtains and bed and table covers, while the heavier versions work well for upholstery and more formal curtains and blinds.

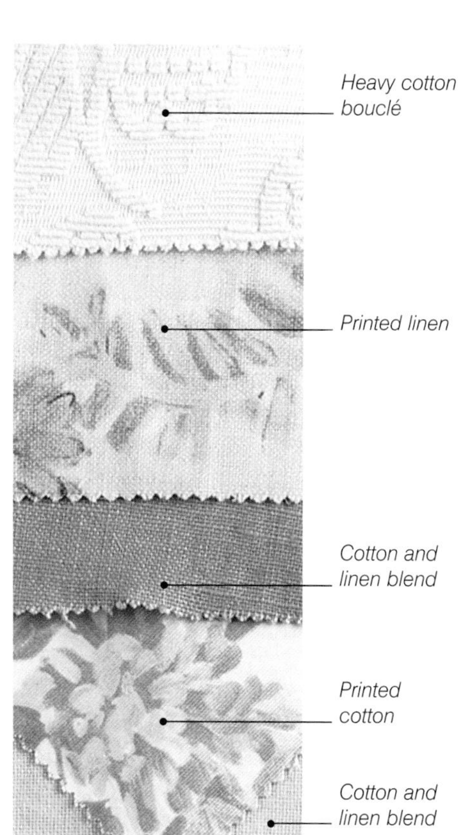

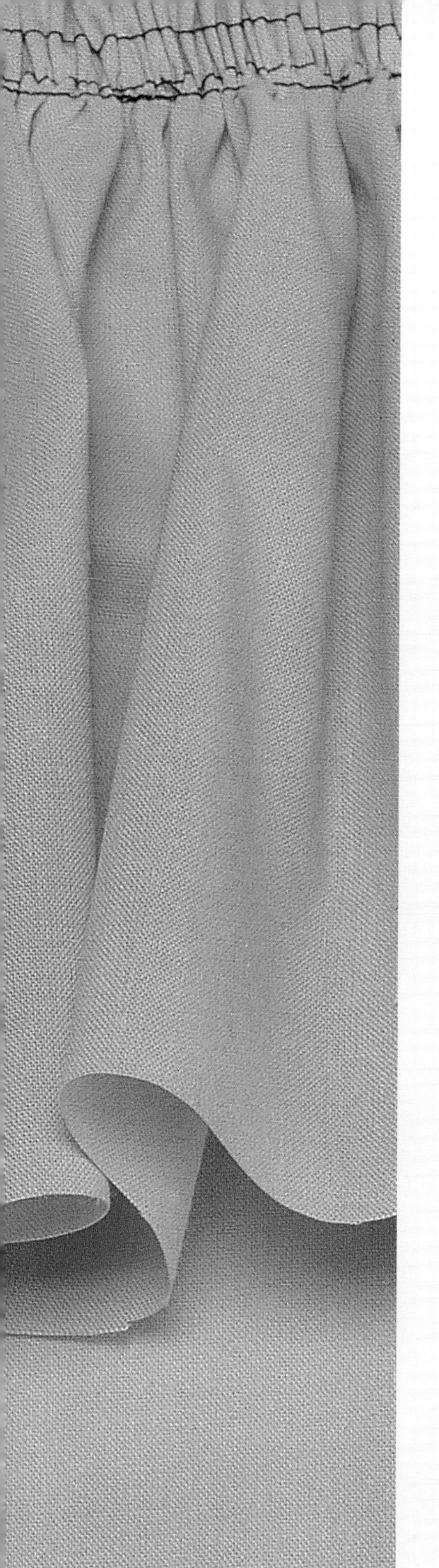

Sewing Basics

Understanding how to carry out basic tasks and using them to their best advantage is the first step to mastering sewing skills. Stitches and seams are the glue that hold an item together. Edges, whether plain hems, mitered corners or ornate frills, finish off a garment or piece of home furnishing, while pressing techniques are a crucial part of any sewing.

Stitches: Hand and machine

Sewing is all about stitches, which are the result of taking a length of thread on a needle through two or more layers of a material to join them. Stitches can be decorative or invisible; they can be made by hand or by a sewing machine. In combination, stitches create seams to secure the pieces that make up sewn articles, from dolls' clothes to curtains.

SECURING A THREAD

A length of thread needs to be secured in some way to hold it firmly in the fabric. The most common method is to tie a knot in the end of the thread before you begin stitching (see below), but if you don't want the small lump created by the knot, tie the thread down with a couple of tiny tight backstitches at the beginning of the seam. Use the same method to tie off at the end of a seam.

Finishing off

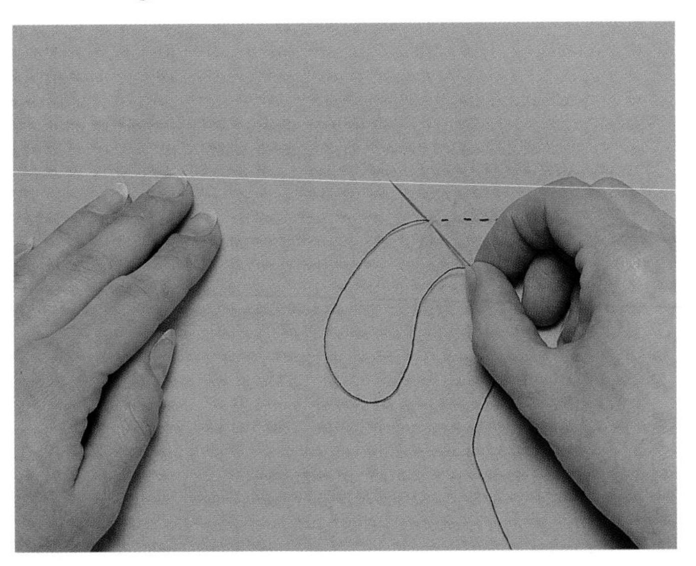

1 When you have reached the end of a row of stitching, or when the thread is not long enough for you to work comfortably any more, take a small stitch next to the last stitch made on the wrong side of the fabric.

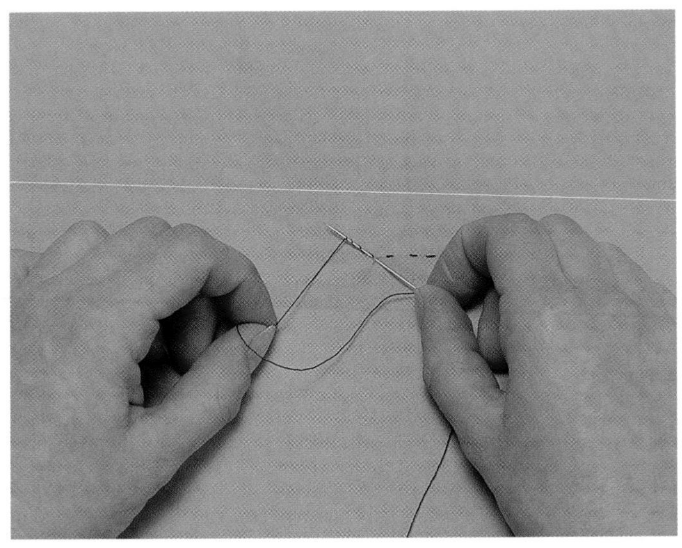

2 Keeping the needle steady in your sewing hand, take hold of the thread with your other hand and wrap it around the point of the needle two or three times.

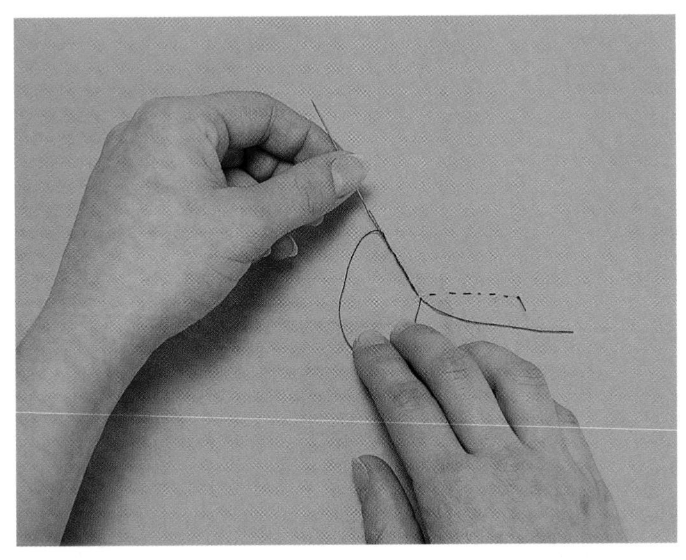

3 Pull the needle through the wrapped loops and carefully pull the thread tight to form a secure knot.

QUICK KNOTTING

Hold the needle in the right hand so the thread cannot slip out. Loop the loose end of thread around the index finger once or twice. Hold the loop securely between thumb and finger and roll it off the finger into a knot.

Basic hand-sewing stitches

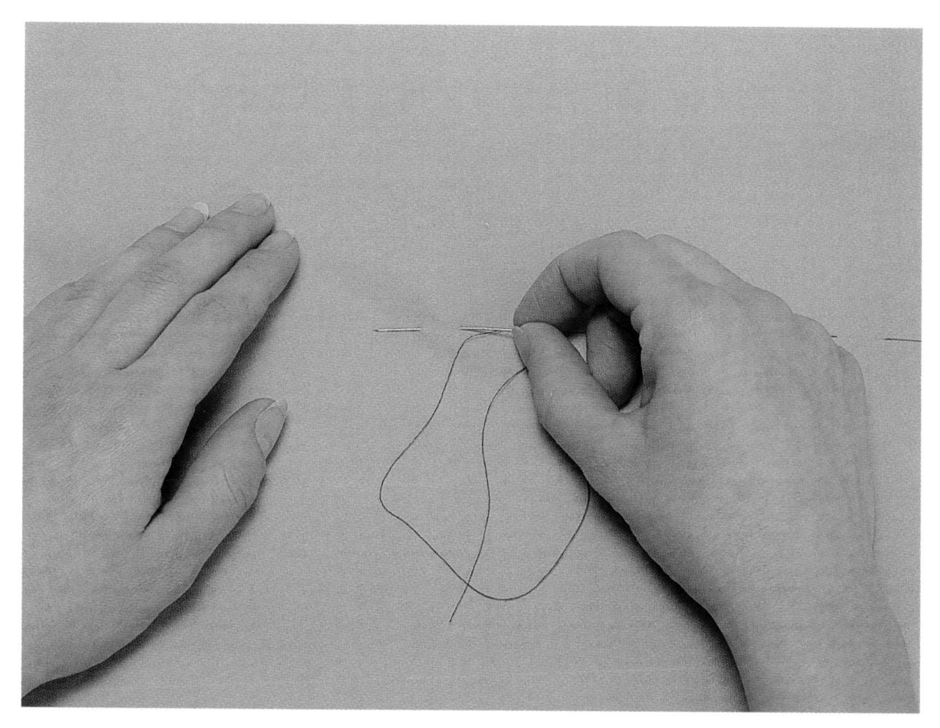

Basting is also known as tacking. It is a long stitch used to hold pieces of fabric in place until they have been sewn together permanently. Basting stitches are removed after the final stitching has been done. Knot the end of a length of contrasting thread and work a long running stitch through all layers of the fabric.

USING A THIMBLE

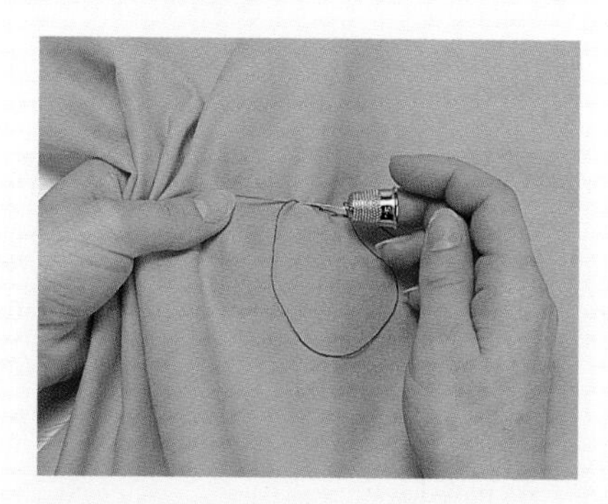

Some stitchers always use a thimble; others never do. If you are sewing a heavy fabric, you are likely to find it particularly useful. Place the thimble over the tip of the middle finger of the sewing hand and gently press the eye end of the needle with it.

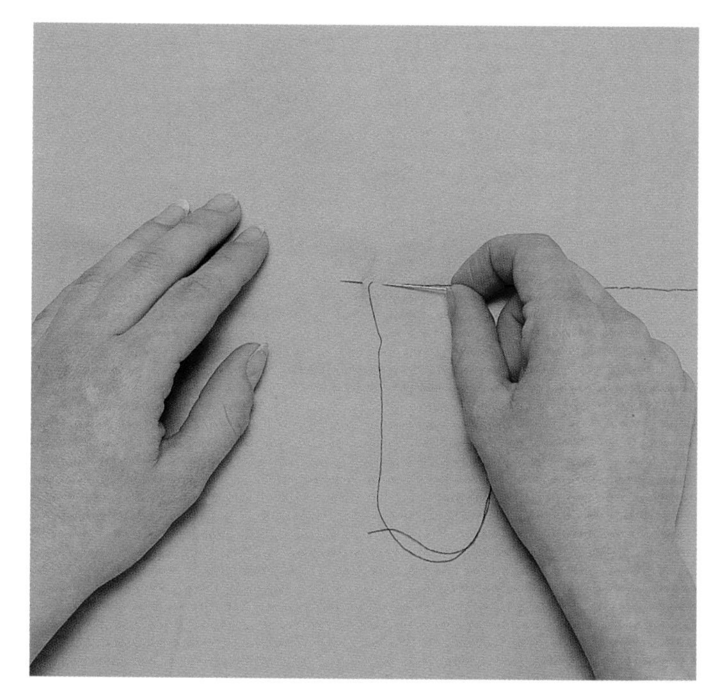

Tacking stitch can be used to join seams that will not be subjected to strain, and for gathering fabric and making tucks by hand. Take the needle in and out of the fabric several times, picking up small, evenly spaced stitches. Pull the needle through the fabric until the thread is taut; repeat to continue stitching.

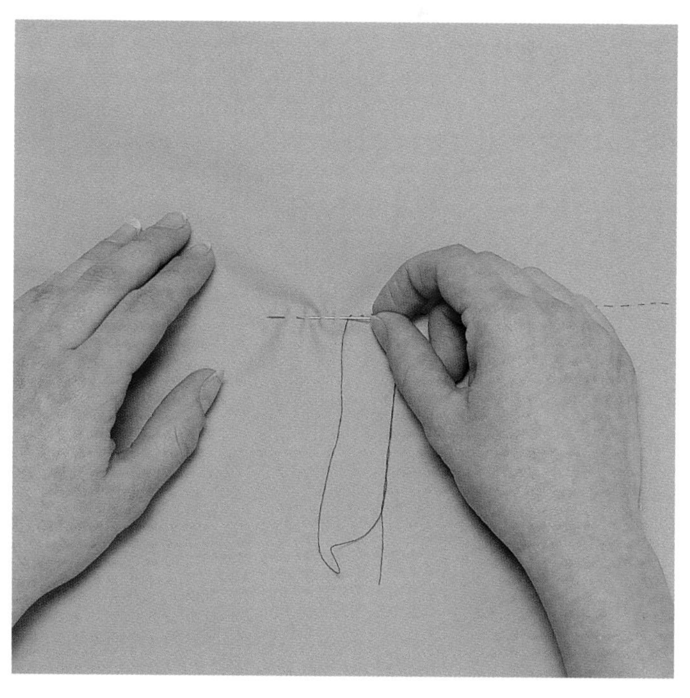

Backstitch is a strong stitch, making it ideal for securing seams and mending. Take the needle and thread it through all the layers of fabric, then bring the needle back a short distance behind where it came out and insert the needle. Bring the point out ahead of the resulting stitch to the same length in front of the needle and continue.

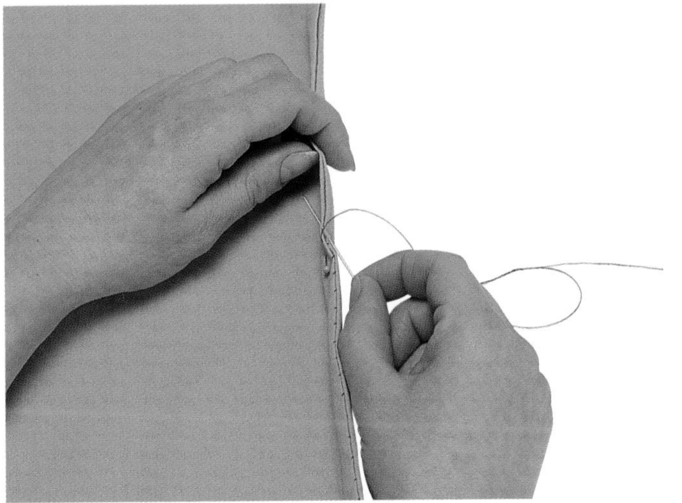

Slipstitch is almost invisible and used mainly to join folded edges of fabric. Knot a single thread and hide the knot in one folded edge. Pull the thread out on that edge and make a stitch ¼ in (6 mm) long through the opposite edge. Insert the needle back in the first side and slide the needle along inside the fold. Repeat to continue.

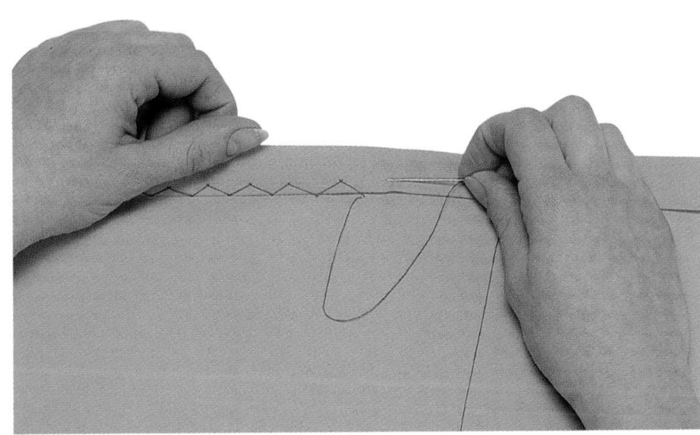

Herringbone stitch is useful for hemming. Working from left to right with the fabric flat, take a long diagonal stitch across the edge being secured, and make a backstitch into, but not through, the folded-up hem fabric. Bring the needle up in the opposite diagonal direction and pick up a few threads of fabric with a single backstitch. Repeat. The stitches will be tiny on the right side.

Buttonhole/blanket stitch makes a firm, strong edge finish that is particularly suitable for use on buttonholes. Its variation, blanket stitch, is worked the same way with the stitches farther apart. Working with the needle pointing toward the fabric and away from the raw edge, insert the needle through the fabric. Loop the thread under the point of the needle and pull it through to create a ridge of thread along the raw edge.

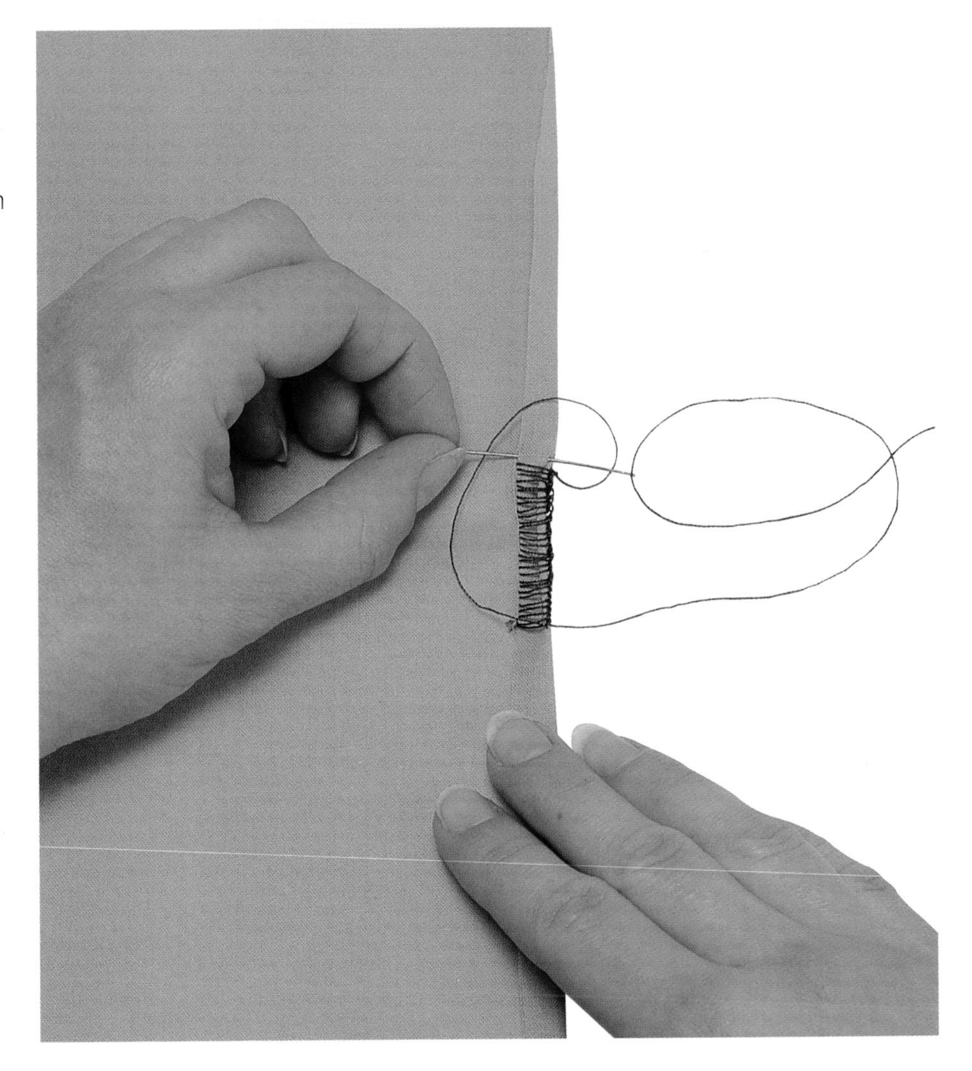

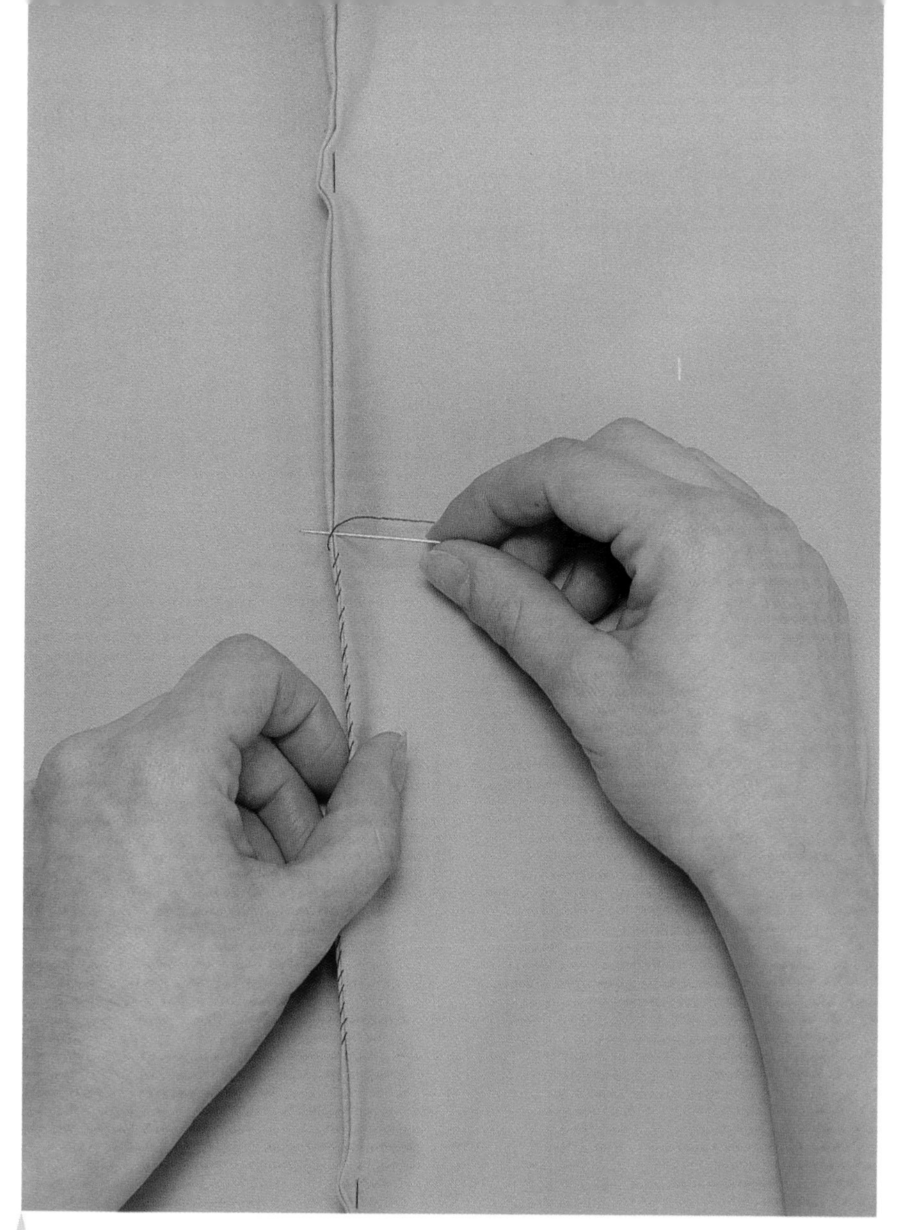

UNEVEN SLIPSTITCH

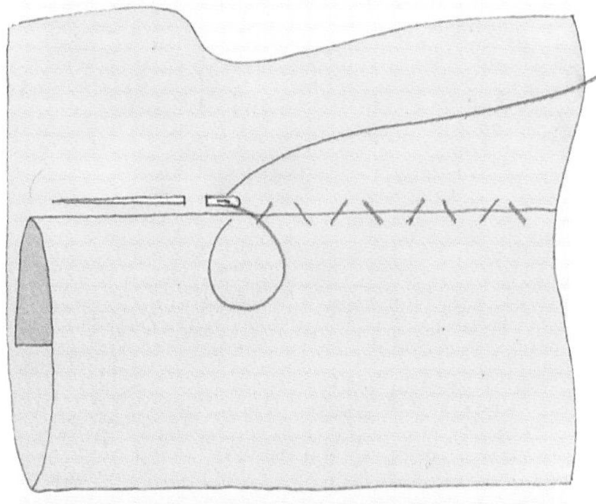

Also known as slipstitch hemming, this stitch is widely used, especially in curtain making. The tiny, almost invisible stitching is used to join a folded edge to a flat piece of fabric. Working from right to left, hide the knot as in slipstitch (opposite) and come up through the fold. Pick up one or two threads in the flat fabric, then make a ½ in (1 cm) stitch through the fold. Repeat.

Overcasting, or oversewing, is used to finish raw edges, particularly on seams worked in fabrics that fray easily. Secure the thread with a few backstitches or a knot and work equally spaced diagonal stitches over the folded raw edges.

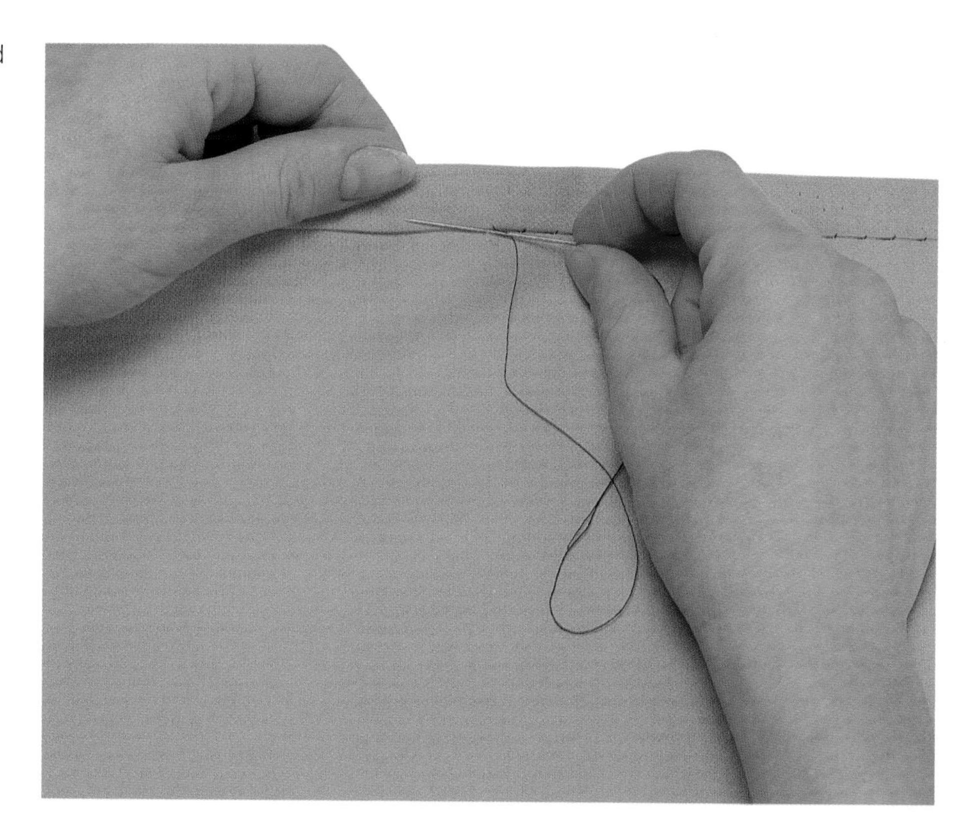

Hemming stitch Hemming stitch is used on most types of hem. Working from right to left, secure the thread inside the turned-under edge of the hem and bring it out. Pick up a few threads from the wrong side of the fabric, then take a diagonal stitch through the turned-under edge. Pull through and repeat.

Hand-sewn thread loop

1 Secure the thread in position at one end of the loop. Take two or three long stitches to the length of loop required, working them side by side on the right side of the fabric, and secure them again.

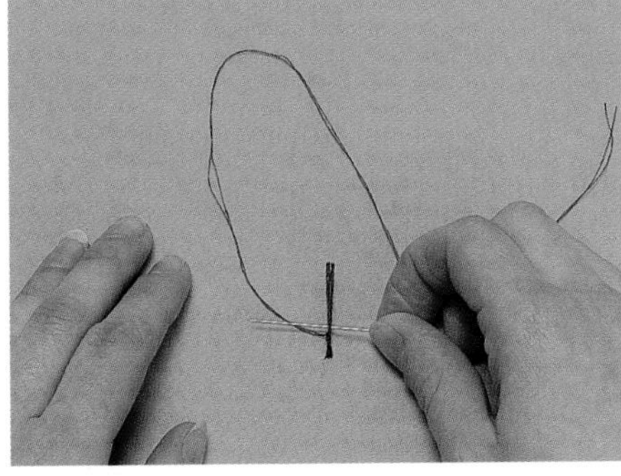

2 Working over the long thread but not through the fabric, make a row of tightly spaced buttonhole stitches (see page 28) along the entire length, taking the thread under the needle point on each stitch. Ease each stitch against the next.

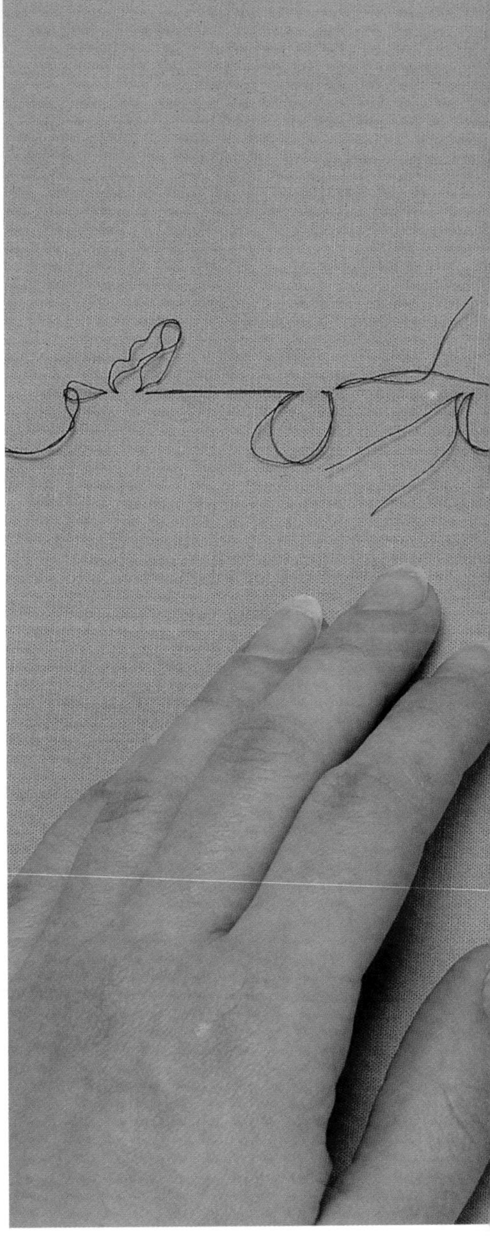

3 Finished loops are strong and lightweight. They make ideal belt loops or can be used with hook fasteners in place of metal eyes or bars. Heavy-duty loops can be made by sewing more long stitches initially, or by using thicker thread.

Hand-sewn bar tack

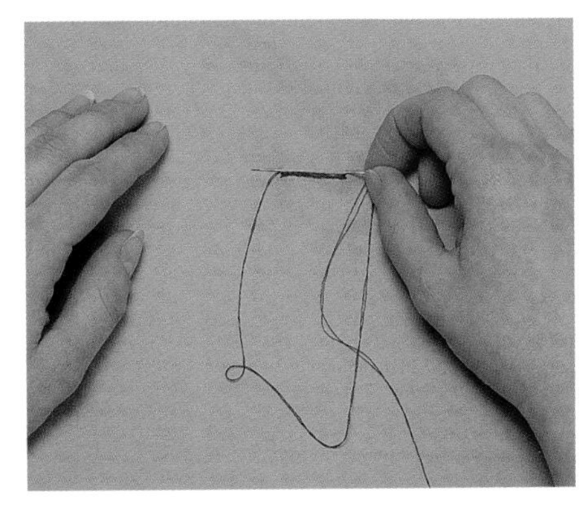

1 Make two or three stitches of equal length in the place where the tack will be worked.

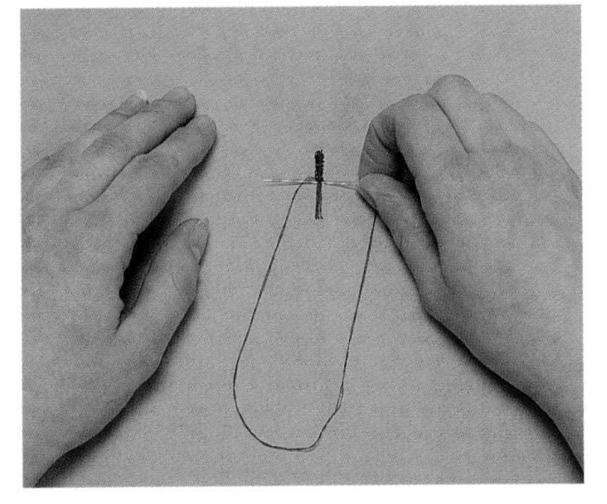

2 Make a row of tightly spaced buttonhole stitches (see page 28) along the first set of stitches. Work each stitch over the laid threads, picking up several threads of the fabric at the same time. Make sure that the thread is looped under the point of the needle on each stitch.

3 The finished bar tack can be made to any length that is appropriate to reinforce small areas that may be subjected to strain and to strengthen slits in necklines or hems.

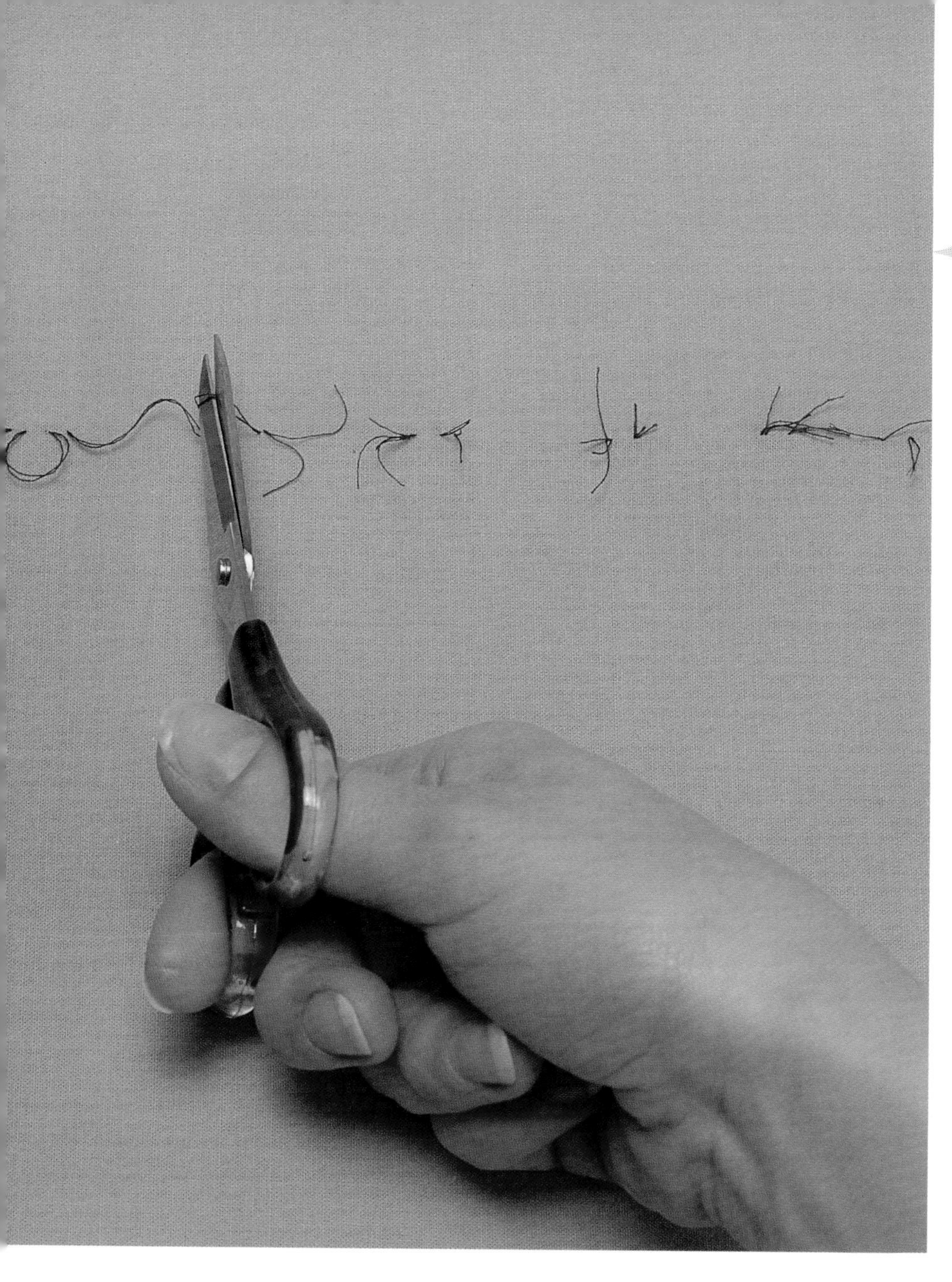

Tailor's tacks Tailor's tacks are used to mark two layers of fabric without drawn lines. They can be worked in a line or at individual points. Pin the pattern in place, and with a doubled thread, stitch through all layers of fabric and pattern paper. Take another stitch in the same spot and make a generous loop. Repeat along the line.

When all the marks have been transferred, cut through the center of each long joining thread. Unpin the pattern, partially separate the fabric layers, and stretch the loops to their limit. Cut each loop between the layers of fabric, leaving the threads to mark the points.

Hand-sewn arrowhead tack

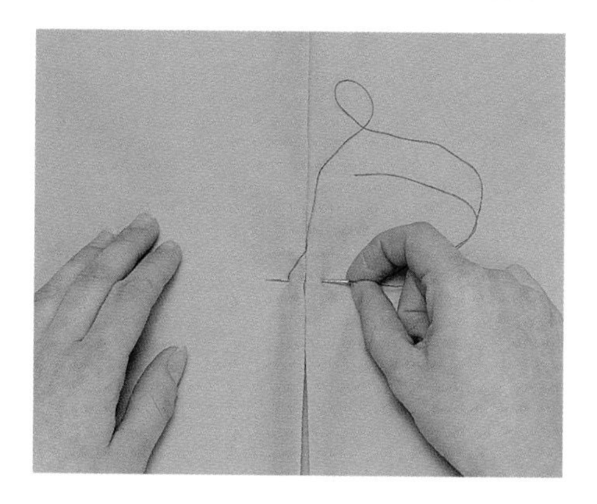

1 Bring the needle from the wrong side so the thread is on the left side of the bottom of the point to be reinforced. Take a tiny stitch at the top of the arrowhead from right to left. Bring the needle down to the right side of the bottom and insert it at the same level as the first stitch.

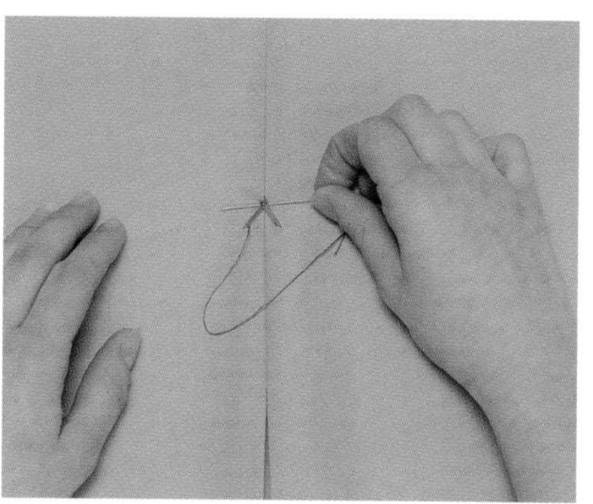

2 Bring the needle out next to the starting point on the inside of the thread triangle. Take a stitch at the top just below the previous one, from right to left. Repeat this pattern of stitches, working toward the bottom center of the arrowhead, until the whole area is fully covered.

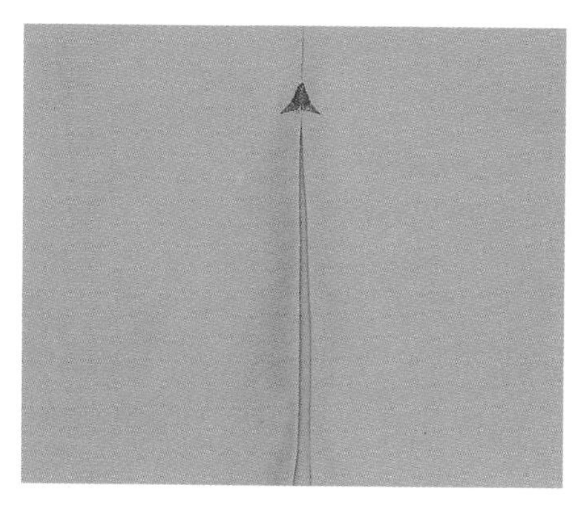

3 Arrowhead tacks give strength to the top of pleats and at the corners of pockets, as well as adding an attractive decorative touch.

STITCHES FOR CURTAIN MAKING

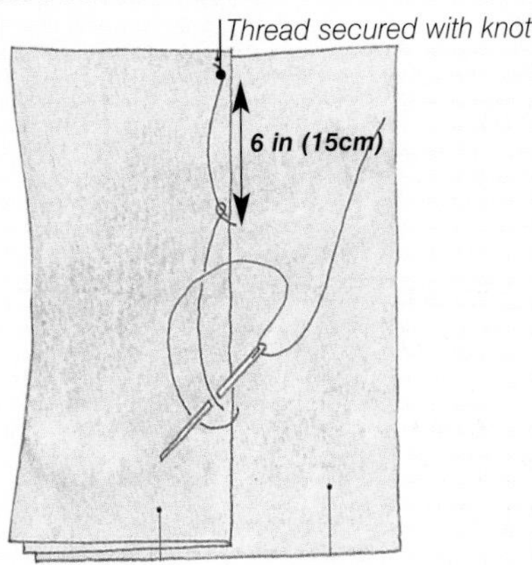

Locking-in stitch

Use this stitch to hold curtains and linings together. Fold back one edge of the lining to 6 in (15 cm). Knot the thread in the fold, take the needle through the edge of the fold and pick up a few threads of the main fabric. Take the needle behind the long stitch and make a small, slack loop. Repeat 6 in (15 cm) down the fold.

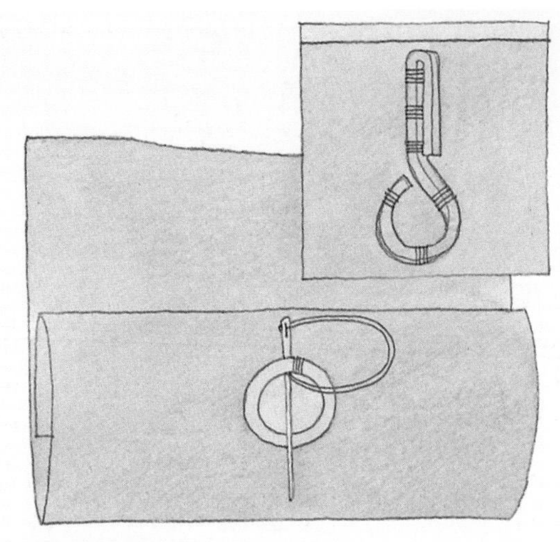

Couching stitch

This stitch is used to attach objects such as hooks or rings. With a doubled thread, make a simple stitch over and over in the same place. Anchor rings in just one place; secure hooks in this way at several places along the length and at the curved end. Keep the thread intact between each group of stitches.

Stabbing stitch

This stitch is used to secure several layers of fabric together in pleated headings. Knot the thread and pull the needle through one or two layers so the knot is hidden within the pleat. Make small stitches in the same place by pulling the needle back and forth through all the layers to create a firm but unobtrusive stitch with the pleat fanning out above and below.

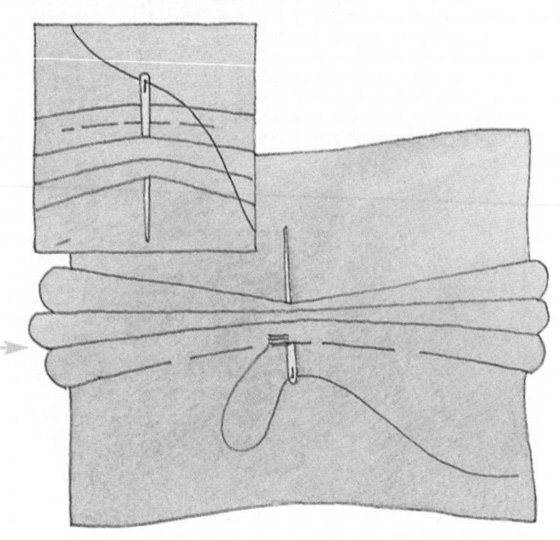

Daisy chain stitch

This stitch is used to tie the bottom hems of curtain and lining together loosely.

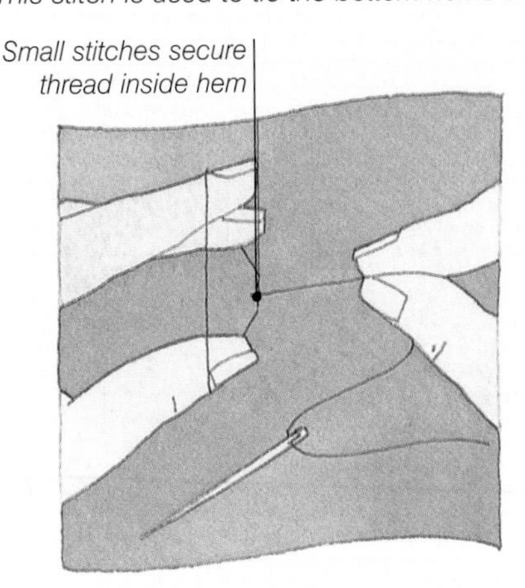

1 Secure the thread in the main hem, then make another stitch but do not pull it through. Hold the resulting loop around the thumb and first finger of your non-stitching hand and keep the thread in the needle in your stitching hand.

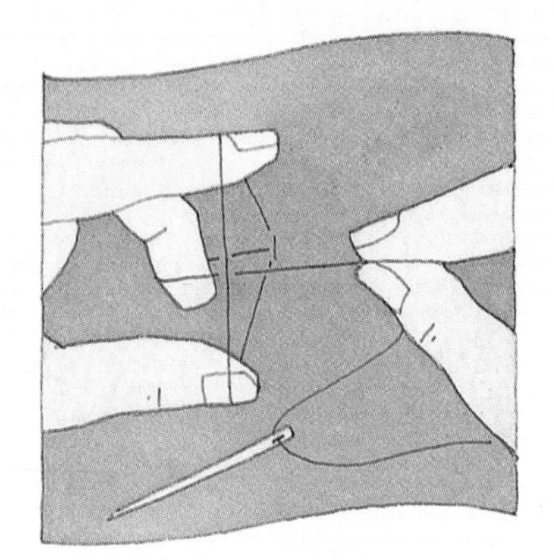

2 Use the second finger of your non-stitching hand to pull another small loop through the first loop near where the thread comes out.

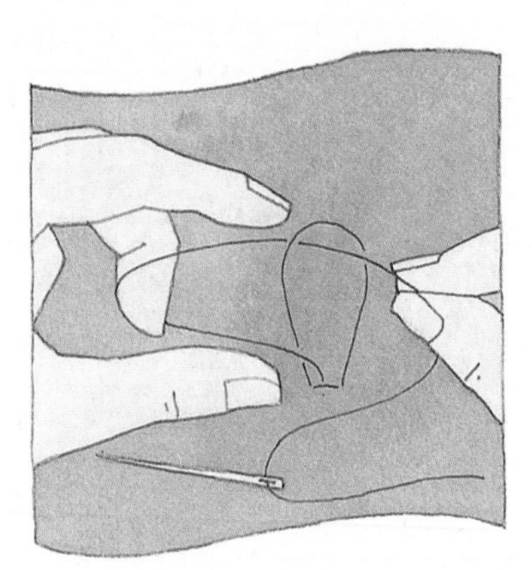

3 Release the first loop, and pull gently with your stitching hand so that it tightens around the second loop. Repeat to make a 2 in (5 cm) chain, then take the needle through the loop and pull the chain tight.

Basic machine stitches

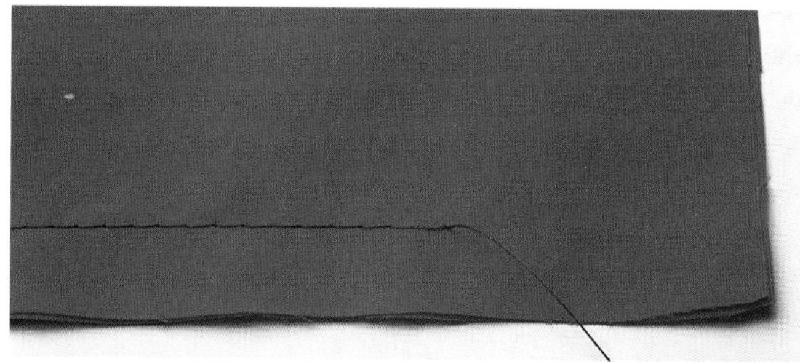

Straight stitch is a line of simple machine stitches. It is the easiest way to join fabric pieces by machine. Practice working straight stitch on different fabrics before beginning work. Follow the marked seamline or the guidelines marked on the machine plate.

Backstitch the ends of machine-worked seams to secure them. Insert the needle ½ in (1 cm) in from the beginning of the seam and use the machine's reverse setting to sew back to the beginning edge. Stitch the seam on the normal forward setting. Use the reverse setting again at the end of the seam to secure the final few stitches.

Machine basting is used to join fabrics temporarily so they can be checked and adjusted before final stitching. Loosen the tension, set the longest stitch length, and stitch a seam. Do not backstitch the ends. To remove basting, clip the thread every few stitches and pull it out.

Staystitching is a row of straight stitches on edges that are liable to stretch such as curved necklines or shoulder points. Work just inside the marked seamline before any other handling of the fabric.

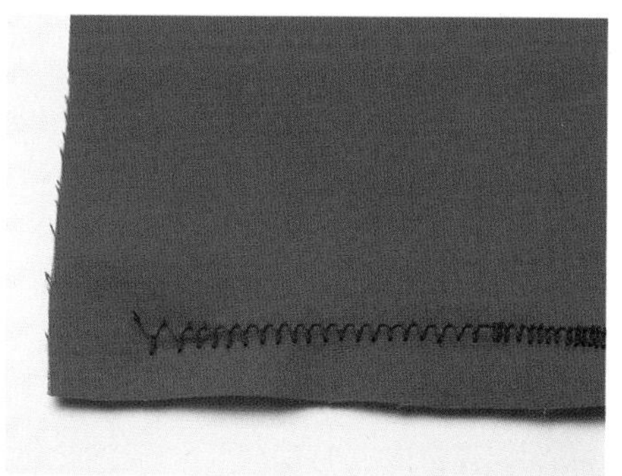

Zigzag stitch is used to finish raw edges to prevent fraying and to make seams in stretch fabrics. Most modern machines have a zigzag function; set it to the desired width and length, and stitch as usual.

Gathering stitch worked by machine makes gathers more evenly spaced than hand gathering. Set the longest stitch and run a line just inside the seamline; then make another row just outside the seamline. Pull up the bobbin threads of both rows together to the desired length. Baste and stitch the seam between rows, then remove the gathering threads.

Seams: Hand and machine

Seams are rows of stitching used to hold pieces of fabric together. Though they are usually stitched by machine, they can be worked by hand. The neat strength of backstitch makes it the best stitch to use for handsewn seams.

The type of fabric and the design of the item determine the type of seam and the way the raw edges are finished. Between the seamline and the raw edge is the seam allowance, usually ⅝ in (1.5 cm) on commercial patterns. (All seams are stitched in a contrasting color for clarity).

Flat seam

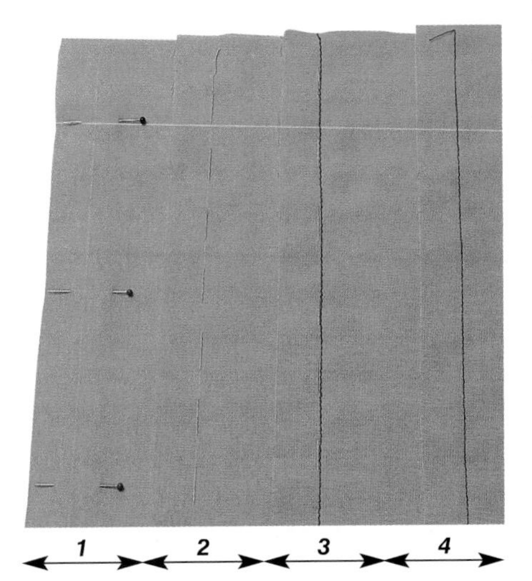

A plain seam worked in machine straight stitch is the basic type used for most sewing. Mark the seamline on the wrong side of the fabric and pin the pieces with right sides together (1). Baste along the marked seamline and remove the pins (2). Work a row of straight stitch along the basted seamline (3). Remove the basting theads (4). Then press the finished seam as instructed, either open or to one side.

Intersecting seams

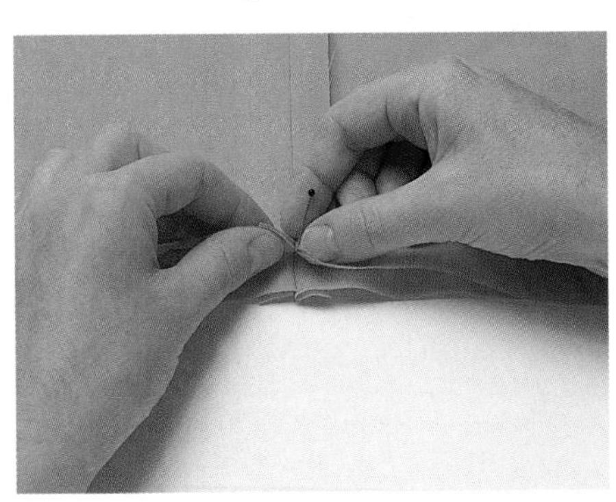

1 To join two seams at precise right angles to each other, make flat seams in the pieces to be joined and press them open. Mark the joining seamline on one piece only. With right sides together, match the stitched seam precisely and place a pin through both stitched seams at the joining point.

2 Pin along the length of the joining seam and baste if necessary. Stitch a flat seam along the marked seamline. To reduce bulk from the intersection, cut the seam allowance away to make a point on both sides of the seam as shown.

3 Press the new seam open (left). The finished seam should form a precise four-cornered right angle at the meeting point (right).

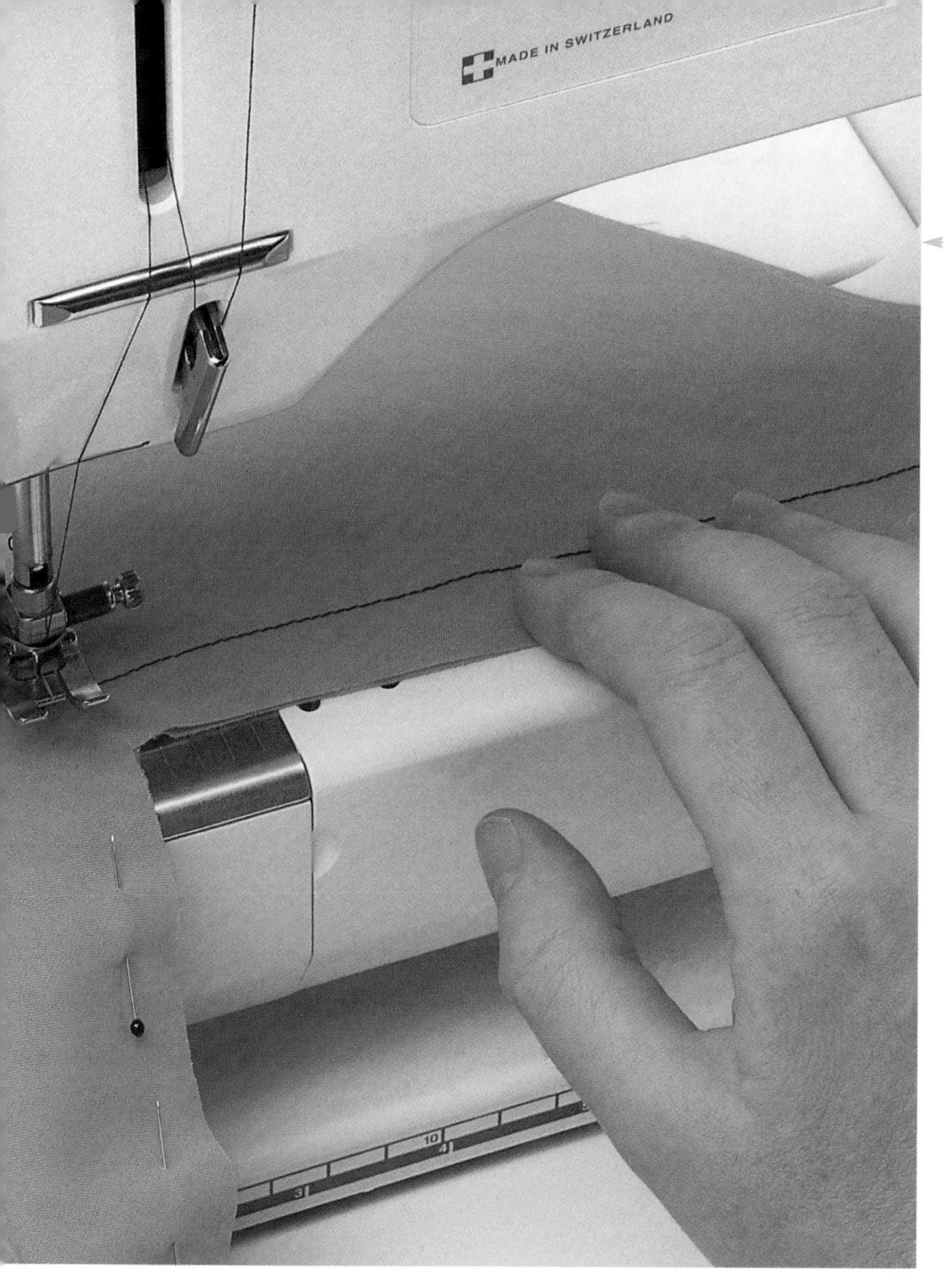

Turning a corner

To turn a corner in a seam in any direction, keep the needle in the fabric when you reach the corner. Lift the presser foot without raising the needle, and swivel the fabric so the new side of the corner is lined up. Lower the presser foot again and continue stitching.

Single-topstitched seam

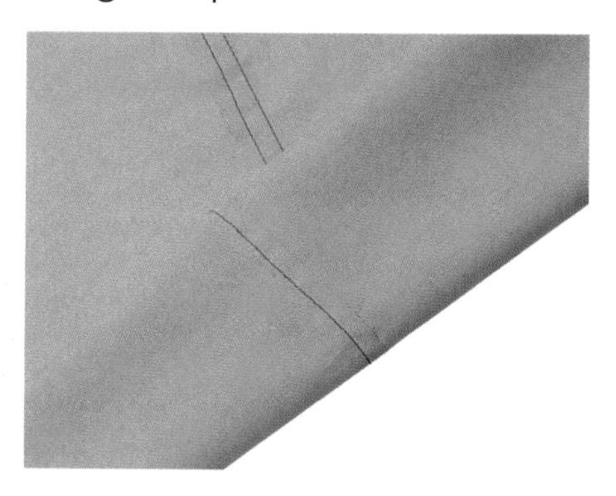

Press a flat seam to one side and work a line of straight stitch along the seam allowance on the wrong side. This holds the seam allowance firmly in place while finishing the raw edges so that they do not fray easily. It also gives a decorative line of topstitching on the right side of the piece.

Double-topstitched seam

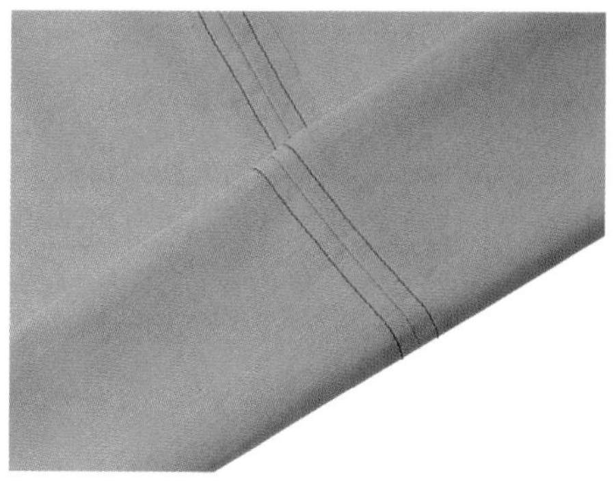

Press a flat seam open and work a line of straight stitch first down one side of the seam allowance and then down the other, equidistant from the seam. On the right side the flat seam will lie in the center of the double row of topstitching, and the seam needs no other finishing.

MAKING A LAPPED SEAM

A lapped or double seam combines the stitching and finishing of the seam, making a narrow double row of stitching on the wrong side that is particularly useful on sheer or lightweight fabrics. Stitch along the marked seamline and then stitch in the seam allowance of about ⅛ in (3 mm) in from the seamline. Trim away any excess fabric from the raw edge close to the stitching and press the seam to one side.

French seam

A French seam is a very narrow seam that looks like a plain seam. The right side is used mainly on delicate fabrics like silk, rayon, chiffon, or other sheer fabrics that fray easily.

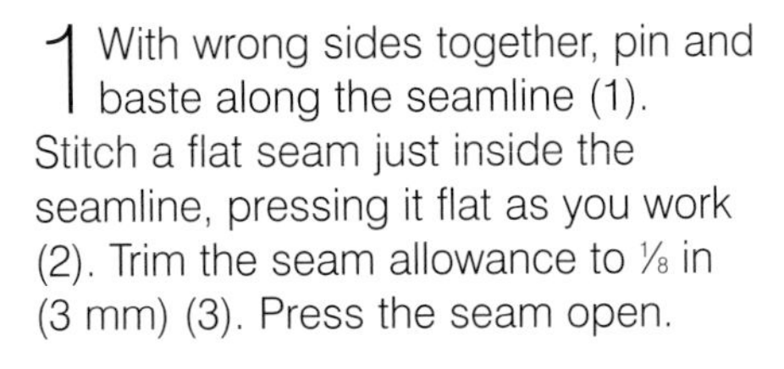

1 With wrong sides together, pin and baste along the seamline (1). Stitch a flat seam just inside the seamline, pressing it flat as you work (2). Trim the seam allowance to ⅛ in (3 mm) (3). Press the seam open.

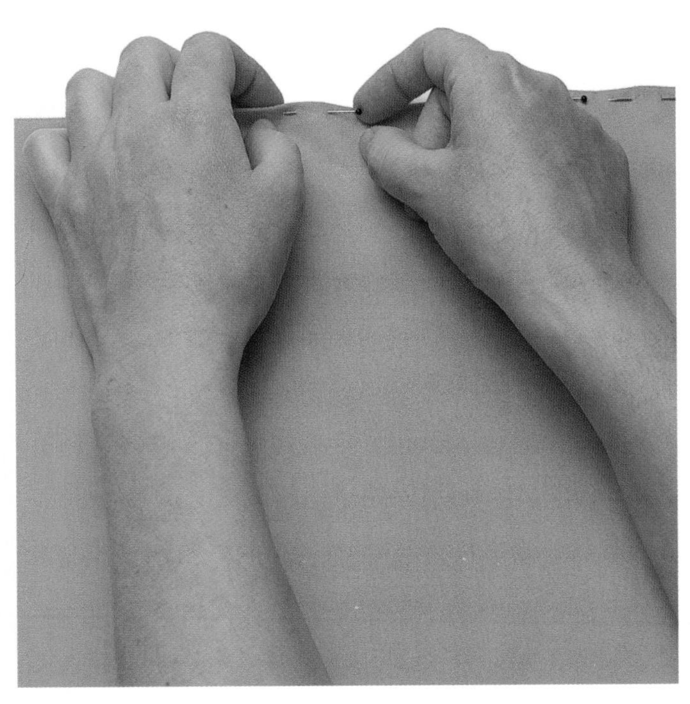

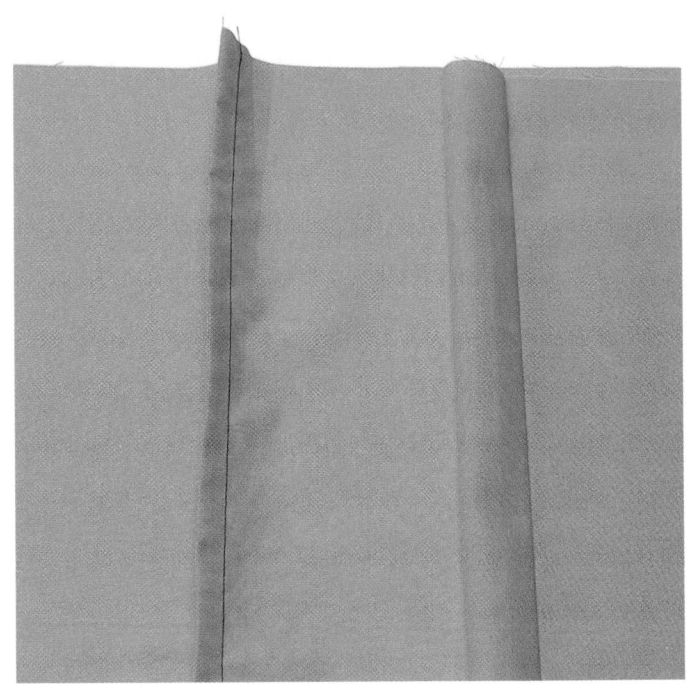

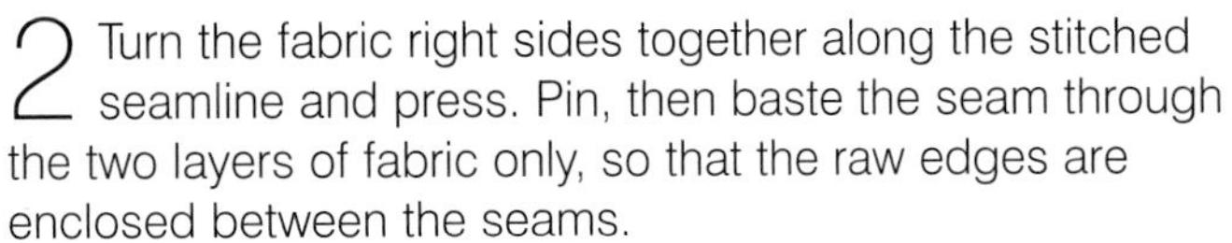

2 Turn the fabric right sides together along the stitched seamline and press. Pin, then baste the seam through the two layers of fabric only, so that the raw edges are enclosed between the seams.

3 Stitch along the basted seamline and press to one side. The finished seam encloses the raw edges completely on the wrong side and looks like a small tuck, as shown on the left above. From the right side of the garment, it looks like a flat seam, right above.

Flat fell seam

Like the French seam, this seam encloses the raw edges, but it also incorporates a line of decorative stitching. It is widely used in making clothes that will be subjected to heavy and frequent use, such as sportswear, children's clothes, and jeans.

SEAMS ON JERSEY

Seams on knitted fabrics can be zigzagged (left) with a short narrow stitch to ease tension and provide strength, overlocked (right) to prevent fraying where the seam will not be subjected to strain, or both (right), which will provide some "give" with strength and prevent fraying. Always sew with a ballpoint needle.

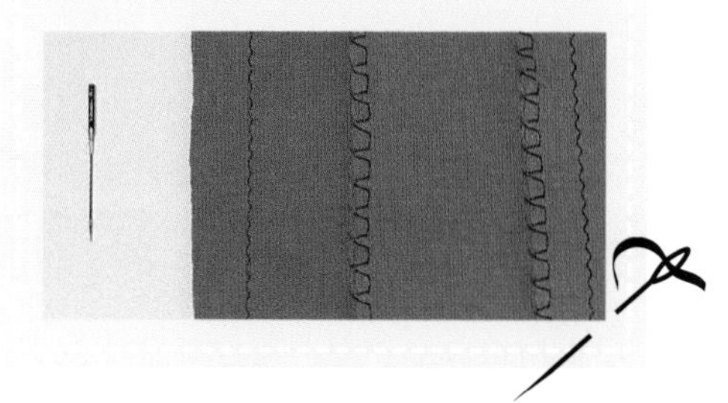

1 With wrong sides together, pin and baste the seamline; then stitch a flat seam. Press the seam open, then press it again to one side. Trim away the seam allowance on one side, the under layer, to half its width.

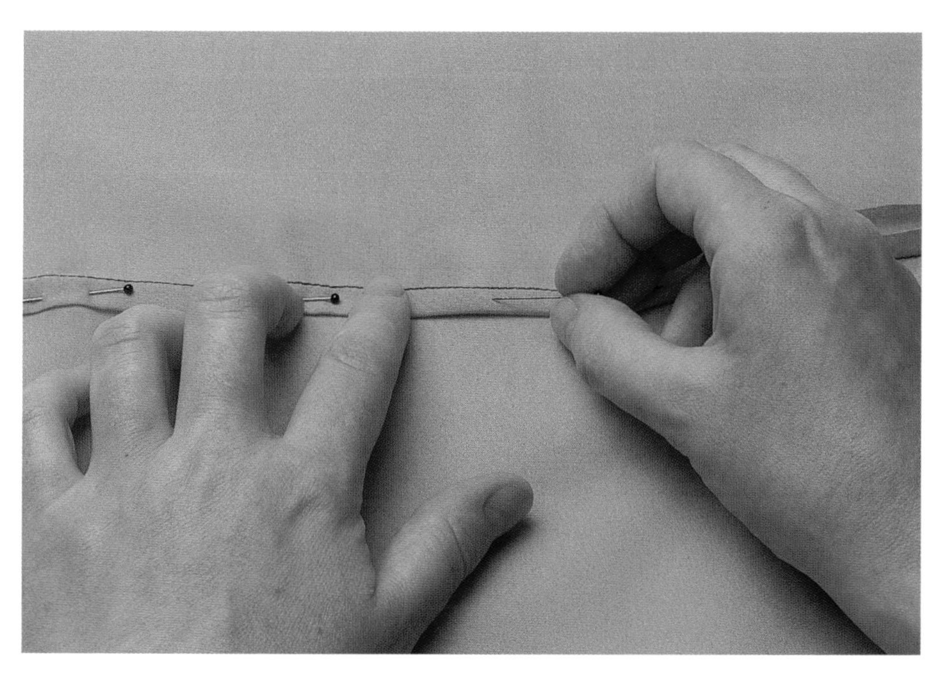

2 Open the piece out flat and fold the wider seam allowance, the upper layer, over to enclose the trimmed layer. Pin in place along the fold. Stitch along the edge of the fold, removing pins as you work.

3 The finished seam is double-stitched on the right side of the garment, as shown top right. Below that is the seam shown from the wrong side, where it appears as a flat seam with a single row of stitching alongside it.

Seam finishes

By stitching or securing the raw edges of the seam allowance, you will give your seam a more professional appearance. Finished seams will also help to prevent fraying as well as general wear and tear.

FINISHING SEAMS

Selecting the correct finish for the raw edges of a seam allowance can make all the difference to the overall look of a piece of work. Check the information in brackets after each entry below to help in choosing.

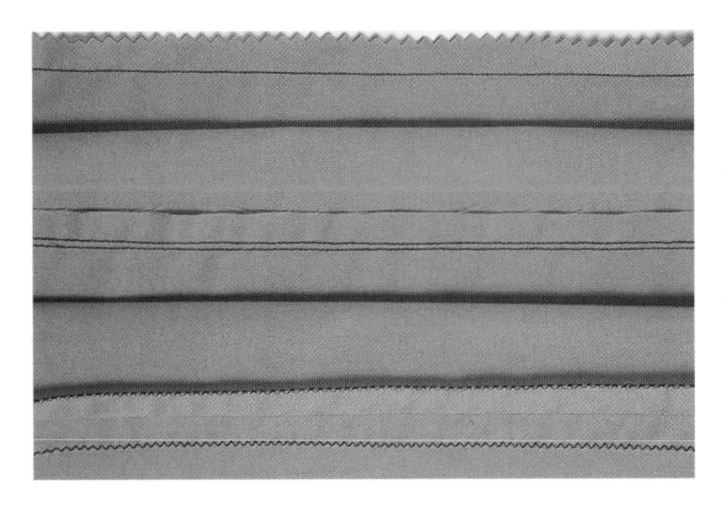

Simple finishes

Top The seam is pressed to one side, and the doubled raw edge is trimmed with pinking shears to prevent the fabric from raveling. (Most seams and fabrics)

Center The seam is pressed to one side, and a second row of stitching is made in the seam allowance close to the seamline. (Subject to strain)

Bottom The seam is pressed open and the raw edges are sewn separately with a zigzag stitch, taken as close to the edge as possible. (Tendency to fray)

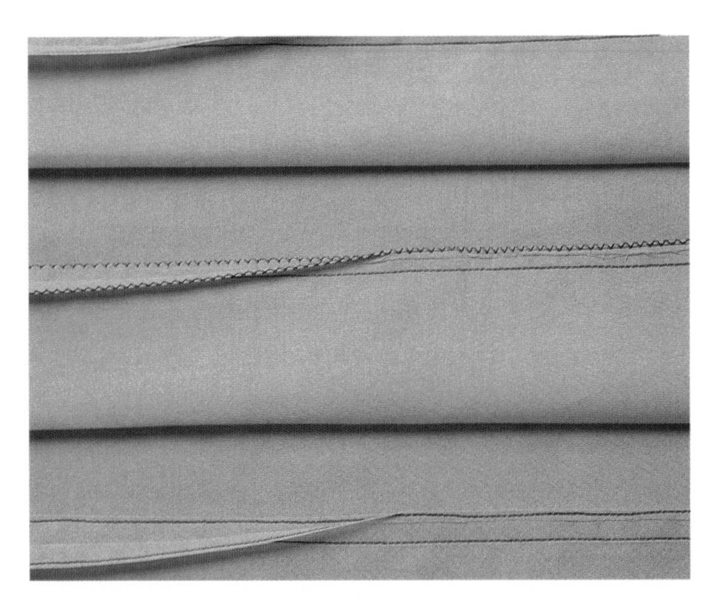

Tailored finishes

Top Pin a length of narrow bias binding over each raw edge to enclose it and stitch close to the edge of the binding. (Most seams and fabrics)

Center Turn under a single hem along each raw edge and zigzag along each folded edge. (Lightweight and sheer fabrics that have a tendency to fray)

Bottom Turn under, pin, and stitch a single hem along each raw edge of the seam. (NOT for heavyweight fabrics)

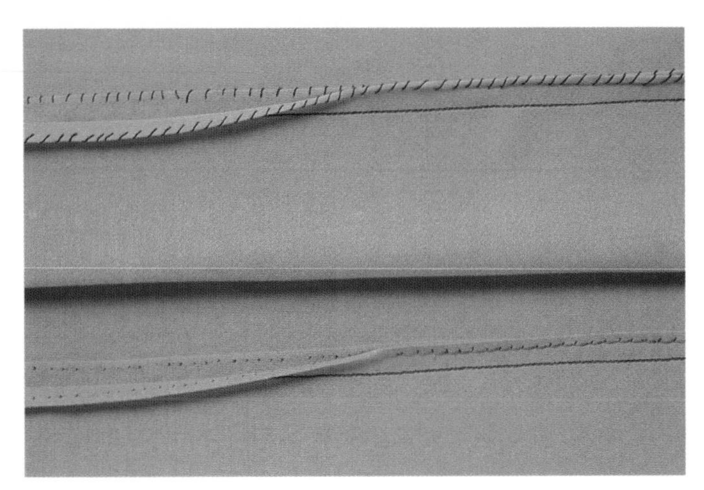

Hand-sewn finishes

Top Stitch a row of evenly spaced overcasting along each raw edge. (Heavyweight fabrics)

Bottom Turn under a double hem along each raw edge and work a row of hemming by hand. (NOT for heavyweight fabrics, good for delicate fabrics)

Clipping corners

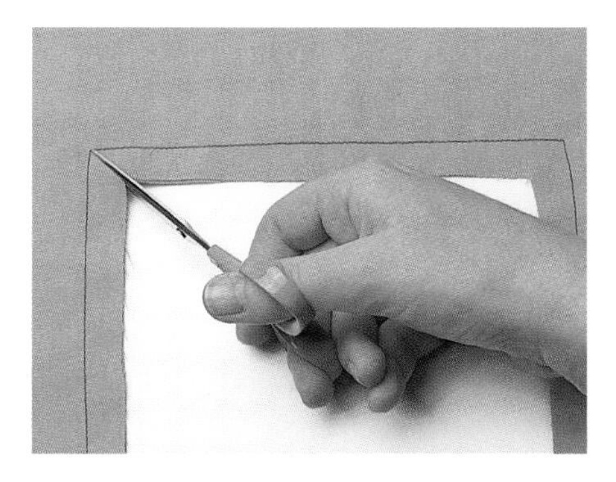

Right angle Hold a pair of small sharp scissors at a 45-degree angle to the corner and clip into the seam allowance, taking the cut up to but not through the stitching.

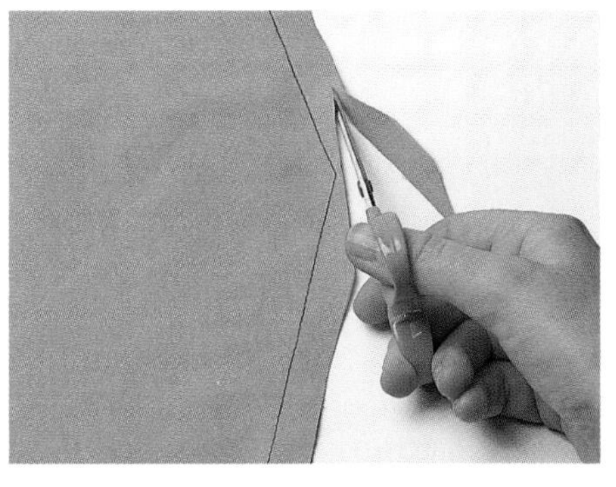

Wide (obtuse) angle Use sharp scissors with blades long enough to cut off the point of the angle in one snip. Cut as close to the stitching as possible without cutting through it.

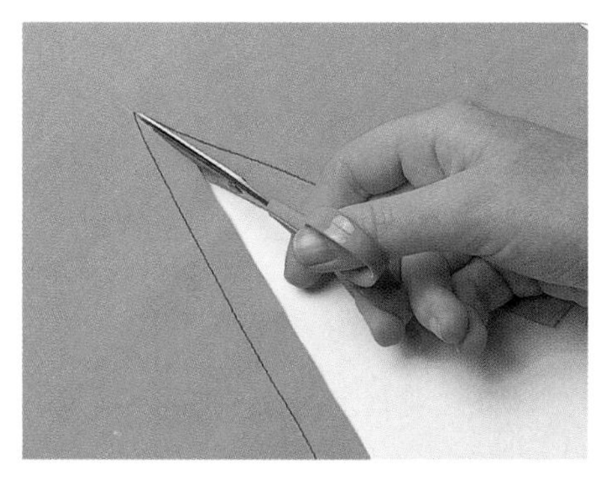

Sharp (acute) angle Use small sharp scissors to cut into the center of the stitched point, up to but not through the seam.

Clipping curves

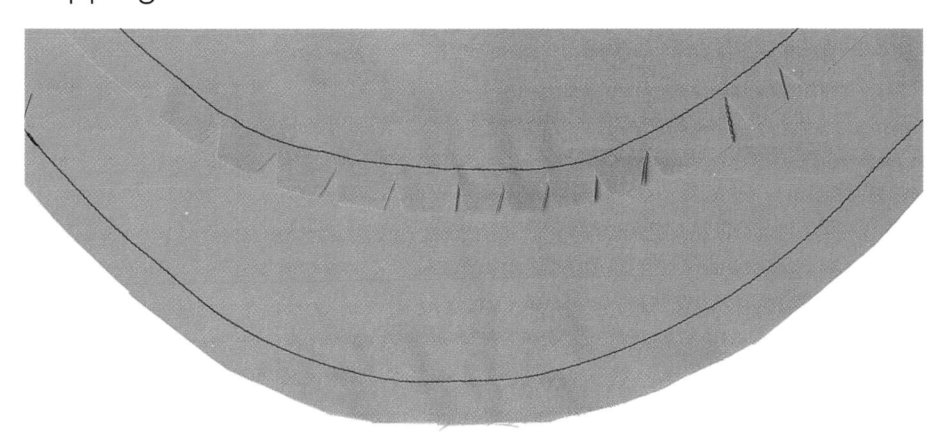

Convex curves need to have fabric removed to reduce bulk in the seam allowance. Using small sharp scissors, cut a series of notches up to but not through the stitching. The fabric will be flat when turned right side out.

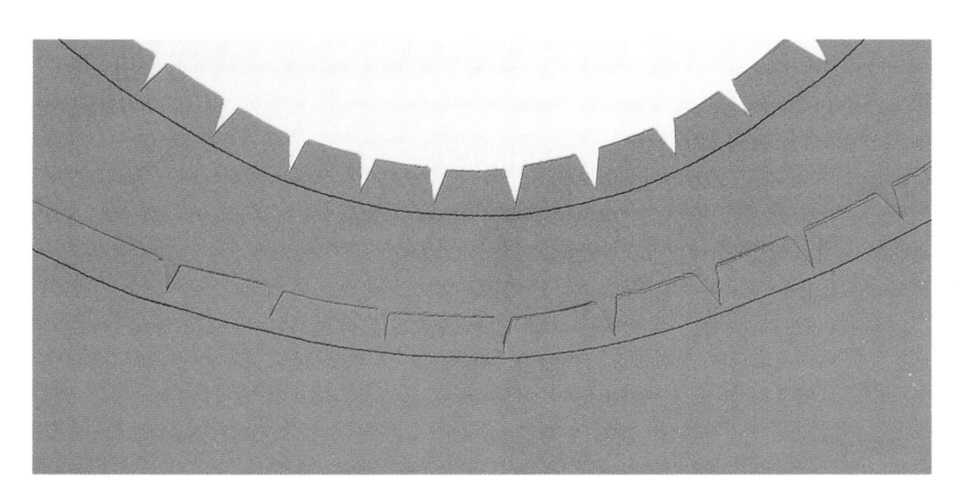

Concave curves need to have the tension eased, so use small sharp scissors to clip the seam allowance up to but not through the stitching. The seam can be pressed flat when the piece is turned right side out.

COMBINATION CURVES

To ease tension in a seam joining a concave curve to a convex one, clip the seam allowance at a right angle to the stitching and press the seam toward the convex side to make the piece lie flat.

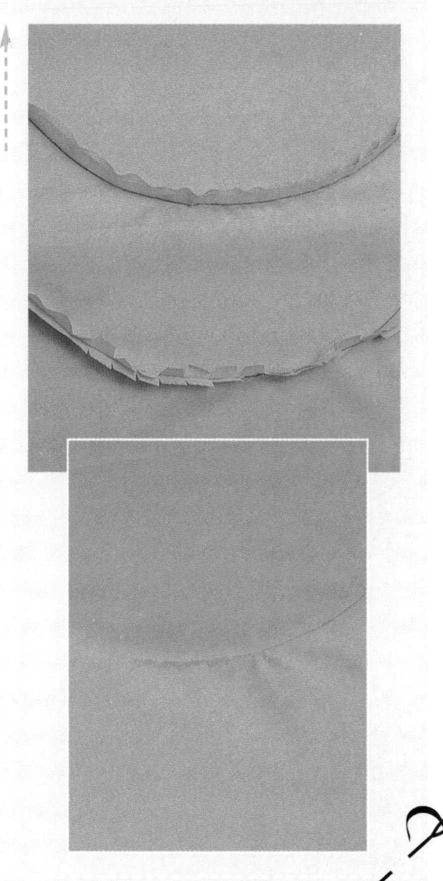

Edges

The raw edges on garments, accessories, and home furnishings must be finished to prevent them from fraying; often the finishing can be decorative. Although hems are the most usual way of finishing, binding with bias or straight strips of fabric is another useful method. Trims and borders such as piping, cording, and ruffles also make simple and attractive finishes for edges and seams. Creating your own edgings allows you a much greater choice of fabric, color, and pattern.

Making bias binding

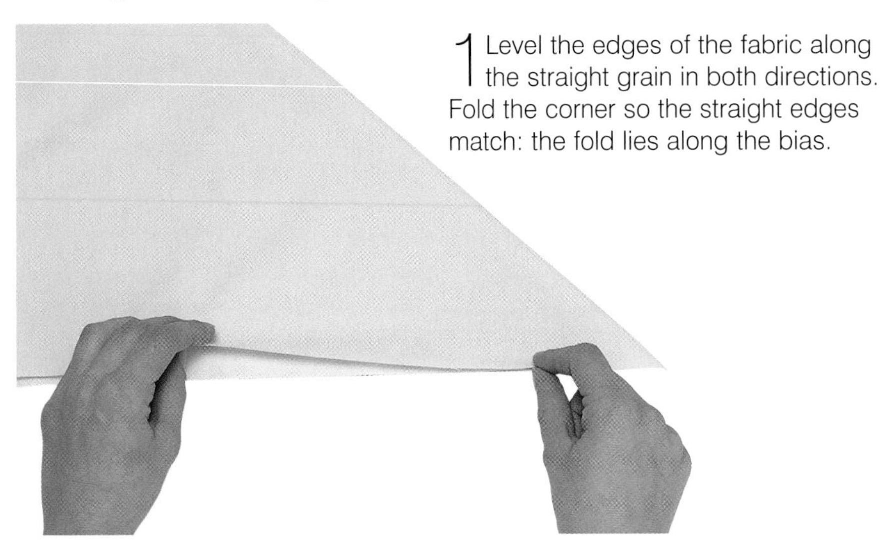

1 Level the edges of the fabric along the straight grain in both directions. Fold the corner so the straight edges match: the fold lies along the bias.

2 Cut along the fold. Mark parallel lines along the bias to the required width of the binding. Using a removable marker, number the rows as shown, staggering the numbers so the first row on the left-hand side is 1, the first row on the right-hand side is 2, the second row on the left is 2, the second row on the right is 3, and so on.

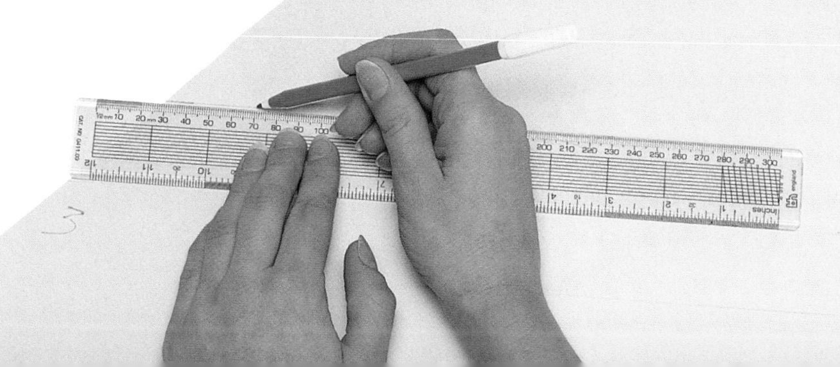

3 Fold the piece with right sides together. Stitch to join the numbered edges, matching the numbers—2 to 2, 3 to 3, 4 to 4, etc.—to make a tube. The strip numbered 1 and the final strip on the opposite side will not be stitched.

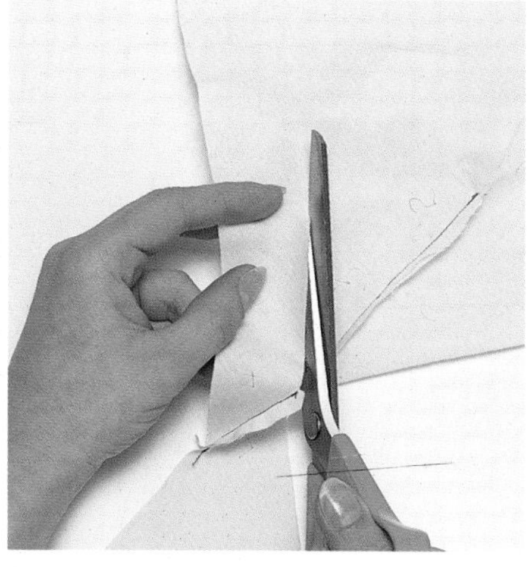

4 Press the seam open. Cut along the marked line on the tube, which is now marked as a continuous spiral running from one end of the tube to the other.

5 The finished bias binding strip is numbered in order at each seam. Remove all of the markings made on the fabric and press the seam again.

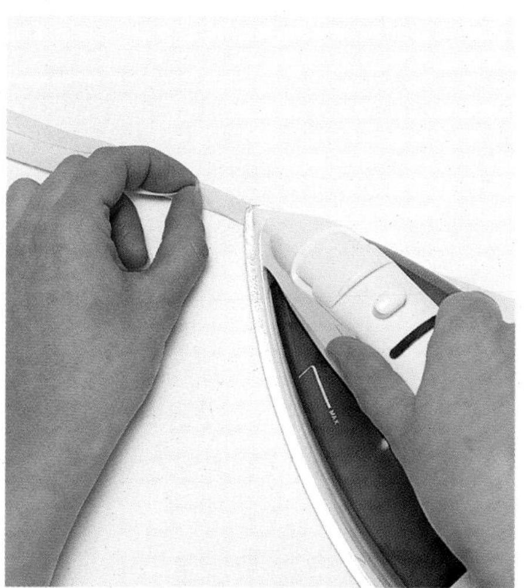

6 To finish, fold both long edges to the center and press them in place. Work carefully to prevent stretching. Fold and press the strip again, lengthwise along the center.

JOINING INDIVIDUAL STRIPS

1 To join two bias strips, pin the ends with right sides together. One strip will lie at a right angle to the other. Stitch a ½ in (1 cm) seam to join the strips.

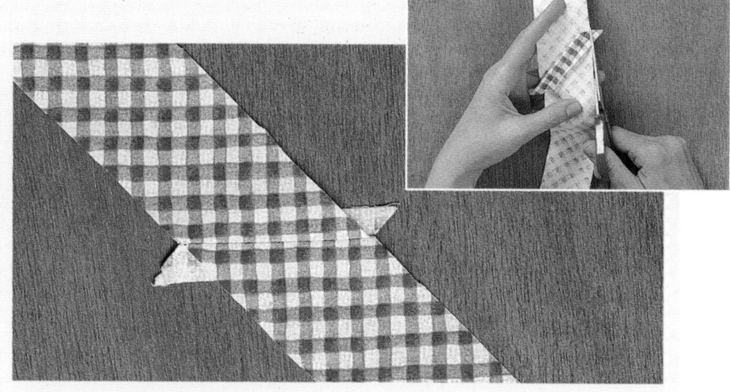

2 Press the seam open. Note that here the checked pattern was matched before the seam was stitched. Trim the points that stick out on each side (inset).

Binding a straight edge

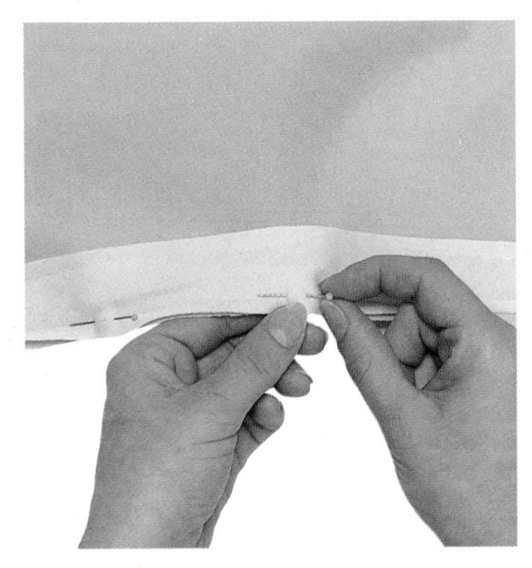

1 With right sides together and folds open, pin one edge of the binding to the raw edge of the fabric to be bound. Be careful not to stretch the binding or the fabric.

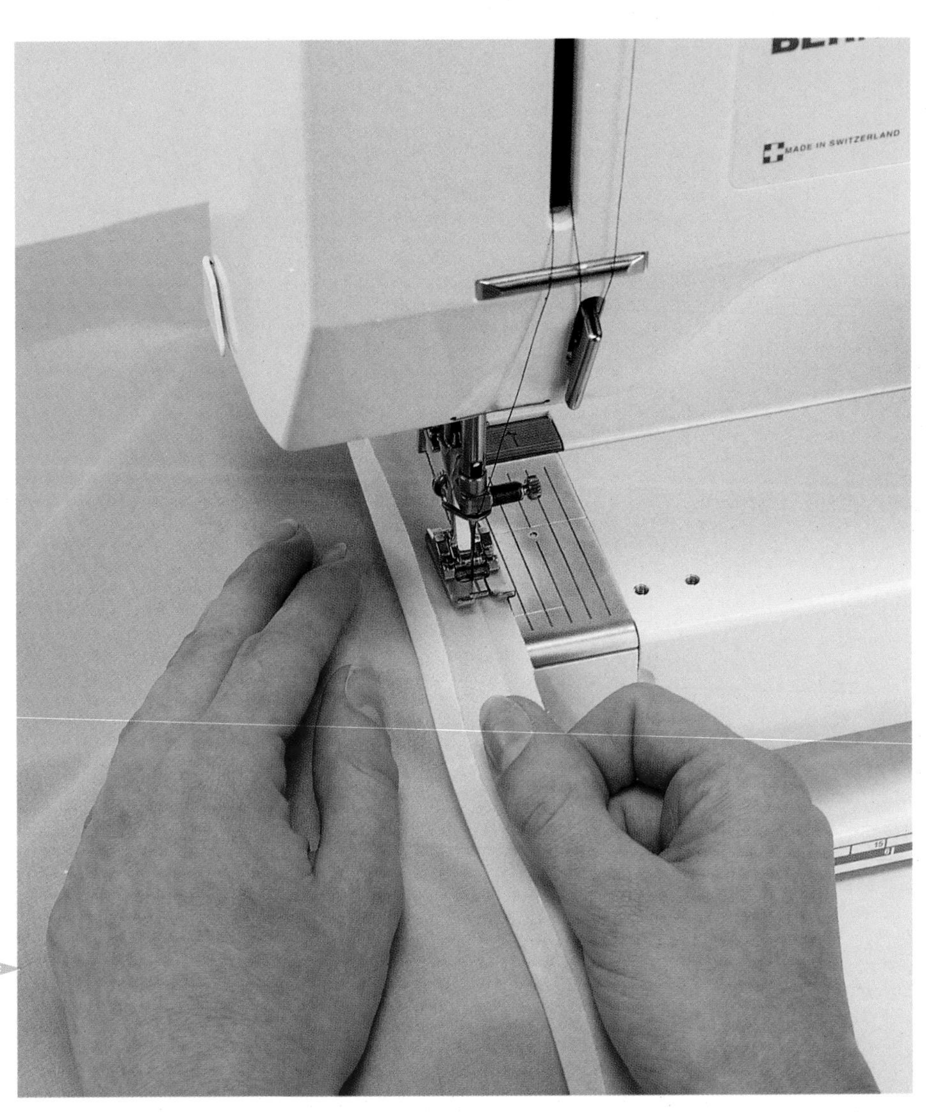

2 Machine-stitch along the foldline, taking care to remove the pins as you work. Gently press the seam toward the binding.

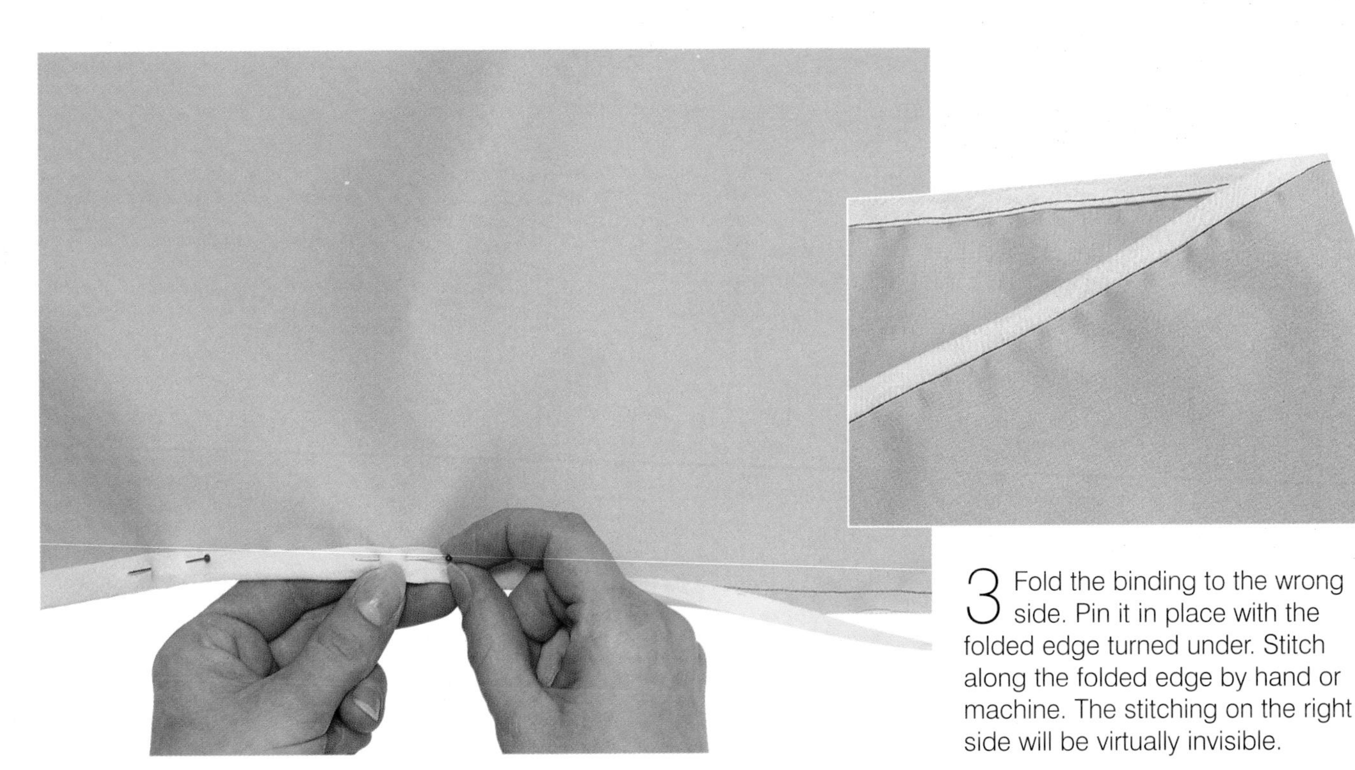

3 Fold the binding to the wrong side. Pin it in place with the folded edge turned under. Stitch along the folded edge by hand or machine. The stitching on the right side will be virtually invisible.

MAKING CURVED BORDERS

This edging is a border, not a binding. It is trickier to work than a binding, but it can give a highly professional finish to many home furnishings.

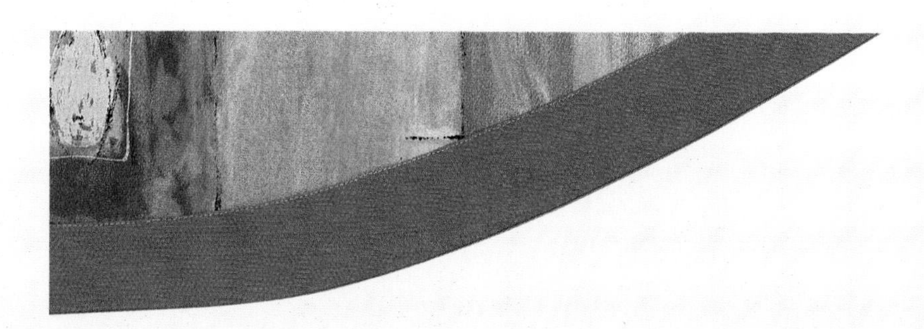

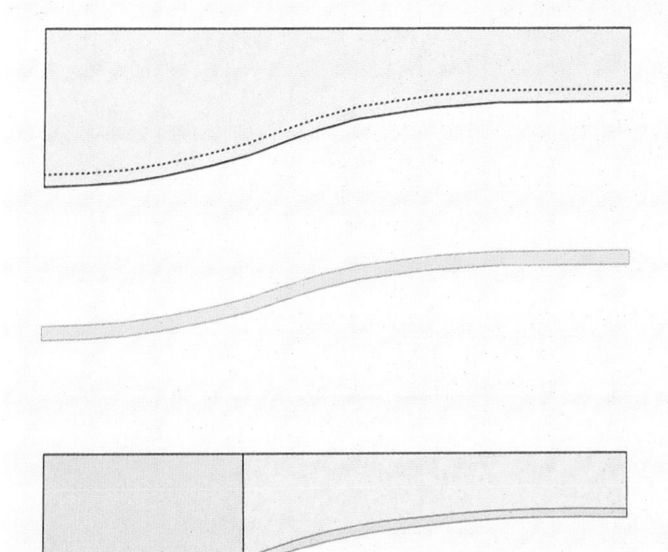

1 *Prepare a template from heavy paper and carefully cut out the main piece and the lining. Then draw a line along the curved edge of the template, measuring the final width of the border together with a 1¼ in (3 cm) seam allowance, ½ in (1 cm) on the top edge and ¾ in (2 cm) on the bottom edge.*

2 *Cut the strip from the template and use it to cut out the border in one single strip. Press under a ½ in (1 cm) fold along the top edge carefully—do not stretch the strip. Aligning the bottom raw edge to the bottom of the main piece, pin the border strip to the main piece right side up and topstitch it in place.*

3 *Repeat the process to make a border on the lining. Then place the main piece and lining right sides together and stitch along the bottom edge of the border to join them. Use scissors to clip the curve where necessary and press the fabric well so that the seam does not show on the main piece.*

MAKING INSERTED BORDERS

This type of straight border gives a neat professional finish to lined home furnishings, provided that the weight of fabric used for the border strip is similar to that of the main fabric. Note that the completed band is wider at the front than it is at the back.

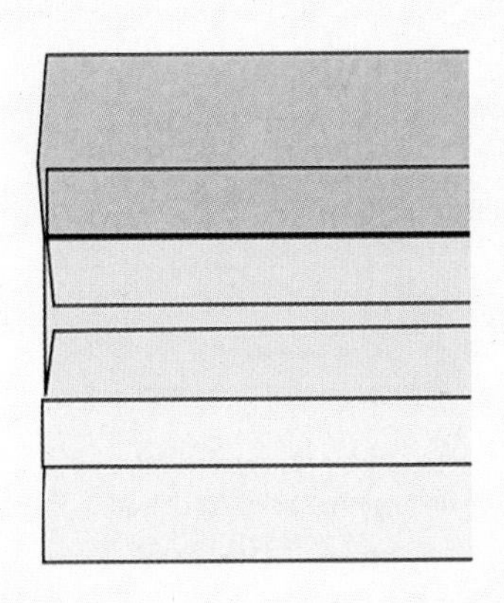

1 *The back side of the border measures 1¼ in (3 cm) whatever the front measurement. Cut the border strip the width of the front, plus the back (1¼ in/3 cm), plus ¾ in (2 cm) seam allowances on each long edge. Pin and stitch the border strip to the main fabric.*

2 *Pin and stitch the other raw edge of the border strip to the lining. Press both seams open. Measure the position of the fold and gently press it in place.*

Mitered binding

1 Join bias strips, cut four times the finished width of the binding, to make enough to edge your piece. Press the strip in half lengthwise.

2 Open out the pressed strip and fold the two long edges to the middle. Press carefully along the entire length of the strip.

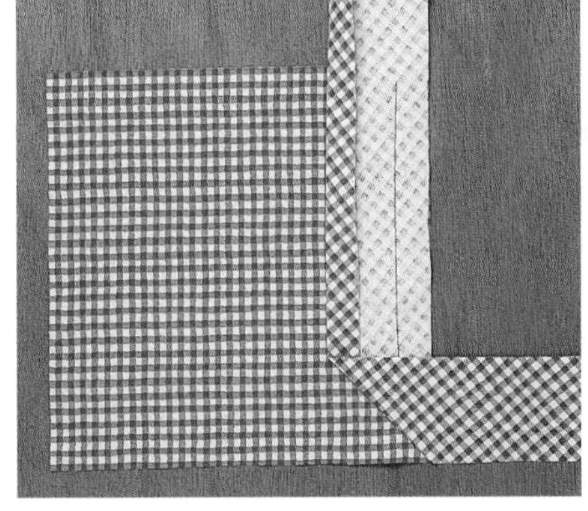

3 With right sides together, pin and stitch along the first fold. At the top of the seam, start stitching the width of the seam allowance down from the edge and stop at the seam allowance on the bottom edge.

4 Remove the piece from the machine and fold the strip away from the corner at a right angle to make a diagonal fold.

5 Fold the strip back over itself, aligning the raw edge of the binding with the next edge of the piece and making sure that the fold is level with the previously stitched side. Pin and stitch this edge as in step 3. Repeat this process to stitch the binding to all four sides of the piece.

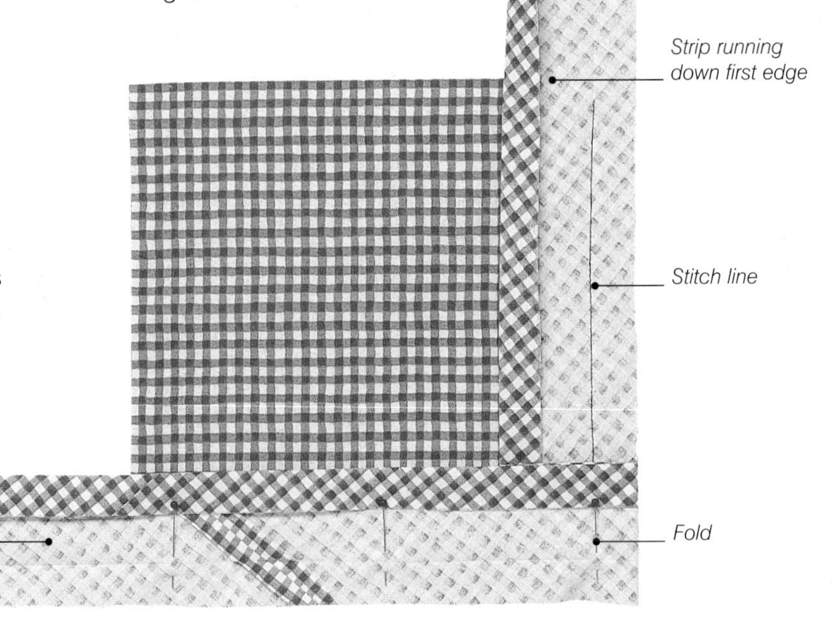

6 At the final corner, fold the binding strip as in step 4 and stitch up to the seam allowance. Place the end of the final strip under the first strip to be stitched.

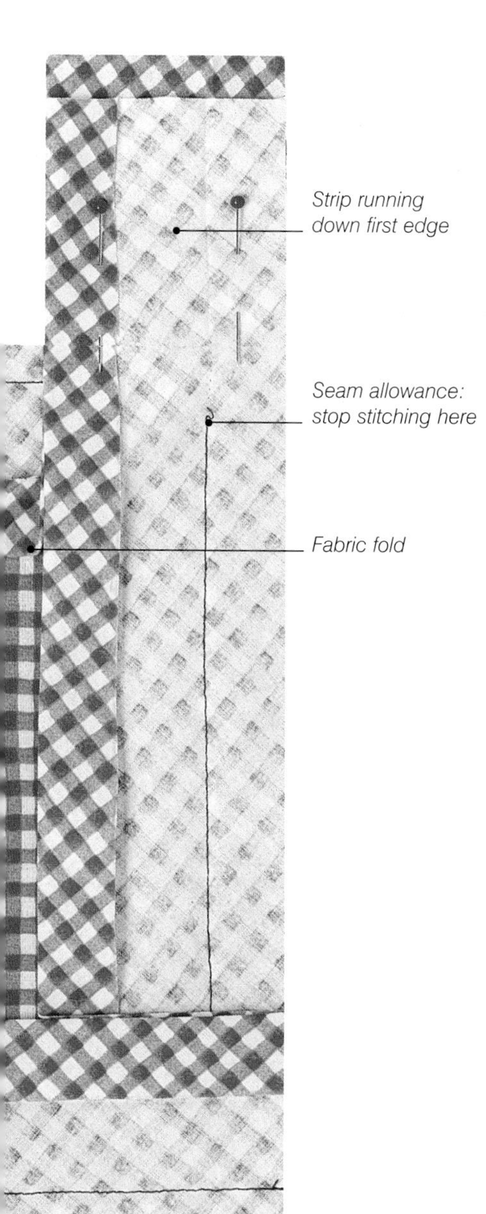

7 Turn the piece over and stitch the ends of the binding together, keeping close to the main fabric edge. Use scissors to trim off any excess fabric close to the seamline.

8 Fold the binding over the raw edges to the wrong side of the piece. A miter will automatically form on the right side of the piece.

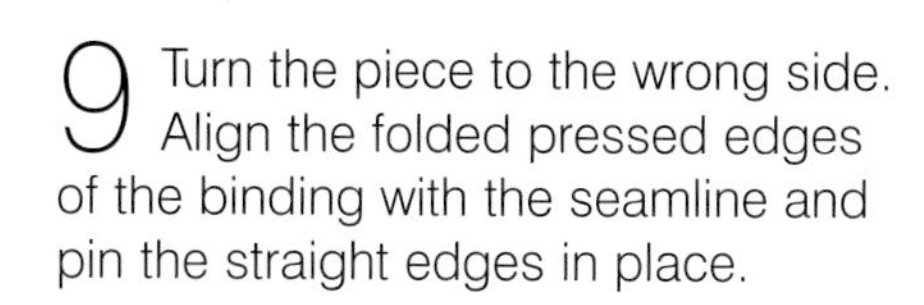

9 Turn the piece to the wrong side. Align the folded pressed edges of the binding with the seamline and pin the straight edges in place.

10 Fold a neat miter at each corner and pin in place. Using slipstitch (see page 28), sew along the folded edges and miters.

Piping

1 Bias strips for piping can be made by any technique you like; this quick method may speed up the process. Cut a square of fabric and mark opposite sides with the same letter, i.e. A opposite A and B opposite B. Then mark one corner 1½ in (4 cm) from the diagonal. Cut the square in half along one diagonal.

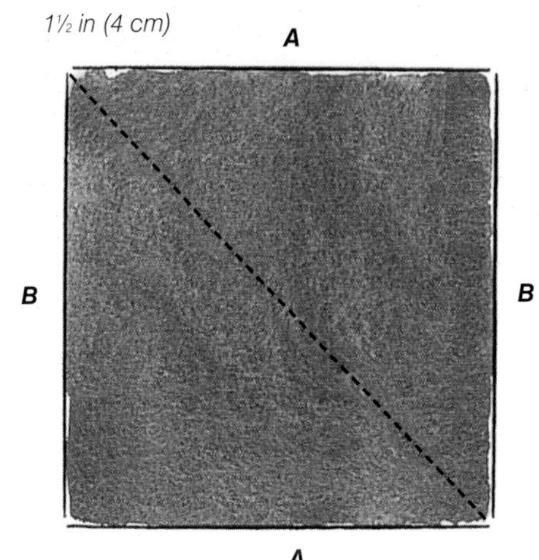

2 Pin with right sides together to join A to A. Stitch making a ⅝-in (1.5-cm) seam allowance.

3 Pin and stitch sides B and B together, matching the corner with the A to A seam, to make a ring of fabric. Press the seams open.

4 With the wrong side out, slip the ring of fabric over the wrist of your non-cutting hand. Starting at the 1½-in (4-cm) marking, carefully cut a strip of fabric at that width. Use a ruler to check the width from time to time, but don't worry if some variation in the width occurs occasionally. This can be easily trimmed to an even level.

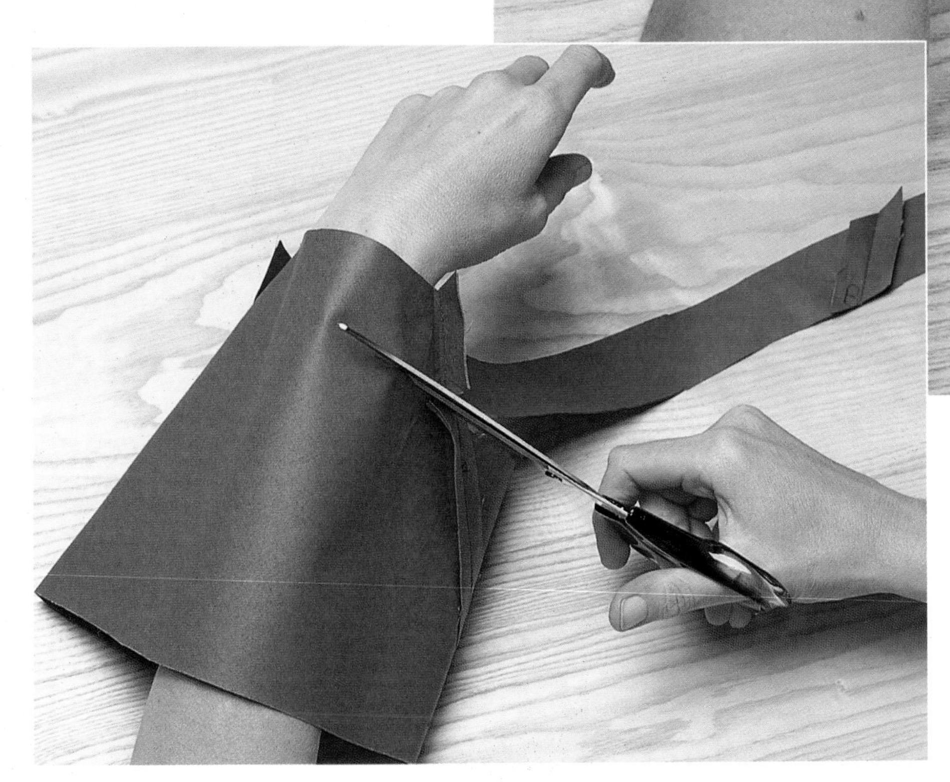

5 Fold the strip around a length of piping cord, with wrong sides together and raw edges aligned. Stitch as close to the cord as possible along the full length of the piping strip, which is now ready to use.

Applying piping or cording

Piping is a flat, doubled strip of fabric that works well with heavy fabrics. Cording is a cord enclosed in a strip of fabric with a seam allowance on one side, and gives extra strength to any edge that it decorates.

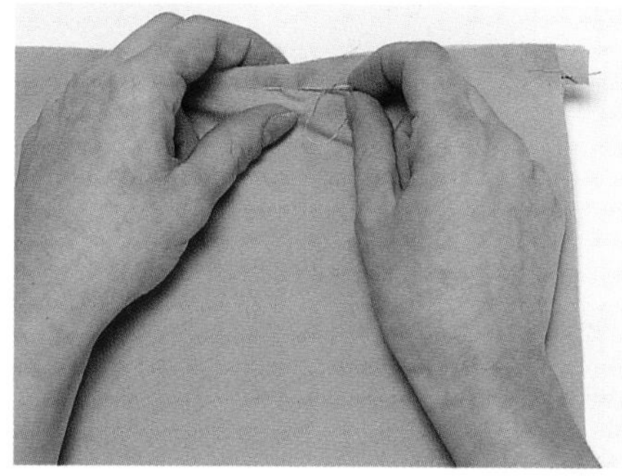

1 With right sides together and raw edges aligned, pin and baste the fabric pieces together along the seamline, with the piping or cording enclosed in the fabric.

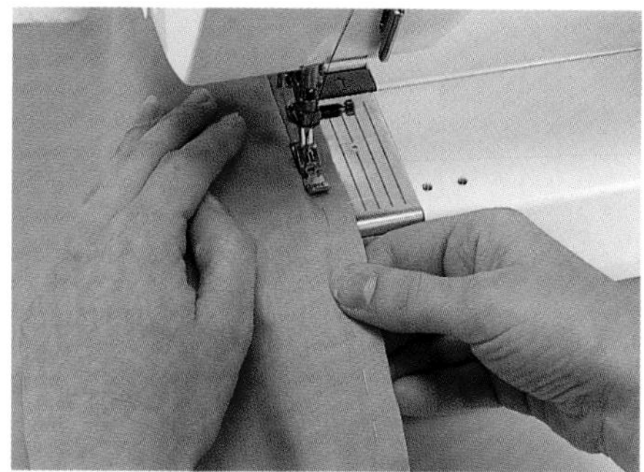

2 On the sewing machine, select a zipper foot for cording or a presser foot for piping, then stitch along the basted line.

3 Cording (top), creates a strong, sculptured edge, while piping (bottom) has a softer look.

Gathering

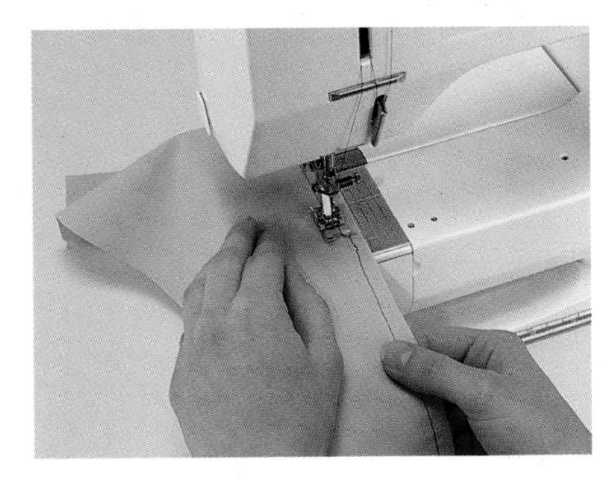

1 Mark and cut the fabric. Set the longest stitch length on the machine and make a double row of gathering stitch along the edge to be gathered (see page 33). Leave the threads long at both ends.

2 Separate each long thread from the others at one end and tie the two top threads together. Repeat with the two bottom threads.

3 Holding the ruffle along the stitched edge, hold the bobbin thread of each row at the untied end and gently pull along the entire length. Adjust the gathers evenly as you work until the fabric is gathered to the required length. Knot the thread ends to secure the gathers.

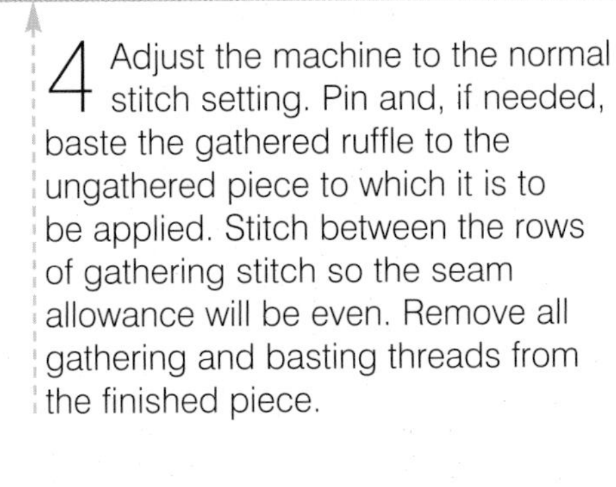

4 Adjust the machine to the normal stitch setting. Pin and, if needed, baste the gathered ruffle to the ungathered piece to which it is to be applied. Stitch between the rows of gathering stitch so the seam allowance will be even. Remove all gathering and basting threads from the finished piece.

Shirring

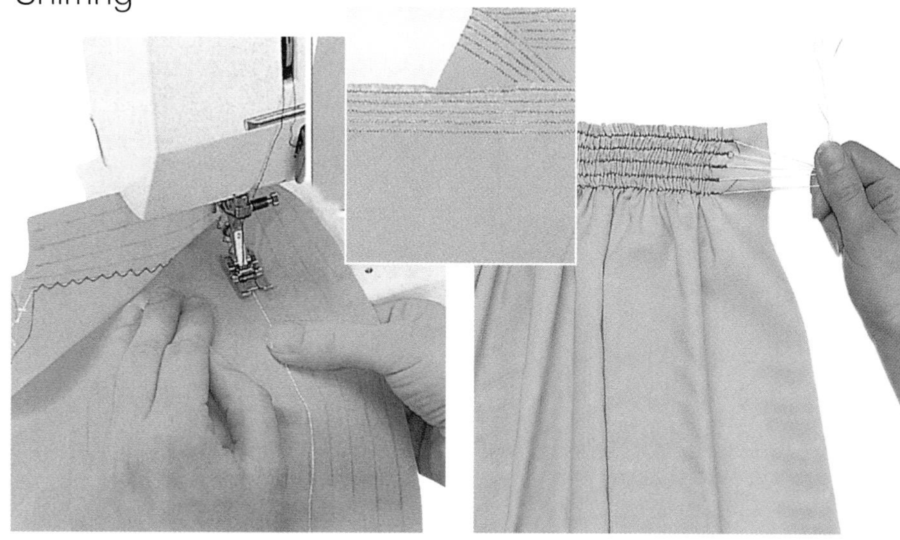

1 Mark the lines to be shirred on the fabric. Cut lengths of fine cord about 6 in (15 cm) longer than the fabric. Set the sewing machine on a wide, open zigzag stitch. Place a cord along each marked line, one at a time, and zigzag over the cord to secure it to the fabric. Backstitch at each end, taking care not to catch the cord in the stitches. Leave a length of cord free at the end of every row, and knot each cord separately at one end of the piece (inset).

2 Hold the fabric firmly at the knotted end and pull gently on the cords at the opposite end. Gather the piece up to the desired length and knot the free ends of the cords to secure the shirring. Then assemble the piece as required.

Double ruffles

Double ruffles can either be pleated or loosely gathered. Cut a strip twice the desired width, plus 2½ to 3 times the finished length. Fold the strip in half lengthwise, wrong sides together, then gather (see opposite) along the raw edges (center right) or pinch up small pleats as you work (top right). Press the finished strip lightly.

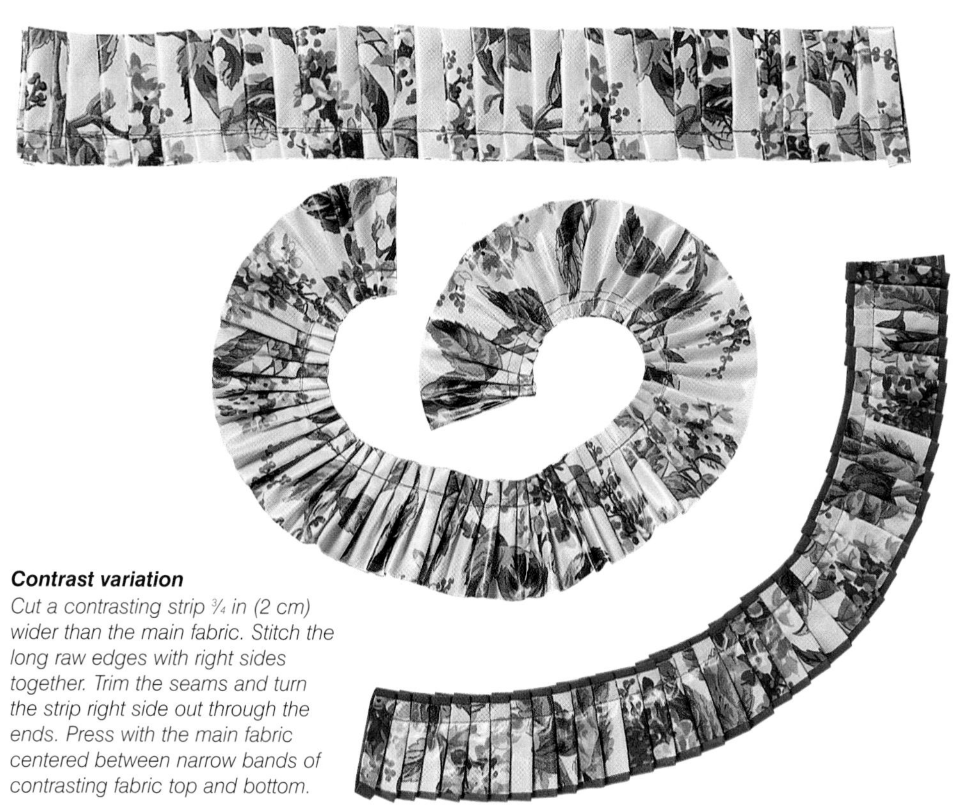

Contrast variation

Cut a contrasting strip ¾ in (2 cm) wider than the main fabric. Stitch the long raw edges with right sides together. Trim the seams and turn the strip right side out through the ends. Press with the main fabric centered between narrow bands of contrasting fabric top and bottom.

Tricks of the trade

BINDING SQUARE CORNERS

Although mitered binding gives a professional-looking finish, there may be occasions when you want corners to be squared, or when you are working with straight rather than bias binding strips, which are more difficult to miter neatly. Make two binding strips the finished length of the long sides of the piece to be bound; the two for the short sides must have a seam allowance added at each end.

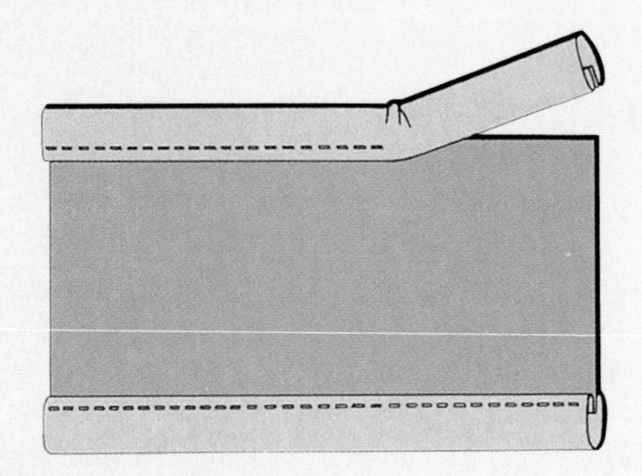

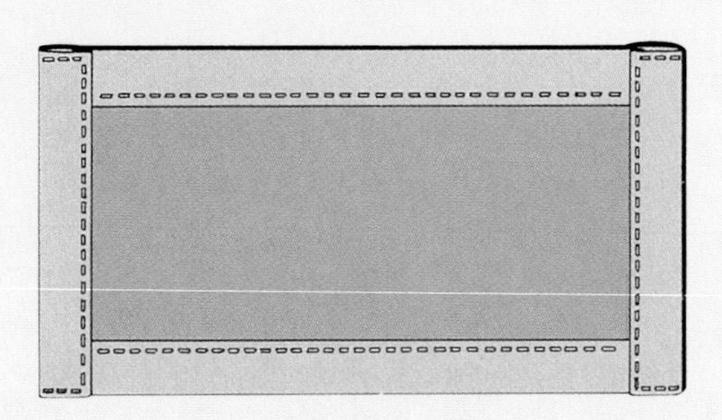

1 *Fold and press the strips in the center and then fold the raw edges into the center and press again (see page 42). Sew a long strip to each long edge (or on opposite sides of a square).*

2 *Sew a short strip to each of the remaining sides, making sure that the long strips are covered at the corners. Tuck the seam allowance under at each end and carefully stitch over each end to secure the corners and make a neat finish.*

INSERTING PIPING

Align the seam allowance of the piping or cording along the raw edge on the right side of one of the pieces to be joined. Pin and baste the other piece of fabric in place, with right sides together and facing the cording. Use a zipper foot to stitch just inside the seamline on the cording. Clip away excess seam allowance from the corners to reduce bulk.

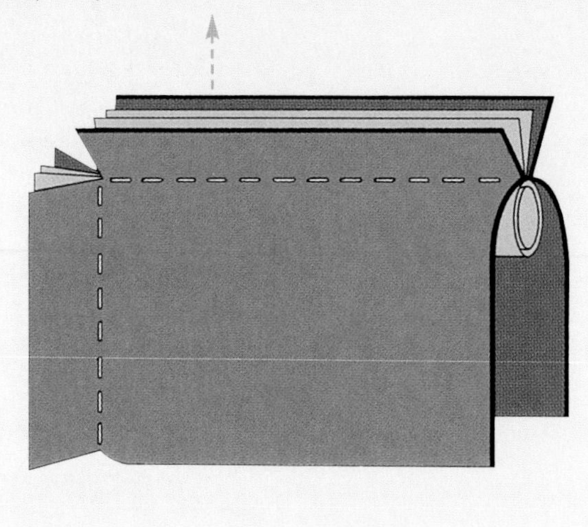

CONTRASTING BINDING

Adding a contrasting binding to home furnishings, particularly to the leading edge of curtains, gives them an attractive look. For best results, work with different fabrics of similar weight. The binding should be added after the pieces have been cut out, before they are assembled.

1 *Cut a strip the same length as the main fabric, plus ¾-in (2-cm) seam allowances, and the desired width, plus 1½-in (4-cm) seam allowances. Turn up the bottom edge of the strip ¾ in (2 cm) and fold it in half lengthwise, then press.*

2 *Pin the strip with right sides together and raw edges level with the leading edge of the curtain piece. Align the lower folded edge of the strip to the foldline for the bottom hem of the curtain or other piece. Stitch the seam from this hem toward the top, making a ¾-in (2-cm) seam allowance.*

3 *Turn the curtain over and press the seam toward the main fabric. Press under the seam allowance on the side hem of the curtain, below the contrasting strip. Working from left to right, use a line of herringbone stitch (see page 28) over the seam allowance to help hold the seam flat.*

4 *Fold the contrasting binding to the back and work a line of herringbone stitch through the folded edge of the strip to the reverse side of the curtain. Fold up the bottom curtain hem and hold it in place with slipstitch (see page 28), then secure the corner with uneven slipstitch (see page 29).*

Pressing

No matter how accurately you have stitched the seams or how fine the finish of the hems, pressing the piece as you work is the key to professional-looking results. Whether you decide to use a dry or steam iron depends on the type of fabric.

Pressing requires a different technique from ironing. It is done lightly, with just the tip of the iron being used on a specific area. Take care not to distort the fabric grain by pressing too heavily, and avoid pressing over zippers, pockets, or thick seams, as these are likely to leave unattractive marks on the right side of the fabric. Accurate pressing is crucial to mitering, while pressing markings such as tucks and pleats before stitching will make the piece much easier to work.

Flat seams are pressed on the wrong side of the fabric, after all pins and basting have been removed, to avoid leaving marks. Open the seam and slide the tip of the iron gently but firmly along its length.

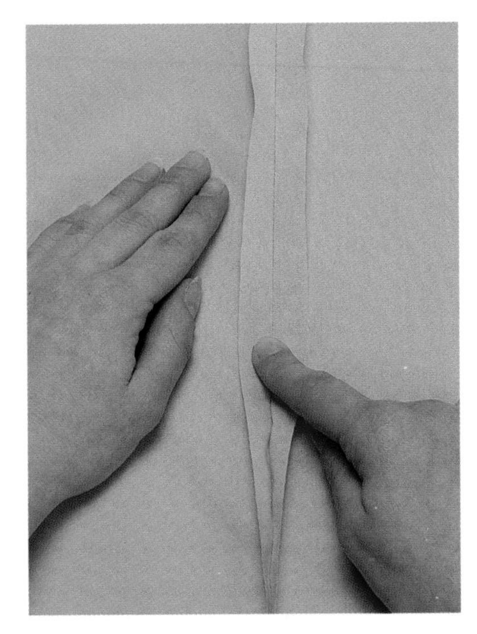

Fingerpressing is widely used in patchwork and when working with firmly woven or pile fabrics. Place the piece on a hard surface and run a fingertip along the length of the seam. Fingerpressing is not suitable for knitted fabrics or those that stretch or fray easily.

Hems of all kinds should be pressed from the fold toward the stitched edge. Leave the basting in place and press with the tip of the iron. Remove the basting and press again to remove any marks left by the threads.

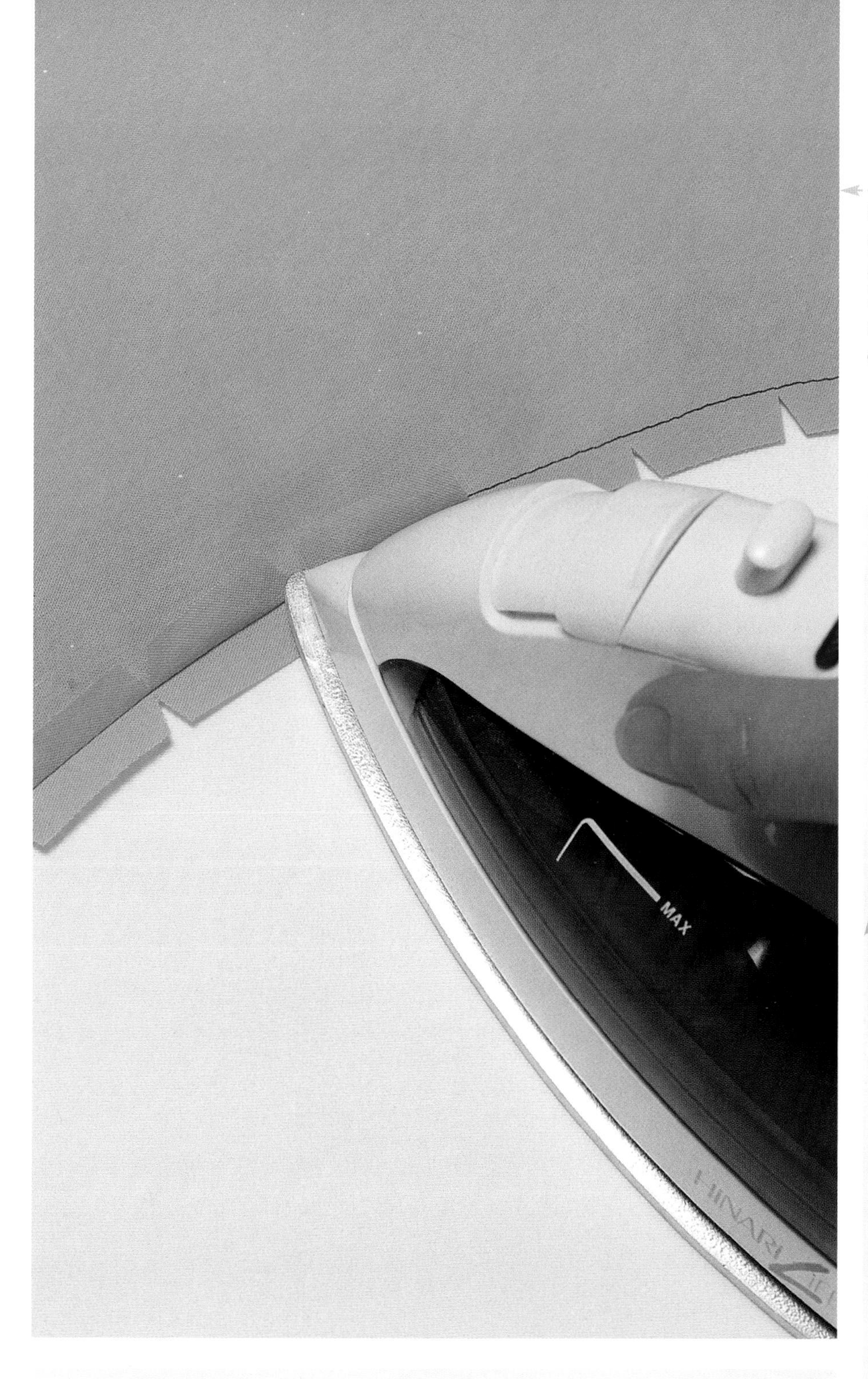

Clipped seams are pressed with the piece lying flat on the ironing board, and the wrong side facing upward. Using the point of the iron, press each section open, pressing the top layer of the seam back onto the fabric.

USING PAPER AND CLOTH

Pressing with paper prevents marks from appearing on the right side. Cut strips of brown paper and place one under the seam allowance on each side or between pleats before pressing.

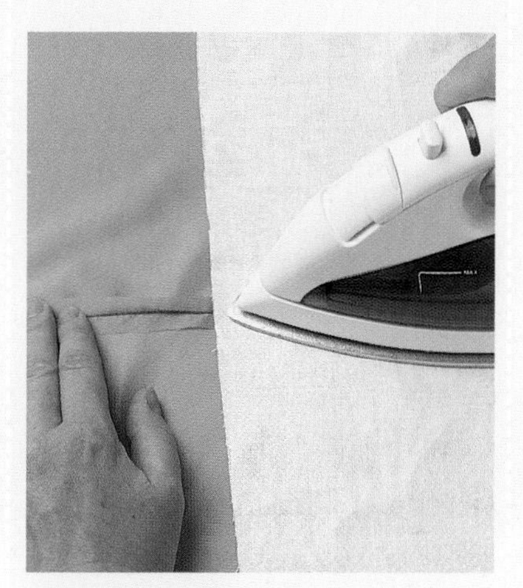

A press cloth can prevent the shine that can appear on many fabrics when they are pressed. Using clean cotton or linen sheeting, place the cloth on the fabric and press as usual. If you use a dry iron, dampen the cloth to create "safe" steam.

PRESSING CHART

HEAT	***FABRIC***
Low	*Acetate, shiny surfaces*
Low to Moderate	*Blends, Nylon, Pile/Nap, Polyester, Rayon, Silk*
Moderate	*Acrylic, Blends, Wool*
Moderate to High	*Cotton*
High	*Linen*

Dressmaking

This chapter breaks a typical garment into its component parts to show, step by step, how to make one of your choice. It starts from reading and cutting out a pattern, to constructing darts and facings, and includes all the other parts, from collar to hem. It also looks at suitable dressmaking fabrics, and includes simple projects with which you can practice your skills.

Patterns

Some people do not need to use a pattern when making garments, but most of us lack either the skill or the confidence to work without one. Certainly beginners in dressmaking are advised to use a commercial pattern until they understand how a piece of work is put together and appreciate the technical aspects of sewing.

Before purchasing a pattern, you have to know what size you need. Use a tape measure to record all the body measurements shown here. Keep your notes up to date, this information will be useful if you ever need to alter a pattern piece.

Front view

A few measurements can only be taken from the front, while those that encircle the body, such as the hips and waist, are taken from the front and the back. Measure sleeve length along the outside of the arm.

Back view

Most measurements taken from the back are simply continuations of encircling ones, but those like the back neck to waist must be measured from the back.

Side view

The outside leg is the most important side-view measurement and should be taken from the waist to the finished length of the trousers or slacks. Make certain that the crotch length is neither too tight nor too loose.

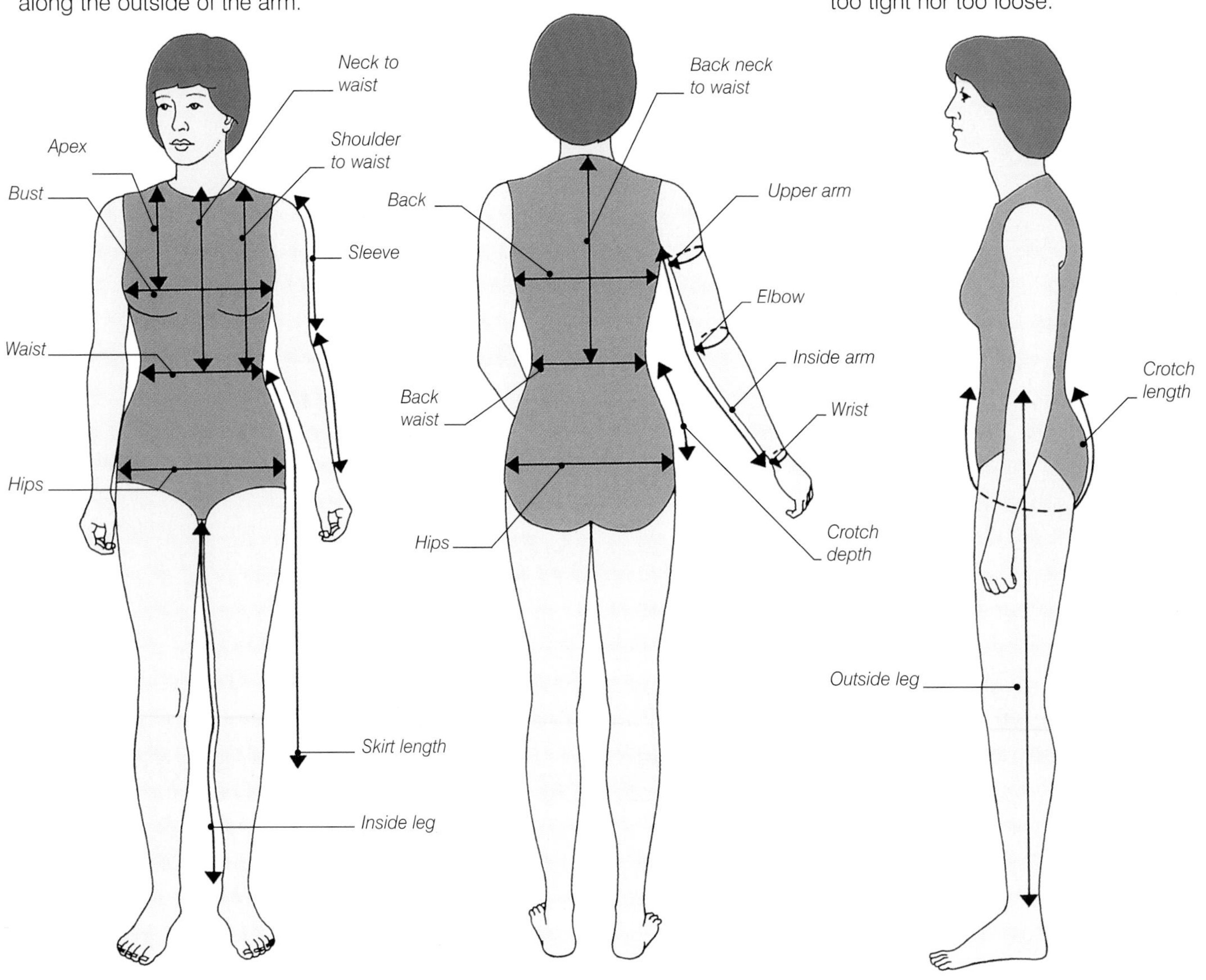

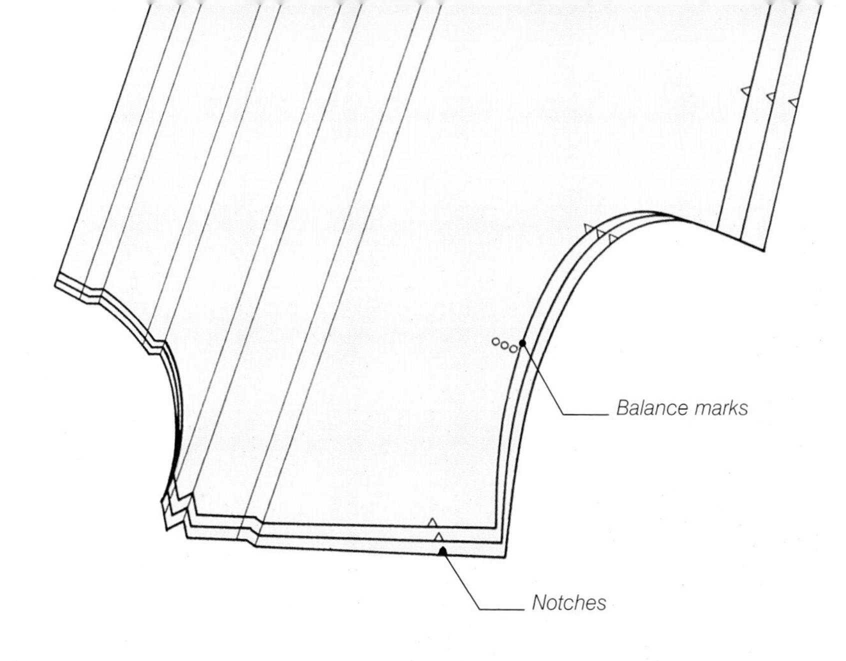

Using paper patterns

Pattern books are published seasonally with pictures of each garment or craft project, and distributed to fabric retailers so customers can choose patterns from them. They are sized according to regularly compiled average statistics and represent an idealized figure, not a totally realistic one. Alterations should be made before you cut out the fabric (see page 58), based on a thorough check of the measurements before you start work.

PLANNING A PATTERN

The instruction sheet that comes with a pattern has suggested layouts for pinning the pieces to the fabric. Make sure you understand the shadings on the layout that indicate right and wrong sides, lining, interfacings, etc. Then lay the fabric doubled with wrong sides together unless instructed otherwise, and arrange the pieces on it with all the pieces lying in the same direction. Make sure they all fit before you pin and cut.

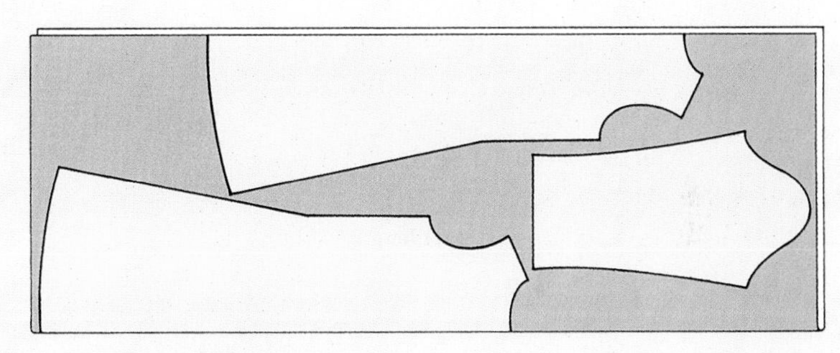

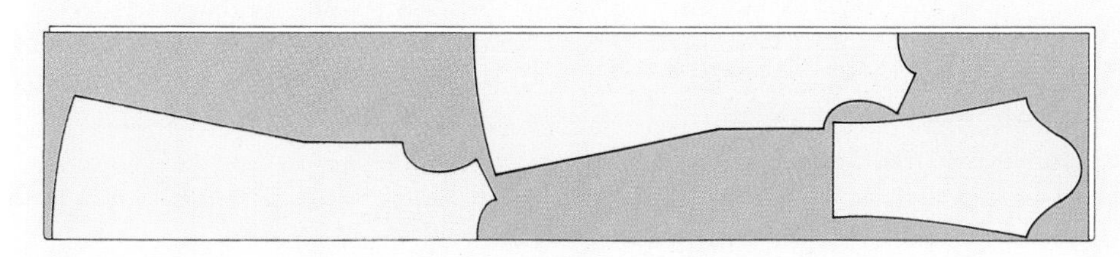

Layouts for different widths

Above is a layout for 45-in (115-cm) wide fabric. The layout below is for the same pattern pieces laid on a 36-in (90-cm) wide fabric.

PATTERN SYMBOLS

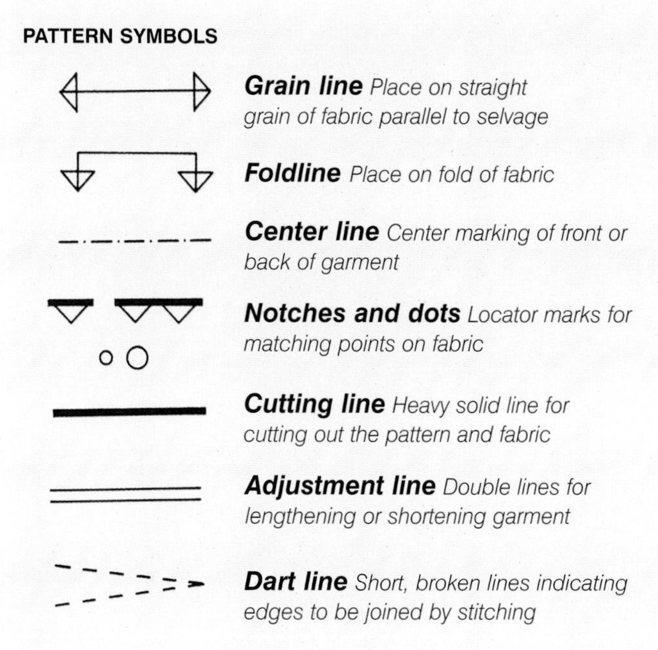

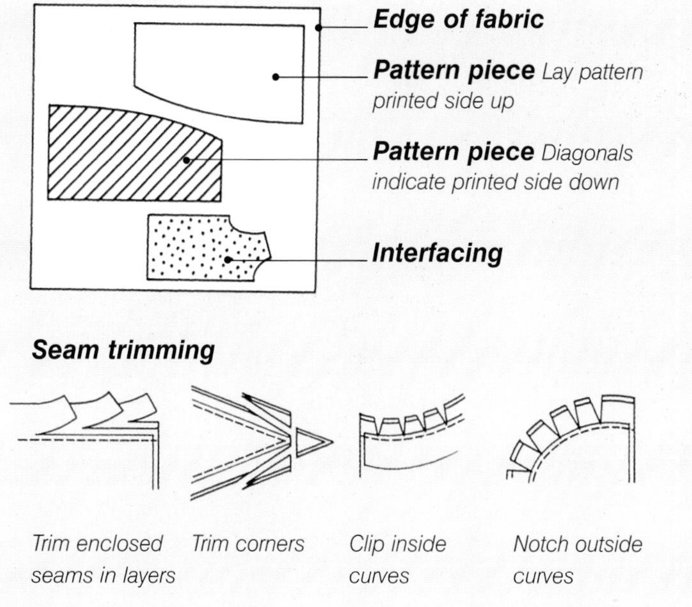

Pinning and cutting

Pattern paper is very delicate and must be handled carefully. Every pattern has a variety of markings (see page 57) to help you follow the instructions included with the pattern. Some, such as notches, are cut into the fabric when you cut out the pattern, while others must be transferred to the fabric (see page 59).

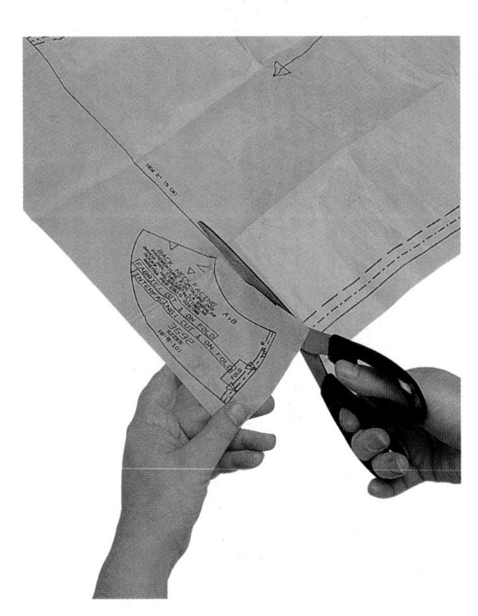

1 Cut out each piece of the pattern from the sheet supplied, but do not cut away the excess paper at this stage. Using the lowest temperature on the iron, press each pattern piece carefully to remove any creases.

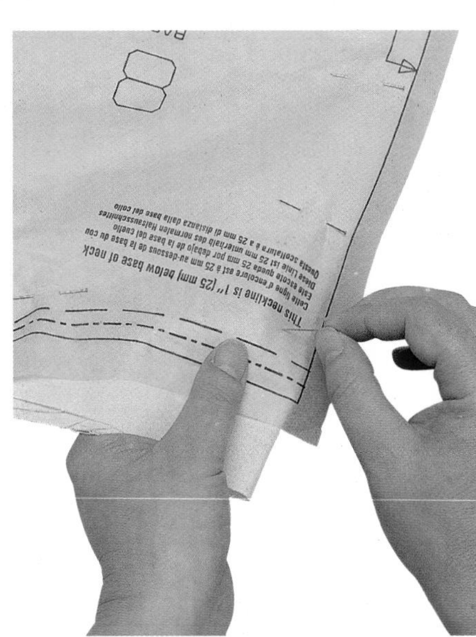

2 Pin each piece to the fabric, following the cutting layout. Pay close attention to the pattern markings to avoid mistakes.

MATCHING PATTERNS

Patterned fabrics should match at certain points to give a professional finish. Vertical stripes, for example, can be positioned to match on the shoulder seam; horizontal patterns should match from the waist seam upward. Always allow extra fabric for matching patterns.

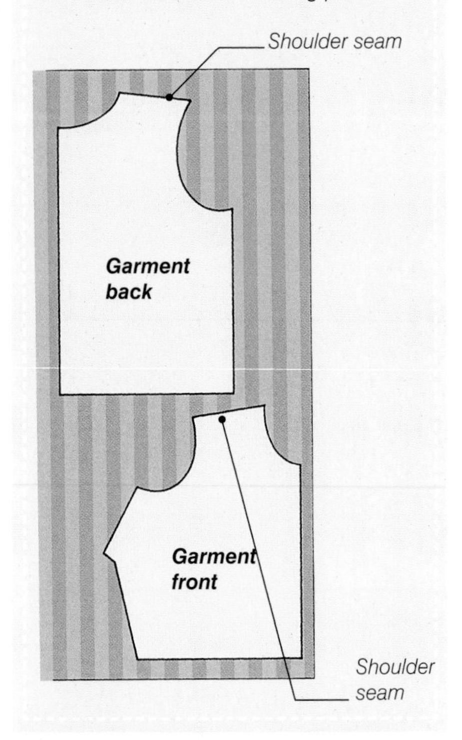

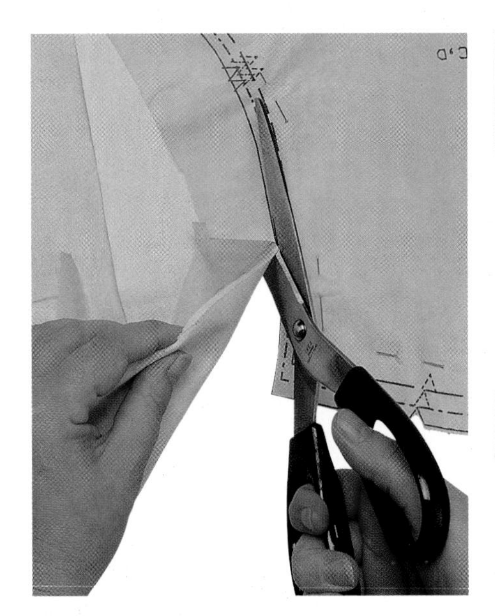

3 Using sharp dressmaker's shears, cut out the pattern and fabric for each piece, following the cutting line for the appropriate size. Discard the excess paper.

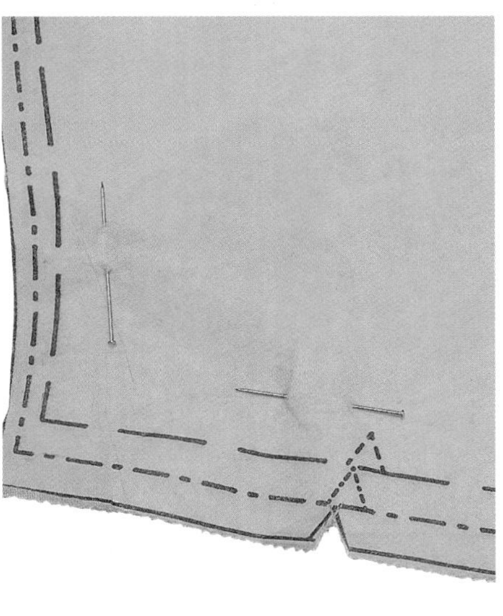

4 Notches may be arranged singly or in groups of two or more on the pattern. They are used to mark matching points in the seamline and will be hidden in the seam.

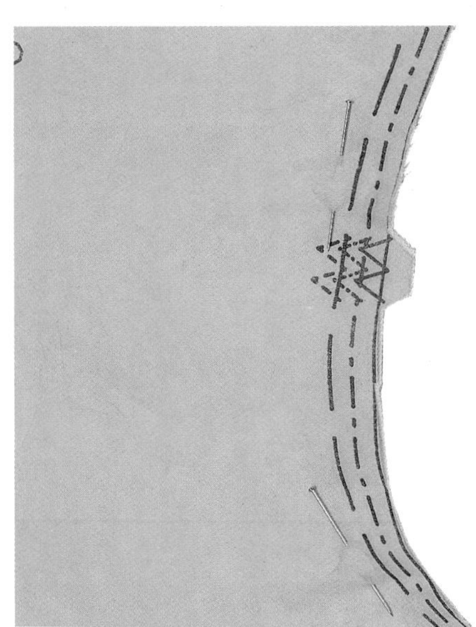

5 Notches can also be cut outward, a good idea for fabrics that fray easily. Double and triple notches can be cut as one unit instead of as two separate triangles.

Marking from patterns

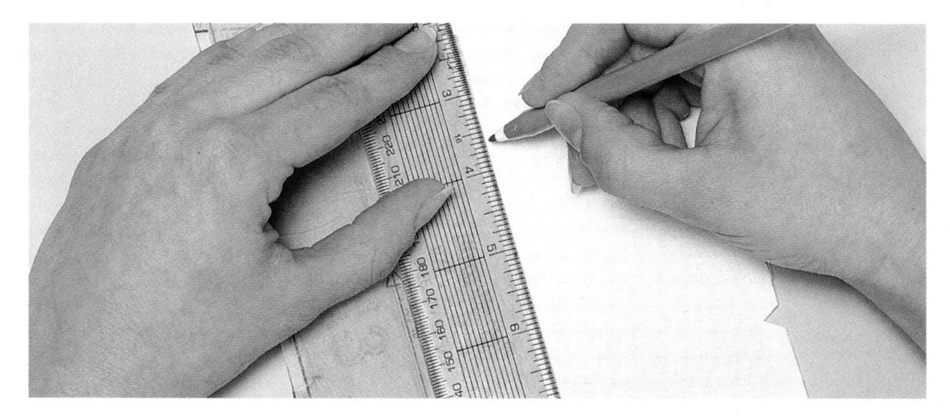

Water-soluble marker

Straight lines, indicated with dashes or dots, can be marked on washable fabrics using a ruler and a removable marker pen. Fold back the pattern along the line to be marked and position the ruler along the edge. Follow the pen manufacturer's instructions to remove the markings.

Tailor's chalk

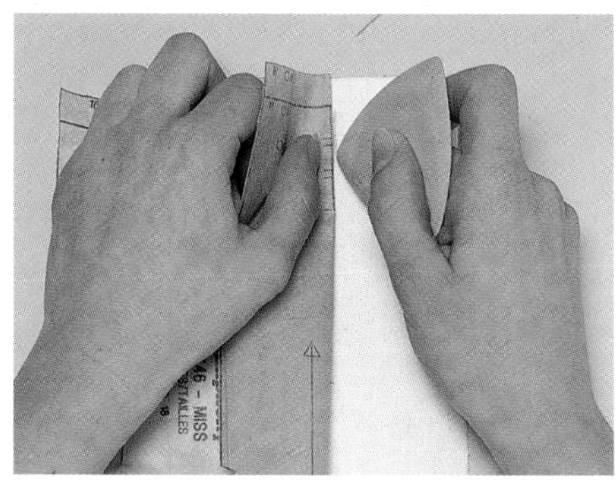

This traditional marker, which brushes off most fabrics, is available in a variety of colors so choose one that will show up on your material. Fold back the pattern and make marks next to the relevant lines.

Tailor's tacks

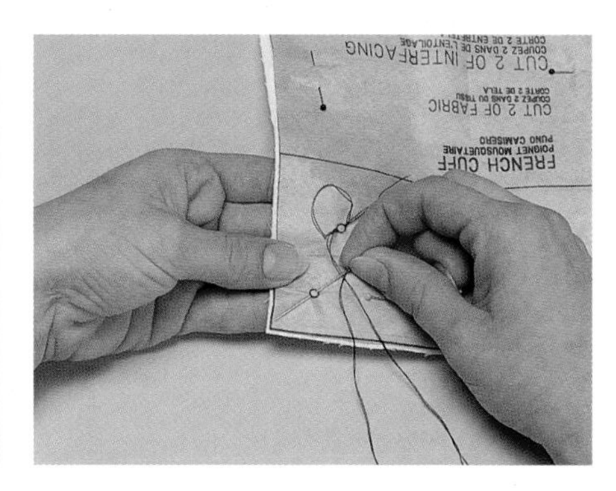

1 Tailor's tacks are useful for button positions and balance marks. Pin the pattern in place and stitch through all layers of paper and fabric using a doubled thread in a contrasting color. Make another stitch in the same spot and pull the thread to make a loop. Repeat to mark all points required.

2 When all the marks have been transferred, unpin the pattern and gently separate the layers of fabric, pulling to stretch the loops as far as they will go. Cut each loop carefully between the fabric layers, leaving the threads to mark the points.

Tracing wheel

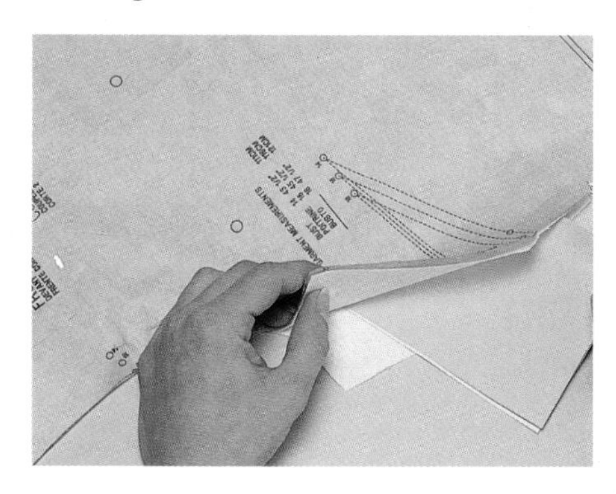

1 Unpin the pattern where the marks are to be made, but leave it attached to the fabric elsewhere. Slide a folded piece of contrasting dressmaker's carbon between the fabric layers on the wrong side as the carbon marks are indelible.

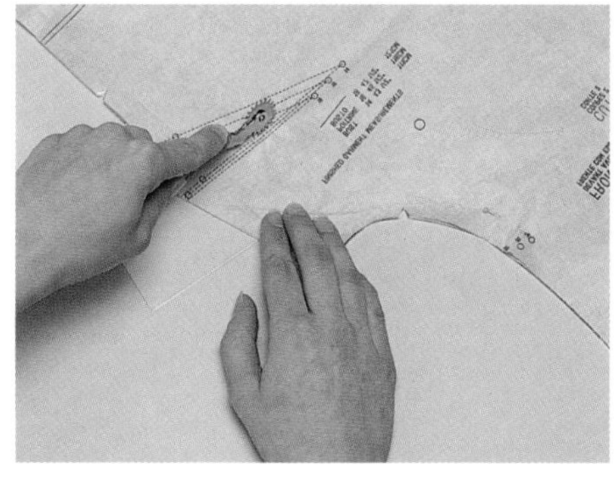

2 Hold the tracing wheel firmly and run the teeth along the seamline, dart, and other points to be marked. The wheel is useful for curved lines and darts, but weakens the pattern by making small holes in it.

Seam gauge

This handy little tool is a miniature ruler with a central slide that can be set to the width of the seam allowance. Hold the flat edge of the slide against the raw cut edge of the fabric and mark the seamline on the wrong side of the fabric.

Alterations

Standard pattern sizes often coincide with individual measurements, but some alteration is usually needed to achieve a perfect fit when you use commercial patterns. Indeed, being able to customize a garment is one of the advantages of sewing. Generally, a cut is made in the pattern and a new piece inserted to enlarge a measurement, or an overlap is folded to reduce a dimension. Each pattern piece has key points where reducing and enlarging need to be done.

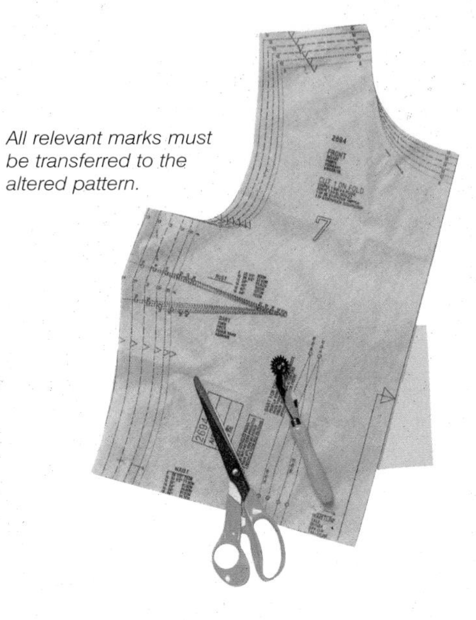

All relevant marks must be transferred to the altered pattern.

Where to measure

To achieve a perfect fit, you need to be aware of the crucial places where a pattern can be altered. Always use a flexible tape measure whether you are measuring people or pattern pieces.

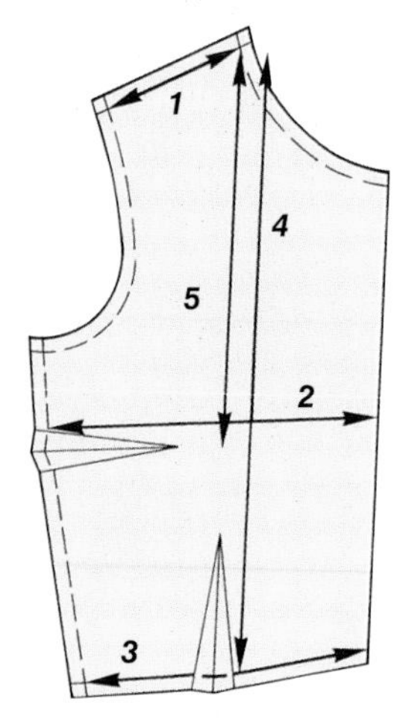

Bodice *Crucial measurements are shoulder (1), bust (2), waist (3), neck to waist (4), and neck to dart point on bust (5).*

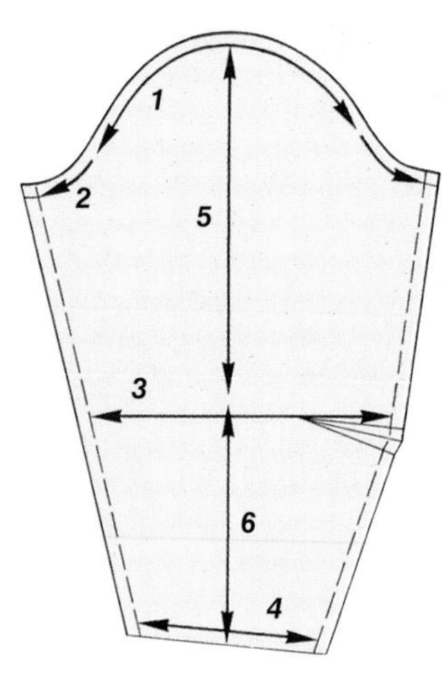

Sleeve *Crucial measurements are sleeve cap to balance marks (1), sleeve cap to underarm (2), elbow (3), wrist (4), shoulder to elbow (5), and elbow to wrist (6).*

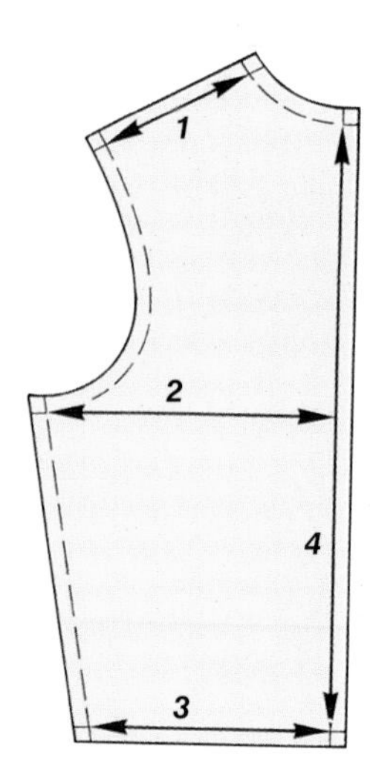

Bodice back *Crucial measurements are shoulder (1), underarm to center back (2), waist (3), and neck to waist (4).*

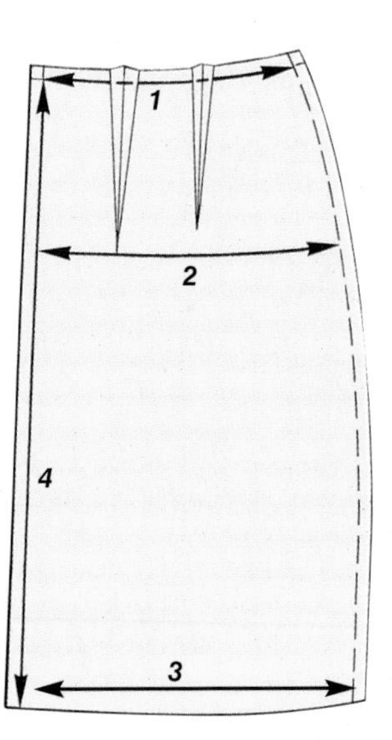

Skirt *Crucial measurements are waist (1), hips (2), hem (3), and waist to hem (4).*

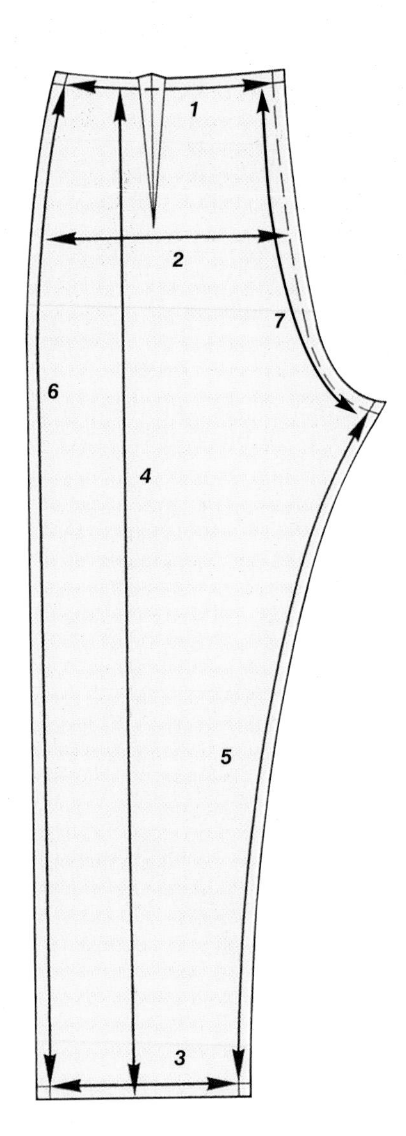

Trousers *Crucial measurements are waist (1), hips (2), hem (ankle) (3), waist to hem (4), inside leg (5), side seam length (6), and crotch (7).*

Altering paper patterns

To reduce the size of a commercial pattern, you can fold a crease in the piece and secure it in place with pins or tape. To enlarge a pattern that will only be used once, you can pin or tape strips of heavy paper carefully to vents cut into the pattern piece. Then pin and cut out as usual.

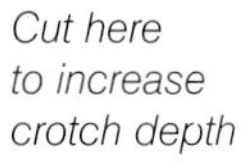
Cut here to increase crotch depth

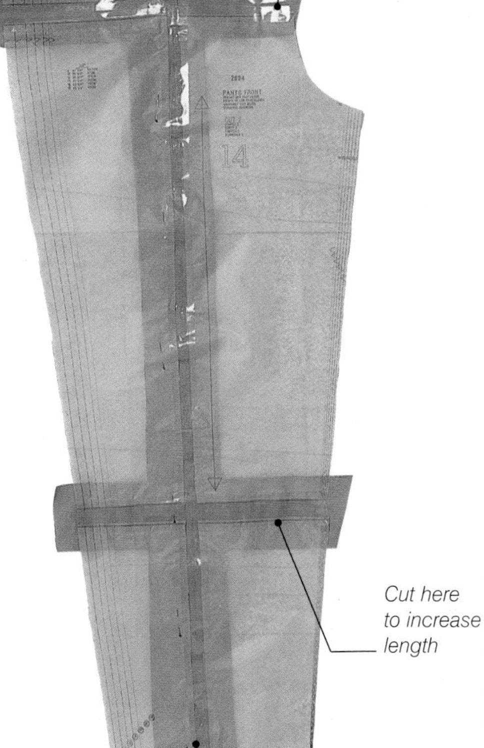
Cut here to increase length

Cut here to increase overall width

Increasing sleeve cap size
To increase sleeve cap size, or to make a full gathered sleeve cap from a more tailored one, cut the pattern from the center balance mark on the sleeve cap. Pin or tape a full width of paper into the full depth of the vent.

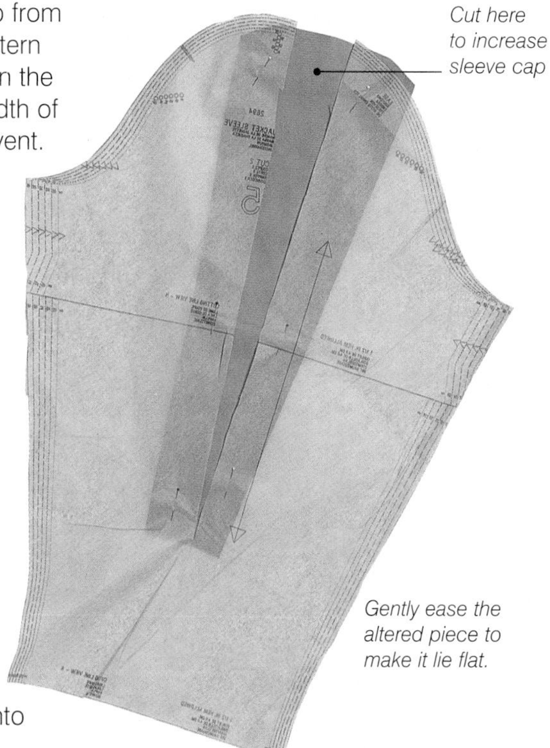
Cut here to increase sleeve cap

Gently ease the altered piece to make it lie flat.

Increasing width and length
To increase width, cut the pattern along the full length from waist to hem. Do not cut into a dart or other waist marking.

TAPING PAPER VENTS

When you enlarge a paper pattern, use transparent tape so that any markings can be read. Make sure the new paper strip is longer and wider than the cut, and tape it on both sides, front and back, to strengthen the altered pattern piece. Smooth the pattern piece carefully as you work to keep it from bobbling.

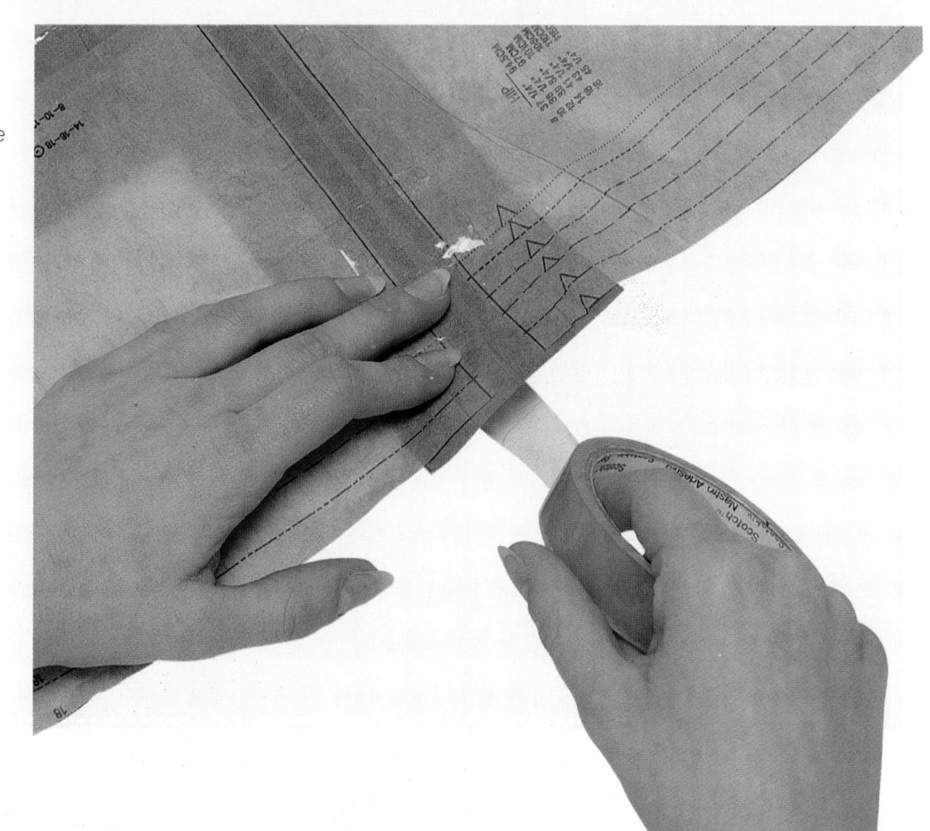

Using a toile

Cutting a pattern from inexpensive cotton fabric means that it can be used more than once. To make a toile, or fabric pattern, pin the paper pattern to the fabric, cut it out, and transfer all the crucial markings. Decide where you need to reduce or enlarge and either cut into the fabric pattern and insert strips of fabric to enlarge, or fold over excess fabric and pin it in place to reduce the dimensions. Try the piece on to check that the fit is comfortable. Note that in the illustrations, a contrasting fabric has been used for the strips to make the method easy to see.

To reduce skirt fullness cut from the hem to the hipline of the pattern. Avoid cutting through any darts or other markings. Overlap the cut edges until the required width is reached and pin or baste them in place (left). The reduced piece can now be pinned to the garment fabric and cut out and marked as usual (right).

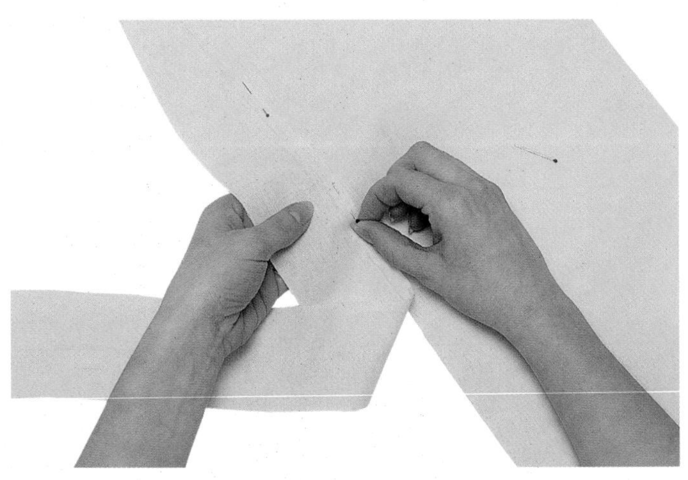

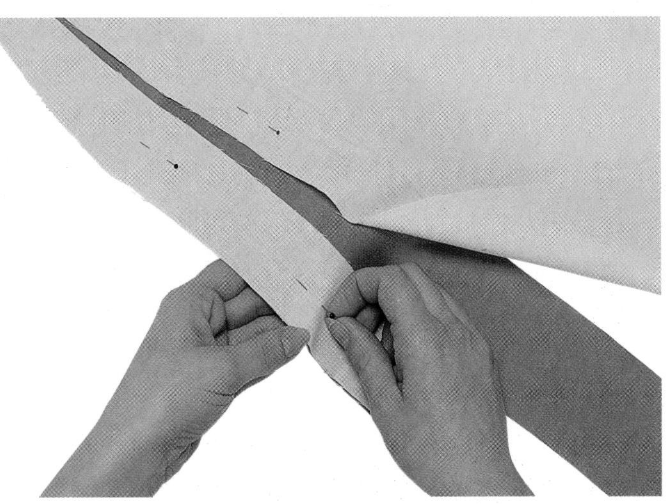

To increase skirt fullness cut from the hem to the hipline of the pattern and cut a strip of similar fabric wider than the required increase. Starting at the top of the cut vent, pin the fabric strip in place along both cut edges until the desired width has been reached (left). Baste the pinned edges to secure them if you wish. The enlarged pattern can now be pinned and cut out as usual (right).

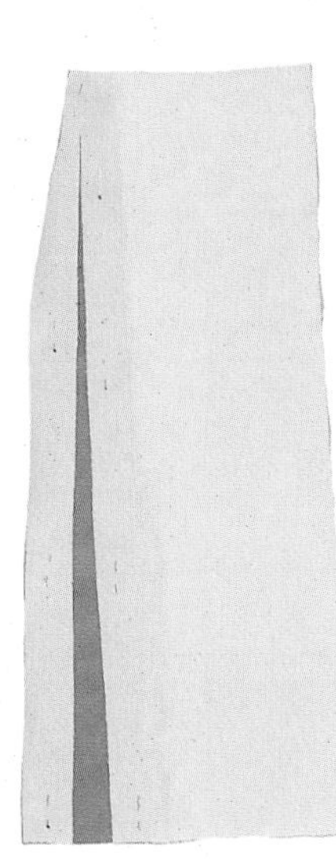

To increase crotch depth on a pattern, cut from the center seam almost to the seamline on the side. Work above the curved area of the center seam and below any darts or other waistline markings. Pin a strip of fabric along the vent until the required depth is reached (left). Even up the cutting line by marking a straight line on the strip and trimming the excess fabric away (right).

Reducing bodice fullness

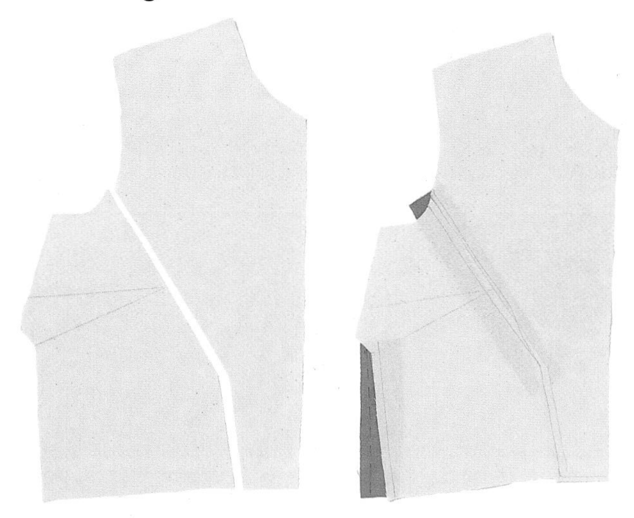

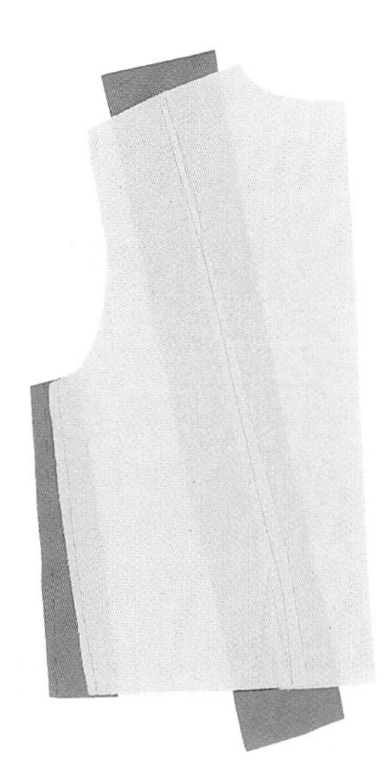

Altering the front Mark any darts and other markings before cutting into the fabric pattern. Cut up from the waist almost parallel to the center seam, then across on a diagonal line that ends above the bottom curve of the armhole and avoids the point of the dart (left). Overlap the cut edges of the pattern and pin or baste it into position. Add an extra strip of fabric to the side seam if necessary to even up the edge (right).

Altering the back Cut from the waist almost parallel to the center back seam. Then cut at a sharper angle to finish near the middle of the shoulder seam, again avoiding cutting through any crucial markings (left). Overlap the cut edges and pin it into position. If the overlap is very narrow, anchor it to a backing strip of fabric to secure it. Add a strip of fabric to the side seam to even it up if necessary (right).

Increasing bodice fullness

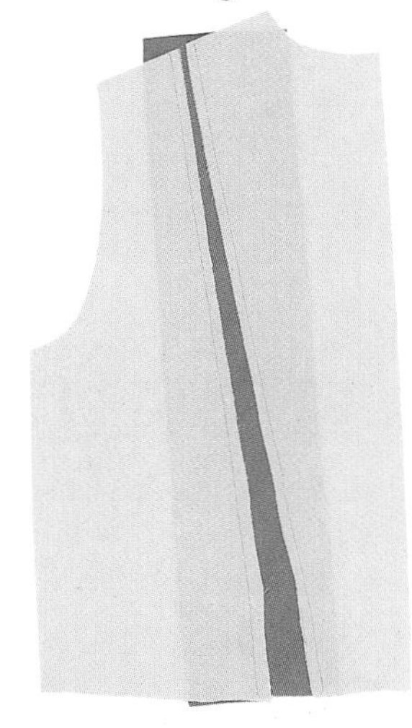

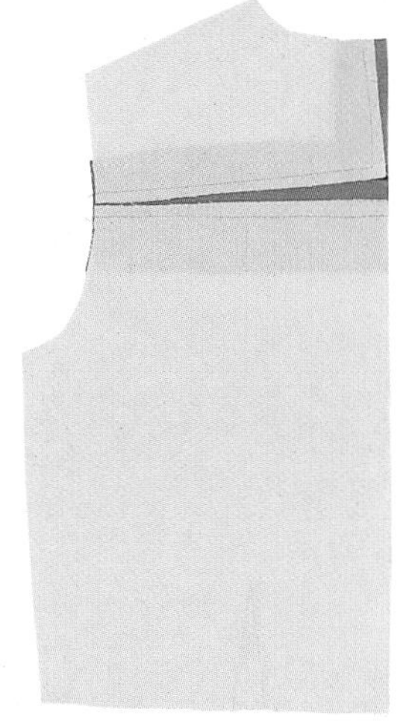

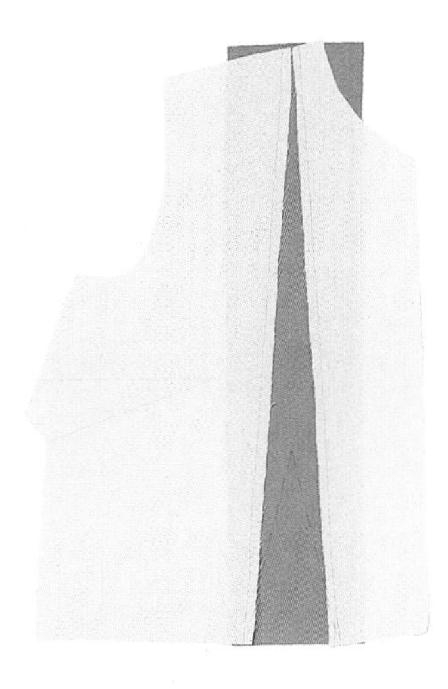

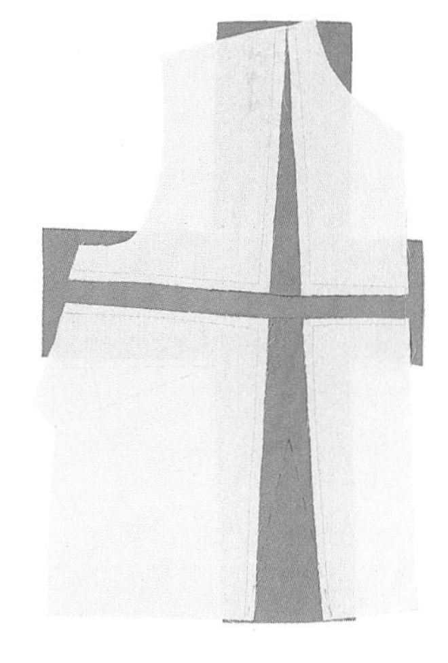

Altering width on the back Always cut from the waist to the shoulder seam. Cut a strip of fabric that is wide enough to lie flat under the cut edges of the pattern. Adjust the size as necessary, then pin and stitch the strip into position.

Altering length on the back Cut from the center back to finish between the shoulder and underarm curve. Pin and stitch a strip of fabric as required. You may find it necessary to add a vertical strip to even the center back cutting line.

Altering width on the front Cut from the waist to the shoulder seam, avoiding any crucial measurements like darts. Cut and pin a strip of fabric to the cut edges of the pattern, then stitch the strip into position as shown.

Altering length and width on the front Widen the fabric pattern as shown above left and then cut it into two pieces between the armhole and bustline dart. Pin a fabric strip in place and stitch to secure it. Even up all cutting lines on the enlarged piece.

Choosing fabrics

Fabric is the dressmaker's creative medium. The choices available are so vast that selecting the right material can be confusing. To produce a garment you will be happy with, it is important to choose the most suitable fabric for the design.

The best way to learn about fabric is to work with it, but first get to know its look and feel. Seek out and visit different suppliers where you can compare and handle a whole range of fabrics, to find out which ones appeal to you most *(see also pages 20-21).*

NATURAL FABRICS

These fabrics are made from fibers that occur in nature: cotton, linen, silk, and the wool of animals such as sheep, llamas, and some rabbits. Each type varies in weight, weave, and use. All can be dry-cleaned, and many can be laundered. Always check cleaning instructions when you purchase fabric.

Wool

Warm and absorbent, wool is produced in a variety of weights and weaves, and can be woven or knitted. Wool for home sewing varies from lightweight Viyella® (which is a blend of wool and cotton) to gabardine for jackets and suits. Wool fleece can be used to make or line coats, and mohair and angora are luxurious, long-fibered wools used for woven and knitted fabrics. Some wools can be washed by hand, but avoid wringing or squeezing them; most types of wool should be dry-cleaned.

Cotton

Made from the fibers of the cotton plant, cotton takes many forms, from sheer gauze (butter muslin) and lightweight lawn to thick, sturdy corduroy and denim. Cotton takes dye well and is easy to launder. It can be woven in patterns, particularly checks and plaids, or designs can be stamped on after weaving. As a knitted fabric, it is soft and supple, and it hangs and washes well.

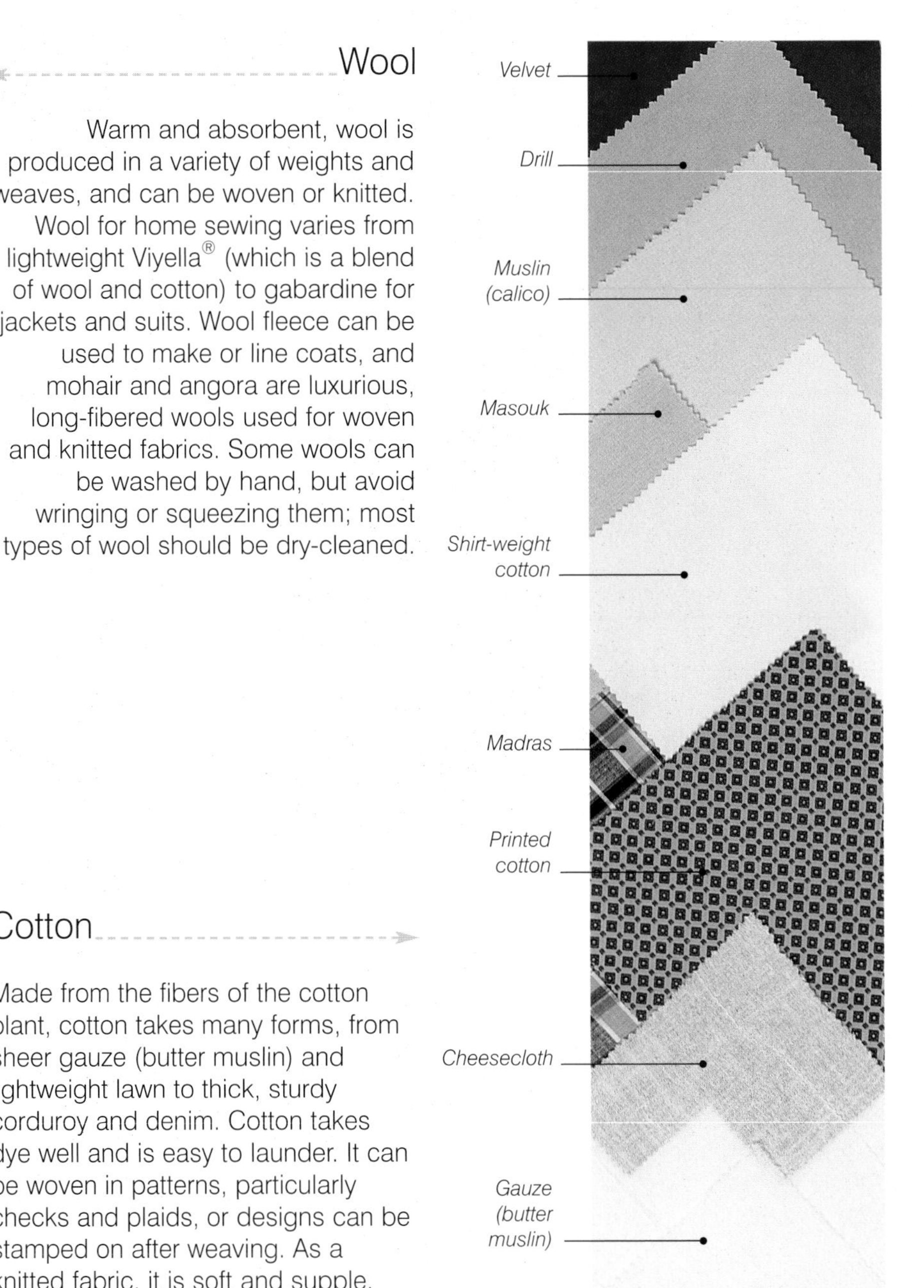

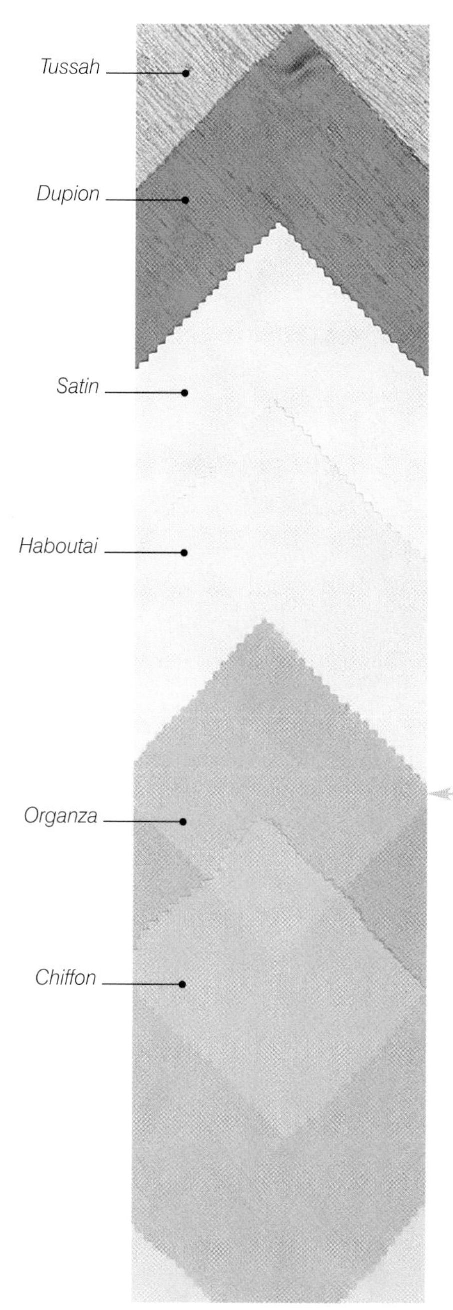

Silk

Woven from long filaments produced by silkworms, silk was so valued in ancient China that its manufacture was a closely guarded secret until a number of silkworm cocoons and seeds of the mulberry tree (the silkworm's only food) were smuggled to the Middle East in a walking cane.

Silk is strong, drapes well, and can be woven into an enormous variety of weights and weaves, from gossamer sheers to heavy slubs. Some silk can be laundered by hand, but most pieces should be dry-cleaned.

Linen

Made from the fiber of the flax plant, linen can be woven into various weights, from fine handkerchief cloth to heavyweight suit fabrics. Its texture varies from a smooth finish to a rough slub. Linen is cool and comfortable to wear and is valued for its characteristic strength and luster, but pure linen creases easily. This crumpled look has a certain fashion value, but is not always desirable. To reduce the problem of creasing, many linen fabrics intended for dressmaking are blended with other fibers.

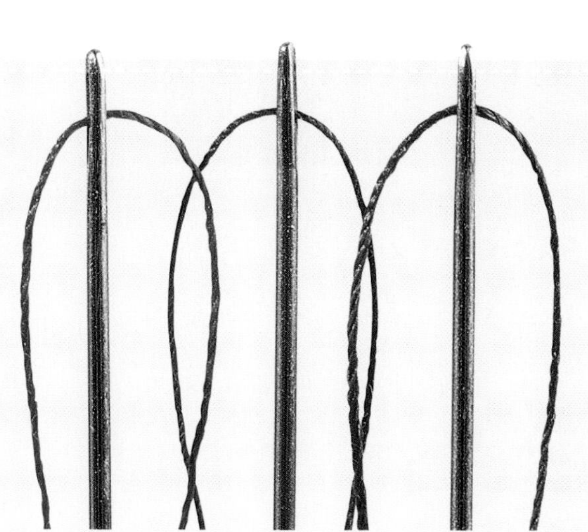

THREADS

The weight and color of a fabric will determine your choice of thread. It is available in a variety of weights and can be spun from several fibers. Cotton, polyester, and a combination of the two are most often used for dressmaking, while sewing silk is more difficult to work with—and more expensive—but it is sometimes used with fine silk fabrics. To be certain of a good match, test the thread on a sample of the fabric to be used.

Man-made fabrics

The wide variety of man-made, or synthetic, fabrics available available is overwhelming. The fibers, chemical compounds that can be spun, include acetate, acrylic, nylon, polyester, and rayon. While many fabrics are 100% synthetic, others are blended with natural fibers (see pages 64-65) to combine the best features of each type. You will find that blends are usually less expensive than natural fabrics.

Most synthetics, and many blends, fray easily. Use very sharp scissors or pinking shears when cutting out, and leave a generous seam allowance to help overcome the problem.

CARING FOR SYNTHETICS

Most man-made fabrics are shrink- and crease-resistant. Most are washable and need little ironing if the care instructions are followed. Use a cool iron when pressing as synthetics scorch easily.

Synthetics

Most 100% synthetics have a silky quality. They fray easily, but are usually washable and hold their shape and body well. Synthetics take dye well and are available in a striking variety of colors. They can sometimes be uncomfortably warm to wear, but good-quality synthetics are virtually indistinguishable from the more expensive silk.

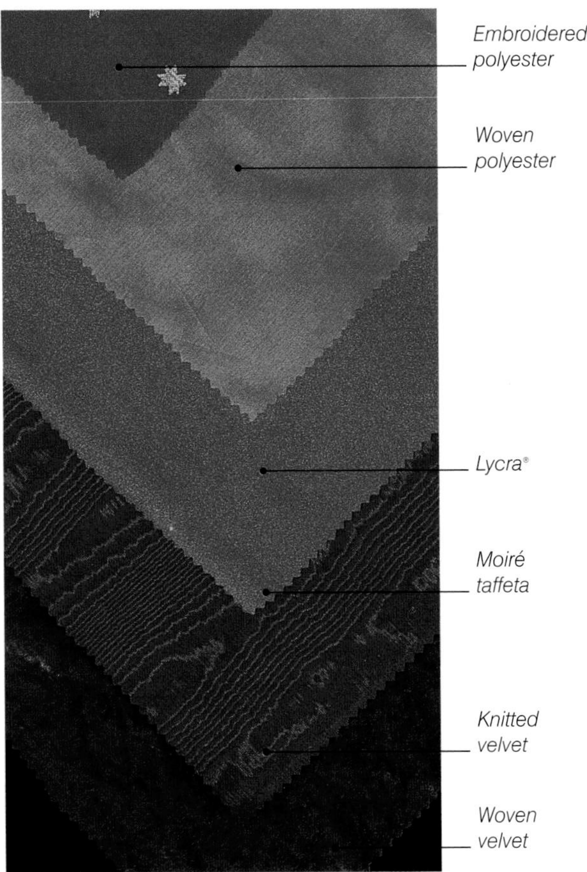

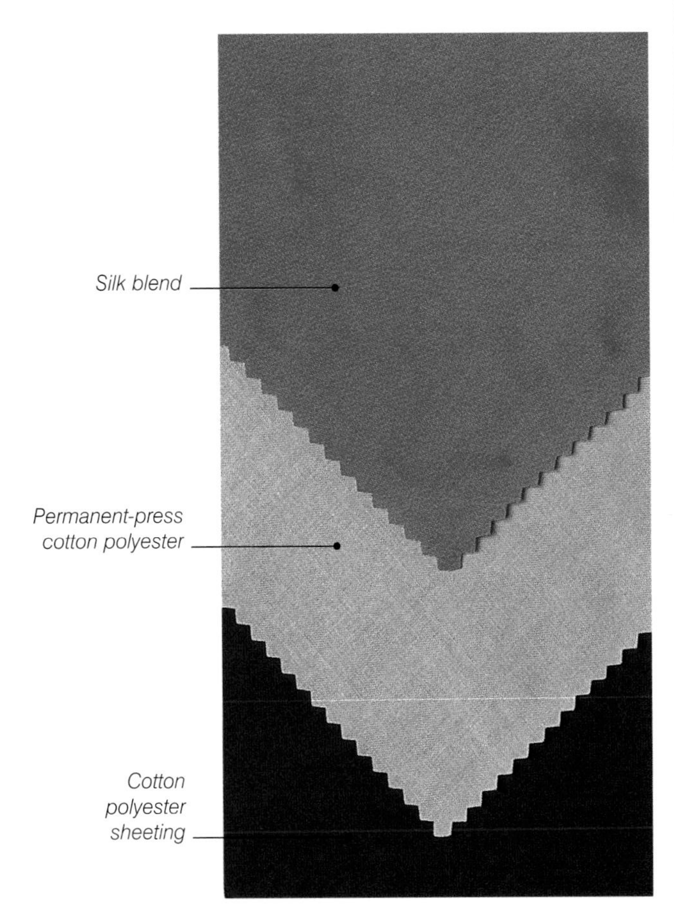

Blends

Blended fabrics are made from a mix of synthetic (often polyester) and natural fibers (usually cotton). Available in an impressive rainbow of plain colors, some blends are woven in patterns or printed with small, medium, or large-scale patterns. These fabrics range from lightweight to heavy and are less likely to fray than pure synthetics.

Most wash-and-wear or permanent-press fabrics are blends, and so should be pressed with a cool iron only.

Vinyls

Supple vinyl fabrics come in a vast choice of colors and textures, from smooth through dimpled to leather-look. They are virtually non-fray, but must not be held together with pins as any hole will be permanent. Instead, use low-tack tape or paper clips to "pin" or "baste" items. Sewing vinyl by hand is difficult and not recommended; invest in a special machine needle to avoid damaging the fabric.

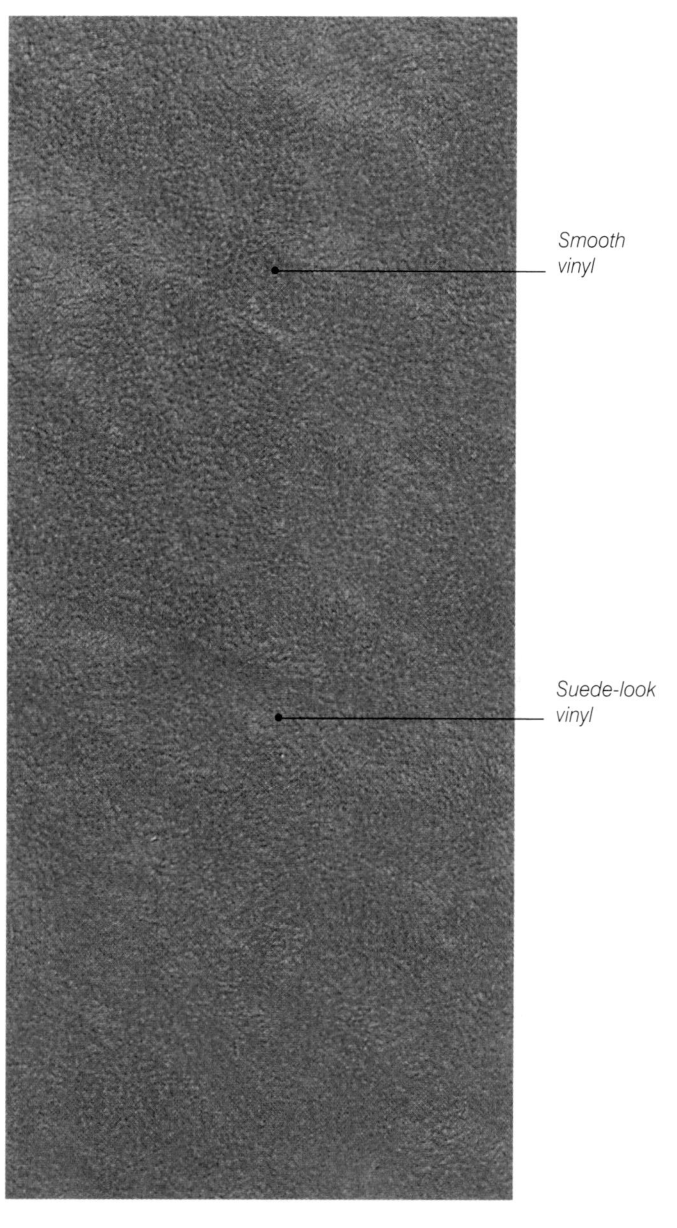

Smooth vinyl

Suede-look vinyl

Plain viscose

Printed viscose

Polyester organza

Synthetic sheers

The array of romantic-looking sheer fabrics found in any good fabric store is due almost entirely to the advent of synthetic fibers. These fabrics are slippery, fray easily, and are generally difficult to work with. They need to be handled with care and given extra-wide seam allowances. Remember to press gently with a cool iron, and baste the piece at every stage, and the results will be worth all the extra effort for making special-occasion garments.

Difficult fabrics

Most fabrics woven from synthetic or man-made fibers, and some natural fabrics, need a certain amount of special handling. These materials can be difficult to work with, and they need extra care both in cutting out and in stitching. Finished garments will also need special attention, but since most of the items made from these fabrics are usually worn for one-off occasions, they are well worth the extra care.

TENDER LOVING CARE

Garments made from the fabrics in this section will need to be dry-cleaned. Few of these fabrics should be folded for any length of time, and some will need to be stored on special padded clothes hangers to prevent marking.

Woven metallics

Metallic thread has been used to weave the two lamé fabrics shown here; both of them fray very easily. Individual sequins have been stitched at regular intervals to a sheer woven backing fabric to make the sequined fabric. Try not to cut or stitch through the sequins, and avoid using this fabric to make structured garments with darts.

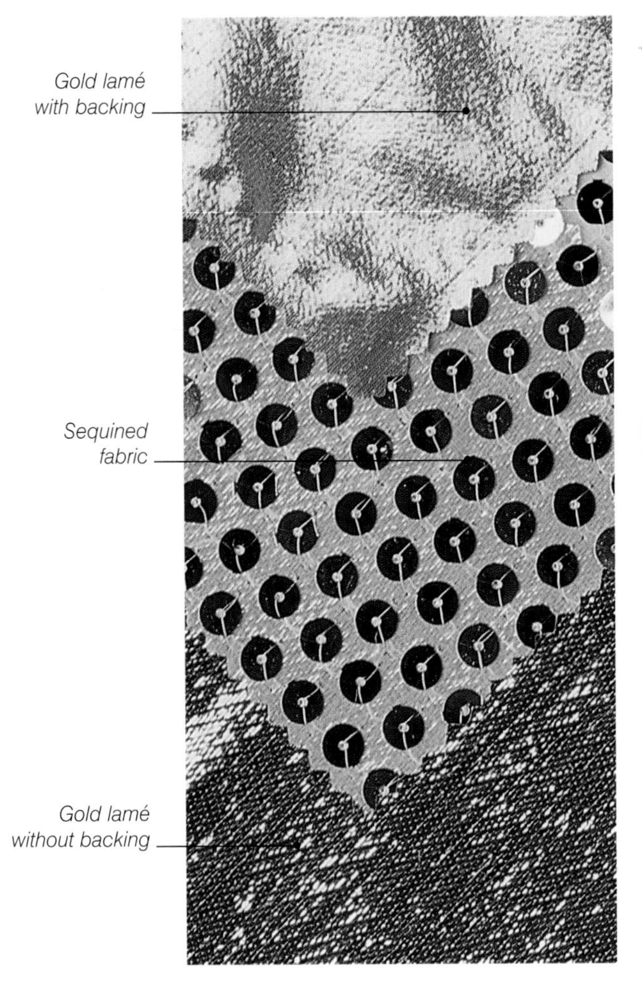

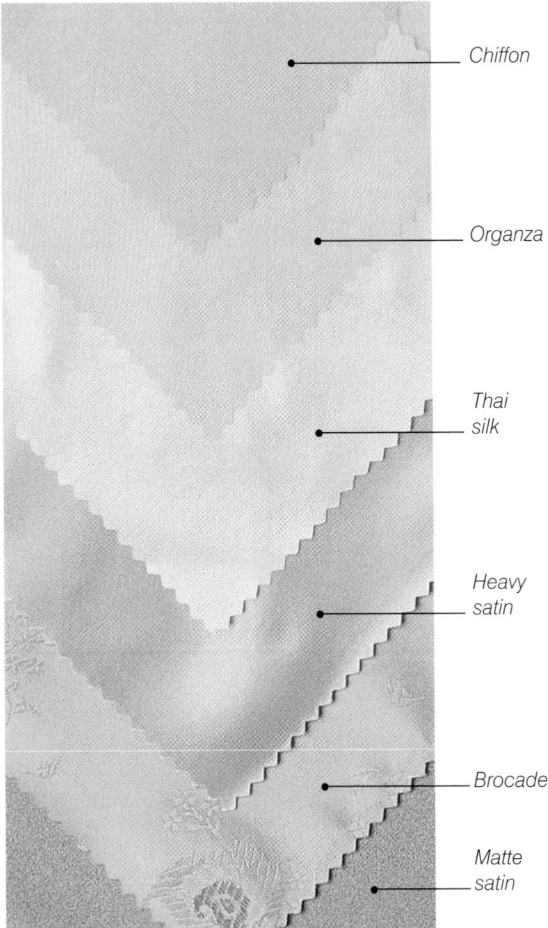

Silk

Though there are a couple of exceptions that are quite easy to work with, most silky fabrics are considered to belong to the "difficult" category. Many silks, and their synthetic cousins, fray easily, and all of them are slippery to handle. Use fine pins and needles to hold them in place, cut extra-wide seam allowances, and baste everything. Press on the wrong side with a cool iron, and protect the fabric using a pressing cloth or brown paper.

Napped fabrics

Because of the way light catches fabrics with a nap or pile, these materials must be cut with the pile running in the same direction on all pieces. These fabrics tend to be thick, so it is best to choose simple designs with few darts, gathers, or pleats. Some of them also fray easily. Use fine pins and needles, and baste everything before stitching.

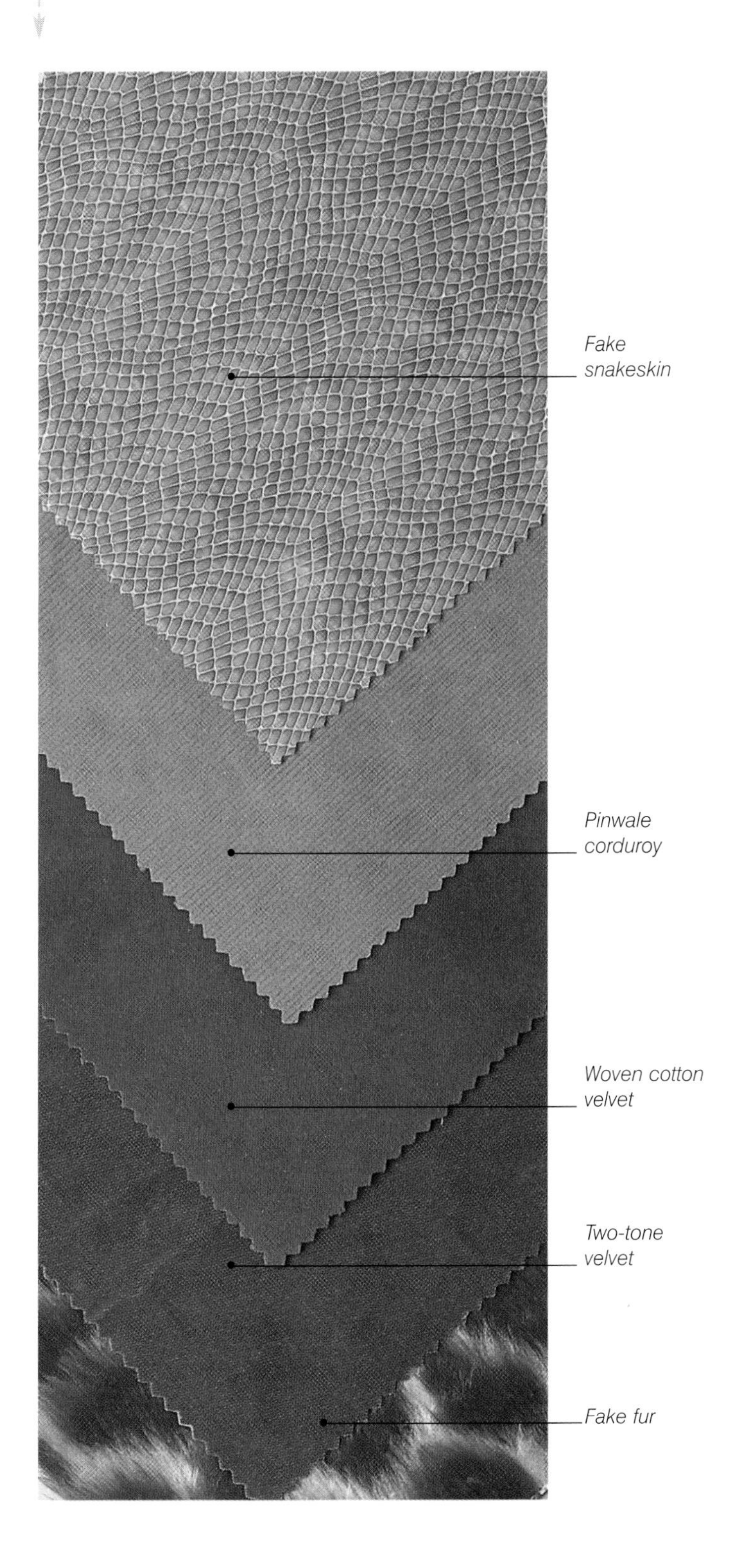

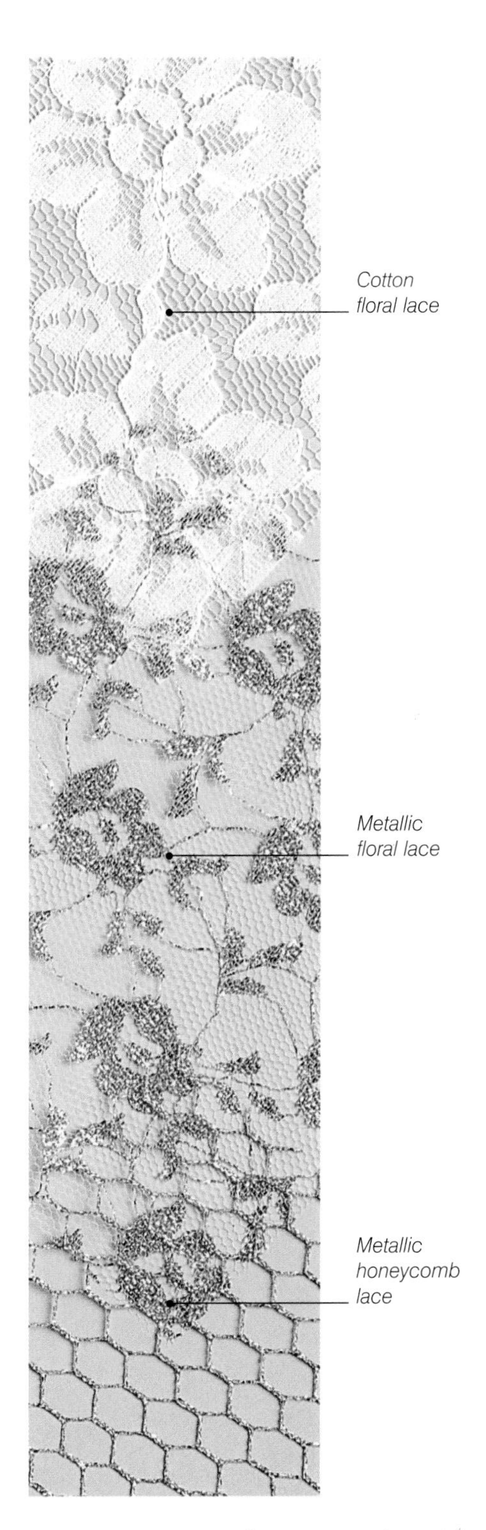

Lace and net

These machine-made fabrics are available in an impressive choice of weights and designs. Unless they are made up into a sheer overgarment, lace and net fabrics need to be lined to add support and to keep the fabric from scratching. Always cut the fabric so the design runs in the same direction.

Knitted glitz

Machine-knitted fabrics are supple and do not fray easily, but they are generally slippery. Use fine pins for holding the fabric together, and sew with fine polyester thread using special ballpoint machine needles. Reinforce all seams with two rows of zigzag stitch. Synthetic knits tend to hold creases, so pressing should be done lightly and carefully. Hang assembled garments on padded coat hangers for a day or two before hemming.

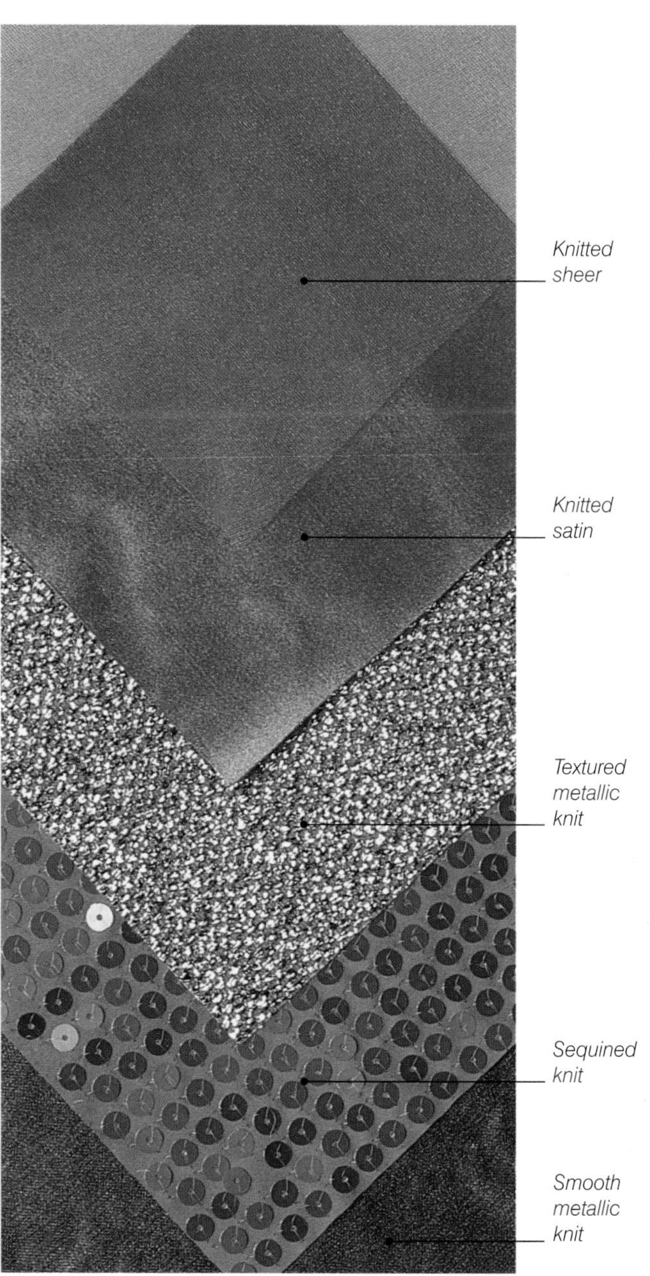

Knitted sheer

Knitted satin

Textured metallic knit

Sequined knit

Smooth metallic knit

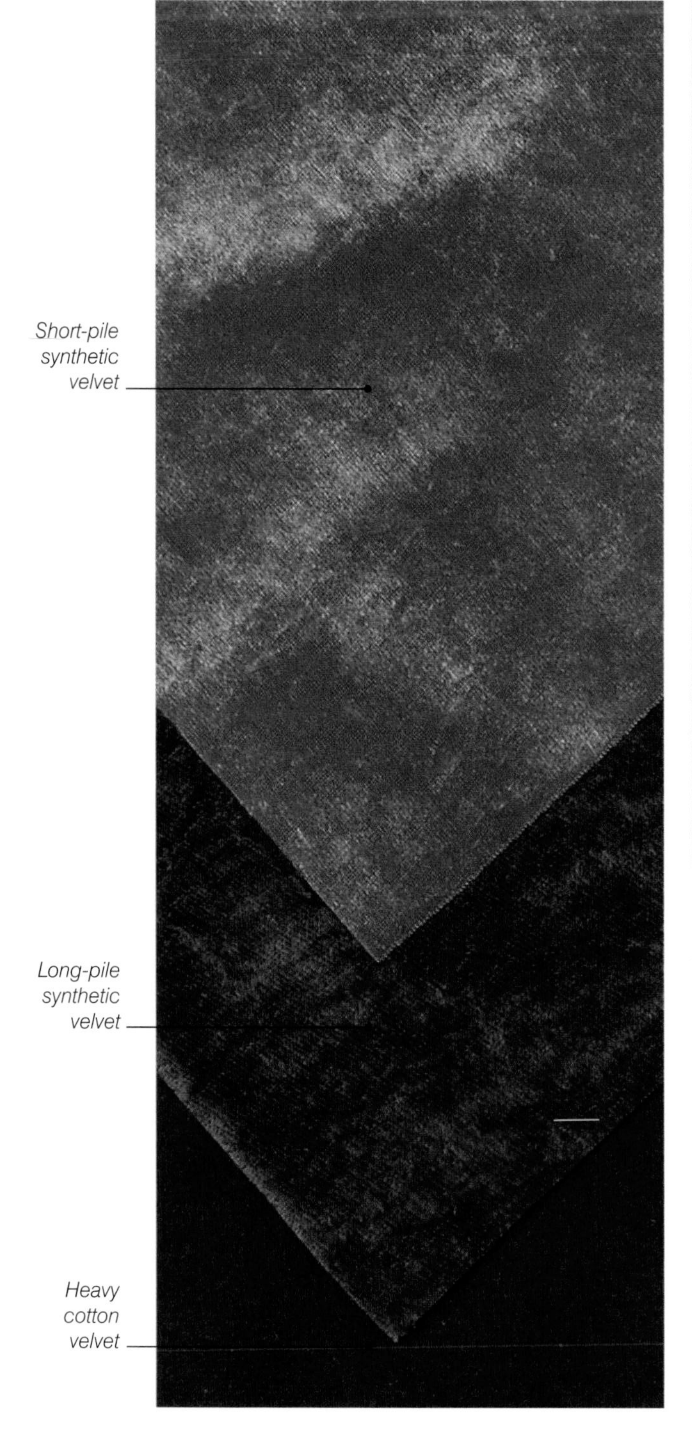

Short-pile synthetic velvet

Long-pile synthetic velvet

Heavy cotton velvet

Velvet knits

Knitted velvet is softer and more supple than its woven counterpart, and it frays less easily. Treat it as a napped fabric (see page 69), cutting out the pieces with the pile running in the same direction (upward if possible). It is advisable to stitch darts and seams in the direction of the pile, and to insert zippers by hand. Finish seam allowances by hand to prevent stretching, and apply hem tape or bias binding to the raw edges of hems. Avoid buttonholes if possible; use loops or hidden fastenings instead.

INTERFACING

An interfacing is a separate piece of fabric inserted between the garment piece and its facing to add strength and stability. The type—woven or non-woven, sew-in or fusible (iron-on)—and the weight, varying from light to heavy, are determined by the garment fabric. The pattern instruction sheet will specify which pieces need to be interfaced.

Most modern interfacings are made from synthetic non-woven material. Interfacings are widely used in home sewing as well as dressmaking.

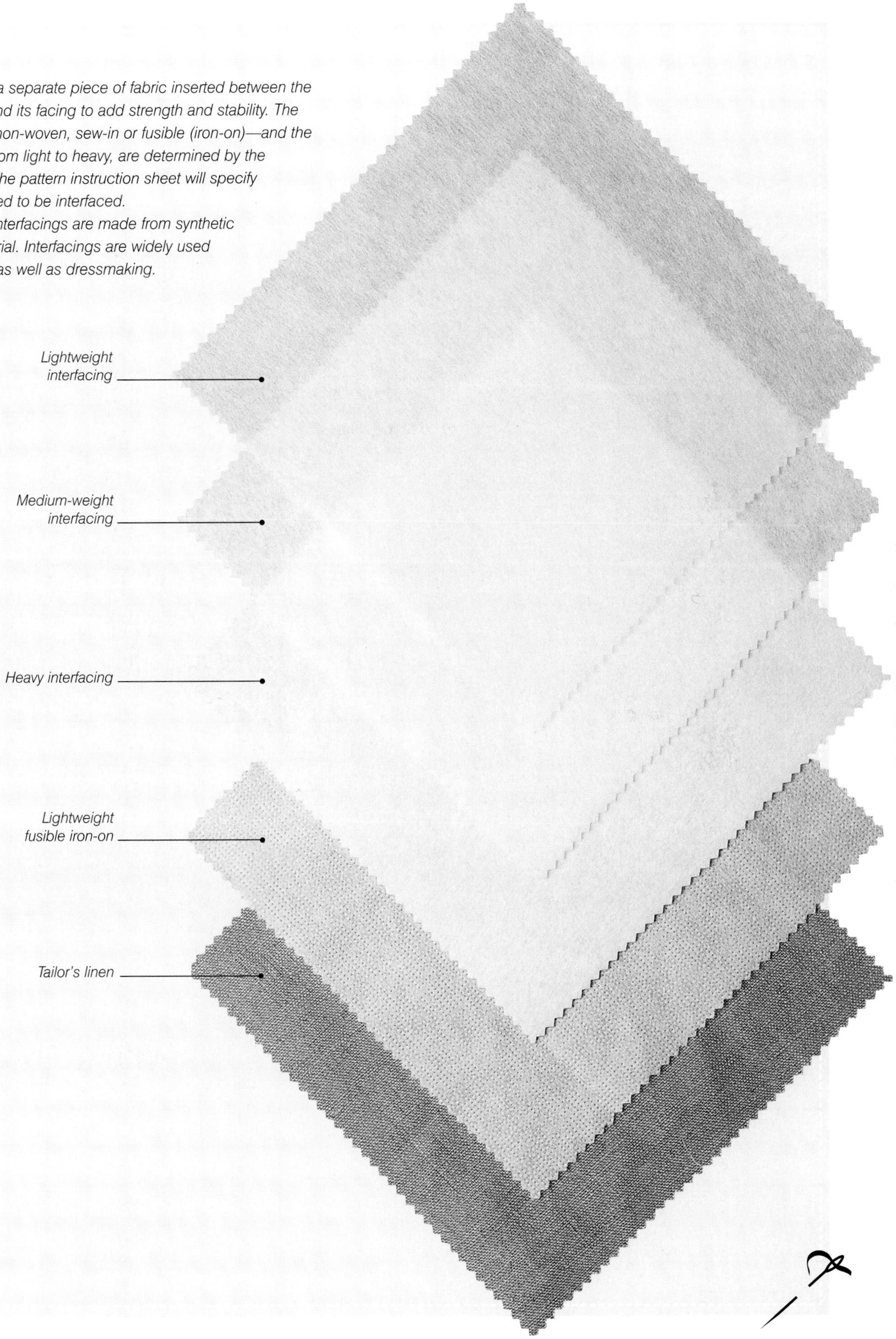

Lightweight interfacing

Medium-weight interfacing

Heavy interfacing

Lightweight fusible iron-on

Tailor's linen

Darts

Darts are narrow pointed folds that give shape and structure to many garments. They create fullness for the main body curves, such as the bust, waist, and shoulder, and are stitched into the fabric and pressed in specific ways. Generally, vertical darts like those at the waist and in shoulder seams are pressed toward the center of the garment. Horizontal ones, such as bustline darts, are pressed downward unless they are to be caught in the stitching (other than the seamline). Darts are usually stitched before the garment pieces are assembled.

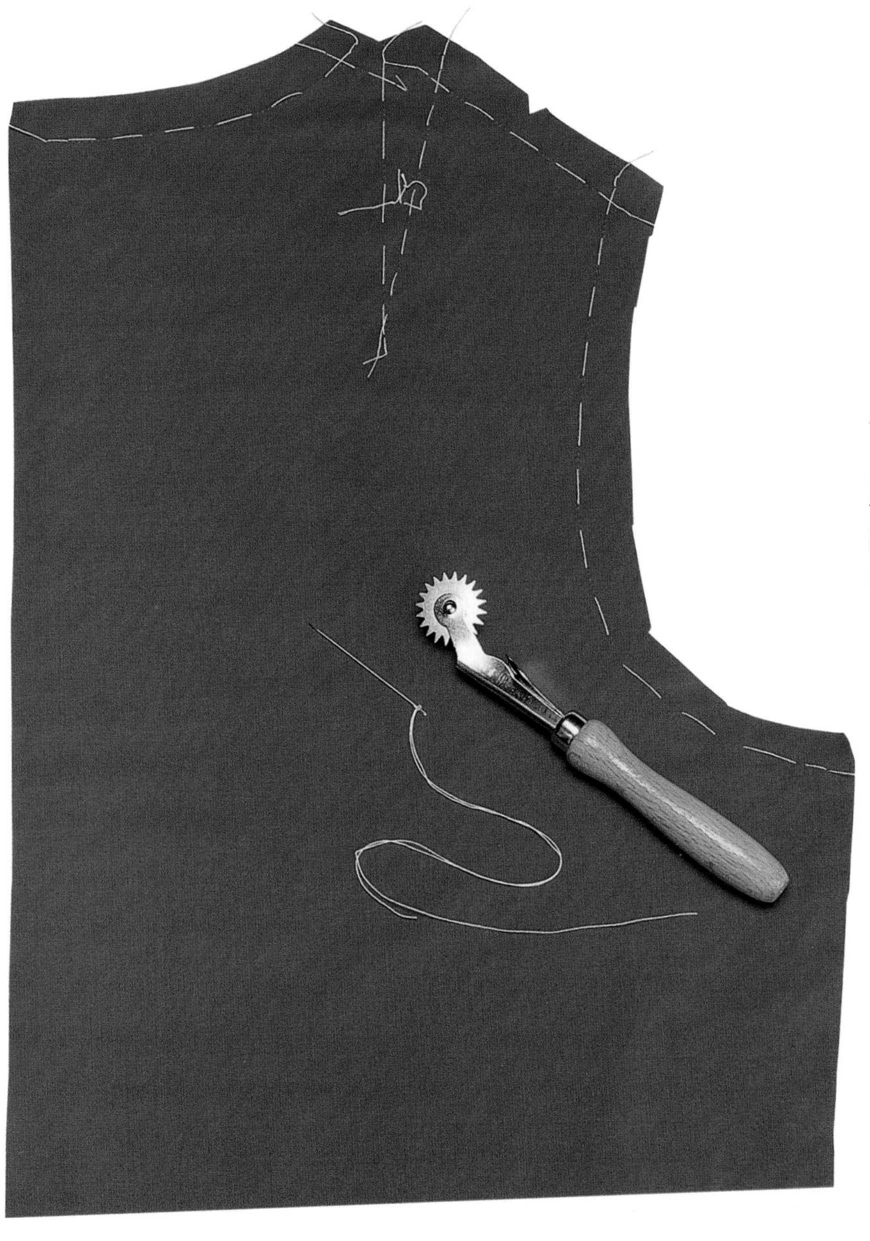

1 Darts are marked on the relevant pattern piece. Following the pattern guidelines carefully, mark and baste all stitching lines.

2 Pin the dart along the basted stitching lines and stitch toward the point. Finish a few stitches beyond the point, leaving about 4 in (10 cm) of thread free at the point.

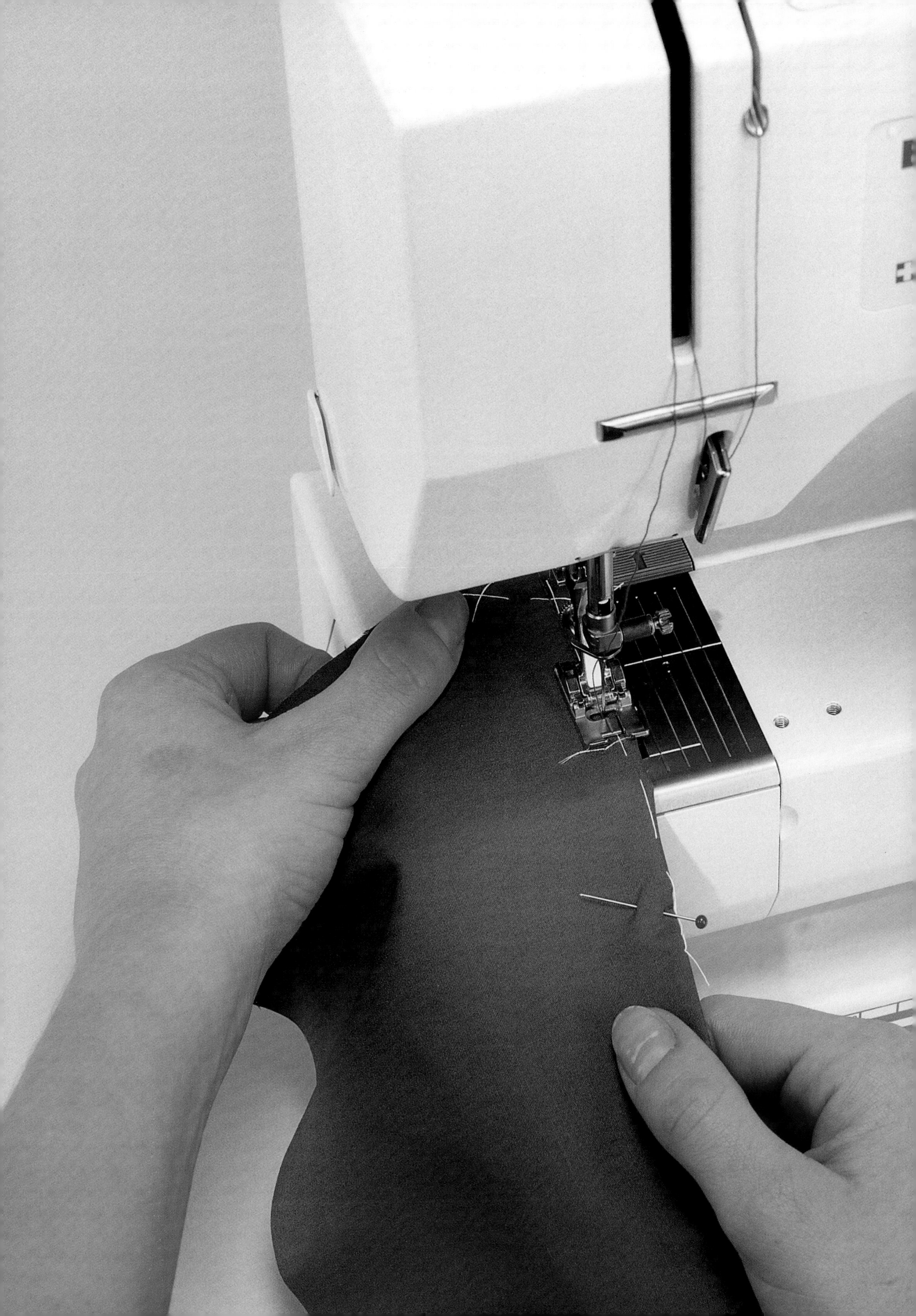

3 Press the stitched dart on both sides of the garment so that it lies flat and to one side. To fasten off, tie the threads left free in step 2 and snip off the ends.

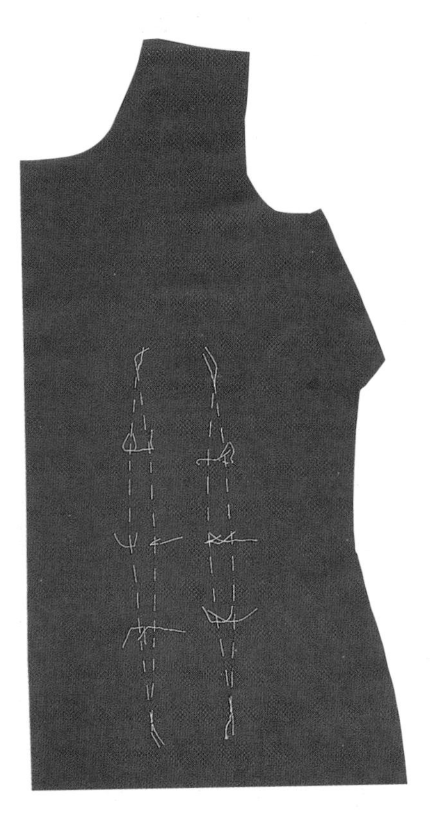

4 Double-pointed darts are made in the same way. Stitch along the basted stitching lines, working from the top down toward the bottom point. Press along the fold of the stitched dart, avoiding the stitching if possible.

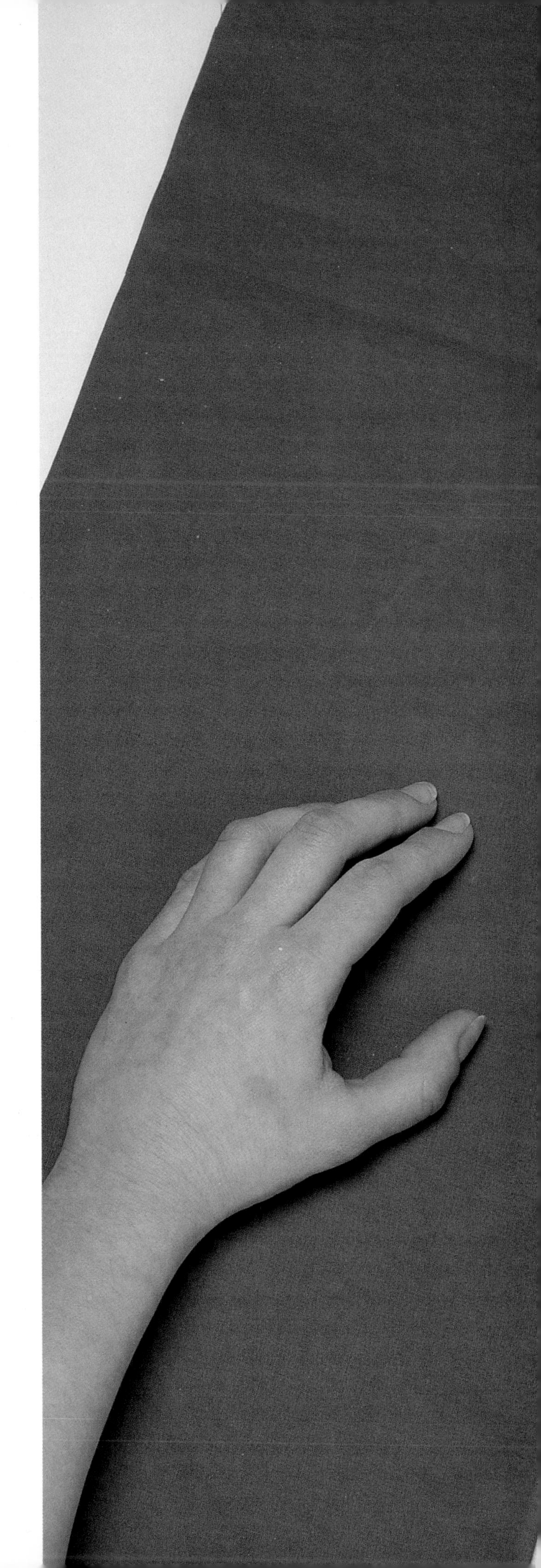

5 Double-pointed darts usually need to be cut. Using scissors, remove a triangle of fabric in the widest part of the dart as shown. DO NOT cut into the stitching. Trim the folded edge of the dart ⅔ in (1.25 cm) from the stitched line in each direction, leaving the point uncut.

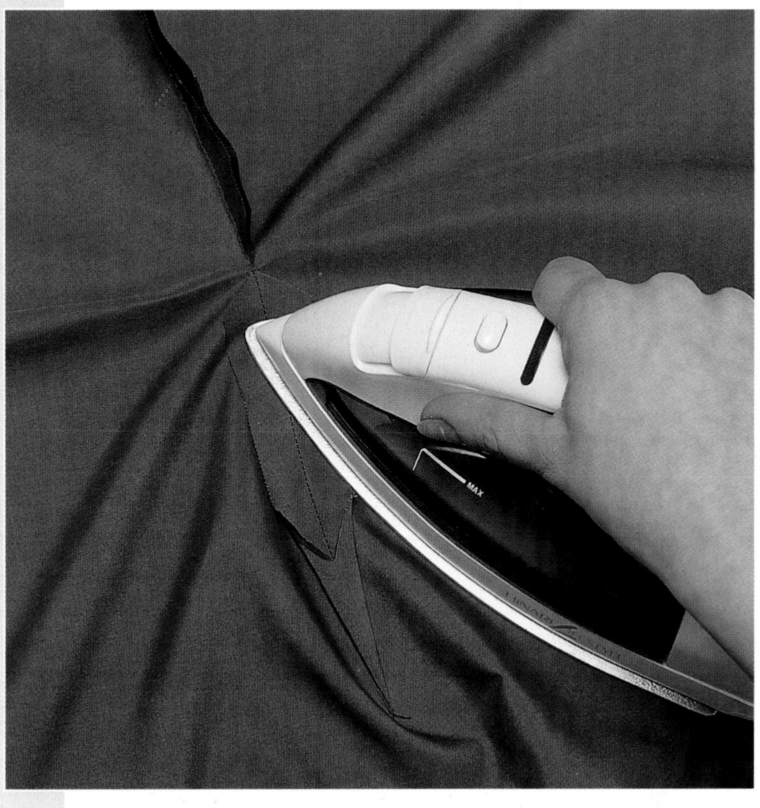

6 Carefully press half of the dart open and flat. Repeat this technique for the other half of the dart.

DOUBLE-STITCHED DARTS

Darts in heavyweight or loosely woven fabric can be double-stitched to make them more secure. To fasten off, tie the threads at the point of the dart separately for each stitching line.

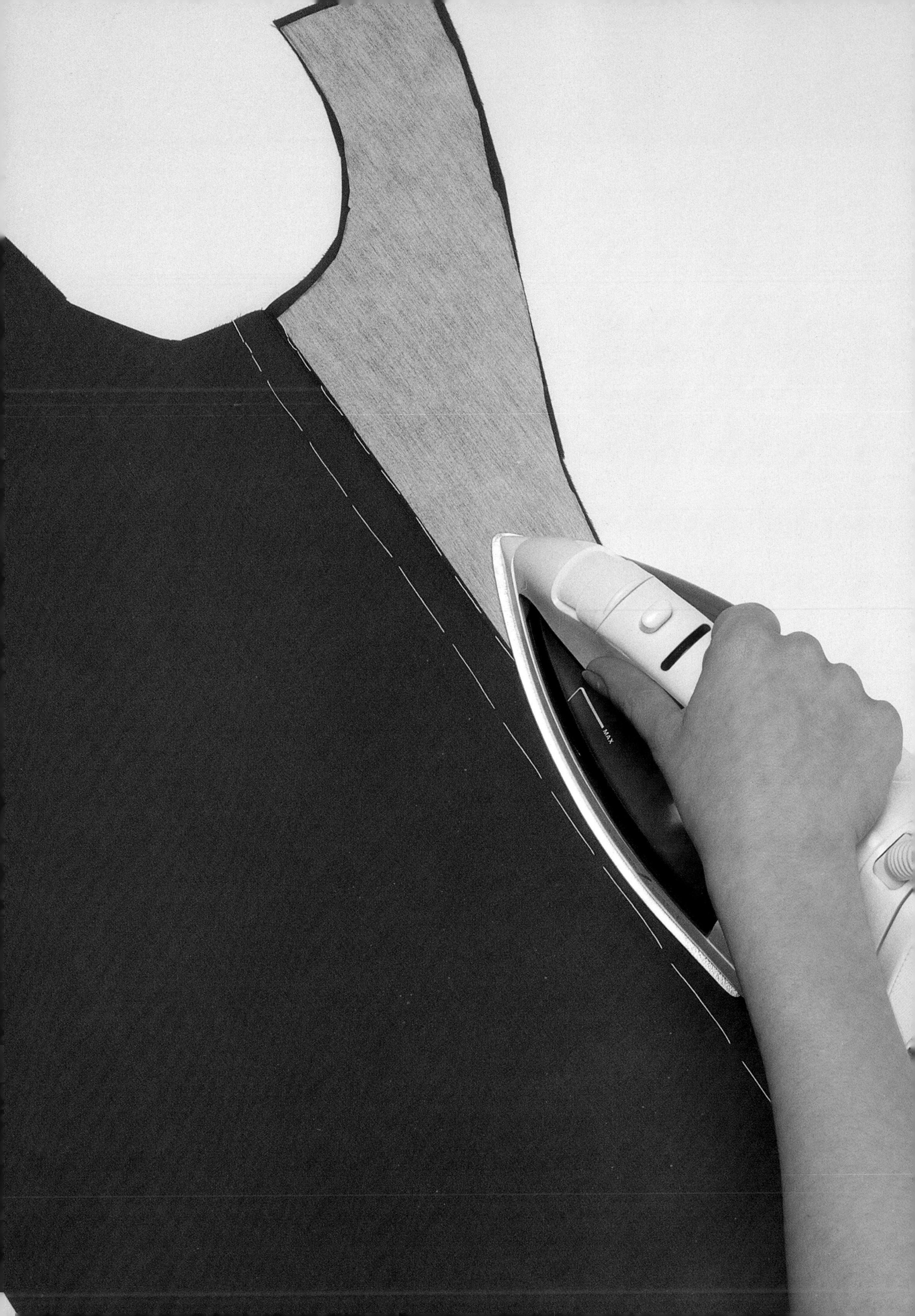
MAX

Facings and interfacings

A facing is a piece of fabric that backs the external edges of a garment and provides a neat finish and added strength. Facings can be separate pieces stitched to the garment and folded under, or cut as part of the garment piece. Most facings are made of the garment fabric, but they can be cut from lighter-weight fabric to reduce bulk. Facings are sometimes backed with interfacing, a very thin layer of fabric that can be sewn or ironed on, to strengthen the piece. Interfacing is available in both non-woven and woven form, and comes in a variety of weights and colors (see also page 71).

One-piece facing

1 Cut out the pieces from fabric and iron-on interfacing. Mark and baste the pieces to be faced.

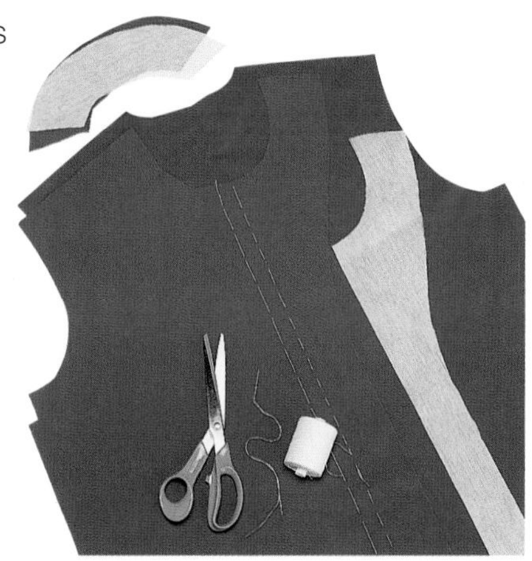

2 Following the manufacturer's instructions, iron the interfacing pieces in position on the wrong side of all the garment pieces. Make sure the iron is set correctly to the recommended temperature.

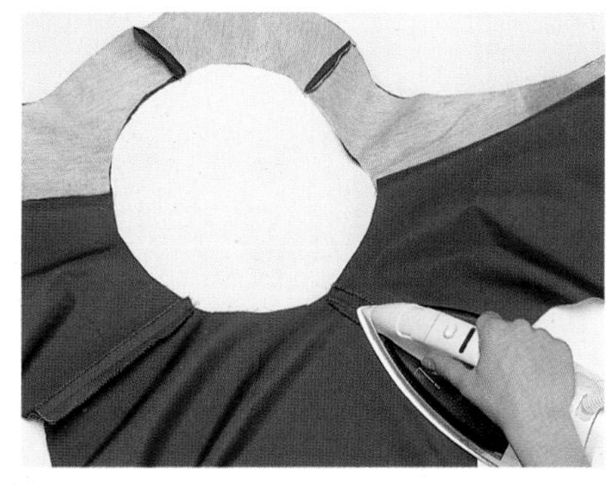

3 Pin and stitch the interfaced pieces together along the marked seamlines. Press all the seams open.

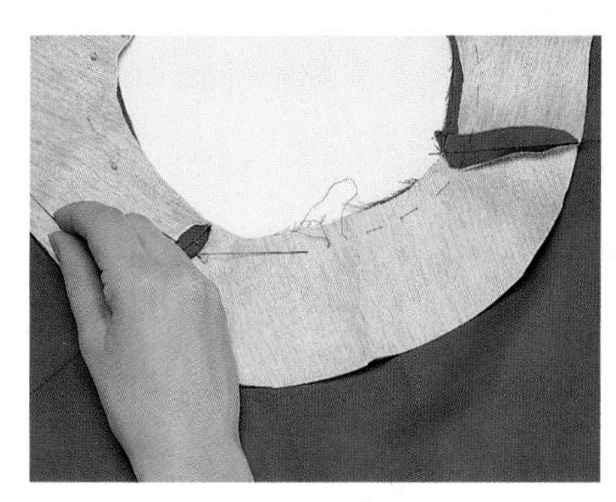

4 Turn back the straight edges along the foldline. Pin and baste the curved neckline seam. Stitch the seam and remove the basting.

SEPARATE PIECES

1 *To make a two-piece facing (shown here in a contrasting color for clarity), first cut out and prepare the pieces, applying interfacing if necessary.*

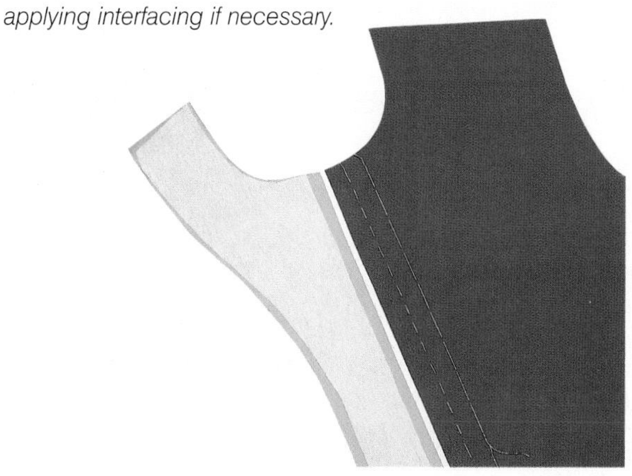

2 *Join the straight seams together to attach the facing to the garment piece, then proceed as described in steps 3 to 7 of making a one-piece facing (see left).*

step 5

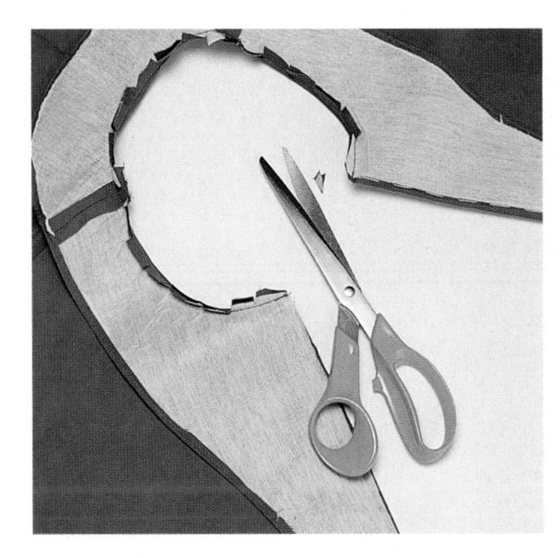

5 Turn under the raw edge of the interfaced pieces and staystitch. Using scissors, carefully trim the corners and clip the curved neckline seam at regular intervals.

6 Turn the interfaced pieces to the inside and press. If you wish, topstitch along the edges.

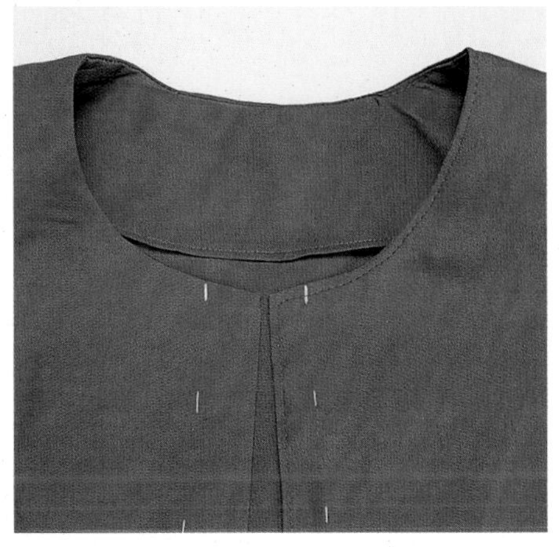

7 The facing neatly encloses the raw edges of the neckline, providing extra reinforcement where it is needed most on the garment.

V-neckline facing

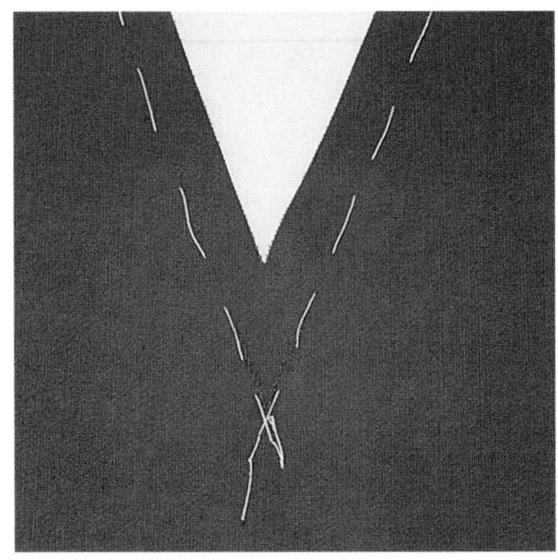

1 Cut out the garment pieces and a bias facing strip. Mark and baste the neck seamline, and staystitch a V about ¾ in (2 cm) long at the point.

2 Stitch the shoulder seams, then baste the bias-cut neckband to the neck, leaving the final 2 in (5 cm) unsewn. Ease the back section between the shoulder seams so the neckband lies flat.

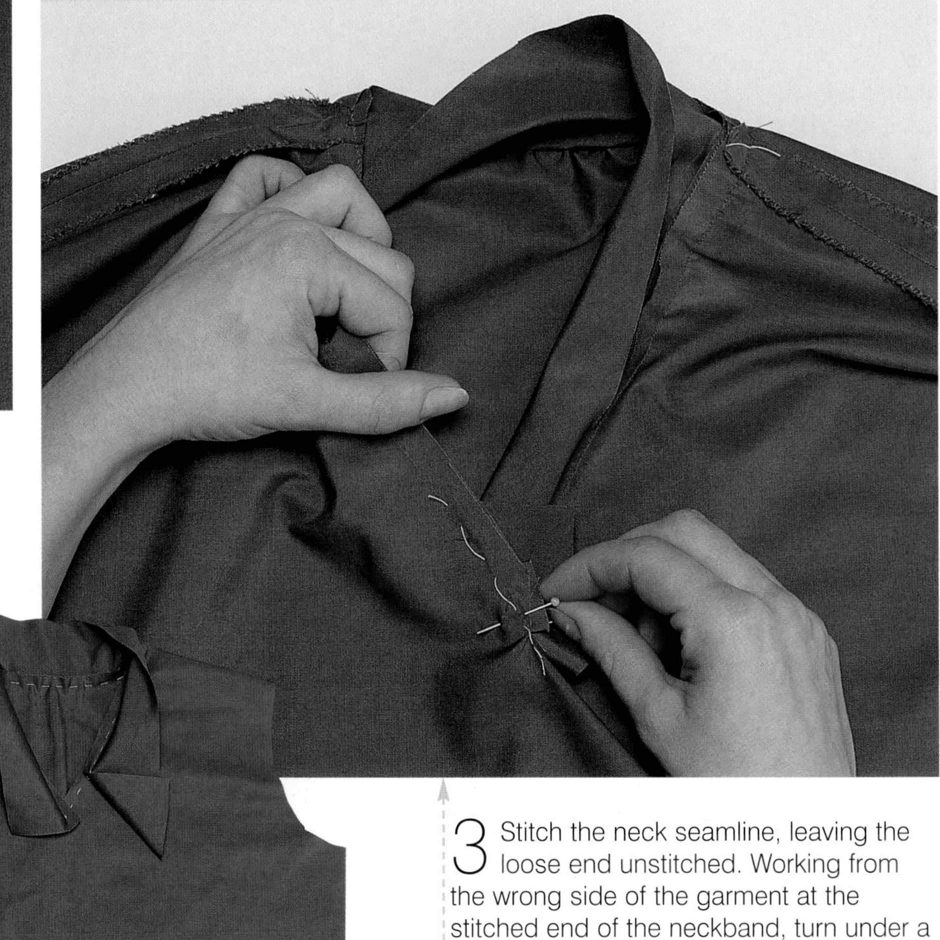

3 Stitch the neck seamline, leaving the loose end unstitched. Working from the wrong side of the garment at the stitched end of the neckband, turn under a doubled hem and baste for 3 in (7.5 cm).

4 Match the unstitched edge of the neckband to the neck edge, enclosing the folded and basted end. Catch the end inside the fold. Pin and baste the V down, past the staystitching. Machine-stitch to the end of the V.

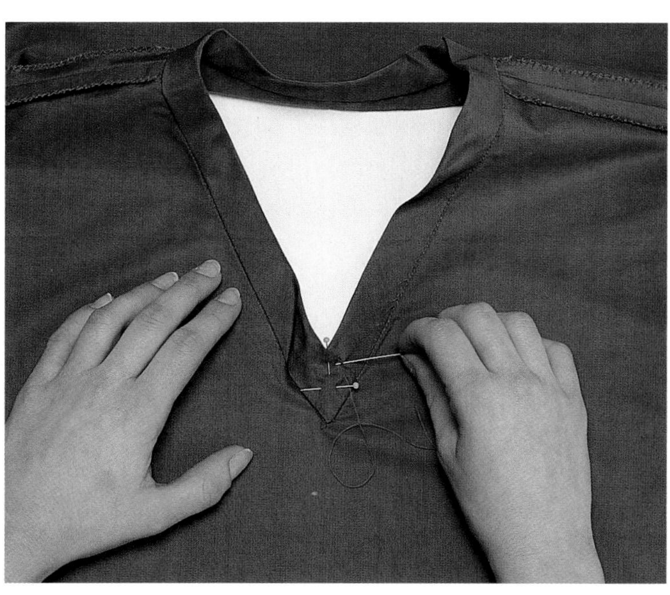

5 Turn the neckband to the wrong side of the garment and hem all around just inside the seamline to finish the edge. Pin and catch down the unstitched edge of the band at the V to prevent it from rolling.

6 The finished faced V-neckline has a sharp overlapped point and is well supported to hold its shape.

EASING CURVES

To ease curves, clip ⅛ in (3 mm) into the seam allowance before staystitching the edge. Cut the seam allowance at an angle as shown.

On either delicate or heavyweight fabrics, herringbone-stitch along the staystitched edge to secure it and prevent the edges from fraying.

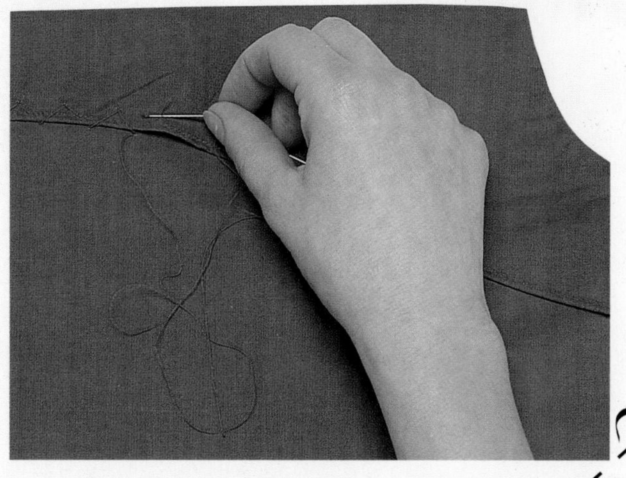

Tucks and pleats

Tucks and pleats are straight folds in fabric. Tucks create a decorative element which add fullness and body to a garment, creating a sense of luxury. Pleats are commonly used to control fullness in skirts and trousers; they are anchored at the top and fall neatly to the bottom of the fabric (see page 52 for advice on pressing tucks and pleats).

Tucks

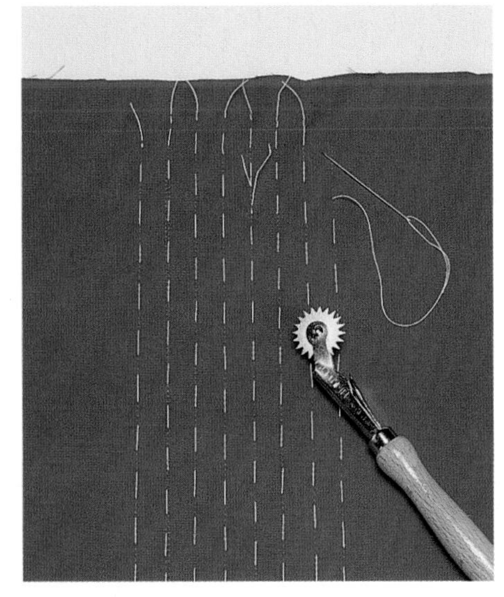

1 Tucks can be vertical, horizontal, or diagonal. Transfer the pattern guidelines to the wrong side of the fabric with a dressmaker's carbon and tracing wheel. Baste each line.

2 Make one tuck at a time. Match two adjoining guidelines and pin the tuck in place. Stitch along the guideline. Repeat for each tuck. Remove the basting and press. Alternatively, you can use the edge of the presser foot or a guideline marked on the footplate to guide the stitching.

STRIPES AND CHECKS

1 Working on striped or checked fabric can create interesting effects. Here the tucks are the same width as the stripes on the fabric. They are folded to leave a narrow band of the contrasting color along each fold, then pinned and basted.

2 This yoke, which was tucked before the pattern piece was cut out, appears as plain green. The tucks are set horizontally and contrast effectively with the wide vertical stripes of the main bodice piece.

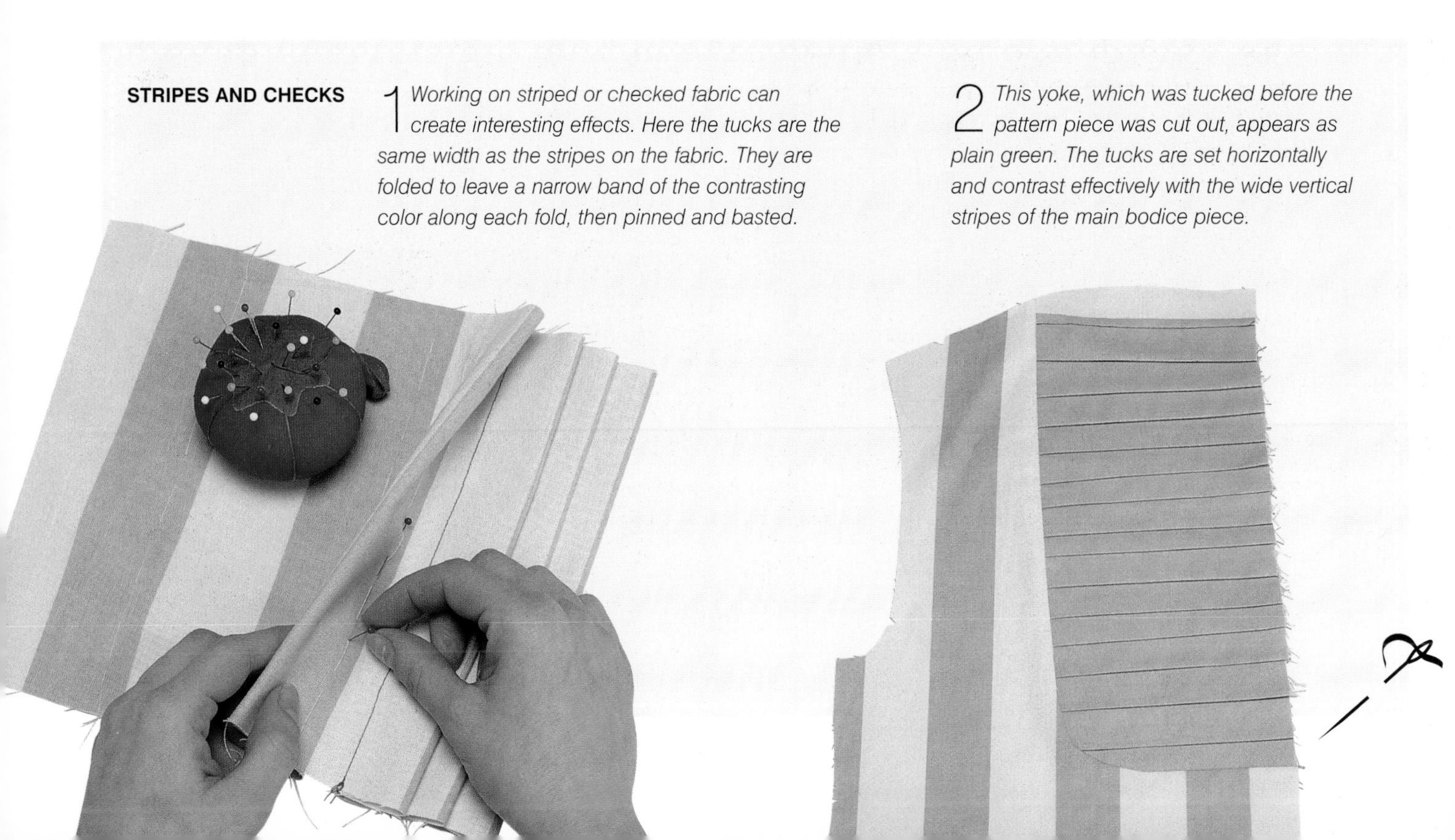

Knife pleats

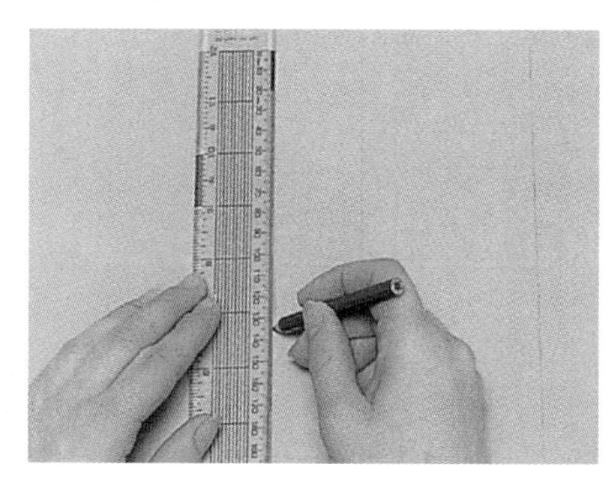

1 Knife pleats are folded in the same direction. Using a removable marker and a ruler to draw lines on the wrong side of the fabric, mark the foldlines and placement lines, and, if necessary, the bottoms of the pleats.

2 Fold the pleats along the marked lines. Pin and baste each one in place on the right side from top to bottom. Pin the top of the pleats well inside the seam allowance. Baste, then stitch to secure the pleats (inset).

3 Topstitch along the top folded edge of each pleat, working from top to bottom. For sharp pleats, press the piece before taking out the basting, but for soft pleats always remove the basting before pressing.

Inverted box pleats

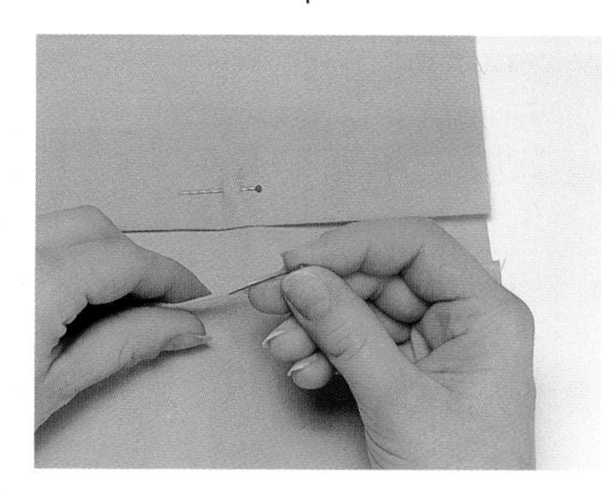

1 Mark as in step 1 above, but on the right side of the fabric. Fold and pin each pleat into the center to meet the one opposite, then pin each foldline with right sides together. Remove the first pins as you work.

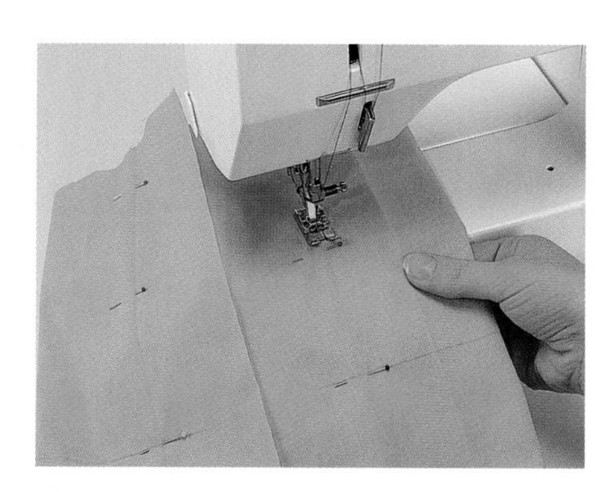

2 Stitch along the length of the foldlines to the bottom of each pleat, removing pins as you work. Backstitch at each end to secure.

3 Press the pleats flat with the stitched foldlines in the center of the underpleats. Baste along the top edge and the folded edge of each underpleat. Finish with a double-topstitched seam along the edge of the center seam to the bottom of each pleat. Remove the basting and press again (inset).

Sleeves

The are two basic kinds of sleeve. The most common is the set-in or mounted sleeve, which is cut with a sleeve cap and can be gathered, pleated, or smooth. The other basic type, raglan sleeves, are cut in one with the bodice piece. In most dressmaking patterns, the sleeve cap has one notch in front and two at the back.

Set-in gathered sleeve

1 Cut out the sleeve pieces and transfer all the markings from the pattern. Work a zigzag stitch along the raw underarm edges and run a double row of gathering stitches between the notches in each sleeve cap.

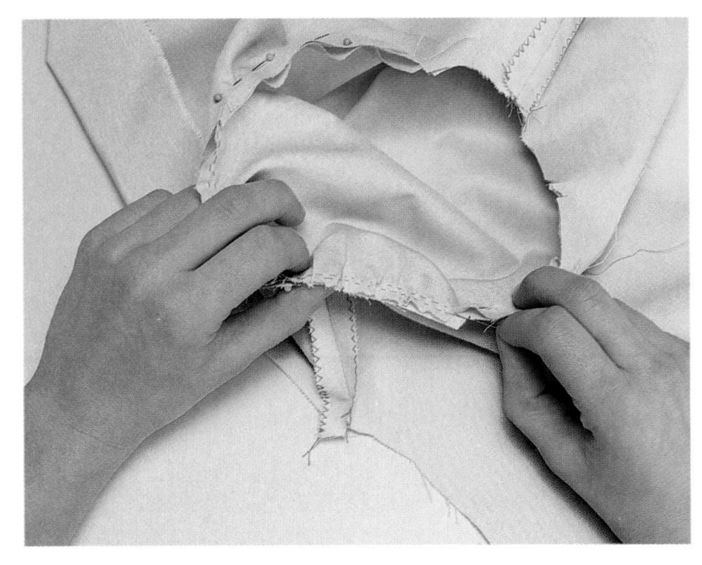

2 Stitch the underarm seam. Match notches on the sleeve cap to the bodice piece and pin the sleeve in place. Pull up the gathers evenly between the notches.

3 Baste the sleeve cap to the garment, matching the notches and underarm seams together. Keep the gathers even over the shoulder area for balanced fullness.

FABRIC THAT FRAYS

For a neat finish to a set-in sleeve made from fabric that frays easily, bind the raw edges of the sewn-in sleeve with bias binding after stitching a double seam all around the armhole.

Set-in gathered sleeve

A set-in sleeve is cut separately from the body of the garment. The gathered style has enough fullness to fit over the arm and allow for normal movement without being bulky.

4 Stitch the sleeve seam to the bodice piece. Zigzag-stitch around the raw edges, about ¼ in (5 mm) from the seam. Clip around the underarm seam, taking care not to cut into the stitching.

Raglan sleeve

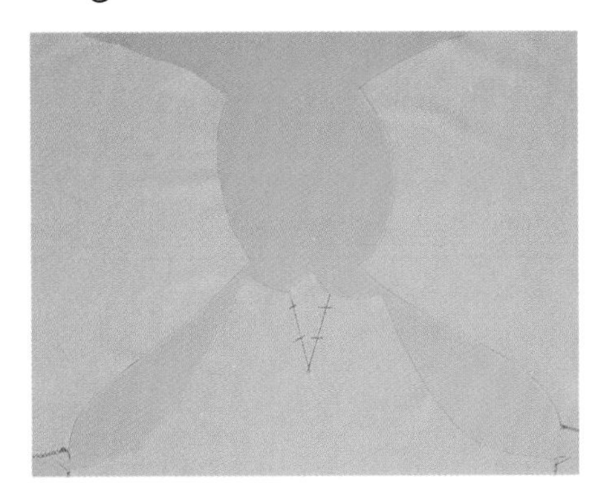

1 Cut out and prepare the front, back, and sleeve pieces by transferring the markings. Work a zigzag stitch along the raw edges.

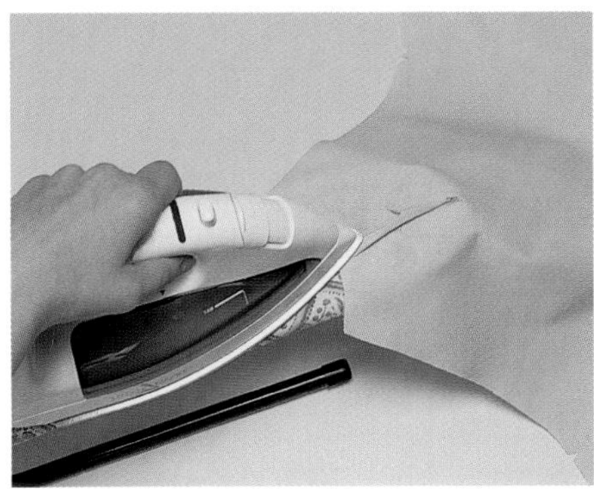

2 Stitch each sleeve cap dart, slash it open, and press it flat.

3 Match the notches, and then pin, baste, and stitch the front and back sleeve seams together. Clip the curves, zigzag-stitch the raw edges, and press the seams open.

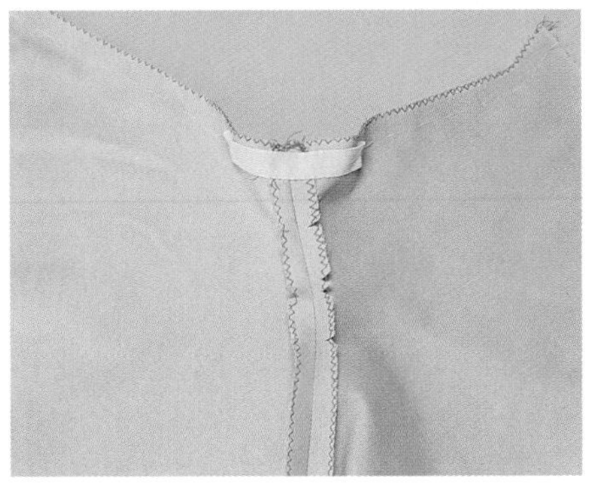

4 Match the sleeve seams. Pin baste, and stitch the underarm seams, catching in a 4-in (10-cm) length of seam tape across the seam to reinforce it. Press the seam open.

PLEATED SLEEVE

1 Cut out, mark, and prepare the sleeve as described in step 1 for making a gathered sleeve (see page 82). Stitch the underarm seam and zigzag-stitch along the raw edges

2 Match the center notch on the sleeve to the shoulder seam and follow the notches to pin pleats in place. Baste and stitch the seam. Finish as in step 4 of making a gathered sleeve (see page 83).

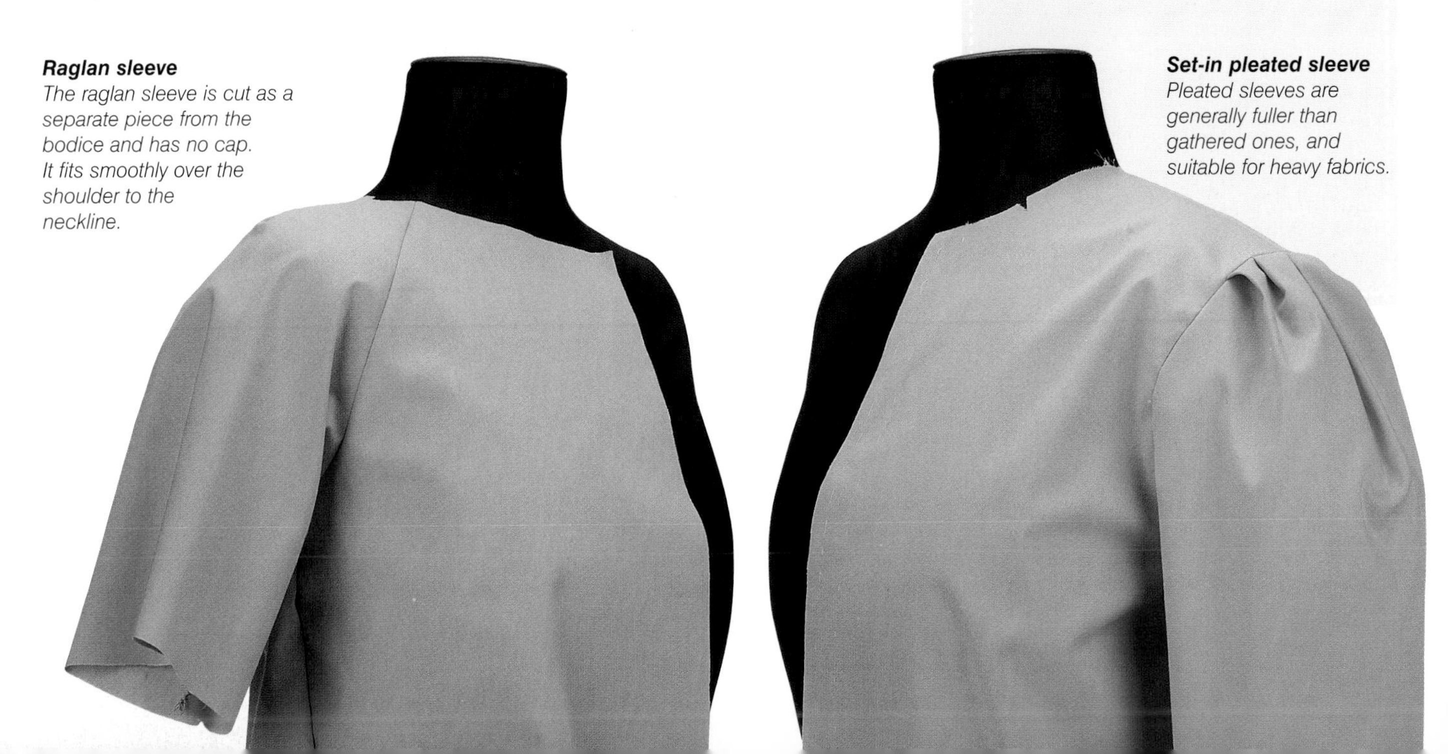

Raglan sleeve
The raglan sleeve is cut as a separate piece from the bodice and has no cap. It fits smoothly over the shoulder to the neckline.

Set-in pleated sleeve
Pleated sleeves are generally fuller than gathered ones, and suitable for heavy fabrics.

Cuffs and plackets

Cuffs are the finished ends of sleeves. They can take many forms, from a simple turned-under hem to an elaborate lace ruffle. A simple gathered cuff with a casing for elastic can be finished with or without a frilly edge.

Snug-fitting cuffs need an opening, called a placket, to allow the hand to fit through the end. Plackets can be faced with a single piece of fabric or bias-cut strip, or finished with two pieces of straight-cut binding for a tailored placket.

SIMPLE GATHERED CUFF

To make a gathered cuff without a frill, place one long edge of a strip of binding right sides together on the raw end of the sleeve, with the short ends of tape on the sleeve seam. Pin and stitch along the long edge. Turn the binding to the wrong side and stitch the other long edge in place. Thread the elastic and secure it as in steps 2 and 3 of making a gathered and ruffled cuff.

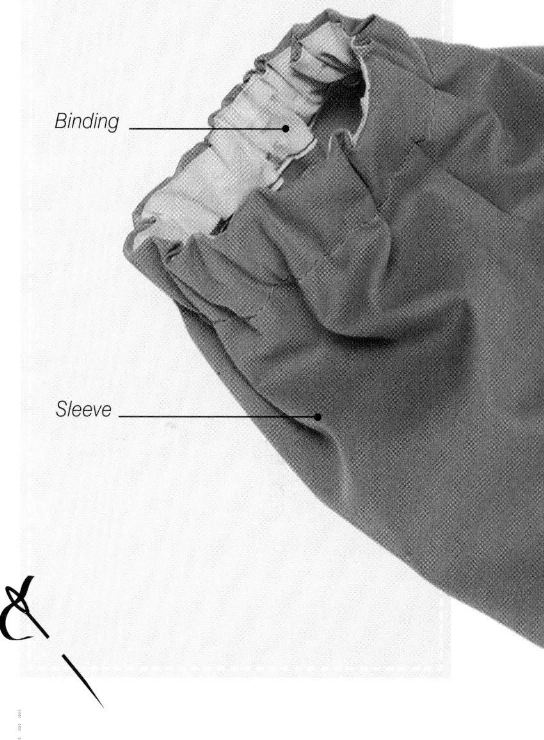

Gathered and ruffled cuff

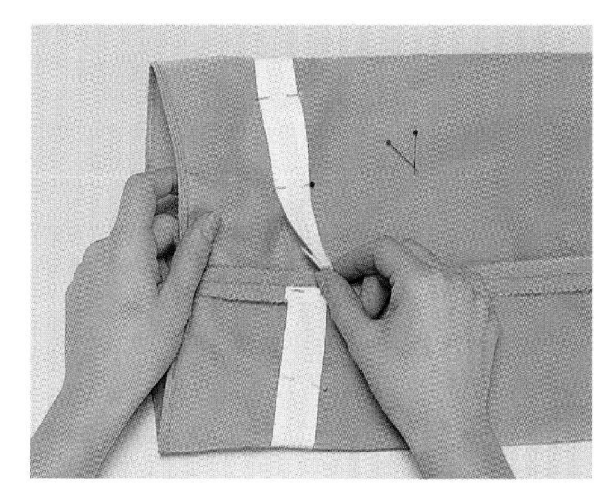

1 Hem the edge of the sleeve and measure the depth of the ruffle from the bottom. Pin the seam tape or binding to the wrong side of the sleeve where the casing will be. Turn under the short ends of the tape where they meet on the underarm seam and pin in position.

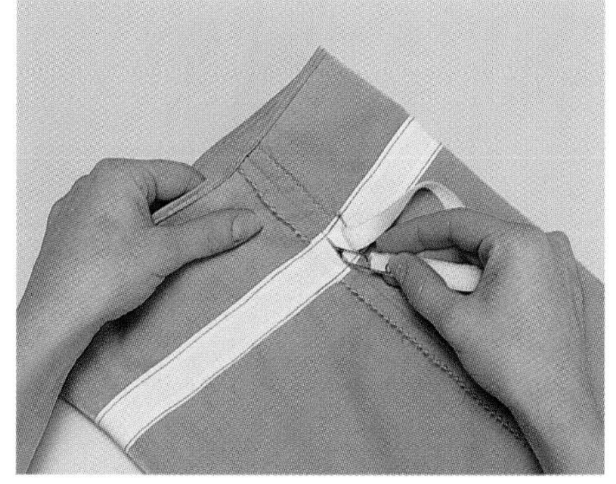

2 Stitch both long edges of the tape to the sleeve. Fasten a safety pin to a wrist-sized piece of elastic and thread it through the opening of the casing.

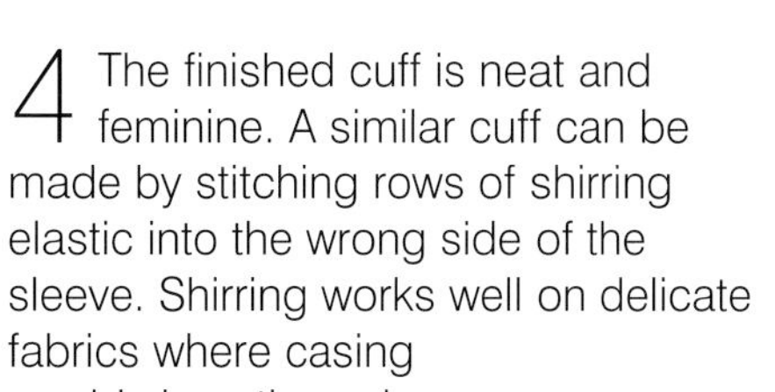

3 Pull the ends of the elastic clear of the casing, overlap them, and stitch them together. Use slipstitch to close the opening in the casing.

4 The finished cuff is neat and feminine. A similar cuff can be made by stitching rows of shirring elastic into the wrong side of the sleeve. Shirring works well on delicate fabrics where casing would show through.

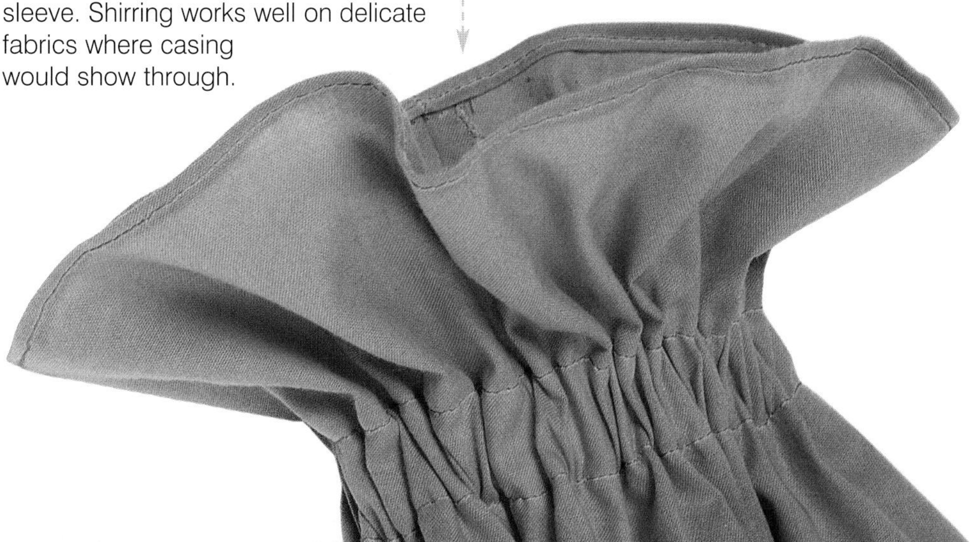

Faced placket

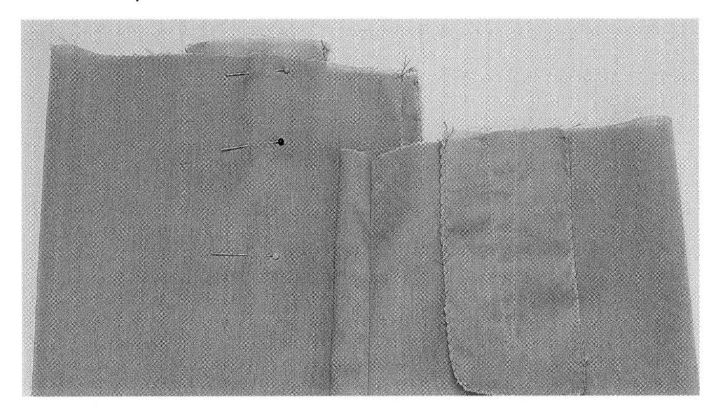

1 Cut out and prepare the sleeve and placket pieces. Pin with right sides together (left) and stitch along the marked line (right). Using small, sharp scissors, slash between the stitching lines to the top of the V.

2 Turn the placket piece to the wrong side and press. Work a row of topstitch around the V (left) to produce a neat overall finish to the piece (right).

Bias placket

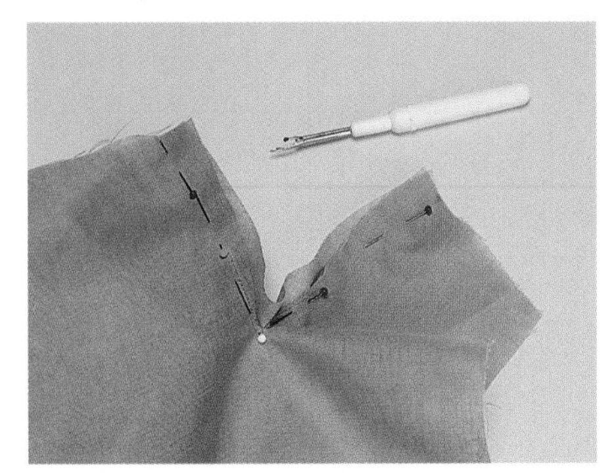

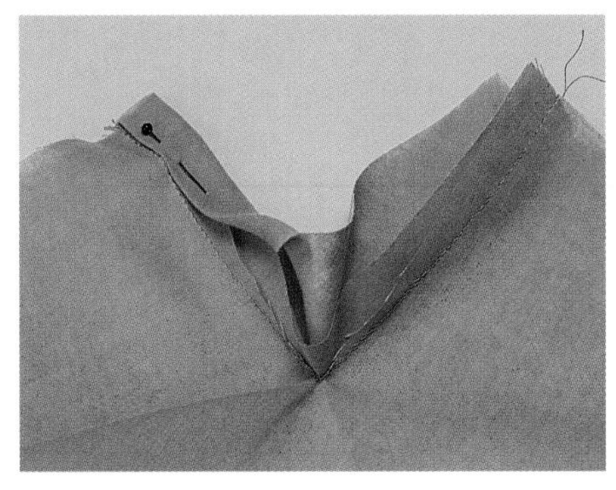

1 Prepare sleeve and bias placket pieces and staystitch for 2 in (5 cm) on each side of the V, making a single horizontal stitch at the point. Using a seam unpicker or small, sharp scissors, slash the placket opening down to, but not through, the staystitching. Pin the bias piece with right sides together to the sleeve piece along the placket.

2 Stitch the placket seam so the bottom edge of the sleeve is level with the corner of the placket. Turn the placket to the wrong side to make a double fold (the placket is wider in the point of the V), and pin it in place along the seam.

3 Stitch the placket in position, removing the pins as you work. Stitch a slanted seam across the top end of the placket. This will help the placket to lie flat once the cuff is attached to the sleeve.

HEMMED PLACKET

This "false" placket is not a slit in the sleeve, but is produced from extra fabric at the end of the sleeve. Notches on the pattern will indicate the placket area, which is turned over and hemmed before the cuff is attached. This placket folds neatly when the cuff is fastened closed.

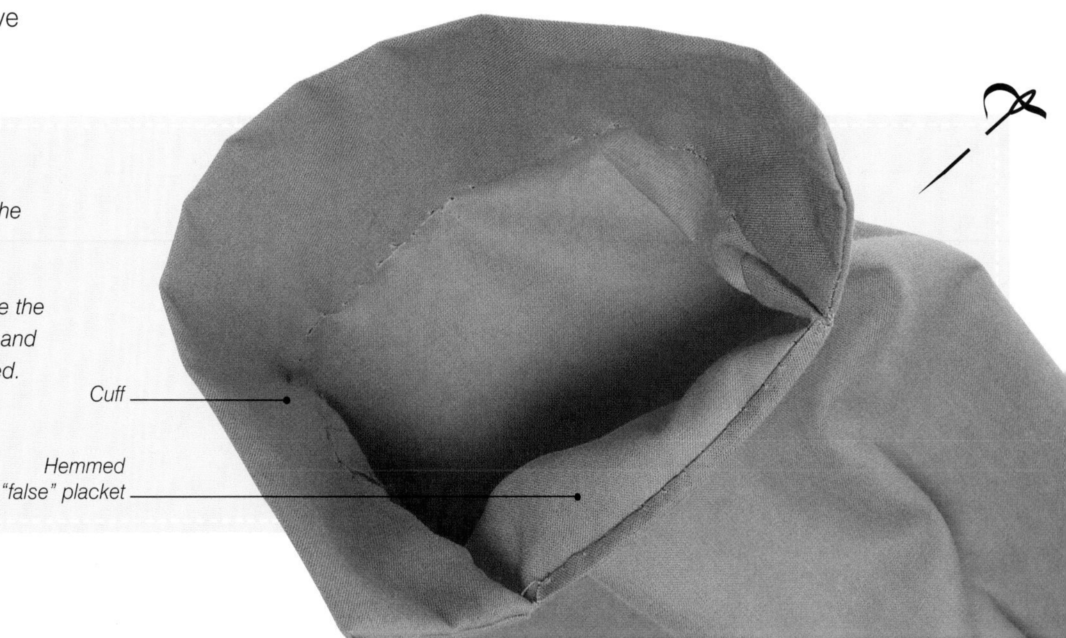

Tailored placket

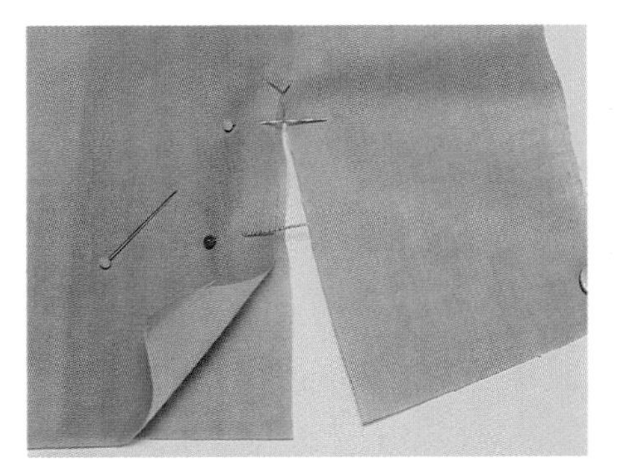

1 Cut out and prepare the sleeve and placket pieces. Cut an inverted V shape at the top of the placket. Pin the right side of the smaller underlap placket piece to the wrong side of the sleeve.

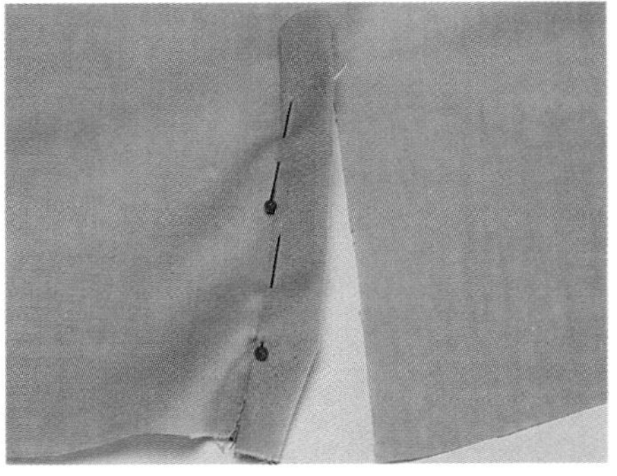

2 Stitch the placket to the sleeve. Turn and press the unstitched placket seam allowance to the wrong side. Turn the pressed placket piece to the right side of the sleeve and pin in place. Topstitch along the seamline.

3 Pin the right side of the larger overlap placket piece to the wrong side of the sleeve. Stitch the seam, then stitch the end of the overlap edge to the top edge of the slash. Press upward.

4 Turn under and press the seam allowance of the overlap placket and baste it in place. Fold the overlap to the right side up to the stitching line and pin. Topstitch along the fold to the top of the opening. Stitch across and up to the point of the placket as shown by the arrows on the inset diagram. To finish and secure all layers, stitch downward, following the seamline (right).

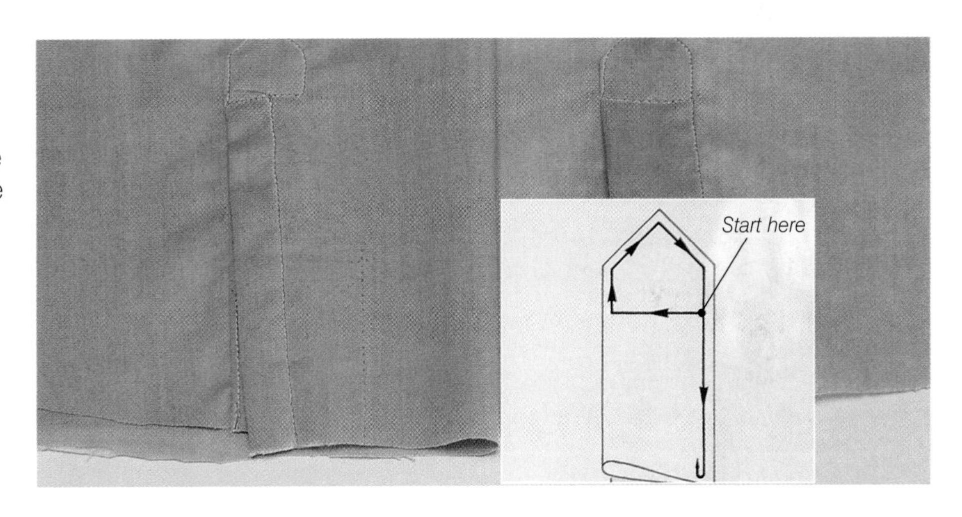

Attaching cuffs

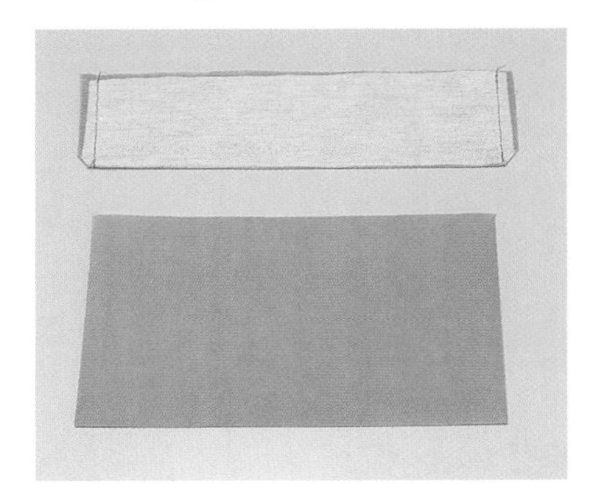

1 These cuffs are ready to be attached. The top one is a single cuff, interfaced, folded, and seamed along the short edges, with clipped corners. Below is a double, or French, cuff, twice the depth of the single cuff, turned out and pressed.

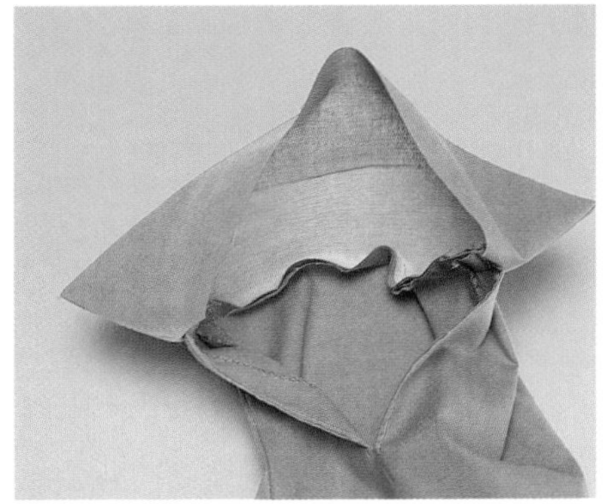

2 Pin one raw edge of the cuff to the right side of the raw edge of the sleeve, easing in fullness according to the pattern instructions. Baste and stitch the seam.

3 Turn the seam allowance of the remaining raw edge to the inside of the cuff and gently press. Pin in place and slipstitch by hand or topstitch by machine to finish.

Collars

Collars are the finishing touch to the neckline of many garments, ranging in style from upright mandarin collars to flat Peter Pan collars. They all share a similar construction and generally consist of two layers of fabric, separated by a layer of interfacing to provide body and shape. In addition, the interfacing helps to prevent the seam allowances inside the collar from showing through on the outside.

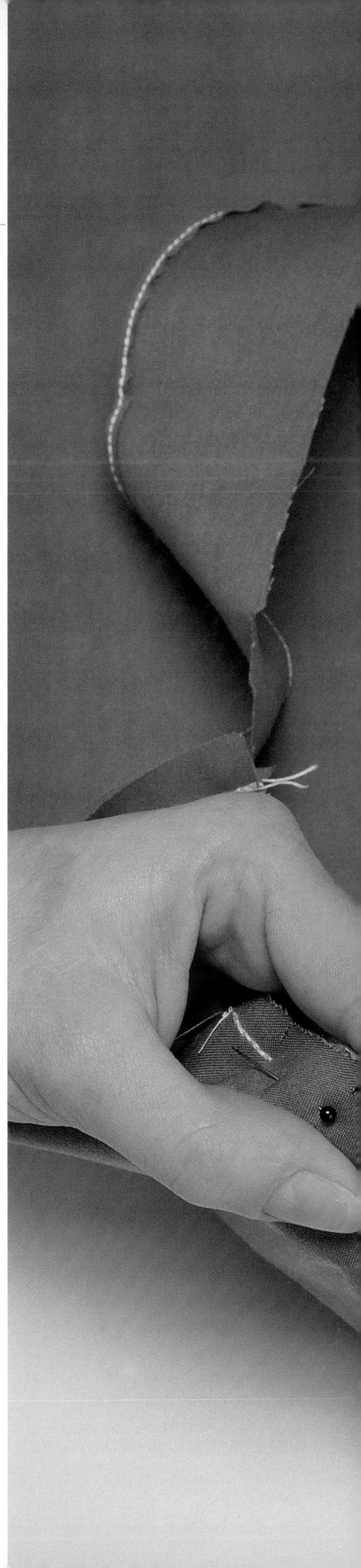

Simple collar

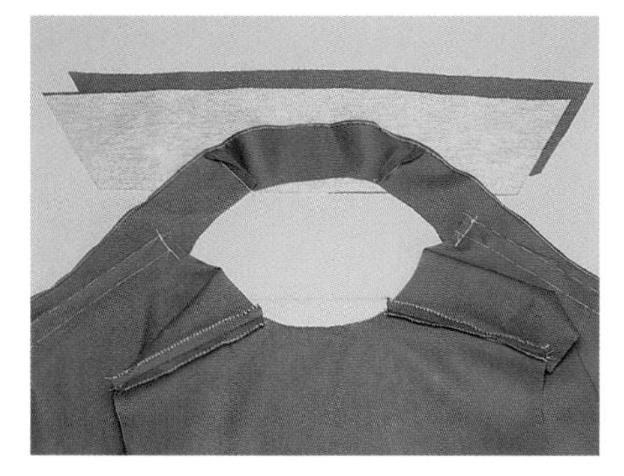

1 Assemble the garment front, back, and facings, following the pattern instructions. Prepare the collar pieces as recommended, and iron on or sew in any interfacings.

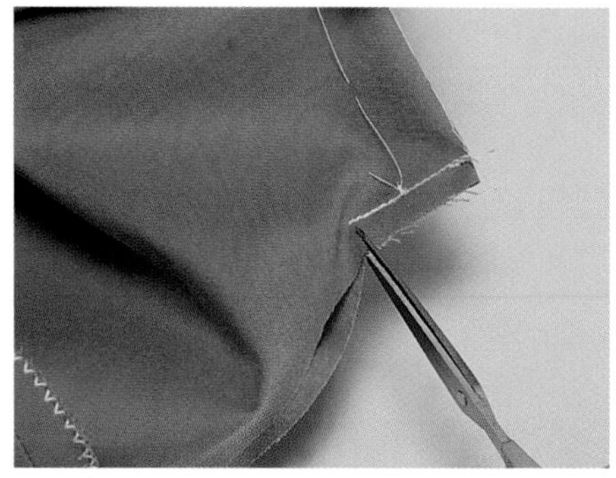

2 If the garment has lapels, fold and stitch this seam to finish the top fronts. Clip into the allowance at the end of the seam, as shown.

Trimmings

For added effect, topstitch a simple collar. Not only will this add a stylish decorative touch, but it will also keep the edges of the collar and garment front from rolling.

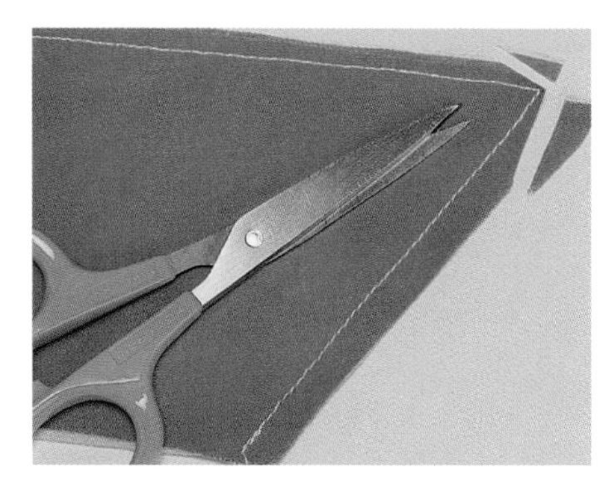

3 Stitch the seam to join the collar pieces. Trim excess seam allowance at the points by cutting away a triangle on each side, making sure you do not cut into the stitches. Turn right sides out and press.

4 Pin the raw edge of the collar to the neck edge, matching notches carefully. Baste in place.

5 Pin and baste the facing in position and machine stitch the neck-edge seam together. Press the facing to the inside.

PETER PAN COLLAR

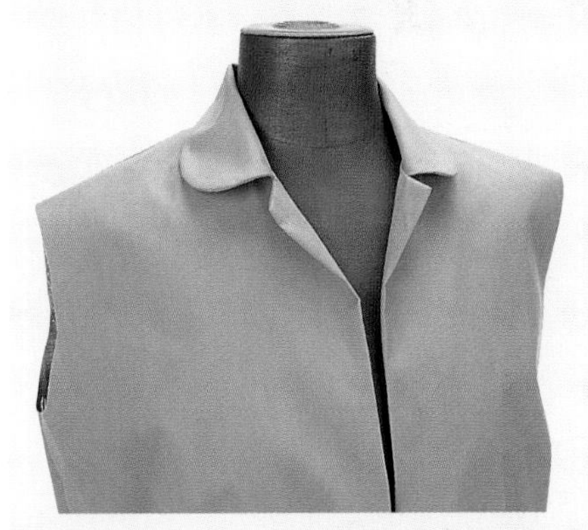

The method shown in steps 1–5 above can be used to apply a simple collar of any shape, such as the Peter Pan collar shown here. For instructions on clipping the curved seam, see page 39.

Shirt collar

A "man-tailored" collar is a combination of a simple collar (see pages 88–89) and a mandarin collar (see page 91). Also known as a "stand" collar, it is commonly used on shirts and jackets, and must fit well to complement the finished garment. Always assemble the bodice of the garment before starting work on the collar.

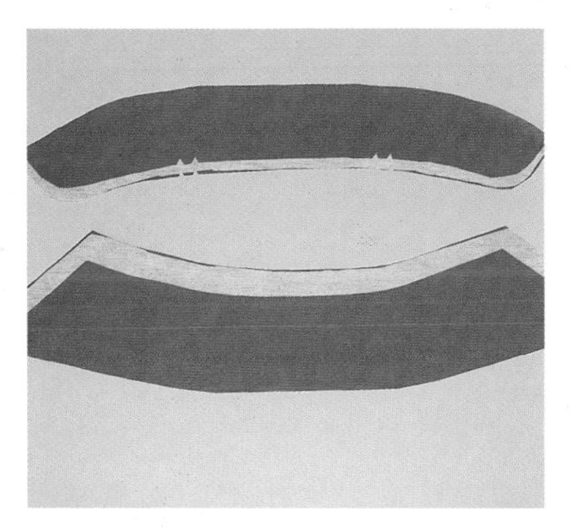

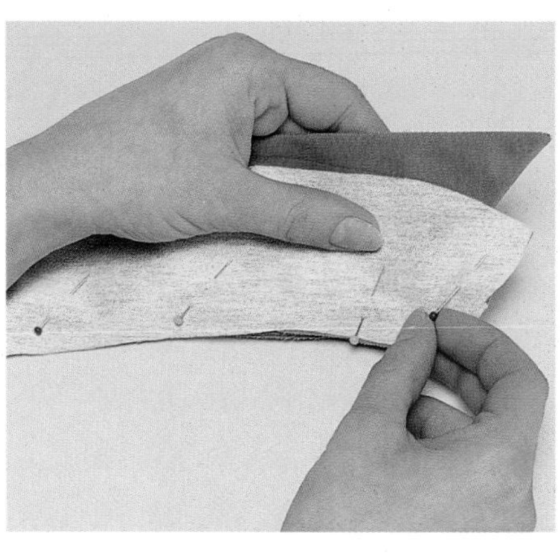

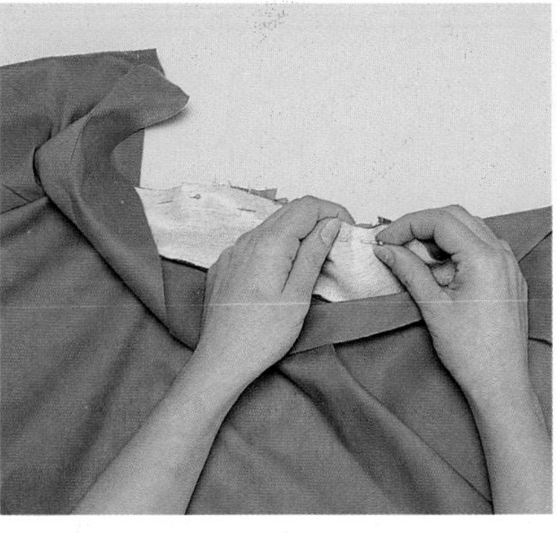

1 Interface one stand piece. Prepare, interface, and assemble the collar pieces. Turn the collar right side out and press.

2 Pin, baste, and stitch the stand pieces to enclose the raw edges of the collar piece.

3 Clip the curves, then turn the collar and stand right side out. Gently press the piece. Pin the right side of the interfaced side of the stand to the garment neck edge.

Shirt collar

The combination of a simple collar with a stand piece creates a neatly tailored shirt.

4 Stitch the seam, removing pins as you work. Finish as in step 5 of making a simple collar (see page 89). Slipstitch inside the raw edge of the stand to cover the neckline seam.

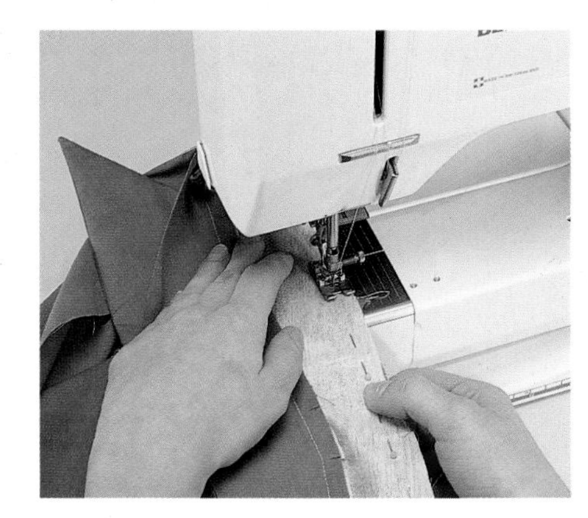

COLLAR POINTS

To make a really sharp point, clip the points (see page 88) and turn the collar right side out. Use the point of a pin to tease out the fabric. Work carefully so you do not pull the stitching or damage the fibers of the fabric.

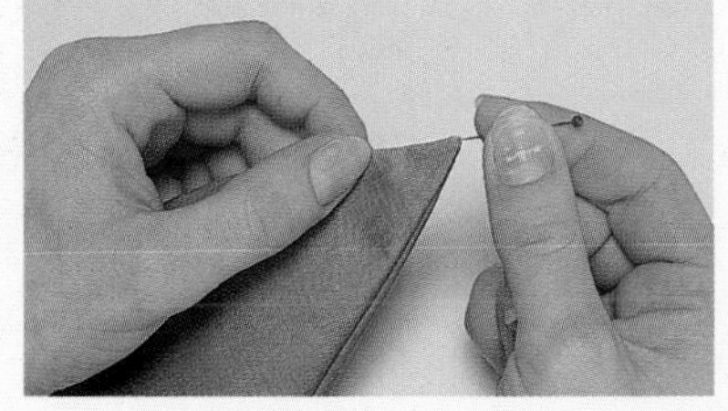

Mandarin collar

A mandarin collar stands up from the neckline seam. Widely used on Chinese garments, from which it takes its name, the collar is usually attached without facings.

1 Assemble the collar pieces as for making a simple collar (see pages 88–89), and clip the curved seam allowances.

2 Pin and stitch the interfaced layer of the collar to the neck edge. Clip the stitched seam and turn the collar to face right side out.

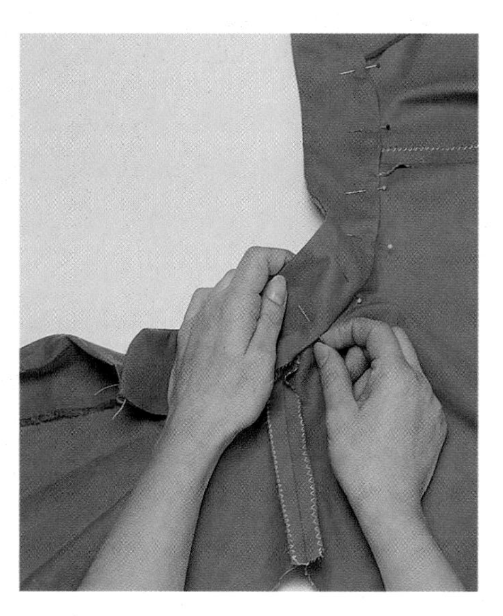

3 Turn under the raw edge of the unstitched layer of the collar and pin it to enclose all the layers and raw edges of the seam.

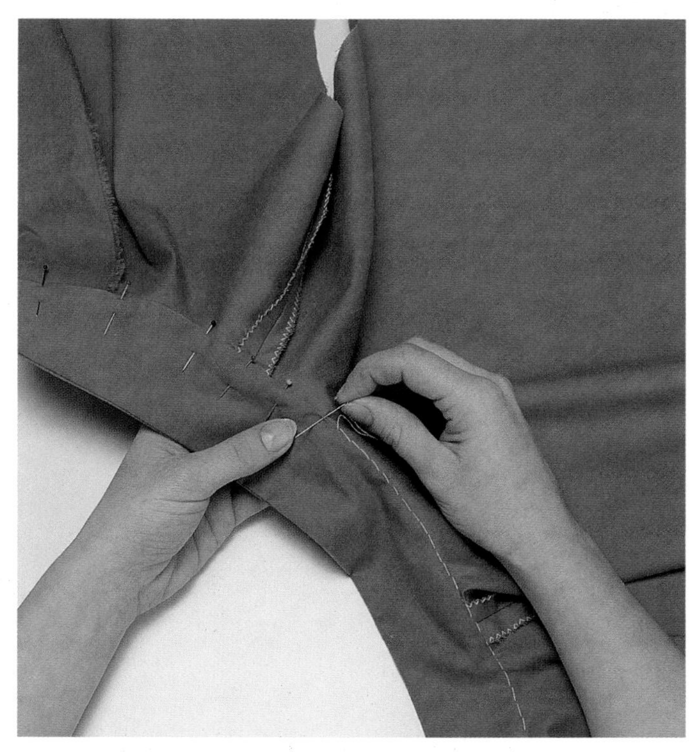

4 Slipstitch the inside neck seam to make a neat finish. Tidy up any loose threads and knots, as well as anything that could be an irritation when wearing the piece.

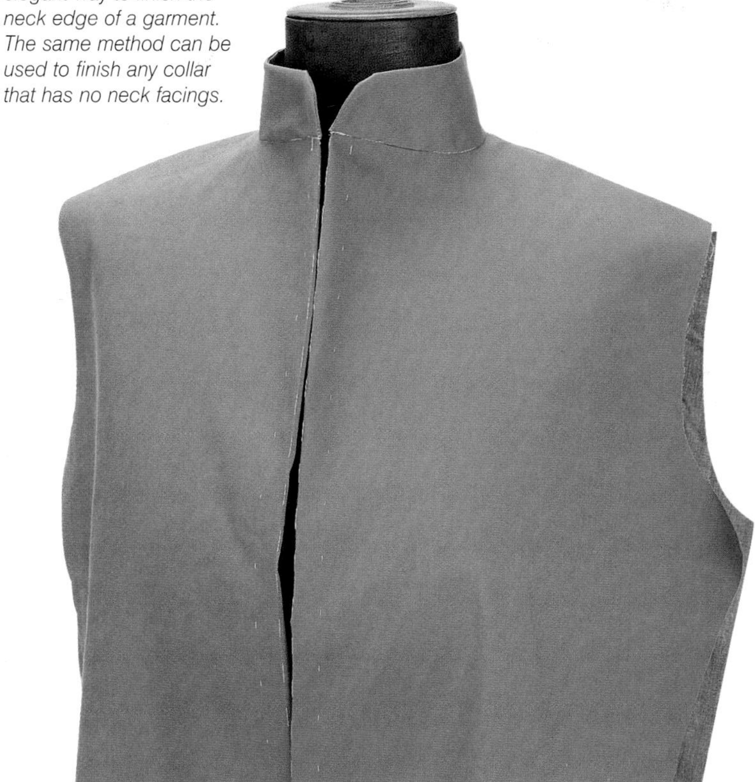

Mandarin collar

A mandarin collar is an elegant way to finish the neck edge of a garment. The same method can be used to finish any collar that has no neck facings.

Waistbands

Waistbands are usually strips made from the same fabric as the garment, cut on the straight grain. They are interfaced and doubled, and finish the top raw edge of skirts and pants, and are sometimes an integral part of dresses. A waistband can be wide or narrow, fitted with elastic or a drawstring, or fastened with buttons or hooks and eyes. The pattern usually contains instructions for assembling the waistband together with suggestions for a suitable closure.

Simple waistband

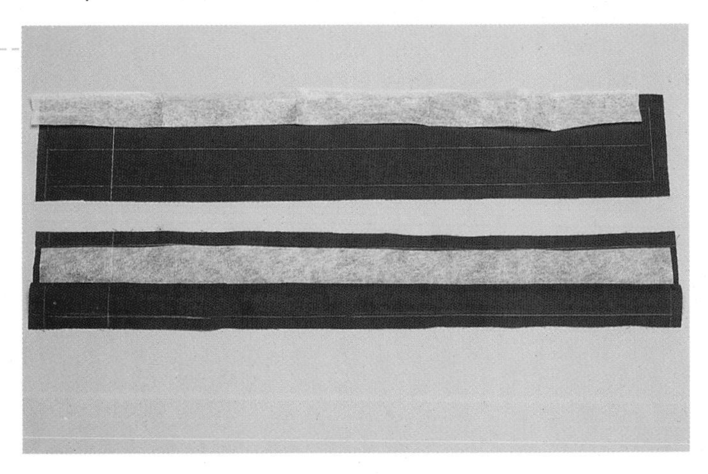

1 Cut out, mark, and prepare the waistband piece and interfacing (top). Iron on or sew in the interfacing and press the center fold lengthwise (bottom).

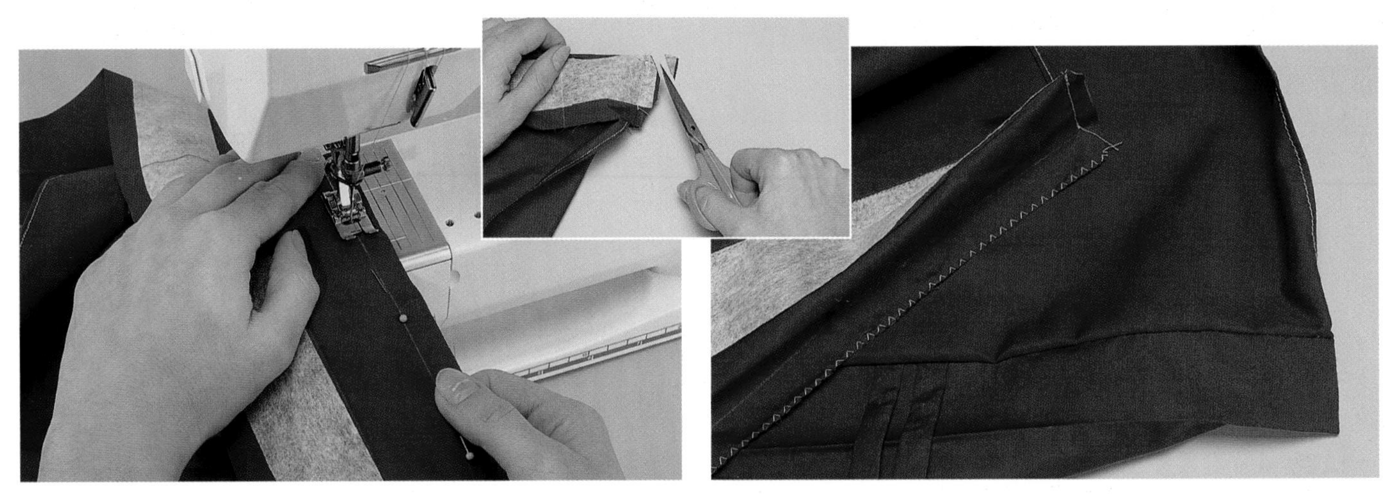

2 Pin the waistband to the garment with right sides together and matching openings. Stitch the seam, removing pins as you work, then stitch the short end seams. Clip all four corners of the piece (inset).

3 Zigzag-stitch along the unstitched edge and turn the band right side out. Pin in place and topstitch the long seam, working from the right side. If desired, a belt loop can be added to the waistband at this stage (see page 93).

FINISHING OFF

On medium- and lightweight fabrics, you can finish the raw edge of the waistband by turning the band right side out and turning the raw edge under before topstitching as in step 3. Add loops at this stage.

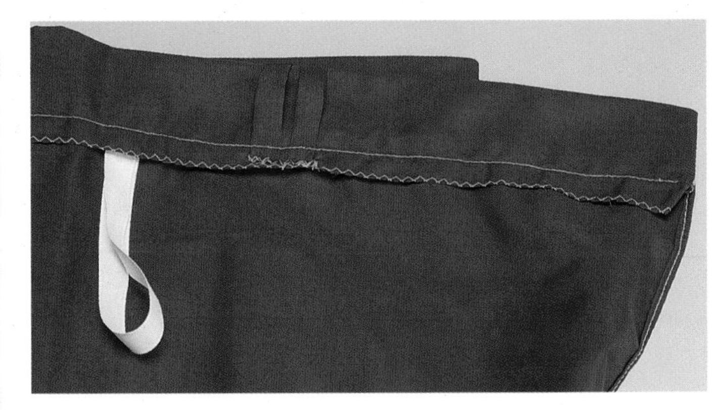

4 The waistband can be fitted with hanging loops made from seam tape. The zipper would normally be put in before the waistband is put on, but has been removed here for the sake of clarity.

Stiffened waistband

1 Prepare the waistband piece as above, cutting a length of grosgrain (petersham) ribbon for a stiffened finish. Pin together and stitch both long edges of the ribbon along one side of the waistband.

REDUCING BULK

Grading seams on thick fabric will help reduce bulk. Stitch the seam and trim the allowance ⅛ in (3 mm) from the seam of the top layer. Trim ¼ in (5 mm) from the next layer. Continue trimming away from all layers in graduated widths.

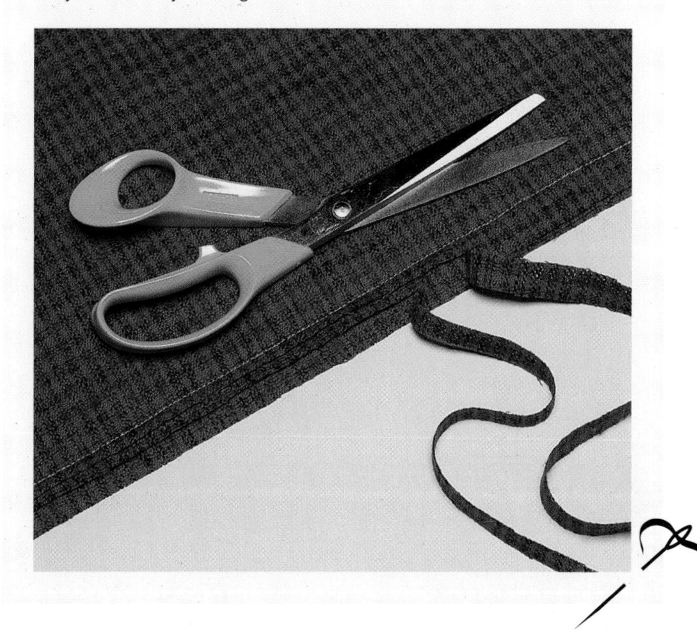

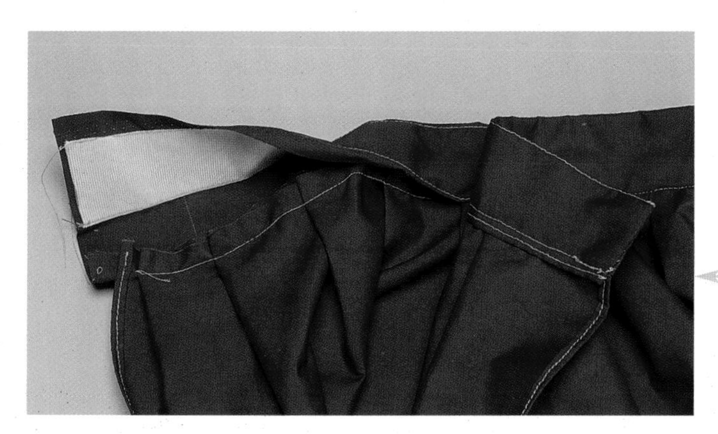

2 Stitch the waistband to the garment as shown in step 2 of Making a simple waistband (page 92). Fold the raw edge under and turn the band to the inside. Pin together and topstitch the long edge. Fold the short ends inside, pin and slipstitch to finish.

BELT LOOPS

It is useful to have some form of belt holder on the waistband of skirts, pants, and some dresses and jackets to hold the belt in place and keep it from getting lost. Carriers should be made from straight strips of fabric. Avoid using bias-cut strips, which have a tendency to stretch out of shape.

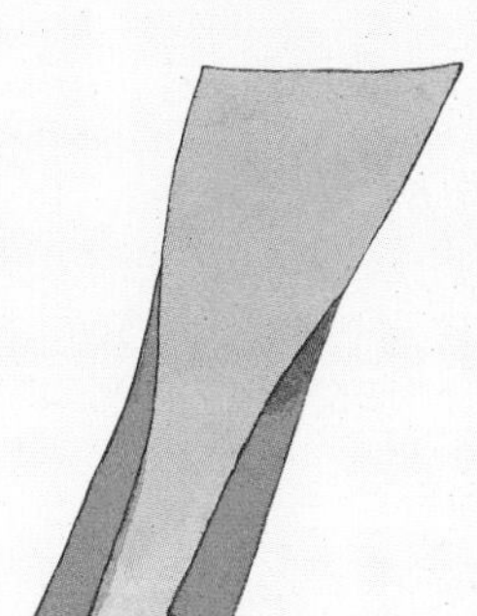

1 For each belt loop, measure and cut out a strip of fabric 1¼ in (3 cm) wide by the width of the belt plus 1½ in (4 cm).

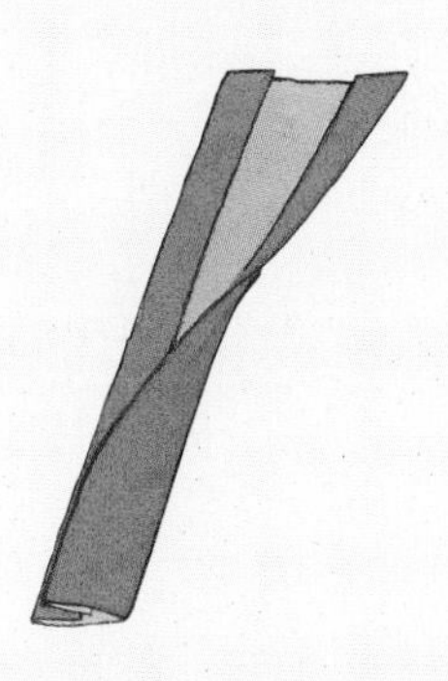

2 Fold ¼ in (5 mm) to the wrong side along each long edge and press.

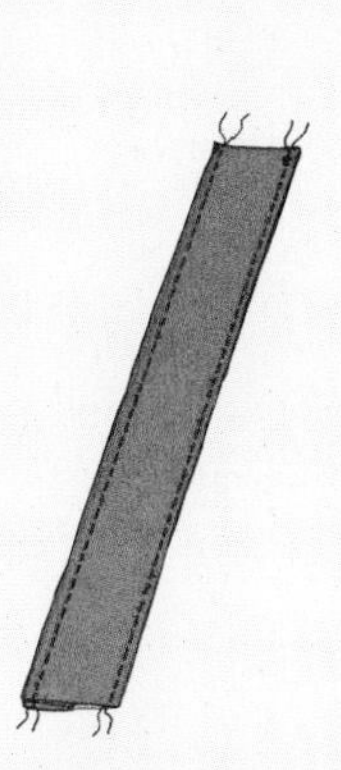

3 Fold the strip lengthwise in the middle and topstitch along the two long edges.

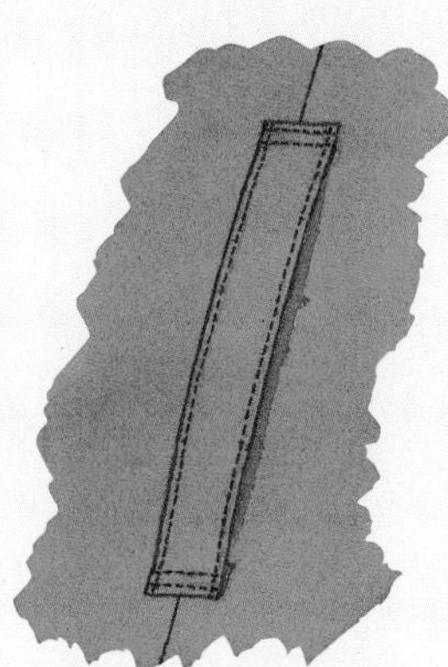

4 Fold the short ends under by ¼ in (5 mm) and pin on the garment. Secure the ends with a double row of stitching close to the folds.

Elastic waistband with folded casing

1 Mark the desired depth of the waistband. Turn the raw edge under ¼ in (5 mm) and fold over to make a casing. Pin and topstitch, leaving a gap in one side seam. Thread the elastic through, overlap the ends, and stitch to secure.

2 Close the gap for the elastic in the folded casing by continuing the topstitch across the seam.

3 To make a drawstring casing, leave an opening in the right side of the garment center seam and thread a suitable length of cord through it.

Elastic waistband with separate gathered casing

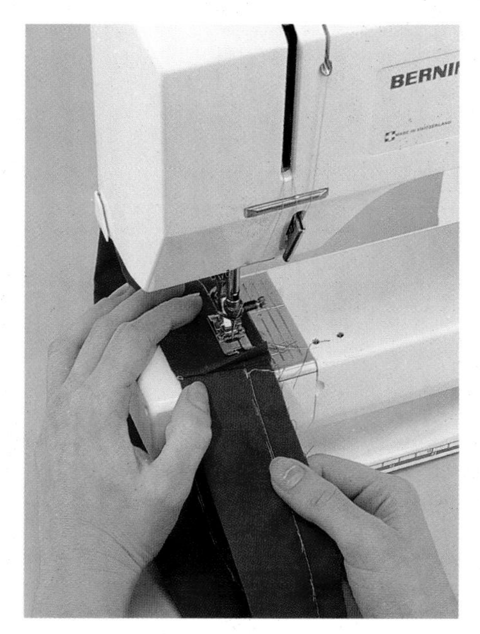

1 Baste the seams on the long edges of the casing piece. Stitch the long edges, wrong sides together, and turn in the seam allowances at the gap in the center seam.

2 Join the seams of the garment. Run two rows of gathering threads along the top edge of the garment and pull up the gathers.

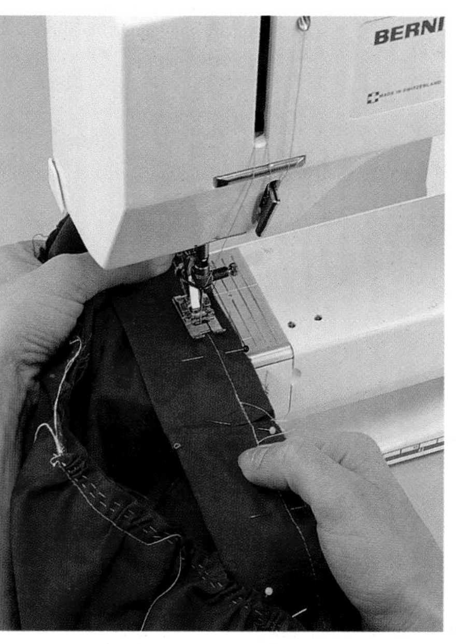

3 Pin raw edge of the casing to top gathered edge of the garment, right sides together and matching center seamlines. Distribute the gathers evenly. Stitch band in place.

4 Thread a length of elastic through the casing, overlap the ends, and stitch to secure. Slipstitch the opening in the casing to close securely.

EVEN GATHERING

To secure the elastic and distribute the gathers evenly at the same time, zigzag along the center of the waistband. Pull the elastic gently to keep the casing smooth as you work.

Pockets

Pockets are functional elements of many garments and should always be strong enough to withstand normal wear and tear. At the same time, they can also provide a striking decorative feature. Pockets are usually made of the same fabric as the garment, but in items made of heavyweight fabrics, internal pockets are usually made of a lighter-weight material.

Basic patch pocket

Patch pockets are placed on the outside of a garment. They are simple to make and have many variations. Using basting or a suitable marker, carefully mark the seamline on both the pocket piece and the garment piece to ensure accurate positioning of the pockets. Patch pockets should be made to work with the design of the item.

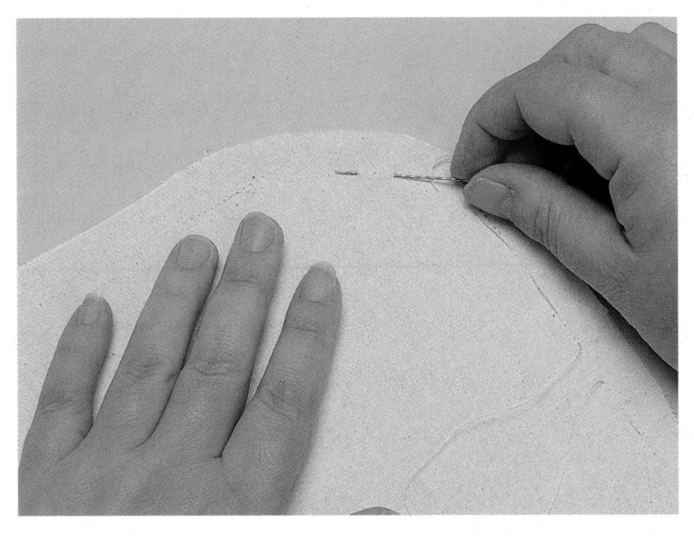

1 Transfer the outline to the wrong side of the garment and pocket pieces. Cut out and baste along the pocket seamline. Zigzag-stitch along the top raw edge.

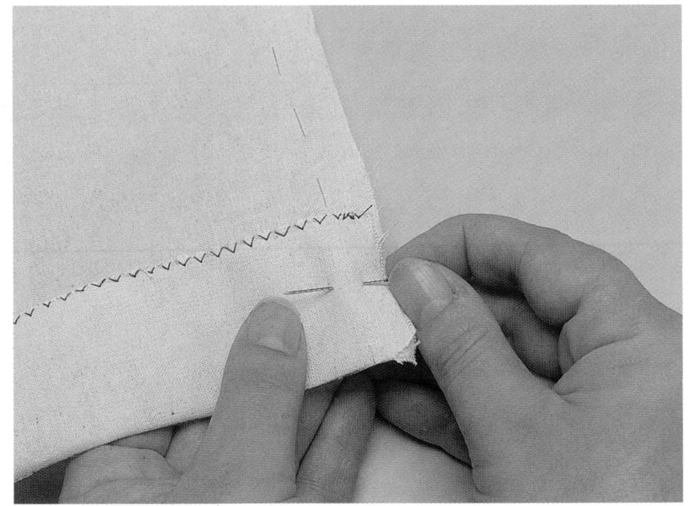

2 Fold the top of the pocket right sides together along the top edge matching the notches. Pin in place.

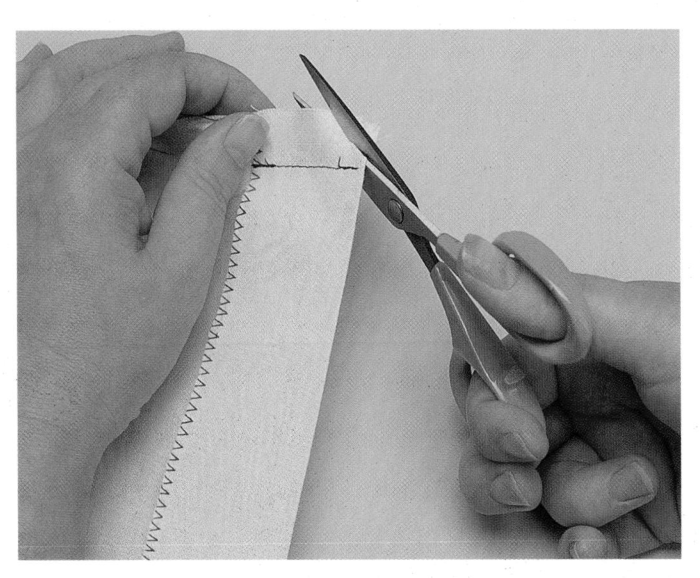

3 Stitch each end of the fold from the zigzag-stitch to the folded edge. Clip the top corners of the pocket.

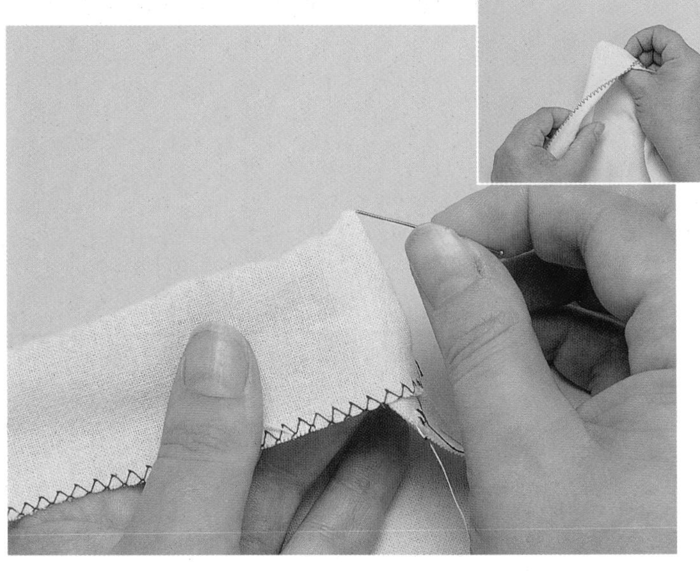

4 Turn the pocket top right side out (inset). Use a pin to tease out the corner to make it sharp and square.

5 Turn the raw edge to the wrong side along the marked lines. Press the piece, then pin and baste it in position, easing the curves as you work.

6 The patch pocket is now ready to be applied. The final stitching has the dual purpose of securing the shape of the pocket and anchoring it to the garment.

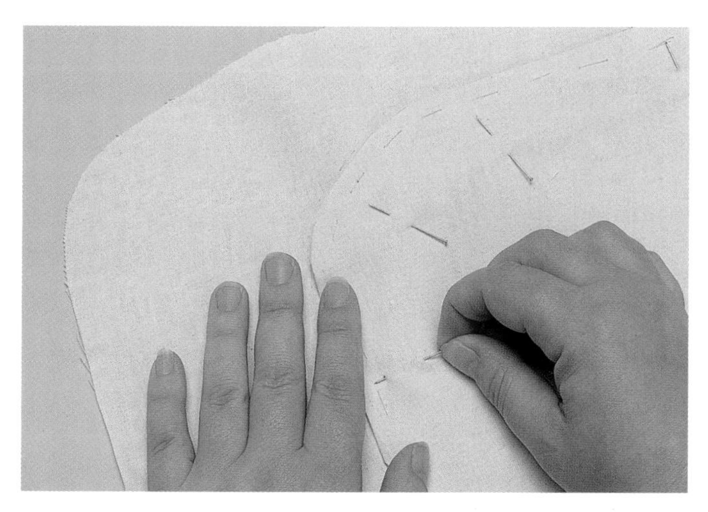

7 Pin the pocket in place on the garment, following the basted outline of the garment.

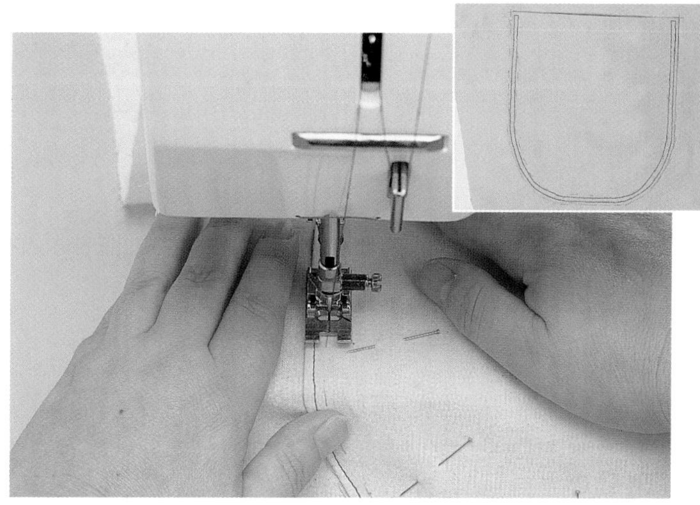

8 Try the garment on to check that you are happy with the final position of the pocket, then sew it in place with a double row of topstitching. Inset shows the final pocket in place.

Lined patch pocket

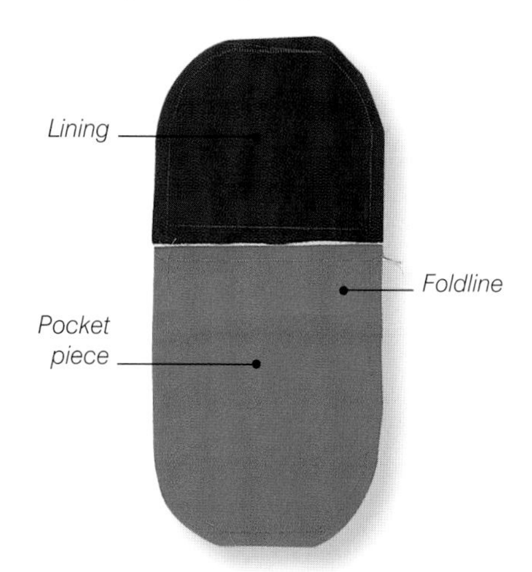

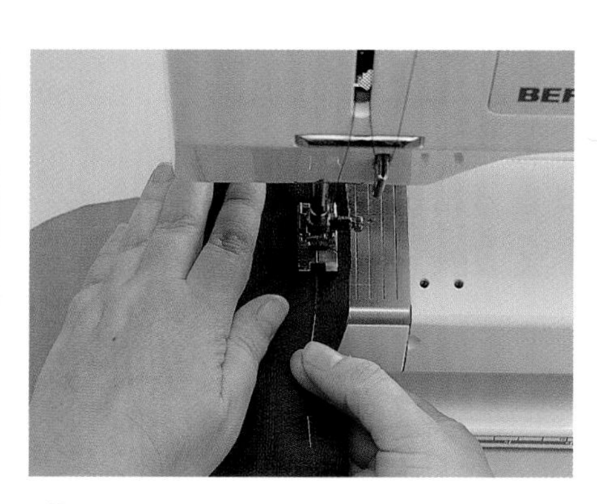

1 Cut out the pocket and lining pieces, then mark the seam allowances with basting.

2 With right sides together, pin, baste, and stitch the top-edge seam of the pocket.

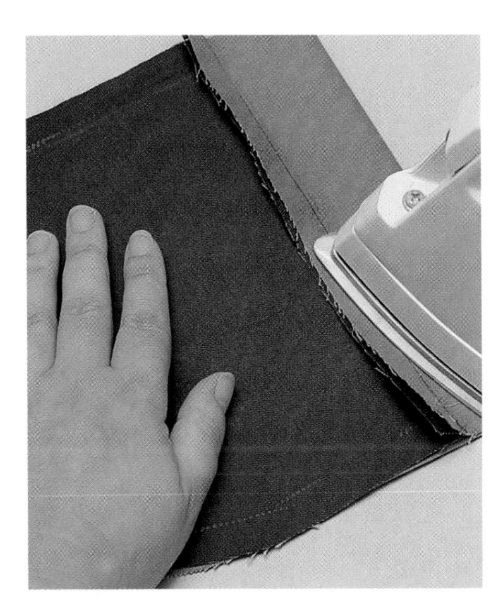

3 Gently press the seam toward the bottom of the pocket. Press the foldline to make the pocket double.

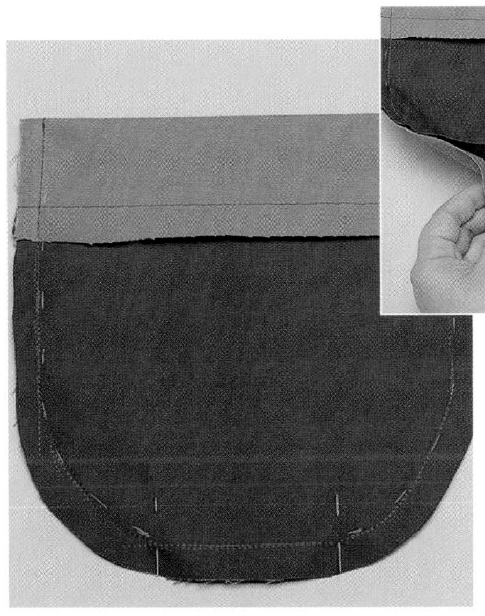

4 Pin and baste the sides and bottom of the pocket, leaving a gap at the bottom. Turn the pocket right side out through the gap (inset), then press the pocket piece.

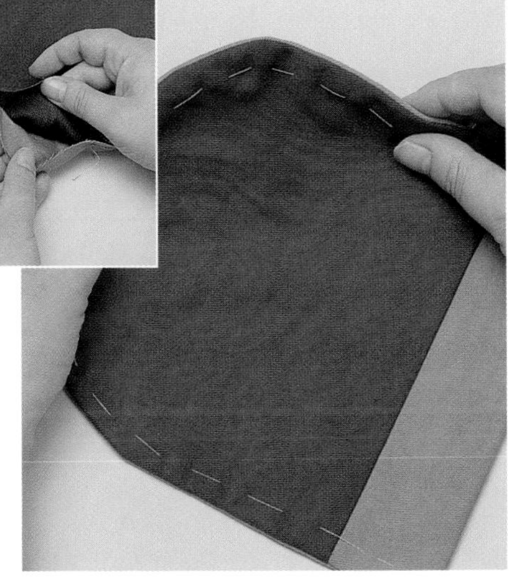

5 Baste all around the edge, closing the gap as you work. Stitch the pocket to the garment as in steps 7 and 8 of making a basic patch pocket (see page 97).

Self-lined patch pocket

The method for making a self-lined patch pocket is the same as for a lined patch pocket, except that no seam is needed to join the lining to the pocket. Cut the double pocket piece and fold it right sides together along the marked line. Then follow steps 4 and 5 of making a lined patch pocket (above).

If you are making small lined pockets, leave an opening in one side edge for turning the piece right side out.

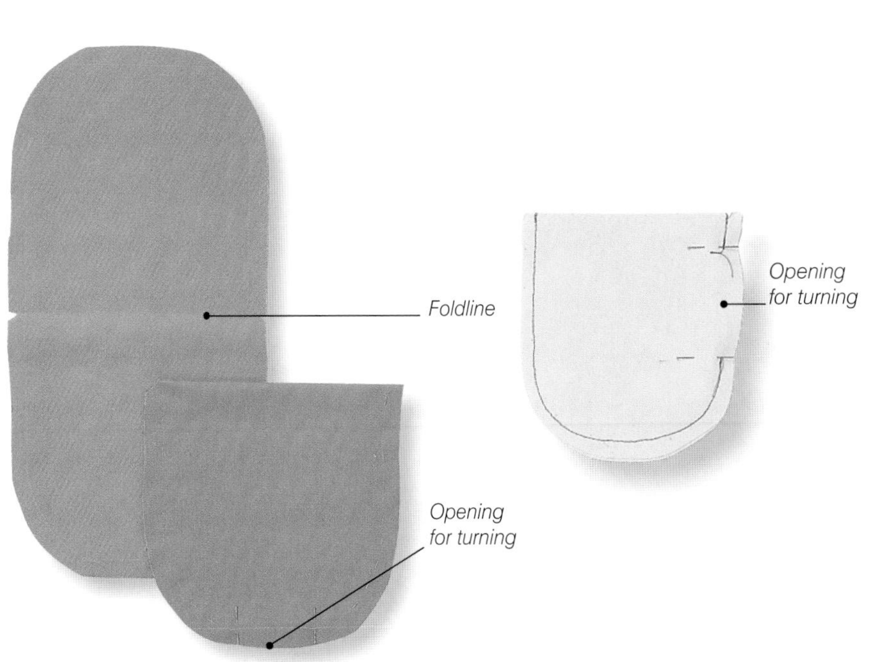

DECORATIVE EFFECTS

There are many ways in which pockets can be trimmed and decorated. This pocket for a child's garment uses a piped edge and a fun iron-on motif.

Front hip pocket

Hip pockets are most commonly used on skirts and trousers. Attached at the waist and side seams, they are made of a front piece that should be the same fabric as the garment and a facing piece that can be a lining fabric. The interfacing gives shape and support to the upper edge of the pocket. Here the dark piece is the pocket front.

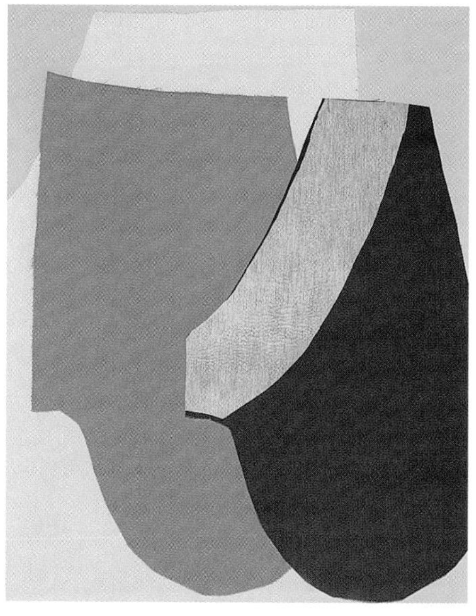

1 Cut out the fabric and mark the garment and pocket pieces. Iron or sew interfacing to the edge of the wrong side of the pocket front piece.

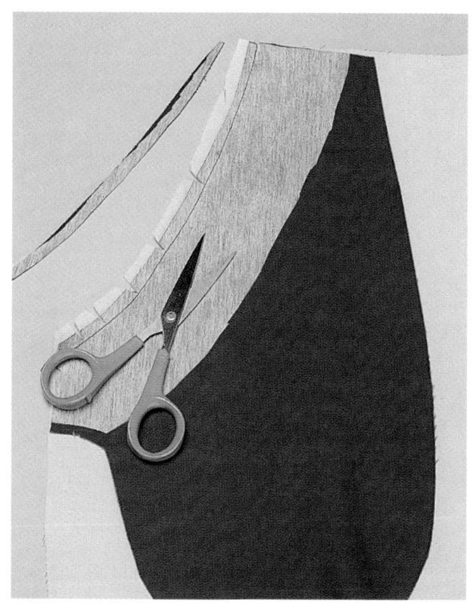

2 Working with the right sides together, pin and stitch the pocket front (dark fabric) to the garment front (pale fabric). Grade and clip the seam allowance.

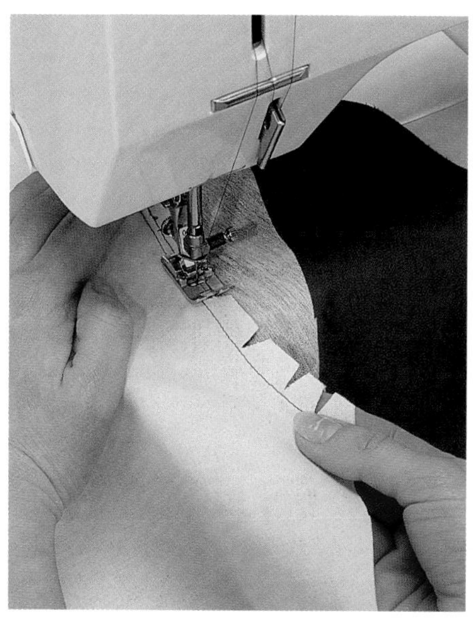

3 Staystitch the inside seam allowance along the clipped seam edge to reinforce the curve. This "understitched" line will appear as a topstitched line on the inside edge of the finished pocket.

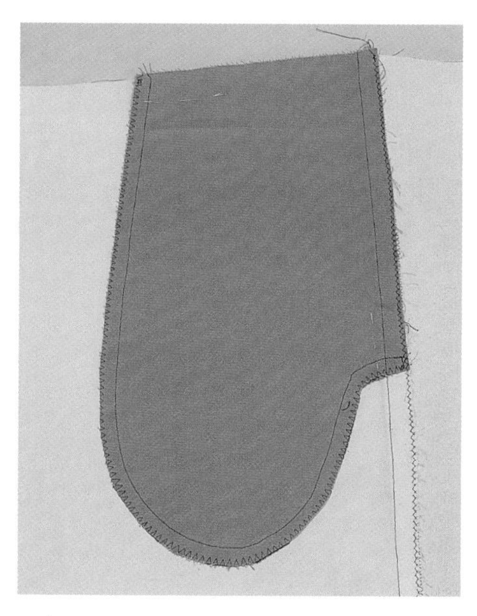

4 Zigzag-stitch the raw edges of the pocket back (mid-color fabric). Press and baste the curved seam. Pin and stitch the pocket back to the pocket front along the curves.

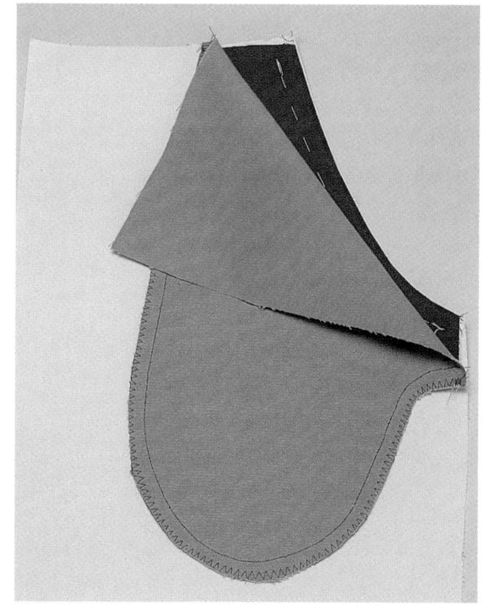

5 Pin and stitch together the garment side seam and zigzag-stitch along the seam allowances. Press to one side so the pocket lies flat against the garment front. Baste in position along the waist.

6 The finished pocket lies smoothly along the hipline of the garment.

MAGIC POCKET

This clever technique works best on a fairly large pocket. It is essentially a patch pocket, but it is sewn so that no stitching lines are visible. The position of the pocket on the garment, and the pocket seamline, must be marked and basted carefully first.

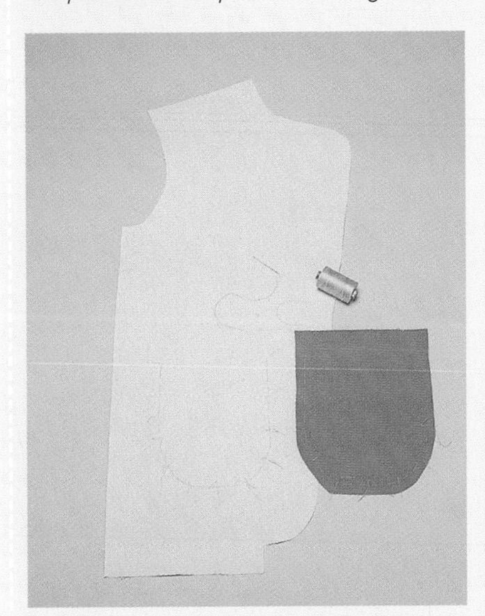

1 Match the basted lines together and place dressmaker's carbon face down on the right side of the garment. Place another carbon face up on it and position the pocket right side up on top. Draw a series of identical balance marks on the garment and pocket.

2 Turn under, pin, and stitch a double hem at the top of the pocket. Match the basted seamlines and balance marks, then pin the pocket's right side to the right side of the garment along one side.

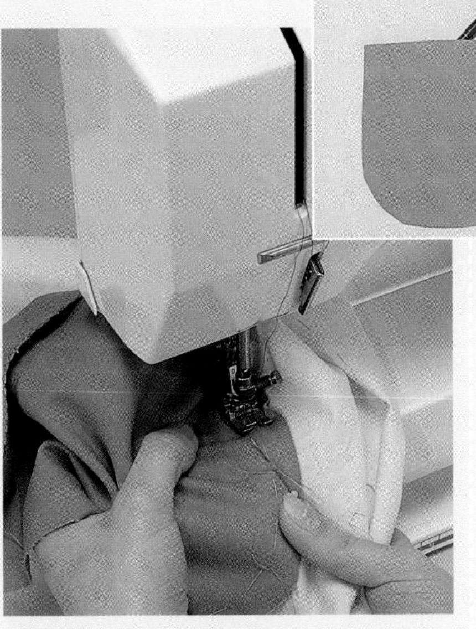

3 Hold both layers of fabric taut and stitch along the seamline. Remove each pin and reposition it farther along the seamline. The finished pocket has no visible stitching on the right side (inset).

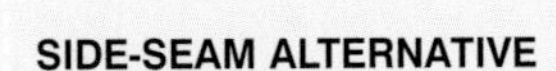

SIDE-SEAM ALTERNATIVE

Patterns offer in-seam pockets in a number of versions. Sometimes the pockets are integral to the garment piece, and elsewhere they are attached to a self-facing edge.

All-in-one integral side-seam pockets are suitable for medium- and lightweight fabrics. Strengthen them with a row of backstitching where they join the side seams.

This self-facing pocket is used mainly on heavy fabrics on which a lighter-weight pocket is needed. The facing strip keeps the line of the garment smooth.

Side-seam pocket

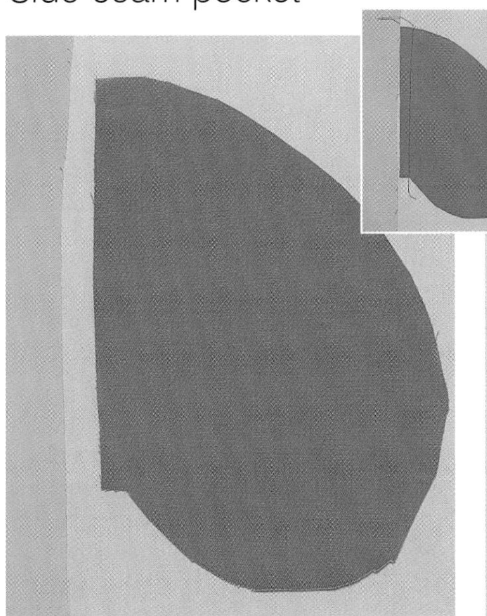

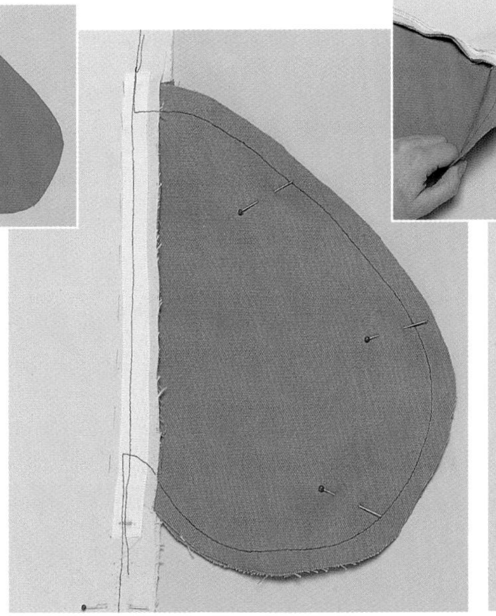

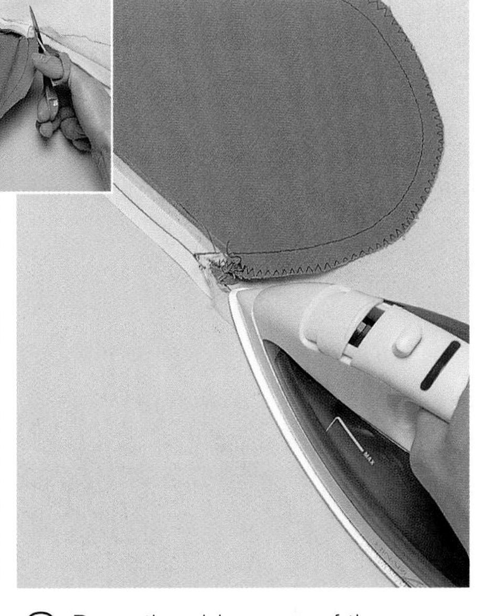

1 Reinforce the pocket edges with two pieces of seam tape slightly longer than the opening. With wrong sides together, pin and stitch one pocket piece to the seam allowance of the front garment and one to the back. Stitch seam tape on the edge of the pocket seam on the wrong side of the garment front and back (inset).

2 With right sides together, pin the garment front and back, and the attached pocket pieces, together. Stitch down the garment seam and around the curve of the pocket, backstitching at the top and bottom of the pocket to strengthen these stress points. Clip the seam where the pocket begins and ends (inset).

3 Press the side seam of the garment open. The finished pocket is a virtually undetectable slit in the right side of the seam.

Welted pocket

Welts are strips of fabric used on the edges of pockets to strengthen them and add a tailored finish. Precision is vital in measuring and marking, and basting is essential to mark positions and to secure the work. To reduce bulk, use lining fabric to make the interior pocket.

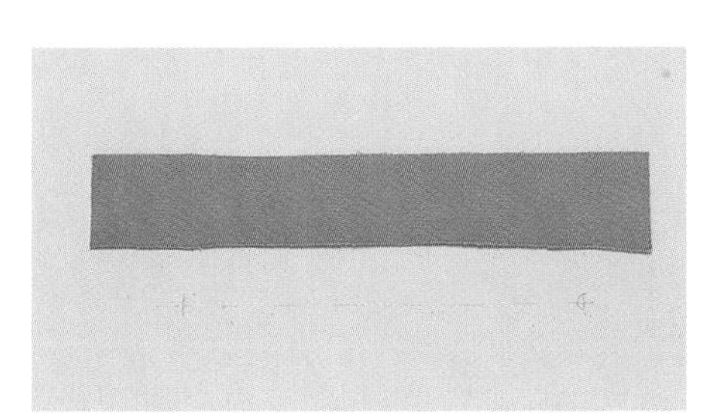

1 Cut out all the pieces. Mark and baste the pocket position on the garment. Fold both welt pieces in half lengthwise and press.

2 Pin the raw edge of one folded welt piece along the top of the basted line on the garment. Repeat with the second welt, pinning it below the basting.

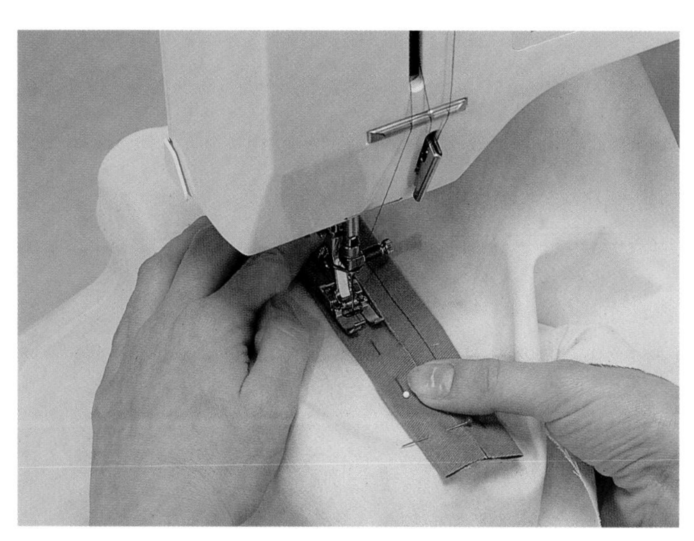

3 Stitch both welt pieces in place along the long edges. Do NOT stitch across the short ends of the welts.

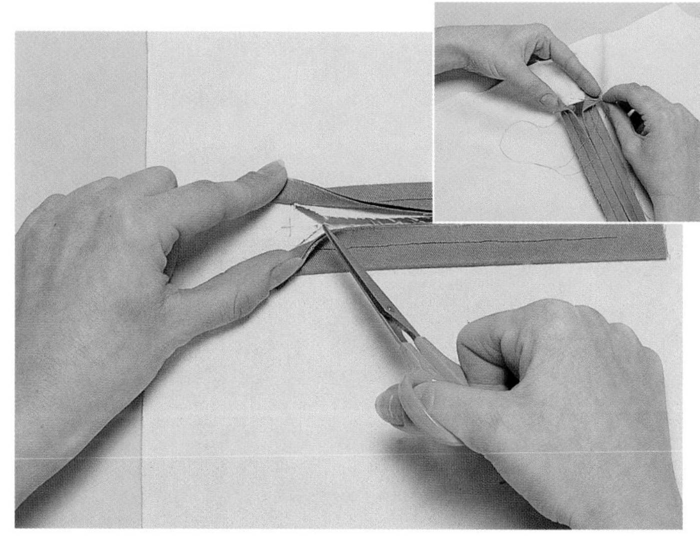

4 Slash the pocket slit from the right side, leaving ⅔ in (1.25 cm) uncut at each end. Clip into each corner of the slash. Turn back a triangle at each end of the slash; then baste and stitch on the wrong side (inset).

5 Turn the welts to the wrong side through the slit. Baste the finished right-side edges together to reinforce them until the garment has been completed. Working on the wrong side of the garment, pin and stitch the top edge of the pocket piece to the raw edge of the top welt. Make sure the garment itself is kept clear of the stitching (inset).

6 Attach the second pocket piece to the bottom welt using the same procedure. Fold down the top pocket piece and gently press.

7 Pin the two pocket pieces together and stitch along the raw edges of the pocket. To finish, zigzag-stitch along the raw edges.

Bound pocket

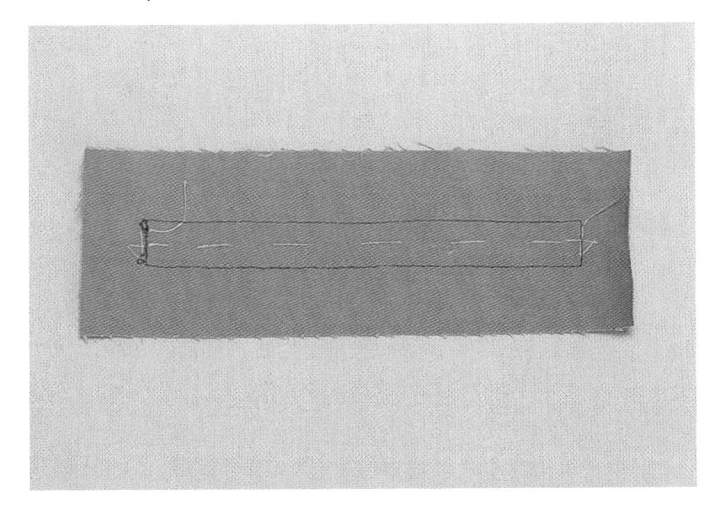

1 Mark the pocket position on the garment piece and baste stitching lines on the pocket binding strip. With right sides together, baste and stitch the pocket binding strip to the garment around all four basted guidelines.

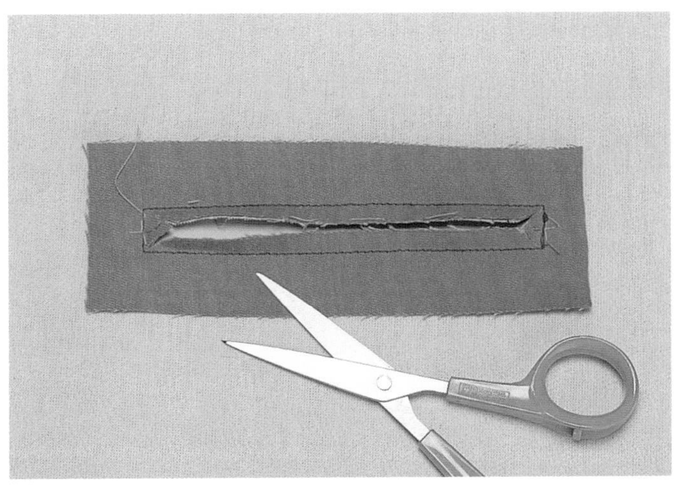

2 Slash through the pocket slit on the garment piece (see step 4 of making a welted pocket, opposite).

3 Turn the pocket binding strip through the opening to the wrong side of the garment. Press, then baste the strip closed. Stitch a pocket piece to each long raw edge of the pocket binding strip.

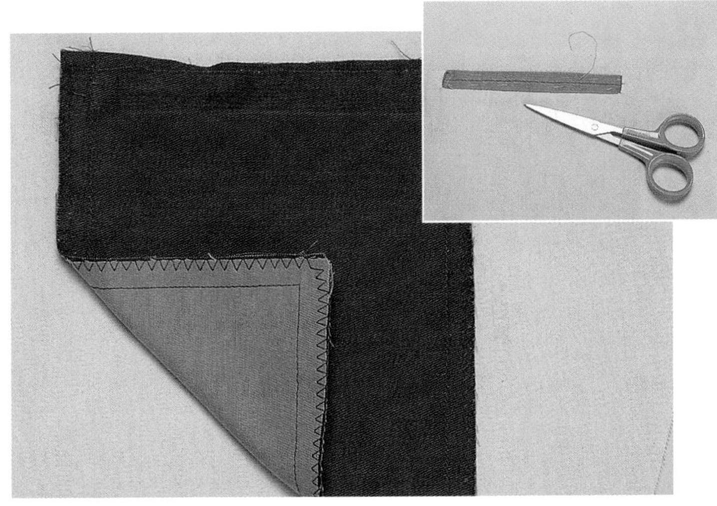

4 Pin and stitch the pocket pieces together along the raw edges, then zigzag-stitch to finish the edges neatly. Remove the basting. The completed pocket is neatly hidden behind the slit (inset).

FALSE POCKET

To make a false pocket or to cover a plain slit pocket, cut two pieces in the shape of a pocket flap. With right sides together, pin and stitch all sides except the top edge. Clip the corners and turn right side out. Press and, if desired, topstitch the edges. Position the right side of the flap upside-down on the garment, fold over to cover the raw edge, and pin in place. Topstitch the flap to the garment.

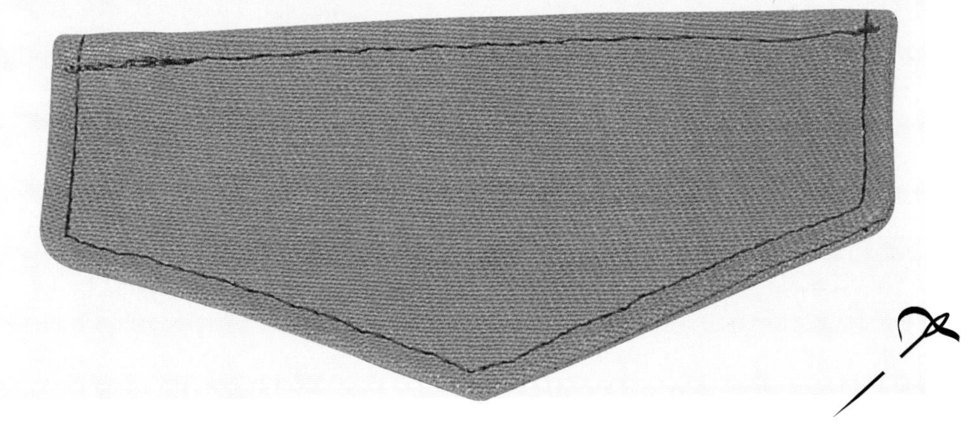

Fasteners

Most garments need some form of fastener. Zippers, perhaps the most daunting to insert, consist of a fabric tape held together by a set of metal or plastic teeth that interlock when a slider is pulled upward to close the garment. Always match the weight of the zipper to the weight of the fabric. Alternative fasteners are buttons, which come in all shapes, sizes, and colors, and more specialized ready-made items like popper snaps and hooks and eyes.

Center zippers

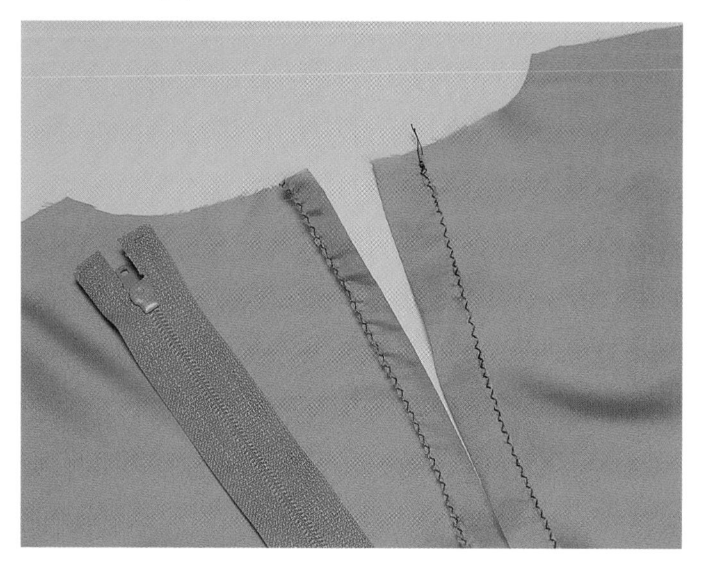

1 Measure and mark the zipper's position on the seams, using the zipper as a guide. Stitch the seam up to the marks, leaving enough room at the top for the facing seam. Zigzag-stitch the raw edges of the seam allowance.

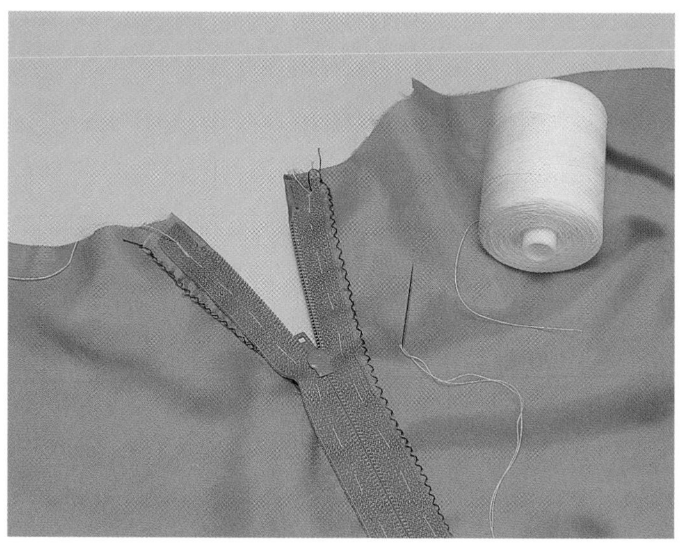

2 Place the closed zipper on the prepared seam and pin it in the correct position. Baste along both sides of the zipper tape to hold it in place on the garment.

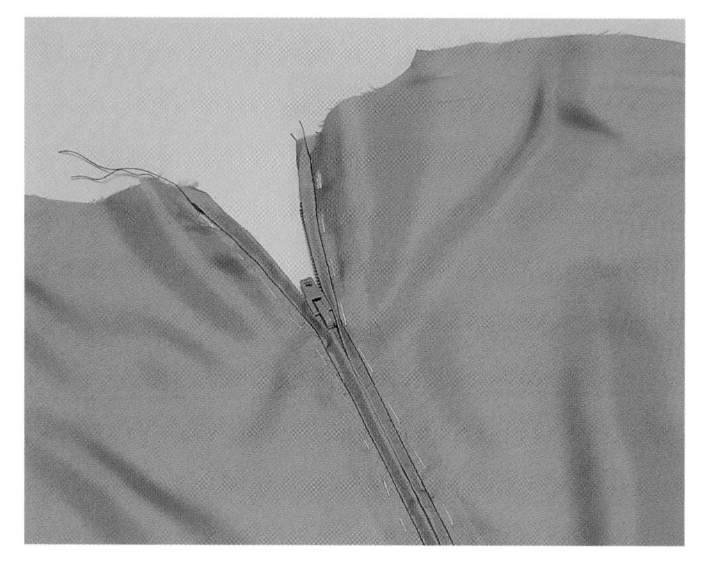

3 Turn the garment piece to the right side. Starting at one top edge of the tape and working around to the other, stitch the zipper in place using a zipper foot. Keep the corners as neat and square as possible.

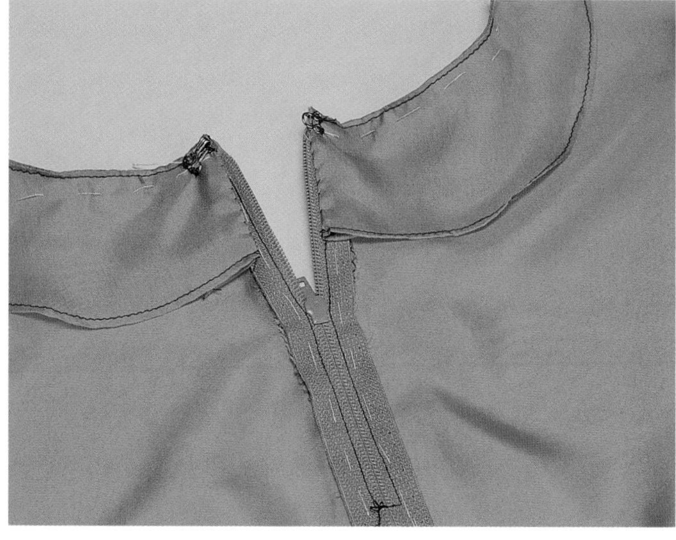

4 Add the facing or waistband piece to the garment and slipstitch the ends to the zipper tape. Avoid letting the stiches catch on the zipper teeth. Add other fasteners if necessary and remove the basting.

Lapped zippers

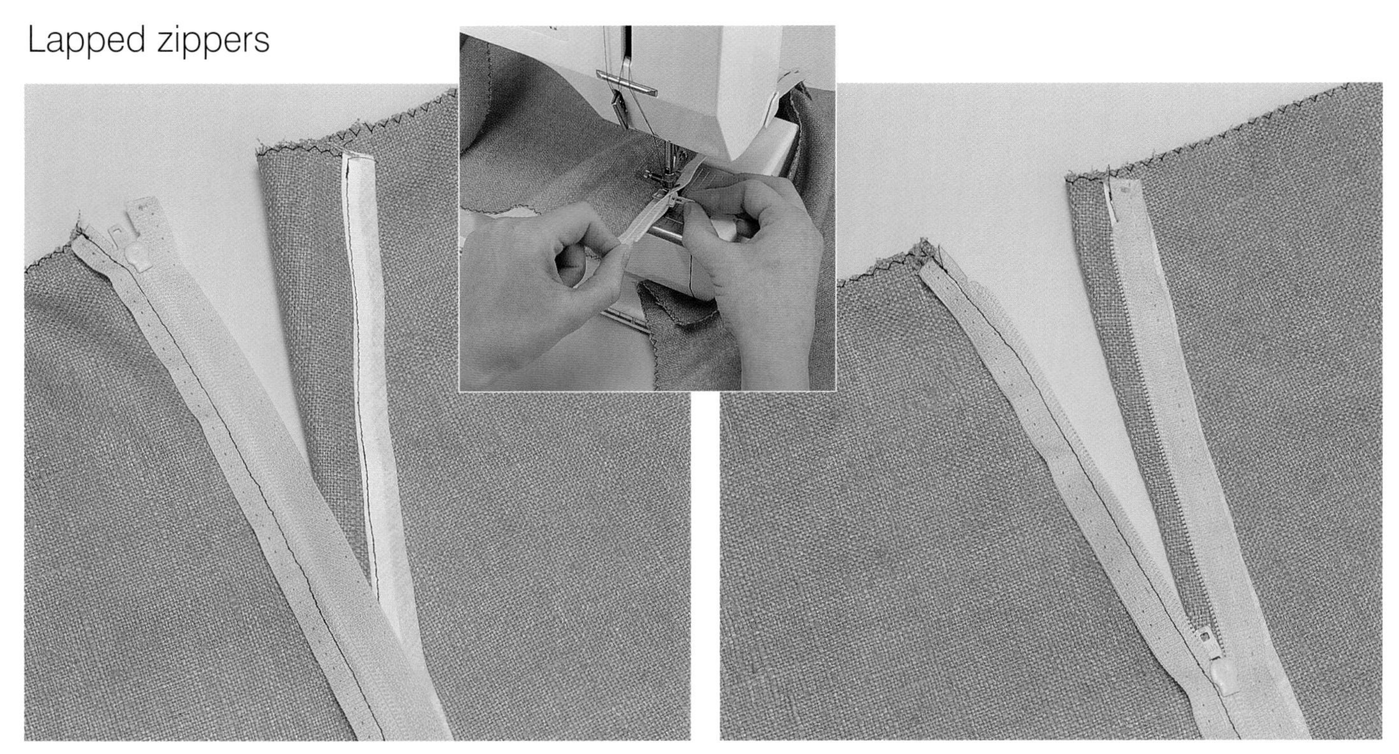

1 Stitch the seam to where the zipper will begin. Zigzag-stitch the raw edges. Open the zipper, and pin and baste it to one side of the seam allowance, which will become the underlap. Then, working from the wrong side, stitch with a zipper foot. Strengthen the raw edge of the overlap side of the seam allowance with seam tape (inset).

2 Fold the overlap edge to the wrong side of the garment. Pin and baste the zipper into position along both sides of the zipper tape, then close the zipper.

3 Stitch the closed zipper in place on the overlap side and across the bottom, then remove the basting. Make sure the zipper slides easily when opened and closed, and check that it is hidden in the seam (inset).

OPEN-ENDED ZIPPER

To insert an open-ended zipper in a garment, fold the lengthwise facings or seam allowances under and baste along the seamline. Insert the zipper as shown for center zippers (see opposite), stitching on the right side of the garment, and then remove the basting.

Fly-front zipper

1 Cut out and prepare the garment pieces. Finish all raw edges with zigzag stitch and baste all the zipper markings shown on the pattern.

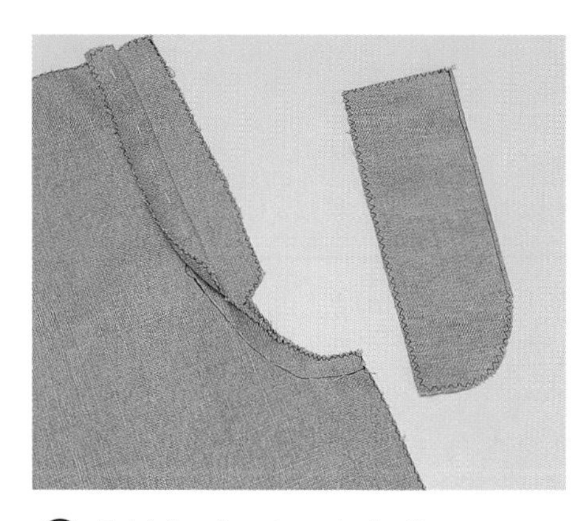

2 Fold the fly piece in half, wrong sides together, and topstitch ⅛ in (3 mm) from the fold. Zigzag-stitch the other edges together. Stitch the curved garment seam. Fold underlap to wrong side. Baste along the fold.

3 Open zipper and align the teeth with the underlap fold. Pin, baste, and stitch the zipper on the underlap. Close the zipper and fold the overlap along the basted line. Baste through all layers on the overlap (inset).

4 Pin the fly piece over the closed zipper, making sure that the curved edges match. Baste in position along the seamline.

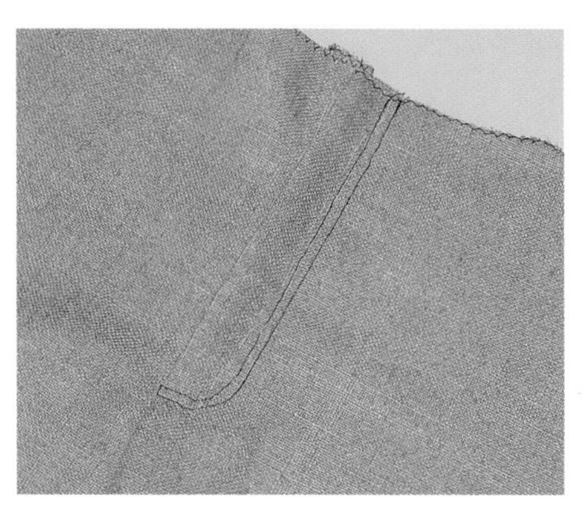

5 Working on the right side of the garment, make a double row of topstitching to follow the curved line of basting on the fly piece.

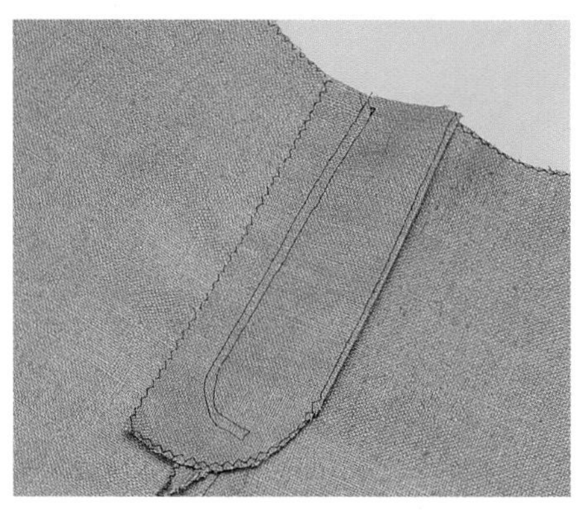

6 Remove all basting. The double row of stitching strengthens the curve of the finished fly. This can be seen on the wrong side.

SHORTENING A ZIPPER

To shorten a zipper, sew the bar of a hook-and-bar fastening securely across the point where the zipper needs to end. Cut the end of the zipper below the bar.

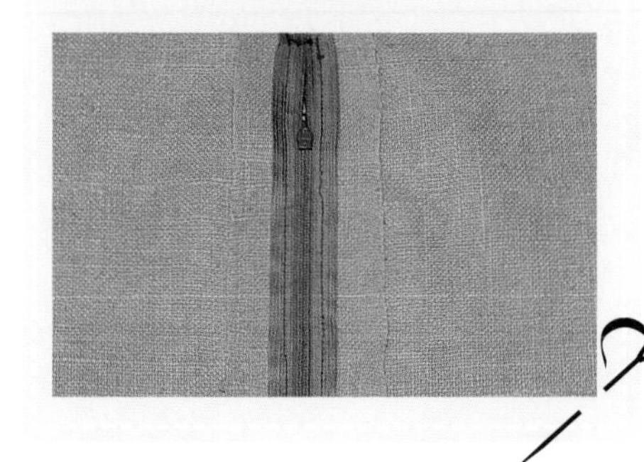

Hand-sewn buttonhole

1 Mark the buttonhole position on the wrong side of the buttonhole band. Baste to mark the center line. Baste along each long side to stabilize the buttonhole.

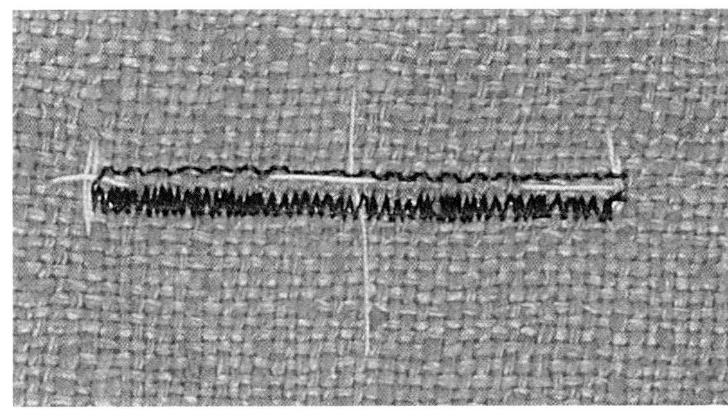

2 Slit the opening. Cut a piece of waxed thread more than twice the buttonhole length. Lay the thread on the top edge and work buttonhole stitch along the edge using a fine needle. Catch the waxed thread in the stitching.

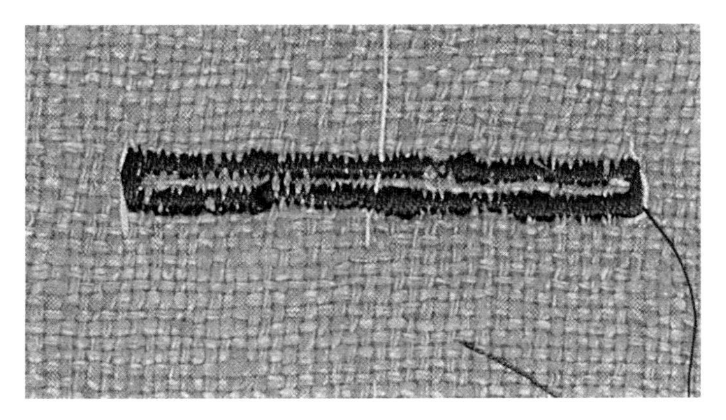

3 Repeat along the lower edge of the buttonhole, always catching in the waxed thread as you work. Keep the stitches small and neat for a professional finish.

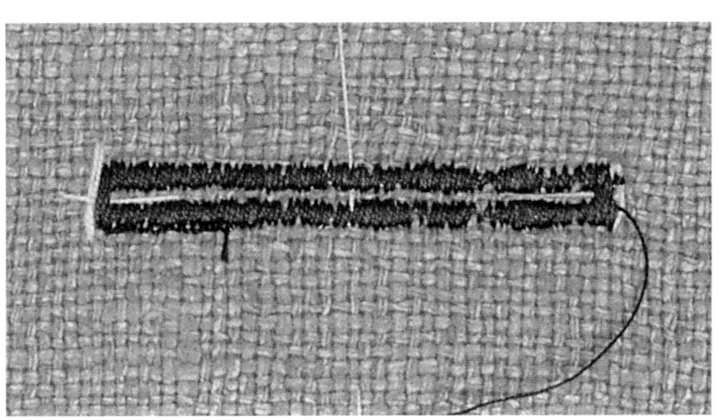

4 Catch down and secure the thread at the end with a few small straight stitches. Trim the ends of the waxed thread and remove the basting.

POSITIONING BUTTONS

To position a button accurately, place the button band and buttonhole band together and insert a pin through the center of the buttonhole. Mark the point clearly on the button band and then sew the button in place on the button band.

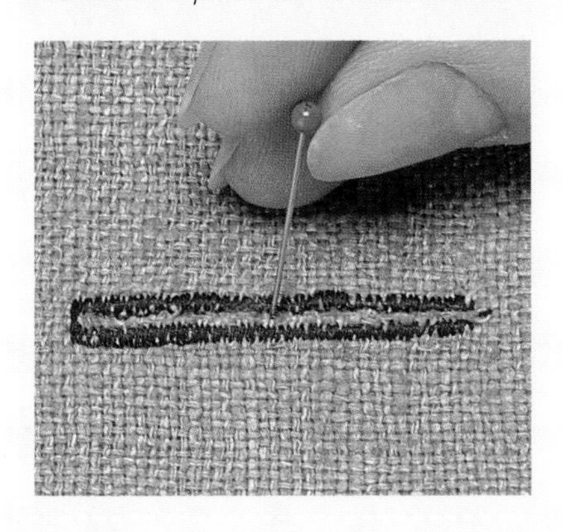

Sewing on buttons

From the top: A two-hole and a four-hole button are sewn by taking the needle into a hole, through the fabric, and back through a different hole from the other side.

A shank button stands above the surface of the fabric. To make a thread shank, cross pins between buttons and fabric, and attach the button, winding thread around the pins between each stitch.

To attach military-style buttons with a metal pin, make a small hole in the button position and buttonhole-stitch around it to prevent fraying. Unclip the pin, insert the shank in the hole, and clip the pin back on the button on the wrong side of the garment.

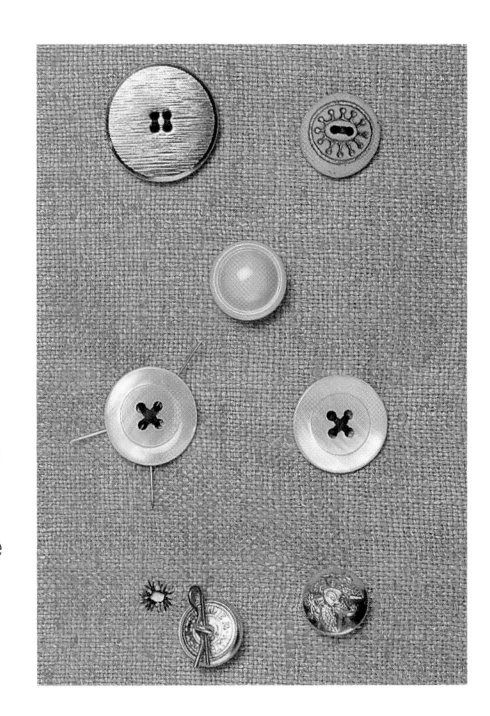

Machine-sewn buttonhole

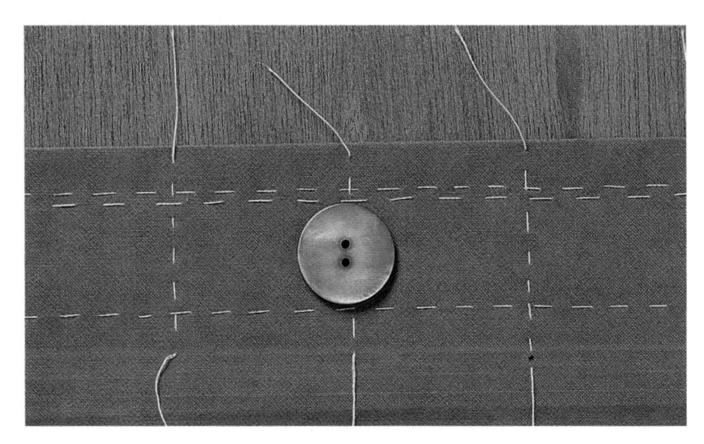

1 Mark the center position and length of the buttonhole with basting on the buttonhole band, using a button as a guide.

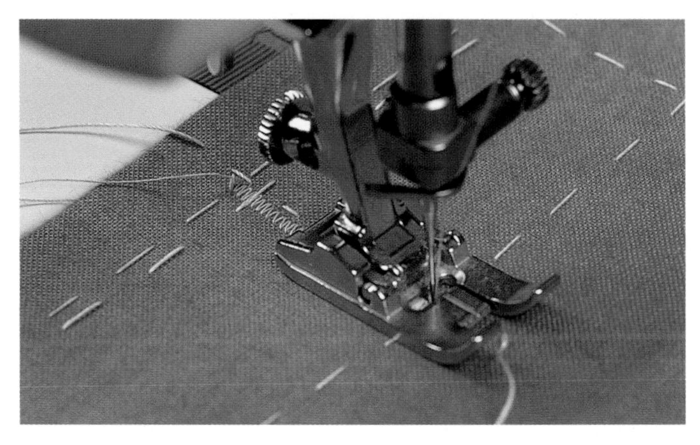

2 Run a line of straight stitches on each side of basted line. Set the zigzag width to medium and stitch a row of tight satin stitch over one line of straight stitches.

3 Raise the foot and turn the work 180 degrees. Make six wide stitches in the same place to form a bar tack, which will reinforce the ends.

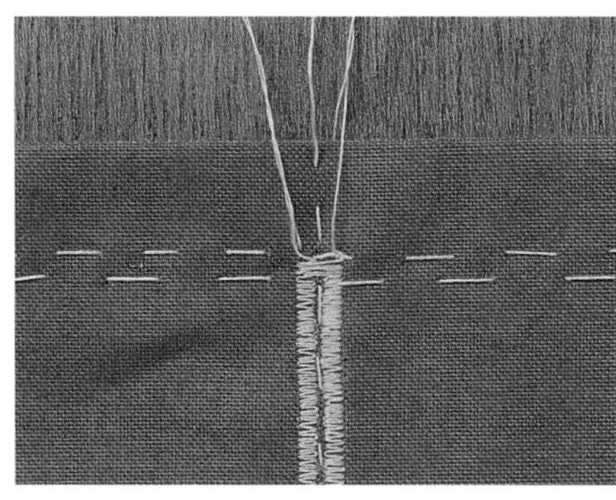

4 Repeat steps 2 and 3 to work the other side and end of the buttonhole. Set the stitch width at 0 and make three stitches to secure.

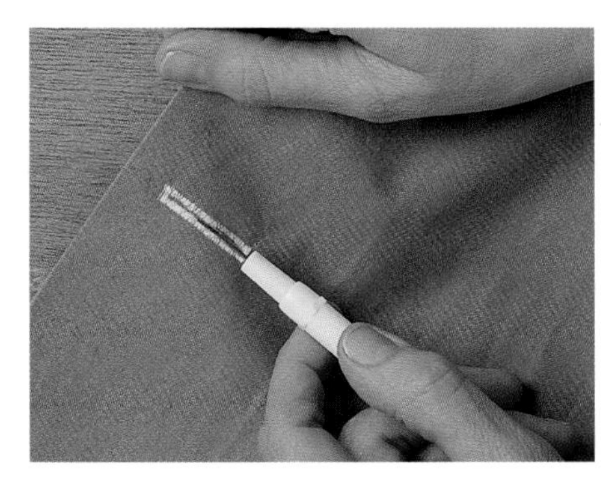

5 Pull the loose ends of threads to the back and trim. Remove the basting and slit open the buttonhole carefully. Avoid cutting the stitching.

COVERING BUTTONS

Self-covered buttons give a stylish finish to garments and are easy to make using special kits. The instructions below may differ from those given with a kit. If so, follow the manufacturer's instructions, selecting the appropriate size and pattern provided with the kit.

1 *Cut the fabric into circles ½ in (1 cm) wider than the button top.*

2 *Place the button top in the center of the wrong side of the fabric. Catch any excess material on the teeth in the underside of the button. Use a pin to even the fabric around the button.*

3 *Push the back piece carefully into position on the button top and snap it firmly in place.*

Bound buttonhole

1 Center a patch 1 in (2.5 cm) wider and longer than the buttonhole over the place marked on the band (right). Baste a line ⅛ in (3 mm) out from the center on each side (left).

2 Fold the fabric patch along the basted lines on each side as shown. Baste again to secure the patch in position on the band, and then stitch along each basted line.

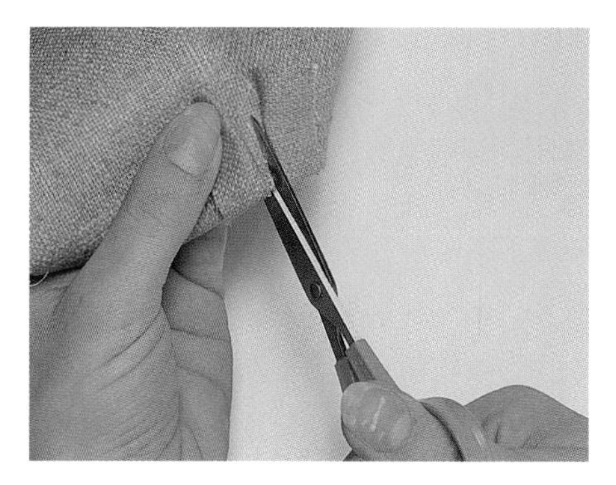

3 Turn the stitched edges back. Fold the buttonhole in half, matching the ends. Use scissors to cut carefully along the center basted line. Clip a small triangle at each end.

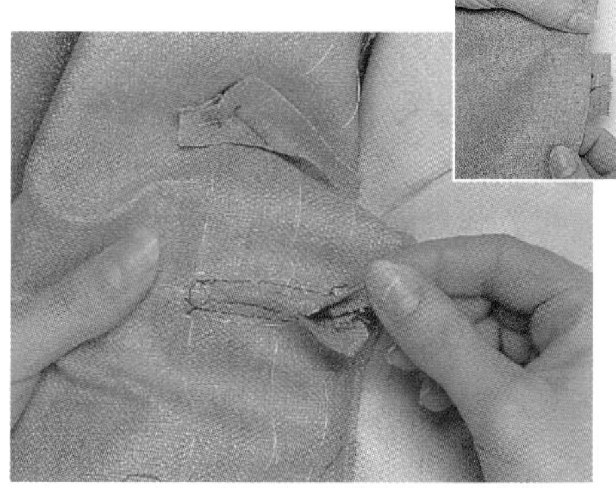

4 Pull the patch to the wrong side of the band. Press and baste the opening closed. Turn back each short end. Carefully stitch to secure the small triangle to the patch (inset).

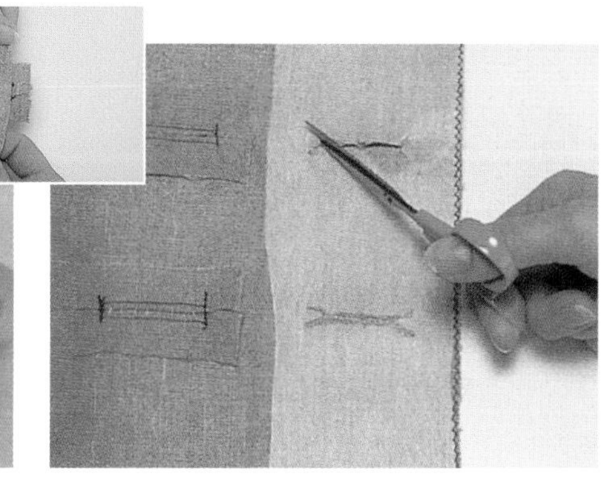

5 Using a pair of small sharp scissors, slit each buttonhole in the facing. Start from the center and cut toward a corner to clip a triangle at each end of the buttonhole.

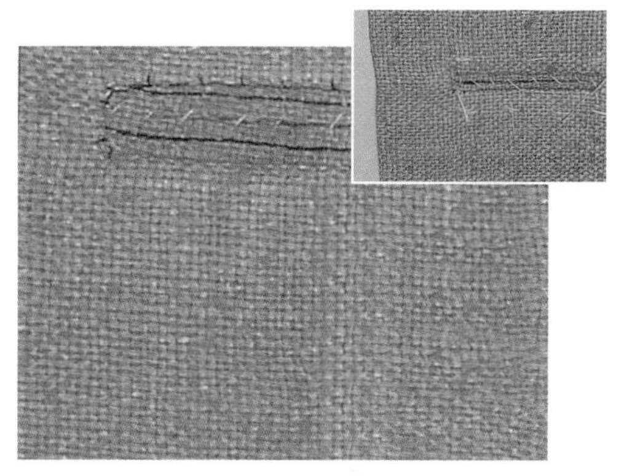

6 Align the facing slit with the buttonhole, folding under the raw edges of each slit. Pin and hand-sew the patch to the facing only. Make all the buttonholes, then remove basting.

Corded buttonhole

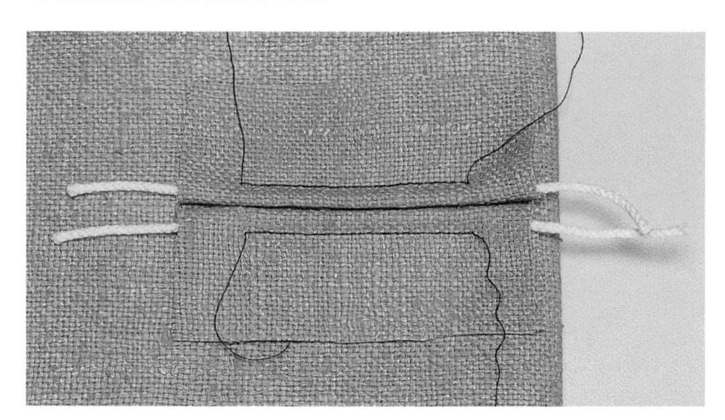

To make corded buttonholes, prepare as in step 1 of Bound buttonholes. Slip a length of cord under each folded edge in step 2 and stitch in place. Then proceed as in steps 3 to 6.

OTHER FASTENERS

Specialized ready-made fasteners (from left): touch-and-close tape; metal popper snap; plastic popper snap; punch-in metal popper snap; heavy-duty hook and bar; lightweight hook and bar; lightweight hook and eye, thread-wrapped hook and eye.

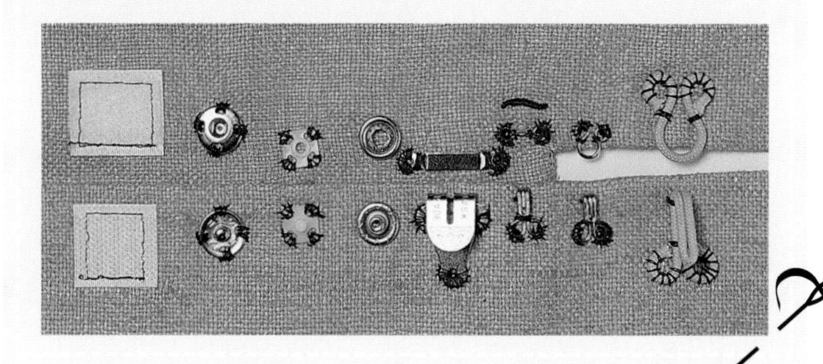

Hems

Hems are used to finish fabric edges on garments and home furnishings, and the examples shown apply to sewing for the home as well as dressmaking. Hems can be worked by hand or machine, depending on the style of the item, the weight of the fabric, and the desired look. The finished hem should be virtually invisible. Hemming usually involves turning under a narrow edge and then turning again to enclose the raw edge completely. Basting the turned hem to mark it helps ensure accuracy, but pinning is usually enough to hold it in place for the final stitching. If the fabric is heavy, or if there is not enough fabric to turn under, the edge can be faced or bound. This method can also be used to create decorative effects.

Simple hand-stitched hem

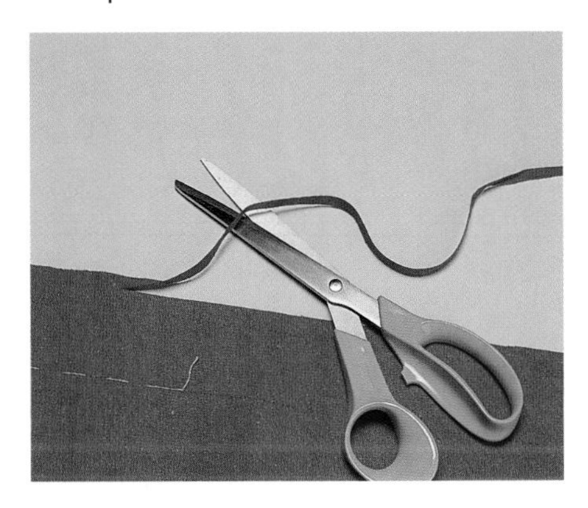

1 Fold and press the top and bottom of the hem to mark it. Baste the bottom foldline. Trim raw edge to ¼ in (5 mm) on the first fold.

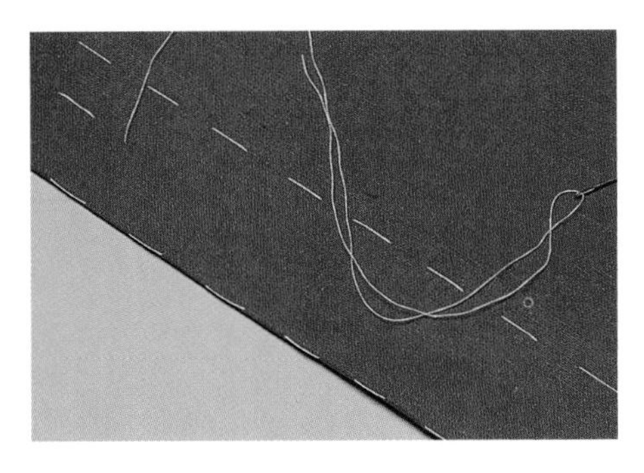

2 Turn up and press the bottom fold. Baste along the marked lines and through the center of the fold. Match all seams together.

3 Turn under the top fold along the basted line and pin the hem in place. The hem is now ready to stitch.

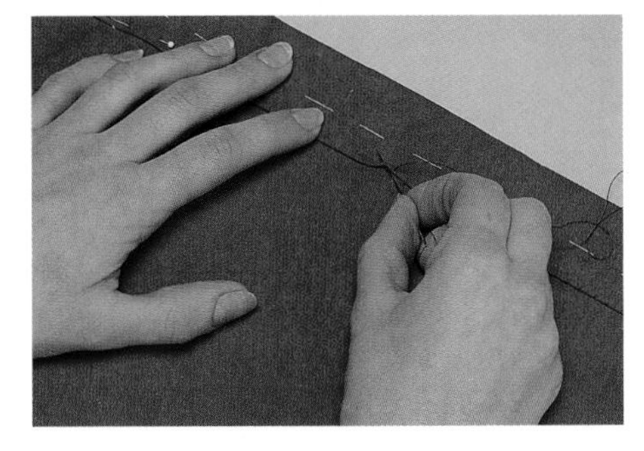

4 Lay the fabric wrong side up on a flat surface. Pick up one or two fabric threads while taking the needle through the edge of the top fold. Remove pins as you work and take out basting when the hem is finished.

TYPES OF HAND-SEWN HEMS
There are a number of methods for working a hem, and you may want to try each technique to see which you prefer and which works best on your particular project.

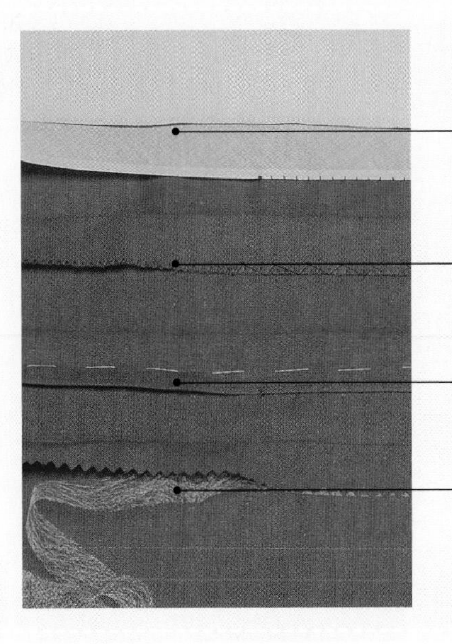

Binding, either bias or straight, is machine-stitched to the raw edge of a leveled hem, then turned up and pressed. It can then be hand- or machine-stitched in position.

The raw edge is zigzag-stitched, then turned up, and the hem is held in place with a row of herringbone stitch.

The raw edge is turned under and machine-stitched, folded up and basted, and then sewn with a tailor's hem (see step 4 of simple hand-stitched hem, above). This method is particularly good for lightweight fabrics.

Fusible hem tape is good for emergency repairs. It can be used on lightweight fabrics, though it may work loose during laundering. Here the raw edge has been pinked and turned up, and the tape inserted into the fold and pressed in place.

Simple turn-up cuff

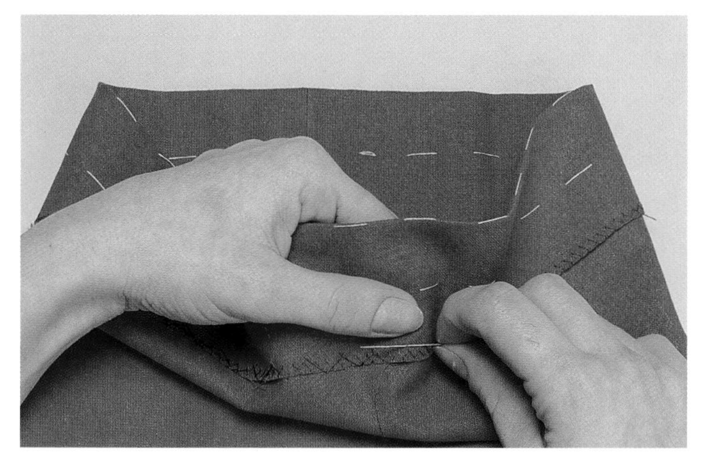

1 With the leg piece wrong side out, fold and baste three lines of the bottom edge of turn-up, top of turn-up, and hemline. Zigzag-stitch the raw edge, turn up the center fold, and press. Herringbone-stitch the zigzagged edge.

2 Turn the leg right side out. Turn up the bottom fold and gently press the piece. Use a catchstitch to secure the seam. Remove the basting.

Curved hem

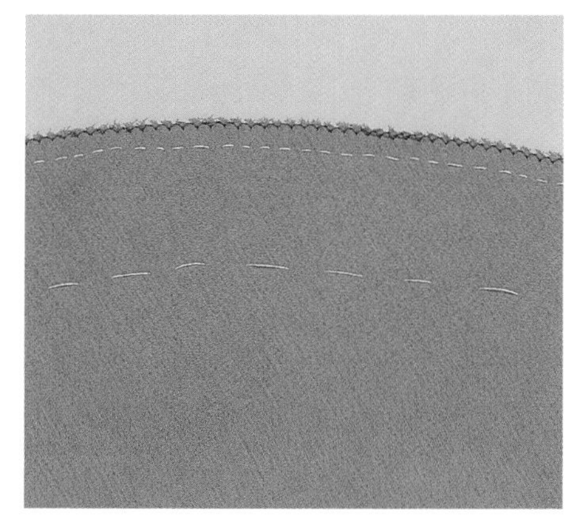

1 Mark and cut the hem. Zigzag-stitch the raw edge and baste the foldline. Run gathering stitches ¼ in (5 mm) from the zigzag stitching.

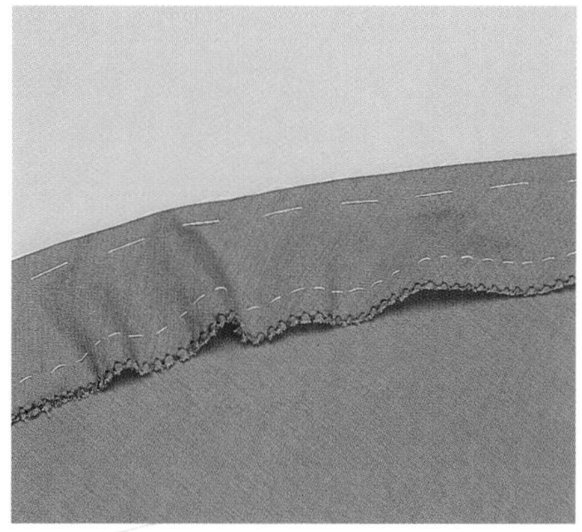

2 Turn up the hem along the basted foldline. Baste the hem in place about ¼ in (5 mm) from the fold.

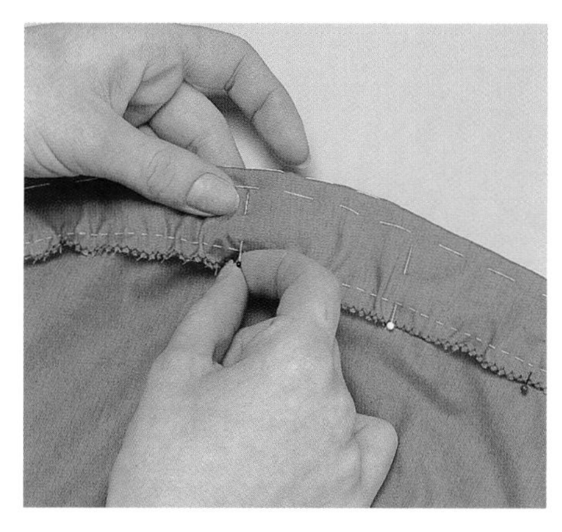

3 Matching the seams, pin the hem in place, pulling up the gathering thread as you work to spread the fabric evenly and ease in the fullness.

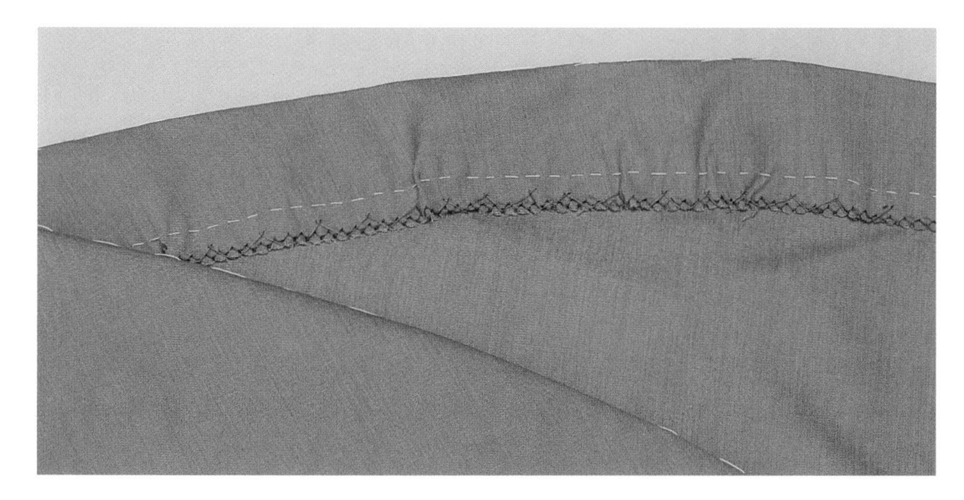

4 Herringbone-stitch the hem in place from the wrong side, removing pins as you work. Remove all basting and press the piece.

Mitered hem

1 At the corner of the piece, turn up the seam allowance and press along the hemlines. Open out the hem flat again and turn up the corner triangle with the pressed marks aligned. Press along the diagonal fold.

2 Open the corner and fold it diagonally with right sides together so the raw edges and the creases meet. Pin and stitch along the pressed line.

3 Trim the triangular piece of seam allowance from the corner and press the seam open. Repeat this process for the remaining corners that are to be mitered.

4 Turn the corners right side out, to the wrong side of the fabric. Turn under the raw edges on each side of the hem and pin in place. Baste, then stitch the hem.

5 The finished miters make neat corners on both sides of the piece. This method is widely used on home furnishings such as tablecloths, napkins, and curtains, and is a good way to finish shirt tails and jackets as well as slits in tailored skirts.

HAND STITCHES

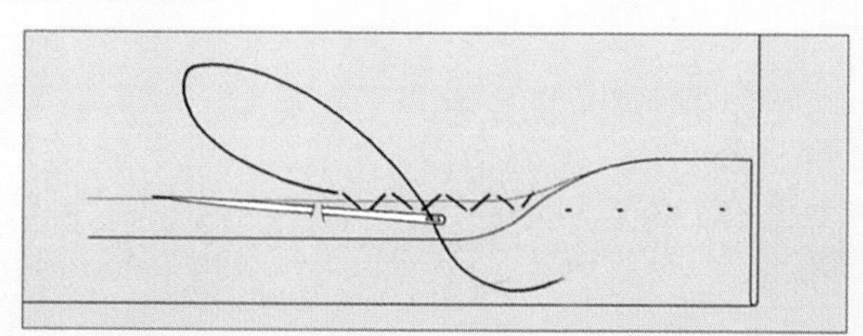

Blind hemming *makes an invisible hem by catching a single thread of the fabric. Finish the raw edge, then make a tiny stitch on the wrong side. Pick up one garment thread, hold the edge down, and pick up stitches on each side of the hem.*

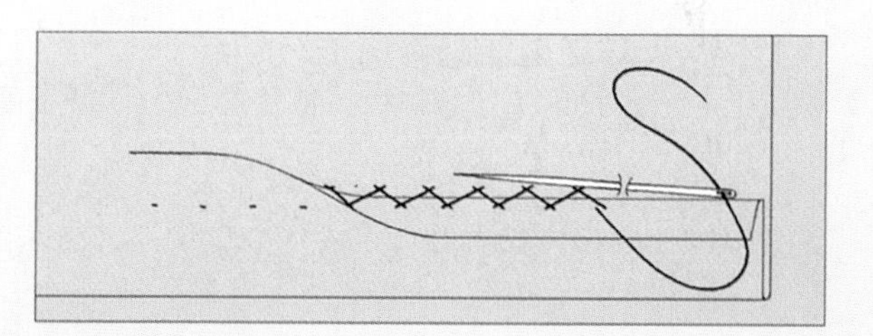

Blind herringbone *is useful for sewing hems on knitted fabrics. Tiny stitches are picked up first on the inside of the fold, then a single thread is taken on the garment, as for blind hemming, but the stitch is worked as herringbone (see page 28).*

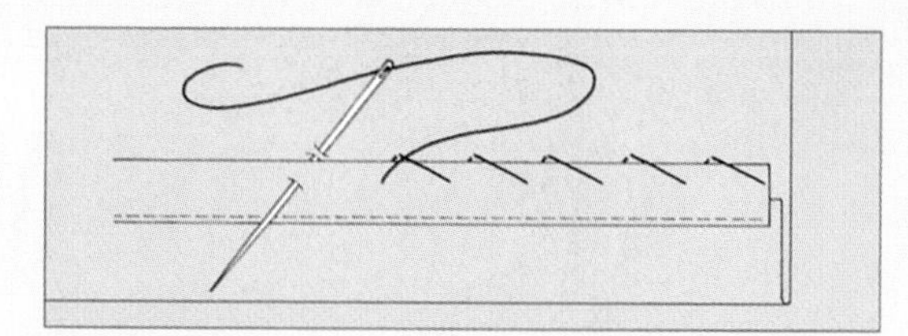

Slant hemming *is used on items that need a fine hem. Take the needle in at a seam and fasten off. Make small evenly spaced stitches along the top edge of the hem.*

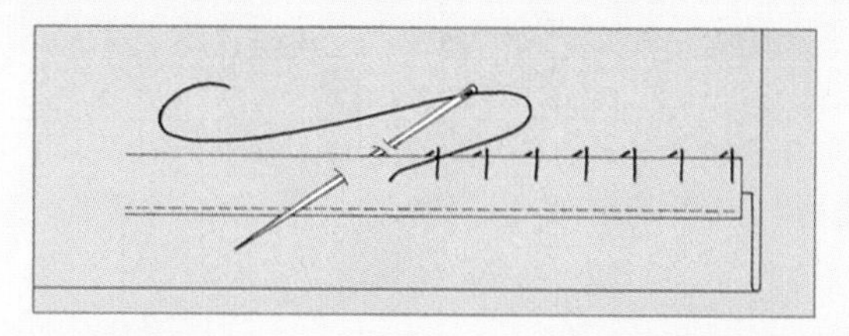

Vertical hemming *is easier to work on heavy fabrics. Start as for slant hemming, but keep the stitches upright. Make the stitches on the right side of the piece as small as possible.*

Simple machine-stitched hem

1 Measure, mark, and baste the two foldlines, one ¼ in (5 mm) from the raw edge and the second ½ in (1 cm) from the first foldline. Turn the first fold under and gently press.

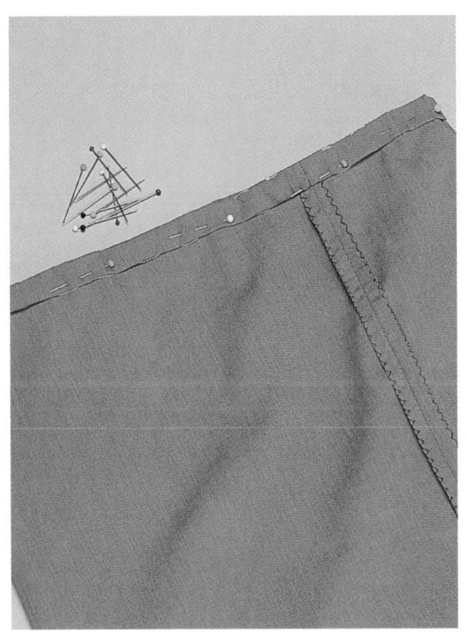

2 Turn the second fold under and press. Pin the doubled hem in position, matching the seams.

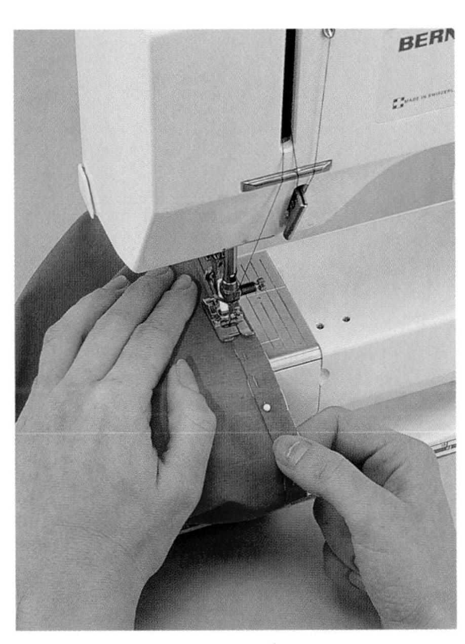

3 On the wrong side of the fabric, stitch along the top fold of the piece, removing pins as you work. Remove the basting and press.

Topstitched hem

1 Measure and mark the hem. Baste along the foldline, then trim the raw edge with pinking shears. Turn the hem under at the foldline and pin in place, matching seams. Baste in place and remove the pins.

2 Working on the right side, topstitch the hem. Follow the guidelines marked on the machine footplate for accuracy. Remove the basting and press the piece.

TWIN-NEEDLE TOPSTITCHING

A double row of topstitching makes an attractive finish. It can be worked using a twin needle, or two rows can be topstitched side by side.

Machine-stitched blind hem

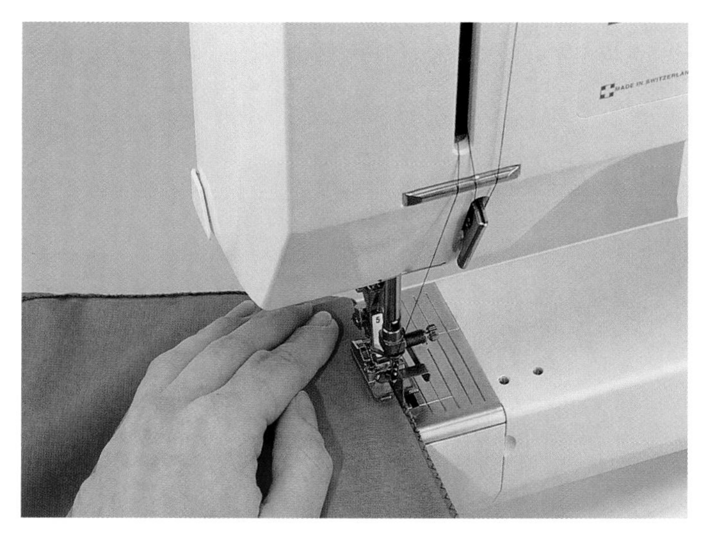

1 Mark the hem and zigzag-stitch along the raw edge. Fold the hem under and baste in place ¼ in (5 mm) from the zigzag-stitching. Using a blind-hemming foot on the machine, fold the hem to the right side so you are working along the zigzagged edge. Stitch the hem.

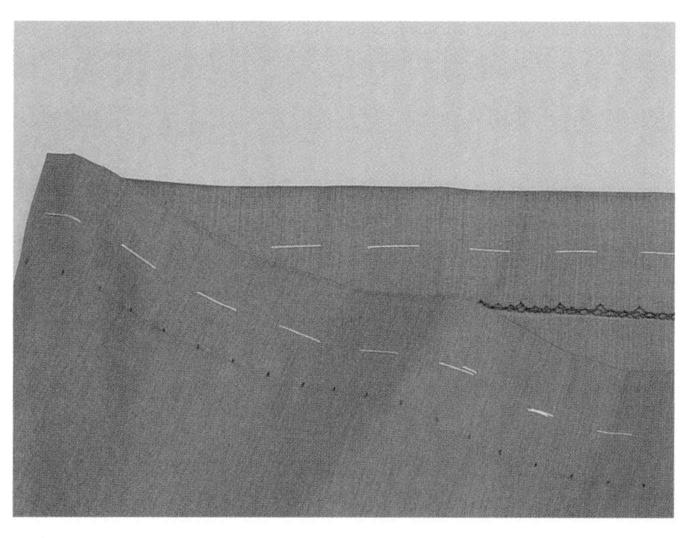

2 The straight stitches follow the edge of the hem while the pointed stitches catch the fabric on the right side. The hem is strong and virtually invisible. The special foot used is available for most modern sewing machines.

Faced hem

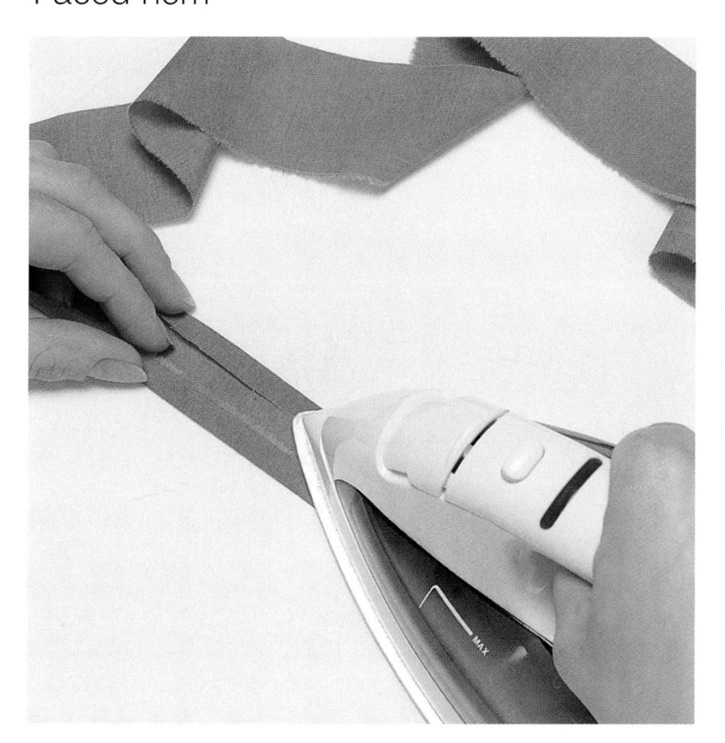

1 Mark the hemline on the raw edge of the piece. Cut a facing strip ½ in (1 cm) wide and the length of the hem plus seam allowances. Fold under and press ¼ in (5 mm) along both of the long edges.

2 Fold under the short ends. Match one short end to a garment seam. With right sides together, pin a long folded edge to the garment along the marked hemline and stitch the seam, removing pins as you work. Overlap the final short end over the sewn folded end as shown and finish stitching. Turn the facing to the wrong side of the garment and gently press it under.

step 3

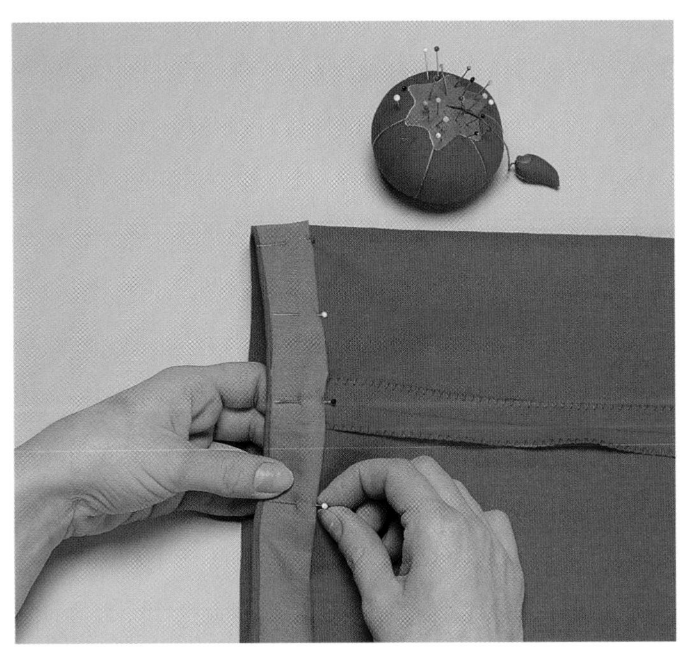

3 Make sure the raw edge of the facing is turned under, then pin the facing in position.

4 Hem along the top folded edge of the facing, working by hand, and press the piece again.

BOUND HEM

This type of hem is similar in construction to the faced hem, but a strip of bias binding is used instead of a straight strip of fabric. It is particularly useful for curved hems and can be turned back as an invisible facing or made into a decorative effect.

If you wish to coordinate the binding and cannot find a ready-made bias binding of the correct color or width, you can make your own from a matching or contrasting fabric by following the instructions on pages 40 and 41.

1 *If you are using handmade bias binding, follow step 1 of making a faced hem (see page 115) to mark and press the edges. Ready-made binding will have folds already pressed in the long sides. Pin and stitch the binding to the bottom raw edge of the garment as shown in step 2 of making a faced hem.*

2 *Turn the binding under halfway if you wish to use it as a decorative feature, and fully hidden if you are using it as a facing. Topstitch on the right side along the top fold of the binding as shown, or slipstitch by hand if you wish.*

Rolled hems

A fine, almost invisible hem that is first rolled and then stitched by hand is the traditional finish on delicate fabrics such as silk, organdy, or chiffon, which all fray easily.

Machine-stitched rolled hems are also suitable for many lightweight fabrics. They give a stronger and sharper finish, and are quicker to work.

Hand-rolled hem

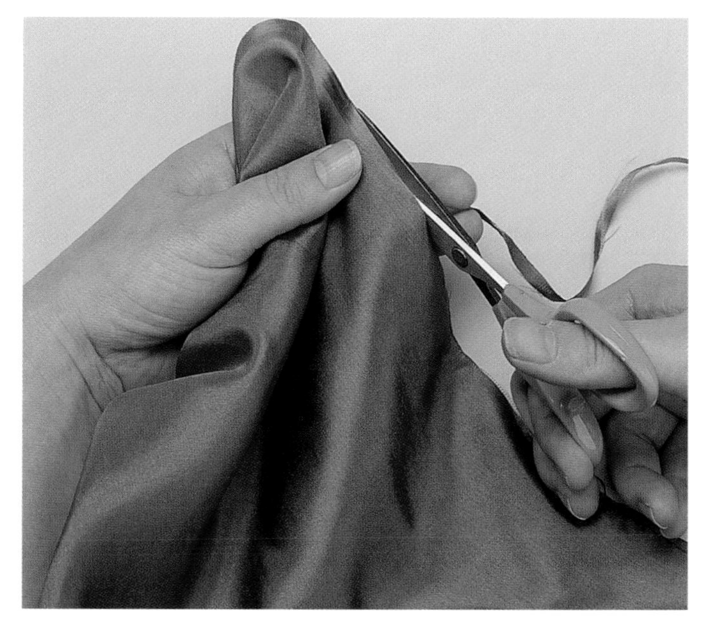

1 Cut the raw edge of the fabric straight, trimming away a little at a time. You may want to mark the hemline with a fine pencil before you begin cutting.

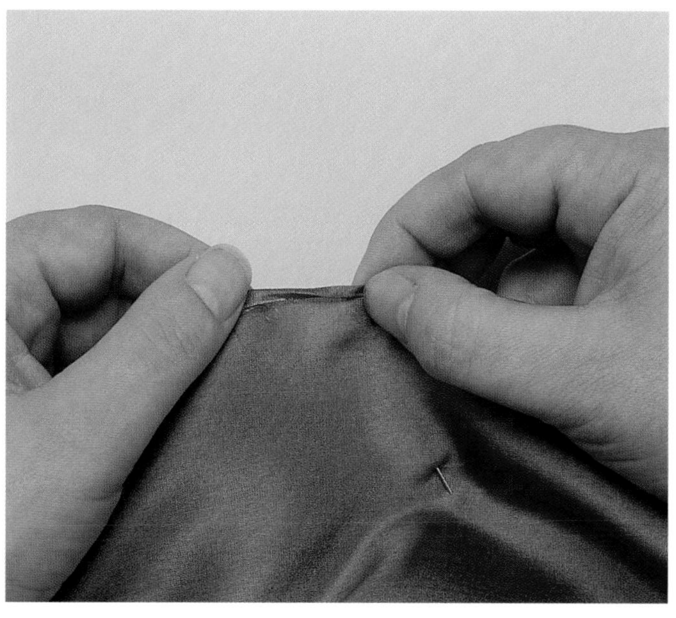

2 Roll the cut edge inward, enclosing the raw fabric completely. Again, work on a small area at a time and keep the roll small—the smaller the roll, the finer the hem.

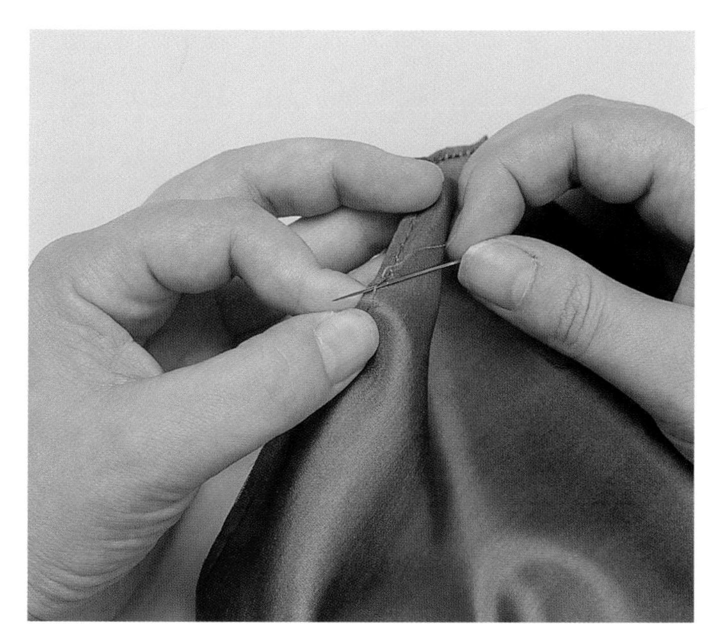

3 Holding the rolled edge tightly over one finger, take two or three evenly spaced stitches onto the needle, picking up only one thread at a time if possible. Pull the stitches gently and repeat.

4 A hand-rolled hem should have evenly spaced stitches and be neat on both sides. To make a sharp, neat corner, clip a small triangle at the corner, then turn and miter it carefully. If necessary, use a fine pin to hold it in position as you work.

Machine-rolled hem—Method 1

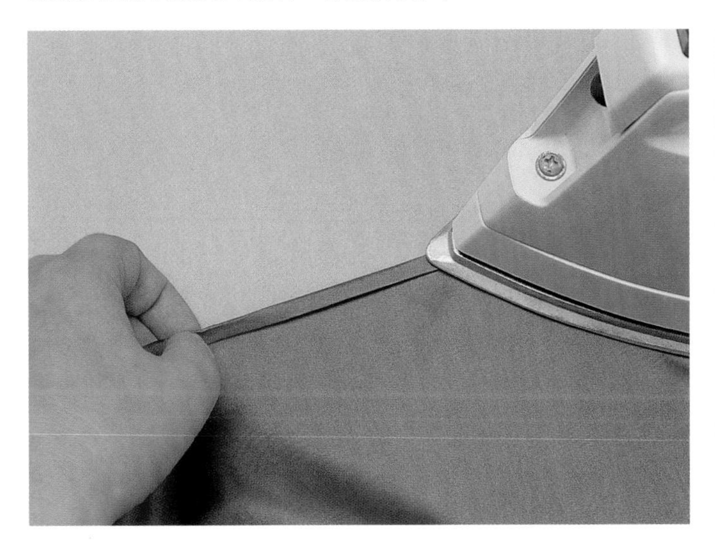

1 Turn under and press a single hem of an appropriate width for the fabric along the edge to be hemmed. Then turn and press a double hem.

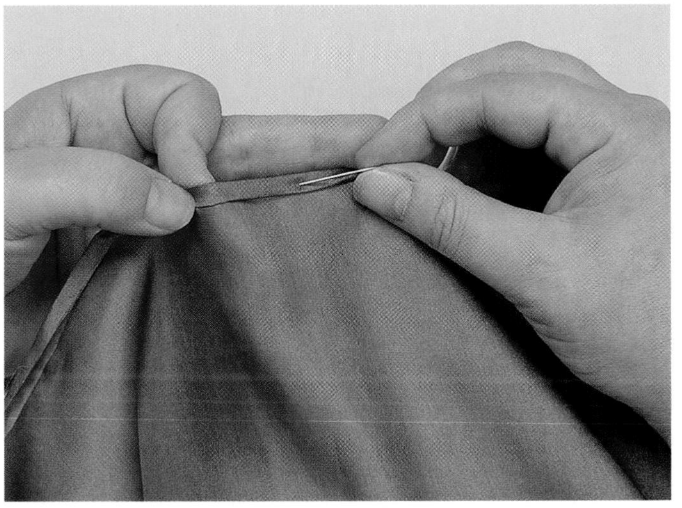

2 Pin the pressed hem in place, matching the seams together. Position the pins parallel to the edge of the hem, pointing away from your stitching hand. Baste the hem in place around any corners.

3 Working with the material wrong side up, machine stitch the hem, removing the pins as you work. When you have finished, press the hem.

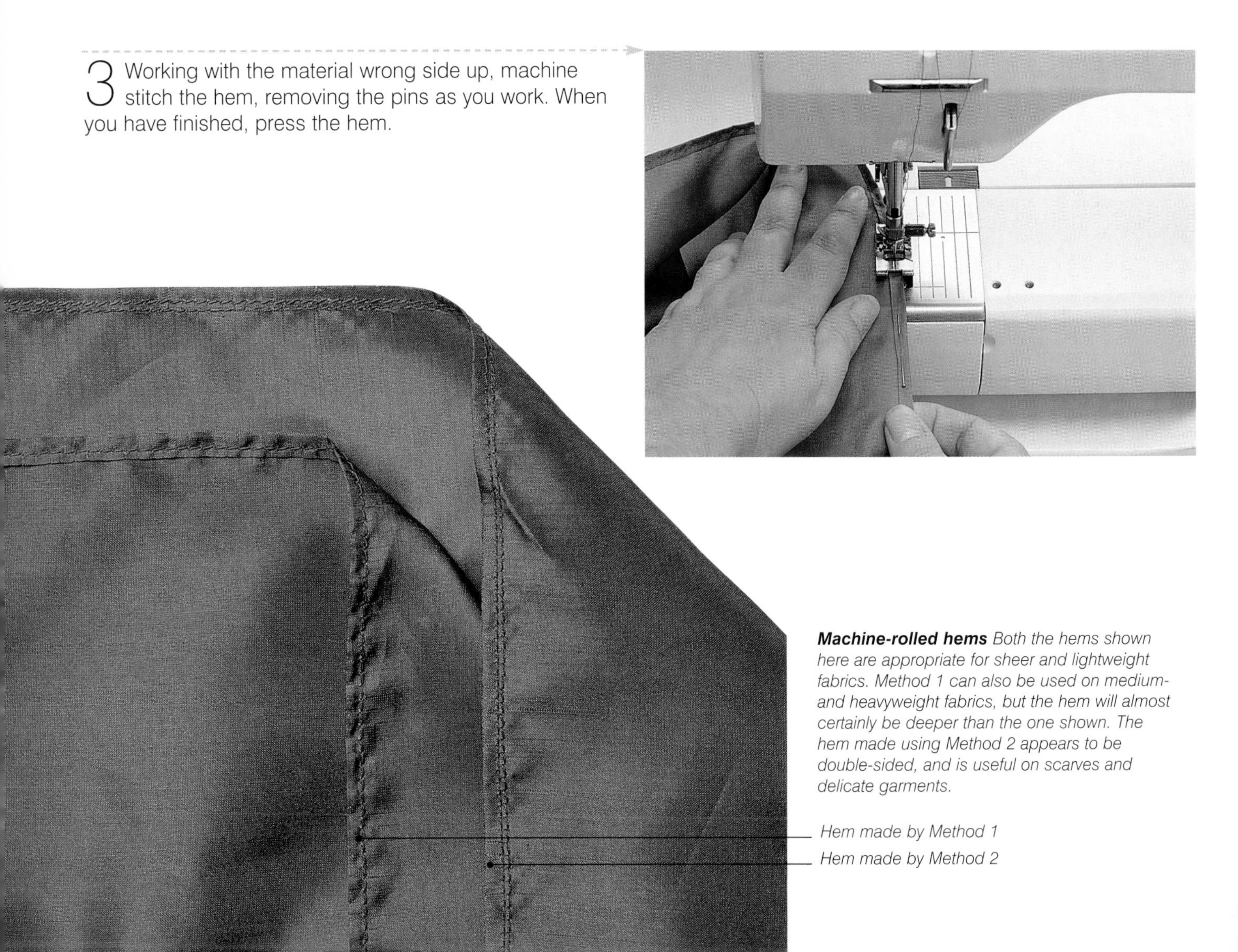

Machine-rolled hems *Both the hems shown here are appropriate for sheer and lightweight fabrics. Method 1 can also be used on medium- and heavyweight fabrics, but the hem will almost certainly be deeper than the one shown. The hem made using Method 2 appears to be double-sided, and is useful on scarves and delicate garments.*

Hem made by Method 1

Hem made by Method 2

Machine-rolled hem—Method 2

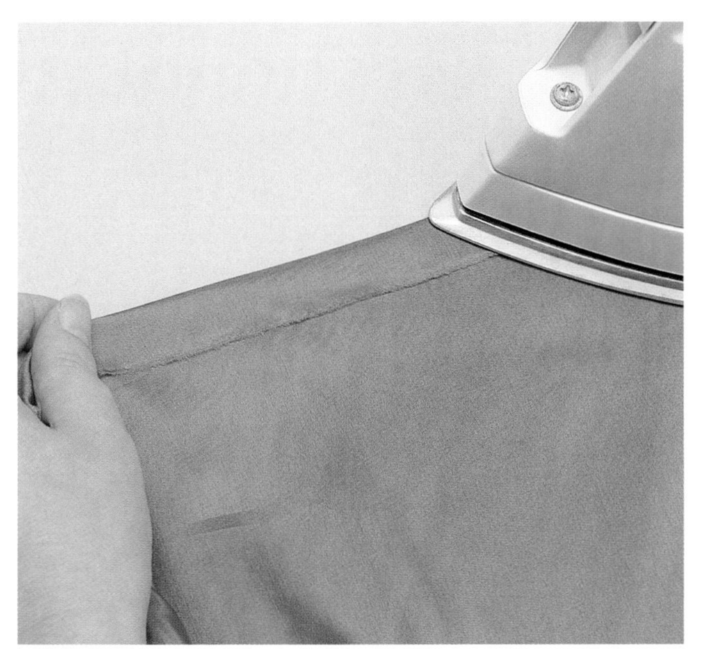

1 Turn under and press approximately ¾ in (2 cm) to the wrong side of the edge of the fabric.

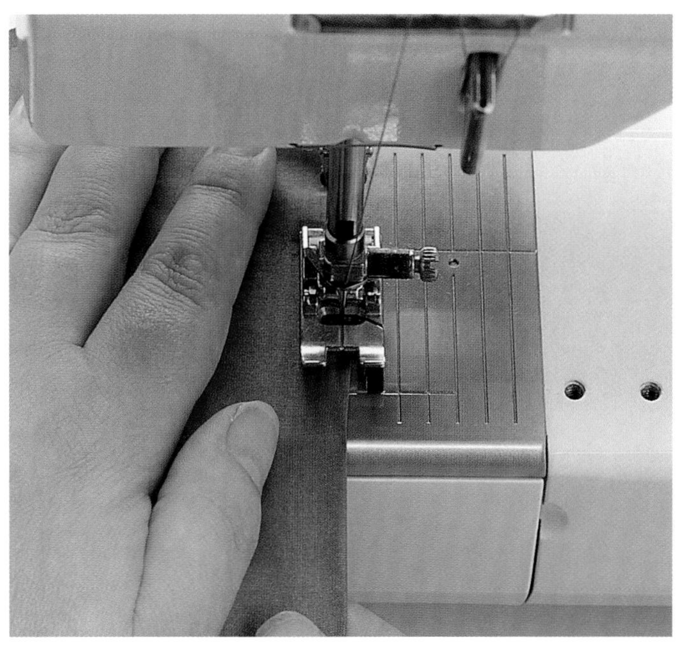

2 With the right side of the garment facing upward, stitch ¼ in (5 mm) from the fold.

3 Hold the stitching line open as shown and use small, very sharp scissors to trim away the excess fabric as close to the stitches as possible.

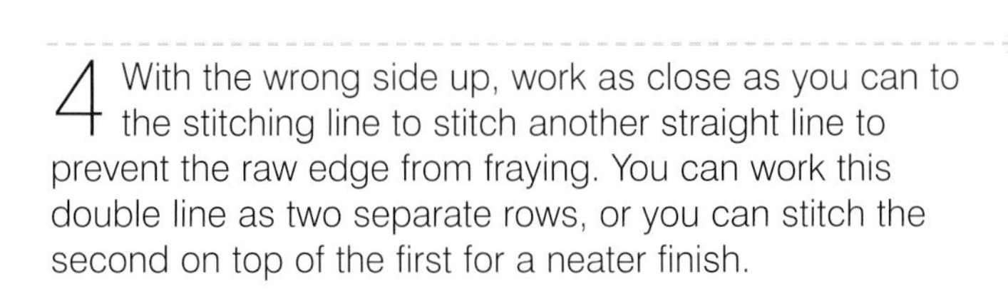

4 With the wrong side up, work as close as you can to the stitching line to stitch another straight line to prevent the raw edge from fraying. You can work this double line as two separate rows, or you can stitch the second on top of the first for a neater finish.

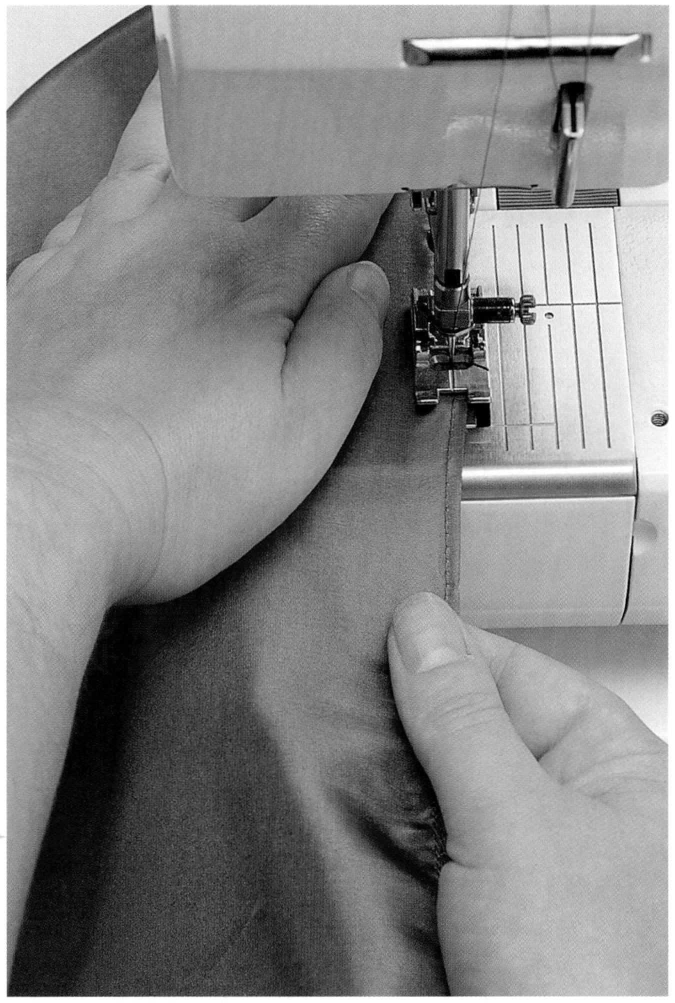

Linings

Many garments are lined to give them shape and to protect their seams and raw edges. A lining increases the bulk of a garment, so lightweight fabrics are preferred. In most cases, linings are assembled in the same way as the garment and then sewn in just before the garment is completed.

ADDING A LINING
To add a lining to a finished garment, turn under and pin the raw edge of the lining in place. Slipstitch neatly all along the edge, taking care not to sew through to the right side of the garment.

Lining a skirt

1 Assemble the skirt and lining pieces, making sure that the zipper aligns with the seam in the lining. The corresponding seam in the lining should be open from the waist to the bottom of the zipper.

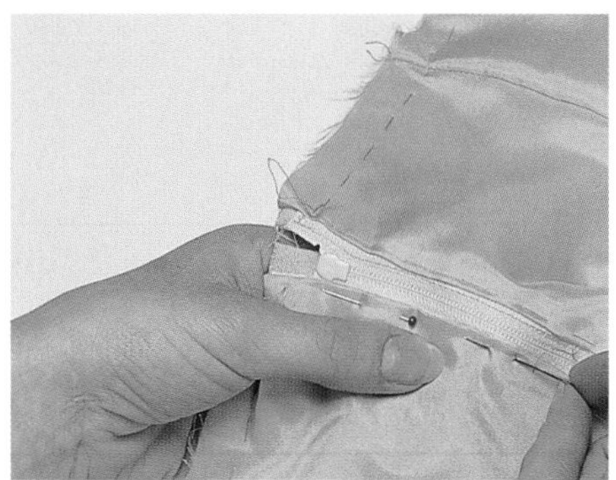

2 Matching darts and with wrong sides together, pin and baste the skirt and lining pieces along the waist. Fold under the seam allowance on the open lining seam, then pin and baste in place around the zipper.

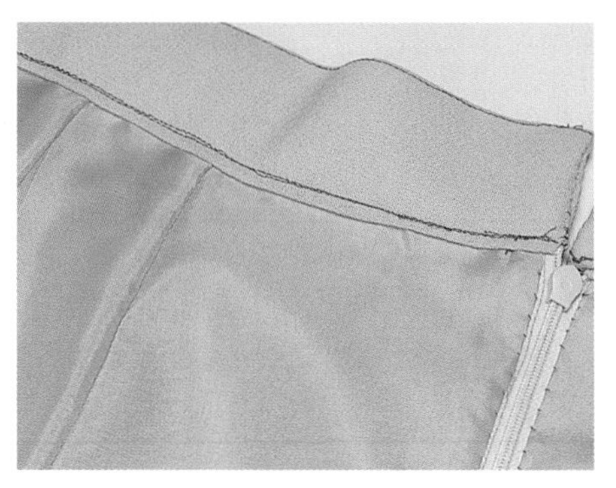

3 Using slipstitch, attach the lining to the zipper tape. Avoid sewing through to the right side of the skirt. Then attach the waistband to the skirt.

FINISHING A BOTTOM EDGE

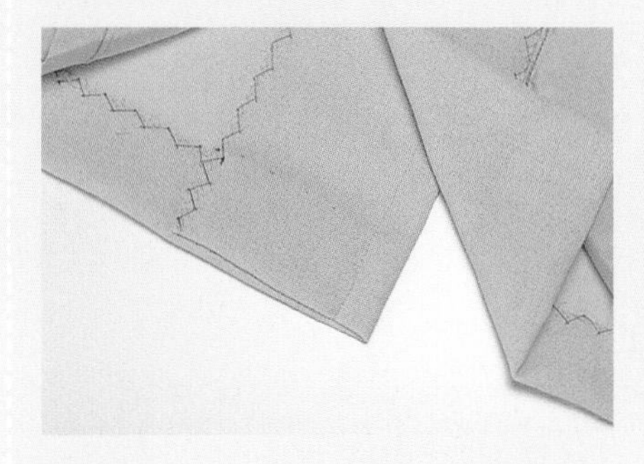

Split skirt
A split is used when the garment and lining have a center back seam. Leave the bottom of the lining's center seam unstitched. Clip the seam allowance on top, then turn under, pin, and stitch a double hem along the length on both sides of the split. Hem the bottom.

Kick pleat
If there is no center seam in the garment, slit the lining to correspond with the pleat or split. Turn under a narrow double hem on both sides of the slit, pin in position, and then stitch. Hem the bottom.

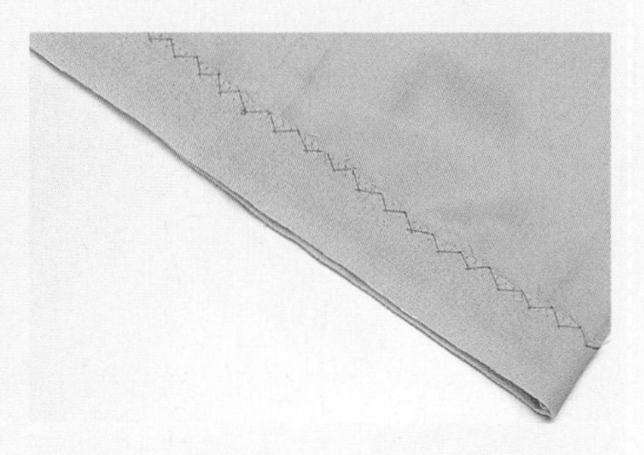

Sewn-in lining
Linings on trousers and skirts can sometimes be secured under the garment hem. Trim the lining slightly shorter than the finished garment and sew the hem to the lining.

Lining a jacket

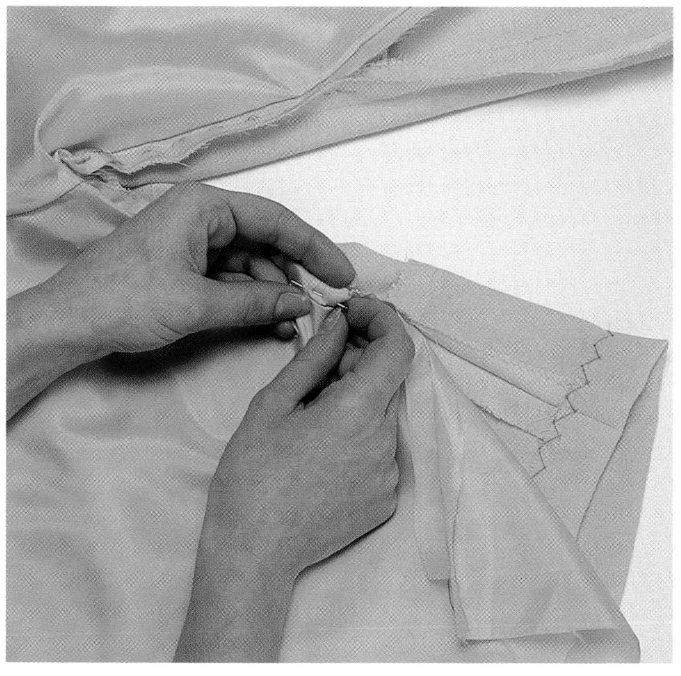

1 Finish the jacket, including all hems. Assemble the lining, adding 1 in (2.5 cm) to the center back. With wrong sides together, match any darts and align the open seams to face each other along one underarm and side seam. Pin and baste the seam allowance on the garment to that on the lining. Stitch together, working from underarm to bottom hem, then from underarm to cuff.

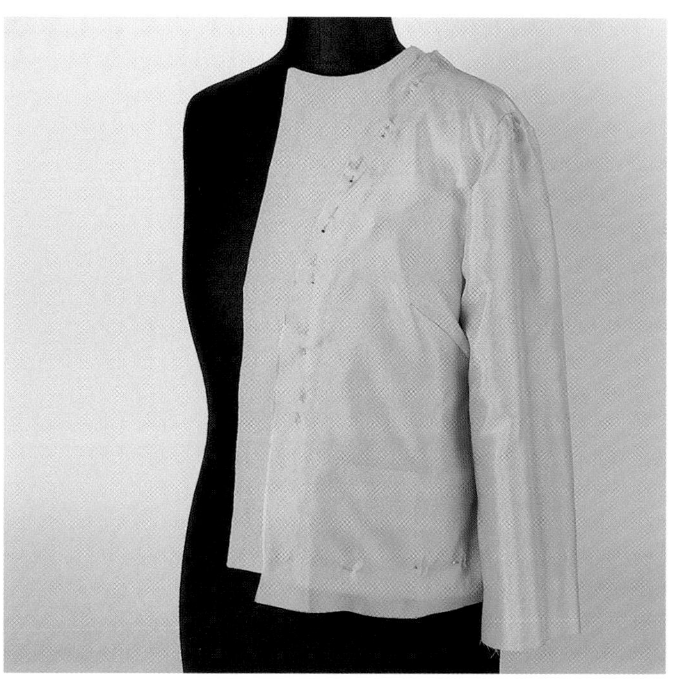

2 Pull the lining through to the wrong side of the garment and pin in place along the edges of the neck and facings. Allow some slack in the lining.

3 At the center back, match the darts on each side and pin a pleat to take up the excess fabric in the lining. Pin a corresponding pleat at the bottom edge.

4 Turn under all the edges of the lining and slipstitch the lining to the jacket all around. The buttonholes can now be worked.

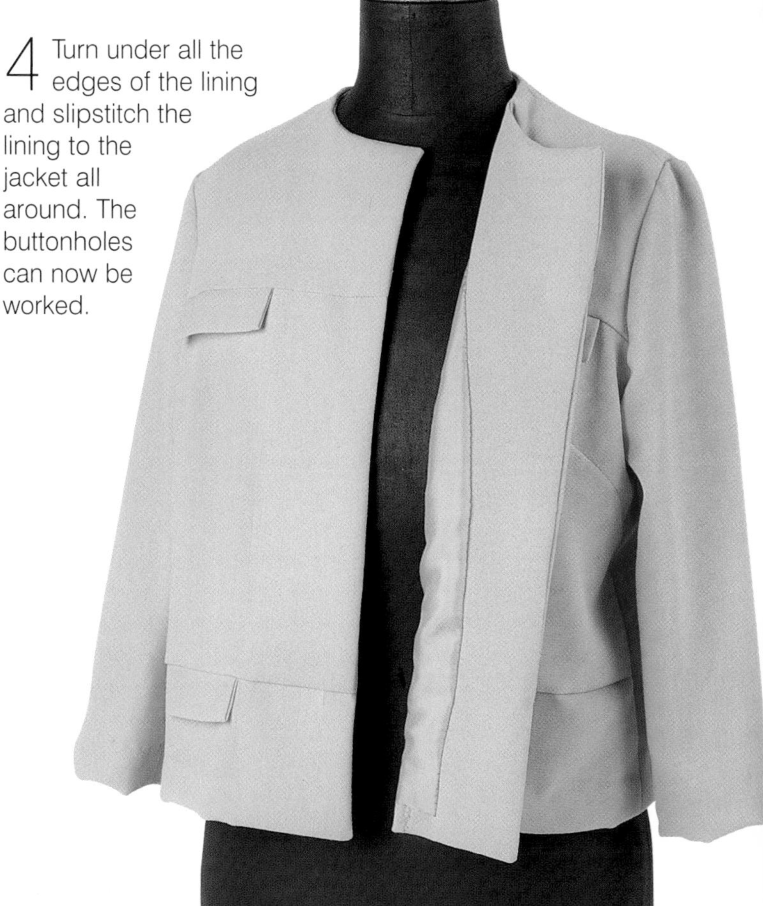

Lining a waistcoat

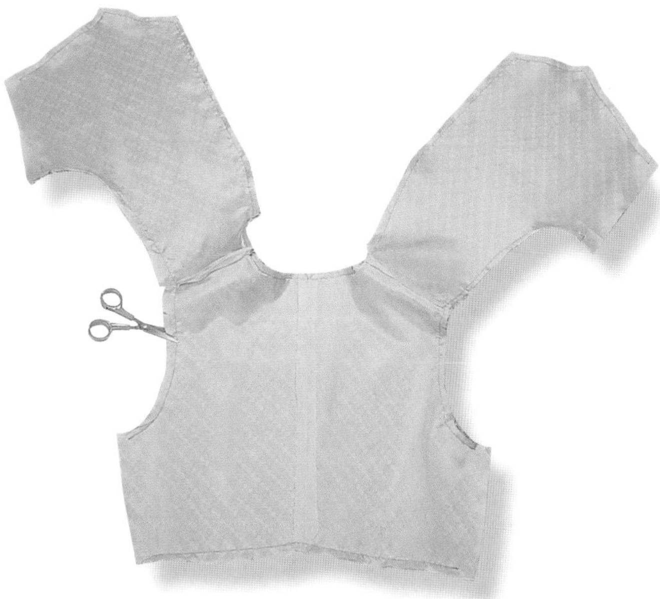

1 Join center back and shoulder seams on the garment and lining pieces. With right sides together and matching seams, pin and baste the lining to the garment. Stitch all edges except the four side seams under the armholes. Trim and clip curved seams and cut off points.

2 Pull the garment right side out through the open side seams. Press the garment carefully, paying particular attention to the edges to ensure a professional finish.

FINAL FITTING

Before a garment is lined and the finishing touches such as hems and buttons are added, always make sure that a final fitting takes place. This allows you to check that the fit is as it should be, and the desired look has been achieved. Alterations can be made without too much fuss if only a seam or two needs to be taken out and restitched. Once a lining has been put in and fasteners attached, it is much more difficult to make changes.

If the shoulder seams are slightly too wide or if the collar is not quite straight, place pins at strategic points to mark the alteration. Then simply unpick the seam, re-pin (and baste it if necessary), and stitch the new seam. When you are completely satisfied with the fit of the garment, then you can add the finishing elements.

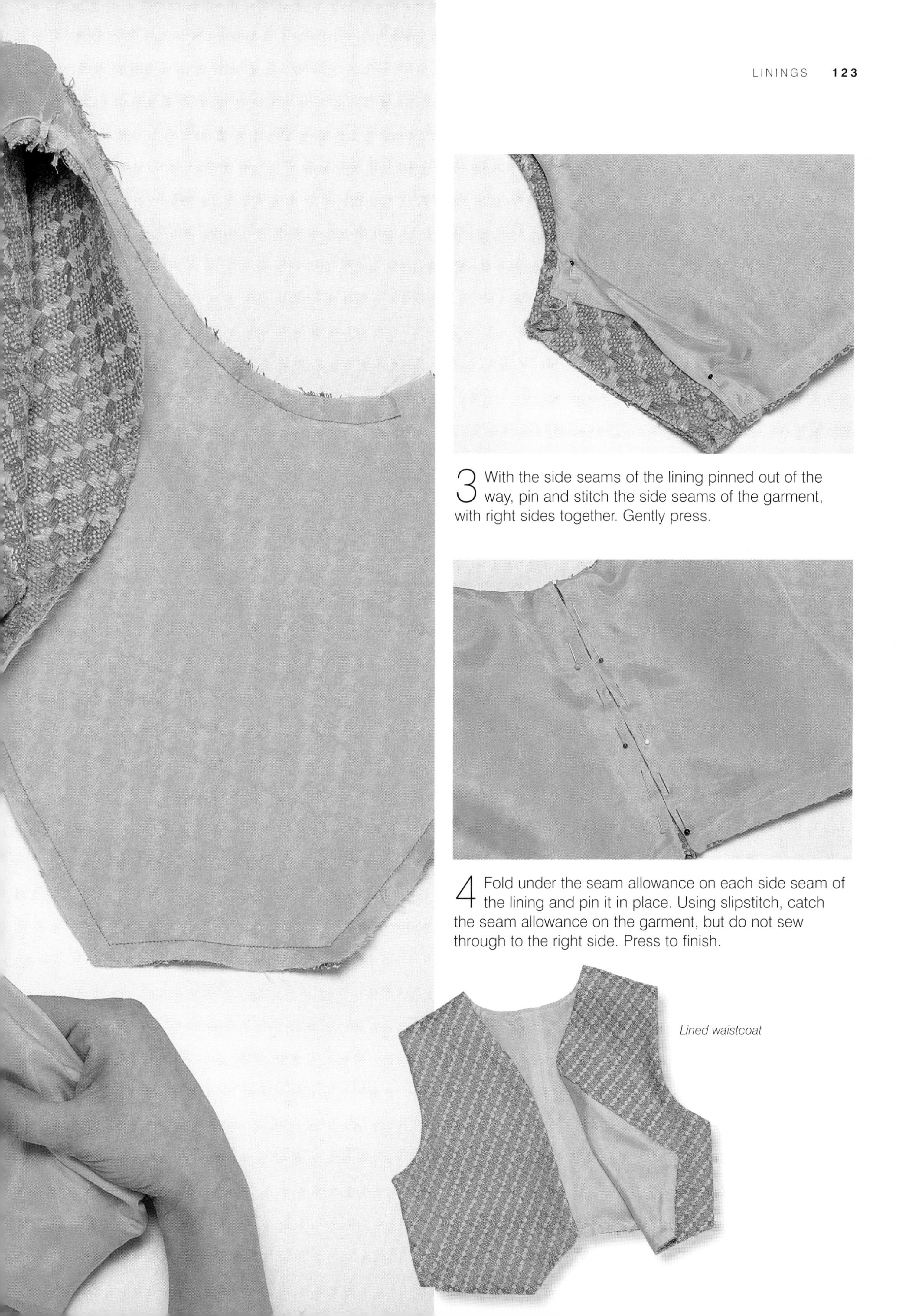

3 With the side seams of the lining pinned out of the way, pin and stitch the side seams of the garment, with right sides together. Gently press.

4 Fold under the seam allowance on each side seam of the lining and pin it in place. Using slipstitch, catch the seam allowance on the garment, but do not sew through to the right side. Press to finish.

Lined waistcoat

Project: Evening wrap

A wrap is a useful between-season addition to any wardrobe. It can be lined or unlined, and padded if preferred. Here a layer of batting is added to provide warmth and softness, and the garment is reversible. The pattern is made as a toile from muslin (calico) that you try on and adjust as necessary. Placed around your neck, it should hang down on each side to just below your knees.

YOU WILL NEED

- *2½ yd (2.2 m) each: muslin (calico), medium-weight velvet, medium-weight silk, batting (wadding)*
- *Removable fabric marker*
- *Scissors, pins*
- *Needle and thread*

1 Cut a piece of muslin to the length required. Mark a quarter circle on one end and cut it out. Fold the fabric in half and cut another quarter circle at the other end to round off the back corners. Try it on again with the straight sides in front and adjust to fit. This becomes the pattern.

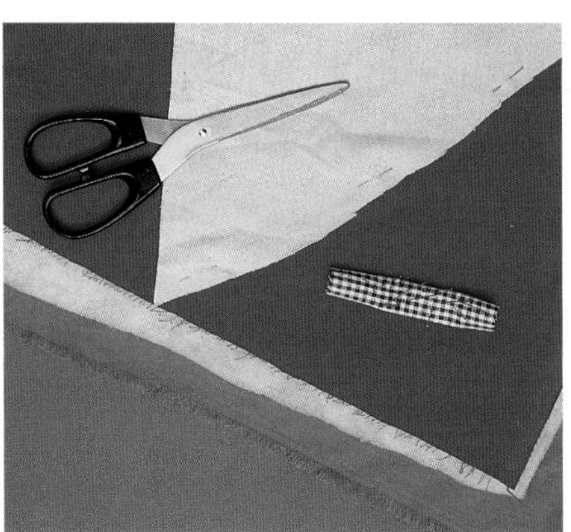

2 Place the batting on the silk and the velvet on top. Pin the muslin pattern on top and cut it out.

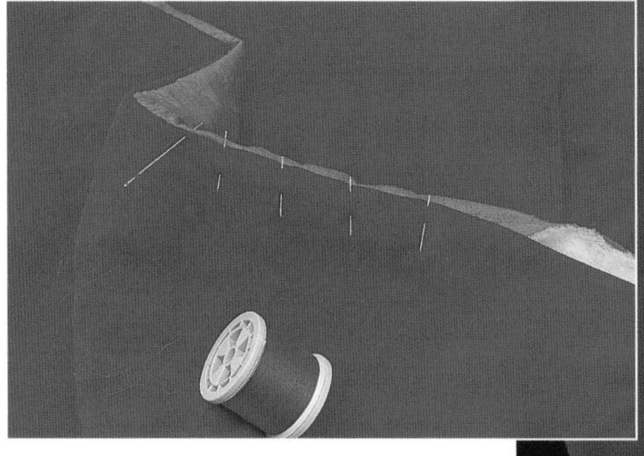

3 Pin and stitch the silk to the batting, close to the edge and right side up. Pin the velvet, right side down, and stitch around the circular edge of the batted silk. Stitch from each end of the straight edge, leaving a gap in the center to be the back of the neck. Remove pins and turn right side out. Slipstitch to close the gap.

Project: Beach bag

This roomy canvas bag is handy for carrying all the gear you need for a trip to the beach or swimming pool, and the rope adds a suitably nautical touch. It is also sturdy and attractive enough to carry shopping or in-flight necessities.

There are borders along the top and bottom which are actually exterior facings that reinforce the bag. The templates are on pages 128–129. Enlarge them according to the instructions and transfer them onto pattern paper.

YOU WILL NEED

- *1¾ yd (1.5 m) canvas, 36 in (90 cm) wide*
- *Pattern paper and pencil*
- *Scissors*
- *Thread*
- *Heavy-duty machine needle*
- *⅜ in (12 mm) eyelet kit*
- *1¼yd (1.1 m) rope, ⅜ in (9 mm) thick*

1 Cut out the canvas pieces using the enlarged templates. Fold under the seam allowance along the bottom edges of both top borders, clip the curves, and press. With the right side of the top border to the wrong side of the side piece, pin in place, matching the side edges. Stitch along top edges. Trim and clip the seams, then turn borders to the right side. Press the seam and pin bottom edge of the border piece in place on the side piece along folded edge. Topstitch close to the fold.

2 Fold under the seam allowances on the top edges of both bottom borders, clip the curves, and press. With the wrong side of the bottom borders facing the right side of the side pieces, pin in position, matching both bottom and side edges. Topstitch close to the border fold, then baste along the other three sides to hold the layers together.

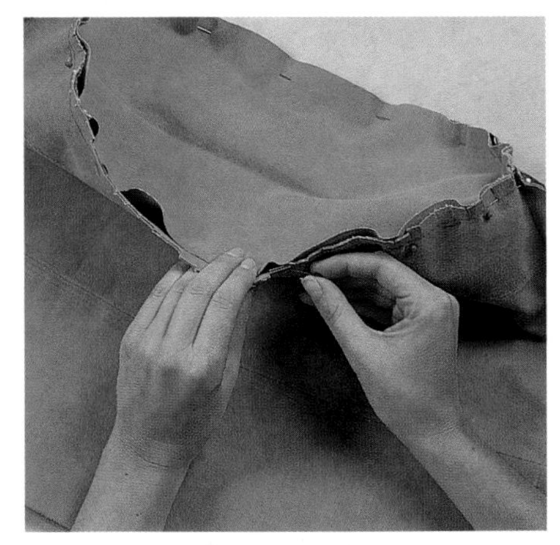

3 With right sides together, pin and stitch both side seams. With right sides together, pin and stitch the base into the bag, matching the notches to the side seams. Bind all the raw seam allowances with bias binding to prevent them from fraying. Turn the bag right side out.

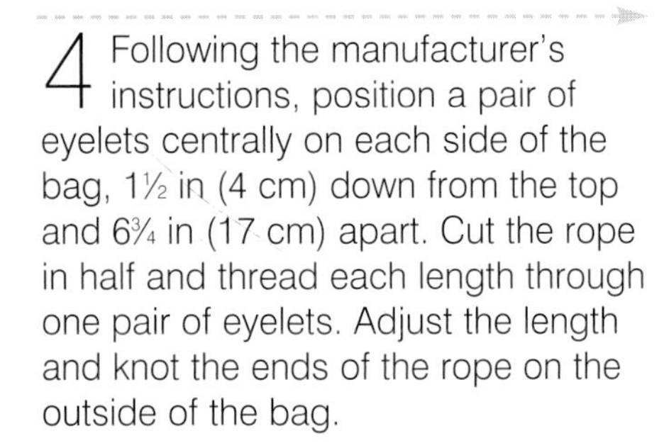

4 Following the manufacturer's instructions, position a pair of eyelets centrally on each side of the bag, 1½ in (4 cm) down from the top and 6¾ in (17 cm) apart. Cut the rope in half and thread each length through one pair of eyelets. Adjust the length and knot the ends of the rope on the outside of the bag.

BEACH BAG

The templates shown here must be scaled up to make a full-size bag. There are various ways of doing this, the simplest of which is to use a photocopier with an enlargement function. Trace each piece separately in the center of a sheet of paper and increase the size. To make our bags, we enlarged the templates by 200%.

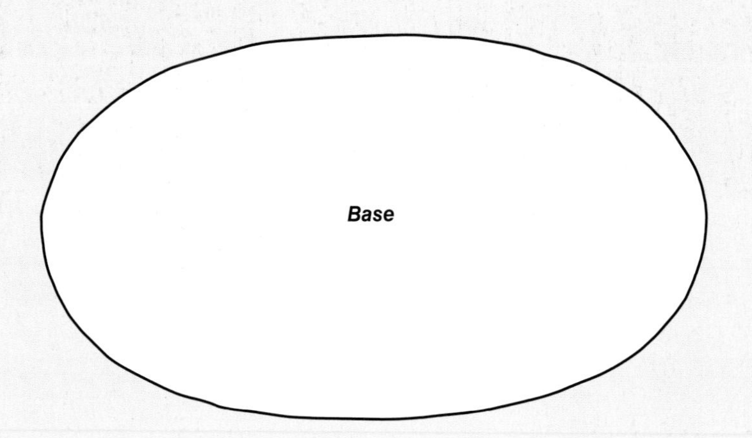

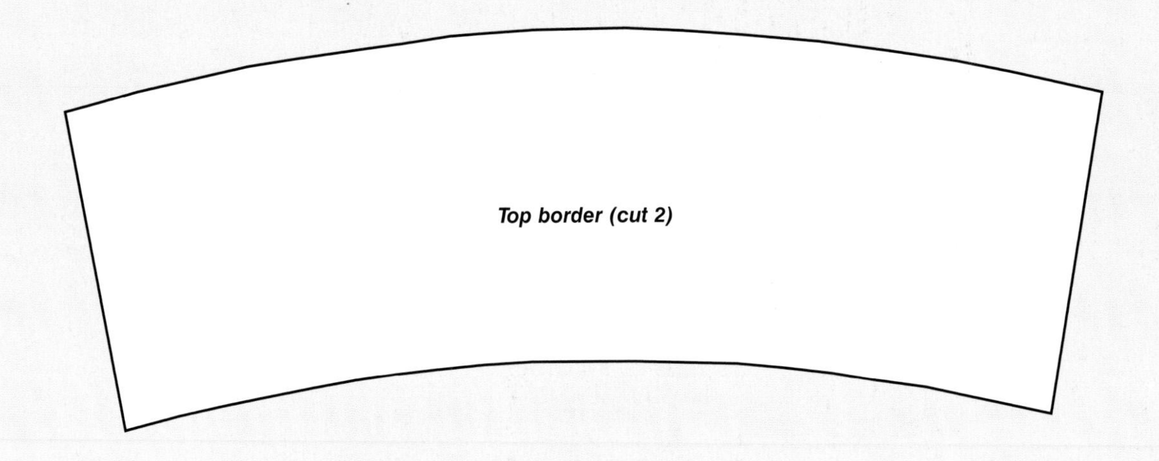

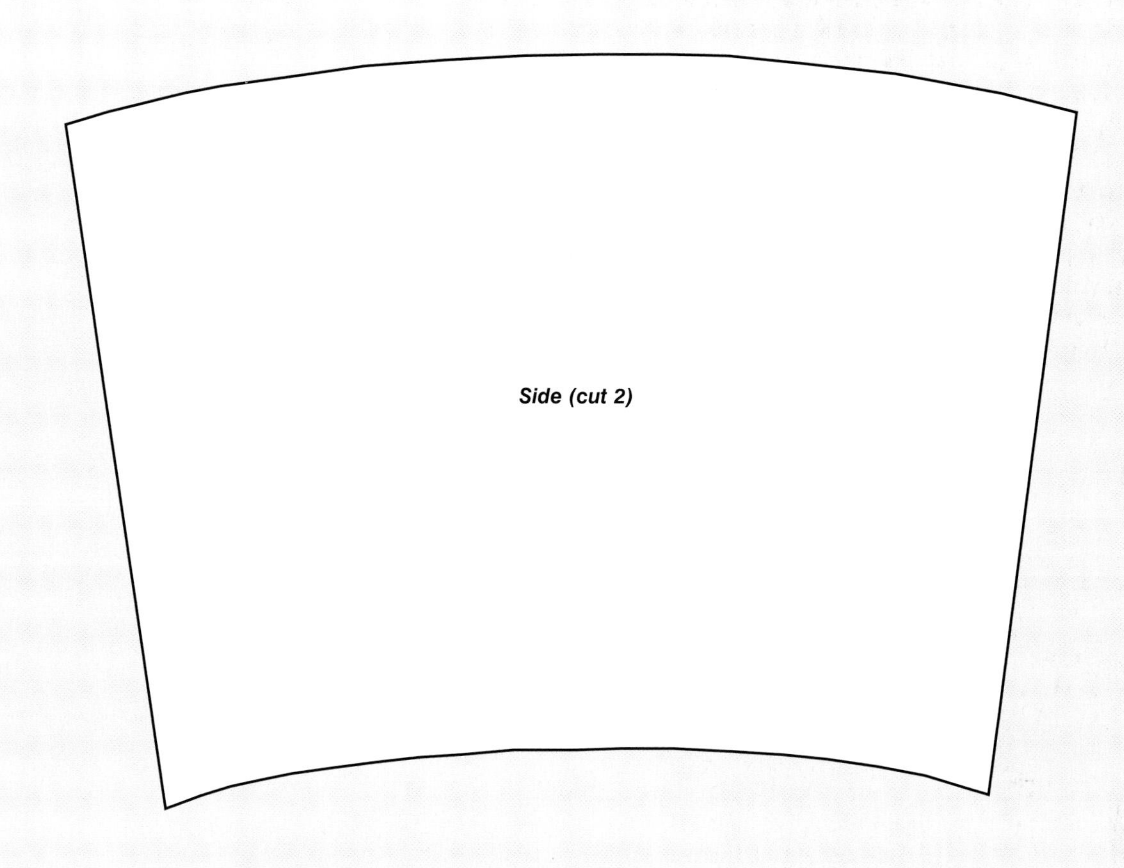
Side (cut 2)

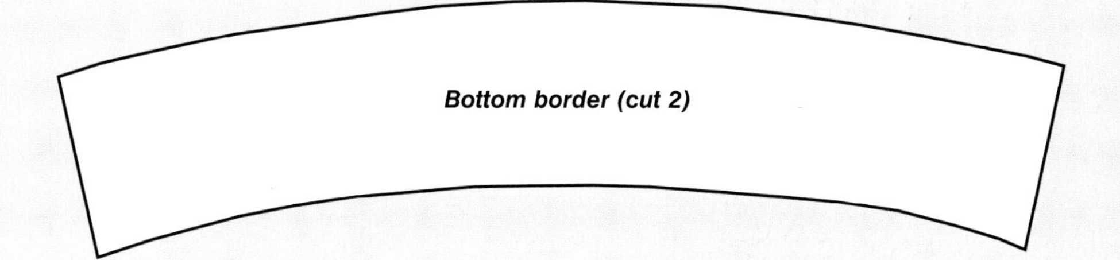
Bottom border (cut 2)

TOLD TO THE GIRLS
NELSON
FIVE GO OFF IN A CARAVAN
FIVE GET INTO TROUBLE
FIVE GO OFF TO CAMP

Home Furnishings

Making your own home furnishings can be satisfying and economical, but the sheer size of many items can be daunting. This chapter helps you to assess your needs and desires, from choosing style and fabric to measuring furniture and windows. It then covers, step by step, how to make curtains, blinds, bedlinen, table linen, cushions, and covers for sofas and chairs.

Assessing furniture

Whether you are decorating a new home from scratch or simply making a new slipcover or curtains, the first step in planning the space is to assess your furnishings in context. Many pieces can be given a new life by adding cushions or a throw, while new window dressings can update a room, but in deciding what work to carry out, you must first look carefully at the pieces of furniture and other furnishings in the room and take account of their style, shape and condition, together with your ideas for the changes you wish to make.

CHAIRS

Chairs come in myriad sizes and shapes, and are found in many different places in the home. Before you can decide what sort of covers or cushions might be suitable for each one, you must look at the style of the seat and its use in its place. Some chairs cry out for a full slipcover that can be removed for cleaning, while others need only a cushion for comfort. Then you must consider its position—an elegant chair in an ornate living room will be covered in a different way from a sturdy wooden kitchen chair, using very different fabrics and trims.

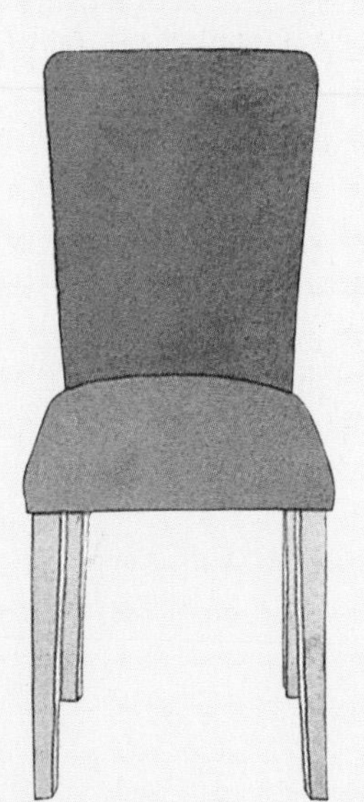

DINING CHAIR

The simple shape of plain dining chairs calls for elegant covers, which will protect them from spills, but should be made from washable or drycleanable fabric.

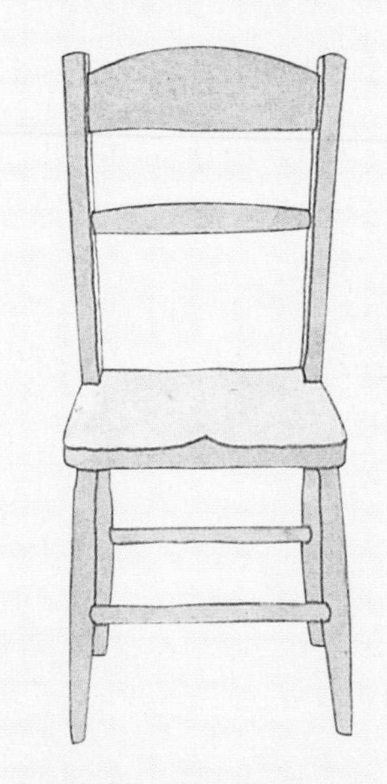

KITCHEN CHAIR

Chairs used in kitchens are often made of wood, with a plain hard seat and simple shape. Fitted squab or box cushions that tie around the back and leg struts will make them more comfortable. Use a sturdy, hardwearing washable fabric.

LINED FOAM BLOCK

Rigid foam blocks make good extra seating in informal rooms. Slip-on covers made from coordinating fabrics turn cubes into stools or seats, and can be used to introduce an accent color into the room.

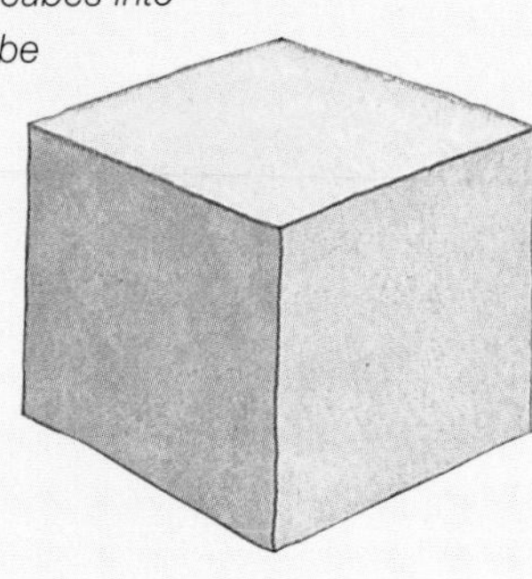

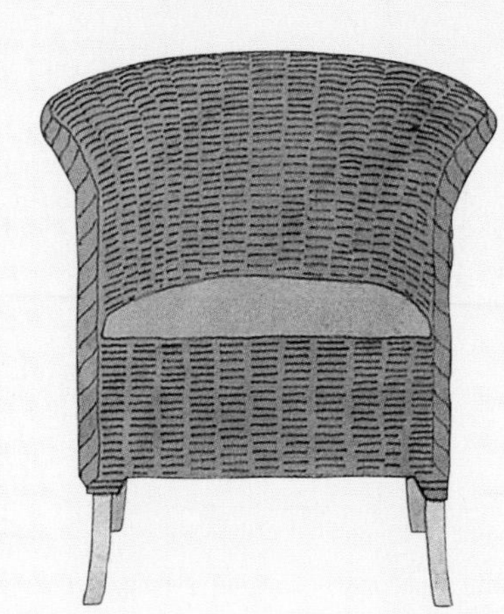

WICKER CHAIR

Traditional wicker bucket chairs are often hard to sit on, and a box cushion made to fit the space will make it more comfortable. Slipcovers can also be created for bucket chairs, a useful way to extend the life of a battered but sound example.

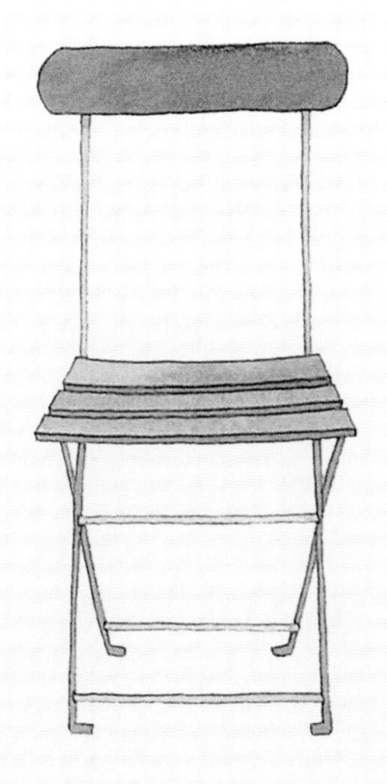

GARDEN CHAIR

Folding chairs designed to be used outdoors can also be brought indoors to provide seating for extra guests. A slipcover or even just a seat cushion can make many examples more comfortable and elegant.

ARMCHAIR

Armchairs are meant to be comfortable and inviting. Slipcovers save wear and tear, but a large throw can also help protect the upholstery and provides a comfort blanket to snuggle up under.

WINDOW SEAT

A bench seat built under a window is useful both as a niche to curl up in and as extra storage under the seat board. A simple large box cushion with scatter pillows or a back cushion will make it comfortable and inviting.

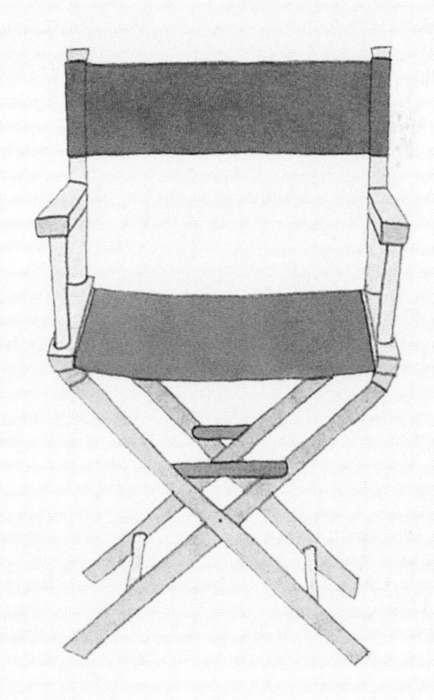

DIRECTOR'S CHAIR

Folding director's chairs are ideal for extra seating, and are often used as the main chairs in informal rooms such as kitchens and dens. The seat and back are easy to replace with sturdy canvas, and they can be hidden under slipcovers made to fit the shape.

TABLES

Tablecloths and other kinds of table linen are usually used to protect the table while providing a decorative surface. On a table used for eating, you will need to choose a fabric that can be laundered easily and that is not a chore to iron. Small tables used in living rooms or bedrooms can be left bare or draped with any fabric that suits the decoration of the space.

DRESSING TABLE

A floor-length tablecloth or skirt will make a dressing table look pretty and will hide the space beneath, which can then be used for extra storage.

BEDSIDE TABLE

Bedside tables are often left bare, but like dressing tables, they look pretty covered with a runner or tablecloth, or a fitted cover.

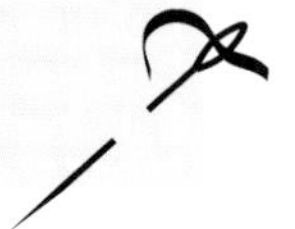

DINING TABLE
Fine dining tables are often dressed with mats to protect the surface, but the elegance of a formal tablecloth is sometimes called for. Heat-resistant undercloths are available. They should be cut to the size of the table and covered with the tablecloth itself.

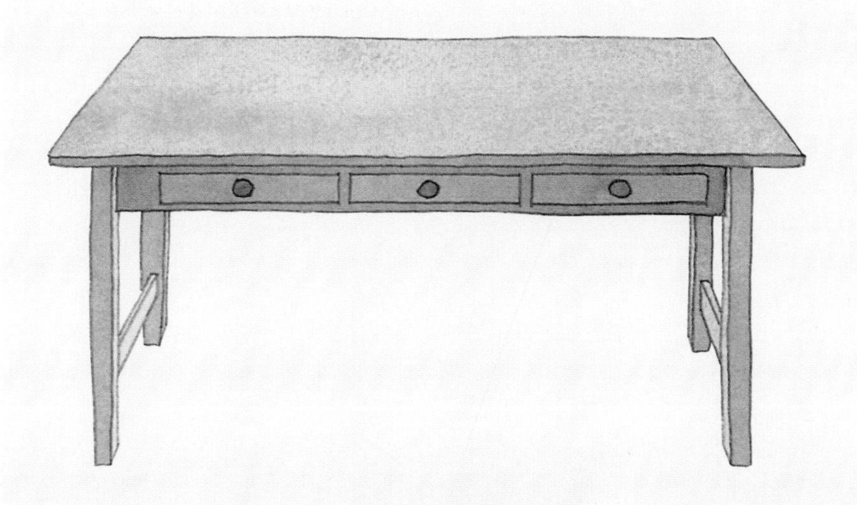

KITCHEN TABLE
The coverings chosen for a hard-working kitchen table, whether they are mats or tablecloths, should be easy to clean. Many wipe-clean fabrics are available, and it is possible to have fabric laminated to match your decor.

OCCASIONAL TABLE
Side tables are used in living rooms, dens, and bedrooms to hold lamps or ornaments, and to place glasses and cups on. Making a full-length cloth provides a way to tie in the table to the rest of the decor, or to introduce an accent color or texture.

SOFAS AND BEDS

Sofas are seating, but are sometimes used for sleeping; while beds are basically for sleeping, but are often used for seating as well. The uses to which these large items are to be put will help determine the type of cover needed and will help make the choice of fabric easier. Beds are often transformed by day into seating by the addition of bolsters and cushions, and sofas can be made more inviting if they are scattered with pillows and a throw.

Most bedding should be made from easily laundered fabric, and slipcovers, blankets, quilts, and comforters should all be drycleanable.

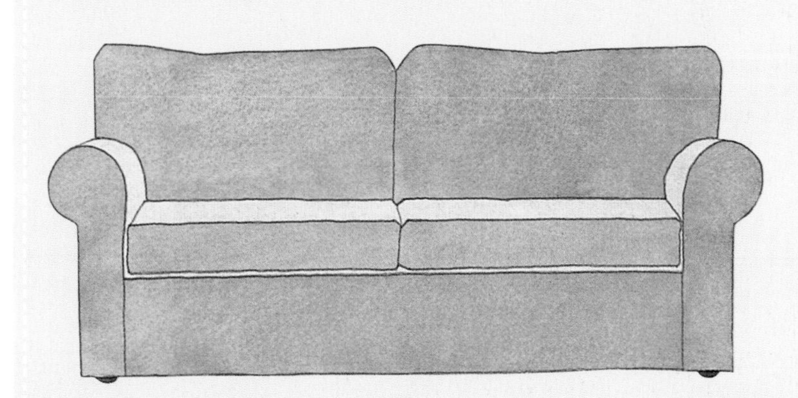

SOFA

As the largest piece of furniture in most living rooms, a sofa is highly visible. It should be attractive and comfortable. Sofa slipcovers should be easy to clean, or a sofa can be covered with a full-size throw and separate seat cushions. Scatter cushions make a sofa look more inviting.

BENCH

Benches are most often found outdoors or in sunrooms and conservatories. Usually made from wood or metal, they can be hard to sit on, but box cushions on the seat and back will transform them into comfortable seating.

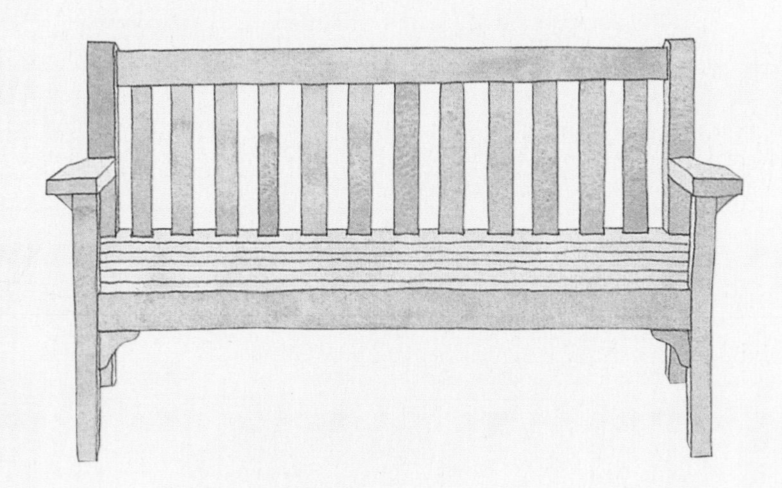

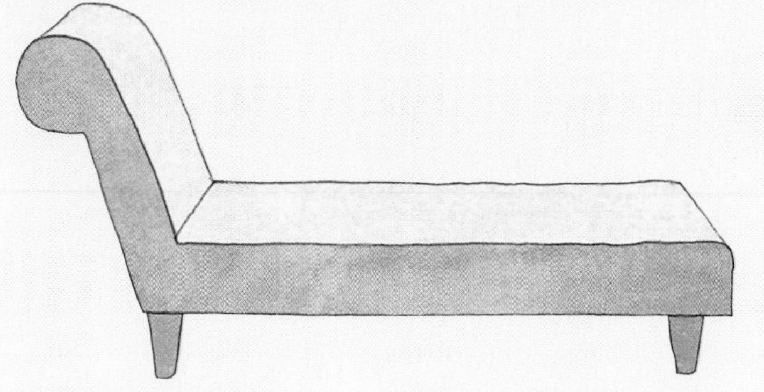

CHAISE LONGUE

Traditional daybeds are usually found in simple, elegant rooms and can be slipcovered or decorated with cushions and a throw.

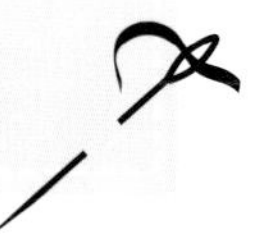

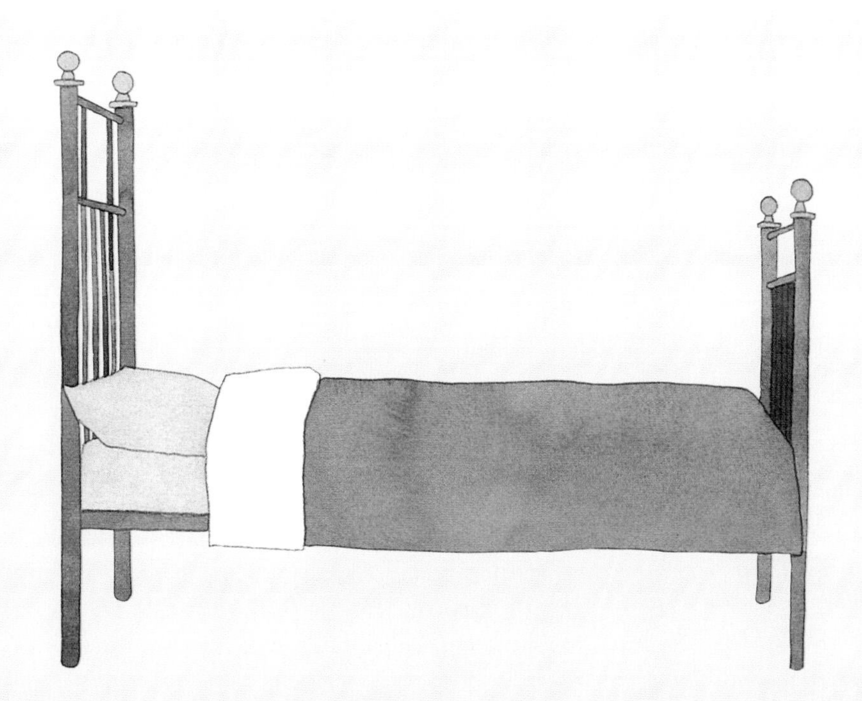

BEDSTEAD

A traditional bedstead, either metal or wood, may be a feature in your bedroom that you do not want to hide under floor-length bedclothes. A neat tucked-in cover is frequently the best option.

DIVAN BED

A divan, or studio, bed is often transformed with bolsters and a sleek fitted cover into a sofa by day. In any case, its simple shape is more interesting if it is covered with a floor-length bedspread or a quilt on top, over a skirt around the base.

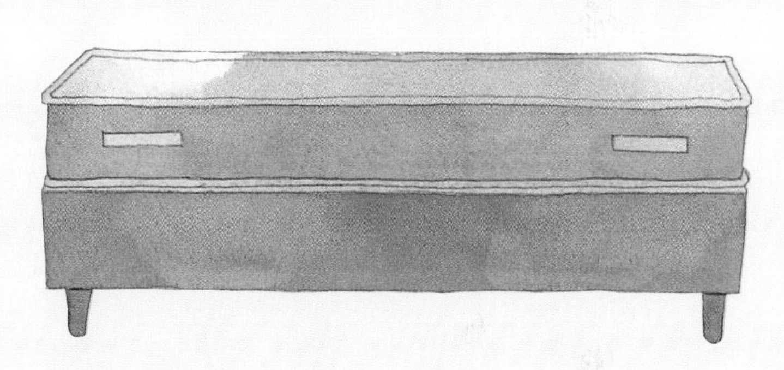

BOX BED

This type of bed is usually found in children's rooms, sometimes in layered bunk beds. A simple cover that tucks in, or a quilt or comforter, is generally the easiest way to dress them.

FUTON

The space-saving futon becomes a chair or sofa during the day, so the mattress is changed into a seat cushion. Other bedding—sheets, quilts, etc.—need to be easy to access and position when bedtime arrives, and must be easy to clean and store.

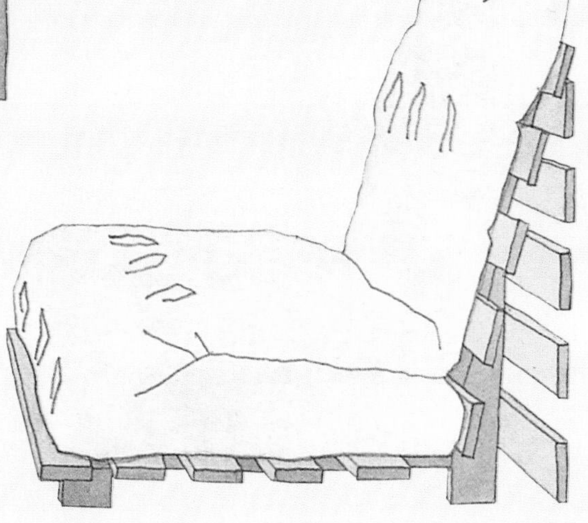

Choosing a style

Before you can plan a home-furnishing project, there are several factors to take into account. If you are making an item to replace or update an existing one, such as new curtains or a chair cover, the style of the room and its color scheme will be known, and a decision will be relatively straightforward.

If you are redecorating an entire room, or a new home, from startup, you will be choosing a style that you and your family like, and one that suits your lifestyle as well as the spaces and furnishings that need to be curtained and covered. Existing architectural features and fixtures can help you determine a style that suits the house or room, but much depends on your own taste. Do you prefer cozy chintz or stark minimalism? There are plenty of options in between, too. Trying to visualize the whole effect can be made much easier if you put together a sample board to bring all the elements into focus in a simple way.

Elements of style
A simple upholstered sofa with a group of scatter cushions in luxurious fabrics and old-fashioned, highly decorative embellishments makes a formal style statement. The same room and sofa with cushions made from more informal fabrics would have a completely different feel.

Creating a sample board

Start a sample board by covering its surface with the chosen wall color. Use an adhesive that allows you to remove and reposition items. Keep swatches and samples in the right proportion as much as possible.

A SAMPLE BOARD FOR A FORMAL ROOM

Dark colors; rich, heavy fabrics; opulent trimmings; deep-pile carpet

A SAMPLE BOARD FOR AN INFORMAL ROOM

Subtle colors; lightweight, natural fabrics; simple trimmings; sisal matting

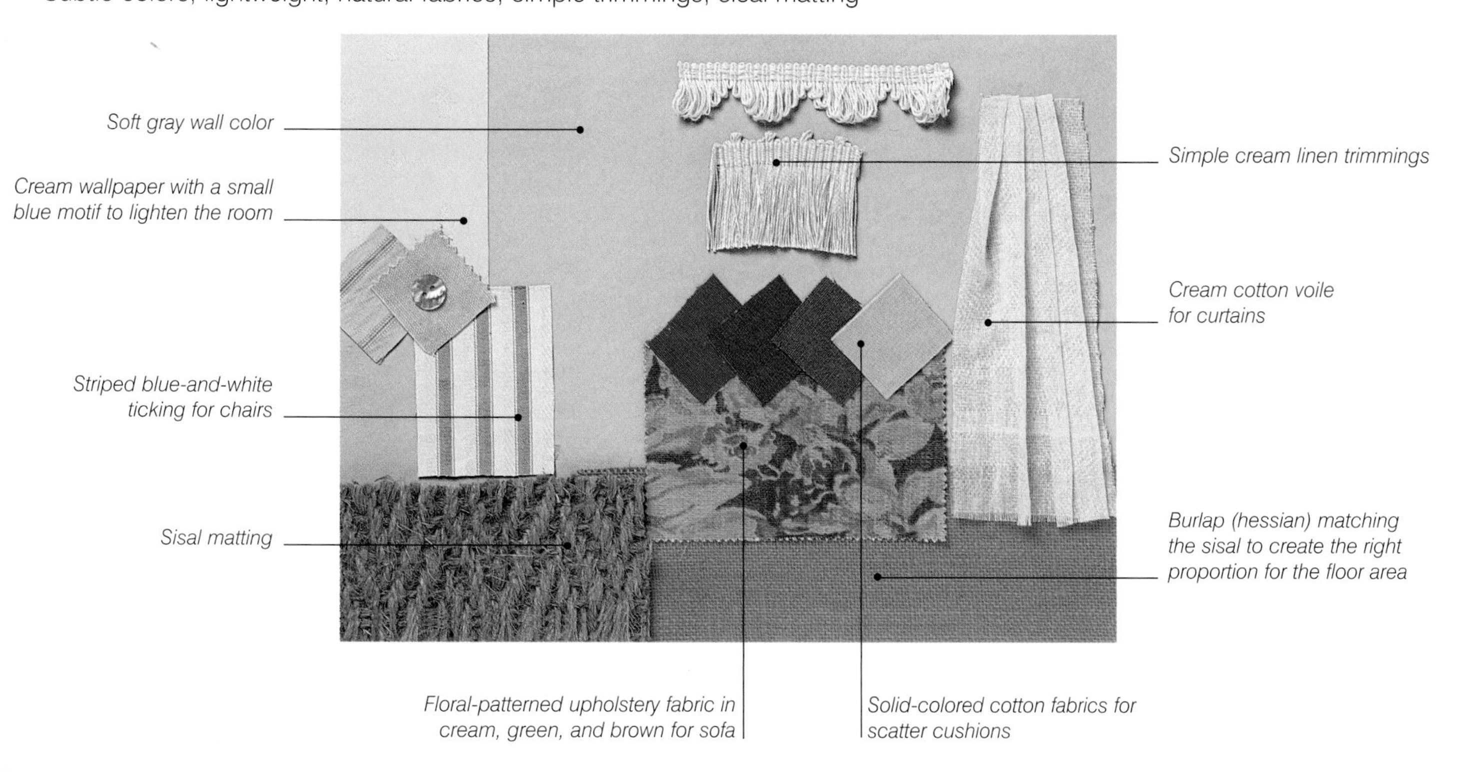

Choosing color

Selecting colors is first of all a matter of personal taste. It is also a question of balance. The size and shape of a room, when it gets sunlight, the architectural style of the house, and the overall impression you wish to create all play a part in color choices.

Colors can be harmonious or contrasting. Harmonious color schemes work best in quiet rooms with a private purpose, such as bedrooms. A room in which shades of one color are used can be bland, but adding a contrasting, or accent, color can liven things up. Colors are described as either warm or cool. A room with several windows and afternoon sun can be cooled down visually with pastel colors from the cool spectrum, while a cool north-facing space can be warmed up with bright shades that make the room seem more cozy. Warm colors such as red, orange, and yellow make colors appear to come closer, advancing visually within a space. Cool colors, such as green, blue, and purple, make a space seem larger because they appear to recede from the eye.

The color wheel

All visual color comes from three primary colors, red, blue, and yellow, none of which can be created by mixing. Secondary and tertiary colors happen when two primaries are mixed to create new colors, such as red and blue to make purple. The color wheel is a device that helps artists and designers to combine, contrast, or blend colors successfully. Harmonious color schemes are based on colors that all appear on the same side of the color wheel, or may be refined further into schemes that use only one color. Both need to be tempered with a contrasting accent.

Successful color schemes based on contrasting colors present more of a challenge, because they depend on colors that are opposite each other on the wheel. Used in pure form they can be brash and visually uncomfortable, but when the base colors are toned down, the more subtle effect can be very exciting.

Harmonious colors *appear on the same side of the color wheel and are contiguous.*

Secondary colors *are achieved by mixing primary colors in various combinations to provide shades in between.*

Contrasting colors *appear on opposites sides of the color wheel.*

Complementary colors *are directly opposite each other on the color wheel. These colors make good foils for each other.*

Monochromatic colors *are tones and shades of a single color. The different values of the color provide visual contrast and can make a space harmonious.*

Neutrals and naturals

We think of all shades of off-white—beige, tan, oatmeal, stone, taupe, cream, sand—as natural colors, while the neutrals are black, white, and shades of gray. Both sets of shades are widely used in decorating, both as background colors and, particularly in minimalist rooms, for furnishings. Indeed, most successful patterned fabrics have a natural or neutral background, because the eye needs to "rest" in the spaces behind the colored design. While the naturals and neutrals can be used minimally, and to play safe, they are also one of the best ways to provide texture and variety. They are particularly useful for toning down bright colors or strong patterns, or for holding together a selection of colors in a scheme. Because they can be warm or cool, though, choose carefully where you use them.

***Harmonious colors** such as this blue-to-green color scheme are successful when a balance of bright and subdued shades is achieved.*

***Contrasting colors** vividly combined—here using red and green with black and touches of bright blue—are ideal for rooms used for socializing.*

Choosing fabrics

The style and colors chosen for a room will determine to some extent the appropriate fabric choices. An opulent bedroom with dark, richly colored walls and heavy curtains would not look right with a ruffled white organdy bedspread, nor would white satin brocade make a good kitchen tablecloth.

Most fibers can be woven into various weights. Silk brocade is very heavy, while silk voile is airy and light. Wool fabrics are generally heavy, but Viyella® is filmy and suitable for curtains and blinds. Linen and cotton likewise can be heavy and slubbed, or lightweight and gauzy; and the range of synthetic fabrics available offers an impressively varied choice of weights.

Fabrics can also be warm or cool, due to their weight and partly to their color. The texture of a fabric is also a factor in its "temperature"—a shiny fabric will feel cooler than a matte one, and pile or napped fabrics will appear warmer, whatever color they are.

Heavy fabrics

This heavy fabric strip is woven 12 in (30 cm) wide in an ornate tapestry pattern. It is good or embellishing or edging a plain fabric.

The ribbed surface stiffens this striped cotton, making it an ideal choice for blinds and borders.

This opulent silky brocade is heavy, but nevertheless drapes beautifully.

This thick wool fabric has a raised surface and is reversible.

This heavy silk damask has a large overall pattern that works well as an upholstery fabric.

When you combine colors, they must be balanced to create a pleasing effect. A warm color can be toned down by a cool one, and vice versa, while a dramatic shade can be cooled or heightened, depending on the color with which it is combined.

The light, natural or otherwise, in a room also affects the color and feel of a fabric, so this needs to be considered carefully. A fabric seen in daylight can appear very different when viewed under electric light.

Heavy and warm

Heavy fabrics are used mainly for curtains and upholstery. As curtains, they keep a room warm, cut out light, and stop drafts from entering a room. Many heavy fabrics can be stiff and bulky, so they do not work well as elaborate curtains. They are better suited to simple curtains and blinds. Heavy fabrics will wear well when used on a sofa or armchair, and give emphasis to the piece of furniture.

For a feeling of warmth, choose fabrics from the warm side of the color wheel. Daylight and sunshine colors, such as yellows, oranges, and reds, will make lightweight fabrics feel warmer. A neutral color scheme can be transformed by the introduction of a warm-colored fabric.

Warm fabrics

This striped cotton fabric is warm in color and also heavy in weight.

The overall tone in this traditional chintz fabric comes from the reds and yellows on a warm cream background.

Another traditional cotton print fabric, this time a paisley, is warmer in color because the background is red.

This striped brocade is soft to the touch and ideal for formal curtains or slipcovers.

This heavy wool damask is woven in two shades of sunshine yellow.

Light and cool

Lightweight fabrics give an open, airy feel to a room. Sheers and open-weaves are the lightest of all, but there are many silk, cotton, and linen fabrics that resemble gossamer but are opaque enough to keep out daylight when they are used as curtains or blinds.

Lightweight fabrics are also widely used for making bedcovers and tablecloths. Sheer curtains can be used to screen a window for privacy while still letting the light through, or they can be combined with heavier curtains to make a dual-purpose screen. Though open-weave lace can be weighty, its effect is one of daintiness and light.

Cool fabrics are often lightweight, but their color is also a determining factor. A heavy fabric in dark shades from the cool spectrum can give the appearance of icy calm, while creamy yellow voile can look warm and sunny.

A reliable rule to follow is that the larger the area, the less intense the color should be; likewise, the smaller the area to be covered, the bolder or brighter the color can be. Try to use subtle variations in tone, as they create a more interesting effect than the repetition of a single color. Remember that light colors are more likely to catch the eye; use them to divert attention from less attractive items.

Blue and white combinations are the quintessential embodiment of cool colors, and are widely used in home furnishings. Sharp whites are often too cool for comfort though, and should be used judiciously. The one exception is pure white table linen, which is always acceptable in virtually any situation, formal or informal, as are white cotton or linen sheets and pillowcases, which tend to be the most popular choice in bedrooms.

Light fabrics

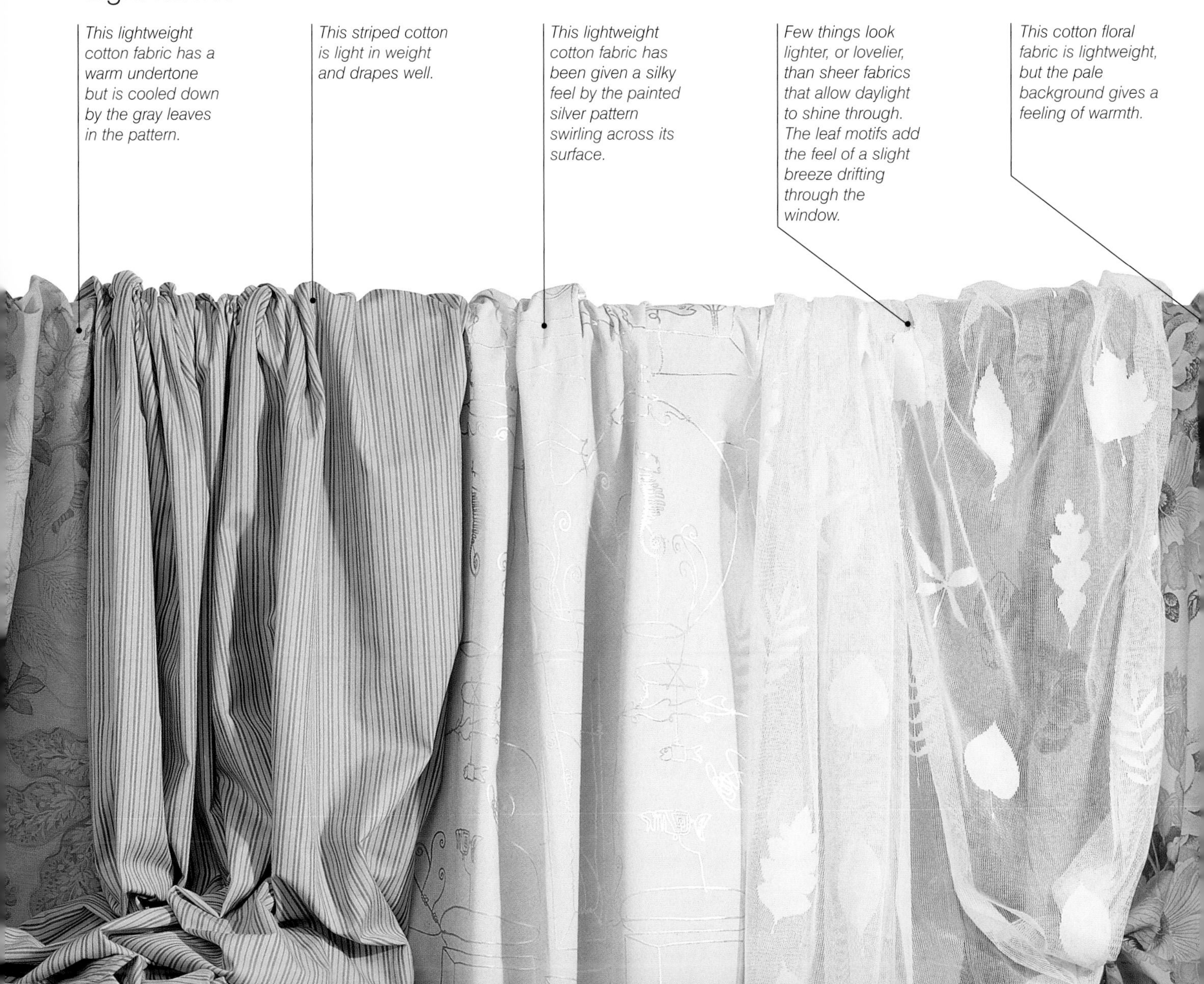

This lightweight cotton fabric has a warm undertone but is cooled down by the gray leaves in the pattern.

This striped cotton is light in weight and drapes well.

This lightweight cotton fabric has been given a silky feel by the painted silver pattern swirling across its surface.

Few things look lighter, or lovelier, than sheer fabrics that allow daylight to shine through. The leaf motifs add the feel of a slight breeze drifting through the window.

This cotton floral fabric is lightweight, but the pale background gives a feeling of warmth.

WORKING WITH SHEER FABRICS

Sheer fabrics are generally woven from cotton, polyester, or silk, and occasionally from linen. Voile and batiste are the most familiar ones used in home sewing. Cotton is the easiest to work with, but it has a tendency to shrink dramatically. Silk and polyester are slippery to handle, fray easily, and can be damaged by a hot iron, but they are both more stable when washed.

Sheer curtains need a great deal of fullness—at least 2½ to 3 times the width of the window. When stitching sheer fabrics, you will need to use a slightly looser tension and a longer stitch than normal. It is also a good idea to start a new project with a new needle in the machine to prevent the material from snagging. Use cotton thread and heading tape for cotton fabrics, and polyester for synthetic and silk fabrics if possible. When making long sheer curtains, finish them with a deep double hem or a narrow hem containing a string of weights.

Try not to join sheer fabrics, because no matter how carefully you make the seam, it will show. If you need more than one width of fabric, try hanging separate panels. The edges will probably be hidden in the fullness of the curtain. If there is no vertical pattern and the height of the window is less than the width of the sheer fabric, you can turn the fabric and hang an uninterrupted length from selvage to selvage.

Cool fabrics

The broken-white pattern of this cotton poplin uses a color from the cool side of the color wheel and drapes beautifully.

The blue and white checks of this classic cotton fabric are the essence of cool.

This lightweight silk fabric is cool in color and weave.

This dark blue velvet is heavy in weight but cool in color. In spite of its weight, it would work well in a cool room scheme.

The equal balance of cool blue stripes and warm red ones is tipped to the cool spectrum by the white background of this cotton fabric.

Plain and patterned

The vast selection of fabrics available can be overwhelming when you need to choose just one. To help simplify the choice, decide whether you want to use a patterned fabric or a plain solid-colored one. Unless you are decorating a room from startup, your decision will depend largely on the style of the room, your overall color scheme, and the type of fabrics already in use.

Combining patterns and plains successfully will create a balanced look that is ideal to aim for, but think carefully about all the elements being used in that particular room or situation. It is probably best to decide on the most boldly patterned fabric first and work the other fabrics around it. It is relatively simple to mix patterns and plains, and combining more than one pattern can be successful if the scales are balanced and the colors are harmonious.

Proportion is crucial. Using a fabric with a small-scale pattern on a large window means that the pattern will be seen as a plain color from a distance, while a large-patterned fabric will look busy on a small window and its impact will be lost. There is a danger that plain fabrics and small-scale patterns used on large windows will be uninteresting, but if the colors are strong, they might be overpowering, so consider adding pattern by putting on a border or mounting a decorative valance. Remember, too, that elaborate curtain headings can blur a complicated pattern, but would look elegant atop a plain fabric.

Plain fabrics

The matte surface of velvet adds to its richness, but it can make a room dark and heavy unless it is toned down with shiny fabrics and some pattern.

A motif woven into the fabric can create light and dark shades of the same color, giving subtle visual texture to the piece.

This chenille is perfectly plain but for the small gold motif that is woven into the cloth.

The balance of blue and white in this checked pattern will make the fabric appear as a plain blue when seen from a distance.

JOINING PLAIN FABRICS

Joining plain solid-colored fabrics is often necessary in curtain-making, and when making bedcovers and tablecloths, because the woven width of fabrics is narrower than the area to be covered. Because the selvage on each edge of a length of fabric is woven more tightly than the main cloth, it will shrink at a different rate and should always be trimmed neatly and evenly before any work is carried out on a project. Some people recommend clipping the selvage all along a length of fabric, but the selvage can still shrink, and may show along the seam.

Joining plain fabrics should be a simple matter of stitching a seam along the cut edges using a fairly tight stitch with a suitable thread for the fabric. Use a sharp needle—it is a good idea to start any project with a new needle of the size recommended for the fabric.

The width of the seam will vary according to the item you are making, but for most upholstery and curtain fabrics, a seam of ½ in (1 cm) to ⅝ in (1.2 cm) is usually recommended. Finish the raw edges of the seam with zigzag stitching to prevent fraying and to add strength.

Plain fabrics can usually be stitched together without pinning, provided the edges are cut straight. Lay the sections, right sides together, as flat as possible with the raw edges level. Guide the layers under the needle at the speed that feels most comfortable. Rather than pull on the fabric, let the machine take it through at its own pace.

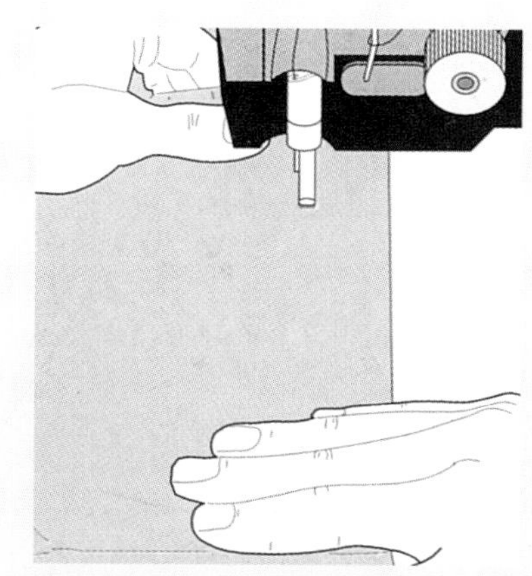

Patterned fabrics

This cotton fabric takes its pattern from a traditional toile de Jouy, but is printed in several colors instead of the usual blue or pink on white.

The large woven motif on this thick cotton is repeated in a bold pattern.

The impact of the architectural design on this fabric will be lost unless the fabric is used flat, say on a blind.

The busy pattern and variety of harmonizing colors in this chintz make it a good choice for blinds, curtains, or cushions.

Traditional stripes are updated on this wool fabric by the thin stripe of gold between each wide stripe.

Subtle and striking

Another aspect of selecting fabrics is similar to the decision between patterned and plain: should the fabrics be subtle or striking, calm or vivid, delicate or bold? The desired overall effect of the room is a crucial factor, but again, the huge selection of fabrics available can make it very difficult to reach a final decision.

On the whole, plains, stripes, and muted colors create a subtle room scheme, while exuberant prints, bright plaids, and vivid geometrics make a striking impression. Subtle should not be boring, but striking schemes must be used with care. The secret as always is to try to achieve a balance, using bold fabrics to add zing and excitement to more subtle background furnishings. On the whole, natural colors and neutrals are subtle and blend harmoniously, while combinations of primary and secondary colors are strong and deliver plenty of drama.

Striking fabrics are usually best used flat or in a place that shows the pattern as a whole. Always try to obtain large samples of any bold fabric that you are thinking of using, even if it means purchasing a pattern repeat or two. A small swatch will not give you a reliable impression of what the overall effect is likely to be.

Remember that if you have chosen a bold pattern with a sizable repeat, it needs to be used on a large area, such as a bed or floor-length curtain, for the pattern to be appreciated. It will also draw immediate attention in a room, so if the item is not in scale with its surroundings, there is a danger of it becoming an eyesore rather than a key feature. Consider using a plain-colored planel as a contrast, to tone down an overbearing color or design. Equally, use a striking design to your advantage if you want to disguise an awkward-shaped feature in your room—scrolling patterns are ideal for hiding contours—or complement an extravagant design with generous swathes of fabric, in the form of valances and swags.

Subtle fabrics

This wool tweed is a plaid in which only the thin red stripe shows as a separate color — the blues, grays, and ochers blend to create a subtle background color.

The narrow self-colored stripe woven into this cotton sheer gives a subtle texture to the fabric.

This thick white cotton has a small, subtle square woven into the fabric to create an even, subtle pattern.

The two-color motif woven into this heavy fabric is made up of muted shades of complementary colors, blue and brown, that give it a subtle impact.

Traditional cotton ticking fabric, here in black and cream, has a subtle country feel.

JOINING PATTERNED FABRICS

Joining patterned fabrics correctly is crucial to the look of a project. The larger the scale of the pattern, the more important it is.

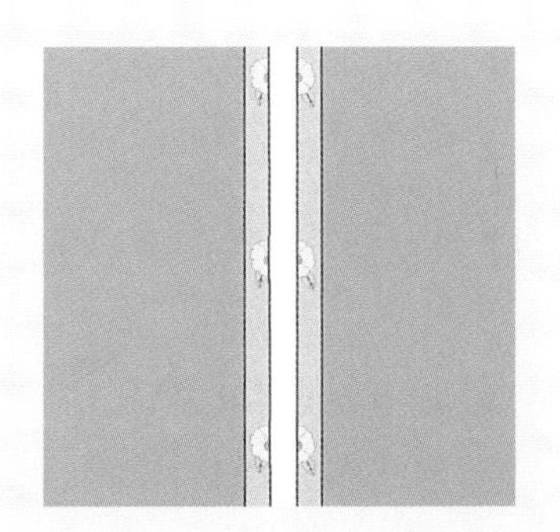

1 Lay the two pieces flat, right side down, with raw edges to be joined together. Fold each edge back until the pattern matches. Press along one fold.

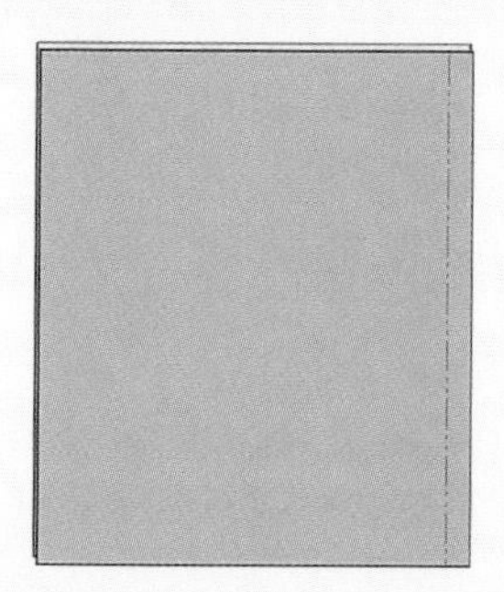

2 Place the pieces right sides together with the pressed piece on top. Line up the pattern with the edges aligned. Pin along the pressed fold if you wish.

3 Stitch along the folded line carefully. As you work, check that the patterns match by lifting up the top piece of fabric.

Striking fabrics

All three primary colors are combined in this flamboyant wool plaid, and a hint of green, the complementary of the dominant red, gives added zing.

This bold pattern is printed on a cream velvet background in iridescent colors.

This heavy cotton with a playing-card motif is made even more dramatic by its black background.

A madras plaid is large in scale and made even more striking by its use of the primary colors toned with occasional squares of cream.

This striped cotton fabric printed with bold citrus colors can be turned in either direction. The effect will be dramatic whichever way the stripes run.

Choosing pattern

Using patterned fabric can be fraught with choice, and great care needs to be taken when selecting a design. Patterns can be printed or they can be woven in stripes, checks, plaids, damask, or tapestry designs.

Designs may be large- or small-scale and repeating. The choices include contemporary or traditional, floral or geometric, busy or bold. Ultimately, as with color and style, the choice is up to individual preference.

Combining patterns successfully requires working to a similar scale. Small, subtle patterns generally work well together, as do strong patterns, provided that you keep to your chosen color scheme.

Looking at the overall effect on a sample board (see page 139) will help you to assess whether the choices go together well. Introduce neutral or natural colors to tie the patterns together in a scheme; stripes and checks, as well as plain colors, can be used in this way with great effect.

Subtle patterns

Subtle patterns, like cool colors, recede visually. They are widely used as backgrounds and make small rooms seem larger. Because they tend to disappear in large spaces, they need to be combined with bolder patterns to create a pleasing balance.

Gingham check
Two-color checks are usually subtle, even when the scale is as large as this linen gingham.

Narrow stripe
Narrow stripes give the impression of being a solid color when seen from a distance, so they are ranked among the most subtle of patterns.

Toile de Jouy
As pure pattern, toiles de Jouy can be described as busy, but because these traditional French fabrics are printed in subtle colors on white or cream backgrounds, they tend to merge into a background area subtly.

Abstract pattern
Abstract designs are often bold, but here the subdued colors and distressed printing technique give this fabric a subtle pattern.

Small print
Small-scale printed patterns tend to be subtle, unless there is a high contrast between the colors used.

Repeated print
Small-scale woven patterns, widely used for upholstery and slipcovers, are also subtle.

ALLOWING FOR REPEAT PATTERNS

Fabric patterns, particularly bold ones, must be matched exactly when you need to join widths, for example when making curtains. Unless you are very lucky, you will need to cut off some fabric from each length in order to match the pattern, so it is important to calculate the amount of extra fabric you will need before buying.

Measure the length of each pattern repeat, which may be written on the bolt or label. Divide the drop of the curtain (or the length of the table or bedcover) by the pattern length. Round the number up to the next full number and multiply by the pattern length. This calculation will give you the total length of the fabric needed for each drop.

For example, if the drop is 146 in (370 cm) and the repeat is 34 in (86 cm), divide 146 (370) by 34 (86) to get 4.3. Round up to 5 and multiply by 34 (86), the length of the repeat, to get 170 in (430 cm), which is 4¾ yd (4.3 m) per drop. Multiply the number of drops by this figure to calculate the total amount of fabric needed.

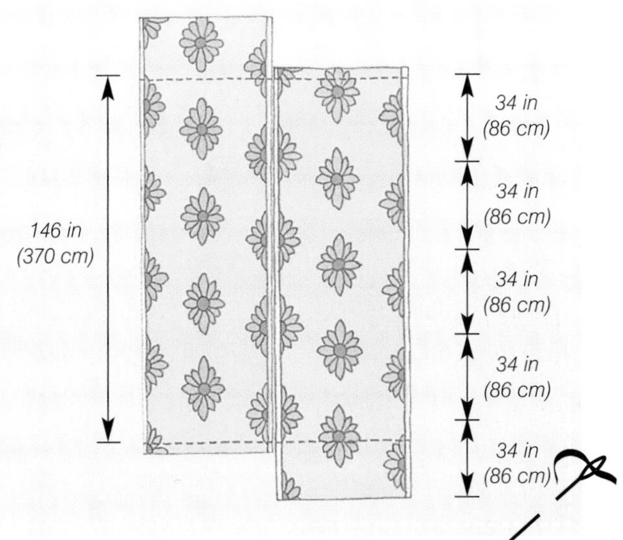

Bold patterns

Bold patterns that are on a relatively large scale and have strongly contrasting colors appear to come forward, like warm colors. They should be used with great care in small rooms, but tend to give large ones a more intimate and welcoming feel. Too many bold patterns in one area can be visually disturbing. Combine them with care and calm them down with plenty of plain neutrals.

Plaid
Plaids, like stripes and checks, can be bold, depending on the choice of colors used in the pattern and the scale.

Woven stripe
Woven stripes can be bold as well as subtle. Here wide stripes are combined with narrow ones, and the subtly contrasting colors create a bold overall impression.

Woven motif
Large-scale woven motifs can be combined with other bold patterns, if the colors are coordinated and the patterns share a similar feel.

Floral print
Large-scale printed patterns, such as this floral design, should be used in a way that allows you to see the motifs clearly.

Ethnic print
Ethnic prints from around the world use abstract symbols to create patterns that can be combined in interesting ways.

Figurative print
Figurative prints on a bold scale are best used on cushions and covers where the pattern can be seen fully.

Choosing texture

The other quality that must be considered when you are making a choice of fabric is texture. Fabric can be shiny or matte, rough or smooth, flat, bumpy, or napped. Each attribute has a bearing on the look and the feel of a piece of cloth, and will affect the room in which it is placed as well as the individual items around it.

Shiny fabrics like silk and polished or glazed cotton reflect light, which makes the colors look brighter and the room feel larger. Matte fabrics like velvet or corduroy and many roughly woven wools absorb light, making the space appear cozy and the colors darker than they may really be.

Smooth textures like silk and velvet are quite different from the rough feel of tweed or hopsacking, and both are quite unlike the crispness of cotton chintz or fine linen. Texture is sometimes woven into the fabric: corduroy has regular ribs, brocade and damask create a raised pattern using just one color, and moiré has a shimmering quality that gives it visual texture on a flat surface.

Informal fabrics

Informal fabrics are most often used in rooms like kitchens and breakfast rooms, dens, and bedrooms to give a practical feel. They can range from slubby linen and tweeds to soft, non-reflective cotton and canvas, and work well in contemporary settings.

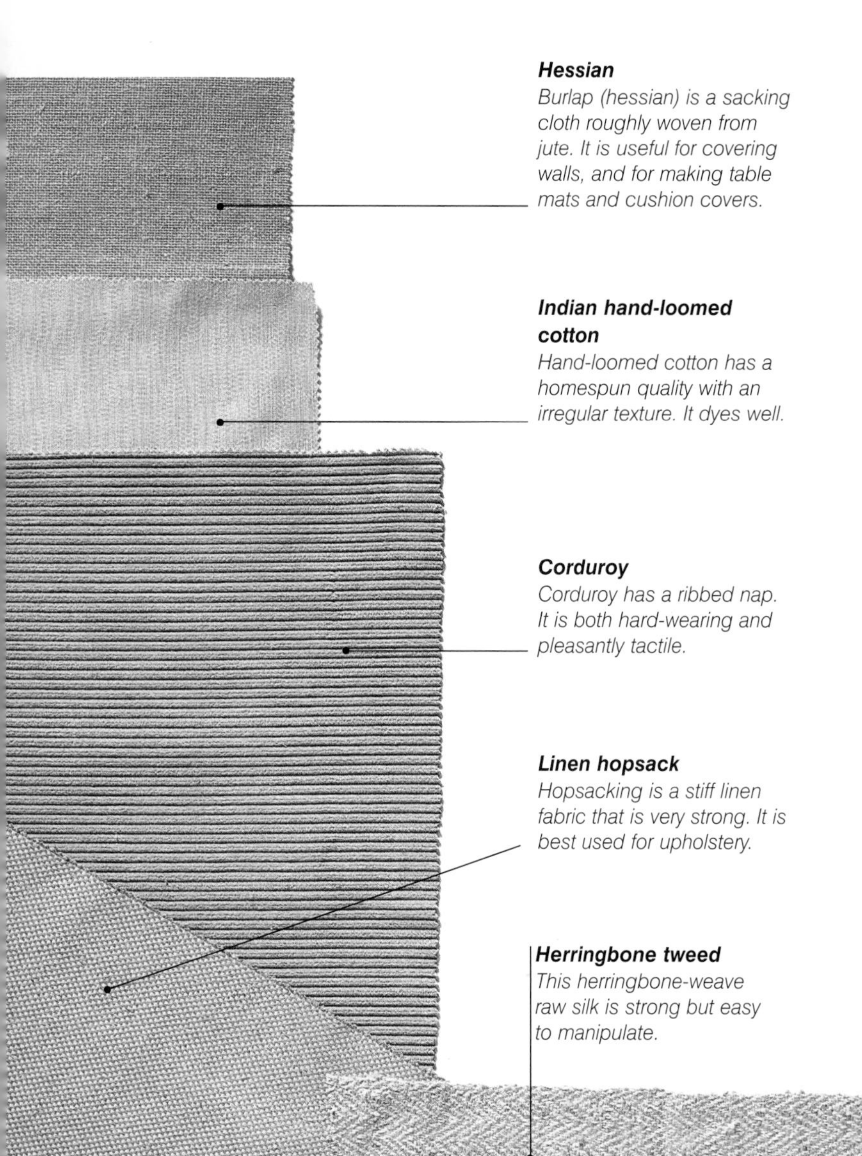

Hessian
Burlap (hessian) is a sacking cloth roughly woven from jute. It is useful for covering walls, and for making table mats and cushion covers.

Indian hand-loomed cotton
Hand-loomed cotton has a homespun quality with an irregular texture. It dyes well.

Corduroy
Corduroy has a ribbed nap. It is both hard-wearing and pleasantly tactile.

Linen hopsack
Hopsacking is a stiff linen fabric that is very strong. It is best used for upholstery.

Herringbone tweed
This herringbone-weave raw silk is strong but easy to manipulate.

Canvas
Canvas is a strong, tightly woven cotton fabric with a stiff but smooth texture.

Linen union
Linen union is similar to canvas in its weave and strength, but has a rougher texture.

JOINING VELVET

To join velvet or other fabrics with a directional pile, you must first make sure the pile runs in the same direction on the pieces to be joined. Stroke the fabric gently with your hand to see which way it feels smoothest, which is the way the pile "runs." If you run your hand in the opposite direction, the pile will stand up. Fabric with the pile running the wrong way will absorb the light and look darker and more drab, so if you join widths running in opposite directions, the piece will always look wrong.

Velvet is one fabric on which the selvages should not be cut off. They are generally soft, made from a single layer of fine fabric, and cutting them off will cause the fabric to fray. If you are joining cut pieces, you will need to overlock the raw edges before you do anything else. Make sure the pile is running in the same direction on both pieces and even up the raw edges. With right sides together, make a generous seam, sewing in the same direction as the pile lies. Keep adjusting the edges as necessary; the layers may slip a little as you work. Because the selvages can curl up over time, anchor them with invisible herringbone stitch.

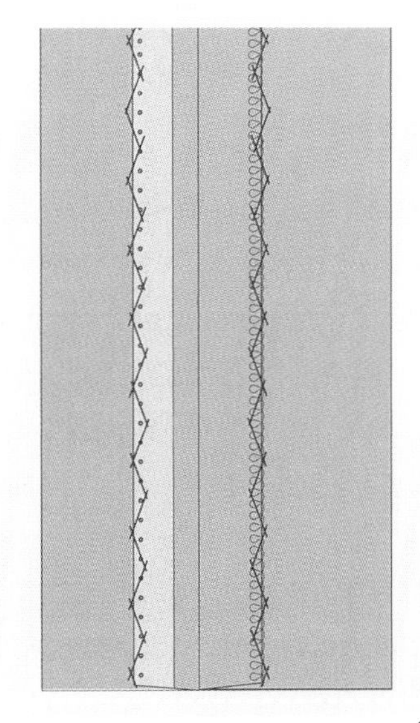

Formal fabrics

Formal fabrics are generally more elaborate and have a rich, traditional feel that works well in rooms decorated in period style. Many of them are luxurious (and expensive), with plenty of texture. They work best in formal rooms used mainly for entertaining, but are often used in elegant bedrooms as well.

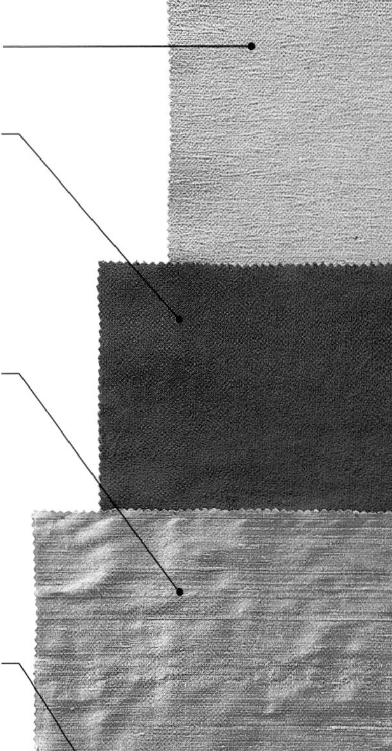

Chenille
Chenille is traditionally made from silk or wool. Its double-sided pile makes it soft to handle and drapes well.

Moleskin
Moleskin is a strong but soft cotton fabric with a pile, which is hard-wearing, an attribute that many formal luxury fabrics lack.

Indian dupion silk
Dupion is a delicate, unevenly textured silk with a rich shine.

Damask
Damask is a rich fabric made traditionally from silk. It has a slightly embossed texture created in the complex weaving process.

Cut velvet
Cut velvet is heavily embossed to create elaborate textural patterns. The designs are cut into the fabric by a chemical process that removes the pile, but leaves the background layer intact.

Velvet
Velvet is a fine matte fabric with a directional pile that gives it a feel of elegance and luxury.

Crewel work
Crewel-embroidered fabric is often stitched by hand. Its usually floral patterns are highly traditional.

Fabric glossary

The best way to learn about different fabrics is to seek out and handle as many different types as possible. The more fabric types that you are familiar with, the simpler will be the task of selecting the one that best suits your project, and complements the style and decor of your home.

The key characteristics of a cloth will have a bearing on your choice of fabric. Do you want a natural fiber, a man-made one, or a blend of two or more? If you are making curtains, you may need lining and interlining, and here, too, there are choices to be made.

Sometimes the situation will dictate to a certain extent the type of fabric you can use. For example, kitchen curtains need a lightweight and washable fabric, whereas a chair cover in a family living room needs a strong and hardwearing type. Even when the fabric type is decided for you though, you will still need to decide on the color, pattern, texture, or even the fiber.

Linings and basic fabrics

INTERLINING
Interlining goes between the fabric and lining in curtains and provides a useful layer of insulation. It is made from combed cotton or manmade fiber, and is available in various thicknesses.

THERMAL LINING
Use this lining fabric when interlining would make a curtain too thick, but where insulation is needed. The side coated with a metallic silver-gray layer faces the wrong side of the curtain fabric, while the other side, which is usually light in color, looks like standard lining fabric.

MUSLIN (CALICO)

This inexpensive fabric is woven from unbleached cotton. It is available in various widths and can be used either as a lining or backing. Muslin (calico) can also be used in its own right for making covers and curtains.

SATEEN

Sateen is a tightly woven cotton fabric with a slight sheen. It is popular as a lining fabric for curtains because it retains its shape after cleaning. It is also useful for backing quilts or bedcovers, and can be made into items in its own right.

BLACKOUT LINING

A popular choice for backing curtains in children's bedrooms, blackout lining is a very effective light shield. It consists of a layer of opaque fabric bonded between two layers of lining fabric.

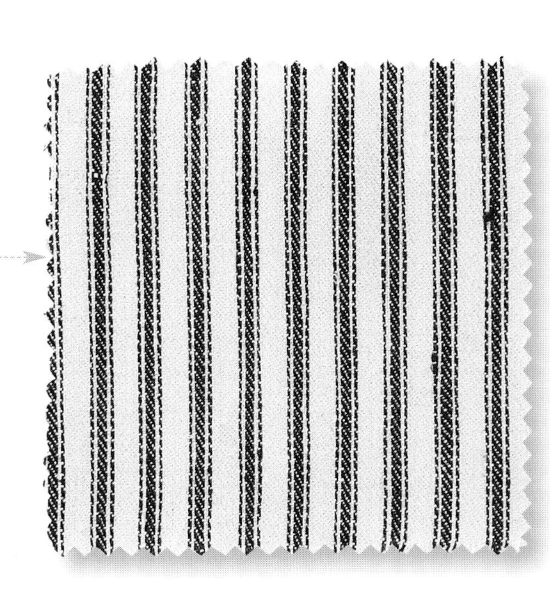

TICKING

Ticking is a hardwearing woven cotton that was originally used to cover mattresses: its tight weave was strong enough to keep traditional stuffings from working through the fabric. It usually has regular stripes of black, gray, or blue with white or cream. Ticking is also available in special soft weaves that are suitable for home furnishing projects.

Neutral and simple-patterned fabrics

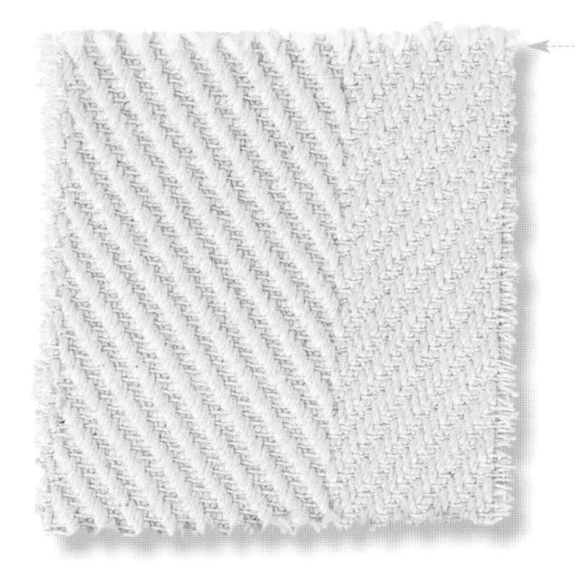

HERRINGBONE WEAVE

This strong cotton fabric is woven in a diagonal rib called herringbone. It is highly textured and quite stiff.

LACE INSET

This sheer cotton fabric has a design of lace insets running through its surface. The openwork embroidery lightens the weight of the fabric.

COTTON CHECK

This medium-weight cotton fabric has a simple two-color checked pattern that is reversible, making it ideal for unlined curtains. Its strong weave makes it useful for all kinds of home furnishing projects.

CHENILLE DAMASK

The soft pile of chenille is woven here into a traditional damask design with fluffy raised motifs surrounded by flat background areas. It makes an ideal fabric for covering chairs and sofas.

FRENCH TICKING

French ticking is another traditional material used to cover mattresses. Its irregular stripes are often two shades of the same color. Its weight and weave make it a practical choice for home furnishings.

VOILE

Voile is a gauzy, very fine, almost sheer fabric. It can be made from cotton, as here, silk, or polyester, and can be plain or patterned with printed motifs as shown or with a self-colored design woven into the cloth.

BURLAP (HESSIAN)

Burlap, or hessian, is woven from jute fibers to make a rough open-weave fabric that lends itself to informal situations. It is usually plain, but sometimes has a pattern woven into or printed on it.

LINEN

Linen is woven from the fibers of the flax plant. It can be rough or smooth, loosely or tightly woven, and comes in a variety of weights. Heavyweight linen is hardwearing, making it ideal for domestic furnishings. It also drapes beautifully when used for curtains.

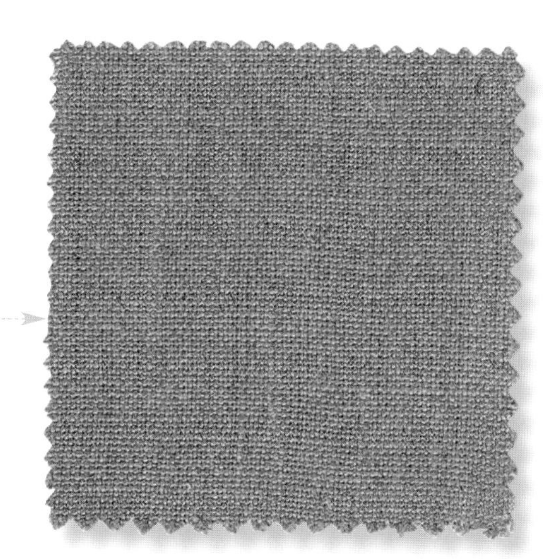

Printed and woven patterns

COTTON AND LINEN BLEND

When linen and cotton fibers are woven together, the resulting blend is stronger and harder-wearing than cotton alone, and has more drape than 100% linen.

HEAVY COTTON

Thick cotton fabric is hardwearing. With a pattern woven in (as shown here), it becomes reversible, making it particularly suitable for unlined curtains or blinds.

WOOL DAMASK

This damask made from heavy wool has the raised pattern woven into a flat background. In spite of its weight, it drapes beautifully, and the nature of its weave makes it possible to use the reverse side, too.

WOOL CHECK

The diagonal weave used on this wool fabric is called twill. It is created by taking each weft thread over one thread and then two alternately. Although twill is not as tight as plain weave, it is still quite hardwearing. The subtle woven pattern can be used on either side.

TAPESTRY

While tapestries are traditionally hand-woven, machine-made versions like this ornately patterned fabric can look very effective. These fabrics are useful for slipcovers and cushions.

WOVEN BLANKET

Soft, cuddly wool blankets are made from combed fibers that provide warmth and good insulating properties.

PLAID

Tartan plaids are woven, usually in wool, into patterns of different colors that represent a clan in Scotland. Their medium weight makes them a popular choice for making clothes and home furnishings. In addition, they drape well and are reversible.

PAISLEY

In the 1800s patterns of swirling shapes were widely used on fabrics produced in Paisley in Scotland, from which they take their name. They were popular as motifs on woolen shawls, and are common on cotton fabrics, too.

CHINTZ
This traditional cotton furnishing fabric is usually decorated with floral motifs printed in several colors on a cream background.

COTTON PRINT
Cotton fabric takes dye particularly well, such that some striking effects can be achieved with different printing techniques. In this example, the colorwashed background has been overprinted with gold.

SILK DAMASK
Traditionally, damask fabric, with its subtle pattern of raised areas and flat background, was woven from silk, which gave it a wonderful texture and hang.

STRIPED VELVET
Patterns can be woven into velvet, like the stripe shown here. The red pile contrasts beautifully with the gold background fabric to create a wonderfully elegant cloth.

PRINTED LINEN

While linen is most often used in its natural colors, it can be printed with elaborate multicolored designs, like the example shown here.

TAFFETA

The crispness of silk taffeta is quite unlike that of any other fabric. Woven using different colors in the warp and weft, it is fine and delicate. There is a continually altering perception of its surface color when it is seen in different lights.

CHECKED SILK

This fabric is also woven with different colors in the warp and weft, but it has additional colors used at regular intervals to create the checked pattern.

VELVET

While many versions of velvet are a single color and others have a woven pattern, the fabric can also be printed, as here, in this contemporary two-color striped design.

Measuring

Accurate measurements are vital if your curtains and blinds are to look good and fit your windows properly. If possible, mount the fixtures before you measure a window. This will make it much easier to calculate the exact position of the top of the track or pole.

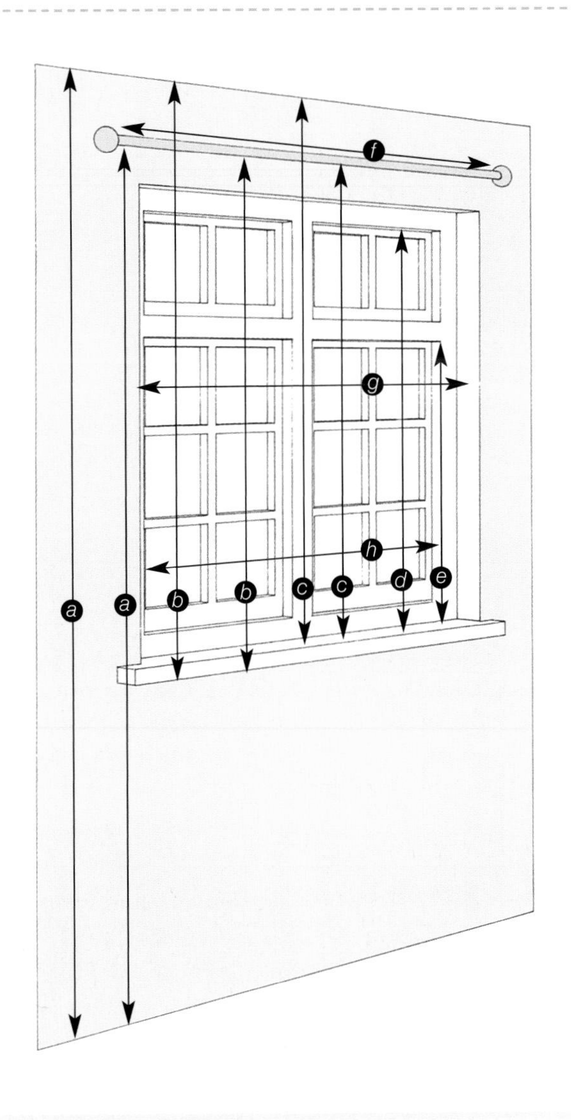

Measuring windows

Make sure when you are calculating the amount of fabric you need that you allow extra for hems, headings, and fullness. The weight of the fabric will be a determining factor: lightweight fabrics and sheers need fullness—up to three times the width of the window—if they are to look right, while heavyweight and heavily patterned fabrics generally need only twice as much. The type of heading also must be taken into account when you are measuring (see pages 212–213).

Height: vertical measurements

a *ceiling or top of pole to floor*

b *ceiling or pole to bottom of window frame*

c *ceiling or pole to sill*

d *top of glass area to sill*

e *horizontal sash to sill*

Length: horizontal measurements

f *ends of pole, track, or rod*

g *outside edge of the window frame to the opposite edge*

h *inside edge of the window frame to to the opposite edge*

GLOSSARY OF MEASURING TERMS

Finished width
The full width of the area that the curtain or blind is intended to cover once it has been completed.

Finished drop
The full length of the curtain or blind once it has been completed.

Selvage
The tightly woven edge of fabric which reacts differently from the main fabric to stitching and cleaning processes, so it is generally cut off before measuring the cut width of curtains and blinds.

Cut drop
The finished length plus hem and heading allowances; the measurements to cut before assembling the curtain or blind.

Width of fabric
The purchased width of the fabric. Unless you are making curtains for a very small window, you will probably need to join more than one width of fabric together to make up the full measurement of your window area.

Drop
This refers to length of the curtain or blind from the very top to the very bottom.

Recessed window
A window that is set into the wall. Curtains and blinds can either be hung inside the frame or on the wall.

Support
The mechanism from which a curtain or blind is hung, including tracks, poles, rods and rails, and laths. The support can be mounted on the wall outside the frame, on it, or recessed inside it.

Cut width
The full length of the curtain or blind once it has been completed.

ESTIMATING FABRIC

There are basic guidelines to follow for calculating how much fabric you need to make curtains and blinds. To the finished length, add 12–16 in (30–40 cm) for hems, plus twice the depth of the heading. If you have chosen a repeating pattern, add one pattern repeat. Full curtains usually look best, so allow 2 to 2½ times the finished width for medium- or heavyweight fabrics, and 2½ to 3 times for sheer and lightweight fabrics. The following example may help you calculate your individual needs.

***For medium-weight fabric**: if the finished length of the curtain is 75 in (1.9 m), the finished width is 48 in (1.2 m), and the heading is 4 in (10 cm) deep.*

Length	*75 in*	*1.9 m*
Headings	*8 in*	*0.2 m*
Hems	*14 in*	*0.35 m*
Pattern repeat	*6 in*	*0.15 m*
Total length required	*103 in*	*2.6 m*
Width	*48 in*	*1.2 m*
multiplied by 2½		
Total width required	*120 in*	*3 m*

***For blinds**: add the seam allowances, returns, pleats, and so on, to the width. To the length, add the bottom hem allowances and enough fabric to attach the blind to the top of its support and to cover it.*

Cut width	*120 in*	*3 m*
Divide by width of fabric	*48 in*	*1.2 m*
Widths of fabric needed	*2½*	*round up to 3*
Cut drop	*75 in*	*1.9 m*
times 3 widths		
Total fabric needed	*225 in (6¼ yd)*	*5.7 m*
Purchase to be safe	*6½ to 7 yd*	*(6 to 6.5 m)*

To calculate the amount of fabric to buy, figure out how many widths of fabric you need to make the cut width by dividing the cut width of your fabric. Round up that figure to the nearest whole number and multiply it by the cut drop of the curtain or blind to give the number of yards (meters) you need to buy.

Measuring for tiebacks

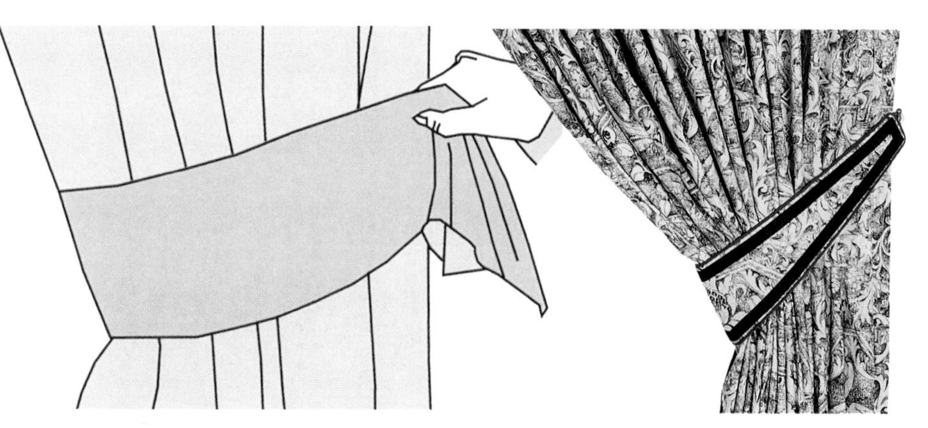

Generally a tieback should be positioned about two-thirds of the way down the side of the curtain from its top. To calculate the size and position of a tieback, hold a length of fabric of the approximate width of the tieback around the curtain at various points until you find the right position. Pull up the tieback until the curtain is neither too loose nor too tight ,and measure that length to determine how much fabric is needed (see page 208).

Measuring for valances or pelmets

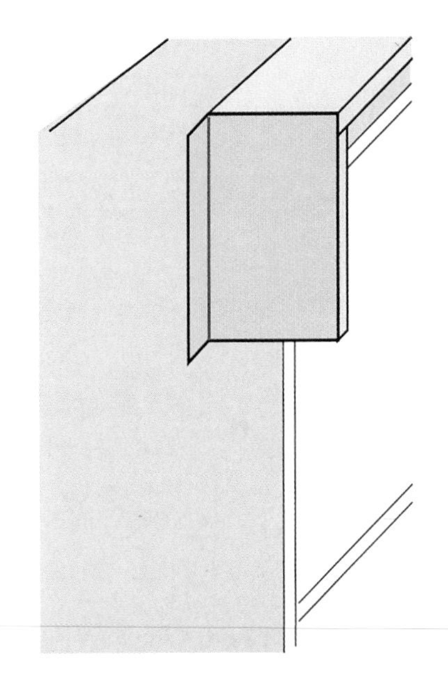

Valances, also called pelmets, are practical and decorative tops that are mounted above curtains and blinds to keep light out and warmth in, to conceal the curtain support, and to add a stylish touch. Accurate measuring is vital for flat valances because it is difficult and time-consuming to alter them after they are finished.

Measure the length and width of the front of the board and the depth of the returns at each end. Allow enough fabric for turning over to hide the edges of the backing board, but make sure the excess fabric will not hinder the opening and closing mechanism of the curtains.

Measuring for different types of curtain and blind

Before finalizing how much fabric to purchase, you will need to consider how the curtain is to be hung: do you want the support mechanism to be inside, on, or outside the window frame? Do you want a floor-length or sill-length treatment, and what type of heading you will use? The type of curtain and blind that you have chosen to make will decide which set of measurements need to be taken.

Always use a steel tape measure of the kind used for home-improvement projects. Tape measures made from flexible cloth are to be avoided because they tend to stretch as you work and give incorrect measurements. If possible, mount your curtain track or pole before you measure for curtains; otherwise, mark the top and bottom ends of the support in some way as a guide.

Measuring for a curtain or blind that hangs from a support on the wall

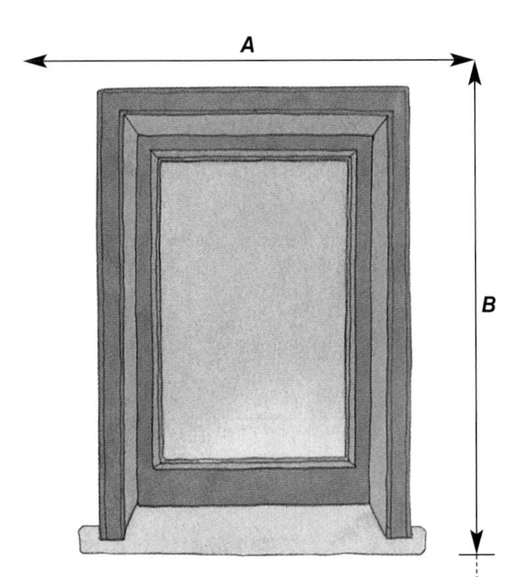

Position a track or pole on the wall 4–12 in (10–30 cm) above the frame and 8–10 in (20–25 cm) to each side. Measurement A is the width of the window plus the side extensions. Measurement B extends from the top of the support to the bottom of the drop, either to the bottom of the sill or B1 the floor.

Measuring for a curtain or blind that hangs from a support attached to the window frame

If the pole or track is to be attached directly to the frame, measurement C, from one edge of the frame to the other, is the width. Measurement D is the drop from the top of the frame to the bottom of the sill. This mounting is most often used for blinds, but if you are making floor-length curtains, extend the drop measurement to the floor D1.

Measuring for a curtain or blind that hangs inside the window recess

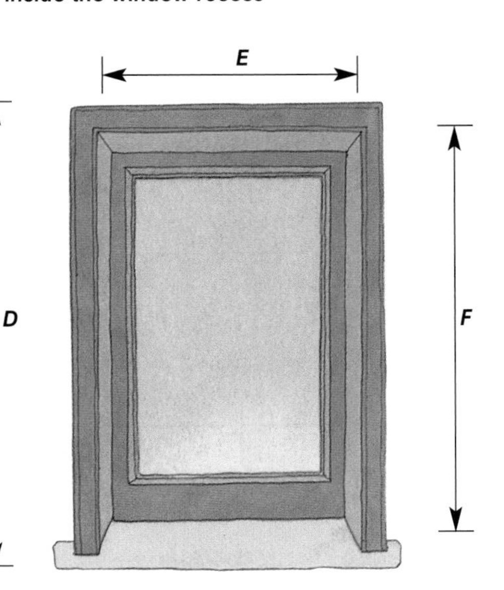

Curtains set inside a recess usually stay drawn, whereas blinds may be taken up and down. Measurement E is the width from one side of the recess to the other. Measurement F is the drop from the top of the recess to the bottom, which is also the top of the sill.

MEASURING FRENCH DOORS

French doors, or windows, are fully glazed external doors. If they open outward, they can be measured and treated as tall casement windows. If they open inward, poles and tracks must be positioned on the wall to allow the curtain to be pulled clear of the door when it is open. Alternatively, blinds or curtains can be mounted on the doors themselves.

MEASURING BAY WINDOWS

A separate curtain can be hung on an individual track for each part of a bay window, but a wide double curtain opening in the middle looks more attractive. A sturdy track designed for the shape of the window is needed and can be ordered from a specialized supplier. Take measurements as for a plain window with the track in place if at all possible.

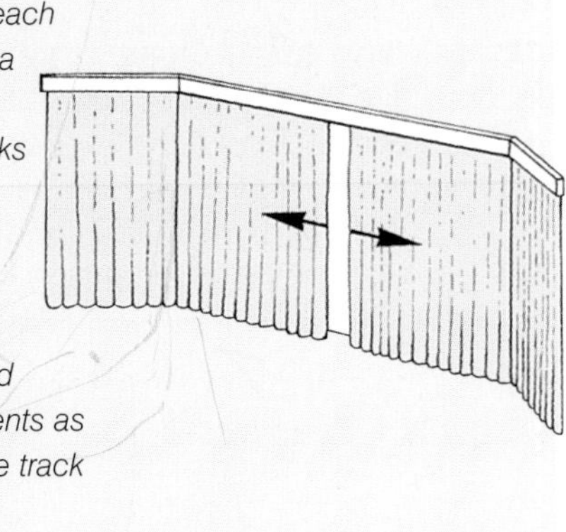

Measuring for blinds

Blinds are usually mounted either on the window frame or inside the recess. To measure inside a recess, follow the instructions on the opposite page, but measure in at least two places in both directions. If the two corresponding measurements differ, use the narrower one; otherwise, the blind will be too wide in places.

Make sure the blind covers the window completely if it is mounted outside the recess. Mount it as near the top of the frame as possible, using a wooden strip attached to the wall just above the frame if necessary. For more information on blinds, see pages 200–207.

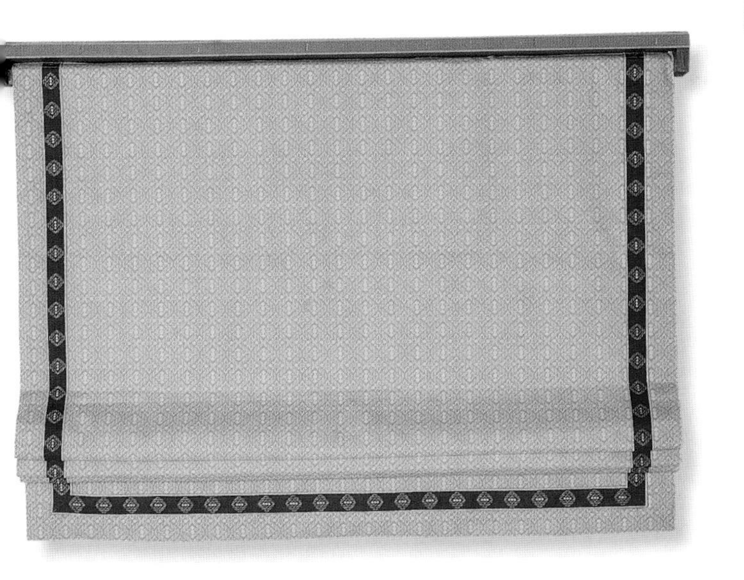

A Roman blind should lie flat against the window. It works well whether mounted inside or outside the recess.

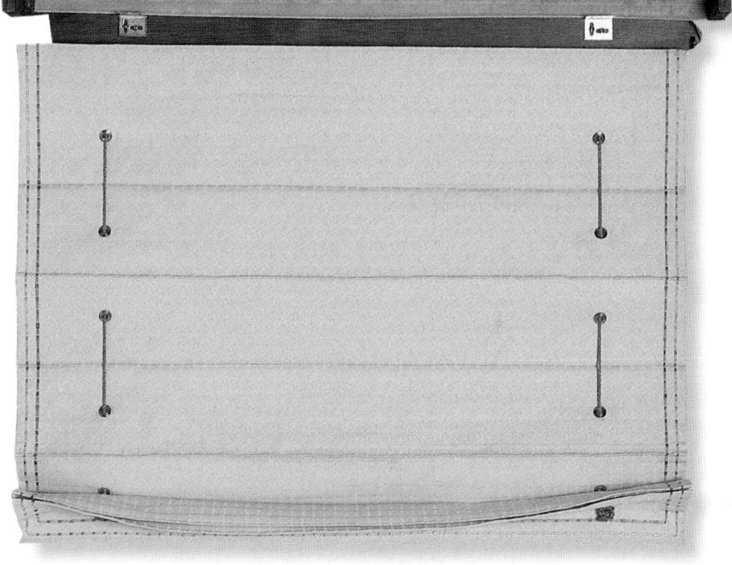

An eyelet blind is a variation of Roman blind and has a clean, modern feel.

A fan blind is a variation of a Roman blind in which the bottom pleats drop down to form a fan shape.

A roll-up blind can wind up to the front from the bottom as well as onto a roller at the top.

Measuring furniture

Measuring and estimating fabric quantities for three-dimensional items, such as seats, cushions, tables, and beds, is made simpler when you view the piece of furniture as a series of flat planes or rectangles. Measure the dimensions of each separate area and then add seam allowances or hems to all edges.

Fabric widths tend to vary, so you cannot estimate how much fabric you will need for a project until you know the width of your chosen fabric. It is worth jotting down the width and pattern-repeat of fabrics when you are collecting samples. To calculate how much fabric you will need, especially for complicated covers, make a scale diagram, preferably on graph paper, to the width of your chosen fabric and arrange the pieces on it. Remember to include elements such as piping or binding in your figures. If you are worried about running out of fabric, it is always better to purchase extra than to regret it later. Leftover pieces can be easily transformed into matching accessories.

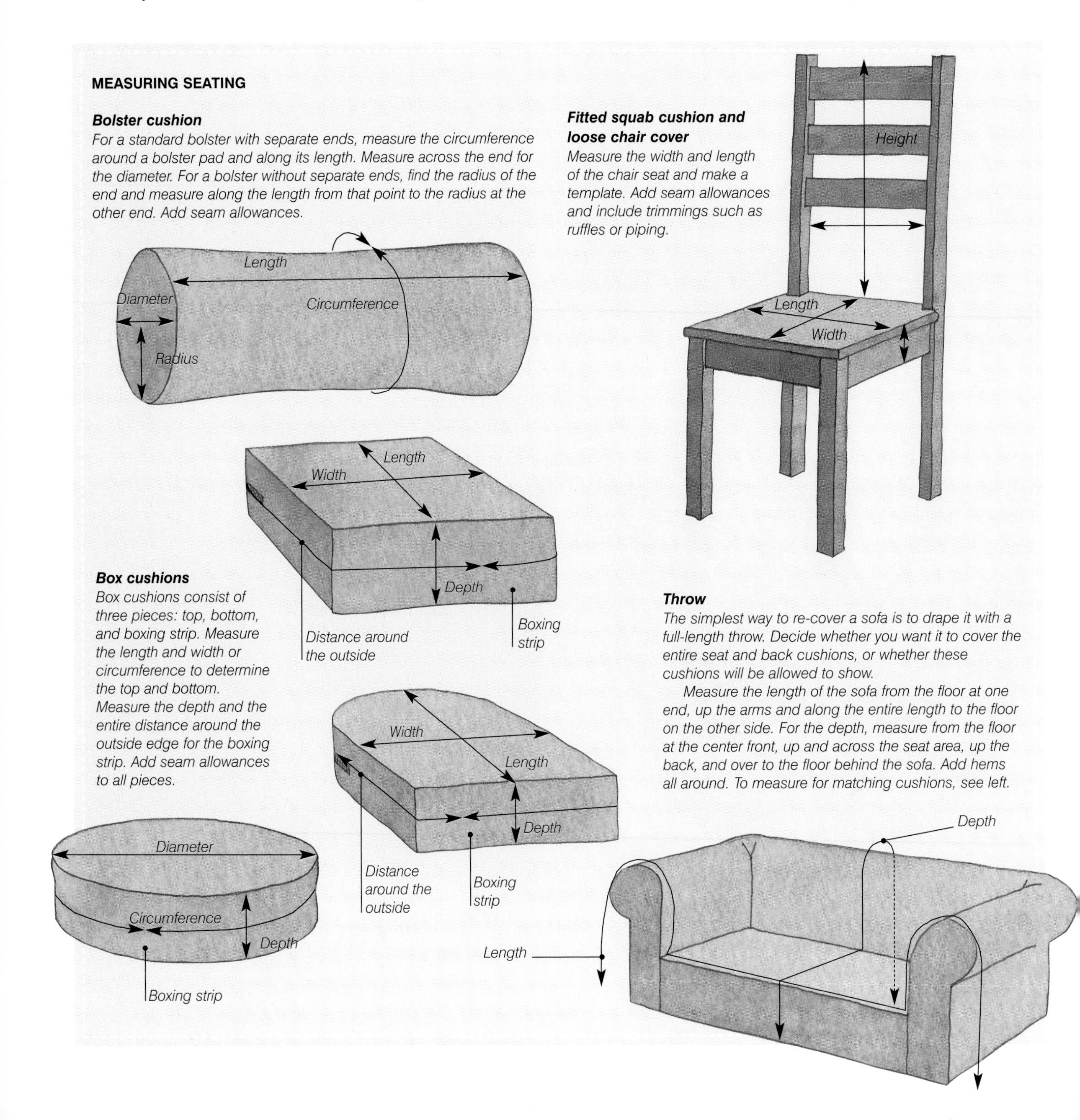

MEASURING SEATING

Bolster cushion

For a standard bolster with separate ends, measure the circumference around a bolster pad and along its length. Measure across the end for the diameter. For a bolster without separate ends, find the radius of the end and measure along the length from that point to the radius at the other end. Add seam allowances.

Fitted squab cushion and loose chair cover

Measure the width and length of the chair seat and make a template. Add seam allowances and include trimmings such as ruffles or piping.

Box cushions

Box cushions consist of three pieces: top, bottom, and boxing strip. Measure the length and width or circumference to determine the top and bottom. Measure the depth and the entire distance around the outside edge for the boxing strip. Add seam allowances to all pieces.

Throw

The simplest way to re-cover a sofa is to drape it with a full-length throw. Decide whether you want it to cover the entire seat and back cushions, or whether these cushions will be allowed to show.

Measure the length of the sofa from the floor at one end, up the arms and along the entire length to the floor on the other side. For the depth, measure from the floor at the center front, up and across the seat area, up the back, and over to the floor behind the sofa. Add hems all around. To measure for matching cushions, see left.

MEASURING FOR SLIPCOVERS

Chairs sometimes have curved shapes, which should be measured using a cloth tape measure. Use a metal tape measure on straight sections. The methods shown here can also be applied to simple sofas.

Simple wooden chair

Measure every area of the chair to be covered, following the arrows. Draw a plan with all the pieces to scale, then make a toile about 2 in (5 cm) larger all around than the finished piece and pin the pieces on the chair to check the fit. Add seam allowances and hems, and include quantities for ruffles, and so on.

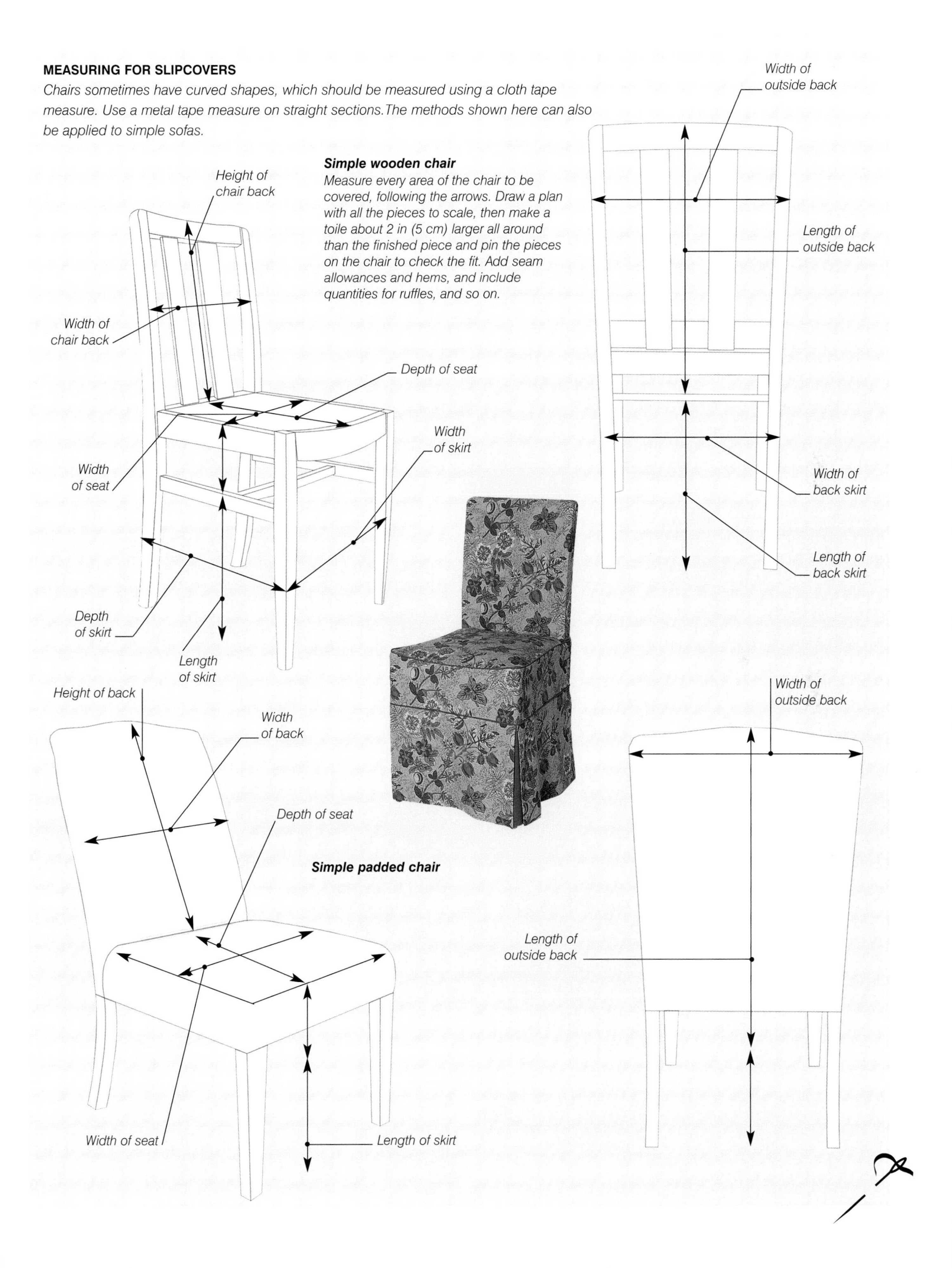

Simple padded chair

MEASURING TABLES

Measuring tables is a simple task, but accuracy is crucial. The length of the drop, or overhang, which creates the skirt of the tablecloth can be any length you choose, from just long enough to drape over the sides of the table to floor length. Oval tablecloths are measured as rectangles, and then the corners are rounded off into the desired curve.

Rectangular tablecloths

Measure the length and width first. The length of the drop, plus hem allowances all around, are added to all four sides of the piece.

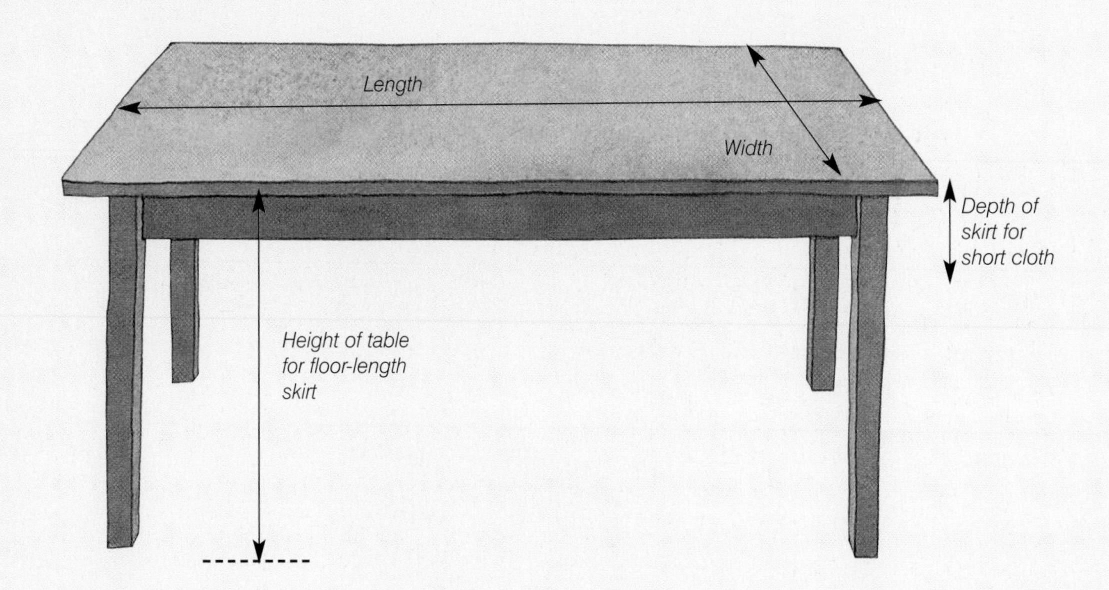

Circular tablecloths

The main measurement for round tablecloths is the diameter of the table plus drops and hems.

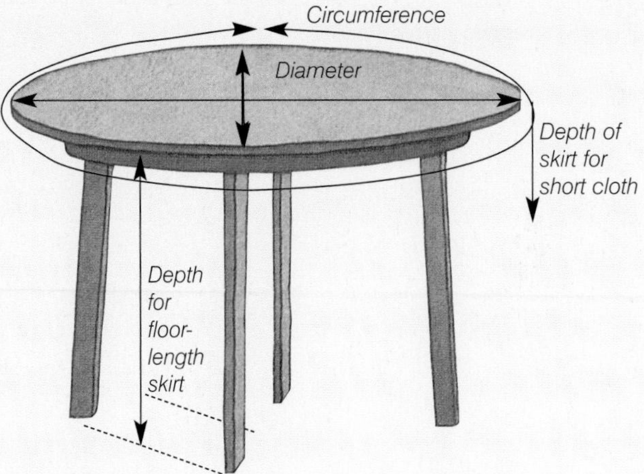

MEASURING BEDS

Headboard cover
Measure the width of the headboard and from the top of the mattress to the top of the headboard. Double these measurements, and add the thickness of the headboard, seam allowances, and hems.

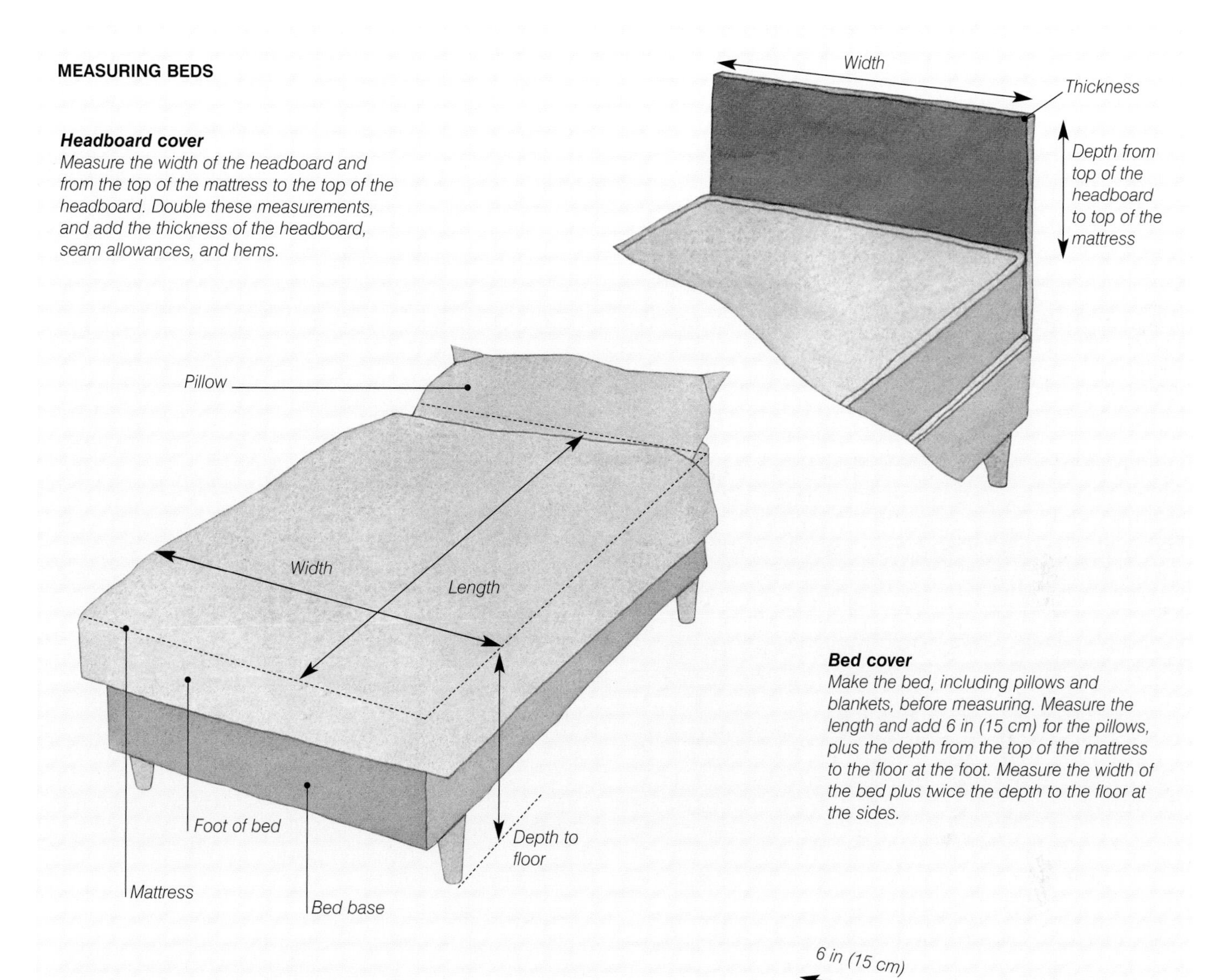

Bed cover
Make the bed, including pillows and blankets, before measuring. Measure the length and add 6 in (15 cm) for the pillows, plus the depth from the top of the mattress to the floor at the foot. Measure the width of the bed plus twice the depth to the floor at the sides.

Bed skirt
To make a skirt to cover the bed base, cut the flat piece separately from the skirt. Measure the length and width of the base for the flat piece. To calculate the full length of the skirt section, start measuring 6 in (15 cm) in at the head, take the tape all the way along the side, across the foot, along the other side, and finish 6 in (15 cm) in at the other side of the head. The width of the skirt is measured from the top of the base unit to the floor. Add seam allowances and hems. The length of the fabric needed for a gathered or ruffled skirt is twice the measurement of the base, and several lengths of fabric may need to be joined to make the required length.

6 in (15 cm)
6 in (15 cm)
Length
Width
Length of skirt
Foot of bed
Depth to floor
Bed base

Preparing and cutting

All fabric needs to be handled with care. Woven fabrics have three directions, or grains: the width across the bolt, the length along the bolt, and the bias, or crosswise, diagonal grain. The grains can be stretched out of shape easily, so it is crucial to get them straight and square before you lay out a pattern or begin to cut. Some fabrics should be washed and ironed before you work on them, especially if the fabric is likely to shrink when washed. Always follow the fabric care advice (see also page 313).

Cutting on the grain

For a professional finish to your piece, always cut fabric on the straight grain—horizontally or vertically—along or across the fabric unless the manufacturer's instructions advise you to do otherwise.

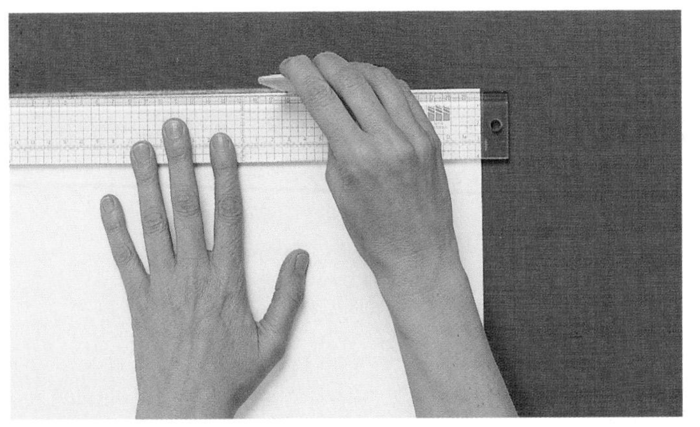

1 Align a piece of paper with the straight selvage and draw along a ruler with chalk to mark the cutting line.

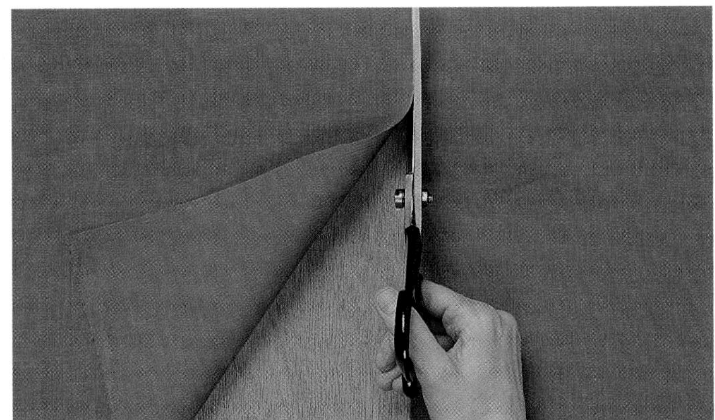

2 Turn the fabric or move around the work surface so that you are facing the cutting line. Use sharp dressmaker's shears to cut along the line.

Cutting on the bias

The cross-grain or bias of the fabric is used to give more flexibility to your piece. It stretches more than the straight grain so it needs to be cut, handled, and worked on with great care to avoid distorting the shape of your piece.

1 Make sure both selvage and bottom edge of the fabric are straight. Mark the cutting line as shown above. Align the bottom edge with the marked line and press.

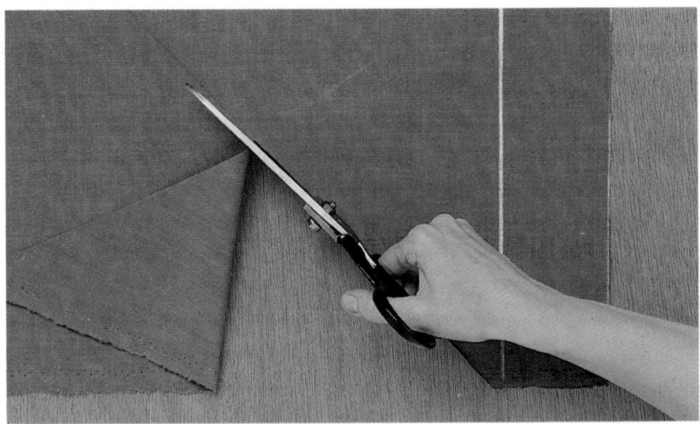

2 Lay the fabric on a flat work surface and cut carefully along the pressed line.

CUTTING FABRIC

Manufacturers wind their lengths of cloth onto tubes or flat pieces of cardboard as the fabric comes off the loom. The inner tube is designed to keep the fabric straight, but always check the fabric carefully before you cut it out to make sure there are no flaws in the weave or the pattern. If the edge of the fabric is not straight, you will need to level it before you begin cutting.

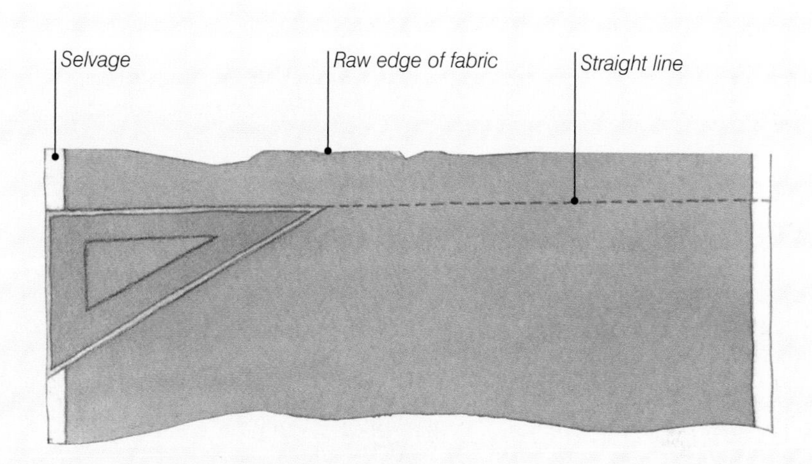

1 Straighten the raw edge using the method opposite, or use a carpenter's square to draw a line at a right angle to the selvage.

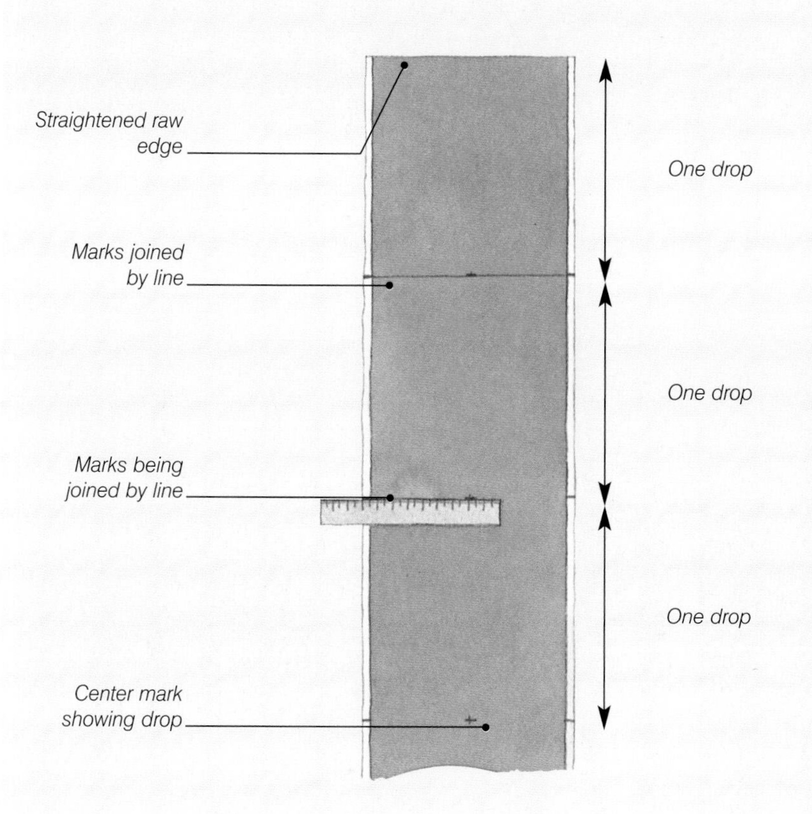

2 The lengths of fabric needed for each drop in a curtain must be measured and cut very carefully. Measure and mark each drop along the selvage and in the center of the fabric. Using a long ruler and chalk or pencil, draw a line across the full width of the fabric to mark each cutting line. Mark all the drops and then cut along the lines.

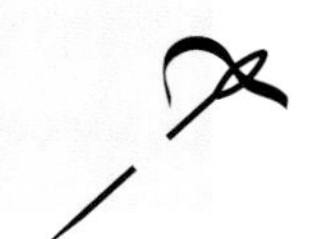

Cutting curves and circles

This method is a quick and easy way to cut circles or part-circles for corners on bedcovers or tablecloths. You need a piece of string, a marker, and a pin. Before you begin, lay out the fabric and level all the edges.

1 Fold the fabric in half and then in half again to make four layers. Measure the radius of the circle required and cut a length of string a little longer than that.

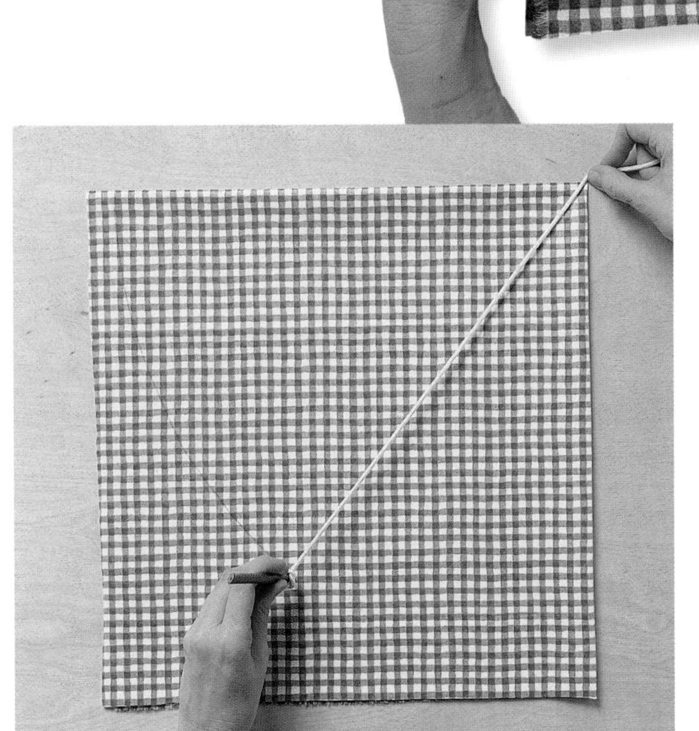

2 Tie one end of the string to a marker pen or pencil and position the other end at the folded corner of the fabric. Hold the string taut or pin it in place securely, and draw a quarter circle with the marker held upright.

3 Pin the layers of fabric together along the inside of the drawn line and cut all four layers along the line.

CUTTING DIFFICULT FABRICS

CUTTING SHEER FABRIC

To cut loose-woven fabrics, including sheers, choose a thread along the cutting line and pull it out. This creates a "path" in the fabric that acts as guideline to cut along.

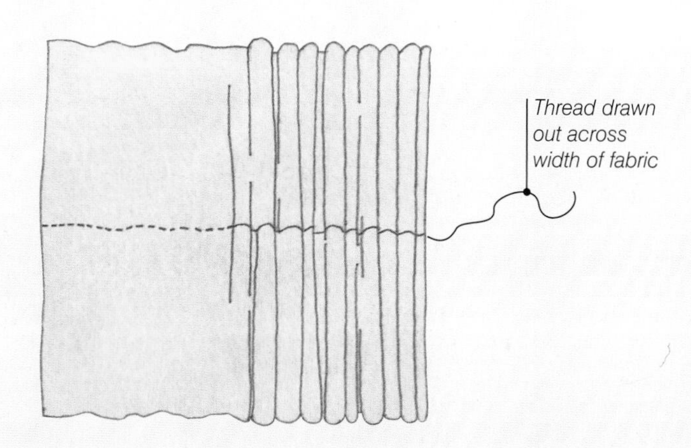

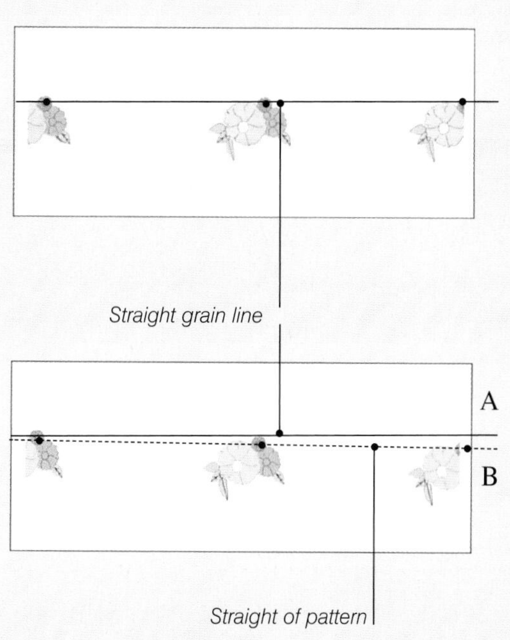

CUTTING PATTERNED FABRIC

Cutting a patterned fabric on the straight grain can be awkward. In a woven pattern, you must make sure that the selvage is on a straight right angle to the widthwise threads. On a printed fabric, the pattern may not run true to the straight grain of the fabric. If the design is small in scale or the pattern busy, it may not make a difference that the grain is slightly off. However, in fabrics where it will be obvious, you must mark the line of the pattern and cut straight along the pattern rather than the straight grain.

A good way to check the grain is to clamp one end of the fabric to a table with the edge overhanging slightly. Run the flat side of a metal ruler along the edge of the table to make a crease at a right angle to the selvage and check the widthwise threads against it.

CUTTING VELVETS

The luxury and expense of velvet fabric means that many people worry about cutting into a piece in case they spoil it. The best advice is never to use the points of the scissors. If you keep the cuts short and deep in the V where the blades join, the scissors will follow the path of one width thread and keep the cut straight.

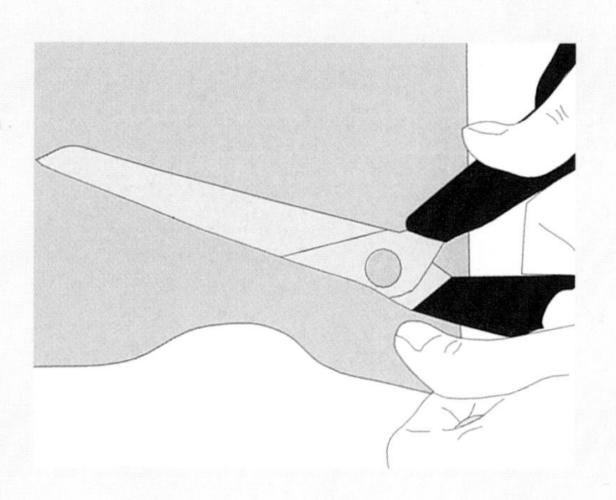

Zippers in furnishings

Zippers are commonly used in home furnishings such as cushions and seat covers. They are almost always inserted before the item is assembled, and should be positioned at the bottom of a cushion cover that is made from fabric with a one-way pattern or design. Zipper weights should always be matched to fabric weights.

Inserting a zipper

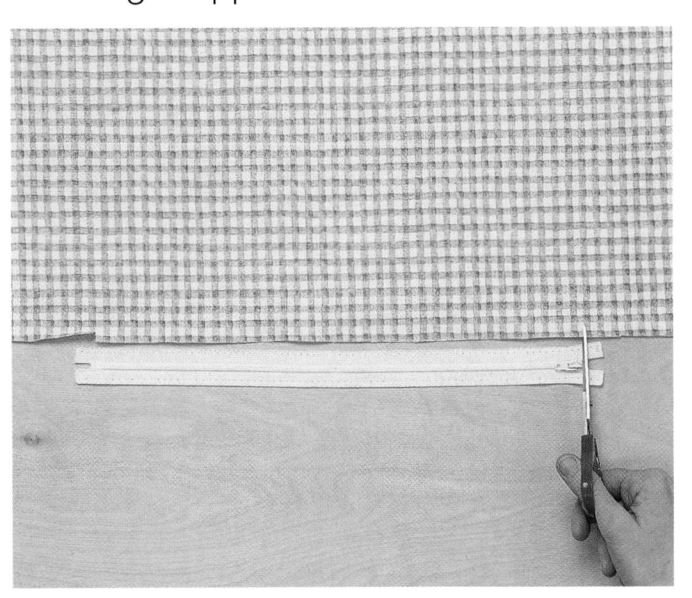

1 Line up the zipper in its position and clip the seam allowances of the top and bottom fabric to mark the start and finish. Aligning the cuts, pin the pieces with right sides together, and stitch from each cut to each side edge, backstitching at both ends to secure.

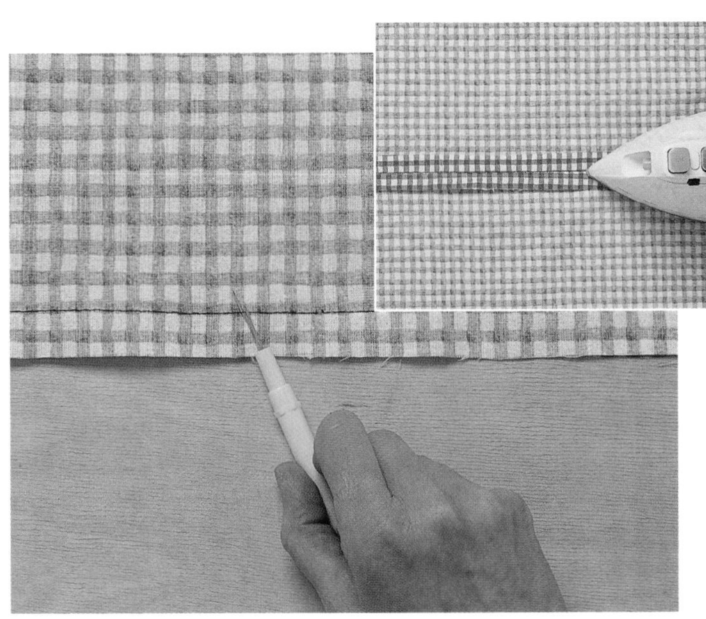

2 Machine-baste along the zipper opening with right sides together. Breaking a stitch every 1 in (2 cm) or so will make it easier to unpick the basting later. Press the basted seam open (inset).

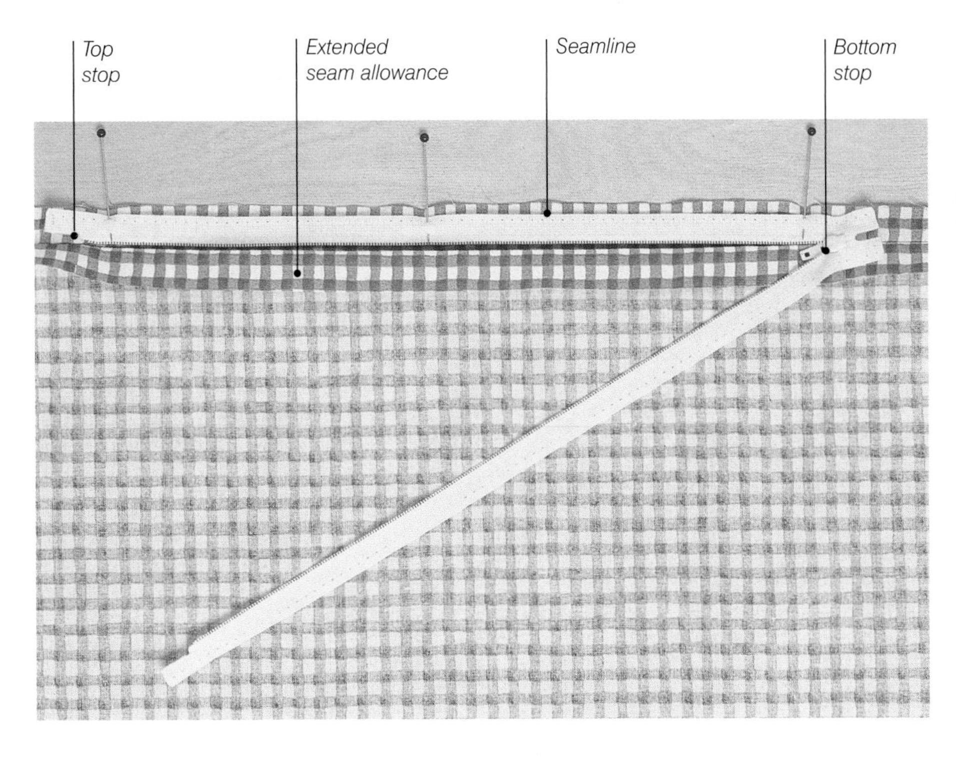

3 Lay the fabric with the seam allowance on the bottom piece extended. Open the zipper and pin it face down, with the teeth close to the seamline. Make sure the top and bottom are aligned with the top and bottom of the zipper position where the cuts were made.

4 Using a zipper foot, keep the needle on its left, stitch close to teeth, and backstitch each end. Turn the work and repeat steps 3–4 on other side of zipper (inset).

5 Remove the basting and turn the work to the right side. Continue to assemble the item.

Putting in a continuous zipper

Continuous zippers are purchased by the yard (meter) to use in extra-long openings. They are easy to cut to the correct length, and the stop is made by stitching back and forth over the end of the zipper.

1 With top and bottom fabrics right sides together, cut a length of zipper to match the opening exactly. Machine-baste the opening (see step 2 opposite). Press seam open.

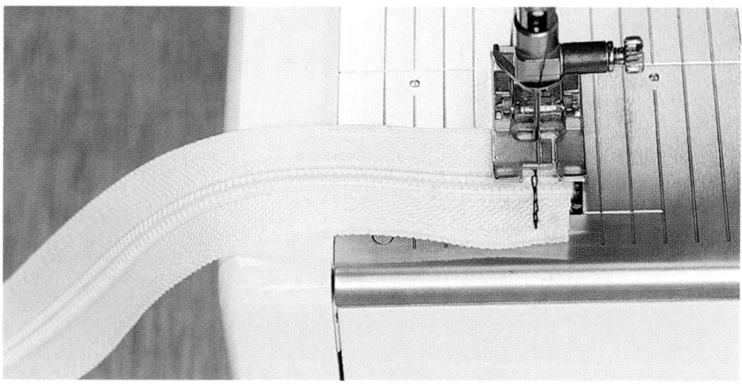

2 Make a stop at the end of the zipper by stitching back and forth several times across the end.

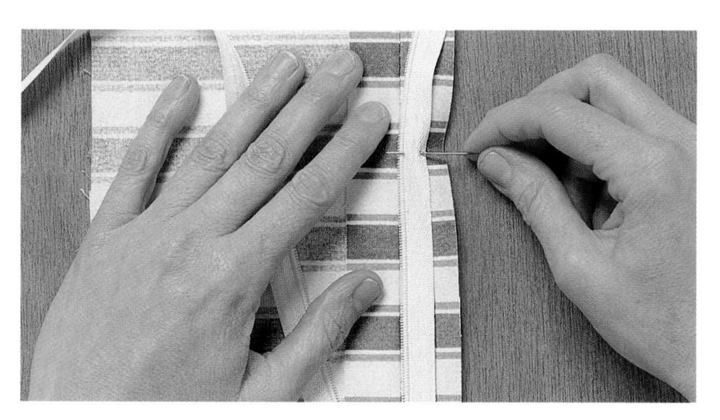

3 Open the zipper and pin it face down along the seam allowance, with the teeth along the seamline, then stitch in place (see steps 3–4 of inserting a zipper). Close the zipper and repeat to stitch the other side.

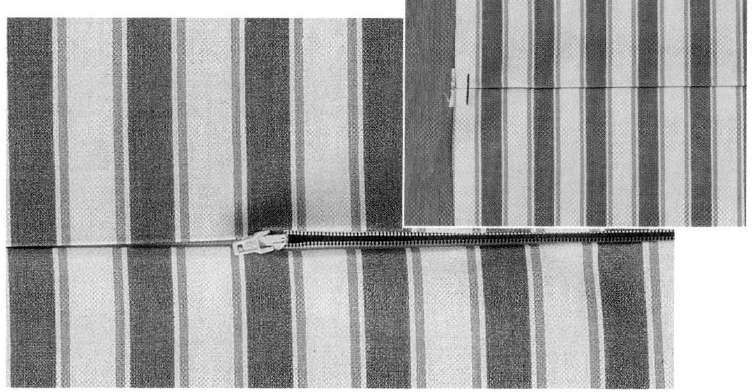

4 Remove the basting to open and close the zipper. Topstitch at each end of the opening to secure (inset).

Making a lapped zipper

A fabric fold hides the opening of a lapped zipper for a neat finish. Lapped zippers are usually inserted between two separate pieces of fabric.

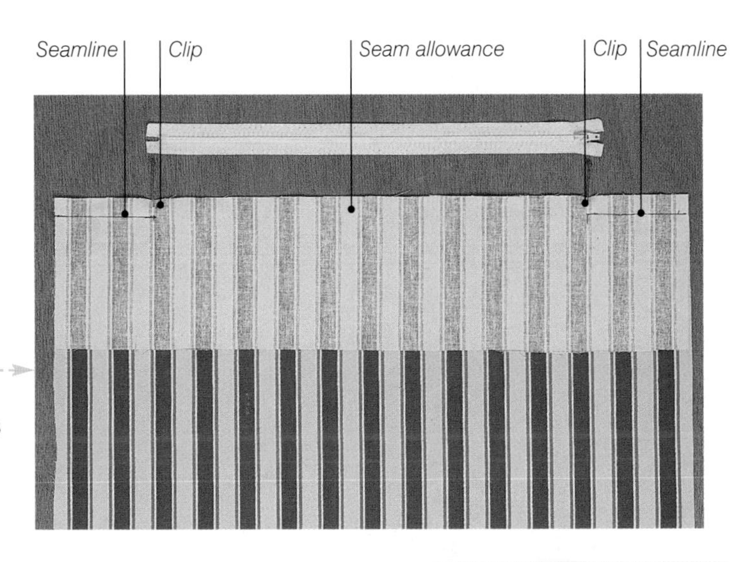

1 Clip the seam allowance of both pieces of fabric to mark the length of the zipper opening. Stitch the pieces right sides together from the side edge to each cut and backstitch both ends. Follow step 2 of inserting a zipper (page 174) to machine-baste along the opening.

2 Open the zipper. Pin one edge face down along the seam allowance on one side, as shown in step 3 of Inserting a zipper, with the teeth along the seamline. Using a zipper foot with the needle to the right, machine-baste in position, ¼ in (5 mm) from the teeth.

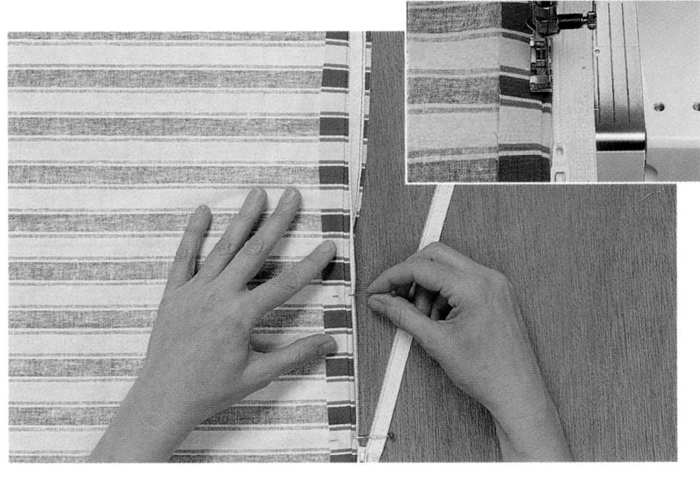

3 Turn the zipper face up and fold under the stitched side of the zipper. Stitch very close to the edge of the fold through all thicknesses (inset).

4 Turn the work around and lay the other seam allowance flat. Close the zipper and machine-baste the unstitched side in place.

5 Working on the right side and with needle to the left of the zipper foot, topstitch over the bottom of zipper, then along the side ½ in (1 cm) from the seam. Topstitch at the top of the zipper as well. Remove basting (inset).

INSERTING A ZIPPER IN A PIPED SEAM

This technique is widely used on cushion covers, but it works on any item where one piece is piped.

1 Zigzag-stitch along the raw edges of the fabric and mark the position of the zipper with pins. With right sides together, stitch the front and back pieces from the corner to the pins, working as close as possible to the piping cord.

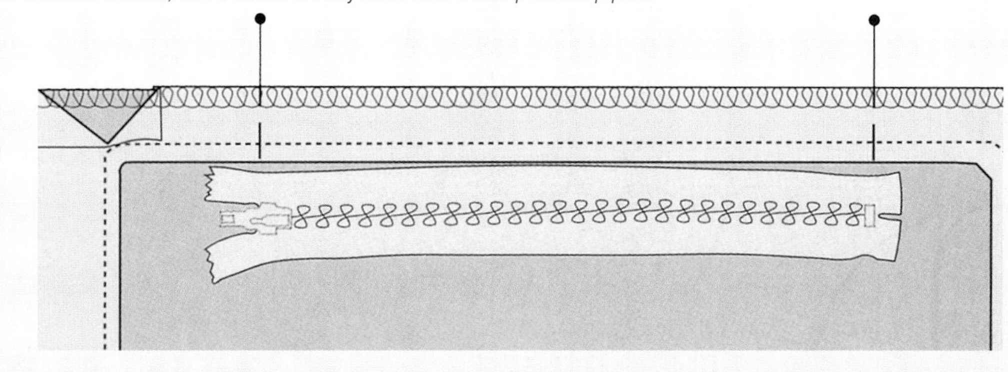

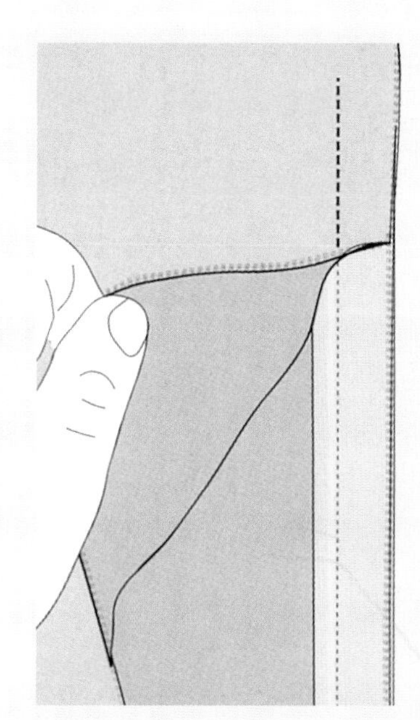

2 Fold back the unpiped piece of fabric.

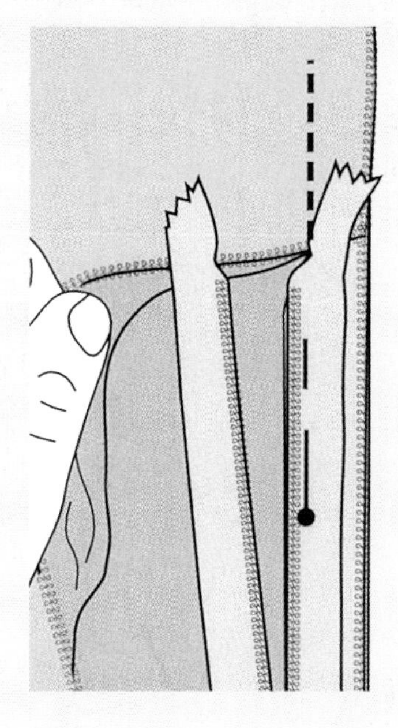

3 Open the zipper and place it face down on the piping with the teeth of the right-hand side of the zipper in the center of the cord. Use pins to hold the zipper in place at the top.

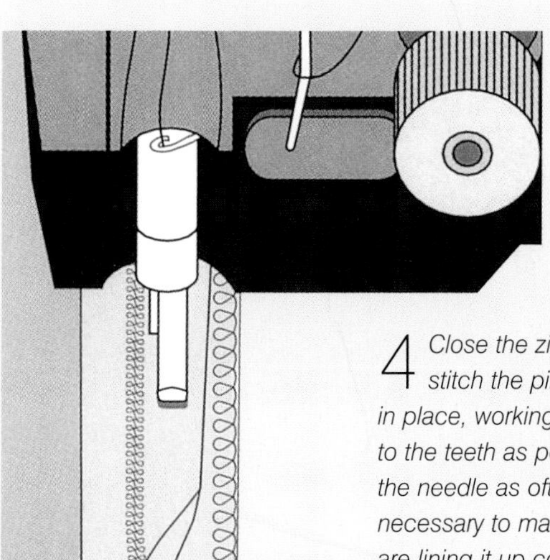

4 Close the zipper and stitch the pinned side in place, working as close to the teeth as possible. Lift the needle as often as necessary to make sure you are lining it up correctly.

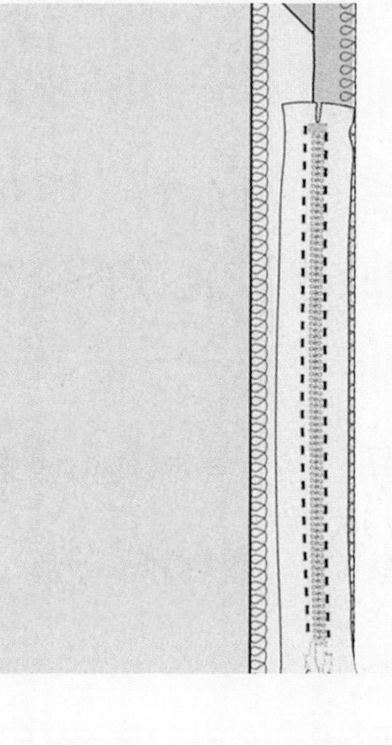

5 Turn the work around and line up the zipper with the inner edge of the zigzagging. Stitch the second side as close to the teeth as possible, but make sure you can move the sliding mechanism freely. Remove the basting and assemble the cushion.

Trims and embellishments

Trims and embellishments can be added to any home furnishing item, but the choices—matching or contrasting, smooth or textured, patterned or plain, simple or elaborate—are largely a matter of personal taste. Tassels, braid, fringe, lace, embroidery, appliqué, tufts, and buttons all add an individual touch to fabric surfaces. When used appropriately, they can help to liven up regular items by defining seams and edges and adding extra weight to hems.

TRADITIONAL TRIMS

Braid and fringe are widely used to trim traditional furniture, curtains, and valances. Most types can be sewn on by machine, but a few of them will need to be added by hand.

Rope (1) is sewn along edges by hand. Rope with an inset (2) can be set into seams in the same way as piping. Decorative braid (3) is available in an impressive choice of sizes and colors. Gimp braid (4), often found on upholstered furniture, makes a good understated finish. Fan braid (5) and looped fringe (6) can be added to furnishings by machine or by hand.

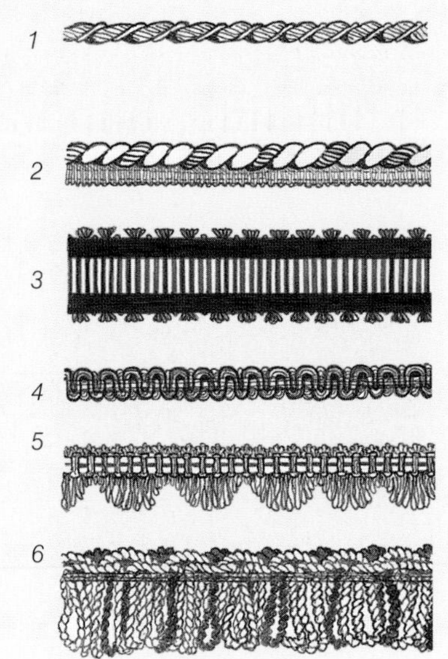

Rope border
Rope braid has been added by hand to edge and outline a luxurious throw.

Fan-edged fringe
Fan-edged fringe chosen to match the navy stripe in the fabric softens the ends of a table runner.

Double border
A double border of brightly contrasting linens frames a boldly patterned main fabric.

Deep linen fringe
Linen fringe enhances the lightweight fabric of a palampore-style printed bedspread.

Self-piping and tassel
Piping and a tassel in the same color as the main fabric give an understated elegance to a velvet throw.

Bobble fringe
Bobble fringe adds a casual 1950s feel to curtains, table linen, and cushions.

SURFACE DECORATION

Ornaments applied to the surface of an item give a professional finish, add interest and texture, and can turn a bland cloth or cover into a stunning accent. They provide you with an opportunity to use your creative expression to make a highly individual item.

Tufts
Tufts can be made quickly and easily from silk, cotton, linen, or wool thread or yarn to hold layers of fabric together.

Appliqué
Appliqué, like embroidery, can be worked using simple shapes and methods to create surface interest.

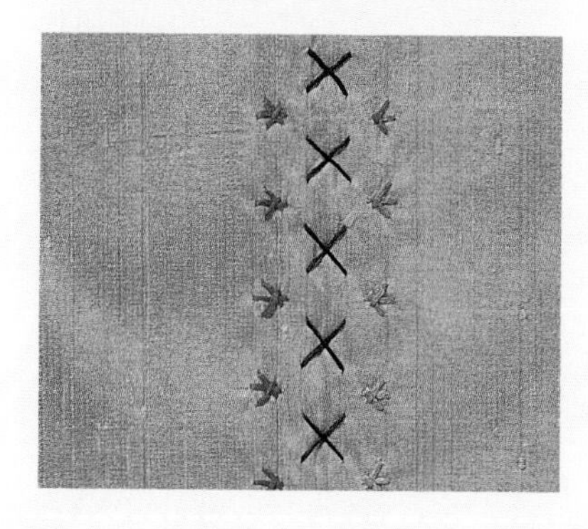

Embroidery
Embroidery, executed with panache using simple stitches, can be an effective way to add texture to a plain surface.

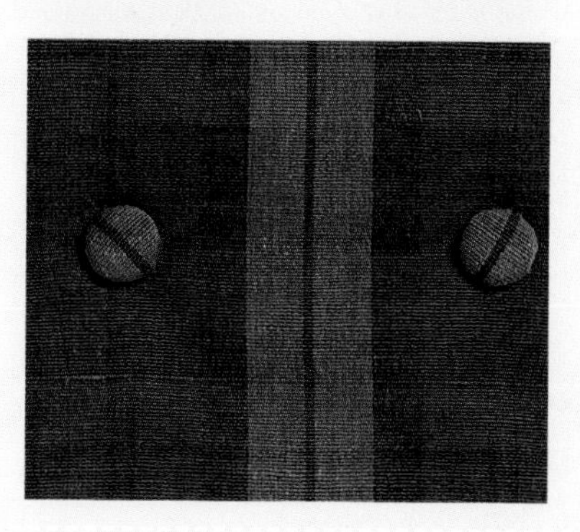

Buttons
Buttons can be used to hold layers together, or to join pieces in a decorative way.

Bullion fringe
Bullion fringe is made from fine threads and gives a formal, traditional edge to period furnishings.

Deep border
A deep single border in a coodinated color sets off a bold print tablecloth or throw. A solid-colored main fabric framed with a matching print fabric works well, too.

Antique lace
Lace gives a delicate edge to traditional lightweight natural fabrics such as linen and cotton.

Ornate tassel
Coordinated tassels and a contrasting narrow single border provide weight and a good finishing touch to an exotic striped fabric.

Gimp braid
Gimp braid outlines and defines edges and adds weight to lightweight fabrics.

Patchwork border
Patchwork borders can highlight the fabrics used in pieced projects like quilts, table mats, and cushions.

Shaped border
Shaped borders of points or scallops can be used to great effect on curtains, table linen, and cushions.

Making rouleau ties

1 Cut strips on the bias to four times the finished tie width. Fold each tie in half lengthwise with right sides together. Stitch ½ in (1 cm) in from the folded edge.

2 Trim the seam allowance to measure exactly ¼ in (5 mm) from the line of machine-stitching to create a straight, even shape for the tie.

3 Attach a safety pin to one end of the tie or use a rouleau turner to turn the tie right side out.

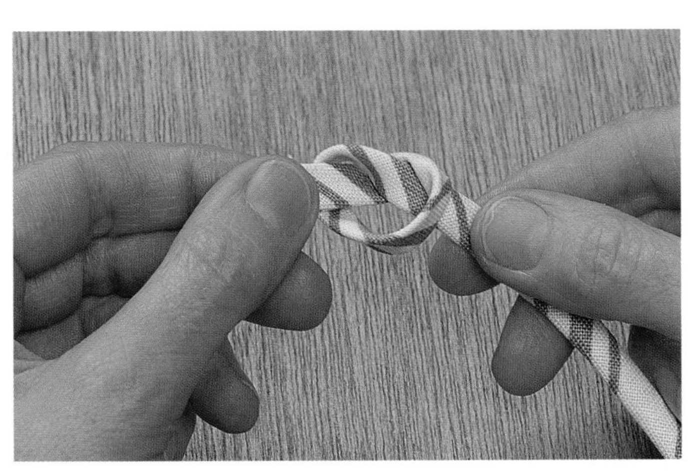

4 Pull the end through the full length of the tie, and finish neatly with a knot in each end of the tie.

Making folded ties

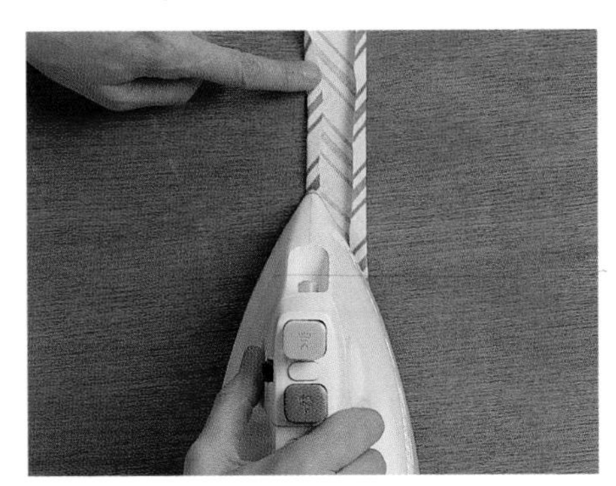

1 Cut bias strips twice the required width, plus a ¼ in (5 mm) seam allowance on each side. Press in a ¼ in (5 mm) allowance to the wrong side along each long edge.

2 Fold the pressed strip in half lengthwise with wrong sides together and press, aligning the folded edges, without pulling or stretching the strip.

3 Fold in one end and stitch close to the fold. At the corner, raise the foot and pivot the needle. Stitch close to the fold along the long edge to the end. Fold in the other end and repeat.

Making tufts

1 Hold two fingers of your free hand about ½ in (1 cm) apart and wind the yarn or thread around them tightly until the tuft is the desired thickness. Do NOT cut off.

2 Keeping the loops in shape, loosen your fingers and slide the yarn off. Wind the loose end of yarn tightly around the center of the tuft.

3 Knot the end of the yarn securely to prevent the loops of yarn from unraveling.

4 Cut the end off, leaving a tail long enough to sew the finished tuft in place when you are ready.

USING TASSELS AND BUTTON TUFTS

Tufts can be used individually or in rows or bunches to embellish many household furnishings. The ones shown here are made from heavy cotton thread and look much like buttons, which also make effective trimmings. Tassels (see page 182) can be added to decorate edges and corners, and make useful pulls for blinds.

Making tassels

This simple tassel is constructed on a piece of folded cardboard cut twice the desired length of the tassel. Simple tassels can be made using several different colors for a striking effect. A more elaborate tassel can be made using a wooden bead as the top.

1 Cut out a piece of cardboard to twice the finished length of the tassel. Fold it in half and wrap thread or yarn around it until the tassel reaches the desired thickness.

2 Using a blunt needle, insert a separate long thread at one end of the tassel and pull it underneath the wrapped threads at the folded end. Wrap the thread around several times, pulling it tightly, and secure with a knot.

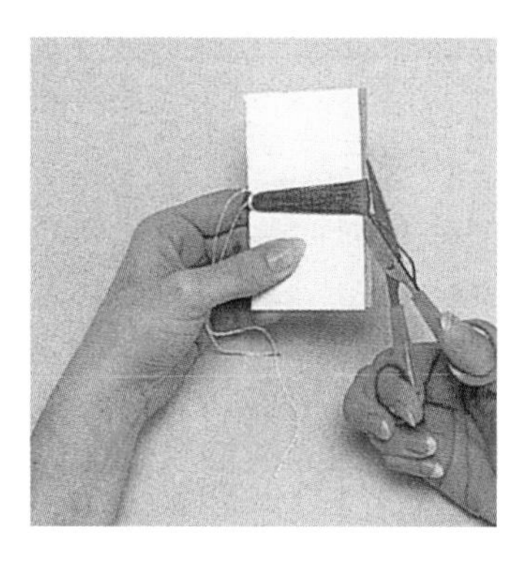

3 Slide a pair of scissors carefully into the open end of the cardboard and cut through the wrapped threads. Do not cut through the top of the tassel or allow the knotted thread to slip.

4 Wrap a new, long thread around the top end of the tassel to make a "neck." Tie it tightly, then thread the ends into a blunt needle, and slide them up through the top of the tassel to make a cord. Trim the bottom edge evenly.

TASSEL VARIATIONS

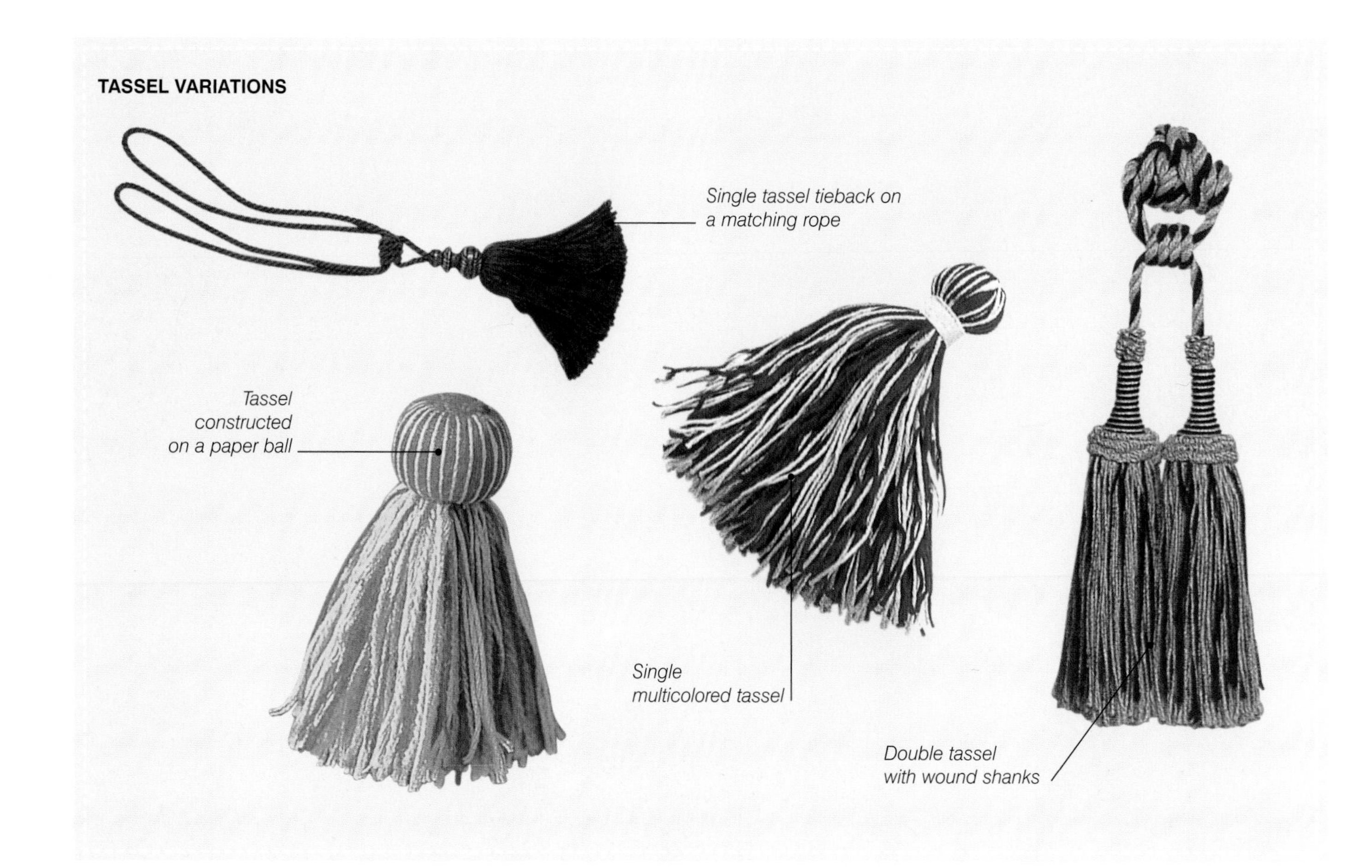

Single tassel tieback on a matching rope

Tassel constructed on a paper ball

Single multicolored tassel

Double tassel with wound shanks

JOINING AN INSET CORD

This method of bringing together the ends of a decorative cord makes the join virtually invisible. Cords that are attached to an inset strip can be sewn into seams or along edges by machine, while plain cords must be added by hand.

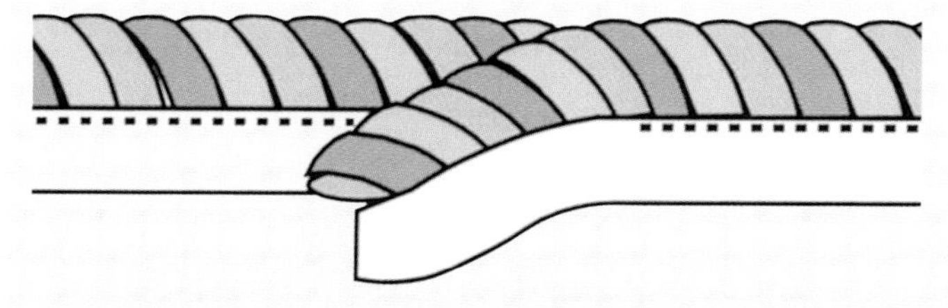

1 *Leaving a 1 in (2.5 cm) cord end, stitch the cord into the seam. Leave a ¾ in (2 cm) gap between the two ends and a 1 in (2.5 cm) end on the cord as before.*

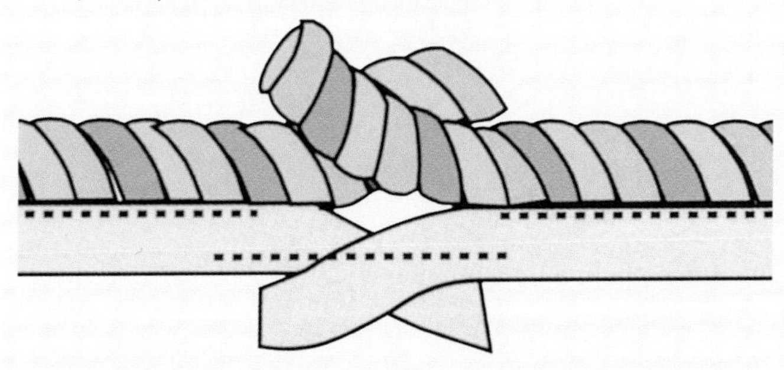

2 *Carefully separate the cord and the inset strip at both loose ends. Cross the ends over each other and stitch them in place to keep them out of the way.*

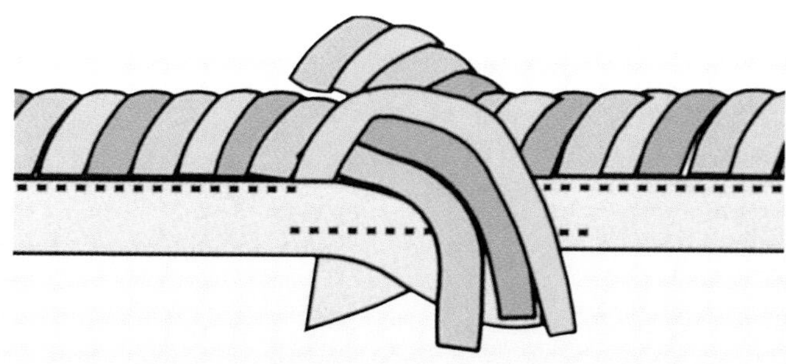

3 *Untwist into individual strands at one end of the cord and gently smooth the strands flat by hand.*

4 *Untwist the other end of the cord and smooth the strands flat as before, covering the previous set of strands as shown.*

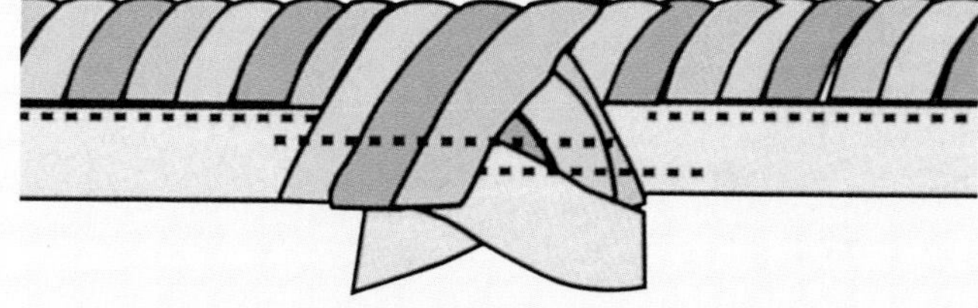

5 *Stitch across all the strands by machine, or sew them in place by hand if your machine is unable to handle the thickness. Trim off any excess ends.*

Caterpillar trim

1 Make a tube from a strip 3½ in (9 cm) wide and four times the finished length. Interline with a 6½-in (17-cm) wide strip. Stitch and clamp one end, then ruche up the fabric.

2 When the trim is the correct length, stitch the open end. Cut a piece of binding 2¼ in (6 cm) square and place it with right sides together along one edge and centered.

3 Stitch the binding in place. Turn in the side edges and fold the binding strip in half over the end. Hand-stitch in place. Repeat to bind the other end.

4 A caterpillar trim in a coordinated or contrasting fabric adds a sophisticated detail to curtain or valance headings.

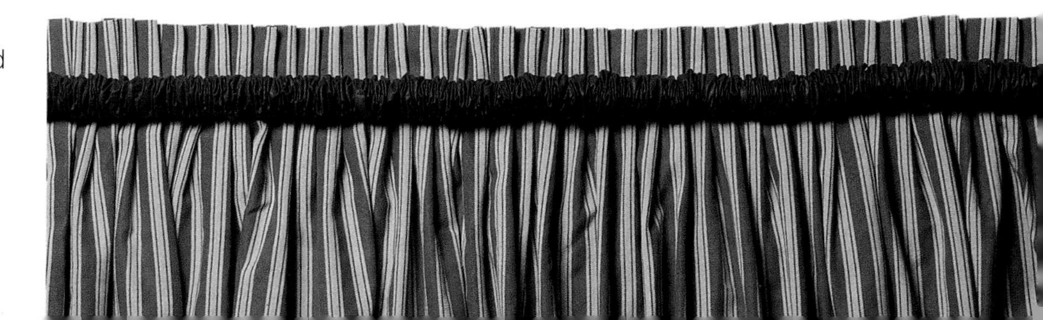

Pads and fillings

Making a choice for the padding in pillows and cushions depends on the purpose to which the item will be put, and on personal preference. Pillow pads, or forms, are available ready-made, filled with natural materials like feathers and down, or with a synthetic fiber or substance such as chips of foam or tiny hard granules of styrofoam (polystyrene). If you want a firm, well-filled pillow, buy pads one size bigger than the cover. Scatter cushions usually need a soft shape, while seat cushions are generally filled with a firmer block of foam that can be cut to the exact size and shape needed. The padded layer in quilted items is usually a non-woven fiber batting (wadding), which is available in several versions. Synthetic batting is available in a variety of weights. Sometimes batting, especially woven batts called bump and domette, is used as padding wrapped around firm foam blocks. Natural batts, used mainly in quiltmaking, include cotton, wool, and silk (which is very expensive and generally used only in clothing to make them warm but lightweight). Check that your choice is suitable for its intended use.

Domette and bump
Both of these are woven from cotton. Both feel like a blanket and are used in quilting and to interline curtains. Always take into account their tendency to shrink dramatically. They are sold by the yard (meter).

Polyester batting (wadding)
Sold by the yard (meter), this comes in different weights from 2 oz, the thinnest, used mainly in quiltmaking, to 12 oz, which can be substituted for bump and domette when padding foam blocks.

Polyurethane foam
The blocks are available in a choice of density and thickness. They can be cut to fit, and firmer versions can be covered with padding if desired. Make sure they are fire retardant.

Foam chips
These have a tendency to lump together and gradually disintegrate, but they are an inexpensive way to fill large floor cushions.

Polyester filling
Inexpensive, washable, and non-allergenic, polyester stuffing is especially suitable in children's rooms and for small cushions, but it will compress and become lumpy over time. It is usually sold by the bag.

Pure goose down
Soft and fluffy goose down is the king of fillings. Given a good shake, the fibers will puff up again. It is sold in bags.

Cotton filling
This stuffing will also become hard with use over time. Used mainly by mattress makers, it is sold by weight.

Down and feather
This is sold in various mixtures by the bag. The higher the percentage of down to feather, the better the quality.

Kapok
This is a natural plant fiber also used by furniture makers. Light, lustrous, and vermin-proof, it has the tendency of natural fibers to become lumpy, but since it tends not to absorb moisture, it is useful for outdoor cushions. It is sold by bagged weight.

Feather
Feathers without a leavening of more expensive down tend to flatten over time. Sold by the bag, they are popular for filling decorative cushions.

Assessing windows

Windows provide us with our outlook on the world around us and let in light from outside. Windowless rooms, dark and enclosed, are avoided by architects and builders. Natural light is good for both mental and physical health. As architectural features, windows must be considered carefully before you decide how to cover them. The style of the room has a bearing, as do the shapes of the windows themselves and their sizes in relation to the proportions of the room. Once these have been assessed, you need to determine whether their position in the room creates any problems that might limit the

***Pairs of identical windows in the same wall** can be treated as a pair, or as one large window. Consider a single curtain on each window, possibly meeting in the middle between them. A pair of identical curtains or blinds can also be used.*

***Two different windows in the same wall** should be treated as though they are the same height, with the top of both at the same level. Blinds or shades could be very effective. Headings are best kept simple.*

***Two or more different windows in the same room** can be treated individually, but are best made using the same fabrics and accessories, both trimmings and fixtures.*

***French doors** or windows usually work best with a pair of simple curtains, one on each side. Blinds may work better if the doors open into the room. It is important to keep access firmly in mind.*

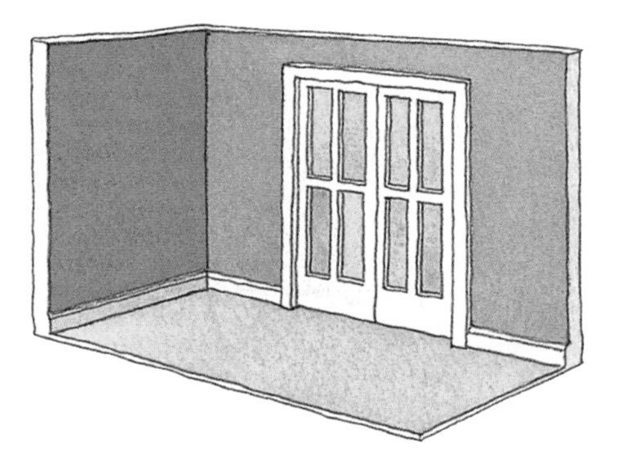

***Windows or sliding doors taking up all or most of a wall** may leave little room for curtains at the sides. If so, lightweight fabric and a simple heading will be less bulky. Blinds or shades mounted on the frame may be the best solution.*

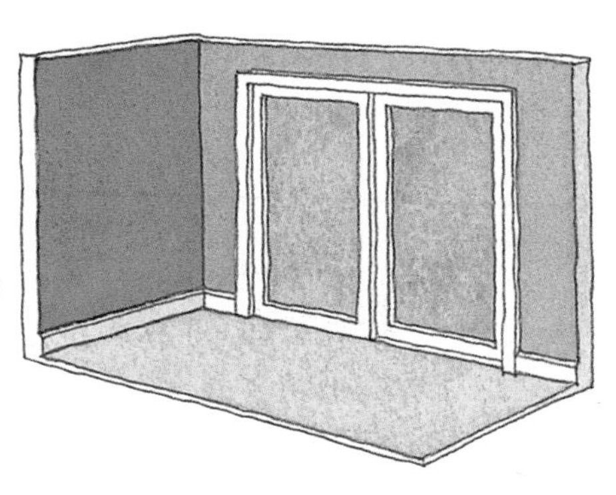

***Bay windows** are usually covered as one unit on a curved track, but again a simple blind mounted on the frame of each window can be quite successful.*

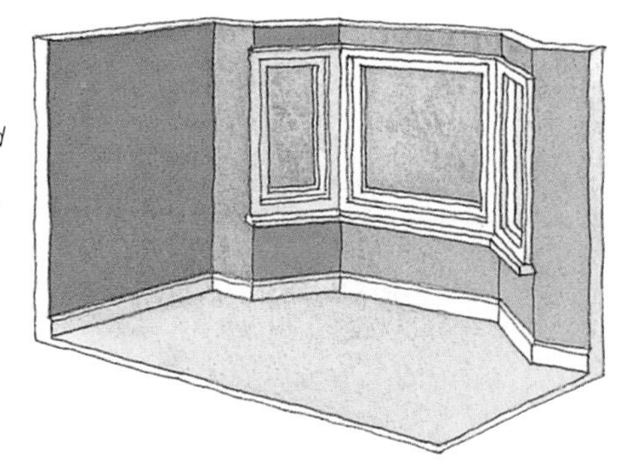

choice of window dressing. Upright windows are the most frequently seen shape; windows that are wider than they are tall, such as picture windows and sliding doors, are also widely used. Square or round windows are more specialized and need extra attention. Upright windows are highly versatile and are suitable for blinds or shades, as well as ordinary curtains and drapes, in every style imaginable, from pretty frills to formal. Wide windows can often be covered with a pair of curtains, but you may need to resort to blinds on extra-wide windows *(see also pages 162-165).*

***Single windows in a wall** will accept virtually any window dressing you wish to use, as long as it is in keeping with the proportions of the window and the style of the room.*

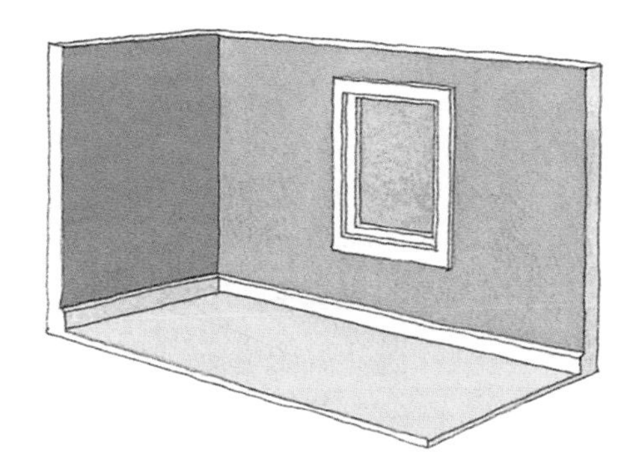

***Windows close to an adjacent wall** can be tricky. Because the window is off-center, a single curtain or a simple shade can be used effectively.*

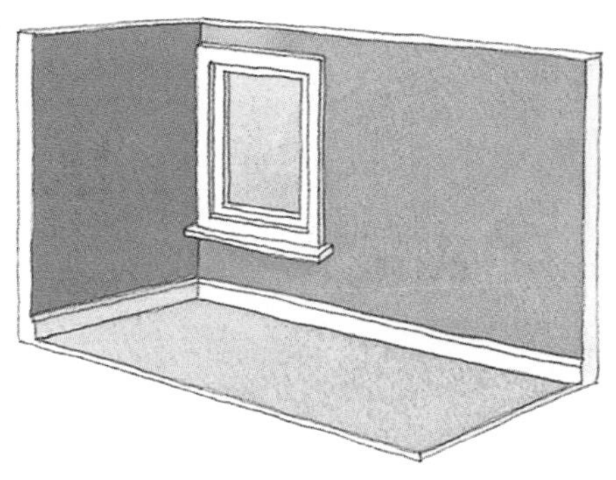

***Windows close to a ceiling** can be covered in a way appropriate to the style of the window itself and the room, but the curtain or blind may need to be mounted on the ceiling to provide enough room for a support.*

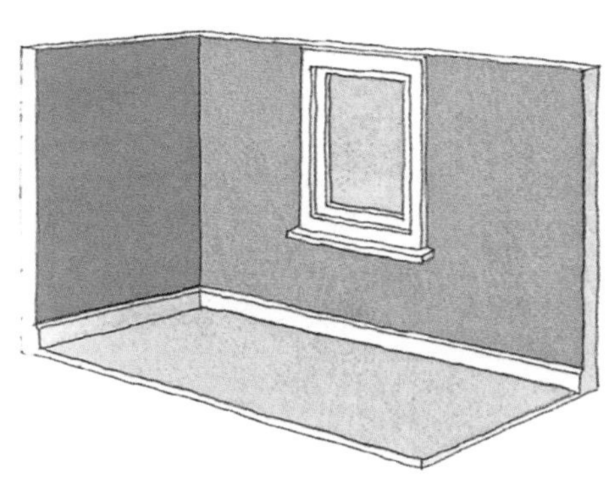

***Windows in a deep recess** are usually best dressed with a treatment mounted on the window frame. The fixtures and headings should be simple, and fabrics lightweight.*

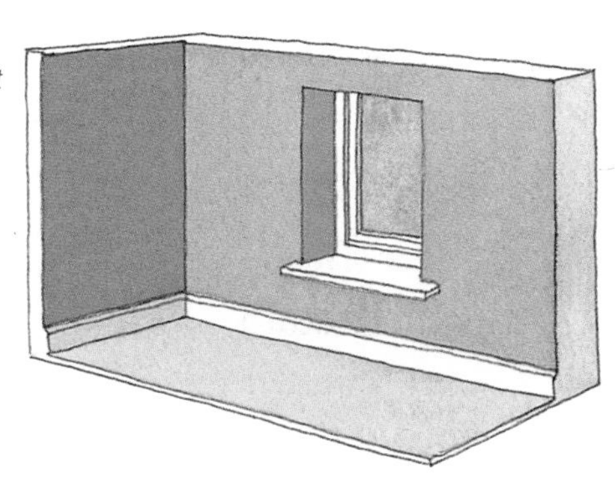

***Windows with a radiator beneath** can be dressed with sill-length curtains or blinds, or floor-length curtains can be hung in such a way that they can be pulled clear of the radiator to let the maximum heat through.*

***Windows on stairs, where the floor is uneven,** are generally best covered with blinds or single curtains that can be opened and closed from the top level.*

Curtains

Making a traditional curtain

This classic curtain is lined and interlined using traditional techniques that give it a highly professional finish.

ESTIMATING FABRIC FOR CURTAINS

Once you have measured the window (see page 162), calculate the cut drop and width, and estimate how much fabric you need to buy. Always allow extra for matching patterns (see page 163).

CURTAIN FULLNESS depends on the type of heading and the weight of the fabric. Allow 1½ to 2 times the width of the window for café curtains; 2 times for a plain gathered heading; and 2½ to 3 times for all other types of heading and for sheer fabrics.

To calculate the cut drop, add 10 in (25 cm) for the top and the bottom hems to the finished drop measurement.

To calculate the cut width, add 4 in (10 cm) for the side hems to the finished width measurement.

LINING should be 4 in (10 cm) narrower and shorter than the curtain measurement.

INTERLINING should be 4 in (10 cm) shorter, but the same width as the curtain measurement.

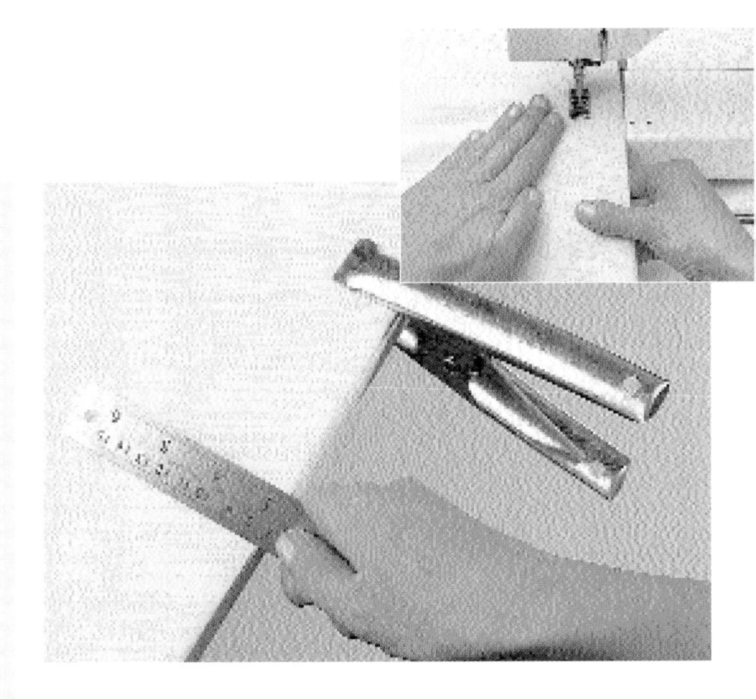

1 Join the drops for the lining, right sides together, as necessary. Fold up 1¼ in (3 cm) along the bottom edge and scrape along the edge of the table with a metal ruler to set the fold. Turn up another fold the same width and scrape again. Stitch this double hem (inset) and press.

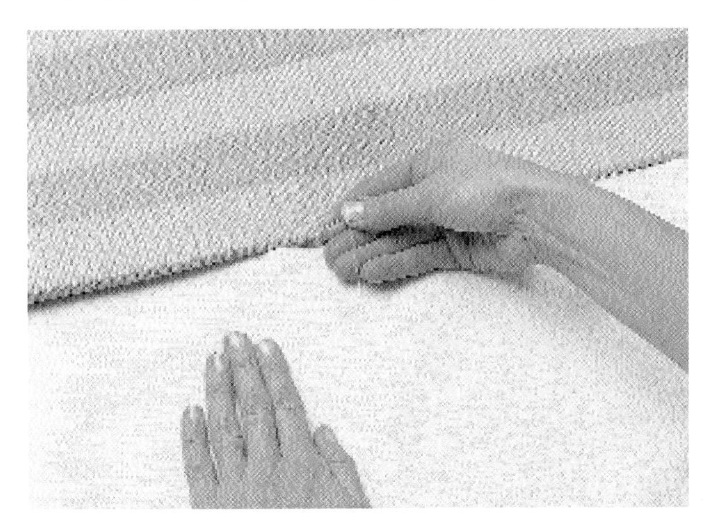

2 Lay the interlining flat and lay the main fabric, right side up, on top of it with the top of the fabric 3 in (8 cm) above the top of the interlining with the side edges aligned. Fold the main fabric halfway back and make interlocking stitches 4 in (10 cm) apart along the vertical center of the interlining, 8 in (20 cm) from the top and bottom. Repeat the interlocking, in rows 16 in (40 cm) apart, down the curtain on both sides of the center fold.

3 Turn the curtain over so the main fabric is facing right side down. Fold the interlining back 2 in (5 cm) at the leading edge, measuring carefully at regular intervals. Pin the interlining in position.

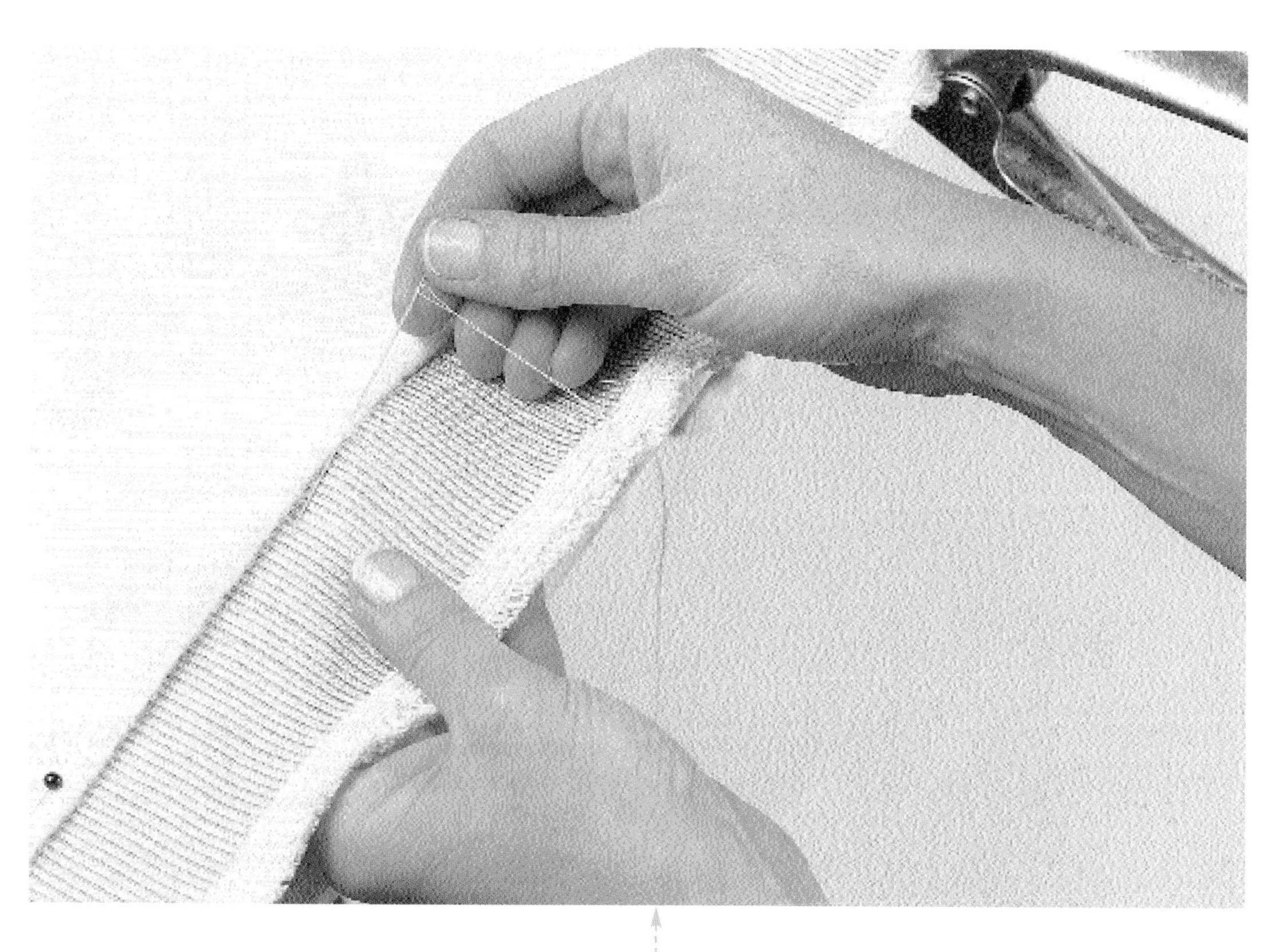

4 Interlock this fold, making the stitches 2 in (5 cm) apart to secure the leading edge.

5 Fold the main fabric over the interlining along the leading edge and anchor it with pyramid stitches. Clamp the edge to the table and work in sections. Repeat on the other side edge of the curtain.

6 Fold 4¾ in (12 cm) along the bottom edge and pin close to the fold.

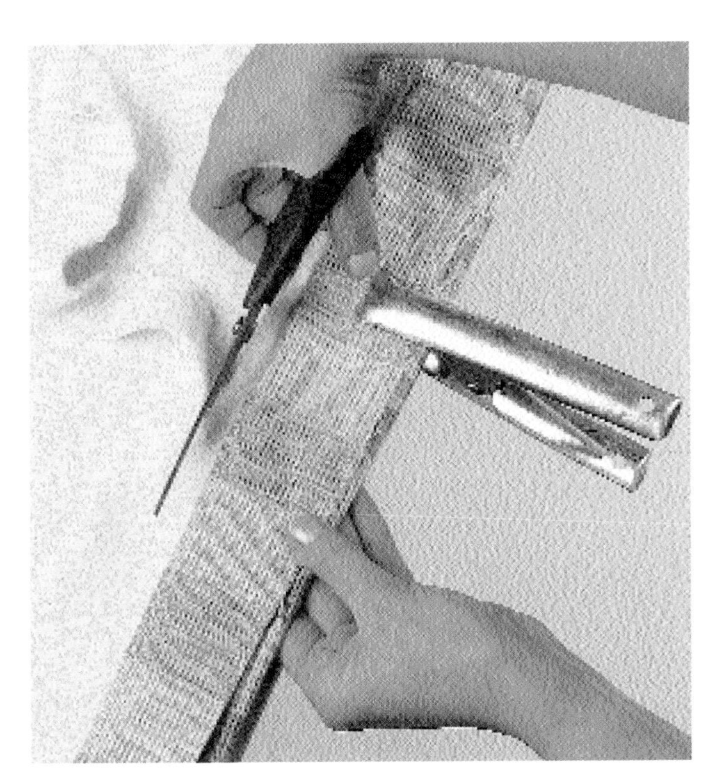

7 Turn the hem back on itself and hold it in position so you can access the interlining easily. Trim off 1¼ in (3 cm) of surplus interlining.

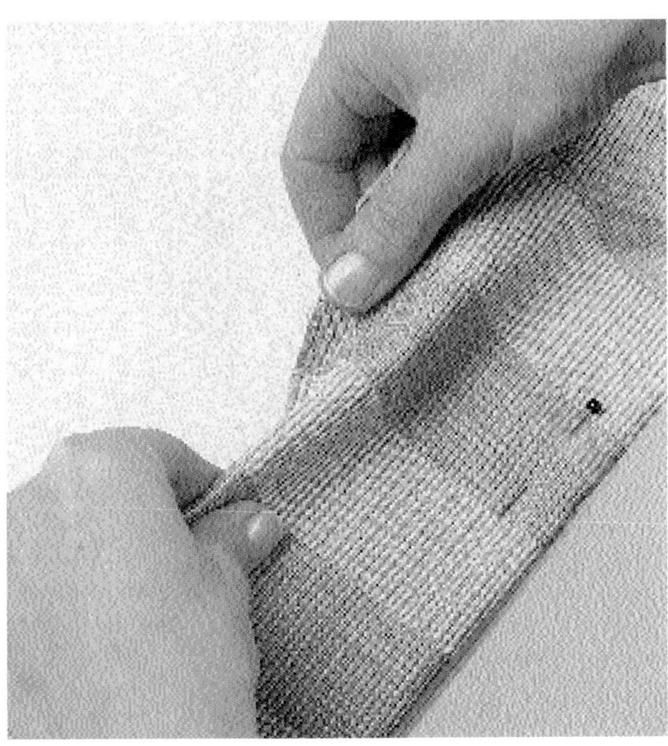

8 Fold 1¼ in (3 cm) under on the main fabric, moving the pins up from the bottom fold. The hem should cover the raw edge of the interlining. Leave 12 in (30 cm) unpinned at the corners.

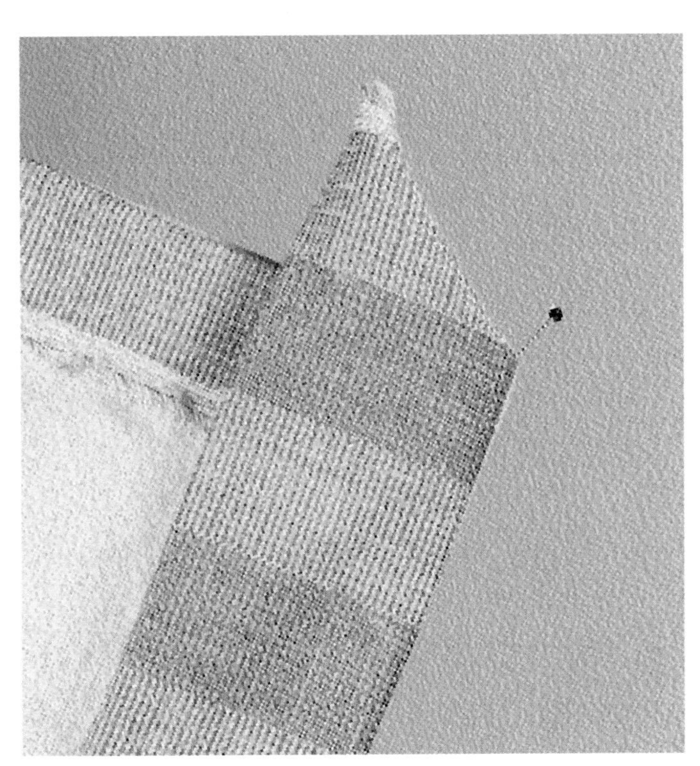

9 Lay each corner flat and make sure that it forms a right angle. Smooth the corner with your hand to remove any wrinkles and mark it precisely with a pin.

10 Open the corner flat and cut away a rectangle of interlining to reduce bulk. Then cut off a triangle at a 45-degree angle where the marking pin is placed (inset).

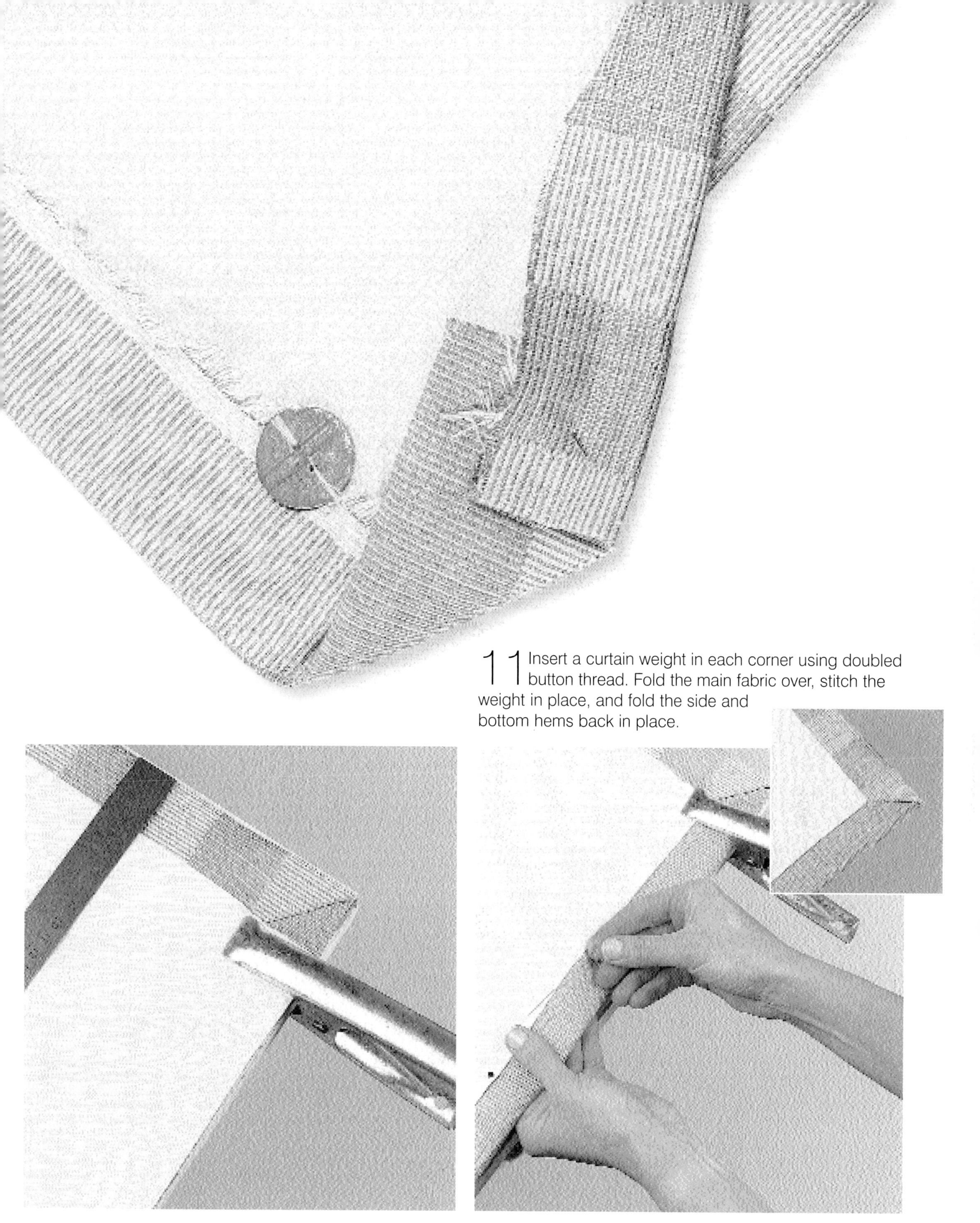

11 Insert a curtain weight in each corner using doubled button thread. Fold the main fabric over, stitch the weight in place, and fold the side and bottom hems back in place.

12 Align one raw edge of the lining with the leading edge of the curtain. Leave 1¼ in (3 cm) of the main fabric hem showing below the lining hem. Clamp in place.

13 Fold the side edge of the lining under 1¼ in (3cm) and align the corners with the corner fold of the main fabric. Slipstitch the lining to the main fabric, starting 1¼ in (3 cm) from the corner of the hem and working up the side edge to a point 8 in (20 cm) from the top.

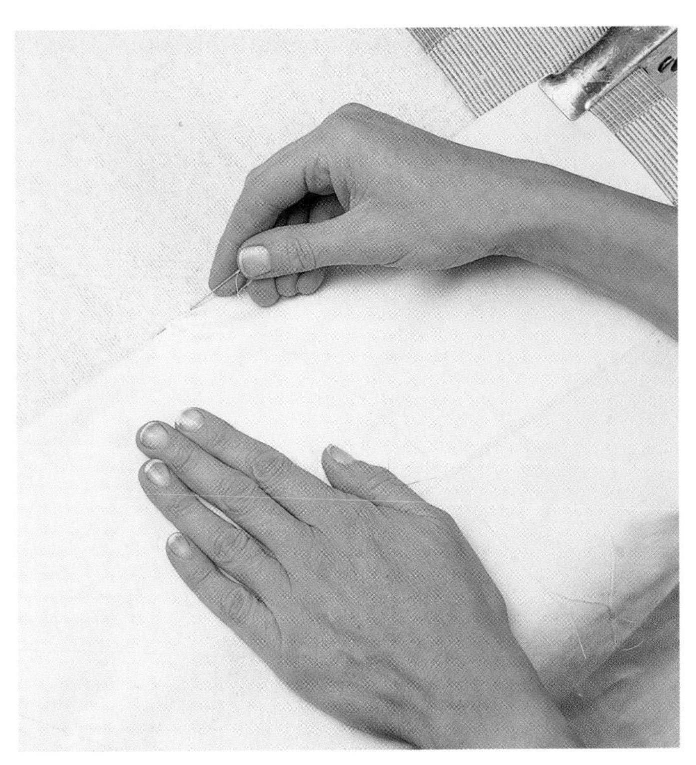

14 Interlock the lining to the interlining, working from the leading edge, and join the bottom edges together with a few anchoring stitches. Trim off the extra lining on the unjoined side of the curtain, align the raw edge of the lining with the edge of the curtain, and repeat steps 12 and 13 (see page 191) along this side.

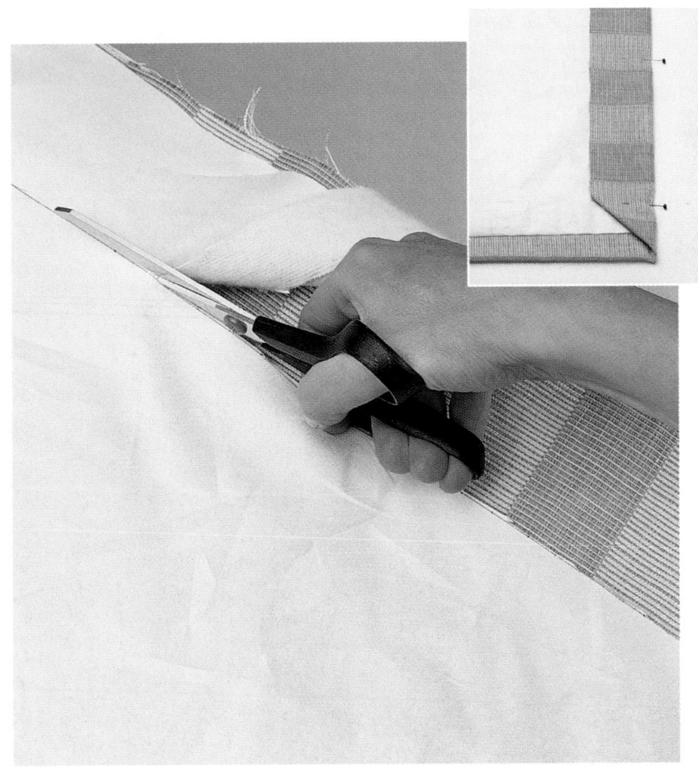

15 Measure the finished drop of the curtain from the hem up. Mark a clear line across the back of the curtain at this point and cut away the extra lining and interlining. Do NOT cut into the main fabric. Fold the top of the main fabric to the cut edge and turn the corner under at a 45-degree angle. Pin along the fold as shown (inset).

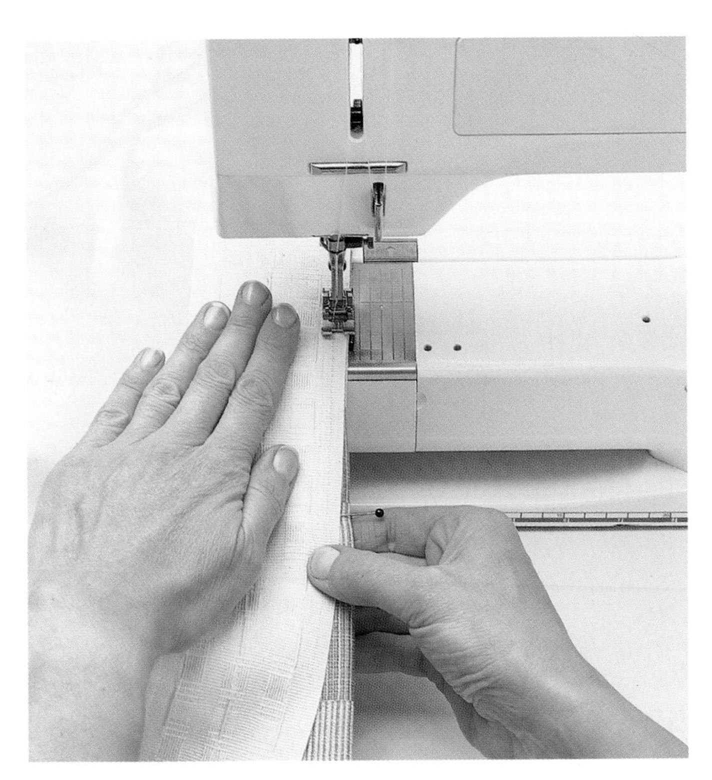

16 Stitch the heading tape in place with the top edge aligned to the top of the curtain (see page 212).

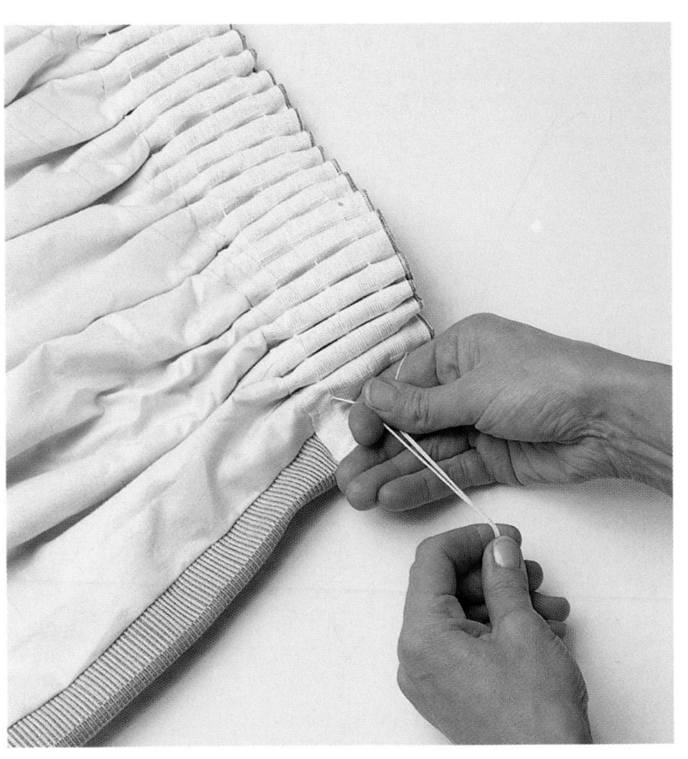

17 Pull up the cords together to obtain an even gathering, until the curtain is the desired width. Knot the cord securely and even up the pleats.

Tube lining

1 Measure and cut the curtain and lining the same length, but with the lining 8 in (20 cm) narrower than the curtain. Stitch the side seams, right sides together, stopping 6 in (15 cm) from the bottom.

Measure each side and turn back the edges of the main fabric evenly so the lining is centered on the curtain. Turn right side out and press.

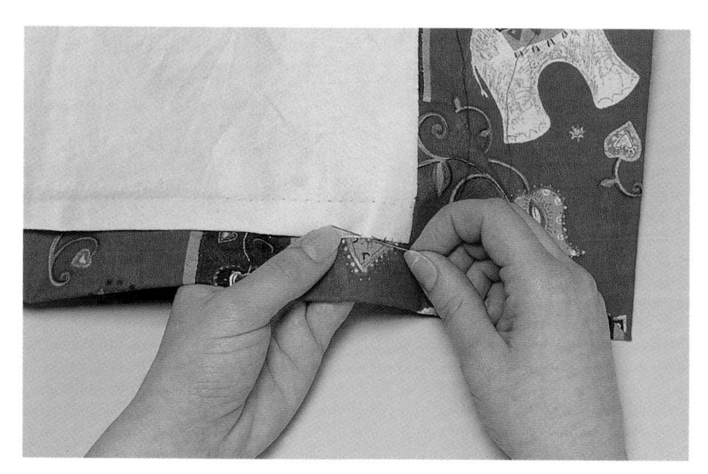

2 Measure the finished length and pin the bottom edge of the main fabric in place. Repeat to make the lining 1½ in (4 cm) shorter than the curtain. Machine-stitch a double hem on the lining. Miter the corners of the main fabric and hem it with hand-stitching.

3 Slipstitch the unsewn side edges of the lining to the curtain, catching in the bottom corners neatly. Add the chosen heading as shown on pages 212–217.

Loose lining

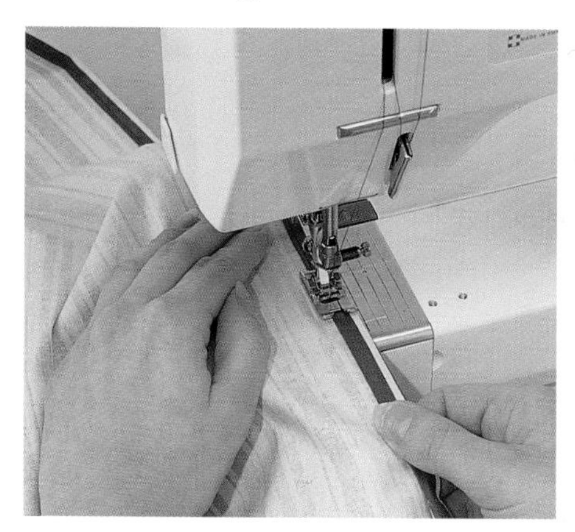

1 Cut out the curtain and lining to the same length, but subtract the side hem measurement from the lining. Turn under a double hem on both sides of the lining.

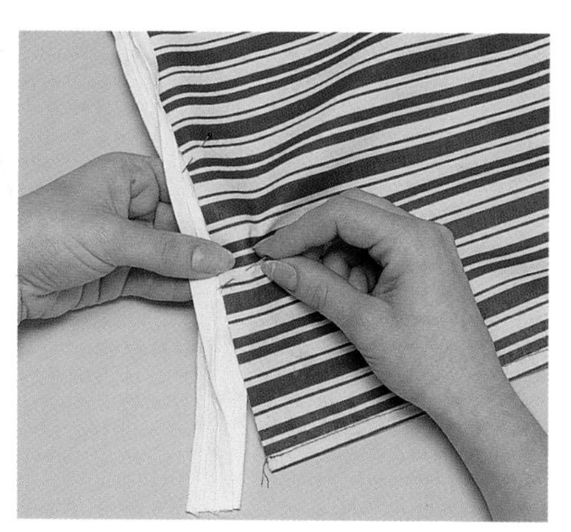

2 Pin and baste a length of gathered heading tape along the top of the lining to enclose the raw edge. Stitch the tape in position.

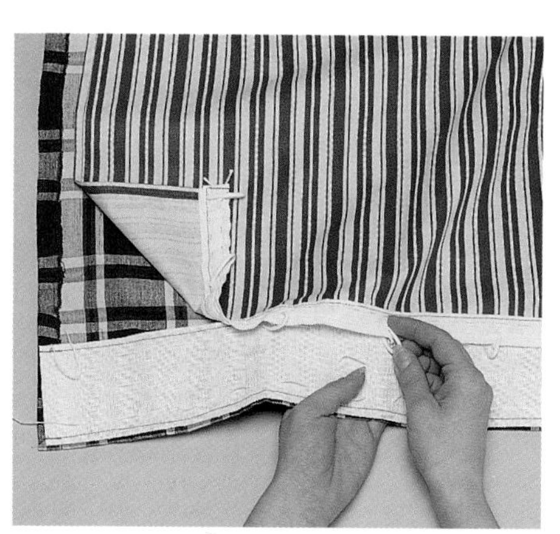

3 Insert hooks securely into the lining tape and then mount the lining onto the back of the finished curtain. You can now hem the lining to the required length.

Traditional café curtain

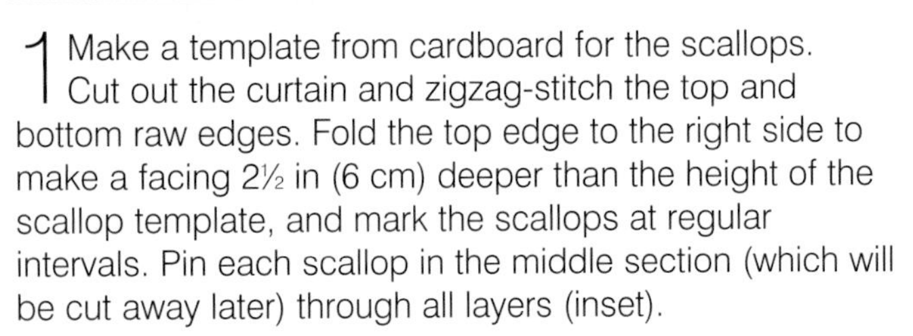

1 Make a template from cardboard for the scallops. Cut out the curtain and zigzag-stitch the top and bottom raw edges. Fold the top edge to the right side to make a facing 2½ in (6 cm) deeper than the height of the scallop template, and mark the scallops at regular intervals. Pin each scallop in the middle section (which will be cut away later) through all layers (inset).

2 Stitch each scallop along the lines marked on the fabric. Using fabric shears, cut out the scallops. Trim back any surplus to ⅜ in (1 cm) inside the stitching. Clip the curves and trim off the corners, taking care not to cut through the stitching.

3 Turn the facing right side out and gently press. Fold each tab to the back and stitch it in position along its top edge. Turn under a narrow double hem along each side edge and topstitch the hem in place.

4 Thread the curtain pole through the fabric loops and mark the bottom hem level of the curtain. Turn up the zigzag-stitched edge and stitch a single hem.

CAFÉ CURTAIN VARIATIONS

Tied café curtains
The scalloped loops have been replaced with ties made from bias binding, which has also been used to edge the curtain on all four sides. Knotted ties or ribbon bows are also effective.

Tabbed café curtains
Tab strips made from the same or a coordinating fabric are stitched separately and inserted inside a facing strip at the top of the curtain.

Triangles
Triangles made the same way as the scallops shown above have been cut out and faced with a contrasting fabric. The triangles are folded to the front, revealing the contrasting fabric, and secured with buttons.

Scalloped curtains with rings
The tops of the scallops are not folded over to make loops, but are attached to café curtain rings that clip on the top of each tab.

Simple sheer curtains

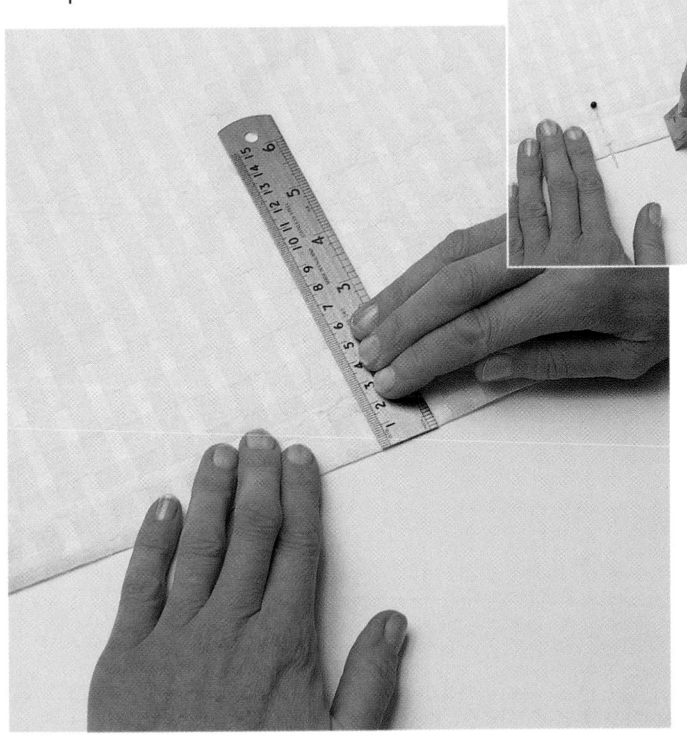

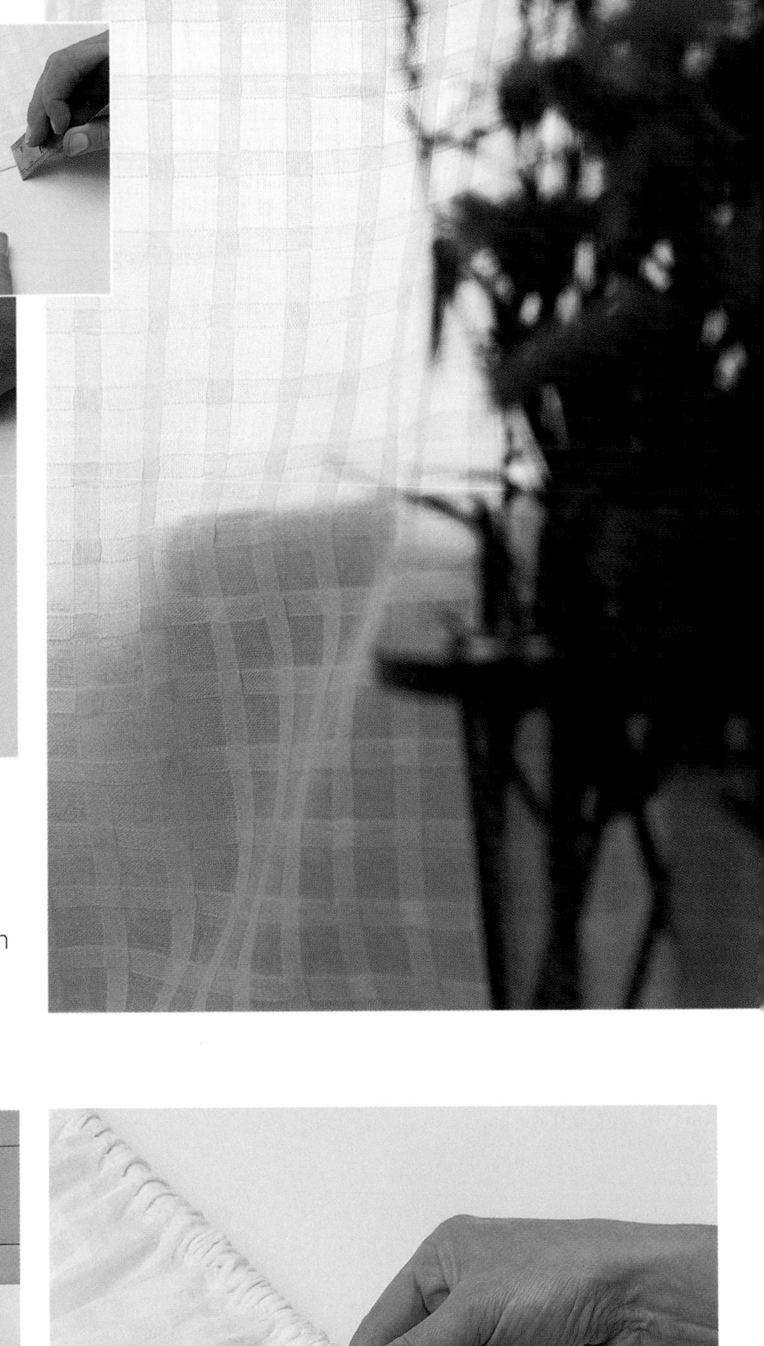

1 Measure and cut out the fabric. The length is the finished drop plus a 2-in (5-cm) hem, plus twice the diameter of the curtain rod plus ¼ in (5 mm) for the heading. The width is 1½ times the length of the pole. Fold up a 1-in (2.5-cm) hem along the bottom and pin it in place. Scrape the folded edge to crease the fabric. Then fold and scrape again to make a double hem (inset).

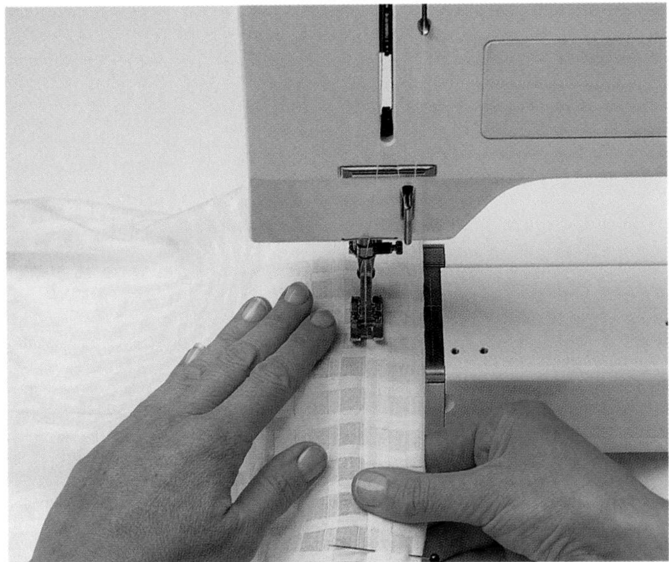

2 Stitch as close as possible to the top folded edge. Make the heading in the same way, folding under half the total heading measurement each time. Finish the raw side edges with zigzag stitching.

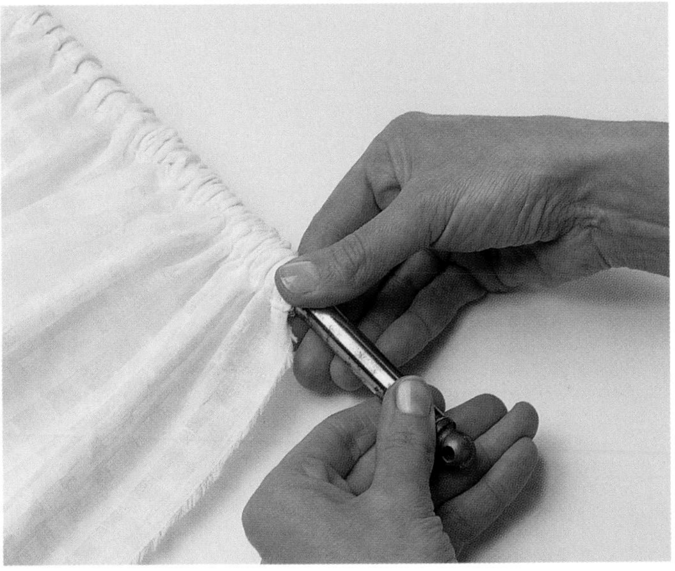

3 Insert the curtain rod through the casing, gently easing the fabric along the rod to avoid any snagging. Take hold of both ends of the rod and hang it in position on the wall. Gather the fabric evenly along its length.

Curtain valances

Valances, or pelmets, need to be long enough to cover the top of the window. Make sure that you allow enough at each end of the pole or track to conceal the curtain support without interfering with the opening and closing mechanism. The depth depends on the style, length, and fullness of the curtains (see also page 163).

Special valance tracks or ordinary curtain tracks are available for hanging valances, or you can custom-make your own flat or boxed valances from plywood or fiberboard.

Flat valance

1 Measure and cut out the backing board, batting (wadding), and fabric. There should be enough fabric and batting to be able to wrap them around the board to cover the top and bottom edges and the ends completely.

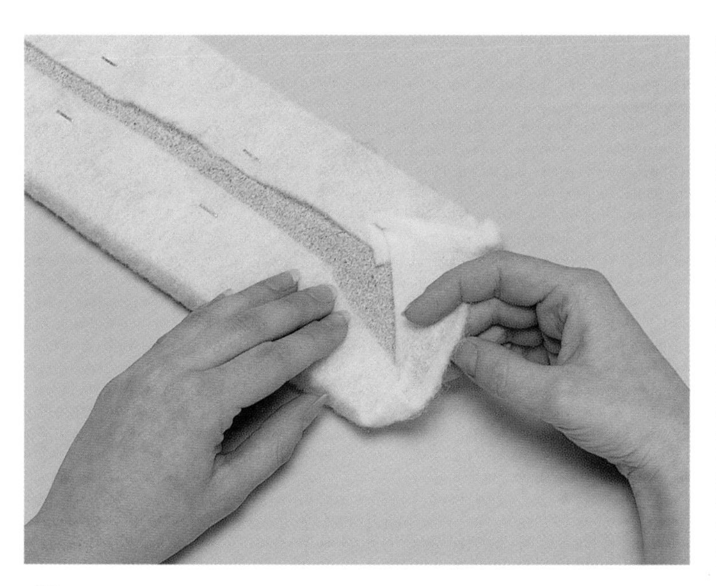

2 Staple, glue, or tack the batting in position on the reverse side of the board. Secure the long edges first, then trim back the corners to reduce bulk. Turn the ends to the back to cover the short end of the board.

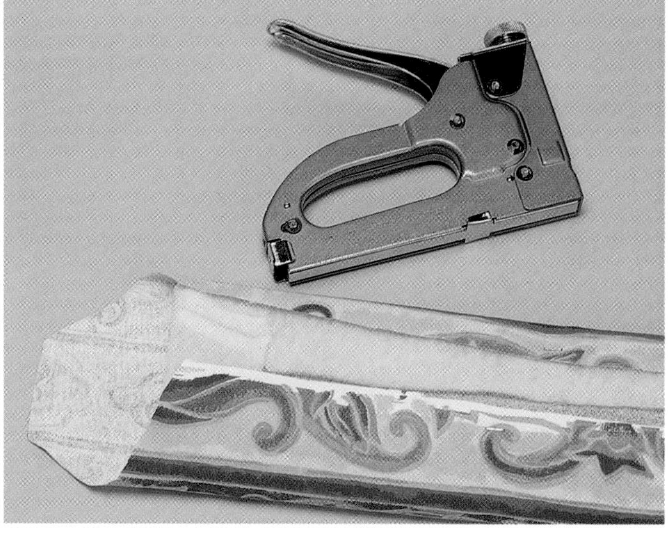

3 Stretch the fabric across the board and secure it in place as for the batting. Trim the corners to reduce bulk and turn them under neatly to conceal all the edges.

4 A valance of this type is most useful for windows set in an alcove where there is no room for a box valance and where the ends of the curtain rod will not be visible. It can be easily mounted on hidden brackets.

Box valance

A box valance can be used with curtains or with blinds, as shown here. The ends are visible, so it is essential to finish them neatly. The top can rest on flat brackets mounted above the window frame. They provide a formal finish to a window and cut out light filtering in at the top of the curtain.

1 Cover the front and ends of the box with batting (wadding) by wrapping it as for making a flat valance (see page 197), or cut separate pieces and glue them in place. Do not pad the edges that will rest against the wall.

2 Cut out a piece of fabric that is large enough to cover the box completely. Staple, glue, or tack it in position along the long edges inside the box, then fold the corners neatly and secure them with staples or tacks.

Box-pleated valance

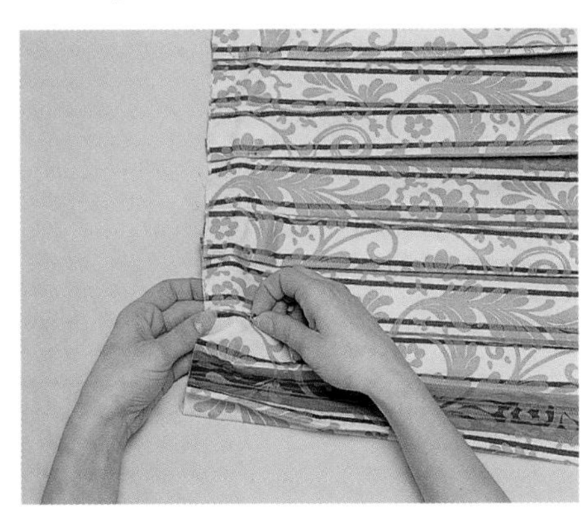

1 Cut enough fabric to cover the box. Fold the short ends to the wrong side and fold the strip in half lengthwise with wrong sides together. Mark, press, and pin the pleats and stitch across the top raw edges.

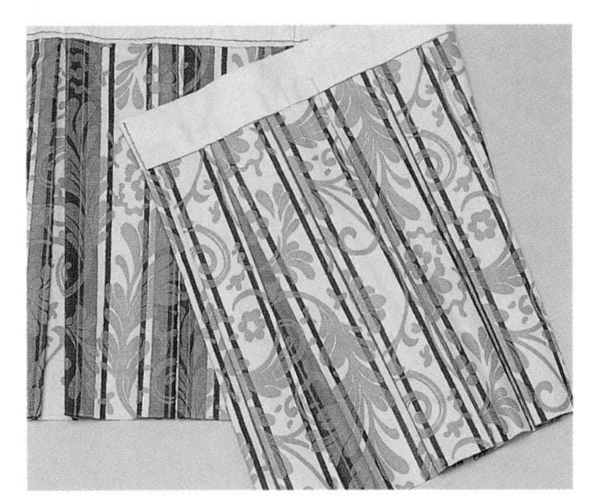

2 Cut a strip of fabric wide enough to bind the top edge. Pin and stitch to the top stitched edge with right sides together. Turn the strip to the wrong side, turn its raw edge under, and stitch the long and short ends.

3 The binding strip folds neatly over the top edge of a valance box and can be stapled in position. Turn the corners carefully, folding the binding before stapling it.

A SIMPLE SWAG

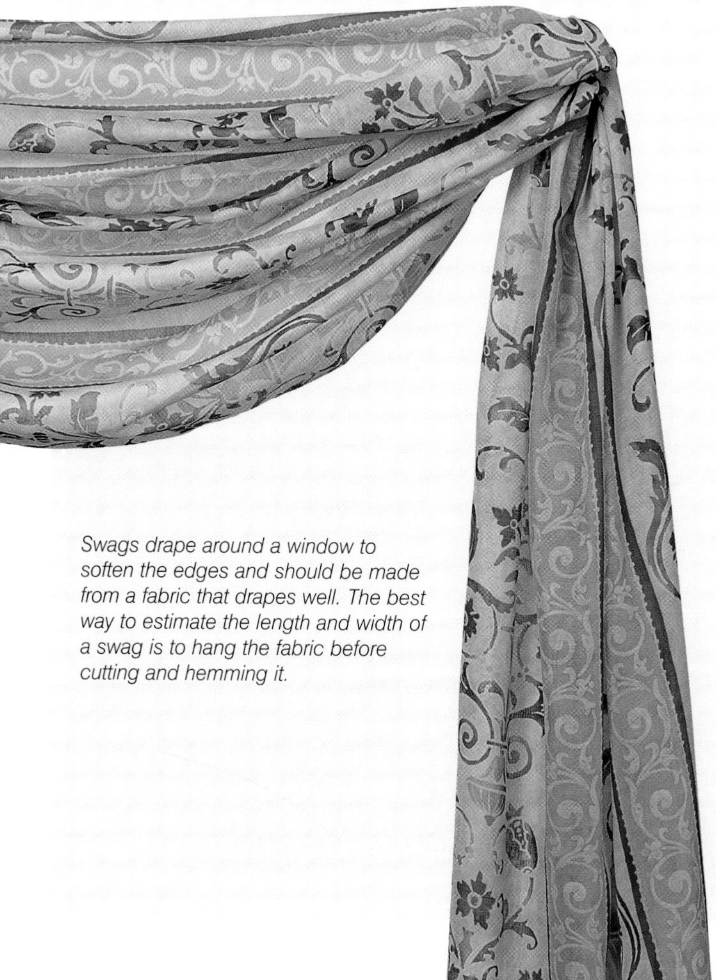

Swags drape around a window to soften the edges and should be made from a fabric that drapes well. The best way to estimate the length and width of a swag is to hang the fabric before cutting and hemming it.

Measure and cut out a length of fabric for the swag. Level the edges and trim away the selvages. Turn the edges under and hem all four sides, backstitching over the corners to secure them.

Gathered valance

1 Measure and cut out a piece of fabric twice the desired depth plus seam allowances, and at least the same width as the curtains plus seam allowances. Hem the short ends. Fold in half lengthwise with right sides together to make a tube.

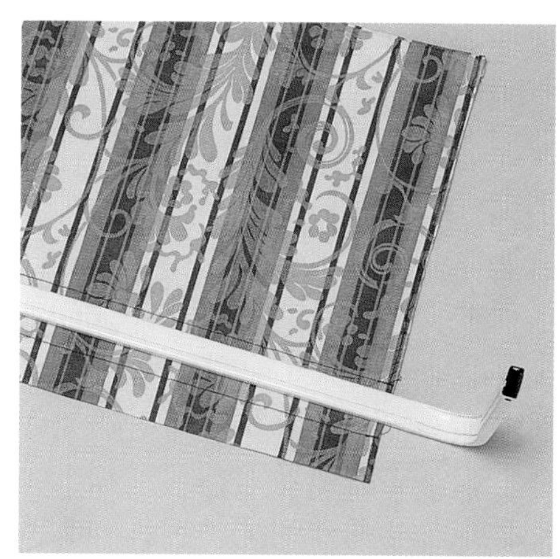

2 Turn the tube right side out and press with the seam at the back. Measure and mark a casing twice the depth of the curtain track. Make sure the casing does not line up with the seam on the back. Stitch along the top and bottom of the casing.

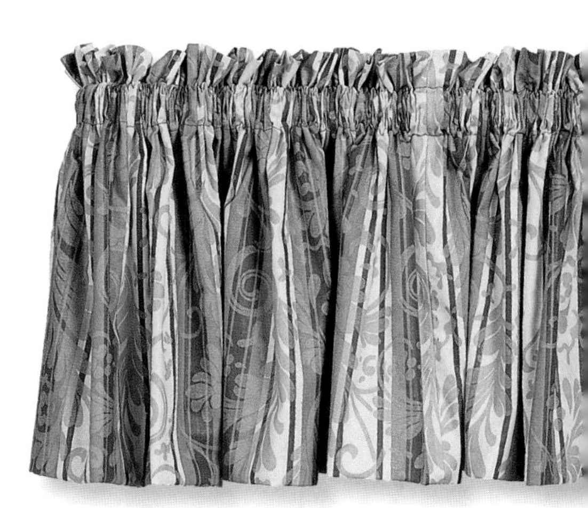

3 Carefully insert the track into the casing, to avoid snagging the fabric. Distribute the gathers evenly. Doubling the fabric means the right side of the fabric shows on both sides of the valance.

Blinds

Window blinds, or shades, are among the simplest of all window coverings. Among the most common types are roller blinds, which are simple panels of fabric that roll up and down on a spring roller bar and can be made from easily available kits; Roman blinds, which pull up into neat pleats when open but lie flat when closed; and lightweight Austrian, or balloon, blinds, which are decorative and frilly *(see also page 165).*

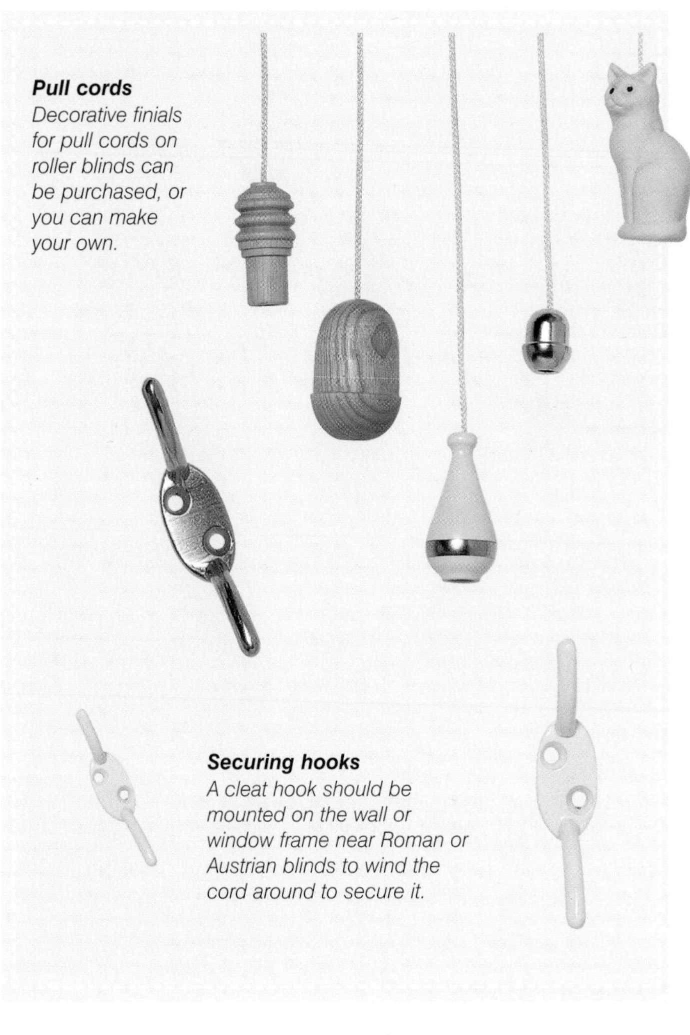

Pull cords
Decorative finials for pull cords on roller blinds can be purchased, or you can make your own.

Securing hooks
A cleat hook should be mounted on the wall or window frame near Roman or Austrian blinds to wind the cord around to secure it.

Roller blind

1 Measure, mark, and cut a length of fabric according to the kit guidelines. Make sure the kit has a spring roller, a slat for the bottom, cord, and small pieces of hardware.

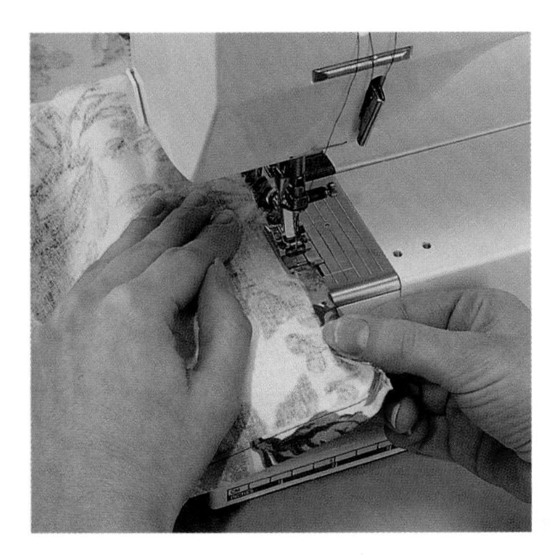

2 Turn under, pin, and stitch a narrow hem on both sides of the length of fabric. Zigzag-stitch a single hem along the top raw edge.

3 Turn up, pin, and stitch the bottom edge to make a casing wide enough to enclose the wooden slat. Insert the slat and slipstitch the ends of the casing.

4 Attach the pull cord mechanism to the center of the back of the slat. Thread a finial on the cord and knot one end. Spray on a coat of protective stiffener if desired.

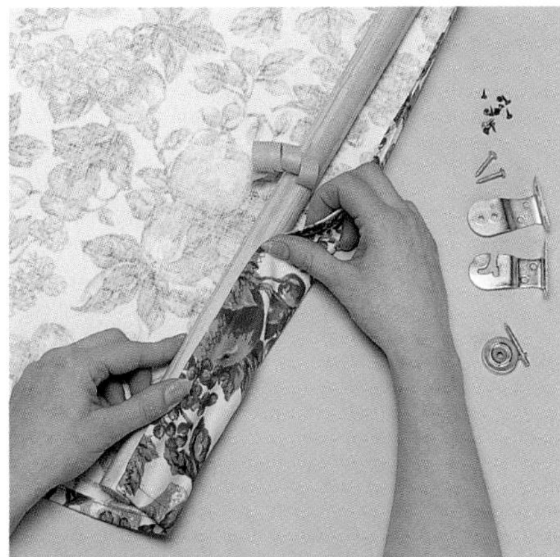

5 Attach the top edge of the fabric to the spring roller carefully. This version has a self-adhesive strip onto which the fabric is pressed; other models may need to be secured with staples or small tacks.

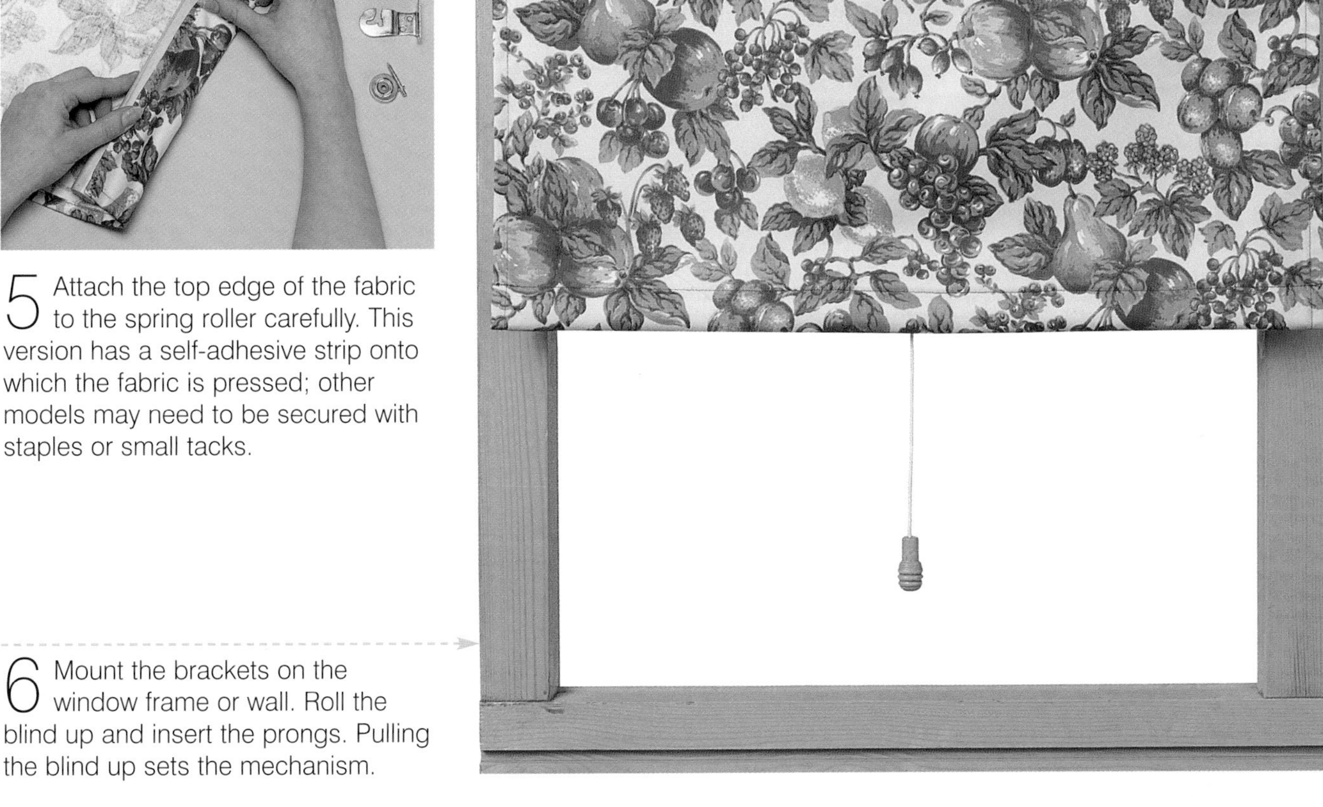

6 Mount the brackets on the window frame or wall. Roll the blind up and insert the prongs. Pulling the blind up sets the mechanism.

DECORATIVE FINISHES

Plain roller blinds can be finished with decorative edges, made from a variety of trimmings, ranging from simple lace or piping to heavy tasseled braid. In some designs, the casing should be made from a separate strip of fabric and sewn onto the back of the blind. In others, the edging can simply be added to the bottom of the casing.

Scalloped edge

A scalloped edge was made and faced, then topstitched. The casing is made from a separate strip.

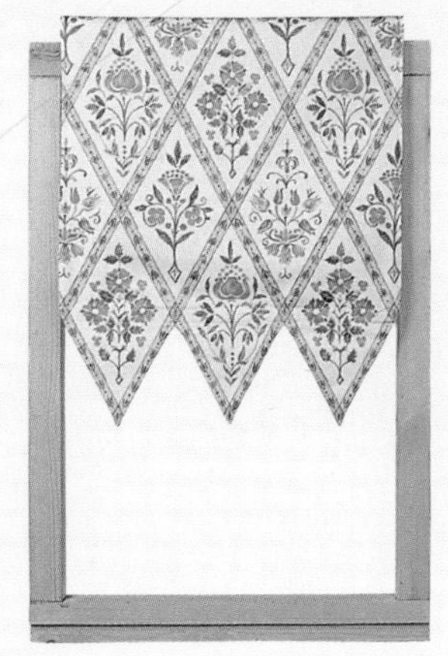

Pointed edge

The pattern of the fabric has been used to make an effective edging. The edges can be faced, or cut wide enough to be hemmed, and a separate casing applied.

Pleated edge

A doubled strip of fabric has been box-pleated and applied to the bottom of the casing to make a stylish tailored edge.

Roman blind

A Roman blind looks similar to a roller blind when it is closed, but it is made with strips of special fabric tape on the back that make the fabric fall into neat pleats when the blind is pulled up. The cords are tied together on one side and can be wound around a cleat when the blind is open. Measure and cut out the fabric to the length and width of the window plus the depth of the top allowance, bottom casing, hems, and seam allowances.

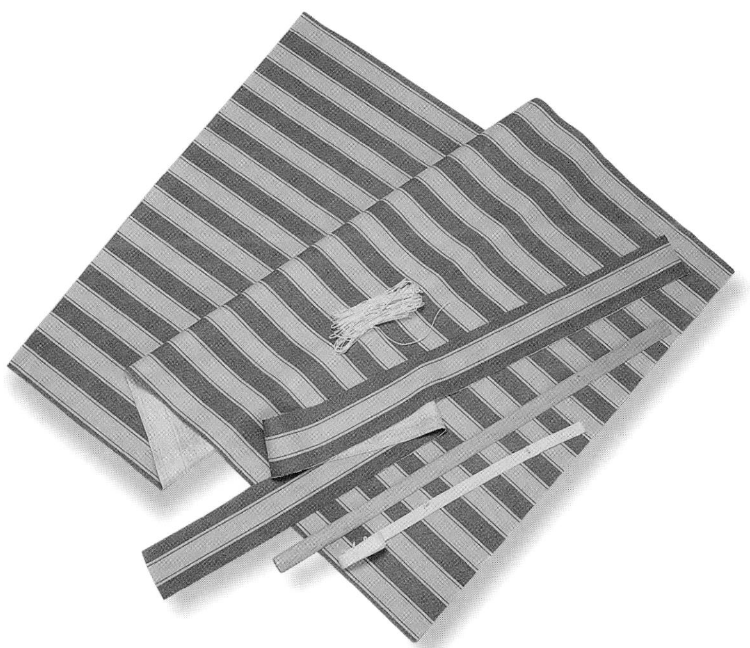

1 Measure, mark, and cut one piece for the blind, plus a heading strip. You also need Roman-blind tape (or plain fabric tape and small curtain rings), cord, a wooden slat for the bottom, and a mounting board.

2 Mark guidelines on the wrong side for three vertical tapes—one on each side and one in the center; use more if the window is wide. Pin the tape in place covering the marked lines and stitch along both long edges. Do NOT catch the loops in the stitching.

3 Turn under, pin, and stitch a narrow double hem along each side edge of the length of fabric.

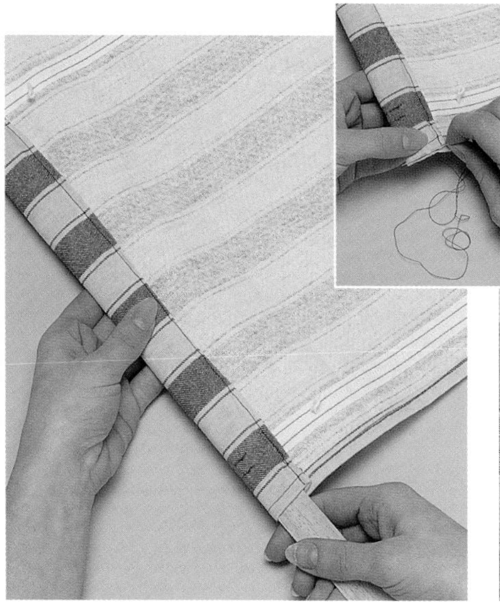

4 Turn up the bottom edges and stitch a casing for the wooden slat. Slide the slat in. Slipstitch the ends of the casing closed (inset).

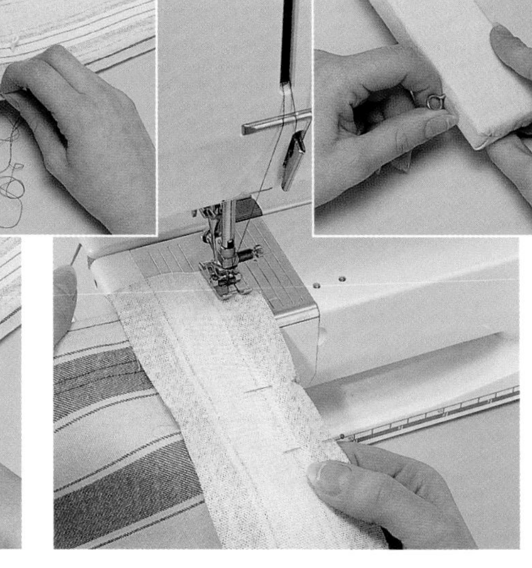

5 Finish the top edge by binding it with the heading strip. On one narrow edge of the mounting board, screw in an eye to align with each vertical length of tape (inset).

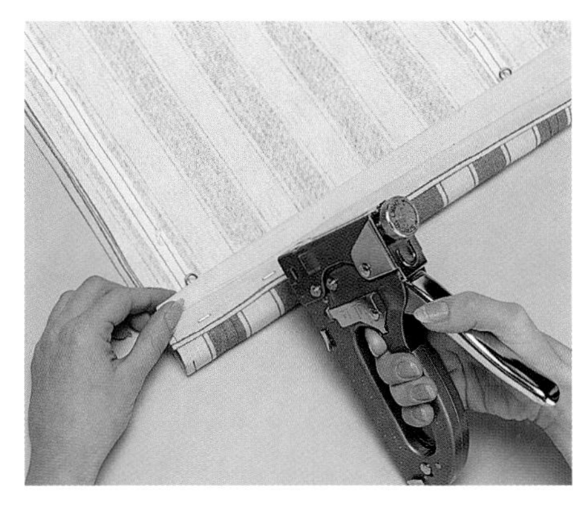

6 Using a staple gun or tacks, secure the top bound edge of the blind to the side of the mounting board that will rest against the wall. Wrap the blind over to hang down the front of the board.

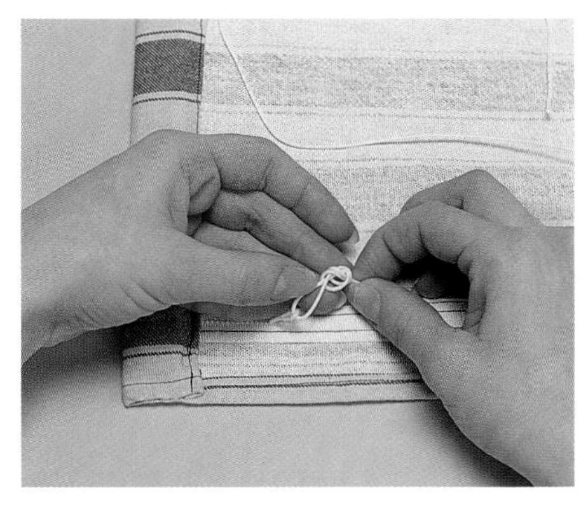

7 Slip the end of a length of cord through the bottom loop or ring on one of the vertical tapes. Secure with a strong knot at the end.

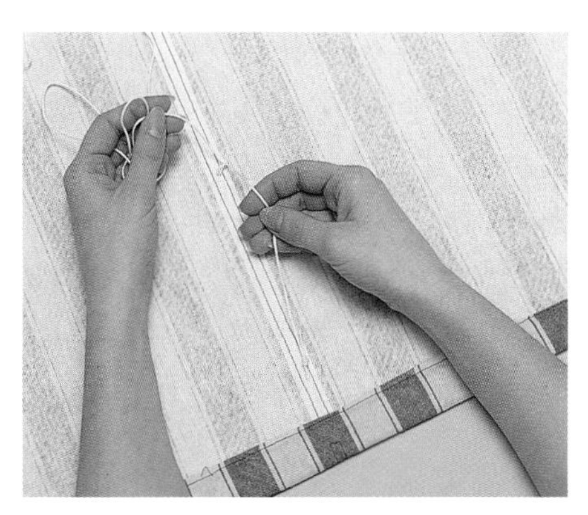

8 Thread the cord up through each loop in the tape. Make sure that you leave enough cord at the top to stretch across the width of the blind. Repeat for each vertical tape, from one side to the other.

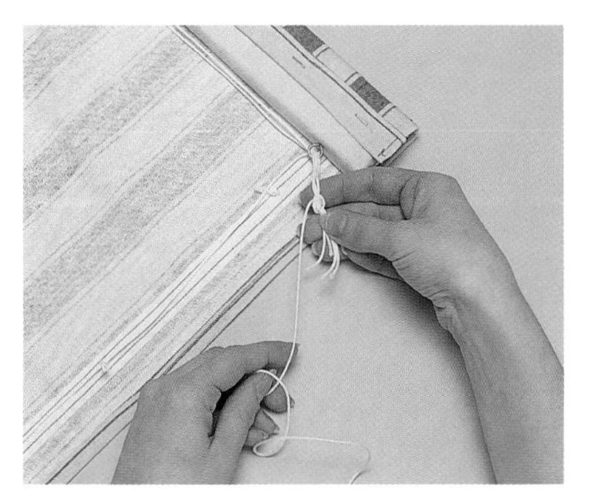

9 Thread the top of each cord through the screw eyes in one direction along the mounting board. Knot them together at the edge. Trim, then attach a separate length of cord to the knotted end to make a pull.

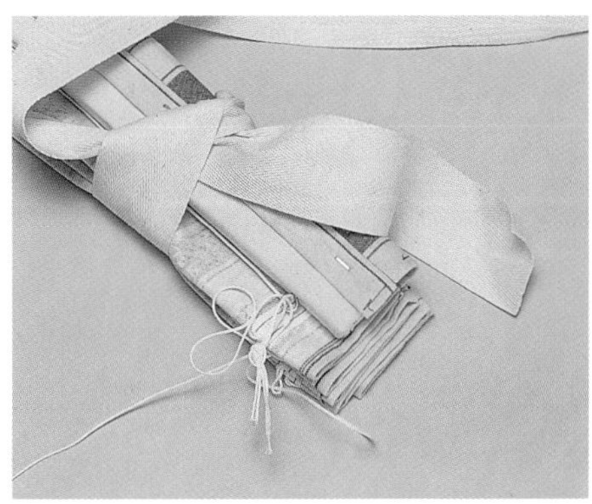

10 Fold the blind into accordion (concertina) pleats, aligning the tape loops, and tie with cotton tape at each end. Leave it wrapped for a day or two to set the folds.

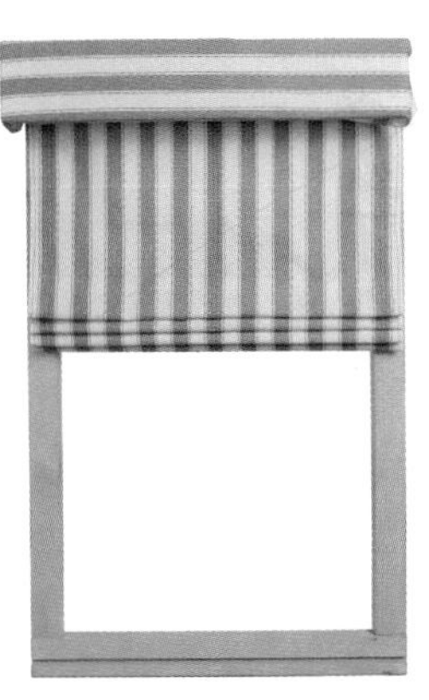

11 Screw through the mounting board directly into the window frame or wall, or mount the board on brackets. Mount a cleat hook on the pull-cord side. Note that the matching valance on this window covers the top to reduce light and drafts.

MAKING A MOUNTING BOARD

1 Cut a piece of 1 x 2-in (2.5 x 5-cm) board to the desired length. Measure the width all around the board and cut a length of lining fabric to that size plus seam allowances.

The length is the length of the cut board plus 2 in (5 cm) seams at each end. Fold the fabric in half lengthwise and sew the long edges. Turn right side out.

2 Slide the board into the fabric tube and turn the ends neatly. Miter the corners and slipstitch to secure.

Austrian blind

This ruched blind, also known as a balloon shade, combines characteristics of lined curtains and Roman blinds. An ordinary curtain heading is generally used across the top, while rows of tape similar to that used on Roman blinds (but without the loops or rings) are stitched to the back of the blind.

The width of the fabric measures 2 to 2½ times the width of the window, plus side seams and seam allowances for joining sections. The length of the fabric is 2 to 2½ times the length of the window, plus hems. Allow more fabric if you are making lightweight blinds.

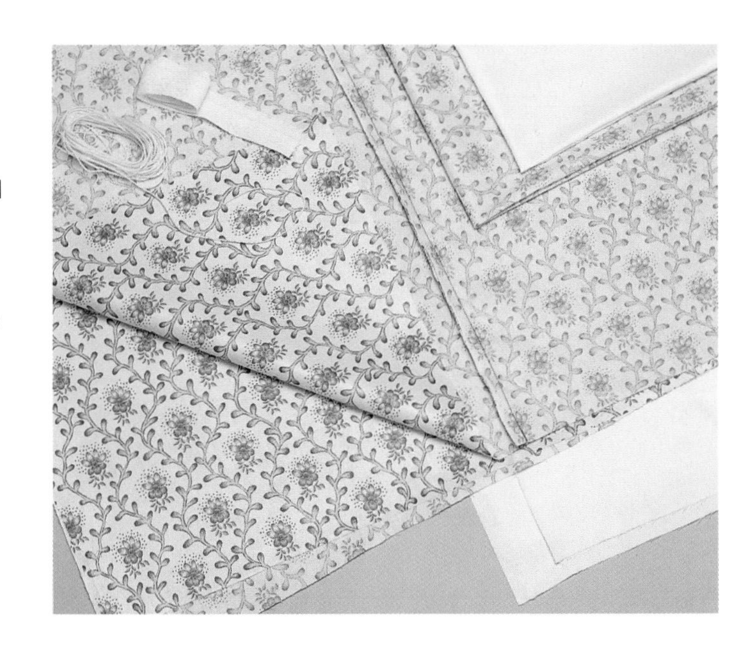

1 Measure, mark, and cut out the front piece, joining sections together to make up the width. Cut a lining piece to the same size, less 2 in (5 cm) on the width. To make the blind, you will also need Austrian blind shirring tape, curtain rings, heading tape, and cord.

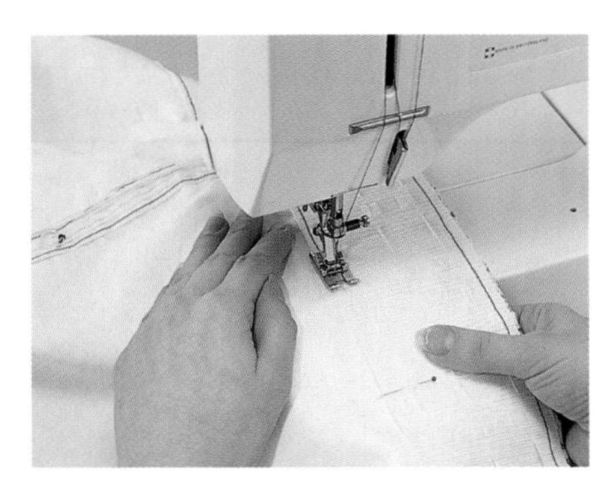

2 With wrong sides together, pin and stitch the front and lining along the two side edges.

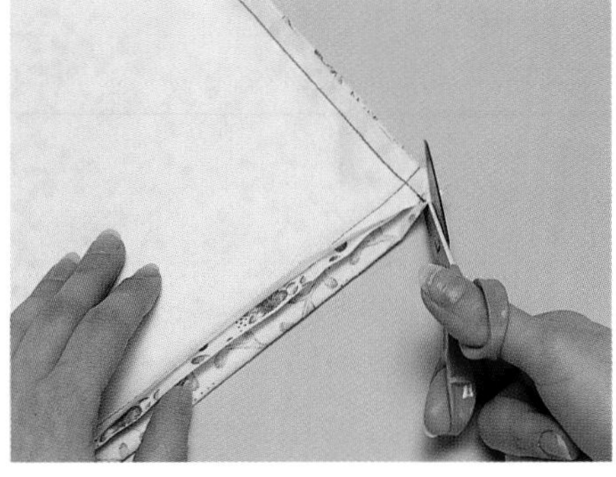

3 Fold the side edges so they are turned back evenly and press toward the outside edge. Pin and stitch the front to the lining along the bottom edge, then clip the corners.

4 Turn the blind right side out through the top. Press carefully, making sure the turned-back edges are equal on each side.

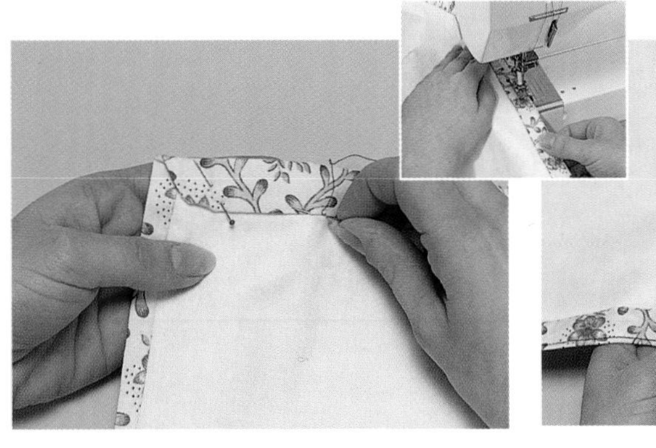

5 Turn up a single hem along the bottom edge, mitering each corner. Pin in place and slipstitch to secure. Topstitch the bottom and sides to create a neat edge (inset).

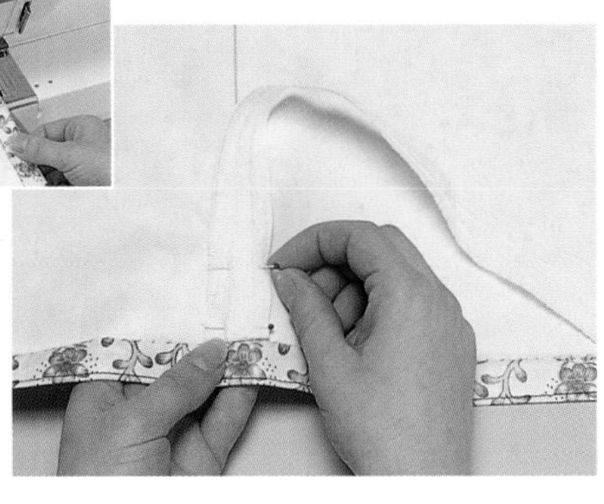

6 Mark vertical guidelines on the lining at regular intervals. Pin lengths of tape over the marked lines, turning under both ends of each tape. Stitch along both long edges of each.

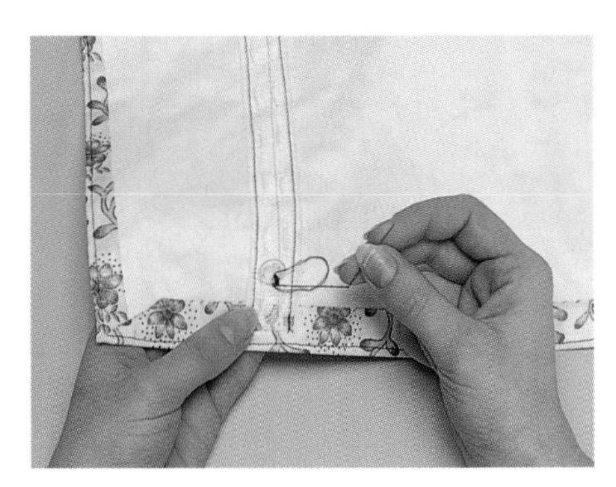

7 Sew a series of curtain rings at regular intervals along each tape. Make sure that they line up evenly across the width of the blind.

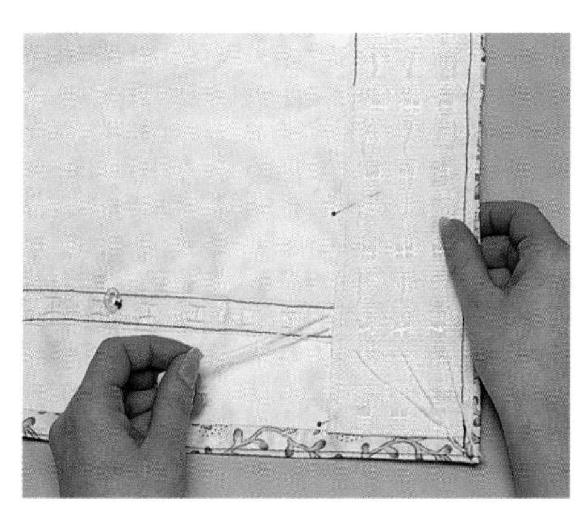

8 Turn under ½ in (1 cm) along the top edge and pin, then stitch the top edge of the heading tape to cover the raw edges. Keep the ends of the cords in the vertical shirring tape clear of the stitching.

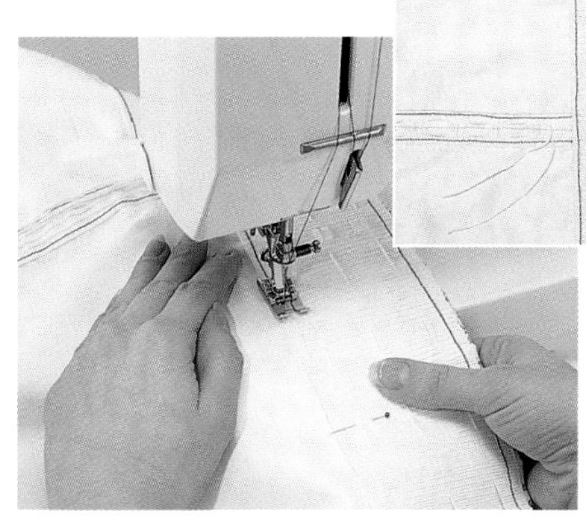

9 Pin and stitch the lower edge of the heading tape in place. Do NOT catch the ends of the shirring tape cords in the seam (inset).

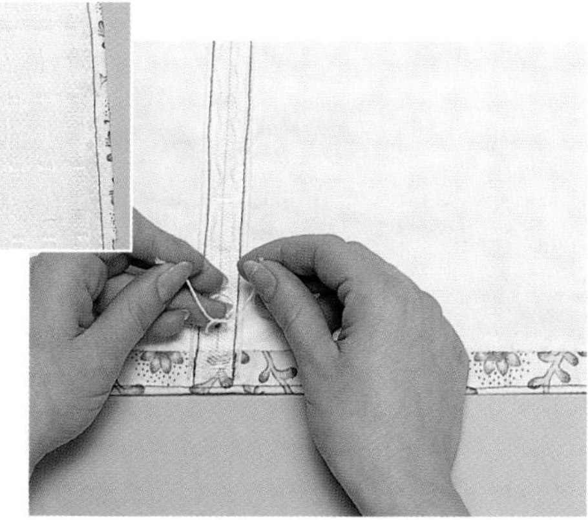

10 Cut a cord measuring the length plus the width of the blind, plus 6 in (15 cm). Tie the cord to the bottom ring on one strip of shirring tape. Repeat to tie a cord at the end of each tape.

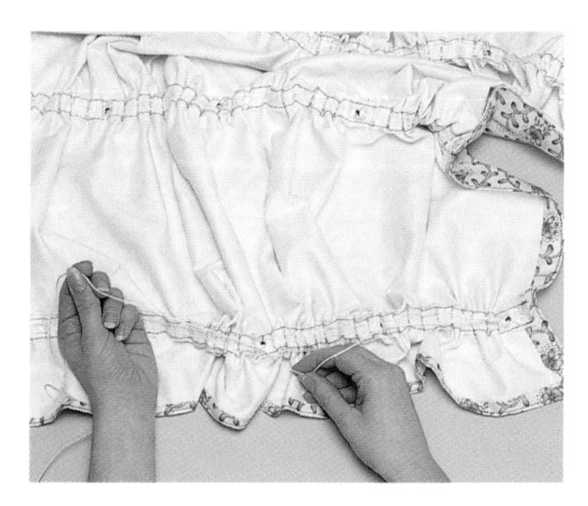

11 Pull up the vertical shirring cords to the finished length. Thread each cord added in step 10 through each ring on its tape and knot securely. Thread the cords through the top rings, knot them together, and attach a pull cord.

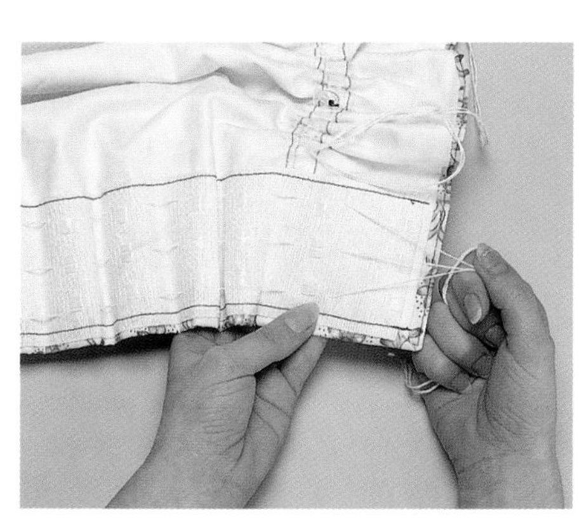

12 Pull up the heading tape to the desired width and tie the ends of the cords securely. Even up the gathering and ruching.

13 The blind is hung like a curtain from a track. Mount a cleat on the wall to secure the pull cord.

Estimating for different blind styles

There are many different styles of blinds. Here are some general guidelines that can be used for measuring your blind to fit before you buy the fabric. They will allow you to make a fairly accurate estimate to follow.

BLIND TYPE	CUT WIDTH	CUT DROP	NOTES
BLINDS WITH ROLLER TOP	*Finished width* *+ 4 in (10 cm) for inside hems*	*Finished drop* *+ 2 in (5 cm) for base hem* *+ 10 in (25 cm) for attaching top of blind to the lath*	*Allow additional lining fabric for rod casings. Each casing measures 4¾ in (12 cm) long by the width of the blind*
PLEATED BLIND	*Finished width* *+ 4 in (10 cm) for side hems* *+ 4 in (10 cm) for returns* *+ amount for each pleat, for example, (8 in) 20 cm*	*Finished drop* *+ (2 in) 5 cm for bottom hem* *+ (10 in) 25 cm for attaching top of blind to the lath*	*Pleated Roman and Austrian blinds often look best with some fullness at the bottom; allow another 8 in (20 cm) on the drop*

Panel blind

Panel blinds are simple and unstructured, without rods. The rings are sewn in rows 4 in (10 cm) from each side edge. The bottom ring should be 2 in (5 cm) from the base, the highest 8 in (20 cm) from the top, and 6 in (15 cm) spaces between each ring.

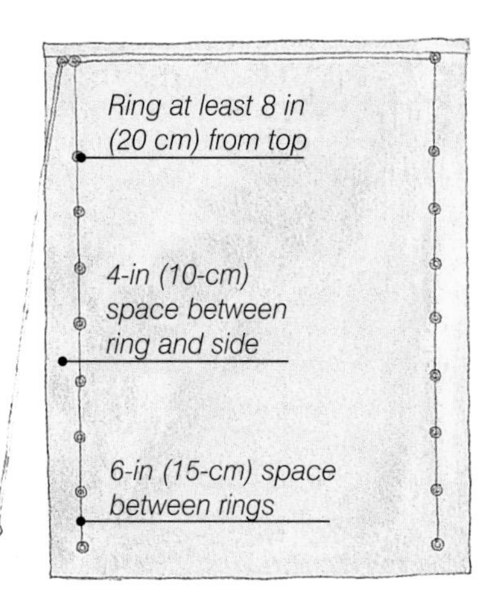

Inverted pleat blind

This blind is looser and fuller, with no rod. It has a row of rings up each side, 4 in (10 cm) from the edge, with the bottom one 2 in (5 cm) from the base, the highest one 18 in (45 cm) from the top, and intervals of 12 in (30 cm) between.

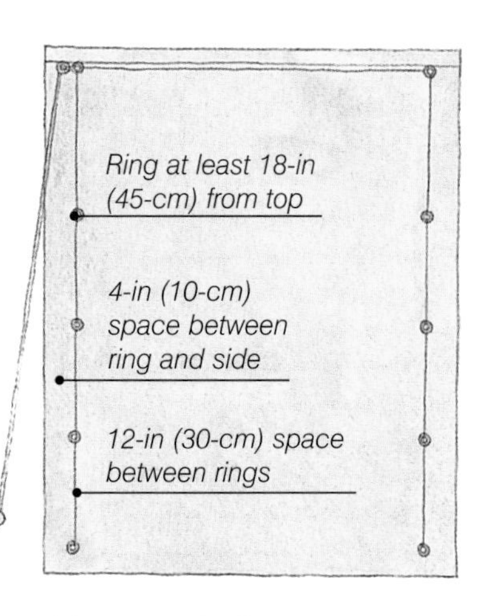

Panel blind with rod

This simple blind has one rod positioned about 6 in (15 cm) above the bottom to give it weight. Sew two rows of rings as for the panel blind (above), with the bottom one 6 in (15 cm) above the rod.

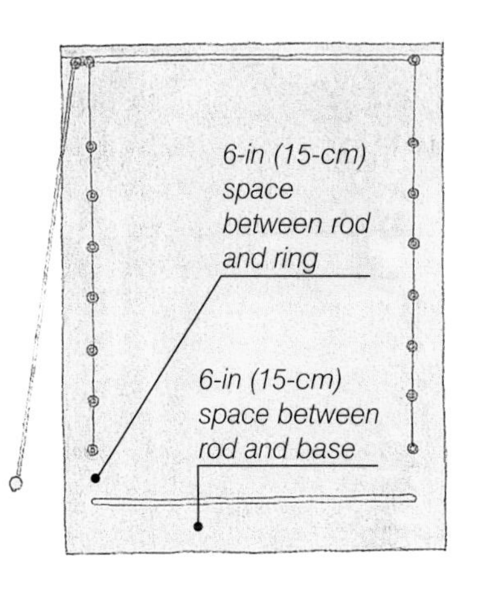

Austrian blind with several inverted pleats

The position and spacing of the rings on this heavily ruched blind is the same as the simpler version above, with the rows running up each inverted pleat as required.

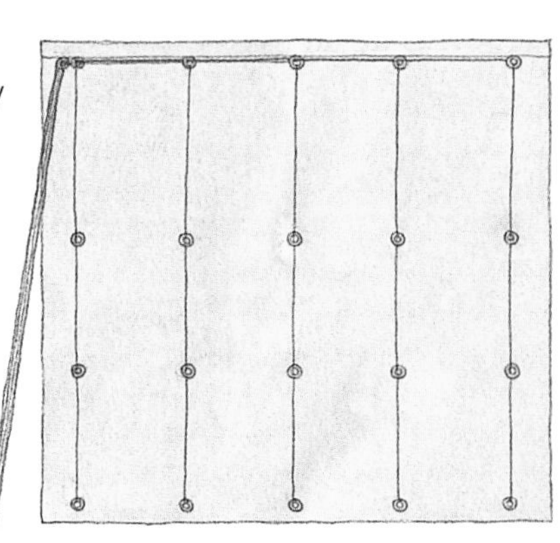

Roman blind with dowels

Dowel rods are inserted in casings that run across the back of the blind to create neat folds. The pockets are stitched into the lining and should be positioned 4 in (10 cm) above the base of the blind with the highest one at least 14 in (35 cm) below the top and intervals of 9 to 12 in (23 to 30 cm) between.

1 Stitch a small curtain ring to each casing all the way up the center. Then stitch a row 2 in (5 cm) from each side. Wide blinds may need additional rows.

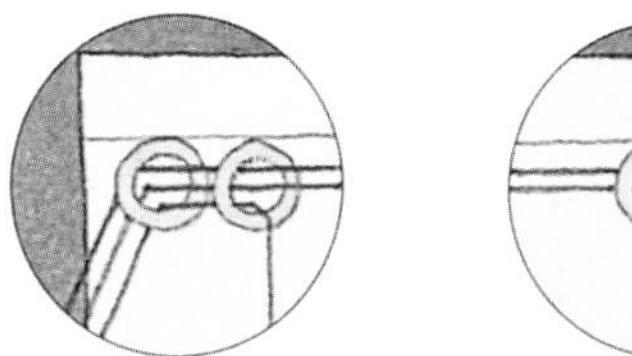

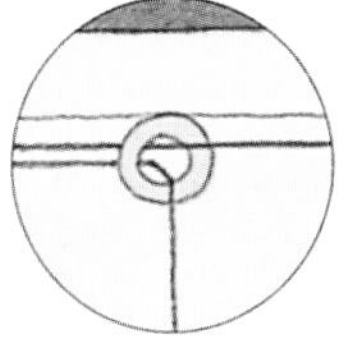

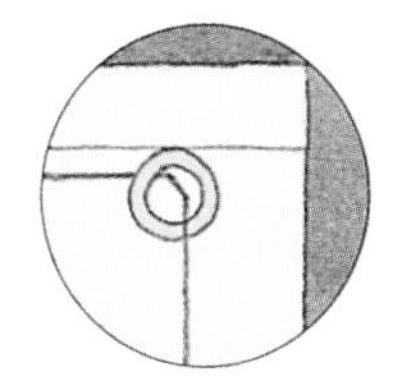

2 Screw an eye into the top lath of the blind in line with the rows of rings. Screw in an extra eye 1 in (2.5 cm) from the edge on the side to which the cords will be threaded.

3 Cut a cord for each row of rings measuring twice the depth of the blind plus its width. Tie a cord to each bottom ring and thread it through each ring in the row. Take it through the extra eye at the side after threading it through any eyes it passes on the way.

4 With the blind fully extended, take the cords through a weight. Trim them evenly and knot them securely. You may need to add a single cord below the weight.

Lath at top of blind

Screw eyes: one for each row of rings, plus one

Rings set 2 in (5 cm) in from blind edge

Dowel rod in rod casing

Cord running up through rings

Cords attached to brass drop weight

Cord knotted to lowest ring

CORDING A BLIND

Roman and Austrian blinds work through a system of cords threaded up the back of the blind. The same principle applies to all types, but the position of the rows of cording varies according to the style of the blind. Cords are secured in small rings anchored at the base of the blind and threaded through rows of rings to its top, where there is another set of stationary rings. The cords are then threaded across the top of the blind to one side and attached to a weight.

Tiebacks and holdbacks

Tiebacks and holdbacks are designed to hold a curtain back in a decorative shape when it has been drawn open. Holdbacks are hardware mounted to the wall or the window frame. Tiebacks are softer, generally made from complementary fabric or cording, and are slipped into a hook next to the window *(see also page 163).*

Making a basic tieback

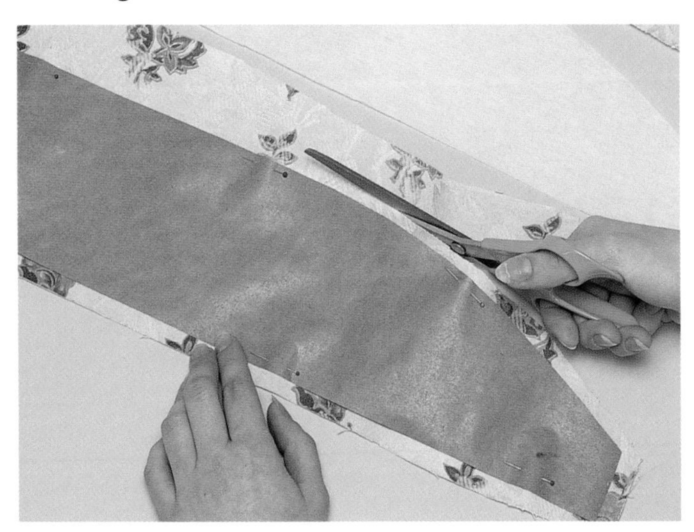

1 Loop a tape measure around the curtain to the wall-mounted hook to determine the length of the tieback. Make a paper pattern of the desired size and shape. For each tieback, cut an iron-on interfacing piece the same size as the pattern, and two larger pieces of fabric that have the seam allowances added.

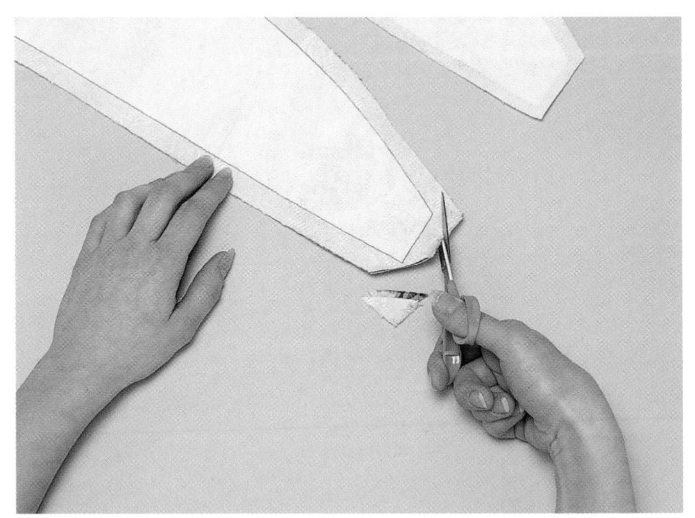

2 Iron the interfacing to the wrong side of one fabric piece. Stitch the fabric pieces with right sides together around all edges, using the interfacing as a stitching guide. Leave a gap for turning right side out and clip the corners.

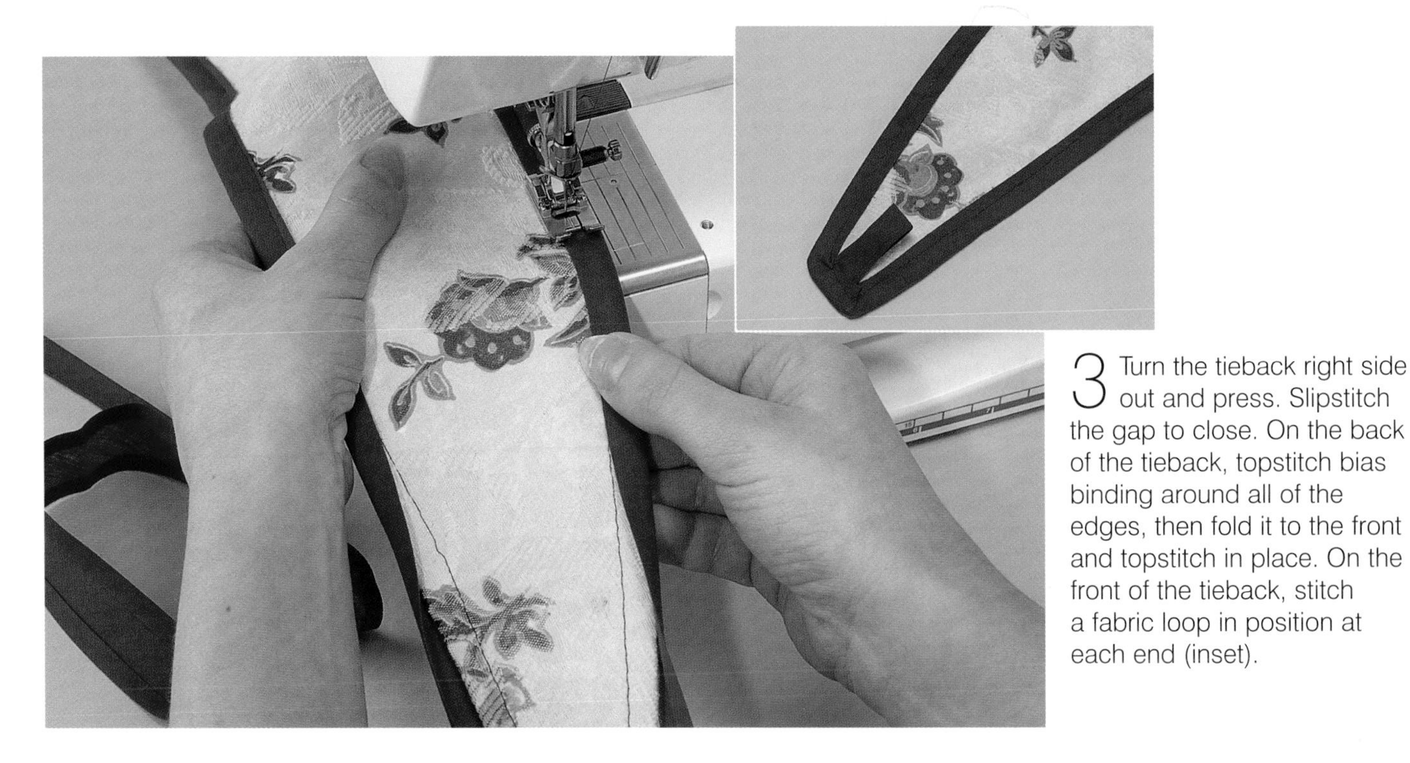

3 Turn the tieback right side out and press. Slipstitch the gap to close. On the back of the tieback, topstitch bias binding around all of the edges, then fold it to the front and topstitch in place. On the front of the tieback, stitch a fabric loop in position at each end (inset).

Tiebacks

Tiebacks can be made in all shapes and from many different materials, ranging from ribbon or braid to plaited cords. They can also be trimmed in a variety of ways.

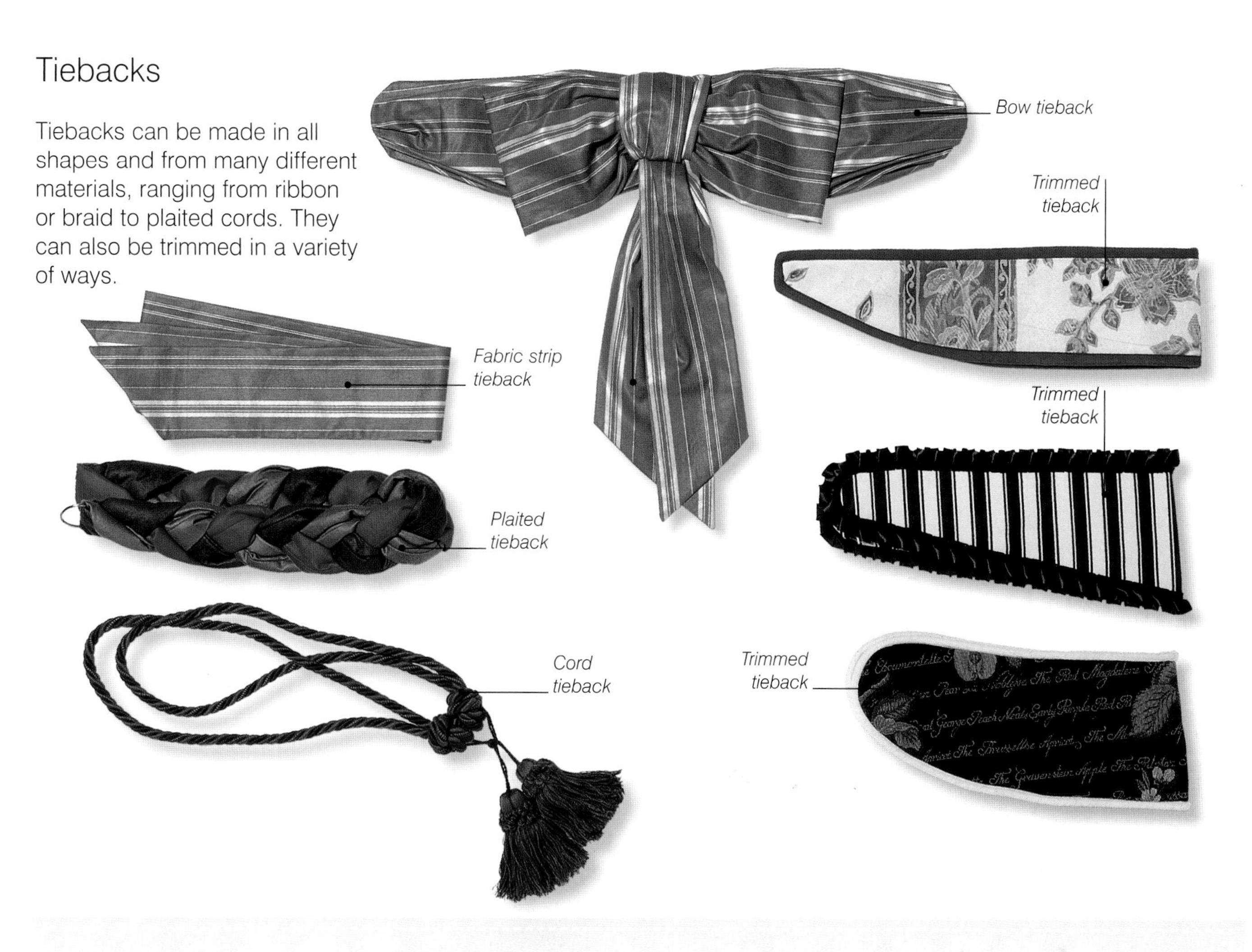

SHAPE VARIATIONS

Tiebacks are at their most effective when they reflect the style of the decor and of the curtains themselves, but with so many possible permutations, the choice can be overwhelming.

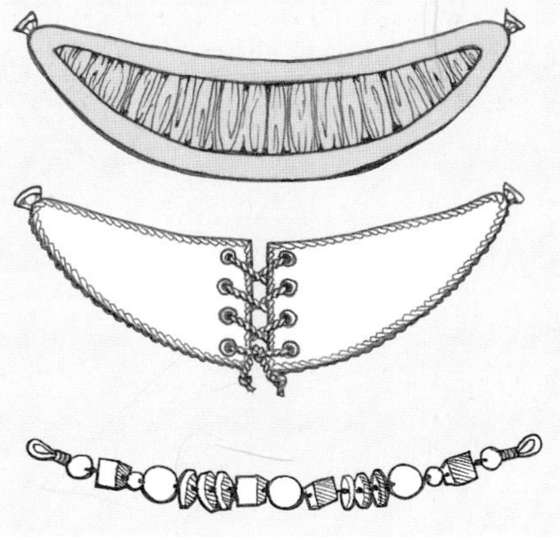

Most tiebacks are crescent shaped, but they can be flat or pleated, and trimmed with binding, braid, cording, or fringe. They can be gently curved or finish in a point. The edges can be scalloped or pointed, and can even be laced together like an old-fashioned girdle.

Cord, braid, and rope lend themselves well as tiebacks, perhaps strung with beads, or plaited or knotted.

Loops need to be added at each end of the tieback so they can be hooked over the holdbacks. Make sure that the ends are finished neatly and securely to withstand daily use.

Making padded plaits

Tubes of fabric can be padded with lining or interlining fabric, or with natural or synthetic stuffing material, and then plaited to make attractive decorative details for curtains. Padded plaits can be used on curtain headings, and tiebacks can be made from plaits, using cord, rope, or simply strips of fabric.

YOU WILL NEED

- *Three strips of fabric measuring 3½ in (9 cm) wide and the length of the finished tieback plus 10 in (25 cm). Cut two strips from main fabric and one from contrasting fabric*
- *Three pieces of string, each 6 in (15 cm) longer than the strips*
- *Three strips of padding fabric 5 in (13 cm) wide and the same length as the fabric strips*
- *Clamp*
- *Binding or cord for making loops, or metal rings*

1 Fold each strip lengthwise with right sides together. In the fold, lay a piece of string level with one end of the strip. Stitch across the end and along the long edge. Pull the loose end of string to turn the strip right side out, then cut the sewn end. Do NOT remove the string. Attach one end of string to each padding strip and tie the other end to a spoon. Pull the padding through the tube.

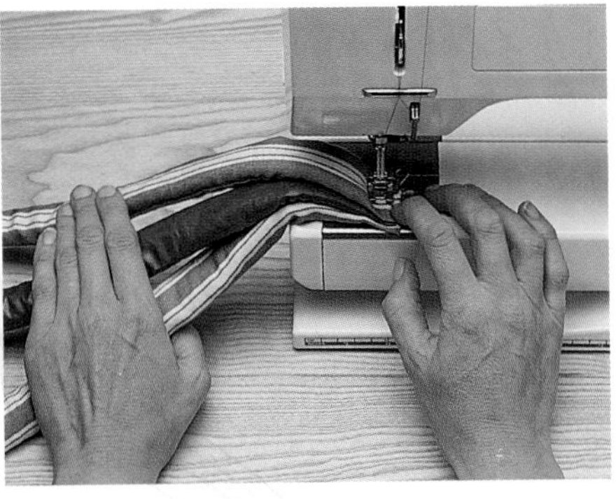

2 When the padding reaches the end of the tube, remove the string. Trim the padding ¾ in (2 cm) shorter than the tube. Stitch the three tubes together at one end. Place one on top of the other with the contrasting fabric in the center, and securely stitch across the tubes.

3 Clamp the stitched end of the tubes to the edge of a work surface and plait them together. Stitch across the unsewn end as in step 2 to secure the loose end and add loops or rings, finishing the ends neatly.

MAKING A PLAITED TIEBACK

The tubes of this tieback are filled with downy kapok to give a soft effect. The width of the strips will depend to some extent on the size of the curtains, but they need to be wider than the version opposite or it will not be possible to fill them with the kapok, which is very fine and tends to "float" away. Do not overfill the tubes—keep the stuffing even and soft. One end of each strip must be securely stitched before filling, and the other end closed tightly before plaiting. The tubes shown here were 8-in (20-cm) wide strips.

There should always be two strips of the main fabric, and only one of contrasting fabric, or the tieback will become the dominant feature of the curtains. The contrasting fabric here was also used as the curtain lining.

HOLDBACKS

Holdbacks are made from wood, metal, or plastic. They are secured to the wall or window frame next to the curtain.

Wooden holdbacks are often round in shape and generally work best in a traditional, even formal setting. Many of the designs available are made to match particular curtain poles.

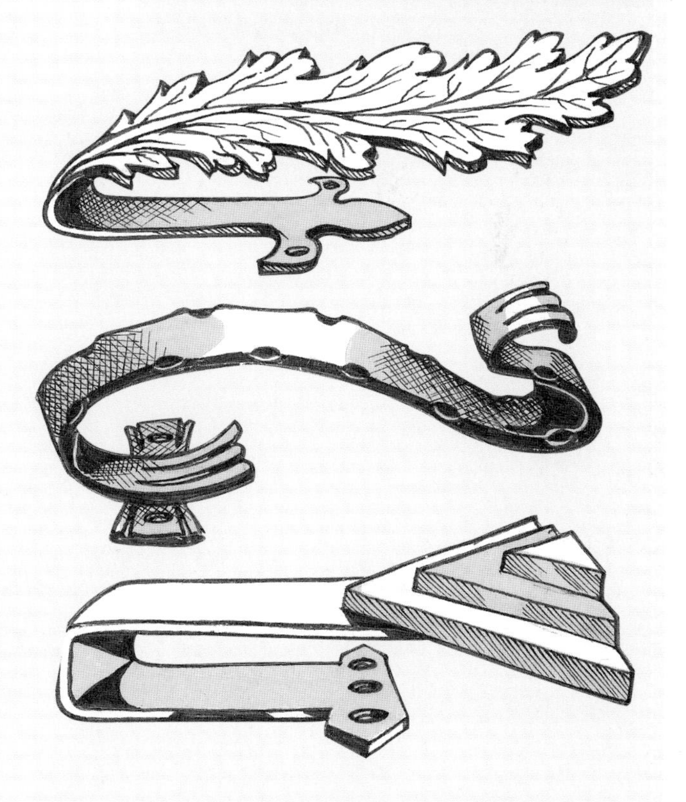

Metal holdbacks are traditionally made from brass or black wrought iron, and like their wooden counterparts, often match specific rods or poles. Other metal finishes, including chrome and steel, are also used. Wrought iron works well with country-style decor, and there are clean-lined holdbacks available to go with modern interiors.

Curtain headings

The heading of a curtain or blind is the edge that runs horizontally across the top. Curtains and Austrian blinds usually contain more fabric than the width of the window to give them fullness, while panel and Roman blinds are generally the same width as the window. Headings can be made by hand, or special heading tapes can be sewn to the wrong side of the curtain panels. These tapes range from simple gathered styles to highly formal designs such as pinch- and pencil-pleats. Some heavy woven tapes have several cords running through them at specific intervals that can be pulled up to the required width; others have pockets woven in, into which special hooks are inserted at regular intervals to make the pleats. All heading tapes have woven guidelines that mark the stitching lines, making it simple to keep the seams straight. The tape length must be as long as the full width of the curtain fabric, plus a generous allowance for turning under the ends.

Casing
This heading is the easiest to make and works best on blinds and lightweight curtains that do not need to be moved. It is especially good for sheers.

Goblet pleats
This formal heading is best on plain, heavy fabrics made into full-length draperies.

Gathered heading
This plain heading is made using a narrow tape and works on long or short curtains as well as Austrian blinds.

Box pleats
This neat, flat handmade heading is particularly suitable for use on lightweight fabrics that have some body.

Pencil pleats
These pleats are made using a wide tape that pulls up into straight folds.

Hand-sewn hooks
These hooks are sewn in individually along the top hem of the curtain to give a simple, flat look. They can be hidden behind the top, or visible, depending on the desired effect.

French pleats
This formal heading is often made by hand, but a triple-pleated tape can be used. These pleats are best for floor-length curtains.

Eyelets
Small holes, or eyelets, punched at regular intervals and bound with special metal rings can be made using a kit. They work well on informal curtains and can also be used on blinds.

HEADINGS AND HOOKS

Heading tapes are available in different sizes, weights, types, and colors. Ask a sales consultant for advice about the best type to use and how to calculate the correct amount when you go to a store to purchase the tape. Always make sure you have selected the right hooks for the type of tape you intend to use.

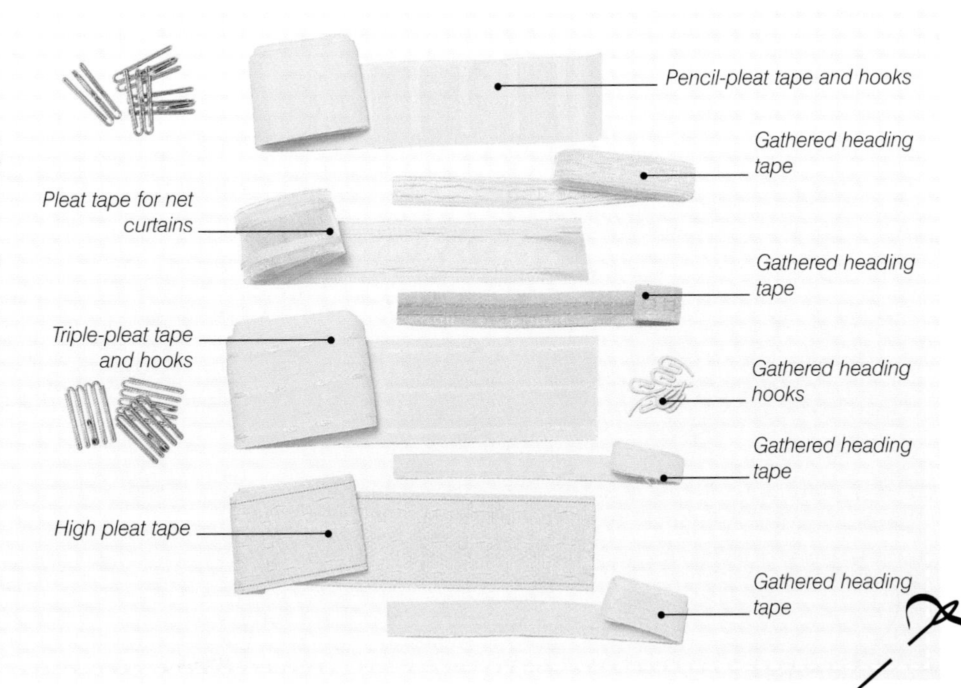

Making a casing

The simplest heading for curtains and blinds is a casing through which a rod or pole is slotted. Lightweight curtains can be gathered up along the rod for fullness. A "slot-headed" blind is a simple panel that lies flat over the window.

1 Turn, press, and pin a double fold along the top edge of the curtain that is twice as wide as the rod.

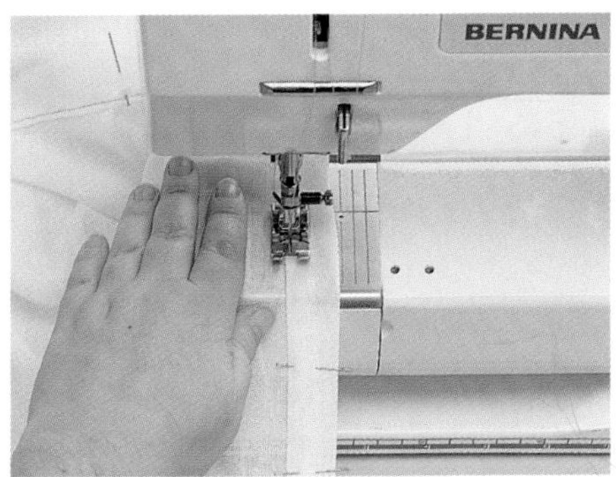

2 Stitch the casing along the inside edge of the bottom of the fold, removing the pins as you work.

MAKING A GATHERED HEADING

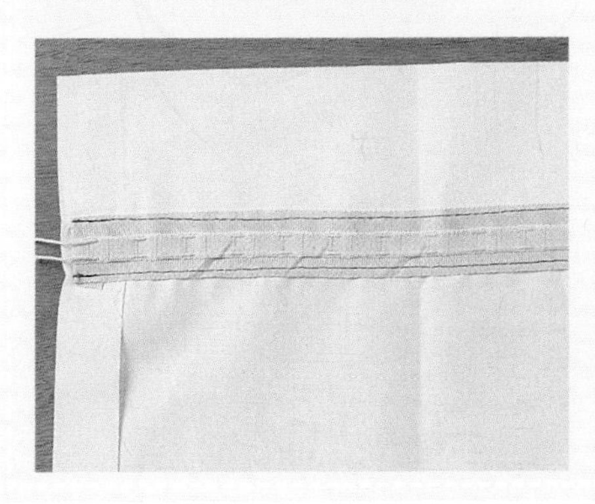

Position gathering tape at least 1 in (2.5 cm) from the top of the curtain or blind; here it is 2 in (5 cm) down. Finish the side edges of the curtain, then fold over the top edge and press the fold. Pin the tape over the raw edge of the curtain and stitch along the guidelines on both long edges. Knot the cords at one end of the tape. Pull up the cords to the required width, and knot, but do NOT cut, the ends.

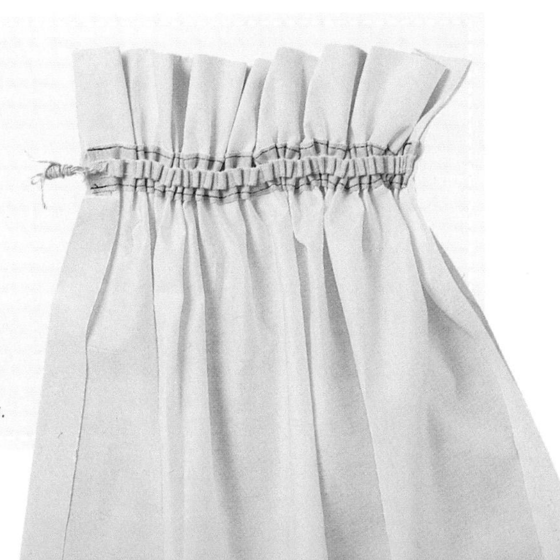

Making a pencil-pleat heading

Pencil pleats can be made using a heading tape, usually 3 in (7.5 cm) wide, that has pull-up cords to make thin, straight, even pleats on the right side of the curtain. They give a generous fullness and body, and hang beautifully.

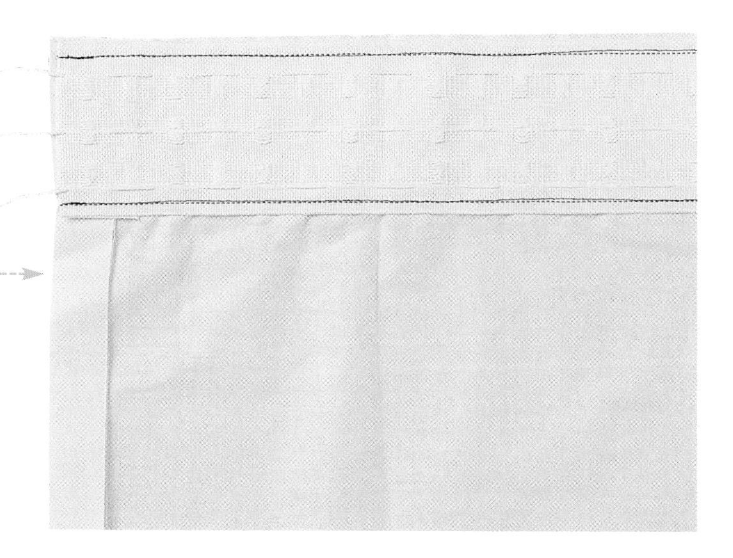

1 Turn a single hem measuring slightly less than the width of the tape at the top of the curtain. Align the heading tape with the top of the curtain, covering the raw edge of the fabric. Tuck the ends under, but pull the cords free first. Knot the cords at the leading edge of the curtain and stitch over them to secure them in place. Leave the cords at the outside edge free. Stitch the top and bottom edges of the heading tape to the curtain.

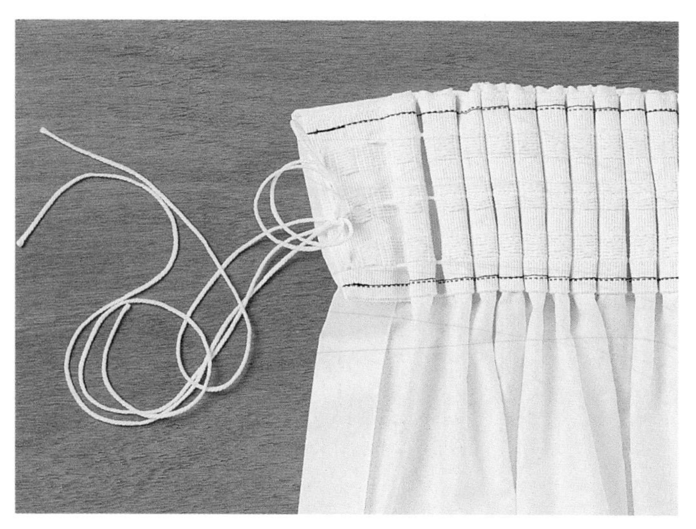

2 Pull on the loose cords to gather up the fabric, until the curtain reaches the finished width. Distribute the pleats and fullness evenly across the width of the curtain. Tie a knot in the cords to hold the gathers securely.

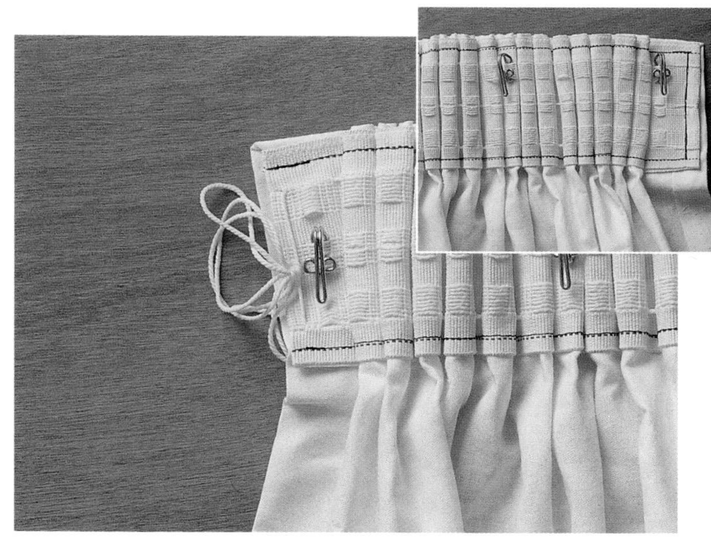

3 Place hooks in the slots in the tape. There is usually more than one possible position for the hooks, but the center row of slots tends to be the most commonly used. Use the bottom or top rows of the heading tape if you want to conceal or reveal more of the curtain support (inset). Put one hook at each end of the curtain, and space the others at intervals of about 3 in (7.5 cm) apart.

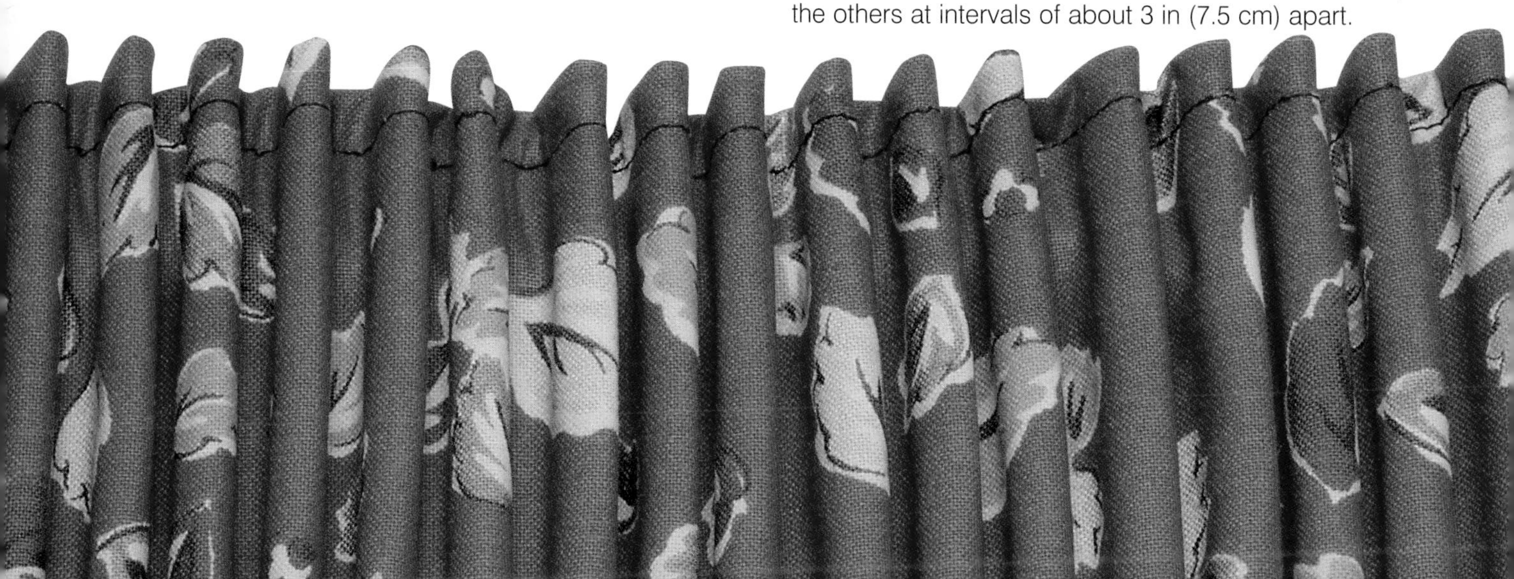

Making box pleats

Box pleats give an even, flat finish to the tops of curtains. They are set up by hand and do not need heading tape. Avoid choosing box pleats for heavy or bulky fabrics, because they cannot be pressed easily.

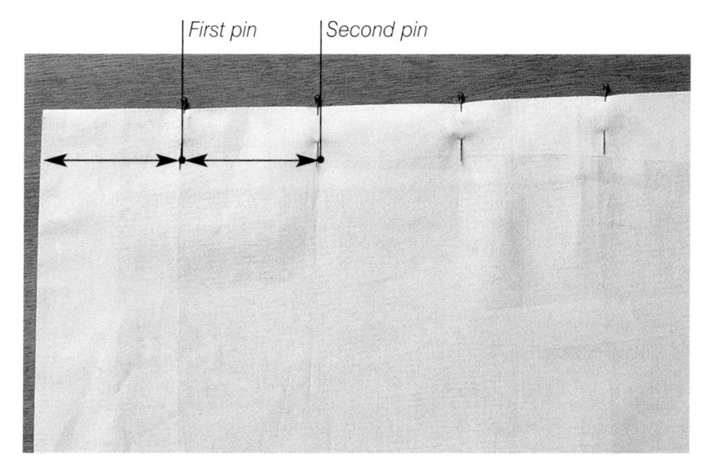

1 Measure the cut width of the curtain and mark equal spaces with pins along the top. The spacing should be generous enough to give fullness, but not too wide.

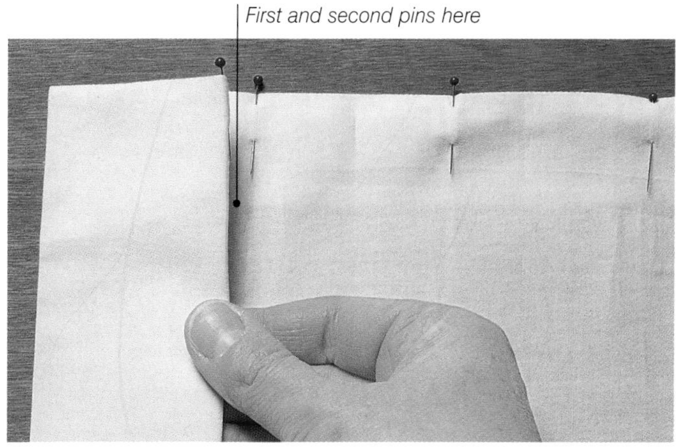

2 Take hold of the first marked pleat and fold it over to align with the point marked by the second pin.

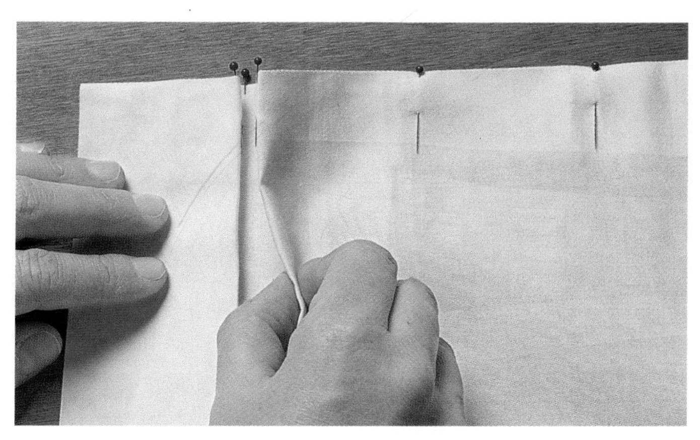

3 Fold the third pin back to meet the second pin as well. Pin both folds in place to make a pleat.

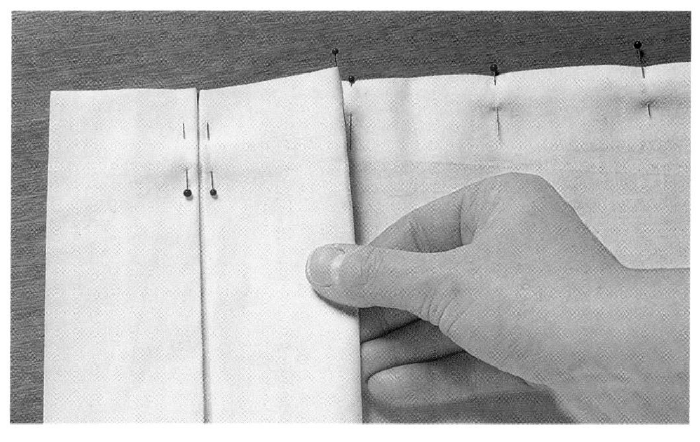

4 Fold the pleats marked by the fourth pin and the sixth pin to meet the fifth pin as before. Pin in place. Repeat across the width of the curtain to pin all the pleats in place.

5 Stitch across the top of the curtain about 1 in (2.5 cm) down to secure the pleats. Keep the folds straight as you stitch. Remove the pins and press the folds. Fold the raw edges of the curtain top to the back or bind them.

Making French pleats

French pleats, also known as pinch pleats, are made up of groups of pleats that are tied together at the bottom and produce a fan-shaped effect at the top. They are especially appropriate for floor-length curtains, and can be decorated with buttons or tassels if desired. It is possible to purchase heading tape that can be made into French pleats, but the hand-worked version is extremely attractive and the pleats are less likely to lose their shape.

1 Mark the top edge of the curtain on the cut and joined length. Fold along this line to the back side and press.

2 Open the fold and align a piece of fusible buckram 6 in (15 cm) longer than the width of the curtain along the marked pressed line as shown. Make sure the bottom edge of the buckram is on the marked line.

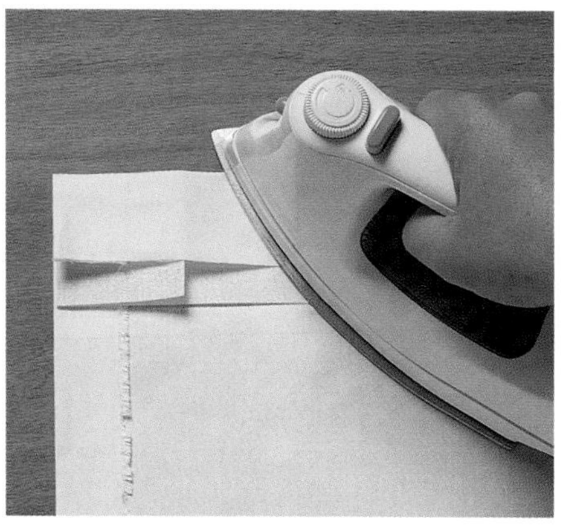

3 Fold in the extra buckram at each end and fold over the extra curtain fabric at the top. Press.

4 Fold the buckram strip so the pressed line is again at the top of the curtain and press again.

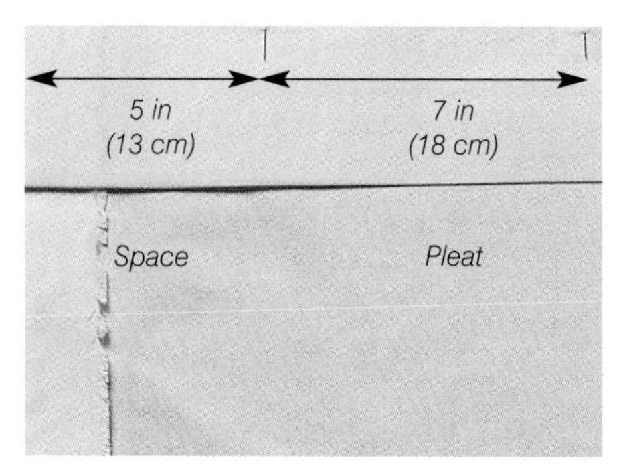

5 Measure the width of the finished curtain and calculate the spacing of the pleats. Using pins, mark the pleats on the wrong side of the curtain. Try to make the spaces slightly smaller than the pleat size. Our pleats are 7 in (18 cm) wide and the spaces are 5 in (13 cm).

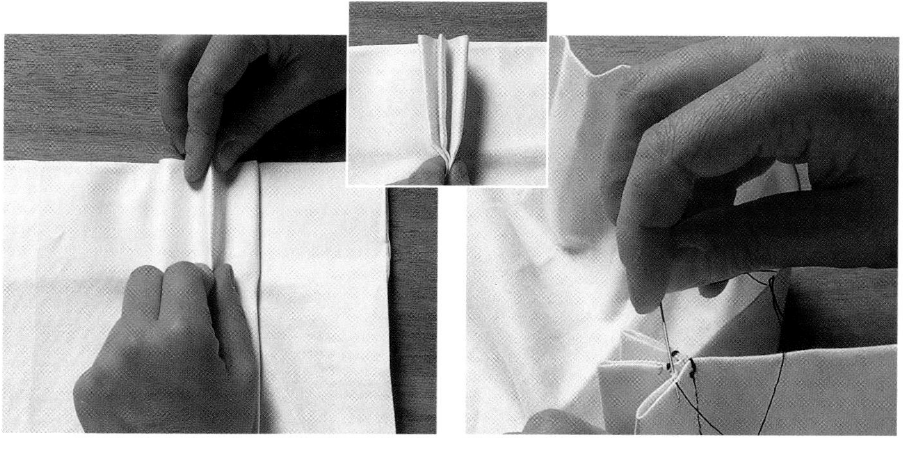

6 Working on the wrong side, fold so the first pin meets the second and pin the pleat along the width of the buckram to secure. Fold the third pin to the fourth and pin. Repeat. Stitch each pleat from the top of the curtain to the bottom of the buckram.

7 Working from the right side of the curtain, flatten each pleat with the center along the seam. Using your thumb and index finger, pinch the middle into a pleat. Pinch each side up to make three equal pleats (inset).

8 Hold the base of each triple pleat firmly in position with stab stitch. Pull the thread up tight and fasten each one securely. Secure the tops of the folds with slipstitch.

Making goblet pleats

Goblet pleats make a formal heading that is elegant but needs to be used in the right setting. Each pleat is padded to give it shape.

1 Follow steps 1 to 5 for making French pleats. Working on the right side, pinch the base of each pleat and secure with stab stitch.

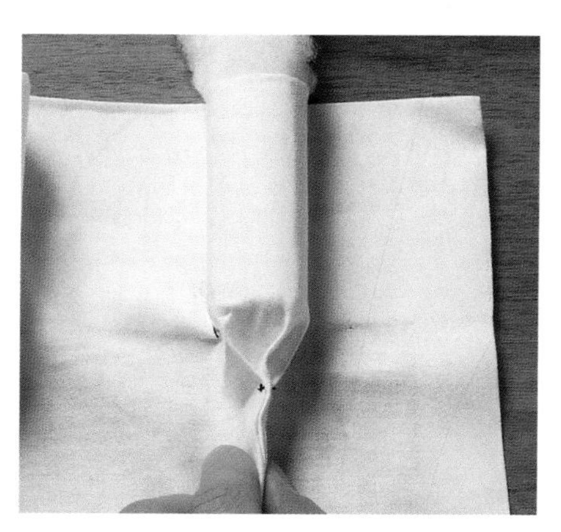

2 Pad each rounded pleat with a small roll of soft stuffing pushed down into the bottom of the pleat.

HAND-SEWING HOOKS

Hooks can be hand-sewn onto the back of a curtain along the top hem. No heading tape is used, and the method is particularly suitable for flat curtains like a café curtain. Depending on the desired effect, the tops of the hooks can be concealed behind the top of the curtain or be allowed to show.

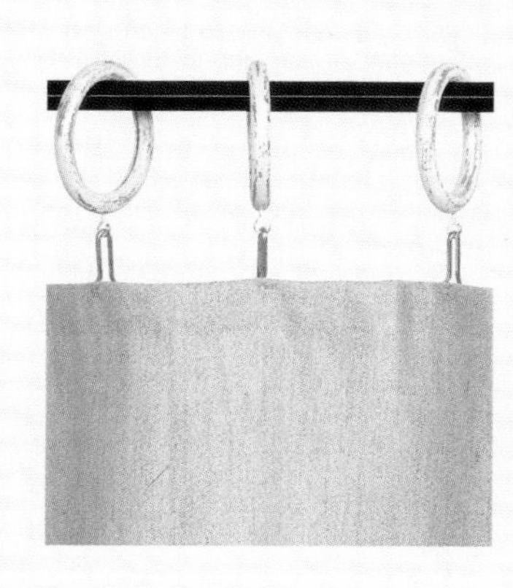

Calculate the spacing for the hooks along the top hemmed edge of the curtain. The spacing will depend on the finished width of the curtain, but should not be more than about 6 in (15 cm); otherwise, the curtain will droop in the spaces. Mark the position of each of the hooks and sew them in place.

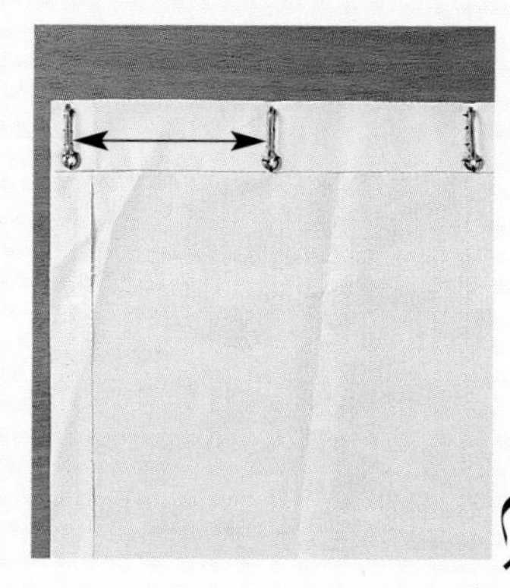

Choosing curtain supports

There are several elements to consider when you are choosing hardware on which curtains and blinds can be supported. The sheer variety of tracks, rods, and poles available can be confusing; and the style of the room, the size, length, and weight of the curtains, and your preferred method for opening and closing them must all be taken into account.

Curtain rods and poles are generally made from wood, metal, or plastic. Track that makes opening and closing curtains easier, especially in the types that have an integral pull cord, comes in metal and plastic in a variety of sizes and forms. Do some research into what options are available to help you decide, but it may also be helpful to have a specific fabric in mind before making your final choice of track or rod.

Ideally, the curtain hardware should be mounted in its final position before you take any measurements for calculating how much fabric you will need.

Rod, poles, and tracks

The curtain supports shown below are a small selection of of what is generally available. Included in this sample are tension-spring rods and spring wires, which are suitable for hanging sheers and very lightweight fabrics only. The rods work under their own tension and are set into the window recess without the need to be screwed in. The wires are attached to a screw-in hook and hold the tension unless they are pulled out of shape.

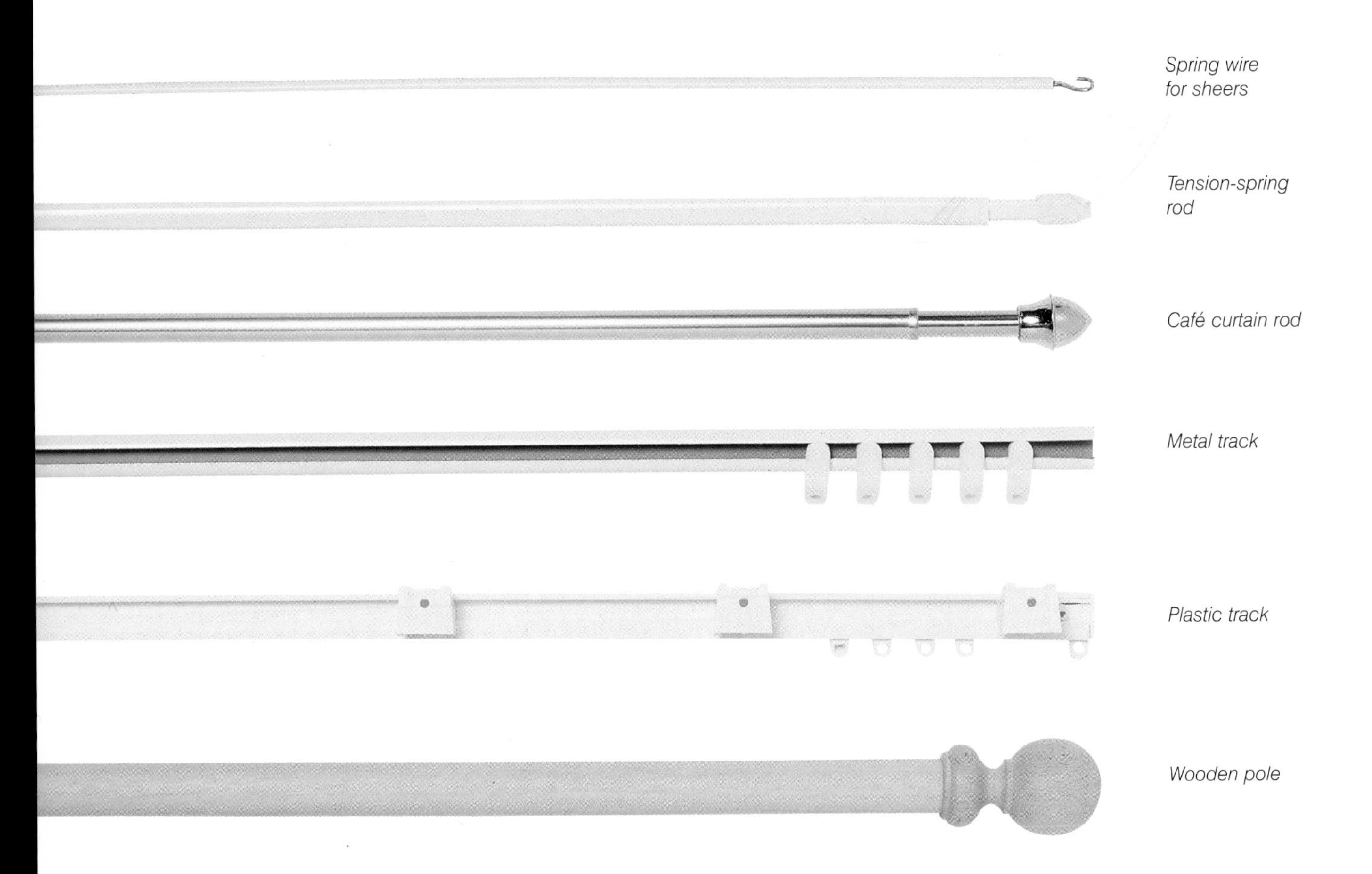

Spring wire for sheers

Tension-spring rod

Café curtain rod

Metal track

Plastic track

Wooden pole

Decorative poles

Poles are generally used for decorative effect, unlike tracks, which are hidden from view behind the curtain heading. The type of poles you choose is determined by the style of the room and by the curtains themselves.

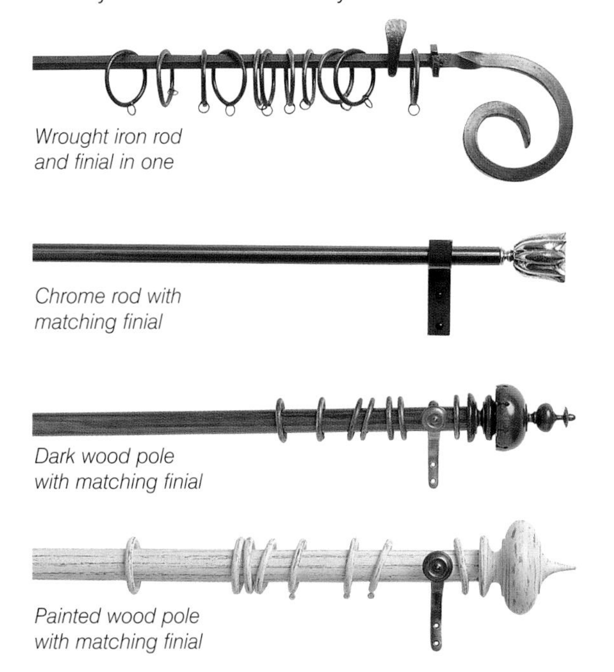

Wrought iron rod and finial in one

Chrome rod with matching finial

Dark wood pole with matching finial

Painted wood pole with matching finial

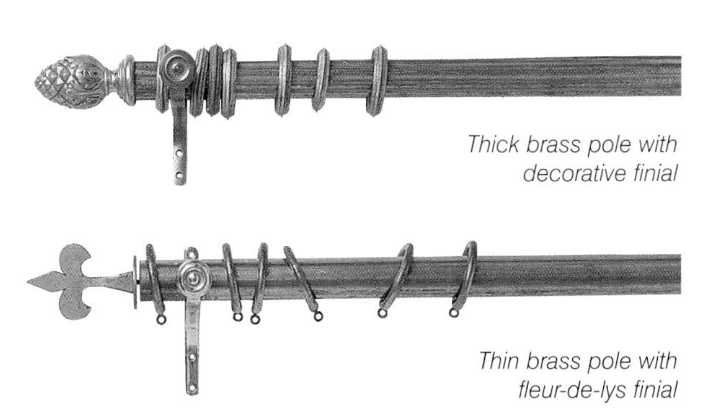

Thick brass pole with decorative finial

Thin brass pole with fleur-de-lys finial

Finials

Finials are the decorative knobs that attach to the ends of curtain poles to keep the curtains from falling off when drawn back. Some finials are an integral part of the pole, while others can be purchased separately.

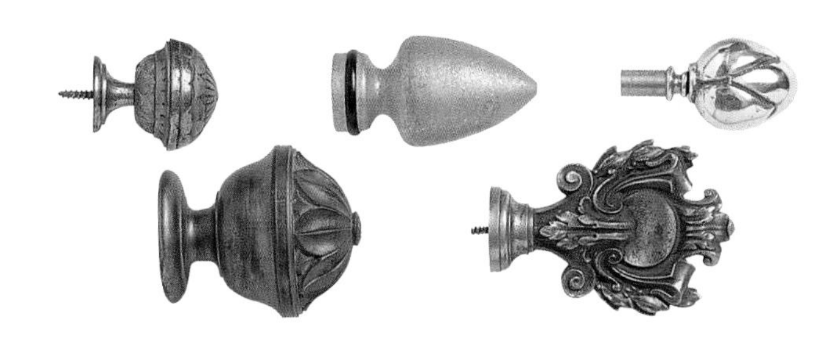

Rings and other attachments

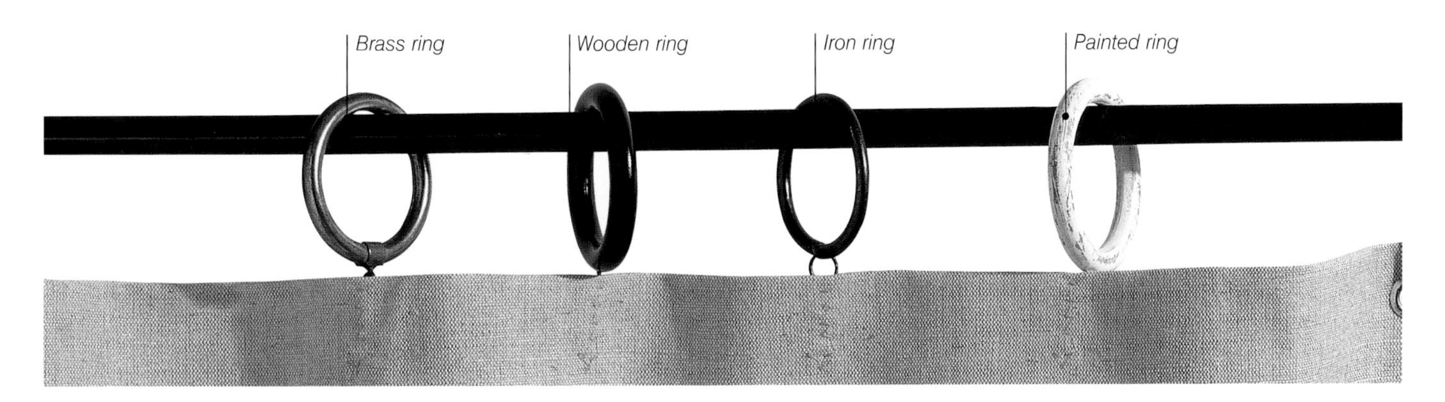

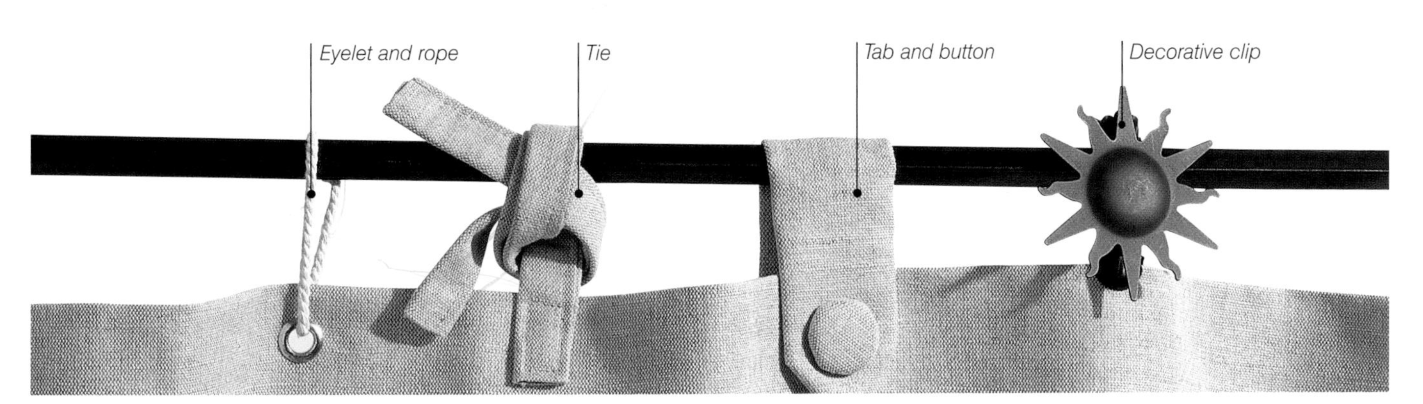

Project: Tab-headed curtain

Shaped tabs give this easy curtain a contemporary flavor. Both ends of the tabs could have been stitched into the seam, but it is fun to add the extra decorative touch of a button selected precisely to enhance the tabs. An alternative treatment is to stitch long thin ties into the seam, which can then be tied in bows over the pole.

These tab heads will always look organized and are guaranteed to behave well, yet they have a charming understated appearance. If you don't use interlining, it may be advisable to add a second dimension to the window treatment, in the form of a roll-up shade, for example. This will help insulate the room and protect the fabric from the sun.

MEASURING

LENGTH: from approximately ¾ in (2 cm) above the window down to 1½ in (4 cm) below the sill. The pole must sit well above the window so that at least 3 in (8 cm) of the tab can hang down below it on top of the curtain.
WIDTH: length of the pole

YOU WILL NEED

- *MAIN FABRIC LENGTH: finished drop plus seam allowance: 4½ in (12 cm) for the hem and ¾ in (2 cm) for the top*
- *MAIN FABRIC WIDTH: half 1½ or 2 times length of the pole plus 2 in (5 cm) at each end for seam allowances*
- *TAB STRIPS AND TOP FACING: see the instructions on the right. steps 1 and 2.*
- *LINING: 4 in (10 cm) shorter and narrower than the main fabric.*
- *Lead weights*
- *Buttons*
- *Tape measure*
- *Pins*
- *Thread*
- *Scissors*
- *Iron*
- *Cardboard for template*

Making the tabs

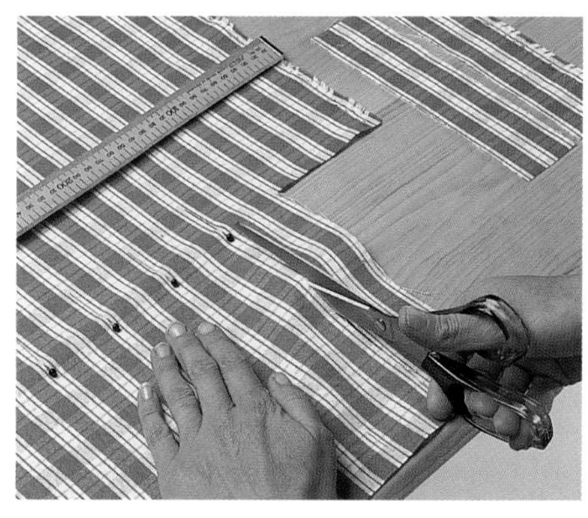

1 For each tab cut two pieces of fabric measuring 8½ × 2½ in (22 × 6 cm). Use sharp fabric scissors and cut along the straight grain.

2 Cut a simple template from cardboard. The template must be the finished size of the intended tab. Place the template in the exact center of a strip on the wrong side of the fabric and draw around it, leaving at least a 1-in (1.5-cm) seam allowance around the sides and point.

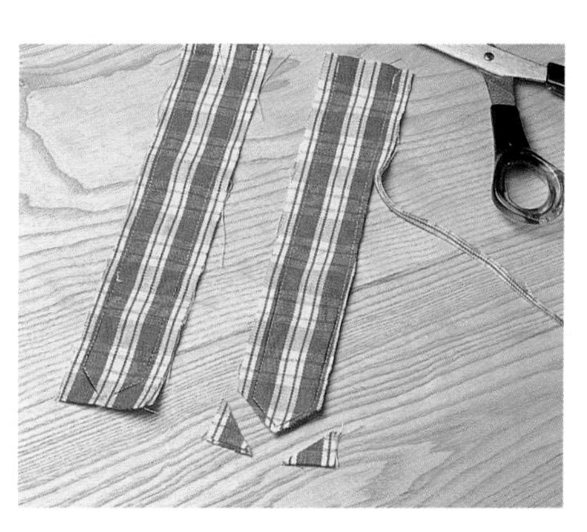

3 Machine stitch the tabs in pairs with right sides together following the template marking, leaving the flat end open. Trim around the tabs, leaving ¹⁄₁₆ in (2 mm) extra.

4 Turn the tabs right sides out (ease the corners by gently pushing each one with a pointed implement such as a knitting needle) and press flat.

step 5

Making the curtain

5 Clamp the main fabric to the edge of the work surface wrong side up. Turn back 2 in (5 cm) at each side seam and pin in place.

6 Turn up 4½ in (12 cm) at the hem, pin, make right-angled corners, and insert a lead weight (see pages 190–191). Slipstitch the hem.

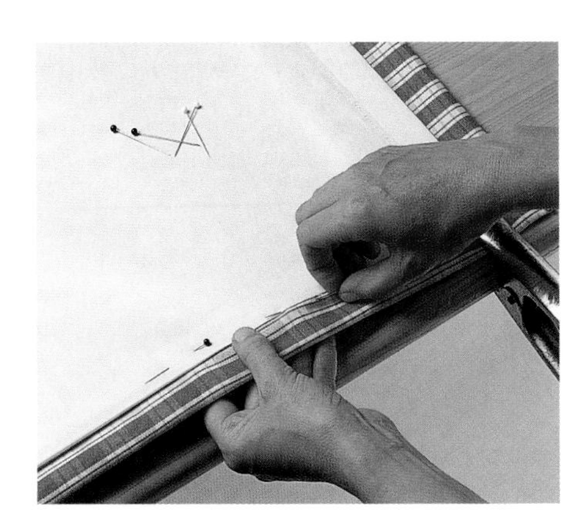

7 Prepare the lining as shown on page 193. Clamp it onto the main fabric wrong sides together, and turn the lining under by 1¼ in (3 cm) at each side. Pin and slipstitch.

Making the heading

8 Pin the tabs in place at the top end of the curtain. Make sure the gaps between the tabs are all equal and regular—here the gap is 1¾ in (4.5 cm). Cut the heading strip 3 in (8 cm) wide and 2¼ in (6 cm) longer than the stitched curtain width.

9 Turn up ⅝ in (1.5 cm) along one long edge. Place the curtain heading on the main curtain with right sides together, tabs in between, and 1¼ in (3 cm) at each end. Pin and baste, then machine stitch along the top edge, making a ⅝-in (1.5-cm) seam allowance.

10 Fold back the heading strip onto the curtain lining and fold in the extra fabric at each end to finish. Slipstitch the folded lower edge of the heading to the lining.

11 Bring the tabs over to the front of the curtain and sew the buttons in place through all the layers of fabric to make the loops.

USING GROSGRAIN RIBBON

Prepare the grosgrain ribbon by cutting 8½-in (22-cm) long strips. Then follow steps 5–10 above, but insert the ribbon folded in half lengthwise between the heading and the top edge of the curtain. Sew an easy-cover button below each ribbon to finish.

Project: Plain Roman blind

Roman blinds are suitable for most types and styles, except windows more than five feet (1.5 m) wide or inward-opening casements. They look neat and work particularly well where there is no room to hang curtains at the sides of a window. Choose a fabric with a simple design. Strong geometrics like stripes and checks work well, as do small-scale patterns that do not become a mess of shapes when the blind is up. Fabrics with some crispness and body work best.

WHAT YOU WILL NEED

- *MAIN FABRIC: finished width of blind plus 4 in (10 cm) for side hems, by finished drop of blind plus 2 in (5 cm) for hem and 10 in (25 cm) for attaching top to lath*
- *LINING FABRIC: as for main fabric*
- *Strip of lining fabric for each rod casing: 4¾ in (12 cm) wide by finished width of blind plus 1½ in (4 cm)*
- *DOWEL RODS: same number as rod casings*
- *1 x 2 in (2.5 x 5 cm) strip of wood, cut to finished width*
- *BRASS RINGS: same number as rod casings, times 3*
- *4 screw eyes*
- *CORD: 3 lengths cut twice the length of the blind plus the width*
- *Drop weight*

The quantities given here relate to a blind with three rows of rings, one on each side and one in the center.

Making the blind

1 Lay the main fabric right side down. Turn 2 in (5 cm) hems to the wrong side at the bottom and along each side. Press, making sure the corners are square.

2 Unfold the pressed hems and turn in each corner so the diagonal fold is at the point where the side and bottom creases intersect. Press the corners.

3 Turn the side and bottom hems again so the diagonal folds meet. Slipstitch the diagonal folds together. Repeat on the other corner.

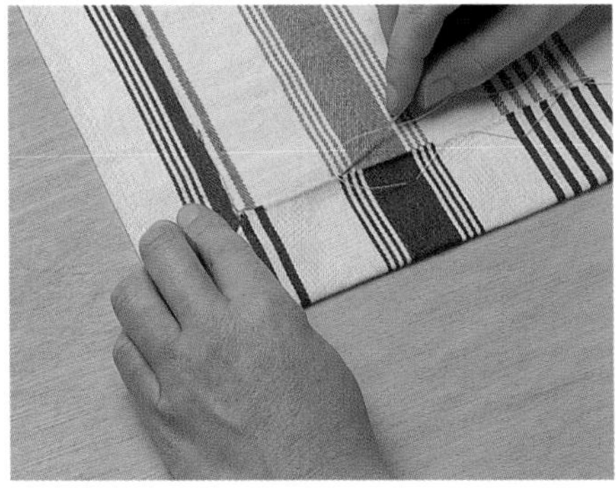

4 Herringbone stitch the raw edges of the side and bottom hems to secure them, keeping the stitches on the right side of the fabric tiny.

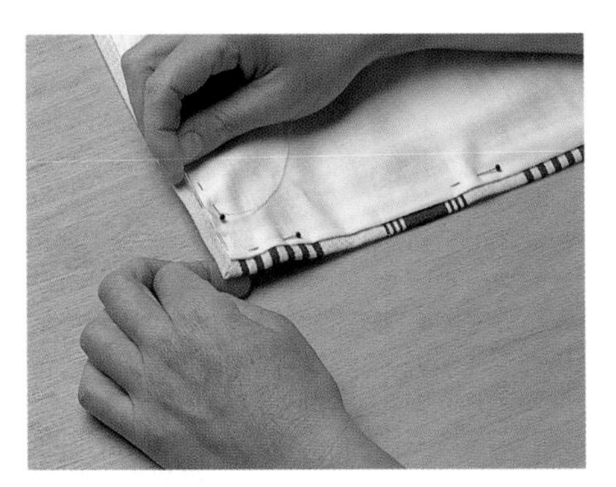

5 Press 2-in (5-cm) hems on the sides and bottom of the lining. Pin the lining to the main fabric with ⅜ in (1 cm) of main fabric showing outside. Slipstitch all three sides.

Making the rod casings

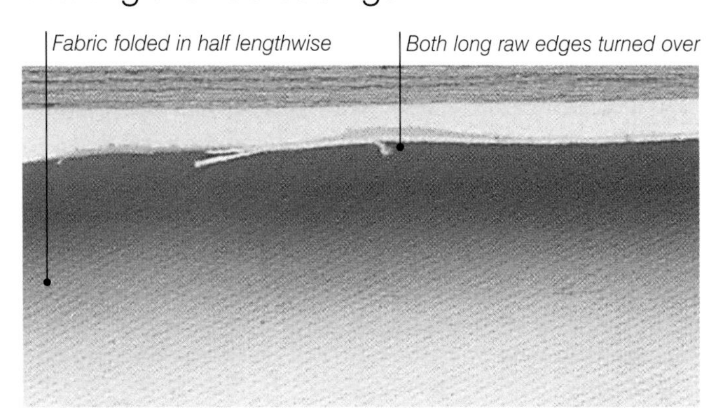

1 Fold each casing strip in half lengthwise with wrong sides together. Turn a ⅜-in (1-cm) hem along the raw edges and press the fabric.

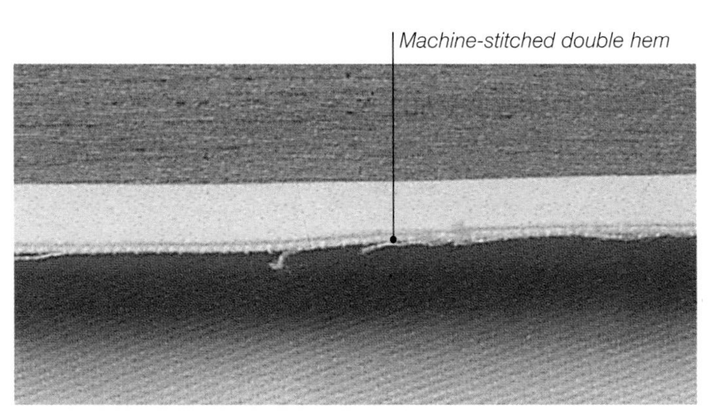

2 Turn the hem again to make a double hem containing both layers of raw edges. Press and stitch in place.

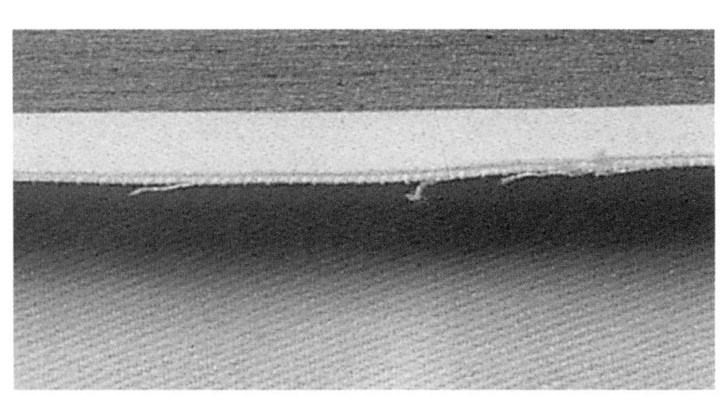

3 Fold over the raw edges at one end twice to make a ⅜-in (1-cm) double hem. Press and stitch this end in place. Make all the casings this way.

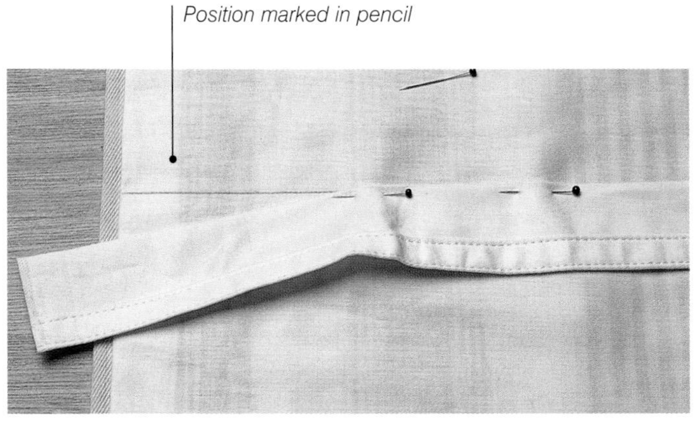

4 Use a pencil to mark the position of the rod casings lightly on the back of the blind. Pin each casing in place along its folded edge to align with the pencil marks.

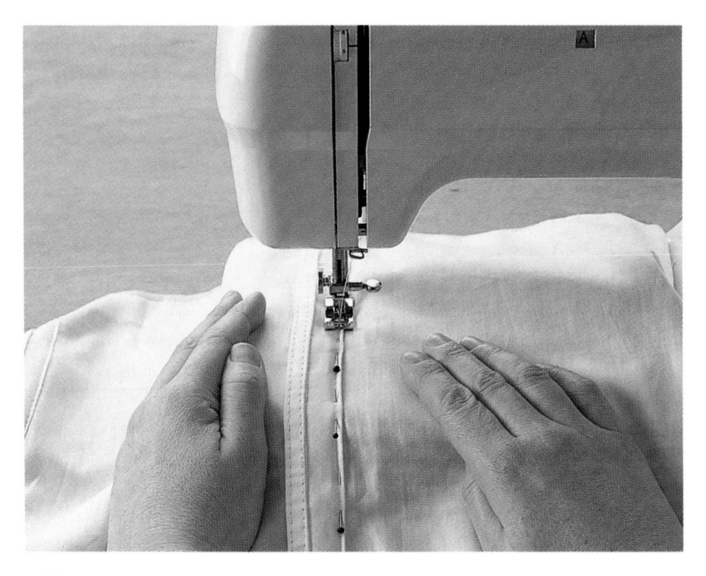

5 Stitch the casing through all the layers. Work as close to the fold as possible, removing pins as you go.

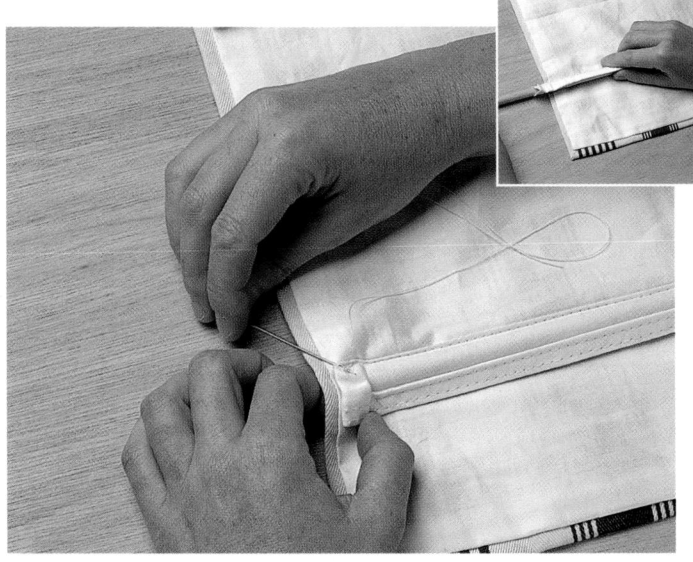

6 Insert a dowel rod in each casing of the blind (inset). Turn a double hem at the open end of each casing and slipstitch it securely to lock the dowel in.

Cording the blind

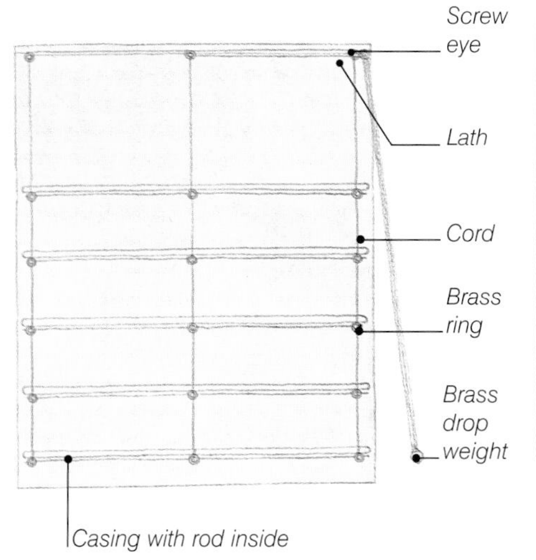

Cording the blind is a simple procedure, but one that is easy to get wrong. When you have finished cording, it is worth testing that the cording works before you hang the blind.

1 Sew a ring 1 in (2.5 cm) in from one side of the bottom casing, then repeat to sew a ring to each casing in line with it. Repeat to attach a row of rings along the other side of the blind, then add a row up the middle. Measure carefully before you attach each ring.

2 Staple the top raw edge of the blind to one side of the wooden lath and roll the top of the blind over to cover the wood. Mark the position of the rows of rings on the lath. Screw the eyes through the fabric into the wood at the top of each row. Add the fourth eye just in from the edge from which the cords will be hung.

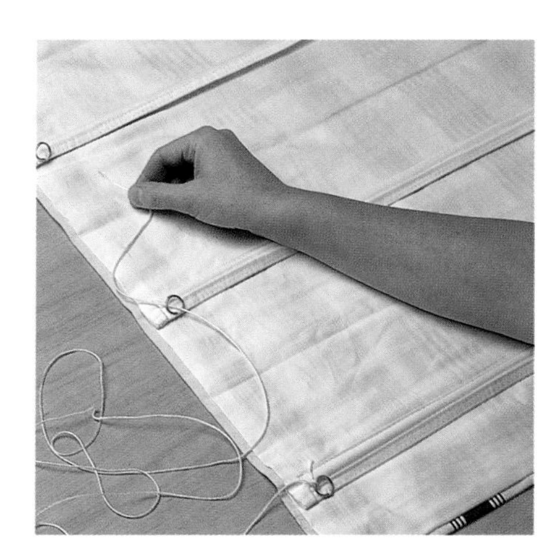

3 Lay the blind flat with the cords straight. Thread the loose end of the cords through the weight and knot them so the weight is level with the bottom of the blind. Trim the ends of the cord. The blind is ready to hang.

4 Tie one length of cord to the bottom ring on one side. Thread it up through the row of rings and the eye. Repeat to cord the other rows of rings. At the top, thread the lengths through the eyes toward the extra eye. Take them all through the extra eye. Do NOT cut them yet.

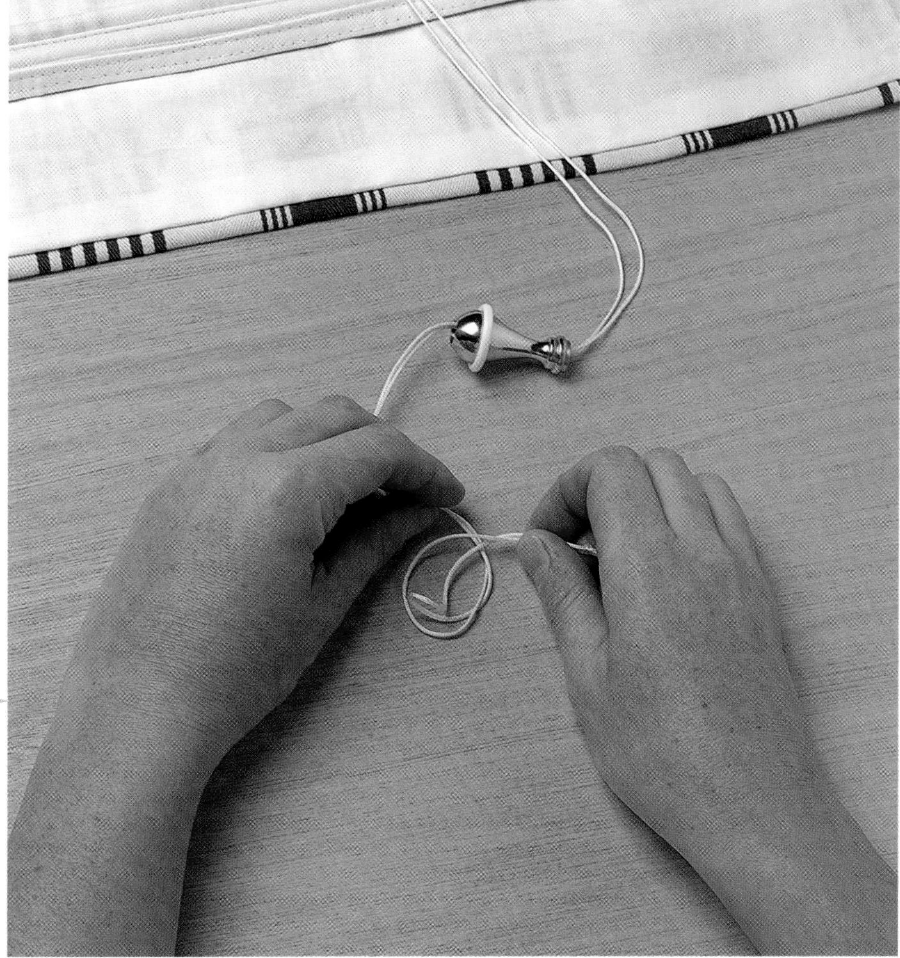

Sheets

Bed sheets can be relatively inexpensive to purchase, but if you want to coordinate your sheets and pillowcases with your color scheme, or have a bed that is not a standard size, you can make your own. Sheeting fabric in various colors and patterns can be purchased in extra-wide sizes and can be used to make pillowcases and duvet covers as well. Plain bed linen, whether purchased or specially made, can be decorated in a variety of ways to coordinate with your decor.

Flat sheet

Making a flat sheet couldn't be simpler, provided the edges are absolutely level along the straight grain of the fabric. Pin a double hem on all four sides. Baste the corners to secure them neatly and stitch all around.

Decorative bordered sheet

1 Measure the desired depth of the border at the top end of the sheet and clip both side edges to mark them. Turn under a double hem on both sides and along the bottom edge and pin. Stitch the hem.

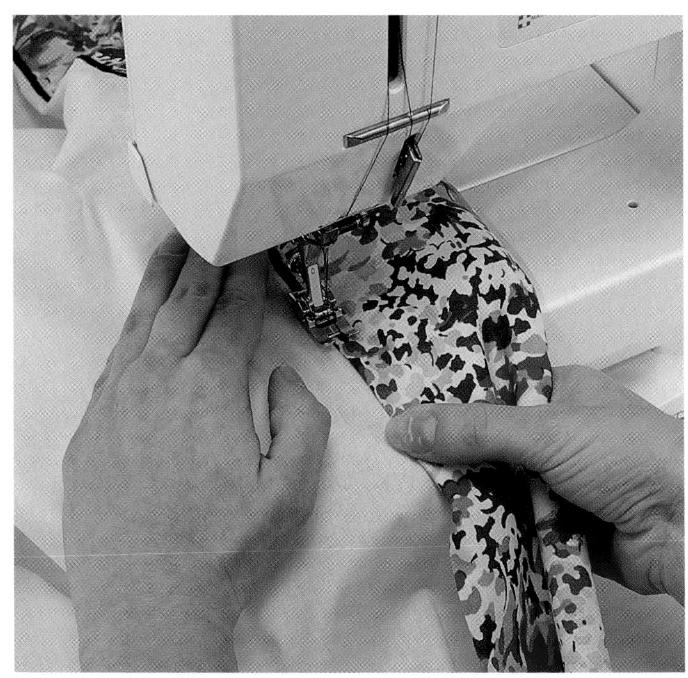

2 Cut the border fabric. The width of the strip is the desired depth of the border and the length is the width of the sheet, plus seam allowances and hems. If required, join strips to make the length. With right sides together, pin the border fabric to the top edge of the sheet and stitch. Make a ½-in (1.25-cm) seam allowance and stitch the side edges of the border level with the edge of the sheet. Turn the border to the wrong side of the sheet and press.

3 Turn under the raw edge at the bottom of the border strip. Pin it in place, then topstitch to secure. Here, a wide satin stitch is used to make a decorative finish.

4 When the bed is made, the border will be folded back onto the right side of the bed and can tie in with your other linen.

DECORATIVE BORDERS

Many different techniques and trimmings can be used to make decorative borders. Shown here are, from the top, a piped corner, which is especially suitable for tailored pillowcases; a piped edge that can then be turned back to make a deep border; a plain contrasting border with a wide lace trim; lace with a contrasting insertion; and eyelet lace (broderie anglaise) threaded with a contrasting ribbon.

Fitted sheet

1 Level all edges and fold each corner as shown. Pin the fold in position and mark a 90-degree angle from the edge of the sheet to the fold. The marked line should measure the depth of the mattress plus a 4-in (10-cm) allowance for underlap and seams.

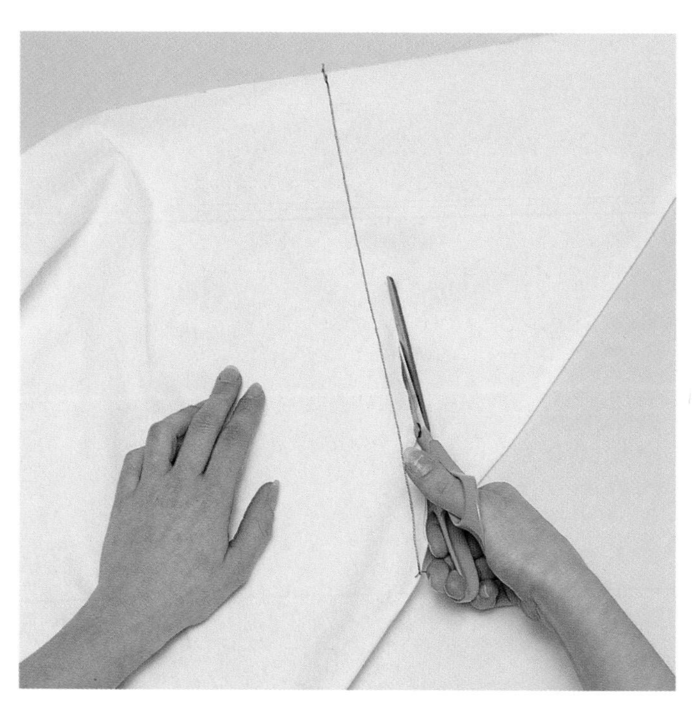

2 Stitch along the marked line at each corner and trim a ½-in (1.25-cm) seam allowance. Press the seam open and finish the edges. Cut a piece of ½-in (1.25-cm) wide elastic to twice the length plus twice the width of the mattress, minus 10 in (25 cm).

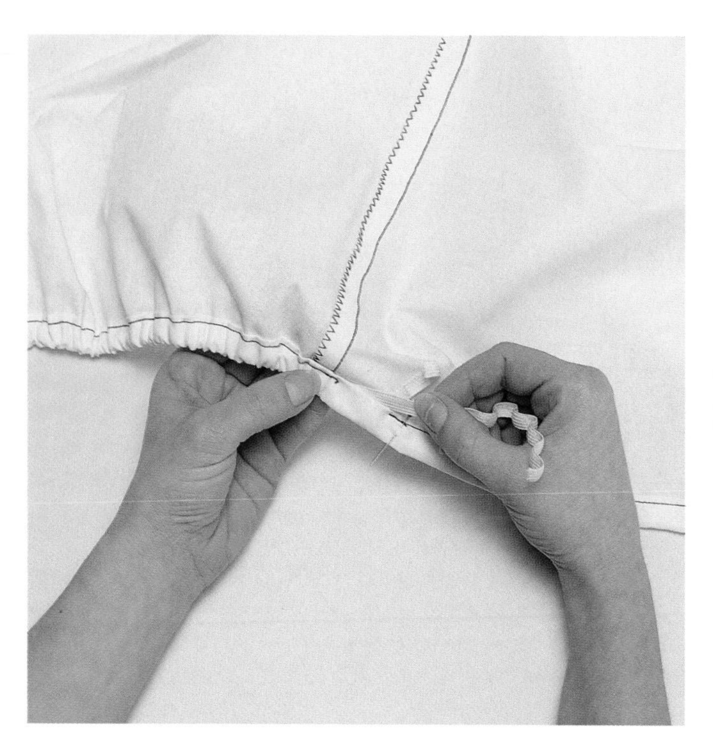

3 Turn up a casing around the bottom raw edge of the sheet wide enough to thread the elastic through. Pin and stitch all around, leaving a gap at one corner. Thread the elastic through and secure the ends by overlapping and stitching them together.

4 The corners should fit smoothly over the corners of the mattress. It is possible to make a fitted sheet using a purchased flat sheet if you first cut off all the hems evenly.

Pillowcases

Pillowcases are mainly used as protective coverings for pillows, but they can be decorative statements as well when displayed on top of the bedcovers. Most pillowcases are inexpensive to buy, but if you wish to match your decor, making your own is simple. Decorated pillowcases, trimmed with pretty lace, braid, ruffles, or piping, make good presents for a bride or a new homeowner.

Top-opening pillow slip

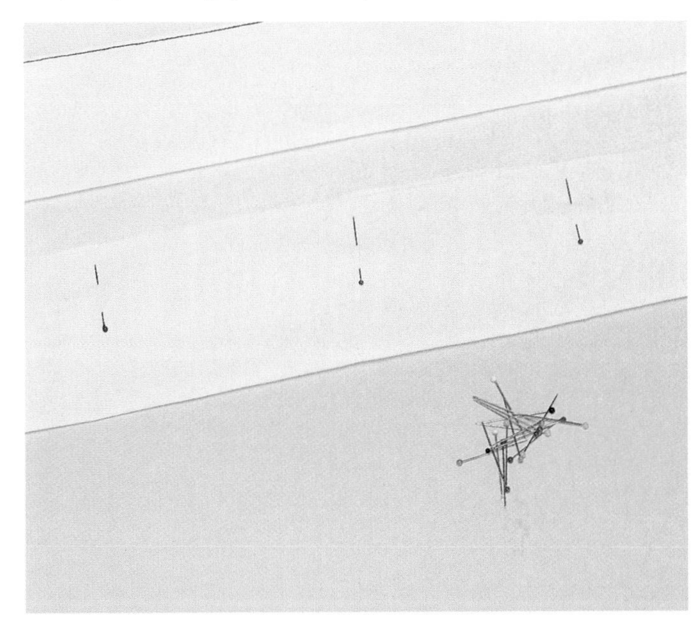

1 Measure, mark, and cut one piece of fabric measuring twice the length, plus hems, of the pillow by the width of the pillow plus seam allowances. Turn a deep hem at each short end, pin, and stitch.

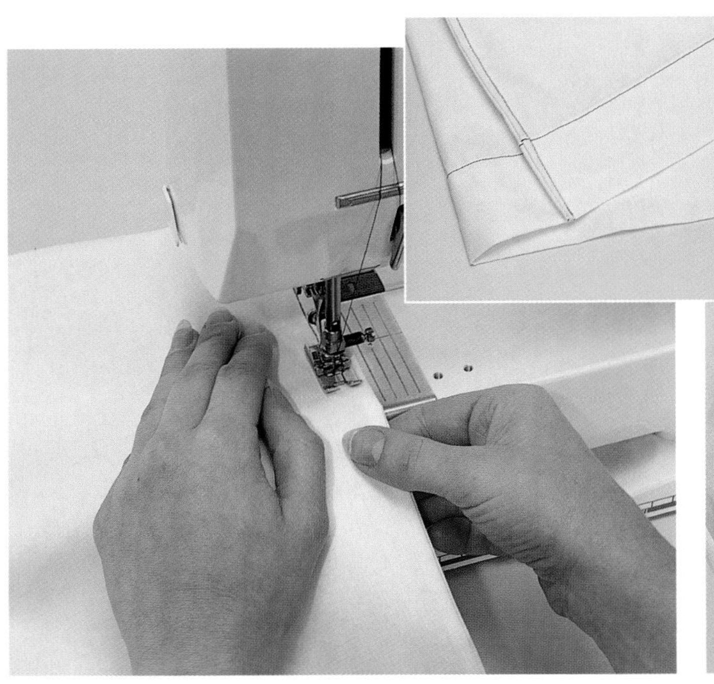

2 Fold in half, aligning the hemmed edges, and bring the long edges together. To make a sturdy French seam, as here, pin and stitch with the wrong sides together, then turn wrong side out and stitch the seam with the right sides of the pillowcase together.

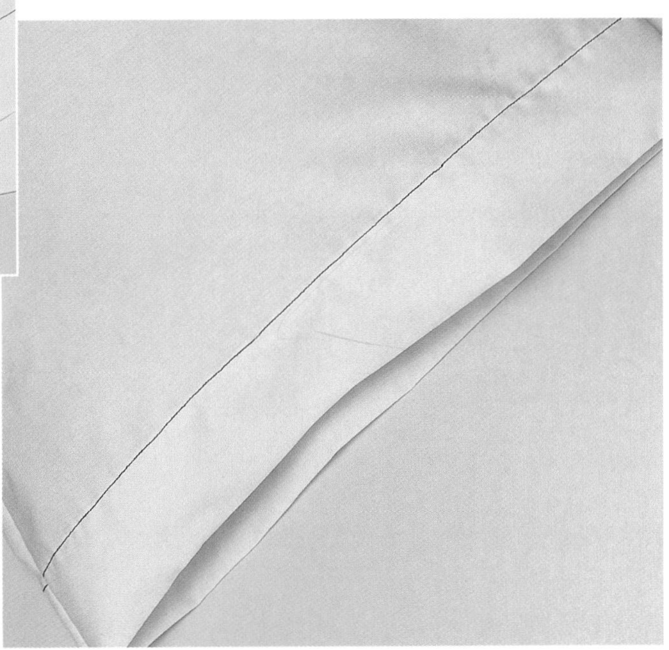

3 The pillow simply slides into the finished pillowcase, which makes an ideal subject for decoration.

Ruffled pillowcase

1 Measure, mark, and cut three pieces. The front piece measures the size of the pillow plus seam allowances. The two back pieces meet in the middle and overlap to hold the pillow in place. They should measure the same length as the front and about three-quarters of its width. Cut a ruffle to the desired width plus seam allowances, and twice the length of the four edges combined plus hem and seam allowance. Join strips together if necessary. Stitch the short ends together, with right sides facing, to make a ring. Make a narrow double hem in one long edge and run a double row of gathering along the other edge. Pull up the gathering and pin the ruffle to the front piece with right sides together.

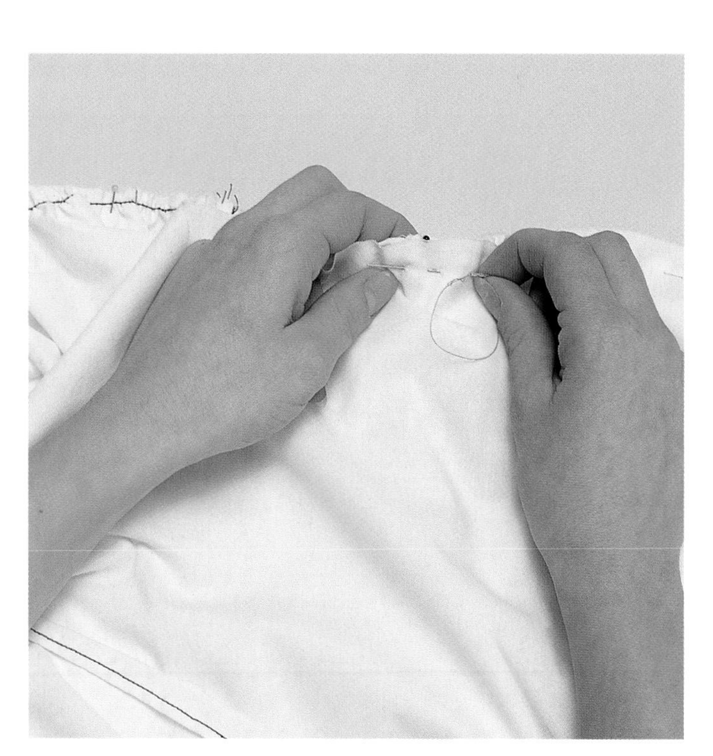

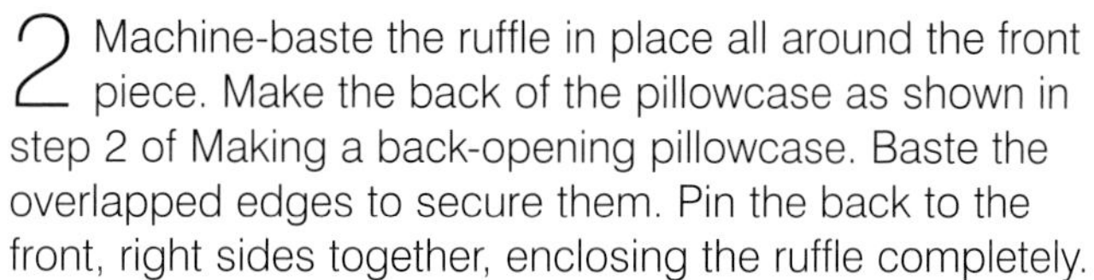

2 Machine-baste the ruffle in place all around the front piece. Make the back of the pillowcase as shown in step 2 of Making a back-opening pillowcase. Baste the overlapped edges to secure them. Pin the back to the front, right sides together, enclosing the ruffle completely.

3 Stitch around all four sides on top of the machine-basted seam. Remove the basting in the back opening, turn right side out, and insert the pillow. A tailored Oxford version (right) can be made by making the pillowcase without the ruffle and stitching a wide mitered border around all four sides.

Back-opening pillowcase

1 Measure, mark, and cut out three pieces of fabric for the front and back as described in step 1 of making a ruffled pillowcase.

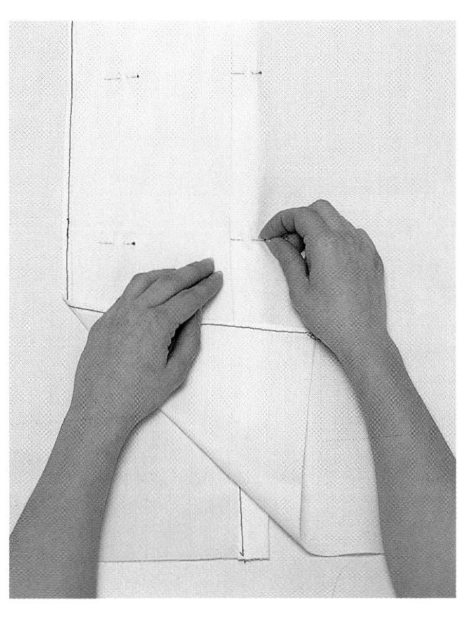

2 Turn under one long side of each back piece and make a (1½-in/ 4-cm) double hem in one end and a narrow double hem in the other. Place the narrow-hemmed piece right side up and lay the deep-hemmed piece right side up on top. Overlap the pieces to match the front and pin.

3 Pin the front piece to the back with right sides together and stitch around all four sides. Zigzag-stitch the seams and remove the pins. Turn the pillowcase right side out and insert the pillow.

"Housewife" pillowcase

1 Cut out one piece measuring twice the length of the pillow, plus hems and 3-in (7.5-cm) flap, and the width of the pillow plus seam allowances. Make a narrow and a deep hem on the short ends. Fold back the narrow hem, right sides together, for a flap.

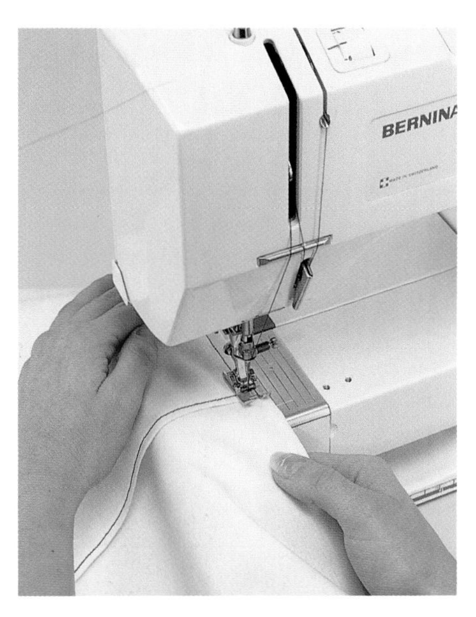

2 Fold in half, wrong sides together, with the deep-hemmed edge along the fold of the flap. Pin and stitch the long seams, then turn and make a French seam as in step 2 of making a top-opening pillowslip (see page 231).

3 The flap, seen here folded inside the pillowcase, holds the pillow securely in place.

Duvet cover and duvet

Duvets, or comforters, and their covers can be expensive to buy, but they are both straightforward enough to make at home. The covers can be reversible or made using a different fabric on each side, and decorated with appliqué or embroidery. For fastenings, the most popular choices are fastener tape or popper snaps, but more elaborate, decorative items are available if you prefer your fastenings to be displayed rather than hidden away.

Duvet cover

1 Cut out two pieces of fabric the length and width of the duvet plus seam allowances and hems. Turn under, pin, and stitch a deep hem at one short end of each piece.

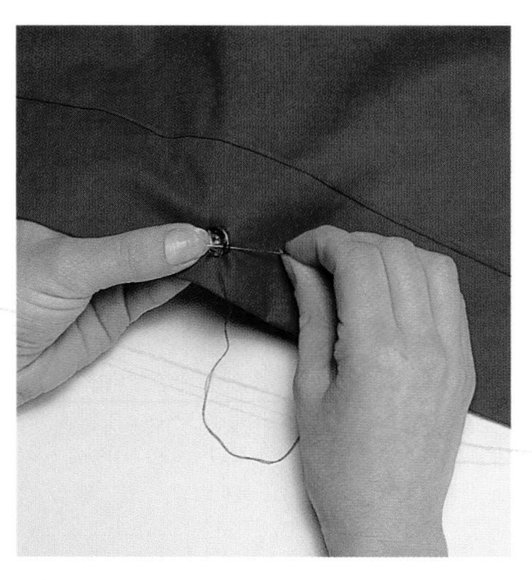

2 Attach half of each snap fastener along one of the hemmed edges, spacing them equal distances apart.

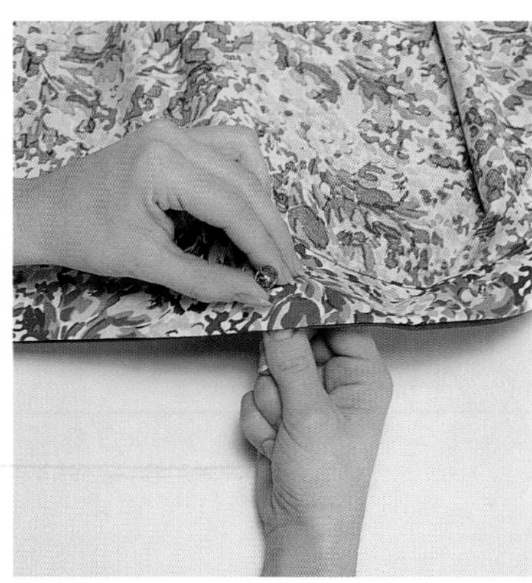

3 Sew the other half of each fastener to the second hemmed edge, carefully matching each pair to make sure they align properly.

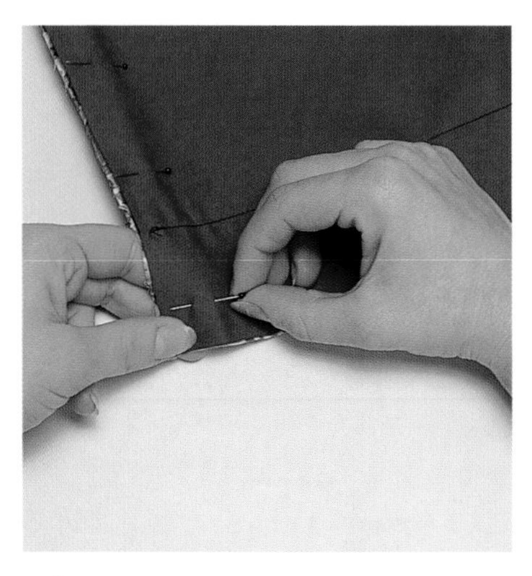

4 Join the fasteners along the edge and with the wrong sides together, pin the three remaining sides of the cover together.

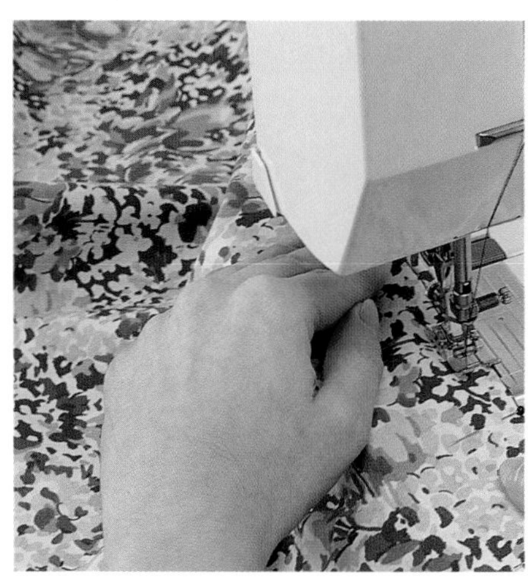

5 Stitch all around the three pinned sides of the cover using a French seam (see page 233) for strength and neatness.

6 The finished cover can be removed easily for laundering.

Making a duvet

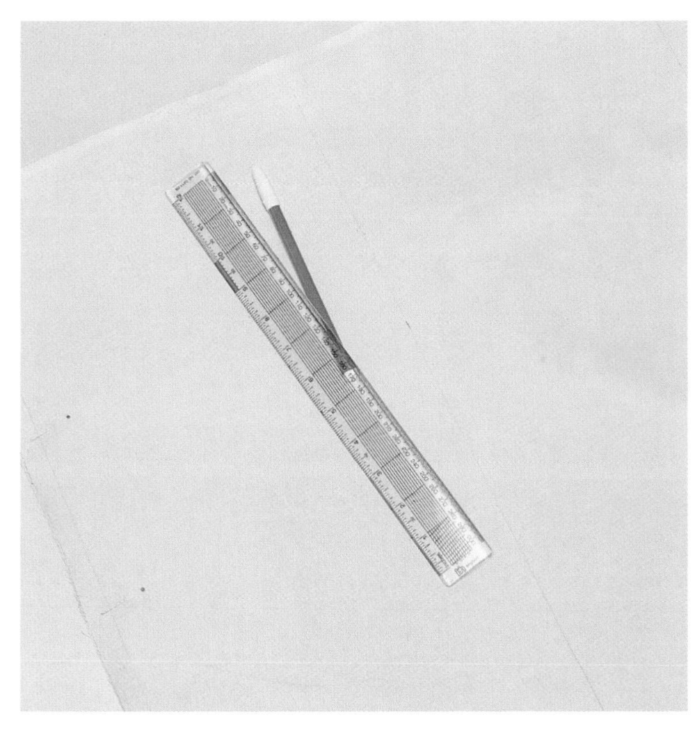

1 Measure and cut out two pieces of sturdy cotton fabric such as heavy-duty muslin (calico) to the desired size of the duvet plus seam allowances. Mark equally spaced stitching lines on the right side of one piece for the channels.

2 Pin and stitch the pieces, with right sides together, around three sides, leaving one short end open. Turn the duvet right side out through the opening. Pin and stitch the marked channels, leaving 1 in (2.5 cm) at the top of each seam at the unstitched end.

3 Fill each channel with a suitable stuffing. To stuff large duvets more easily, hang the open end of the duvet on a clothesline. Fold the open edges to the inside and pin. Topstitch the edge to close the channels.

DUVET FASTENINGS

Buttons, zippers, or the ties and touch-and-close squares shown here can be used to make duvet covers easy to remove for laundering.

Throws and bedspreads

Beds are natural focal points, such that a bedcover or throw can set the tone for the entire room. Plain hemmed bedspreads are simple to make, while fitted and embellished spreads tend to be a little more complicated, but they are well worth the effort.

Curved throw

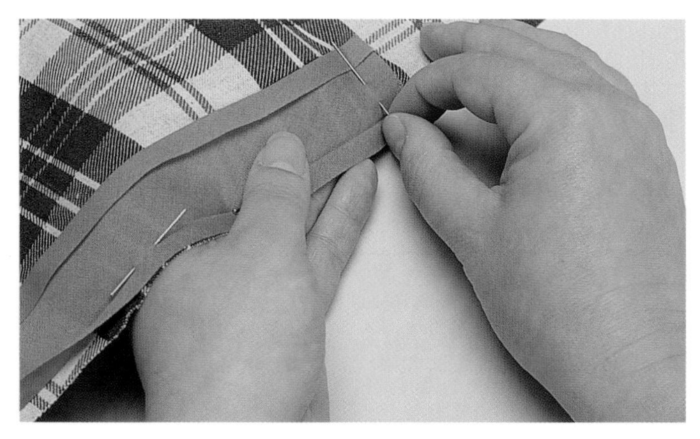

1 Cut the fabric to the desired size and round the corners. Pin bias binding along the right-side edge, joining lengths as necessary by folding the ends under and placing them next to each other.

2 Keep the binding slack as you pin around the corner curves. Stitch the binding along the entire edge. Fold the binding to the wrong side to cover the raw edge.

3 Pin the binding to the edge along the stitched line, then stitch the binding in position.

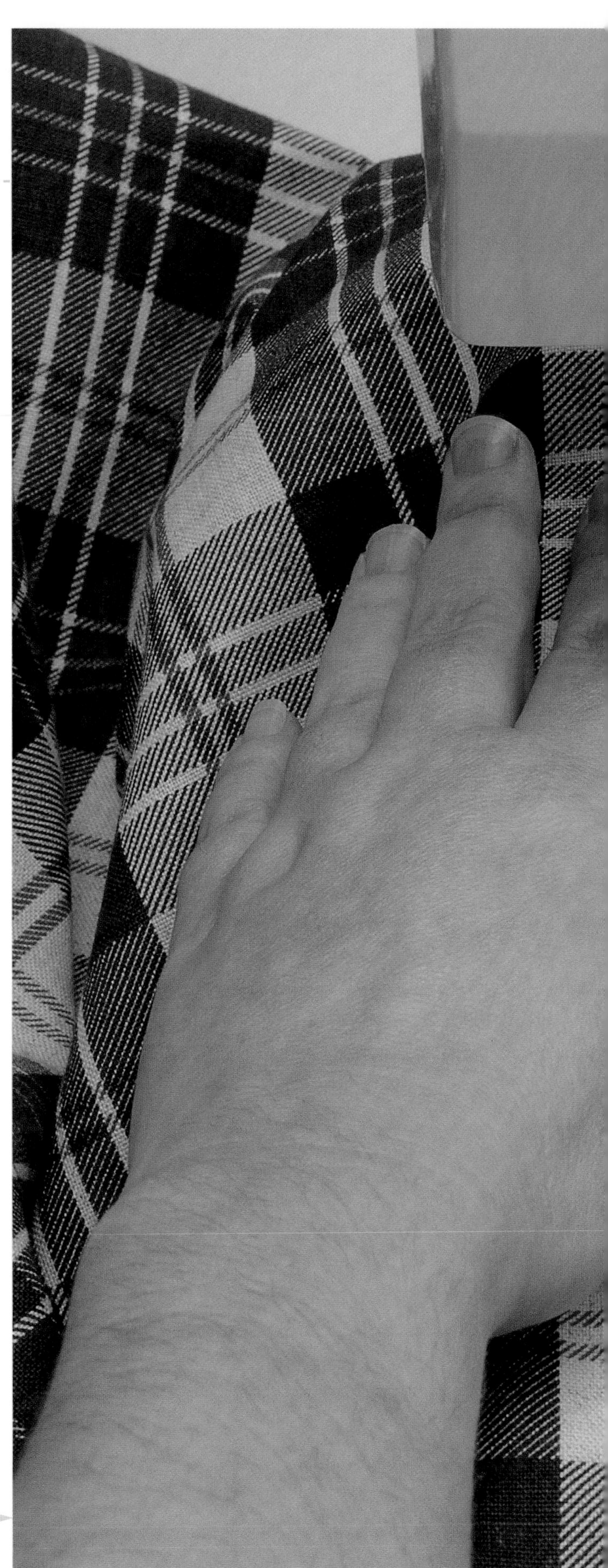

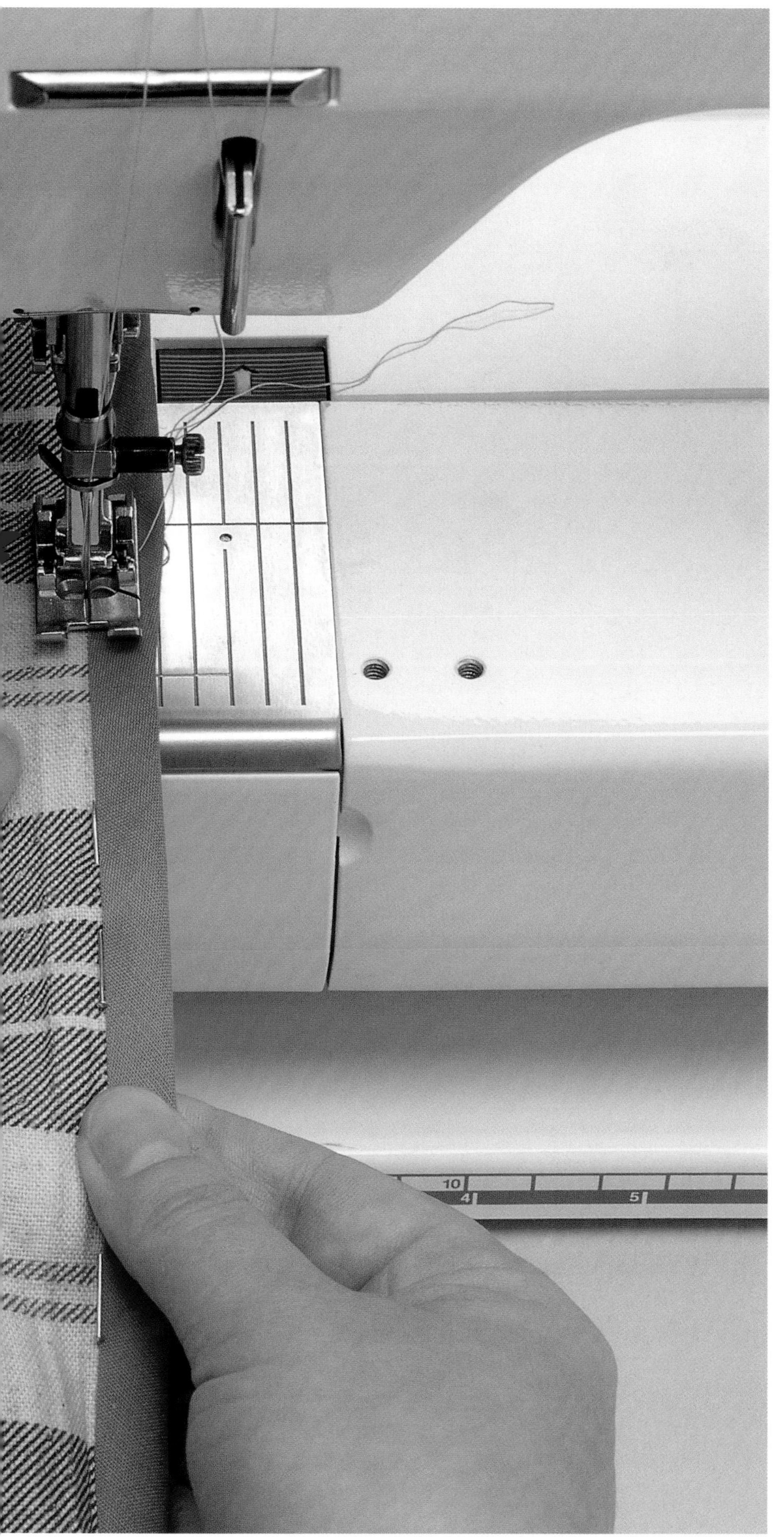

Plain throw

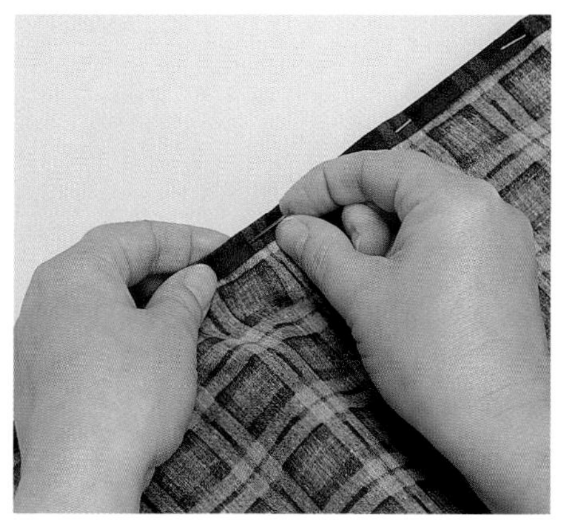

1 Cut the fabric and level the edges. Turn under and pin a double hem along all four sides, except at the corners. Make a mitered hem at each corner and baste it in place.

2 Working from the wrong side, stitch the hem in place. Leave the needle in the fabric at the corners and pivot to give a neat finish.

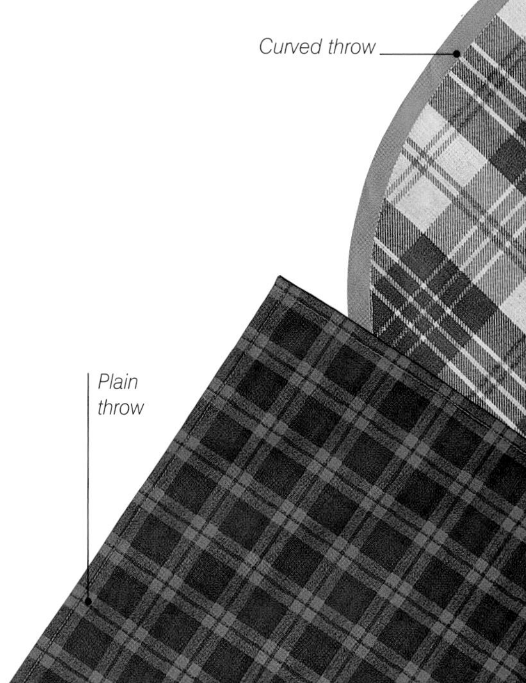

Reversible throw

1 Straighten the edges of the two pieces of fabric and place them right sides together with all four edges level.

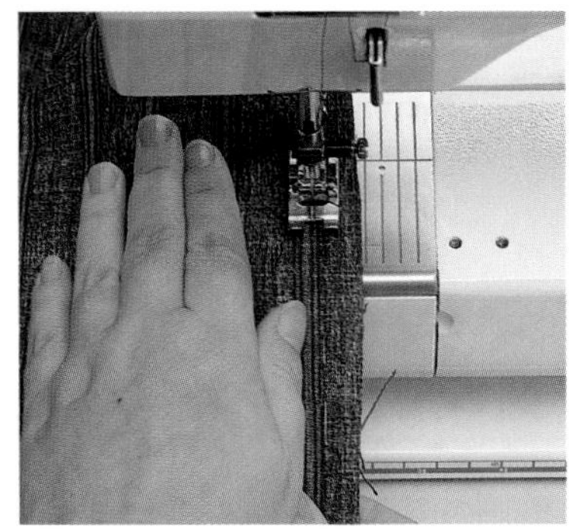

2 Stitch a ½-in (1.25-cm) seam along all sides, leaving a 10-in (25-cm) gap in the center of one side. Turn the throw right side out.

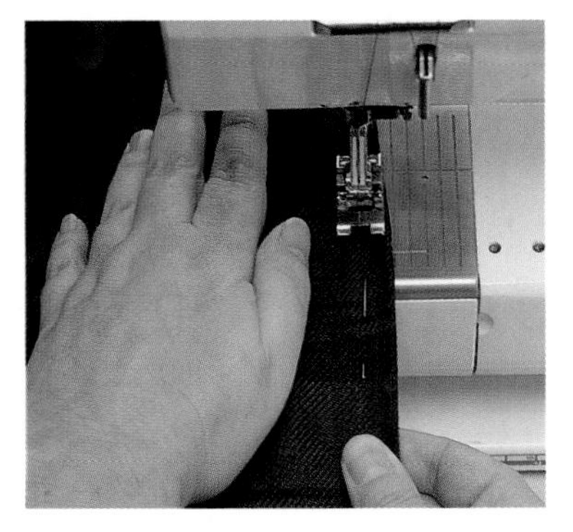

3 Fold the raw edges of the opening to the wrong side and press. Pin the gap and topstitch ½ in (1.25 cm) from the edge to close the gap and strengthen the seam.

Hand-fringed throw

1 Trim each edge of the fabric level, following the weave as closely as possible.

2 Fray each edge to the desired depth. Use a pin to tease out individual threads.

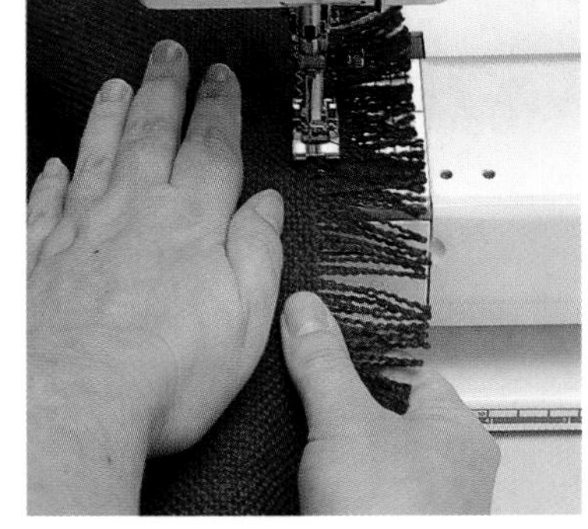

3 Zigzag-stitch as close to the fringe as possible to finish all the edges and to prevent further unraveling.

Ready-made fringing

1 Level the edges of the fabric and pin the fringe to the right side, facing in and overlapping the fabric edge slightly. Stitch along the center of the fringe heading.

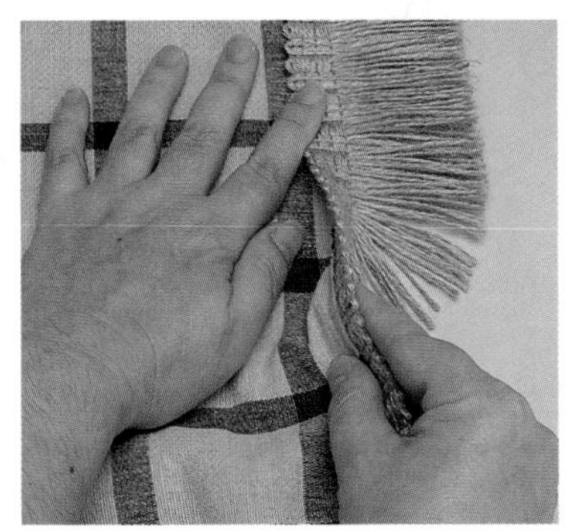

2 Turn the fringe to the wrong side of the fabric, covering the raw edge, then pin it in position. Baste the corners if necessary.

3 Stitch along the top edge of the fringe around all four sides of the piece.

Reversible throw

Hand-fringed throw

Ready-made fringing

Fitted bedspreads

Fitted spreads and bed valances are made by attaching a "skirt" of fabric that drops to the floor to a "deck" piece that covers the mattress or fits underneath it. A valance, or dust ruffle, stays in position most of the time, while a fitted bedspread covers the whole bed and will probably be laundered more regularly.

Flounced bedspread

1 Measure and cut the deck piece to fit the bed, adding 2 in (5 cm) to the length. Turn and stitch a deep double hem at the top.

2 Measure and cut the skirt, joining the short ends as necessary to make up the required length. Press and finish the short seams. Hem the short ends and one long edge.

3 Pin a piece of string the same length as the skirt about 1½ in (4 cm) from the raw edge. Use a wide zigzag-stitch to sew it in place. Pull the ends to gather. Pin the skirt to the deck around the three unhemmed sides, adjusting the gathers evenly.

4 Stitch the pieces together. Trim the top of the skirt to ½ in (1.25 cm) and the raw edge of the deck to 1½ in (4 cm). Fold over and pin the raw edge of the deck to enclose the top of the skirt, then machine-stitch in place (inset).

5 The finished spread gives a soft look to a room.

Headed ruffle bedspread

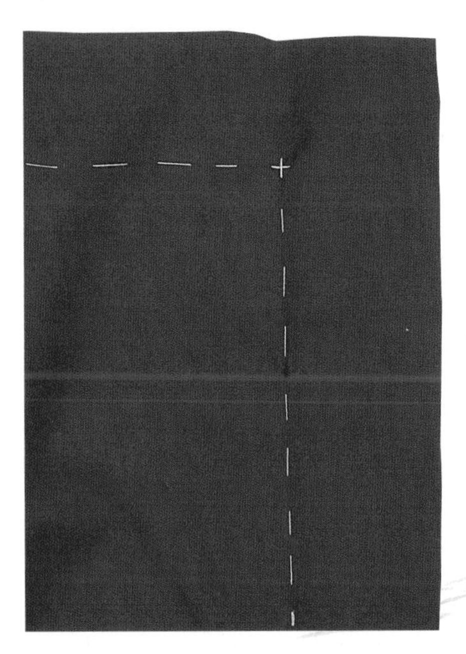

1 Measure and cut the deck, adding 2 in (5 cm) all around. Baste all sides 2 in (5 cm) from the edge to mark the mattress size. Make a double hem following the basted line along the top edge.

2 Make the skirt as in step 2 of making a flounced spread. Fold the top of the skirt once and make a casing through both layers 1½ in (4 cm) deep with two rows of gather-stitch. Draw up the gathers (inset).

3 Pin the wrong side of the gathered skirt to the right side of the deck along the basted line. Position the short ends of the skirt 2 in (5 cm) from the top of the deck.

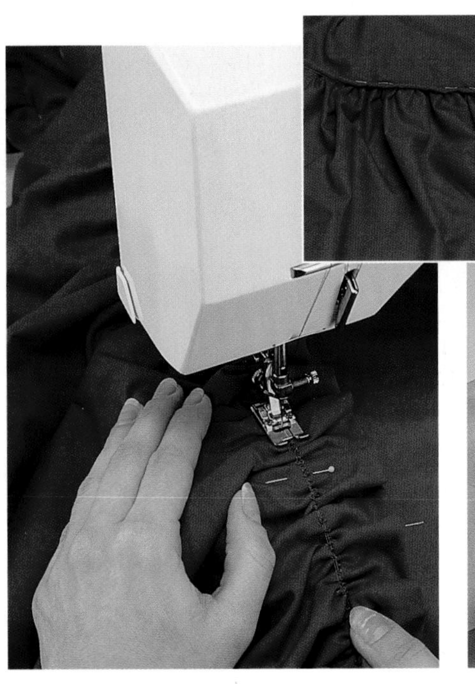

4 Machine-stitch to join the skirt to the deck, carefully removing the pins as you work. Remove the gathering threads from the skirt.

5 Trim the edges of the deck and skirt (see step 4 of making a flounced bedspread). Fold and pin the edge of the deck to enclose the edge of the skirt and stitch it in place. Remove the basting. The inside of the seam is now neat (inset).

6 The eyecatching head of the ruffled skirt makes an attractive feature.

Tailored bedspread

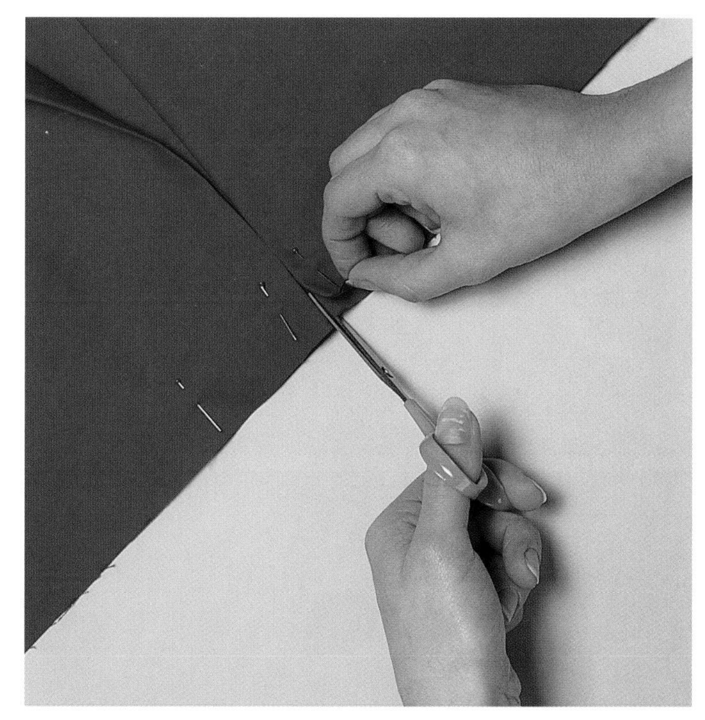

1 Make the deck and skirt as in steps 1 and 2 of making a flounced spread. Mark two corner pleats in the skirt and press the folds. Pin and snip ½ in (1.25 cm) down the center of each pleat. Baste each pleat closed.

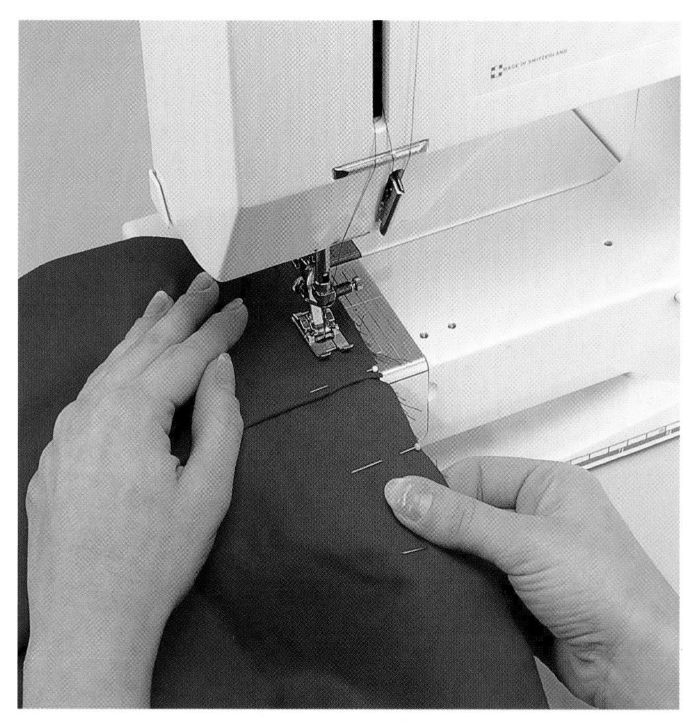

2 With right sides together, pin the skirt to the unfinished short end of the deck. Stitch along the short end only, starting and finishing in the center of a pleat.

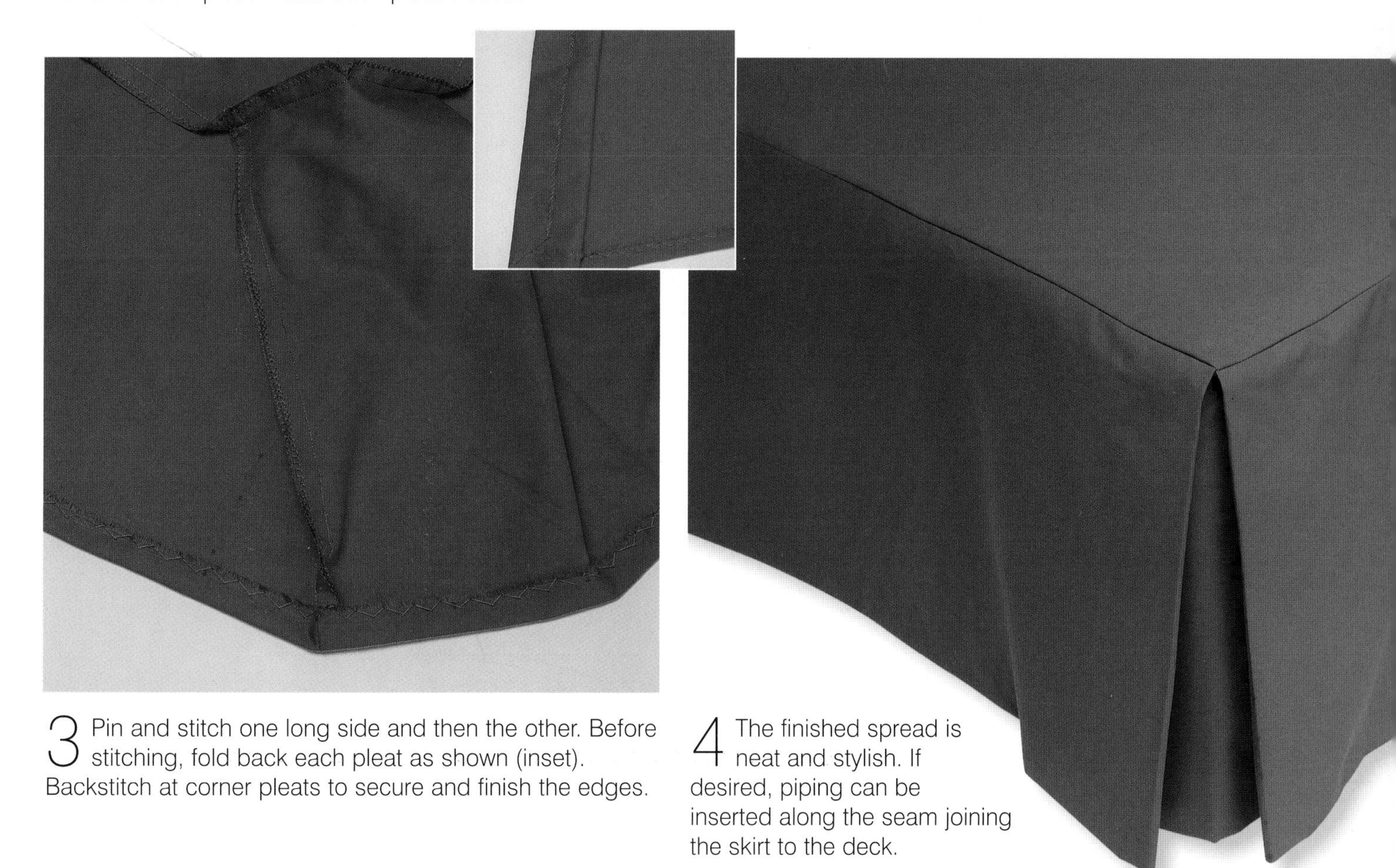

3 Pin and stitch one long side and then the other. Before stitching, fold back each pleat as shown (inset). Backstitch at corner pleats to secure and finish the edges.

4 The finished spread is neat and stylish. If desired, piping can be inserted along the seam joining the skirt to the deck.

Project: Striped duvet cover

Covers for duvets or comforters are straightforward to make and allow you a free choice of fabric to complement your decorative scheme. This reversible cover, measuring 88 in (224 cm) square, uses a simple design—cool, minimal cream and beige stripes on one side and a warm, darker shade of taupe on the other—to give a clean, modern twist in a traditional setting.

YOU WILL NEED
- *Fabric 45 in (115 cm) wide:*
  - *Cotton for light stripes: 2½ yd (2.25 m)*
  - *Cotton for darker stripes, ties, and facing: 5 yd (4.6 m)*
  - *Cotton for darker reverse side, ties, and facing: 5 yd (4.6 m)*
  - *Cotton for piping: 1¼ yd (1.15 m)*
- *Piping cord: 9⅜ yd (8.5 m)*

Making the duvet cover

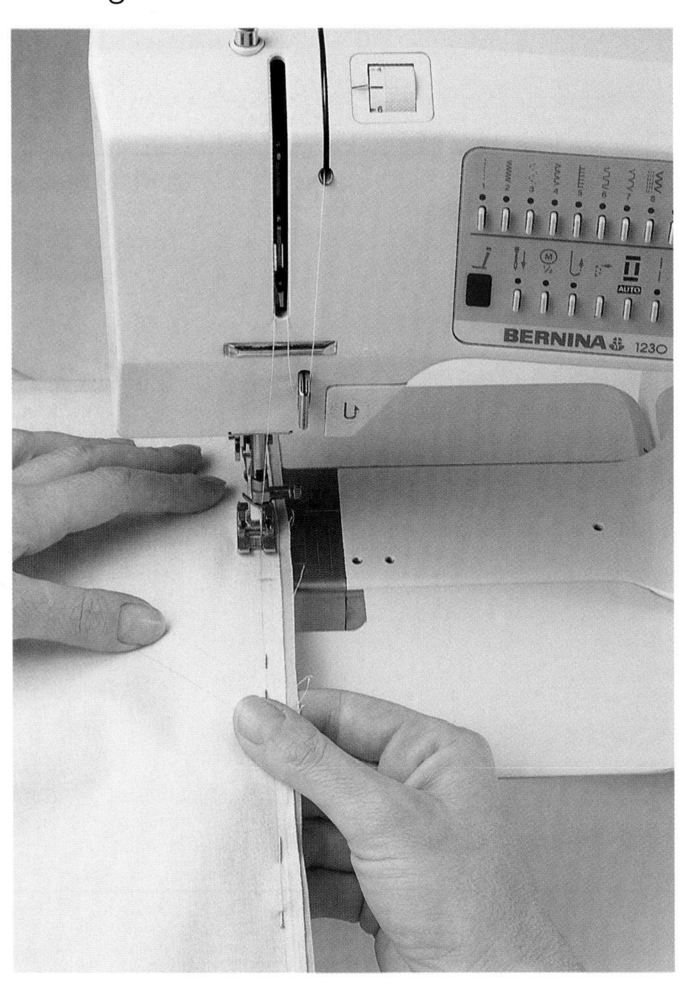

1 Cut four strips of light fabric and five strips of darker top fabric 10½ in (27 cm) wide and 88¾ in (226 cm) long. Pin and stitch strips right sides together, alternating colors and making a ⅜-in (1-cm) seam allowance.

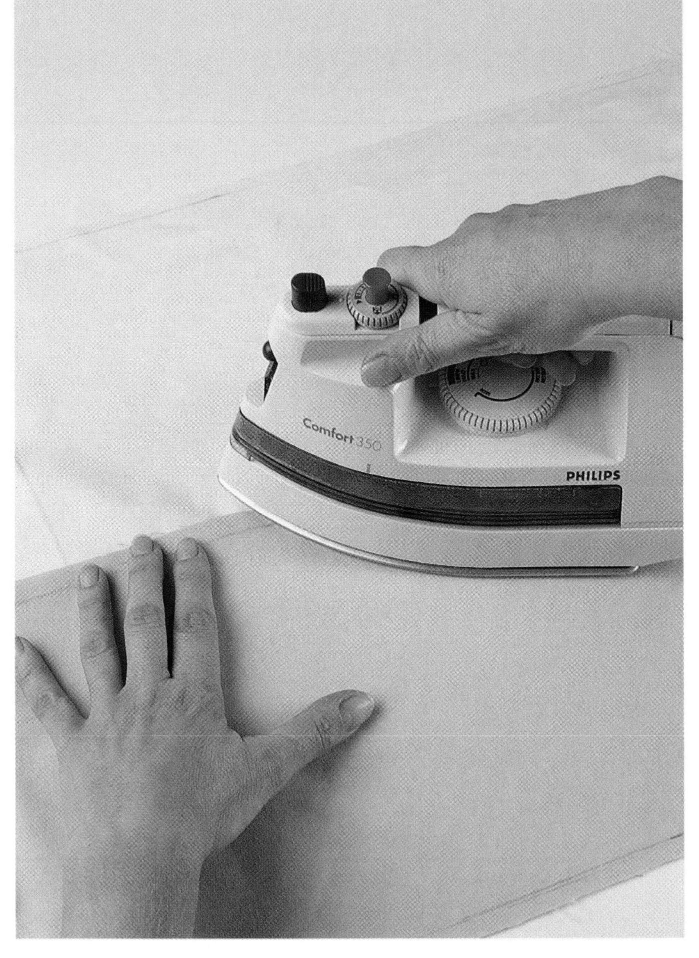

2 Placing the piece on a flat surface, gently press. Make sure that all of the seams are turned to the side, toward the light-colored strips.

3 Topstitch the seams on the right side using thread to match the fabric to strengthen and finish them.

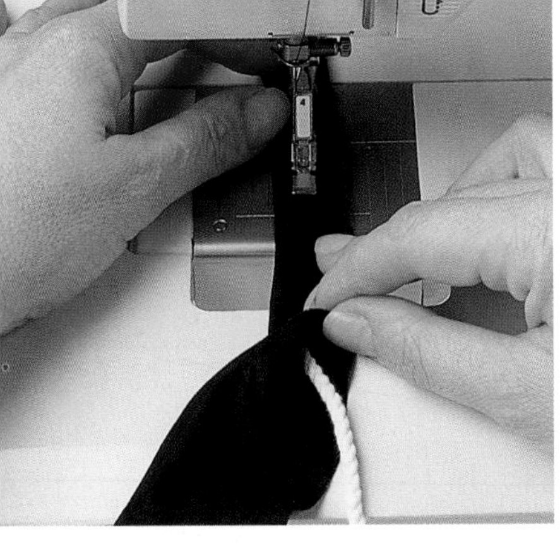

4 Cut bias strips from the binding fabric 2 in (5 cm) wide and join them to make a continuous strip at least 30 ft (9 m) long.

5 For the ties, cut six strips from the top fabric and six from the reverse-side fabric, each 2 in (5 cm) wide and 18½ in (47 cm) long. Fold each in half lengthwise, wrong sides together, and turn the raw edges into the middle down the long side and at the ends. Topstitch along all four sides to make ties ¾ in (2 cm) wide.

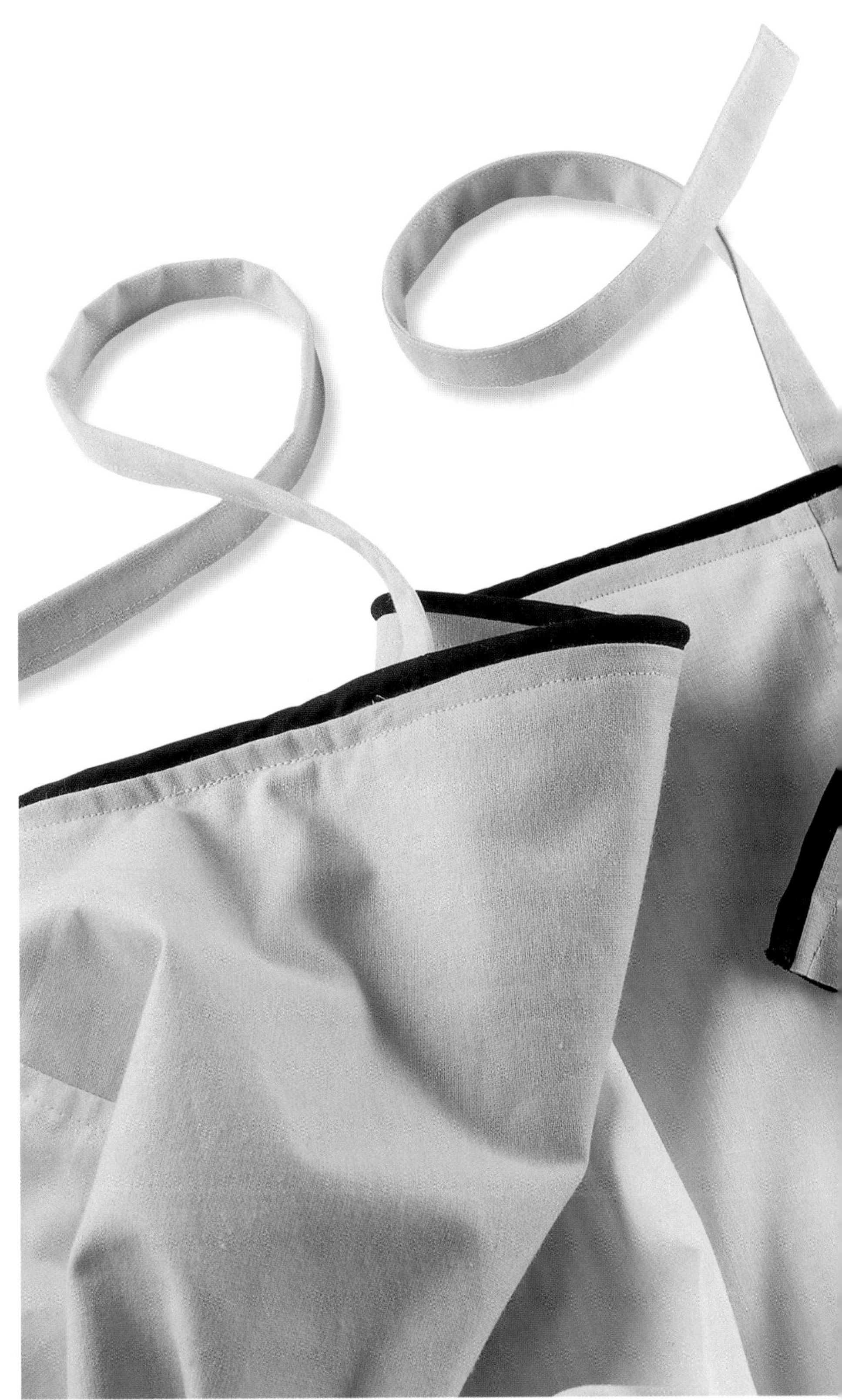

6 Pin piping to the bottom end of the cover top and pin the six top-fabric ties over the piping at 10½-in (25-cm) intervals. For the facing, cut a strip of top fabric 4 in (10 cm) wide and 88¾ in (226 cm) long. Make a narrow double hem along one long edge. Pin, baste, and stitch the unhemmed edge of the facing over the piping and ties with right sides together. Turn right side out, press, and topstitch. Cut the reverse side the same size as the top. Repeat steps 4 and 5 to attach the ties and facing to the reverse side of the cover.

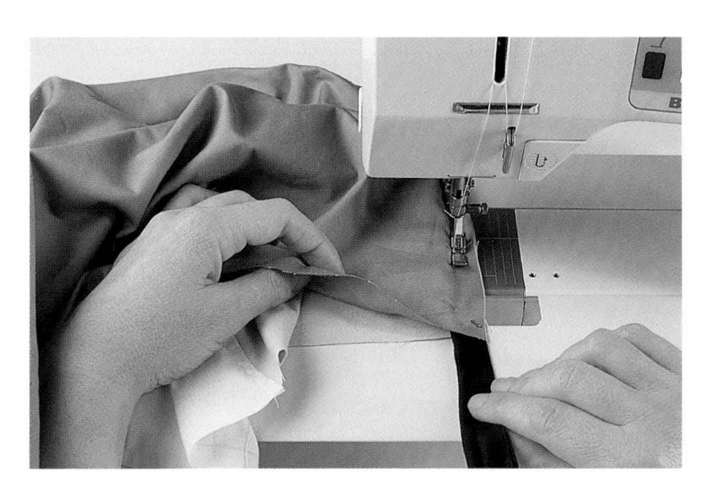

7 Pin the top to the reverse right sides together with the piping between them on the inside. Stitch the three unfaced sides using a zipper foot. Take extra care at the corners.

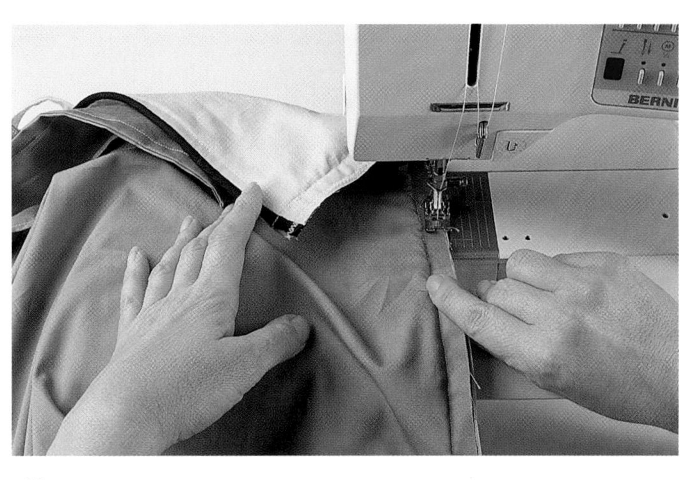

8 Take care not to catch the piping cord in the seam. Zigzag the raw edges on all three sides. Turn right side out and press.

PATTERNED DUVET COVER

Using coordinated prints, or a print and a plain fabric, for the strips on the top side of the duvet cover creates an entirely different look for the duvet cover. The reverse can pick up the same feel and can be either patterned or plain.

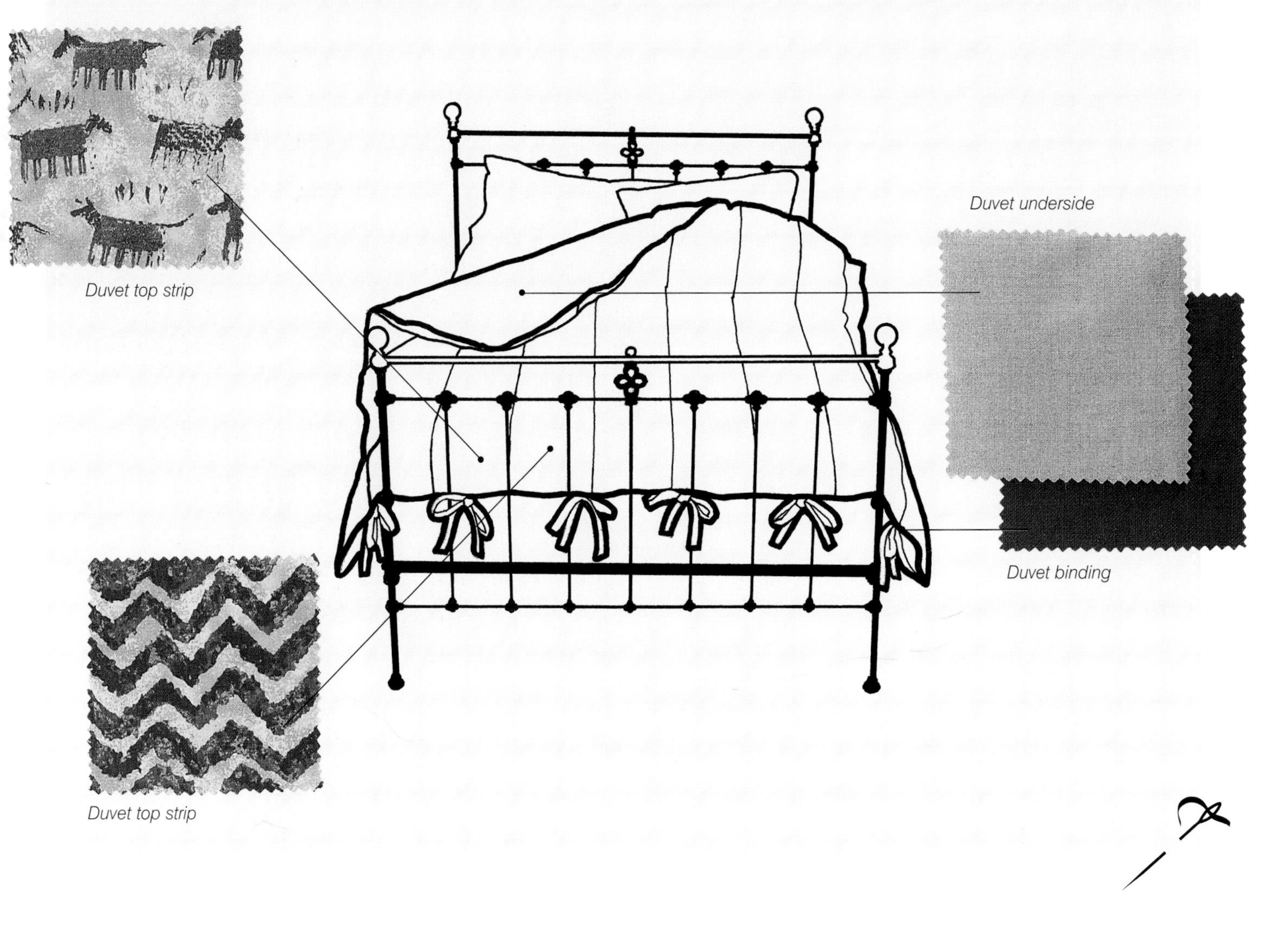

Project: Playmat

This cheerful mat can be used as a baby quilt, or can provide a warm, soft layer on the floor for the baby to play or sleep on during the day. It is made from large scraps pieced together in a variety of ways and appliquéd with simple shapes that will be visually stimulating for an active infant. The measurements have been calculated to make the pieces fit together properly using either the metric or standard system. Use either one or the other—do NOT try to combine them.

YOU WILL NEED
- *Large scraps (up to 10 in/25 cm square) of 16 different fabrics*
- *9 x 7-in (17-cm) squares of cream-colored cotton fabric*
- *½ yd (0.5m) fusible webbing*
- *24 strips of fine cotton fabric (muslin) 5 x 7 in (13 x 17 cm)*
- *40-in (102-cm) square of backing fabric*
- *36-in (92-cm) square 2-oz (56-g) polyester batting (wadding)*
- *Sewing thread, a selection of nine different colors*
- *Stranded embroidery thread to coordinate with fabrics*

Making the playmat

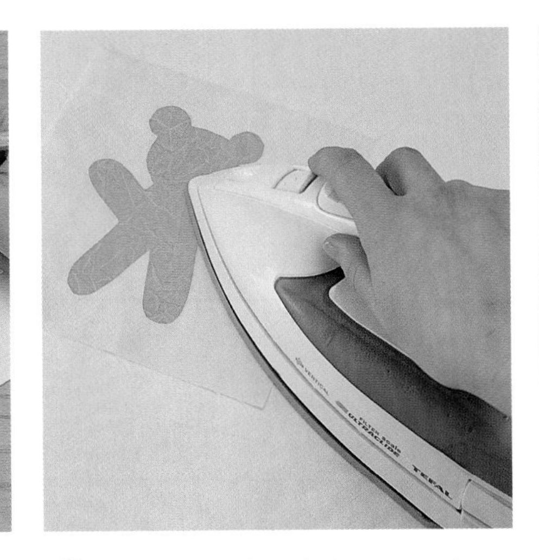

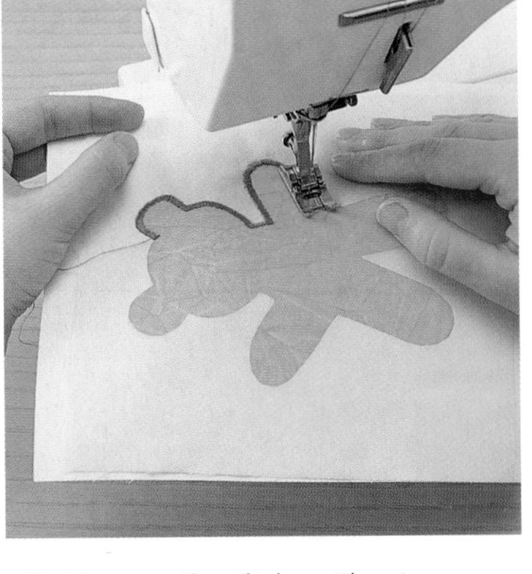

1 Cut a 5-in (13-cm) square from each of the 16 fabrics and set aside. Copy the three templates on page 251 and trace each one three times on the paper side of the fusible webbing. Choose nine different fabrics for the shapes and fuse a shape on the wrong side of each.

2 Cut out the fused shapes and peel off the backing paper. Position one shape in the center of each square of cream fabric, right side up. Fuse the shape to the square following the manufacturer's instructions.

3 Use a satin stitch setting to zigzag-stitch around the edge of each appliqué shape in a contrasting color. Stitch the outside of the lower wings of the butterflies first, then work the upper wings and extend the line to make the body, tapering both ends.

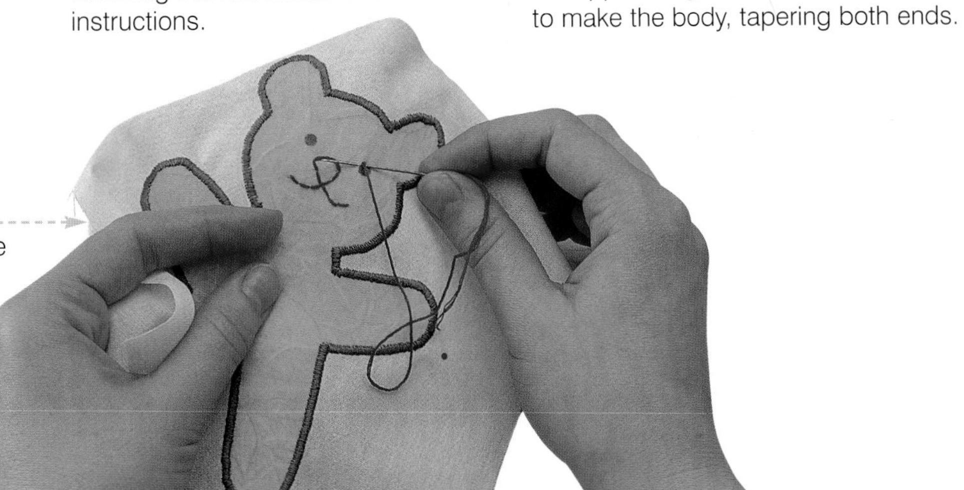

4 Add embroidered details to the shapes using three strands of embroidery floss (cotton) in contrasting colors.

5 Cut the remaining pieces of fabric into random strips of different widths and angles, keeping the edges straight. Use a rotary cutter and mat if you have one; otherwise, cut with scissors. Find a piece of bright fabric to fit one end of a cream strip and position it right side up.

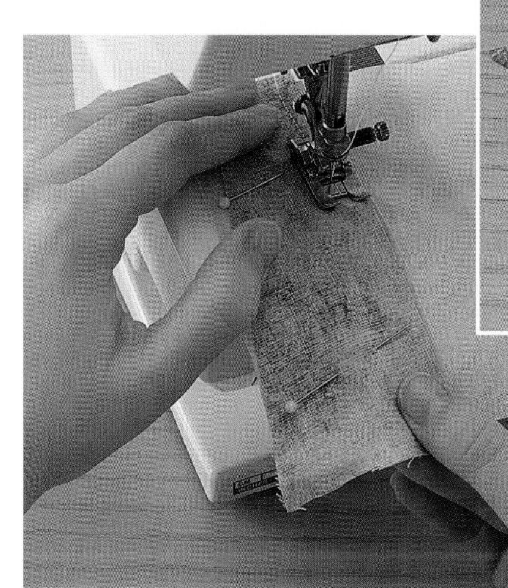

6 Take a contrasting strip and pin it face down over the first with the edges aligned. Stitch a narrow seam along the raw edges. Fold the second piece to the right side and add a third piece in the same way (inset).

7 Continue this "stitch and flip" method of adding strips of varying sizes and shapes until the 24 foundation strips have been covered. Make sure each one is different. Trim excess fabric from each edge so the piece measures 5 x 7 in (13 x 17 cm).

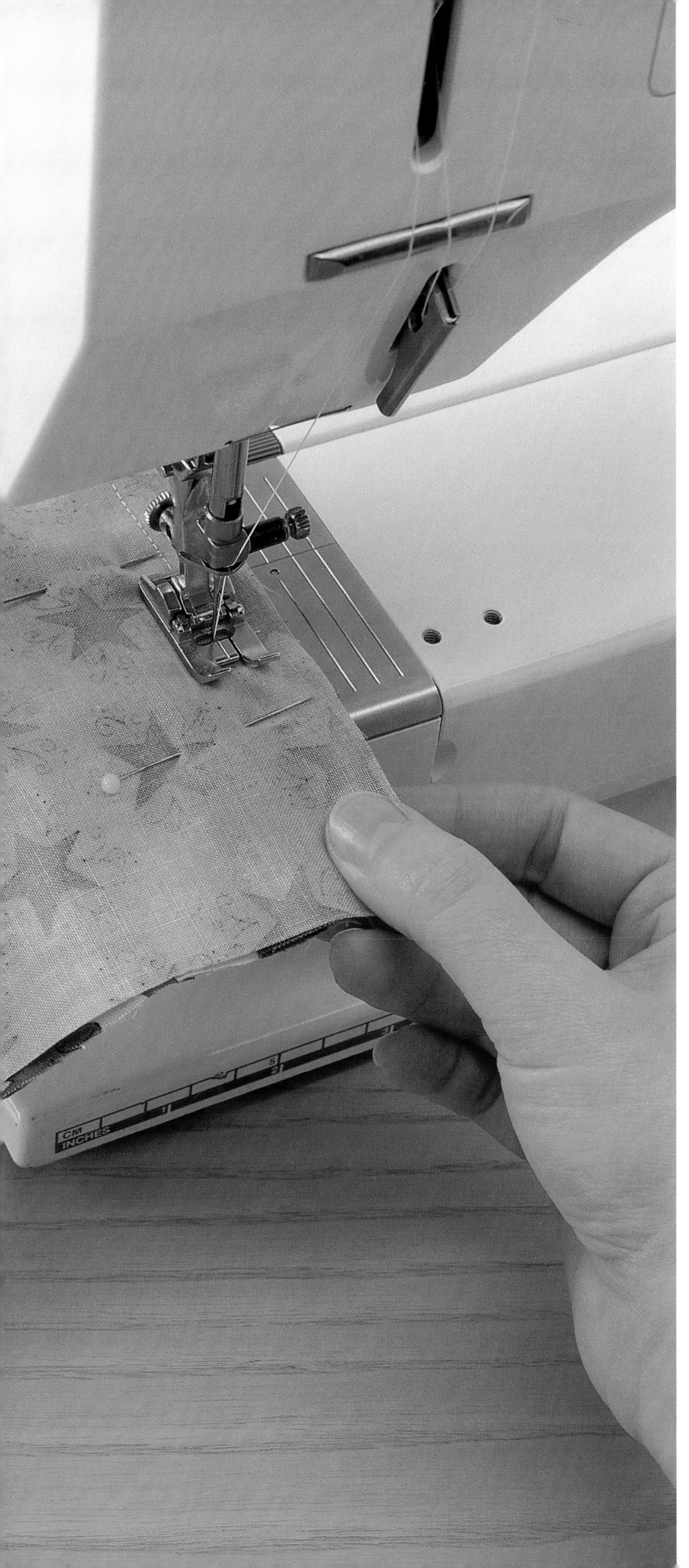

8 Using the diagrams on page 250, arrange the pieces into a pleasing pattern of shape and color across the mat. Piece the horizontal strips for the odd-numbered rows by alternating strip-pieced sections with the 5-in (13-cm) squares made in step 1. Make ½-in (1.25-cm) seams, building up four rows, each with four squares and three strip-pieced sections.

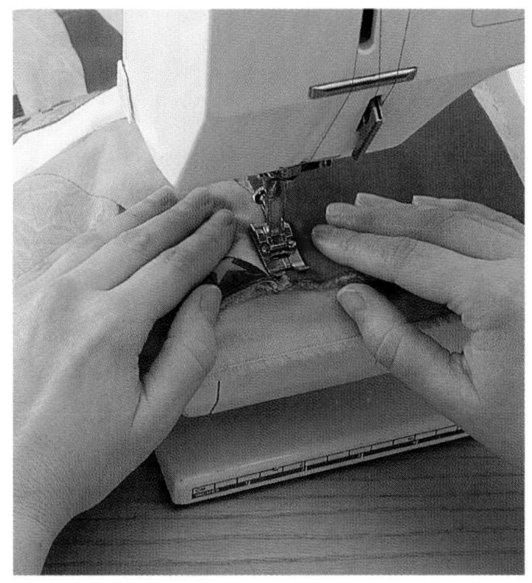

9 Lay the backing fabric right side down on a flat surface and center the batting on top. Lay the playmat on top, right side up, making sure it is centered on the backing. Baste or pin the three layers together, and stitch down and across the seams.

10 Fold the raw edge of the backing fabric to the front of the mat. Pin a double fold to enclose the edge of the mat and the batting. Stitch along the folded edge by hand or machine to finish.

Assembling the pieces

Follow the diagrams to put together the rows of blocks.

Diagram 1

Lay out and arrange four rows of strip-pieced sections, alternating them with the plain squares.

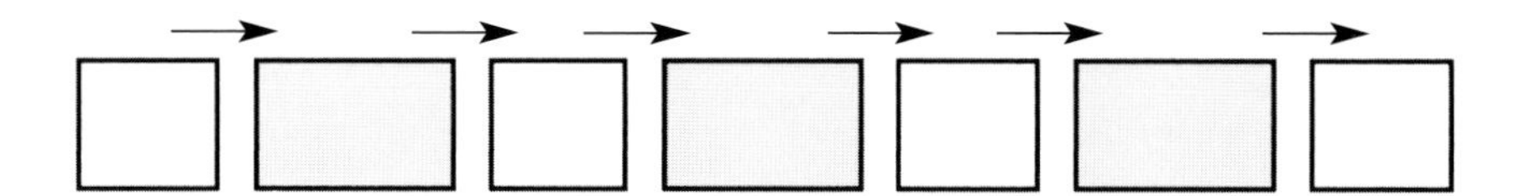

Diagram 2

Make three rows of appliquéd squares, alternating them with the strip-pieced squares.

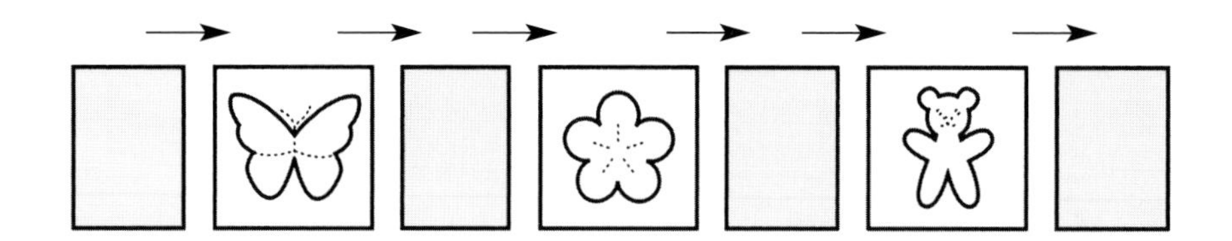

Diagram 3

Lay the rows alongside each other in this order to make the mat.

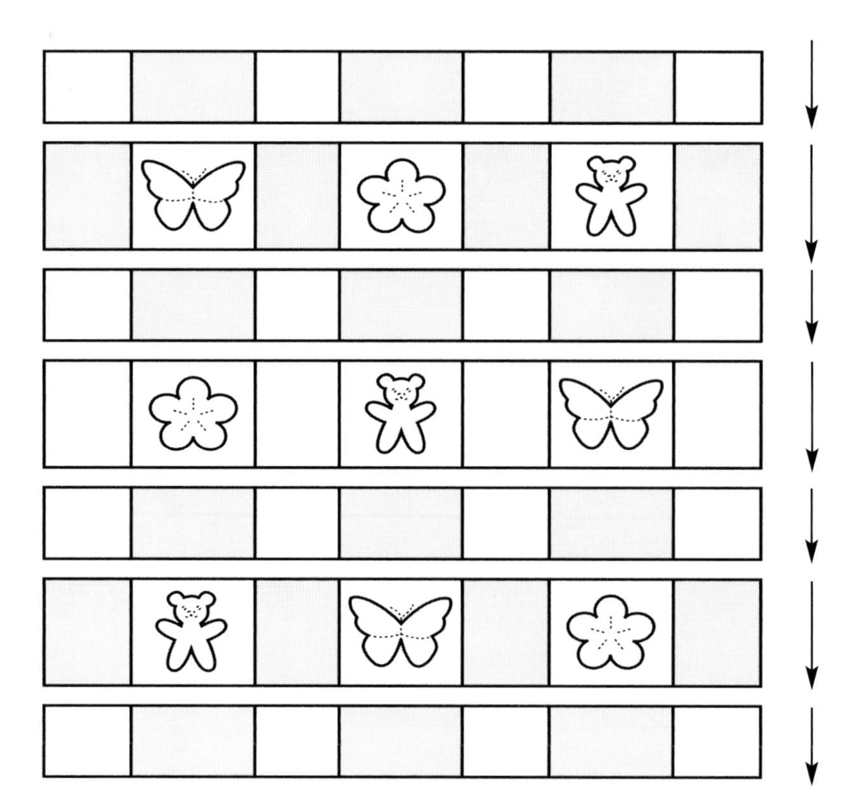

Templates

These templates are the same size as those used in the project and are 100 percent to scale. Trace or photocopy them to make three copies of each motif.

Table linen

Table linen can be expensive to buy and it is often difficult to find them in exactly the size, shape, and color you want. As you are limited by what is on offer, you are better off making your own. A square or rectangular tablecloth can be a simple matter of accurately measuring, cutting, and hemming a piece of fabric. Circle, oval, and rounded rectangle tablecloths involve sewing curves, but are not difficult to make either.

Circular tablecloth

1 Measure and cut a square of fabric the diameter of the table plus twice the drop plus hems. Fold the square in quarters and pin the edges. Cut a length of string measuring the radius of the desired circle plus hems and pin it securely in the folded corner. Mark a quarter circle around the unfolded edges using the string as a guide.

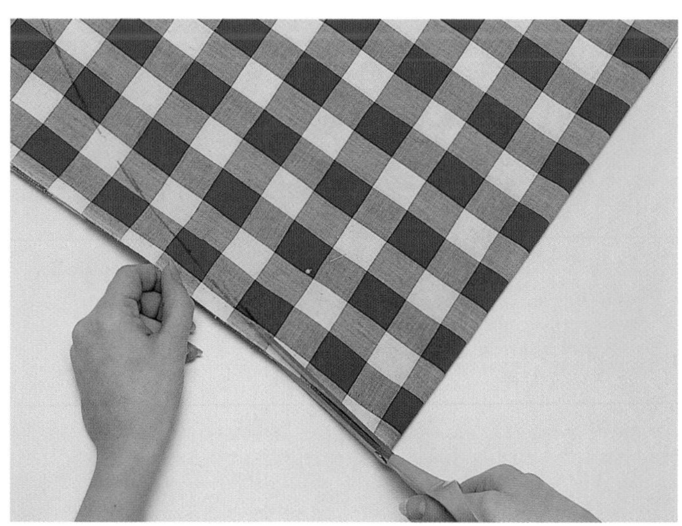

2 Carefully cut along the marked line through all four layers of fabric. Unpin and open out the circle.

3 Pin a double hem all around, close to the edge and stitch it in place, removing pins as you work.

4 A simple circular tablecloth can be made to any length you desire.

MATCHING PATTERNS

To join lengths of printed fabric, you may want to match the pattern to make the seam less noticeable. Identify where the pattern repeats and match the two pieces together before sewing them. This technique is useful for any sewing project.

1 Trim the edge of one piece to be joined and press ½ in (1.25 cm) to the wrong side. Lay the second piece flat and match the folded edge of the first piece to the pattern on the second. Pin in place along the folded edge on the right side.

2 Moving the pins as you work, fold the fabric to work on the wrong side and stitch the seam, using the folded edge as a stitching guide. The seam is virtually invisible.

Long circular tablecloth

1 Cut two pieces of fabric the desired length of the tablecloth. Fold one in half lengthwise, matching selvages. Pin, then cut along the fold to make two pieces the same length as the uncut piece, but only half as wide.

2 Stitch each narrow piece of fabric to one outside edge of the main piece. Trim if necessary to give the correct width measurement. Fold, mark, and cut to make a circle as in steps 1 and 2 of making a circular tablecloth.

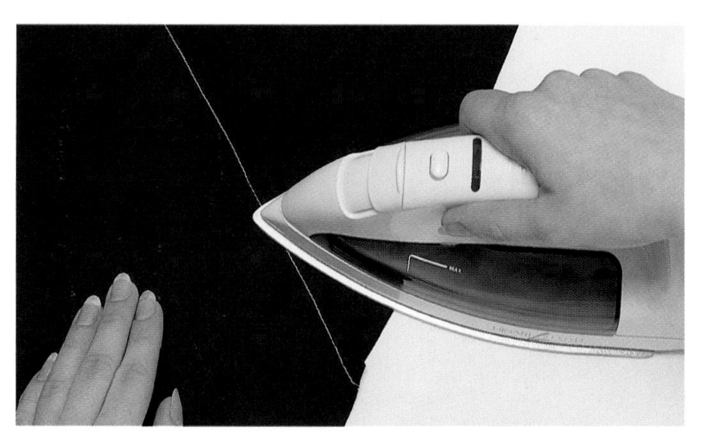

3 Press the seams to the outside edge of the tablecloth. Turn up, pin, and stitch a double hem all around.

4 Seams down the middle of the tablecloth would be unsightly, while this method hides the necessary seams discreetly.

Tablecloth edges

Lace insert border

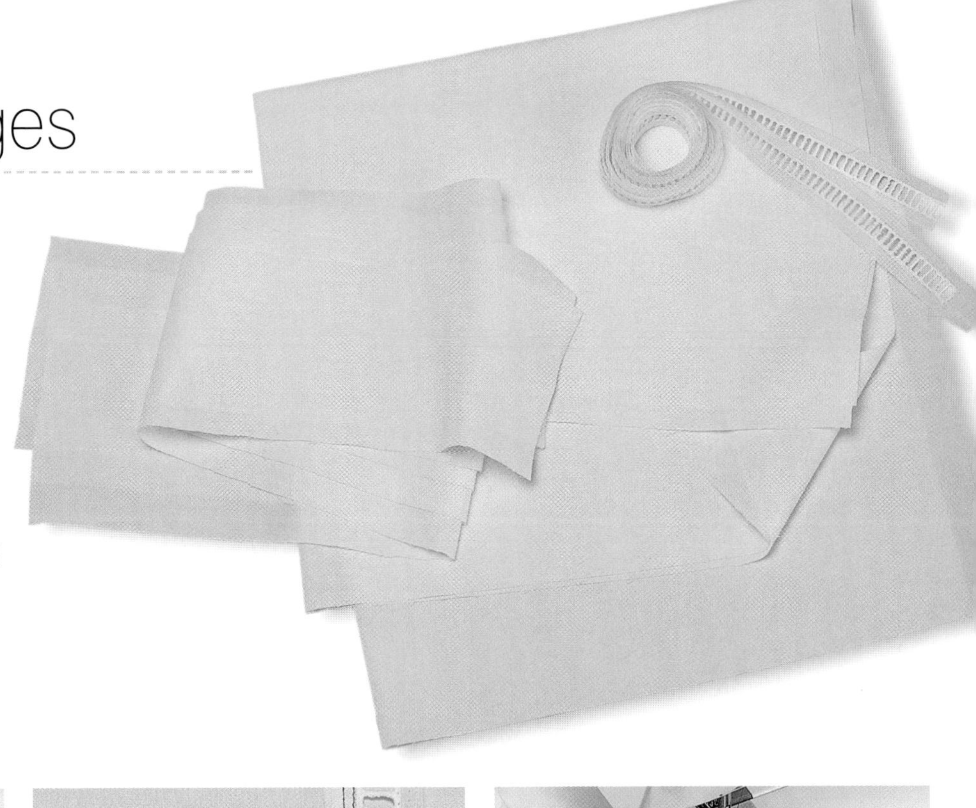

1 Measure and cut the main fabric to measure the width times the length of the table, plus the length of the drop minus the lace and border all around. Cut four border strips twice the desired finished width and four lengths of lace, joining lengths if necessary, the same as the outside edges of the main fabric.

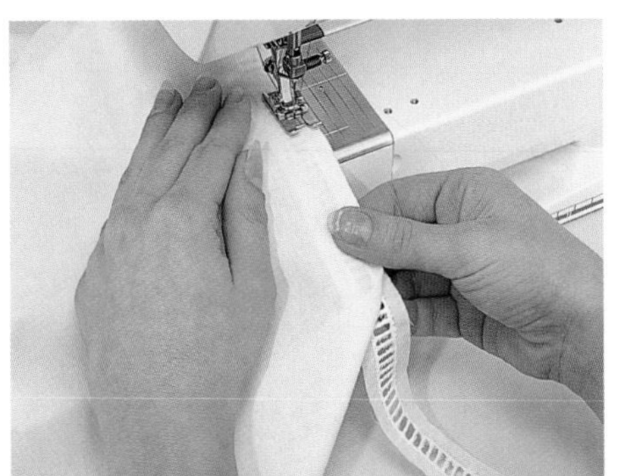

2 With right sides together, pin and stitch a length of lace to the raw edge of the main fabric, leaving a surplus end of lace unstitched at each corner. Work around one side at a time.

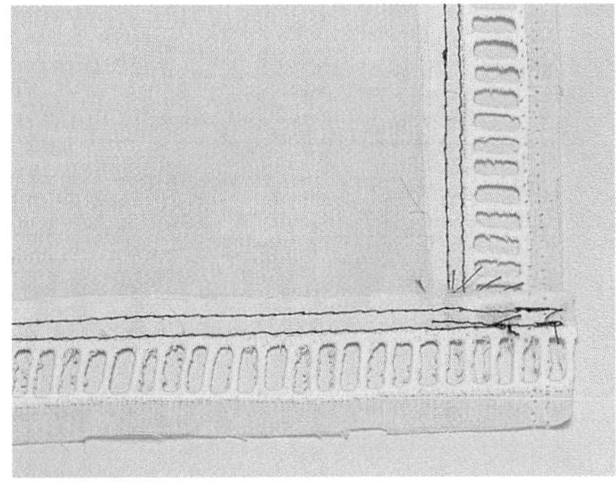

3 Turn the lace out, press it flat, and topstitch the seam, joining the overlapping end of lace to the end of the adjoining strip as shown.

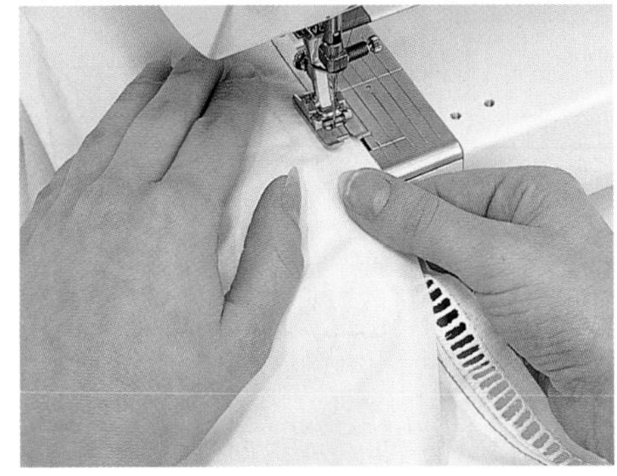

4 With right sides together, pin and stitch the border pieces to the raw edges of lace all around. Leave overlaps at each corner to correspond with the corners of the lace.

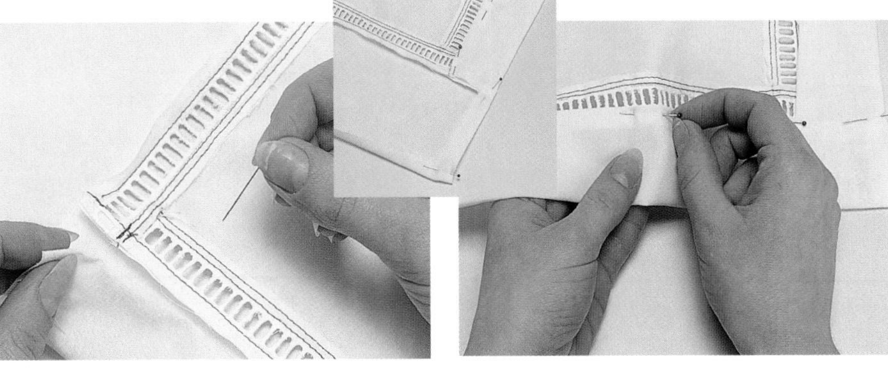

5 Press the raw edge of the border and fold the strip to make a hem covering the outside edge of the lace. Pin the edge. Inset: At the next corner, fold a hem inside the end of the second border strip and pin in place.

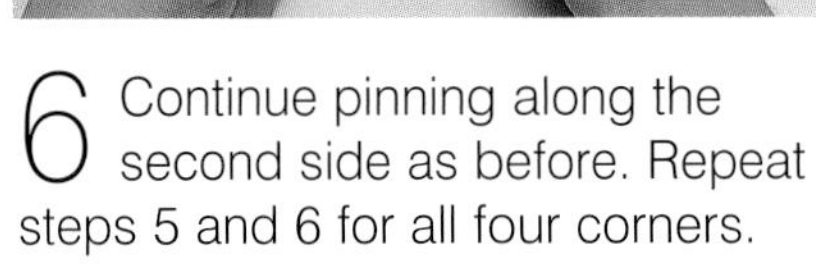

6 Continue pinning along the second side as before. Repeat steps 5 and 6 for all four corners.

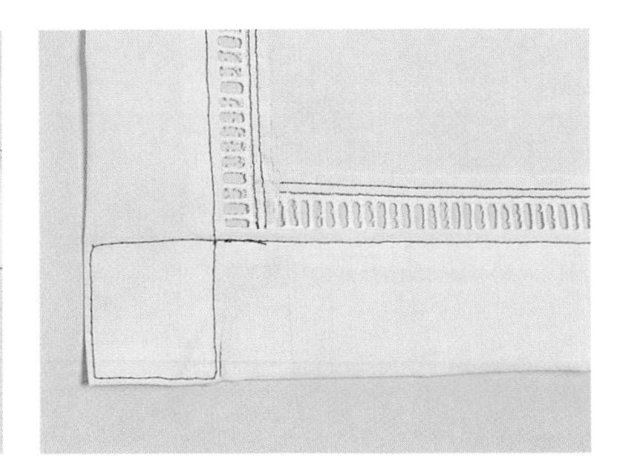

7 Topstitch all sides of the tablecloth to finish the border hem, stitching a square around each corner as shown.

Satin-stitched scalloped edge

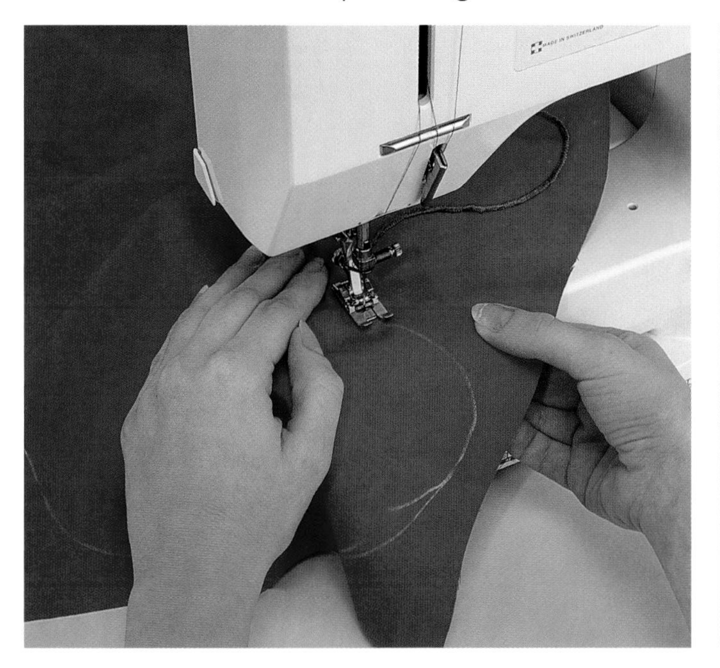

1 Cut the fabric to the desired size and level the edges. Make a template for the scallops from cardboard and mark around it on the edge of the fabric. Satin-stitch through one layer of fabric following the marked line.

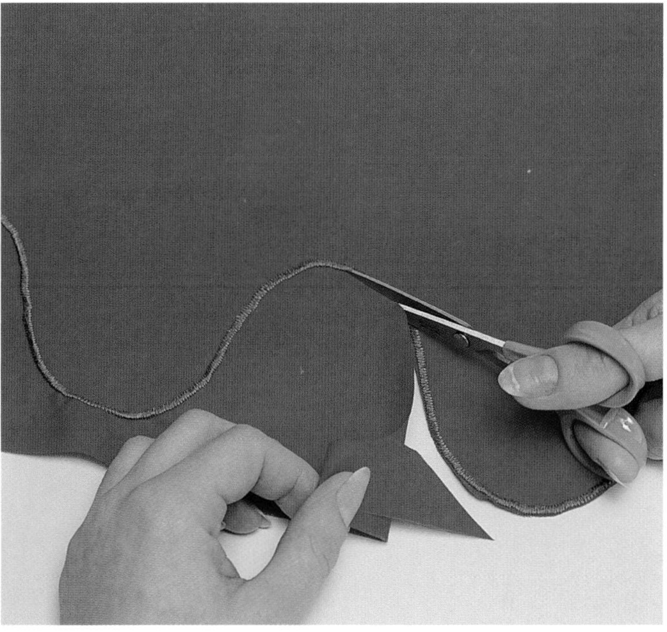

2 Trim carefully along the outside edge of the stitched line. Cut as close as possible, but take care not to cut into the stitches themselves.

OTHER DECORATIVE EDGES

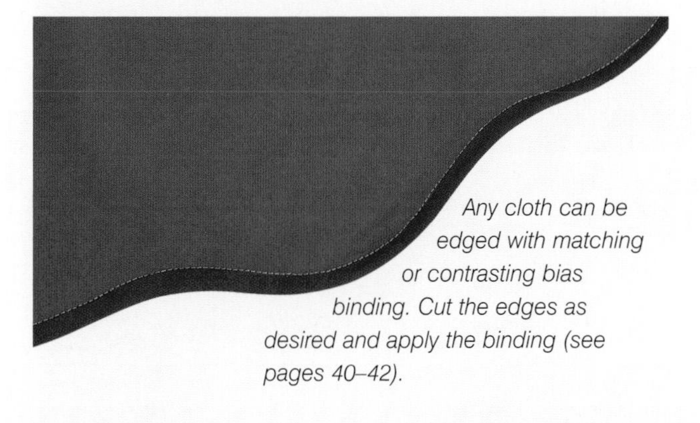

Any cloth can be edged with matching or contrasting bias binding. Cut the edges as desired and apply the binding (see pages 40–42).

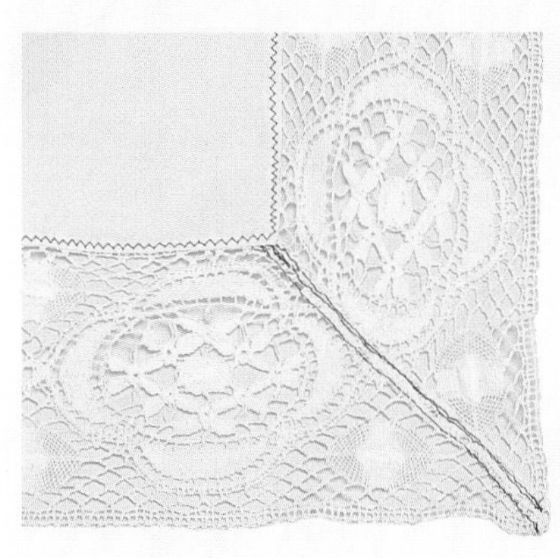

To apply a lace border, make a single hem along the edges of the trimmed fabric. Pin the lace. Zigzag the seam to secure the lace. Here the corner has been mitered using a flat-fell seam.

3 The satin stitching finishes the cloth neatly and decoratively. Simple templates can be made in any shape, from deep curves like these to pointed triangles. Paper patterns of decorative borders can also be purchased.

Napkins and runners

Small pieces of table linen are even easier to make than tablecloths. Extra napkins are always useful to have in reserve and can be coordinated with other table linens. Runners can vary from traycloths to bands of fabric that cover the middle of a long table.

Napkin with mitered corners

1 Measure, mark, and cut fabric as for the plain napkin, but allow a deep double hem. Fold the corner with wrong sides together and stitch a miter (see page 44). Clip the corner. Repeat at all corners.

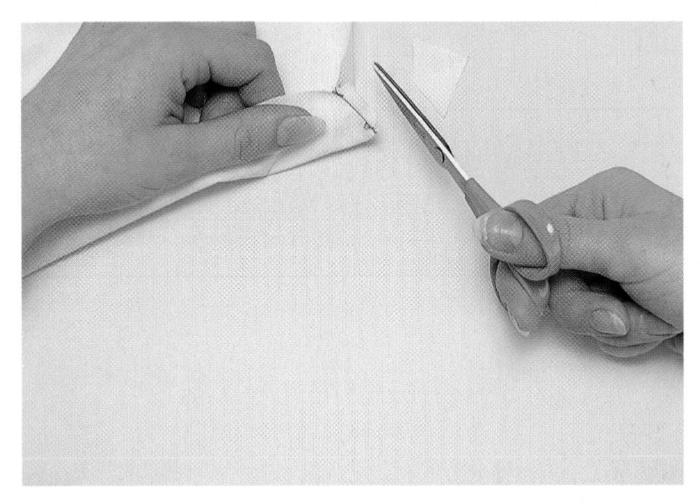

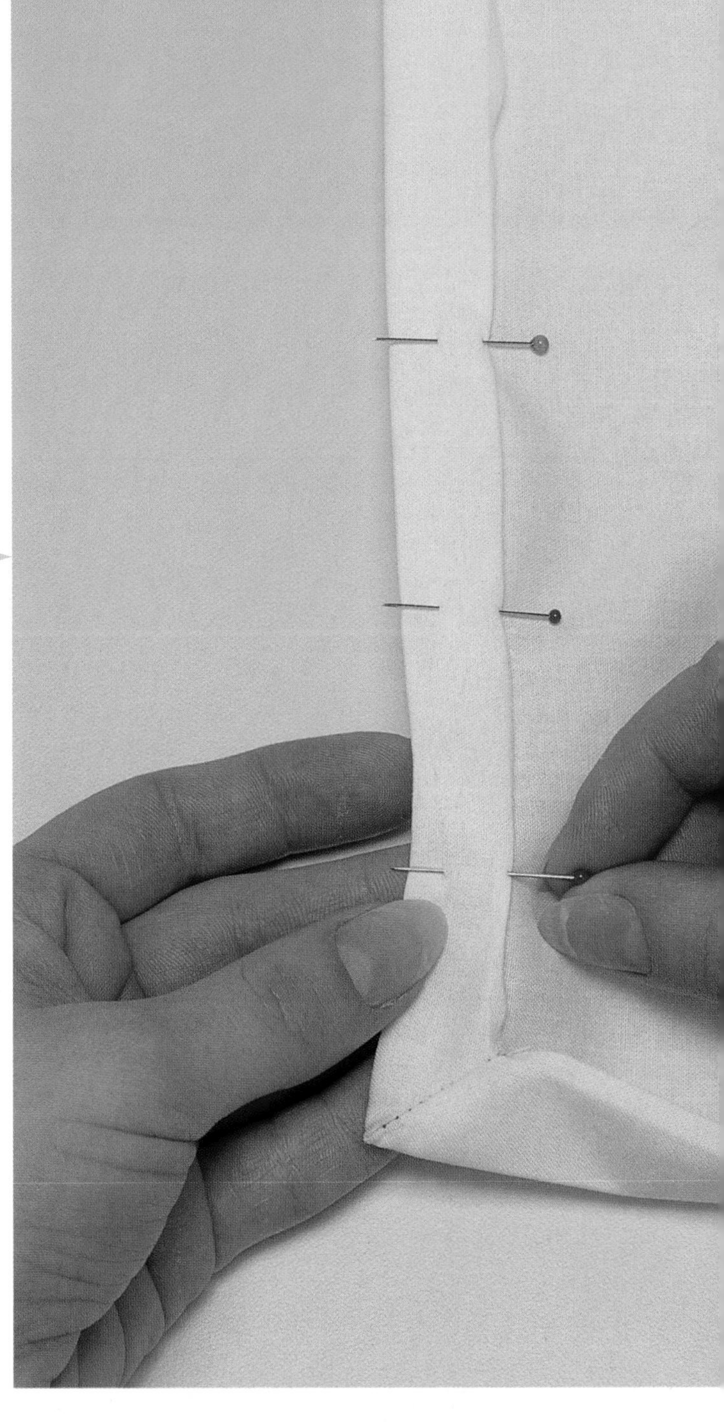

2 Turn the miters to the right side and fold and press the edges of the napkin. Turn under a narrow hem along the raw edge. Pin and stitch from the right side.

Plain napkin

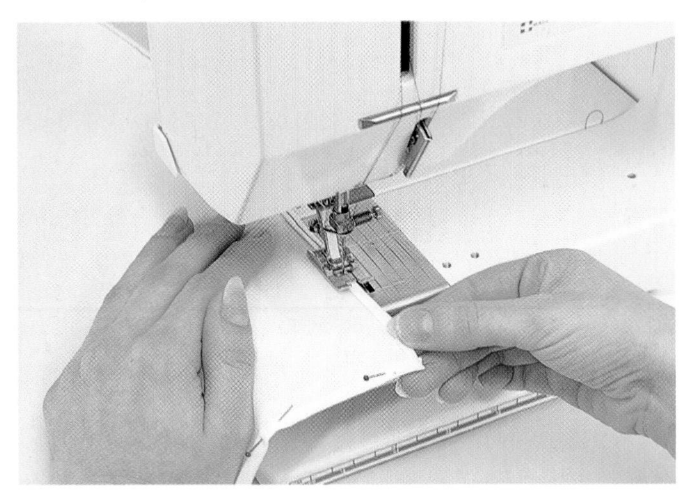

1 Cut a square of fabric to the desired size plus hems. Stitch a narrow double hem. At the corners, stop with the needle in, lift the presser foot, and turn the fabric.

Both plain and mitered edges make a neat finish for napkins. Both the napkins shown here can be embellished if desired.

Padded reversible runner

1 Cut two pieces of contrasting fabric and one piece of batting (wadding) to the desired measurement plus seam allowances all around.

2 Pin all three layers with right sides together and the batting on the bottom. Stitch around all edges, leaving a 4-in (10-cm) gap for turning.

3 Clip all corners (or curves, depending on your shape) and turn the runner right side out through the gap. Press to align all edges, then slipstitch the gap closed.

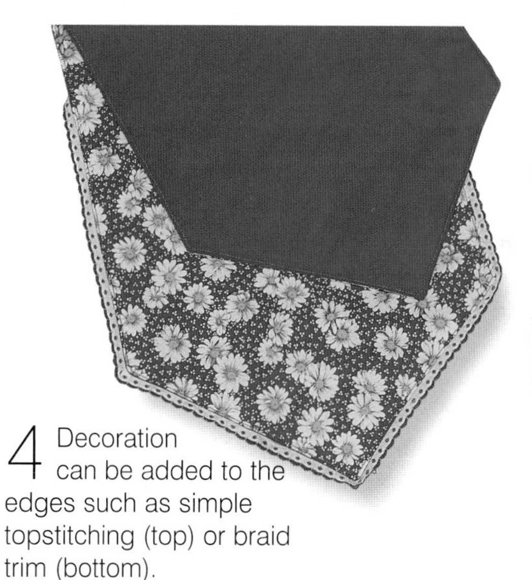

4 Decoration can be added to the edges such as simple topstitching (top) or braid trim (bottom).

Plain runner

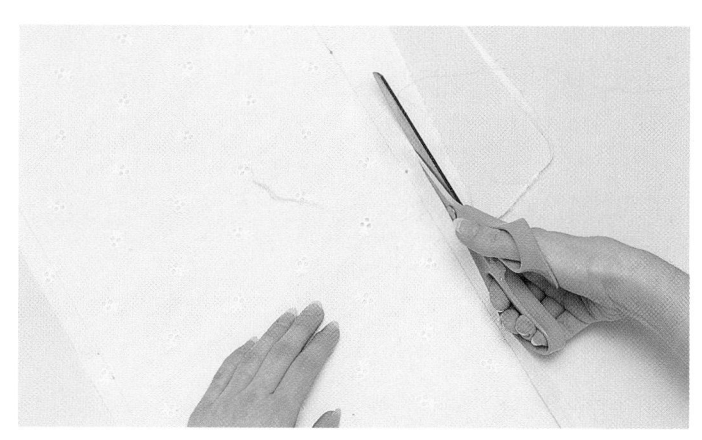

1 Measure and mark the hem foldline on the fabric. Trim the edges evenly ¾ in (1.5 cm) from the marked line.

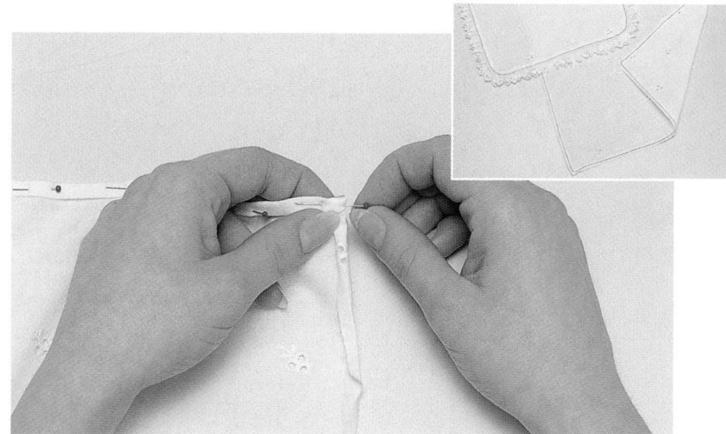

2 Turn under and pin a narrow double hem along the foldline. Stitch in place. The runner can be left plain or a decorative edging can be added as shown (inset).

Placemats

Placemats can be as simple as two pieces of fabric stitched together with a layer of batting (wadding) in between, or as ornate and elegant as you desire. Made in sets with matching napkins, they are ideal personalized presents for a bride or someone moving into a new home.

Reversible placemat

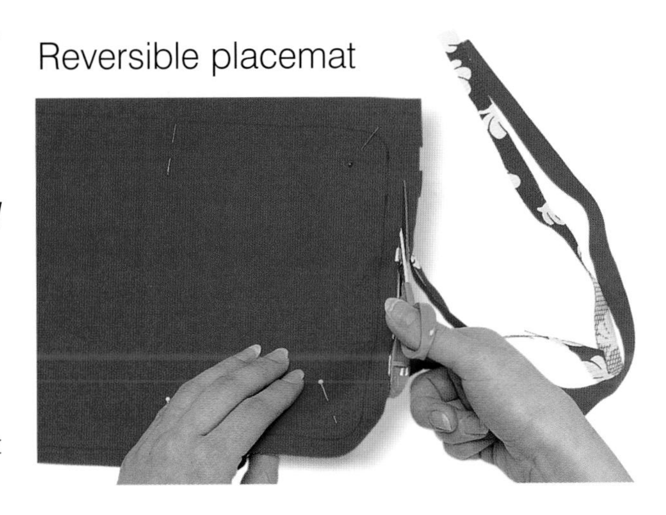

1 Cut two pieces of fabric the same size and pin them right sides together. Mark the shape of the finished mat on one piece, trim ¾ in (1.5 cm) from the marked line.

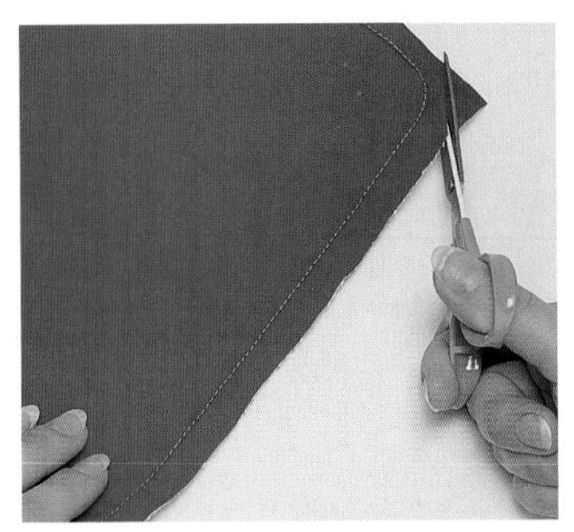

2 Stitch along the marked line, leaving a 4-in (10-cm) gap for turning. Clip the corners.

3 Turn the mat right side out through the gap and press to align the edges. Slipstitch the gap closed.

4 Repeat to make as many placemats as required. The finished mats can be used on either side, or try alternating them around a table.

SELF-BOUND PLACEMAT

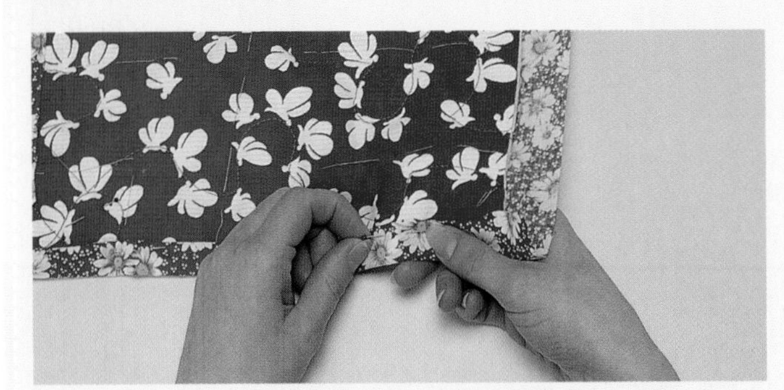

1 Cut fabric for the top and one piece of batting (wadding) the finished size of the mat. Cut the backing 2 in (5 cm) larger all around. Baste the top and batting together. Turn the edge of the backing fabric to the front and pin a hem, mitering the corners.

2 Topstitch along all four turned edges, removing pins as you work. The turned edge of backing fabric has become the binding on the mat.

Appliqué placemat

1 Measure and cut two pieces of fabric and one of batting (wadding) the desired size plus seam allowances.

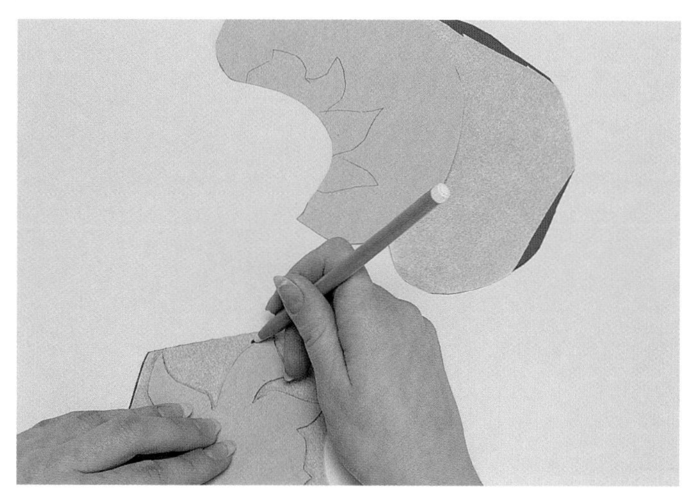

2 Make appliqué templates and draw around them on the paper side of a piece of fusible webbing. Iron the appliqué shapes to the wrong side of the appliqué fabric and cut out along the marked lines.

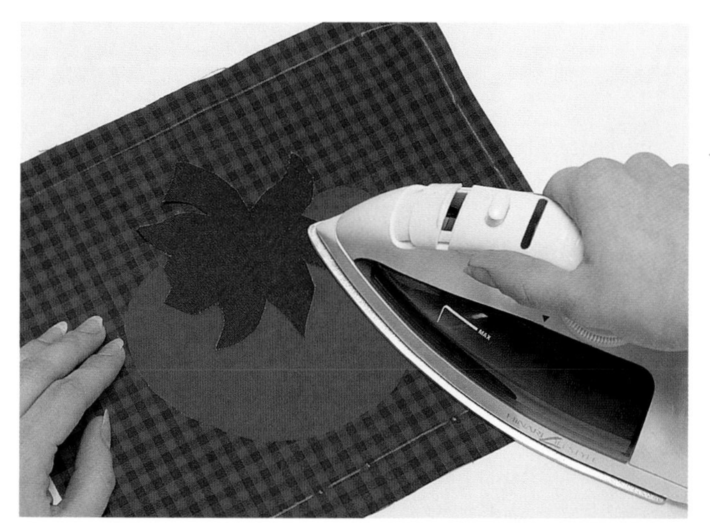

3 Position the appliqué shapes on the right side of the top fabric. When the design is arranged satisfactorily, remove the paper backing from each piece in order and press in place following the manufacturer's instructions.

4 When all the shapes are in place, satin-stitch carefully all around each shape to finish the edges.

5 To finish each placemat, follow steps 2 and 3 of making a reversible placemat, with right sides together and the batting on the bottom.

TIRANT LO BLANC

Project: Double dressing

A floor-length circular tablecloth can cover the most basic or battered of tables to create a highly effective side table to use in the living room or bedroom. This cloth should come all the way to the floor, so measure carefully and cut an extra ½ in (1.25 cm) if necessary to make sure it covers all parts of the table. If the area gets a lot of use, you can cover the long cloth with a protective top cloth in a matching, contrasting, or coordinated fabric.

YOU WILL NEED

CIRCULAR TABLECLOTH

- *A square of fabric the diameter of the table plus twice the drop plus 1 in (2.5 cm) for hems all around. If you join lengths to create the size, add another 1 in (2.5 cm) for seam allowances*

SQUARE TOP CLOTH

- *A square of fabric the diameter of the table plus 10 in (25 cm)*
- *4-in (10-cm) wide strips of border joined to make the combined length of all four edges of the top cloth plus 2 in (5cm)*

ACCESSORIES

- *4 tassels*
- *Pencil or marker pen*
- *String*

Making the tablecloth

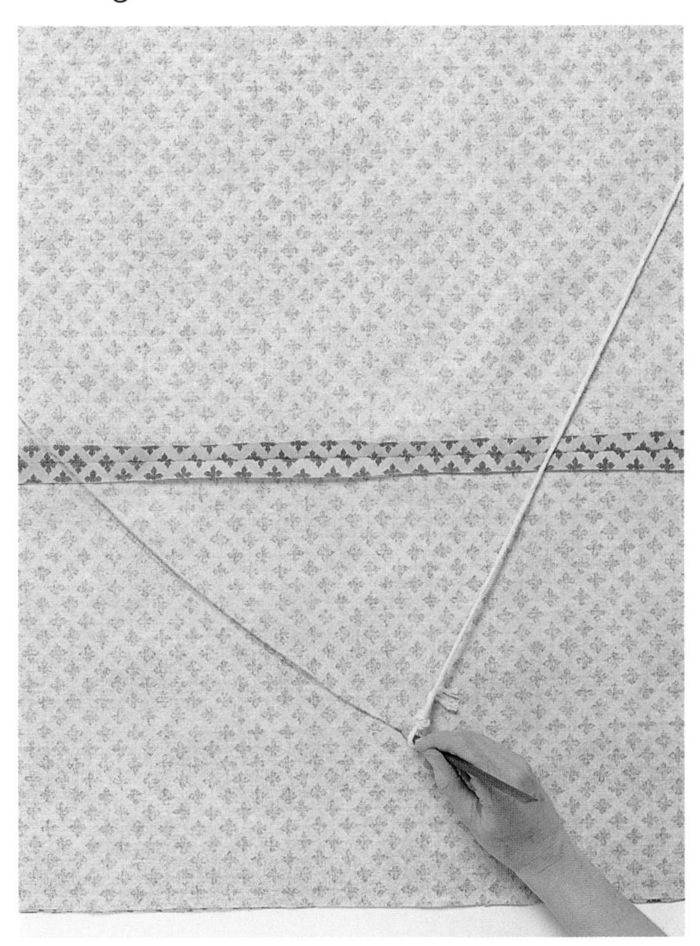

1 Measure and cut the fabric, joining lengths if necessary. Fold the fabric into quarters and secure the edges. Draw a quarter circle along the unfolded edges using a pencil and string.

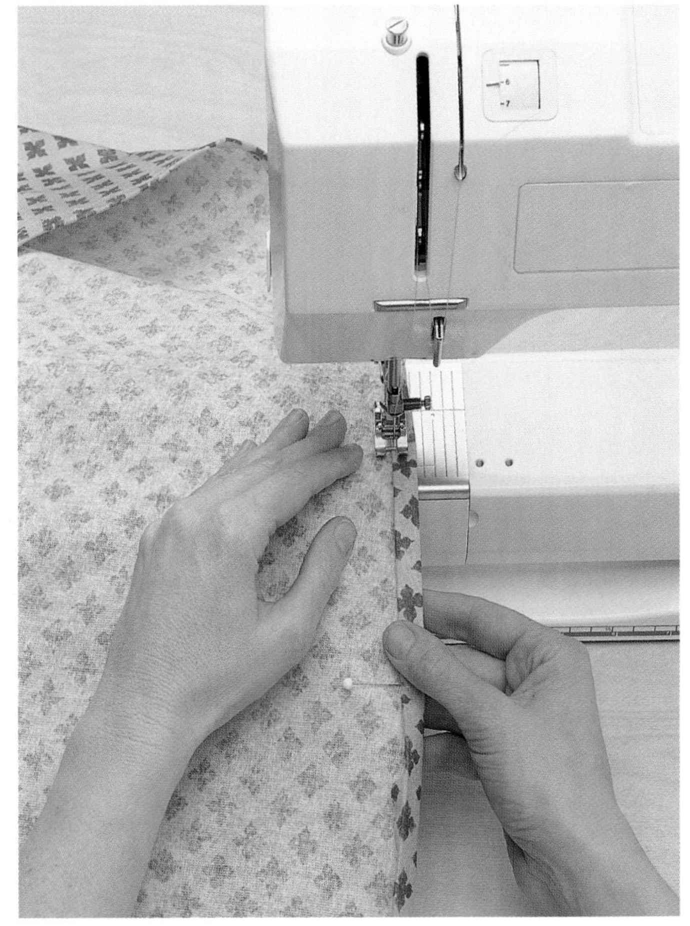

2 Cut carefully along the marked line. Press a narrow double hem around the edge and stitch in place.

Making the top cloth

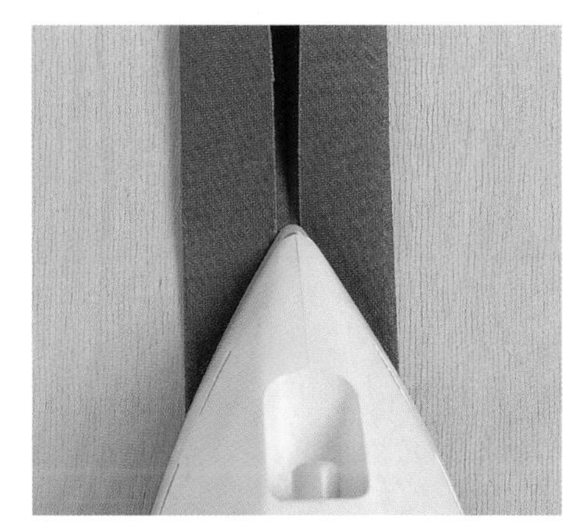

1 Press the border strip in half lengthwise. Open it out and press the raw edges into the center.

2 With right sides together, place the border strip along one side of the square fabric, starting in one corner. Stitch along the first foldline, starting 1 in (2.5 cm) from the end of the strip and stopping 1 in (2.5 cm) before the corner.

3 Fold the border at a right angle away from the main fabric; press.

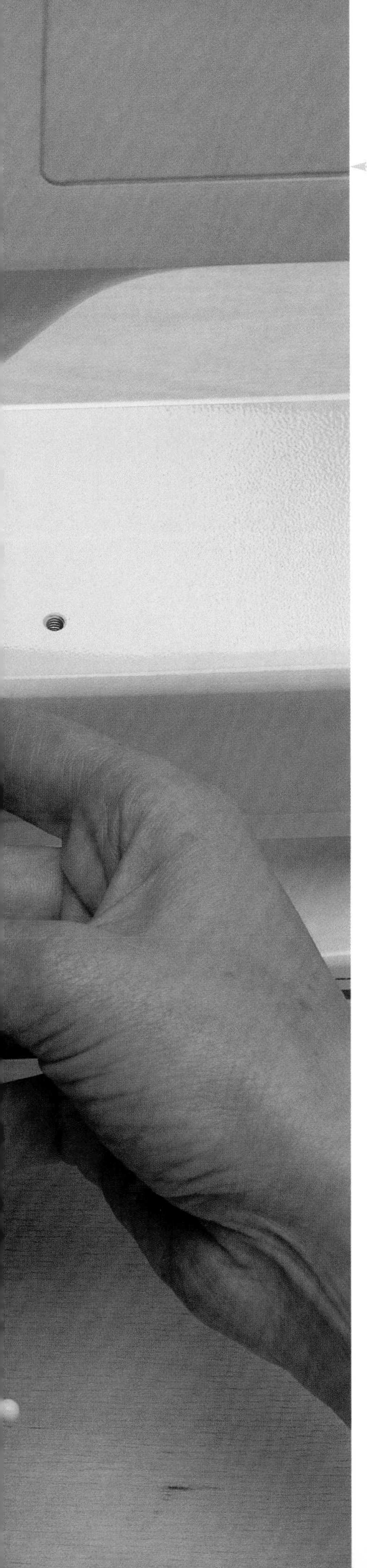

4 Fold the border back over so the fold aligns with the side of the square cloth. Pin and stitch from the fold (following the instructions in step 2). Repeat the process to stitch all sides.

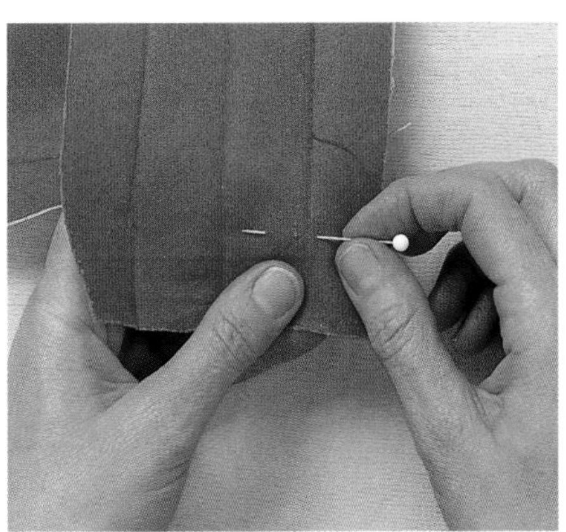

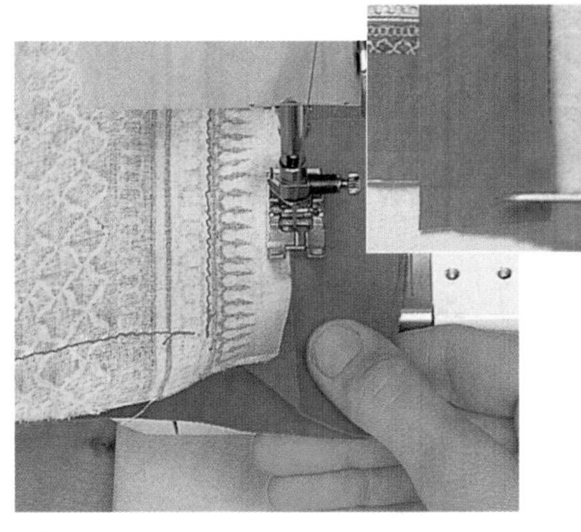

5 Stop stitching 4 in (10 cm) from the fourth corner. Fold the two ends of the binding as in step 3 to create a miter, and pin it in place.

6 Turn the work to the wrong side and stitch the ends of the binding together. (Inset): Trim the seam to leave a ⅝-in (1.5-cm) allowance.

7 Fold the border over to the wrong side of the cloth along the center fold, forming a neat miter at each corner, and press. Pin and slipstitch each miter.

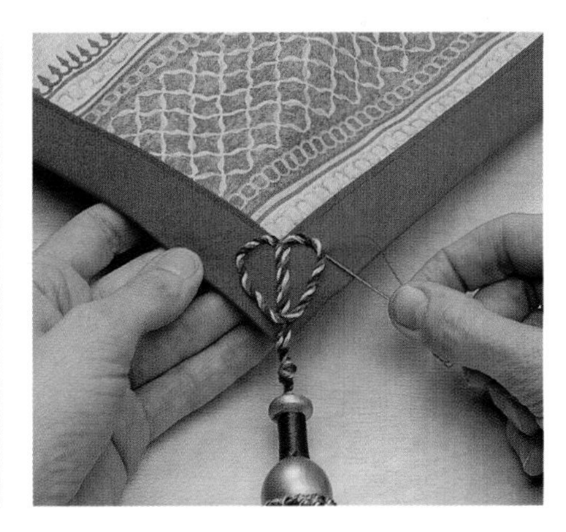

8 Working on the right side, topstitch close to the edge of the border strip, catching in the folded strip at the back at the same time.

9 Handstitch a decorative tassel in place at each corner and press the cloth from the back.

Project: Bordered tablecloth

Adding a border to a tablecloth is a simple but effective way to extend a piece of fabric so that it is large enough to cover a table. If the fabric width suits your table, you may not need seams in the main piece; if you do, add a piece to each side so the seams do not appear across the tabletop (see page 253). If the cloth is to be laundered regularly, choose a washable fabric.

YOU WILL NEED

- *Main fabric: the measured size (length x width plus drops) plus 5/8 in (1.5 cm) all around*
- *Border fabric: two strips the width of the cloth x 6 1/4 in (16 cm) wide: two 6 1/4-in (16-cm) wide strips the length of the cloth*

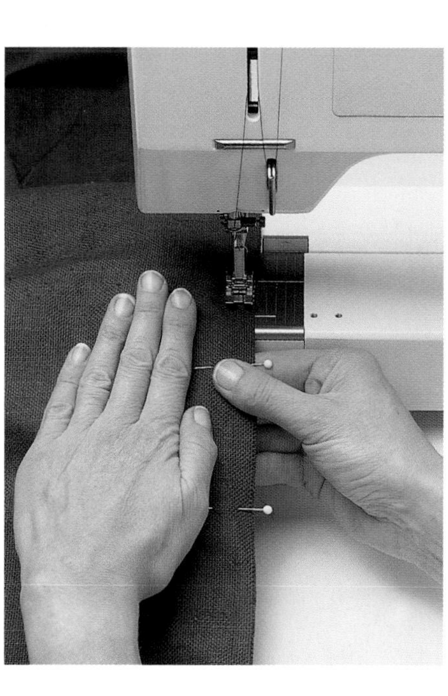

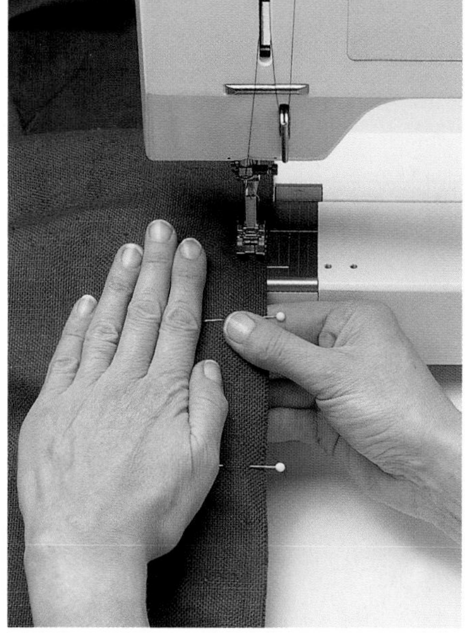

1 Measure and cut the main fabric. Pin the border strips to the main fabric, right side of the border to wrong side of the main fabric. Stitch in place along the four raw edges.

2 Press two opposite strips to the main fabric so the wrong side of the border faces the right side of the main fabric. Repeat with the other two strips.

3 Fold the strips out and trim the ends even with the sides of the main fabric. Cut away an angle at the corners to reduce bulk, but avoid exposing the corner seam. Fold the strips back onto the right side of the cloth.

4 Turn both corners of two opposite strips to make a 45-degree miter and pin it in place.

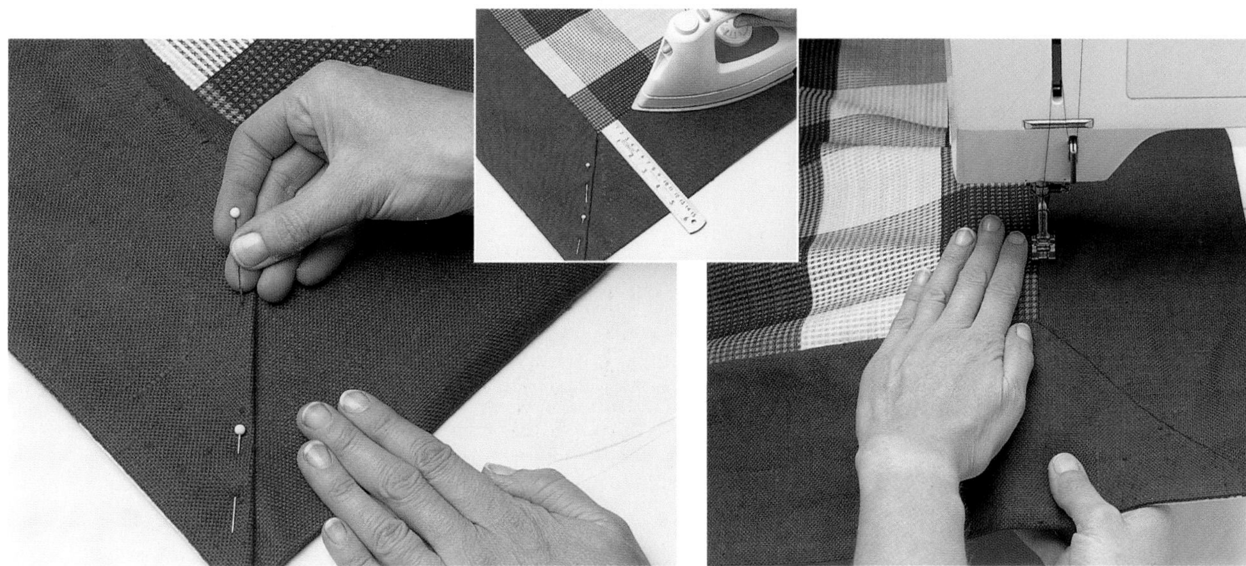

5 Fold these two strips back over the other two strips and pin in place along the mitered seam. Measure a 5-in (13-cm) border from the outer edge. Turn under and press the inner raw edge of the border (inset).

6 Topstitch each mitered corner, then topstitch the turned inner edge of the border to the main fabric.

Project: Quilted table mat

Use these pretty placemats to liven up your table, or give them as a present to a friend. They are quick to make and easy to launder if you make them from a washable fabric and synthetic batting (wadding). The backing fabric is brought to the front to make an attractive self-binding.

YOU WILL NEED

For each mat:

- *Top fabric cut to desired size*
- *2-oz (56-g) batting (wadding) cut to finished size plus ½ in (1.25 cm) all around*
- *Backing fabric cut to finished size, plus 1⅜ in (3.5 cm) all around the edges*

1 Place the backing fabric, wrong side up, flat on the work surface. Center the batting on it, and place the main fabric, right side up, centered on top. Pin the layers together with several rows of pins running diagonally across the mat to hold them together securely for quilting.

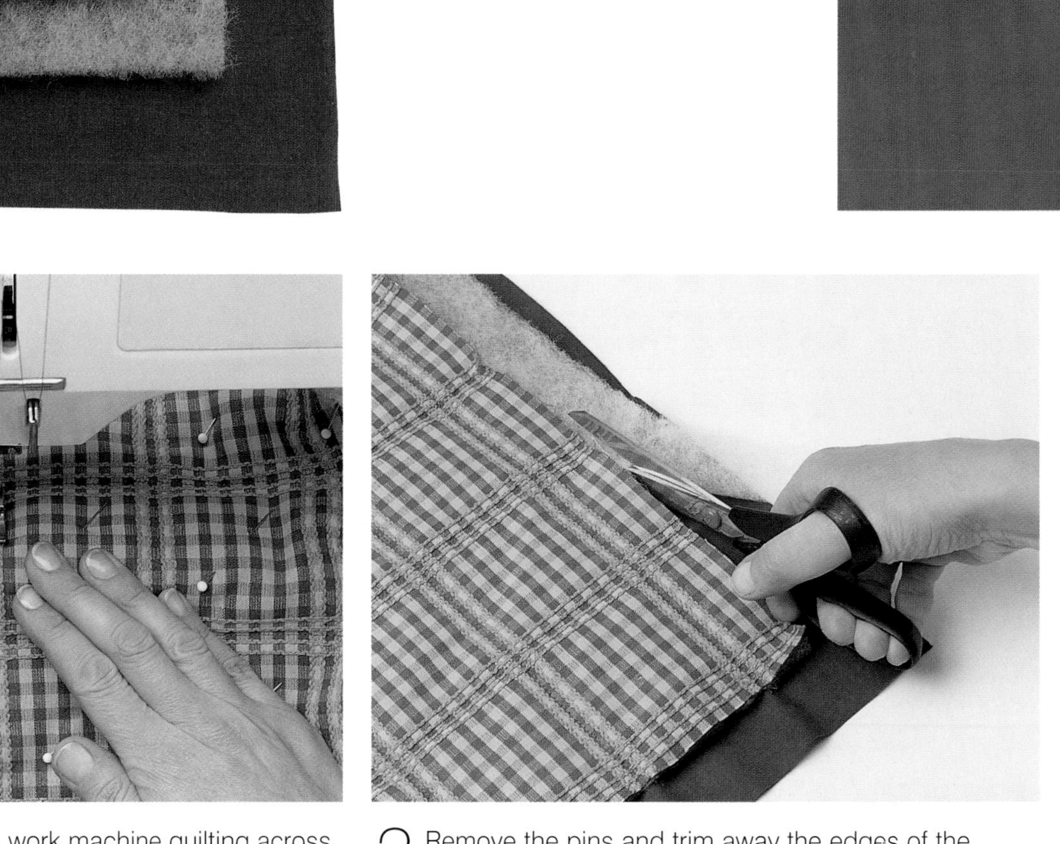

2 Starting from the center, work machine quilting across to one edge, then go back to the center and quilt in the other direction. Make vertical rows of quilting as desired (here the lines follow the pattern of the fabric), then work horizontally across the mat in a similar way.

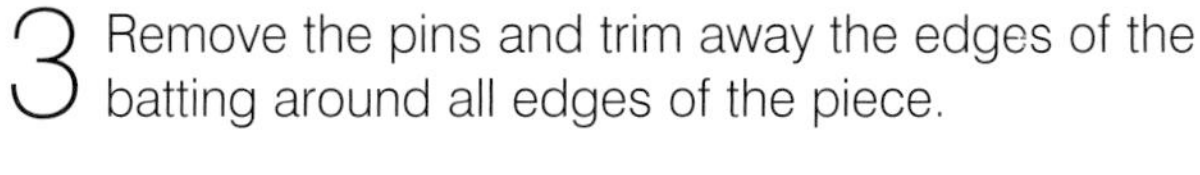

3 Remove the pins and trim away the edges of the batting around all edges of the piece.

4 At each corner, fold the point of the backing fabric over the main fabric as shown. Fold the backing in half along the sides so the raw edge lies along the raw edge of the main fabric. Turn the backing again to enclose the raw edge of the main fabric and pin along the fold. The folded edges will make a miter at each of the corners.

5 Topstitch the inside folded edge of the backing all around, turning sharply at the corners. The small miters should be held in place by the stitching, but slipstitch to secure them if you prefer.

Cushions and pillows

Cushions and throw pillows can make a decorative statement by adding accent colors and softening hard surfaces. They are straightforward to make and can be embellished in a variety of ways. Pads, or forms, can be purchased to fill standard-sized covers, but they are simple to make in almost any shape.

Circular cushion with overlap closure

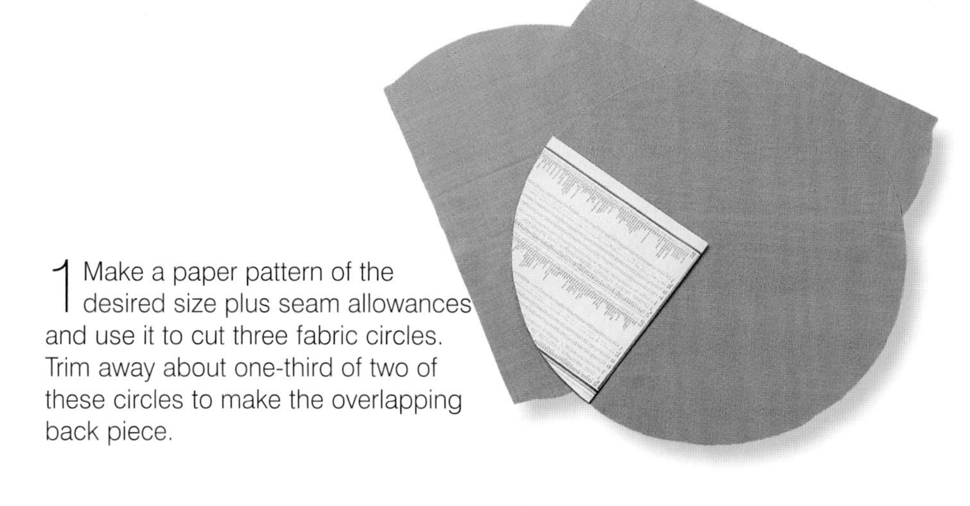

1 Make a paper pattern of the desired size plus seam allowances and use it to cut three fabric circles. Trim away about one-third of two of these circles to make the overlapping back piece.

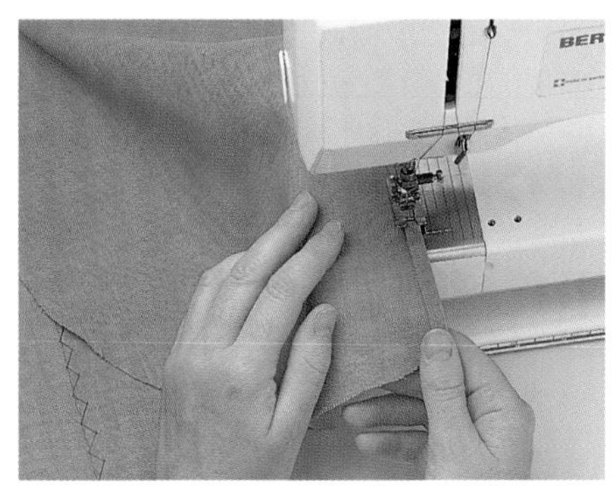

2 Fold back, press, and herringbone stitch a deep single hem on the straight raw edge of one backing piece. Turn under and stitch a double hem on the straight edge of the second piece.

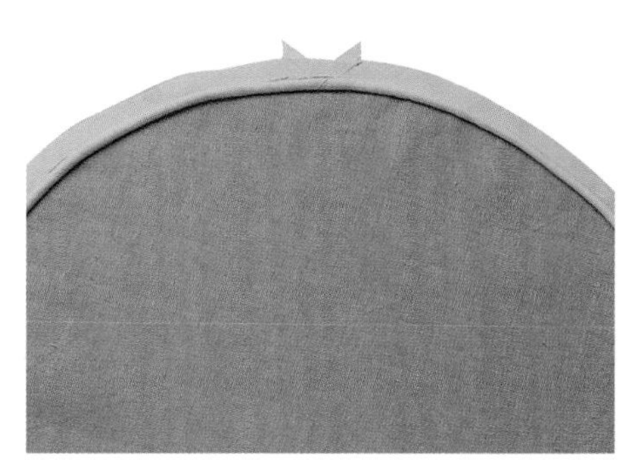

3 Apply piping to the edge of the circular front piece, making sure the piping lies just inside the seam allowance all around. Join the ends of the piping.

4 Lay the front piece right side up, then place the herringboned piece on it, right sides together. Align the hemmed piece right side down on top. Pin and baste all three pieces.

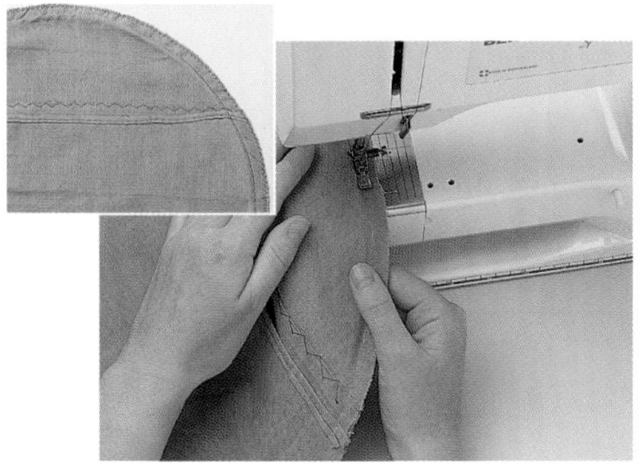

5 Using a zipper foot, stitch all around the edge of the circle. Work as close to the piping as possible. Zigzag-stitch the raw edges of the seam allowance (inset).

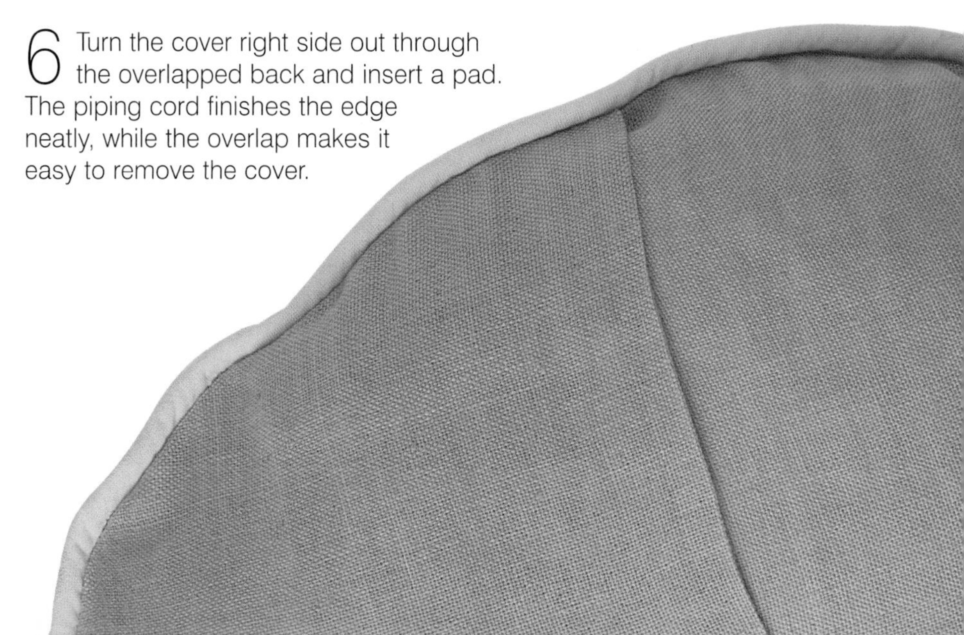

6 Turn the cover right side out through the overlapped back and insert a pad. The piping cord finishes the edge neatly, while the overlap makes it easy to remove the cover.

Square cushion with zipper

1 Cut two pieces of fabric to the final size plus seam allowances. Mark a seamline ½ in (1.25 cm) from the edge on the wrong side of one piece. Use a zipper 2 in (5 cm) shorter than one side of the finished cushion.

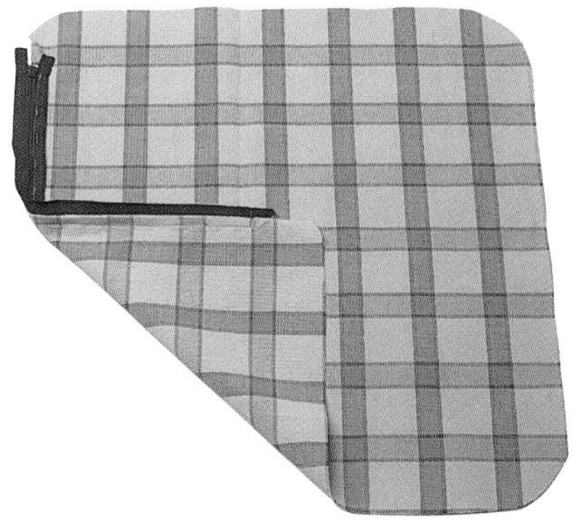

2 On one edge of the marked piece, pin, baste, and stitch the zipper into position. Center the zipper on the seam as shown. Backstitch at both ends to secure.

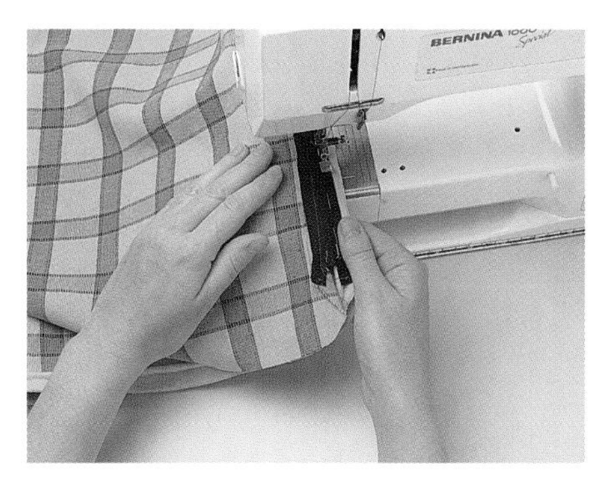

3 If you are using piping or another trim, apply it to the edge of the second, unmarked piece. Baste and stitch the other side of the zipper to one edge of the trimmed piece with the teeth resting against the trimming.

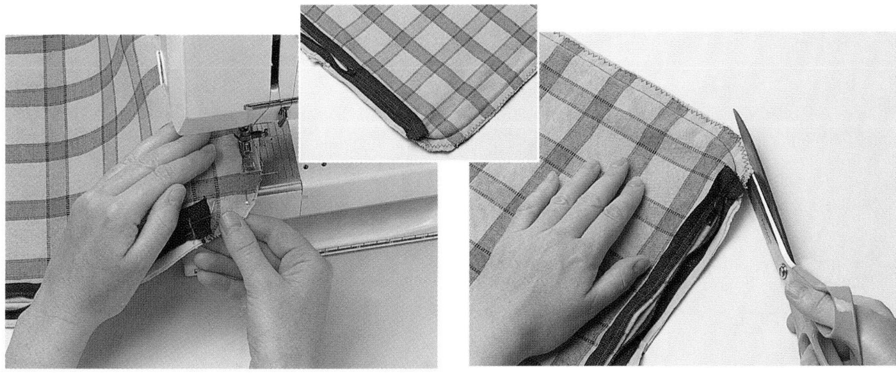

4 Open the zipper, and pin and stitch the two pieces, with right sides together, around the sides. Begin and end just short of the zipper, using backstitch to secure it. Zigzag-stitch the seam allowance (inset).

5 Trim the seam allowance without cutting through the stitching. Turn the cover right side out through the open zipper and insert a pad.

ROUNDING CORNERS

Gently rounding the corners of a square cushion cover will give a more attractive finish on covers that have a decorative edge such as piping or ruffles.

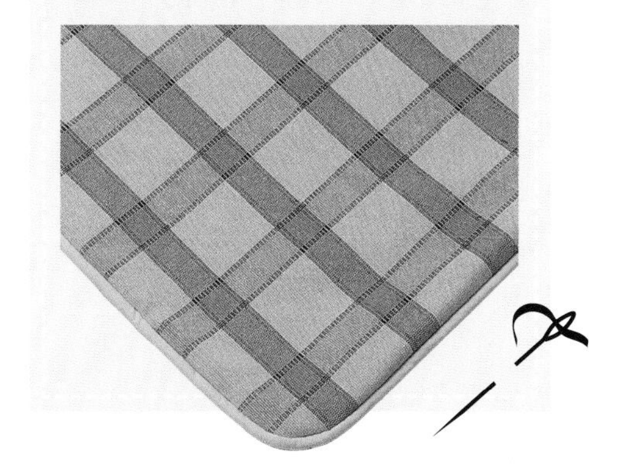

Square and circular cushions

Each finished cover is made using a different method for opening. The zipper and overlap techniques are interchangeable and work for most cushion shapes.

Shaped cushions

Making cushions in geometric shapes is straightforward, but for some complicated shapes you will need to make a pattern for both the pad and the cover, using heavy paper. The pattern for the cover will need to be slightly larger—¼ in (5 mm) all around—than the pad pattern.

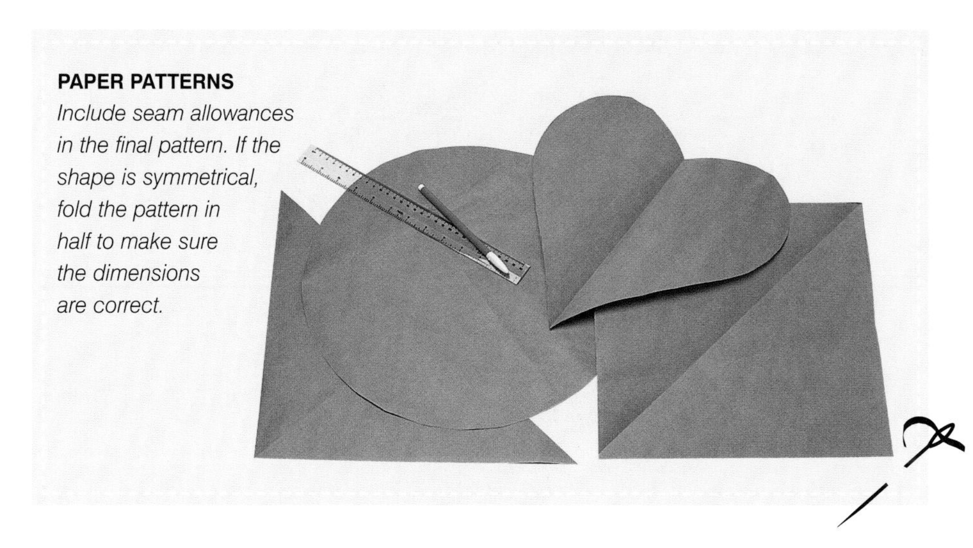

PAPER PATTERNS
Include seam allowances in the final pattern. If the shape is symmetrical, fold the pattern in half to make sure the dimensions are correct.

Heart-shaped cushion pad

1 Measure, draw, and cut out a paper pattern for the heart shape to the desired size of the cushion plus seam allowances. Cut out two shapes from heavy lining fabric and mark the seamline on one piece.

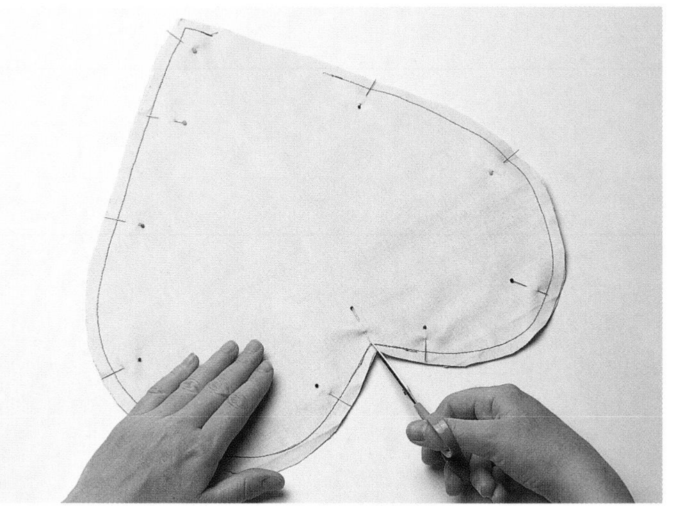

2 Pin and stitch the pieces with right sides together, leaving a 4-in (10-cm) gap along one straight edge for turning and stuffing. Clip the corners and curves.

3 Turn right side out and press. Stuff the pad to the desired fullness and slipstitch the gap to close it.

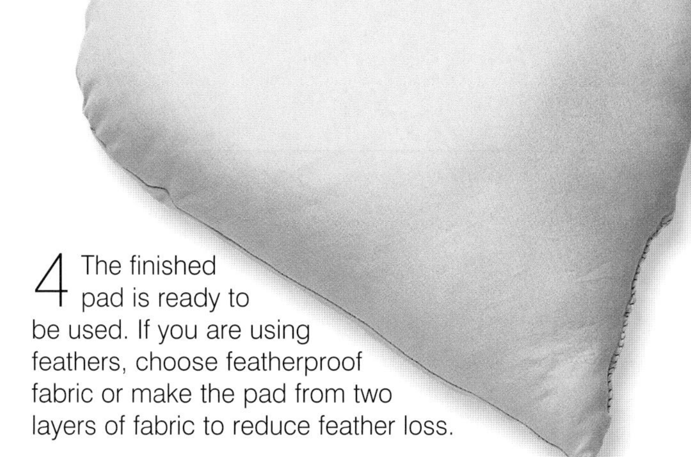

4 The finished pad is ready to be used. If you are using feathers, choose featherproof fabric or make the pad from two layers of fabric to reduce feather loss.

Heart-shaped cover with ties

1 Use the shaped pattern to cut out a second pattern with dimensions that measure ¼ in (5 mm) larger than the pad pattern. Cut one piece for the front. Fold the pattern in half, then fold a generous overlap. Use the folded pattern to cut out two back pieces. Mark the seamline on the front piece. Mark the center foldline on the back pieces.

2 Measure two long strips for the ties. The ties shown measure 2 ½ x 14 in (6 x 35 cm). Mark the seamlines, then cut out the ties. Make sure to include the seam allowances.

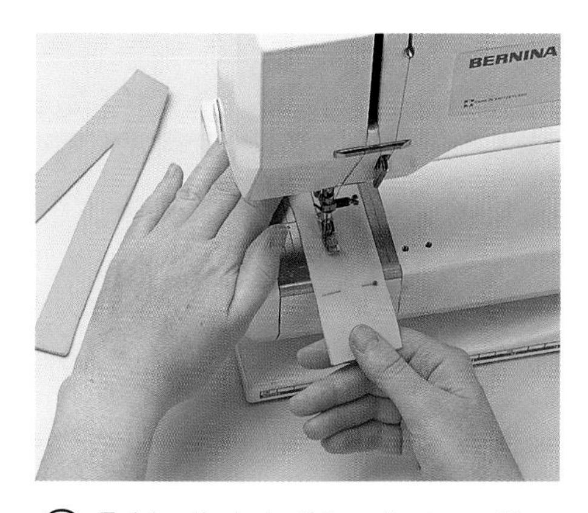

3 Fold a tie in half lengthwise with right sides together and pin. Stitch across one short end and the long edge. Turn right side out and press. Repeat for the second tie.

4 Mark the position of the ties on the back pieces with basting. Position one tie on the overlap piece on the foldline and the other tie on the underlap where the two sides meet.

5 Fold the overlap piece to the wrong side along the center foldline and stitch the raw edge. Turn and stitch a narrow double hem on the underlap piece. Pin and stitch the ties.

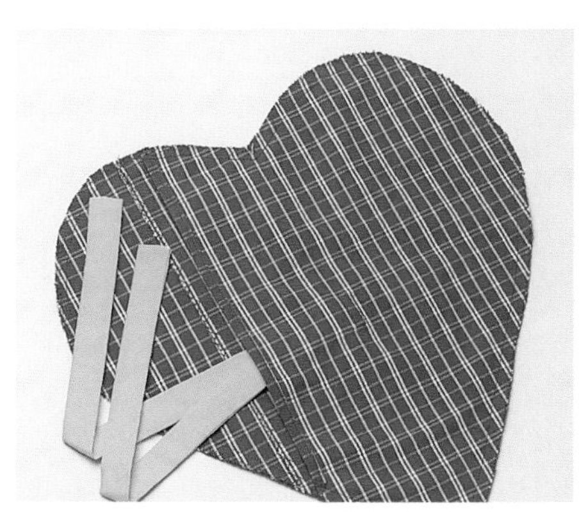

6 Place the overlap, then the underlap on the front piece with right sides together, aligning them carefully. Pin and stitch around the heart.

7 Turn the cover right side out and insert the pad. The tied bow makes a pretty closure.

Decorative techniques

Adding trims, edgings, and other embellishments to cushions makes them unique and coordinates them with a decorative scheme of your own choosing.

Cushion with cord edge

1 To add cord to a finished cushion cover, wrap one end of the cord with masking tape. Stitch the cord along the edge of the cover, making one stitch through the cord and the next through the fabric. Where the ends meet, wrap masking tape around the loose end, allowing for an overlap. Cut through the tape to cut off the surplus cord (inset).

2 Unpick about 1 in (2.5 cm) of the cushion seam. Remove the tape from the cord. Slip the cord ends into the seam, overlapping them slightly. Slipstitch the seam closed, catching in the cord. The join will almost be invisible.

Buttoned cushion

1 Thread an upholstery needle with a long length of doubled quilting or button thread. Sew a button in the middle of one side of a finished cushion. Push the needle through to the other side of the cushion and go back and forth through each button several times. Fasten off the thread securely. You can attach a button on each side if you wish.

2 The buttoned cushion has an attractive roundness that is achieved when the stuffing is not too full.

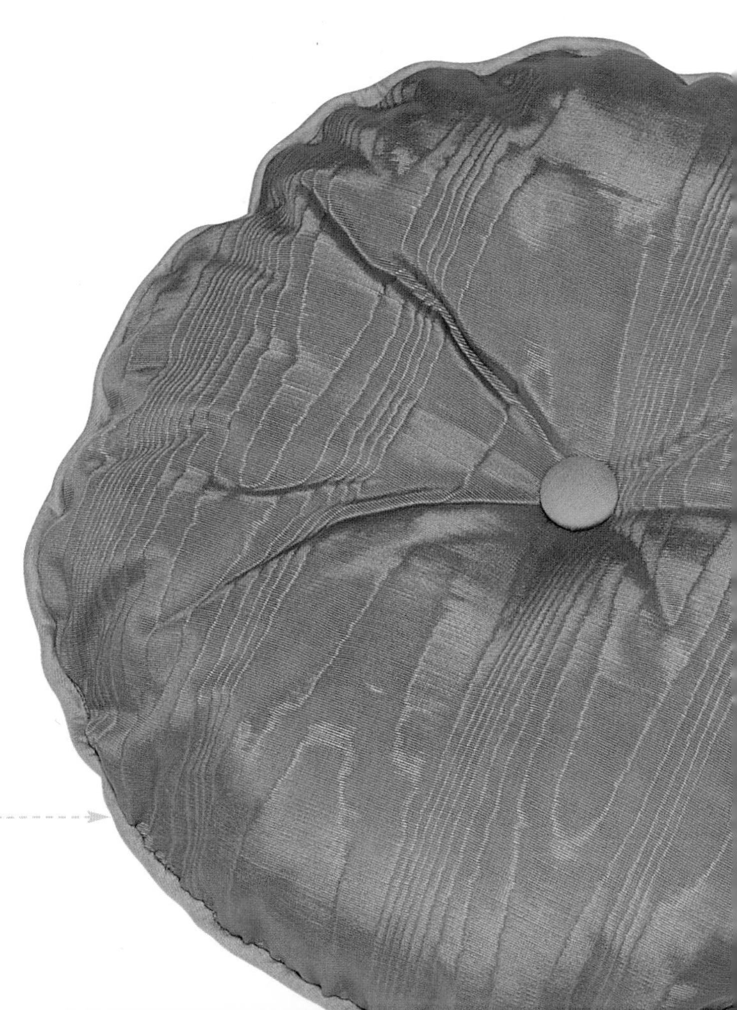

Fringed cushion

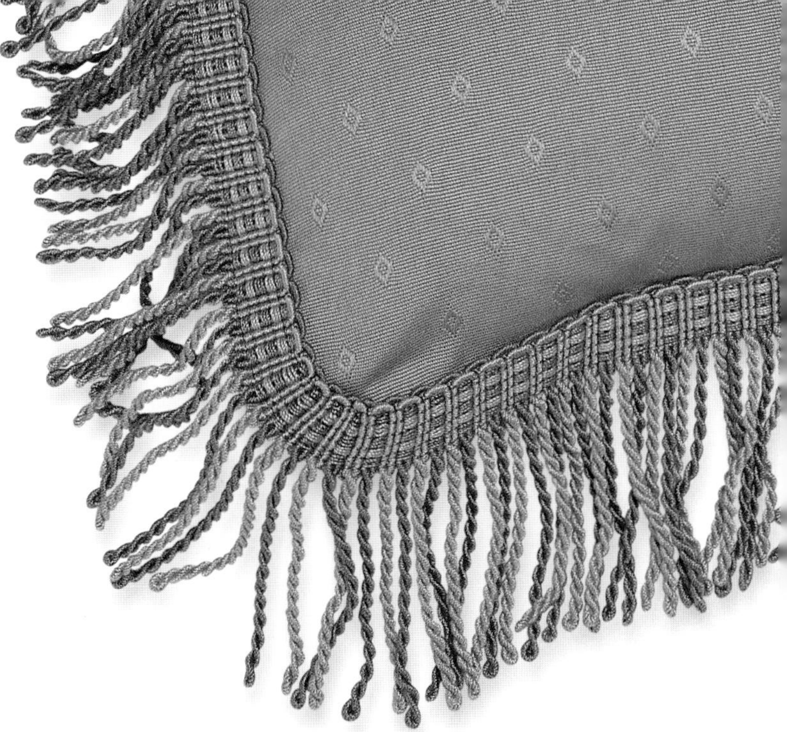

1 Pin the fringe along the front edge of a finished cover. Baste if necessary and stitch in place. Because this fringe has a wide heading, it was stitched along both the top and bottom edges.

2 The sitching lines effectively disappear into the braided heading of the fringe.

Tapestry insert cushion

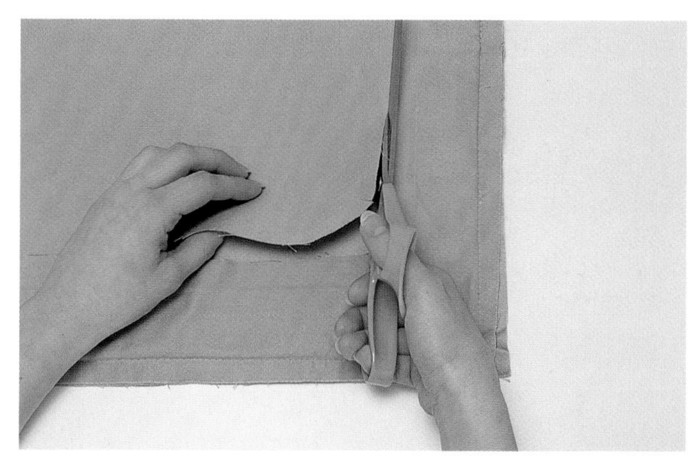

1 On the wrong side of a finished cover, mark and cut out a window the size of the tapestry or needlepoint piece, allowing a generous seam allowance all around. Clip as necessary and make sure the cover's closure is open.

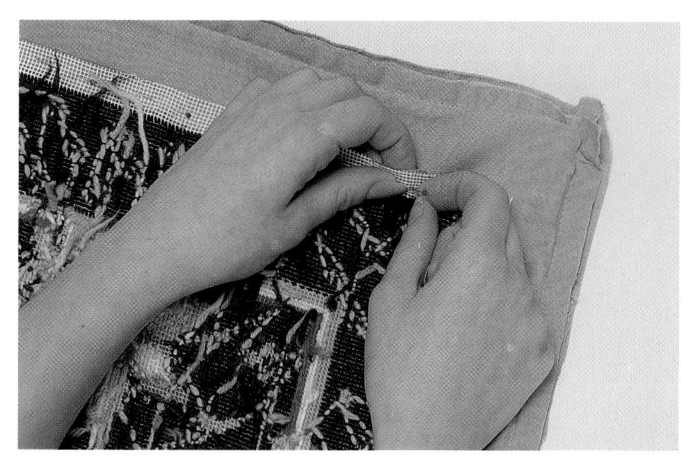

2 Press the seam allowance of the window to the wrong side. Press the insert piece and trim back any edges to 1 in (2.5 cm) or less. Pin the tapestry or needlepoint insert to the allowance along all four sides.

3 Carefully match the edge of the insert to the seamline and stitch it in position. Work backstitch around all four corners to reinforce them. The cover can be turned right side out through the open closure.

Tie cushion

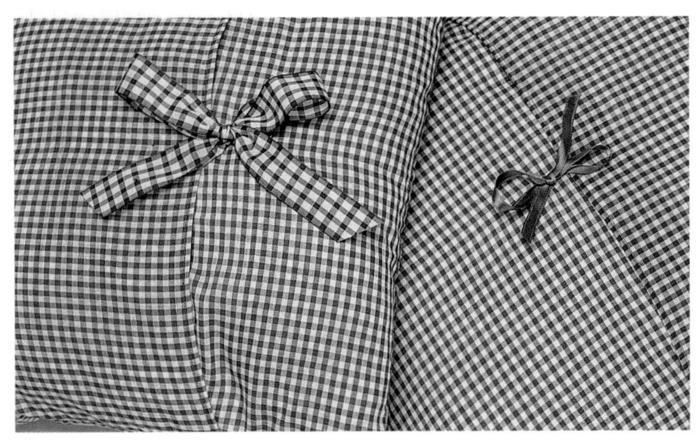

These cushions were both made by the overlap method on page 271 and tied with complementary ribbons.

GINGHAM CROSS-STITCH CUSHION

Simple cross-stitch can be used to enliven inexpensive gingham check. Here, green thread was embroidered in the white squares to make a decorative border with corner motifs.

Ruffled cushion

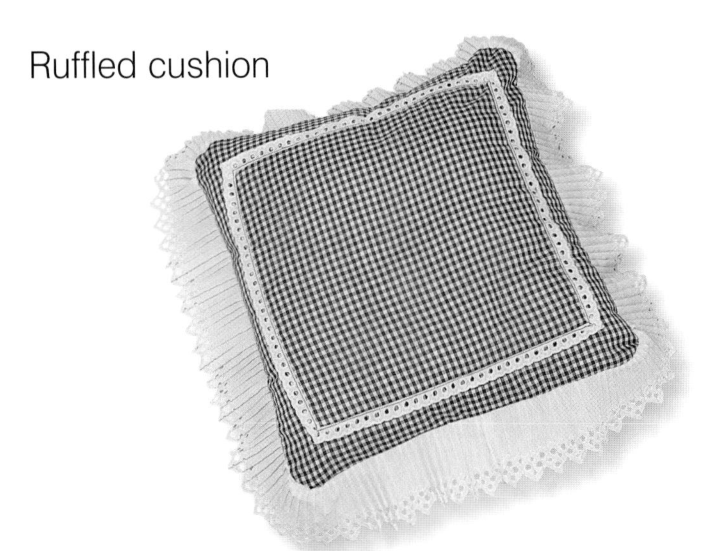

The crisp white ruffle around the edge of this cushion is a ready-made pleated trim, but you can make your own matching or coordinated ruffles if you prefer. The inner border of lace was sewn into position on the front piece before the cover was assembled.

CROSS STITCH

Make a row of diagonal stitches from corner to corner in boxes of the same color. Then work back along the row in the opposite direction.

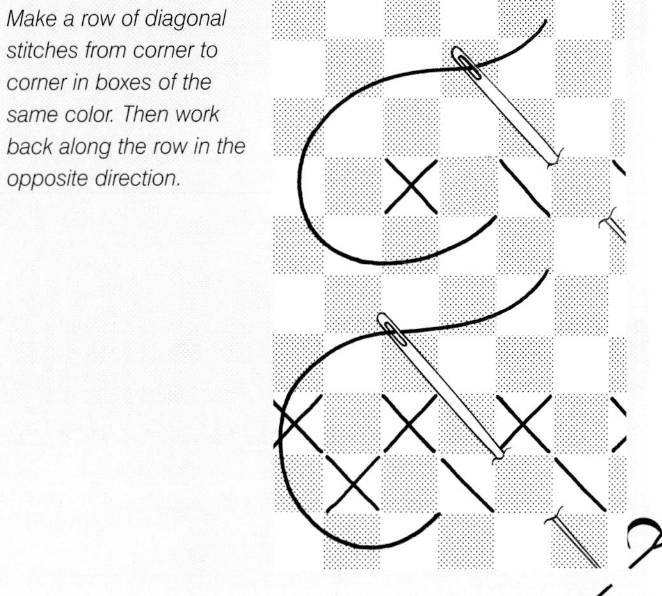

Ruffled tie-on chair cushion

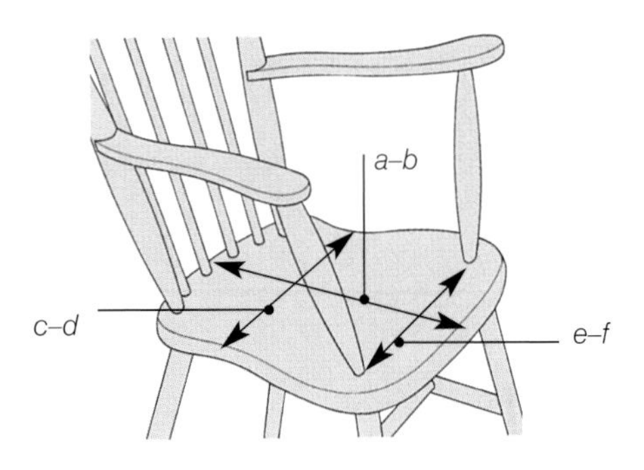

1 Measure the chair seat from front to back (a–b), across the midpoint (c–d), and between the arms (e–f). Make a paper pattern, adjusting it until it is exactly the same size as the chair seat. Add seam allowances.

2 Cut out two seat pieces and four ties, marking the seamlines. Cut a ruffle strip 2 to 2½ times the combined length of the sides and front multiplied by the width plus seam allowance and hems.

3 Make the ties as shown in step 3 of making a heart-shaped cover (see page 271). Turn the ties right side out and gently press them.

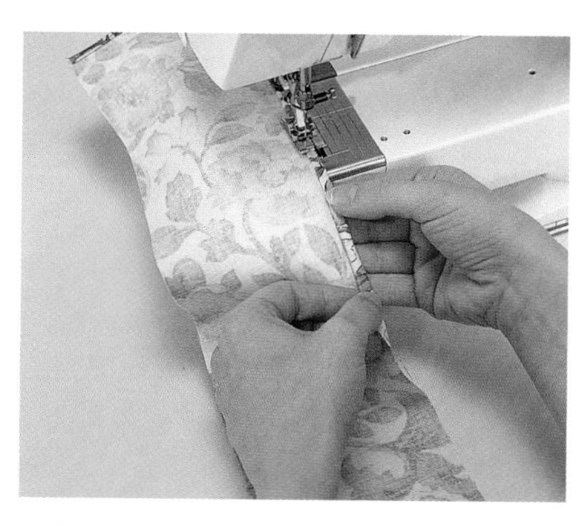

4 Stitch a narrow double hem along one long side and the ends of the ruffle. Run a double row of gathering along the long raw edge.

5 Turn and baste a double hem to the wrong side of each piece between the points where a tie will be positioned on the back edge of the cover. Pin small squares of touch-and-close tape along this hem on each piece. Make sure the squares correspond and align. Stitch on the touch-and-close tape, then stitch along the basted hem on each piece.

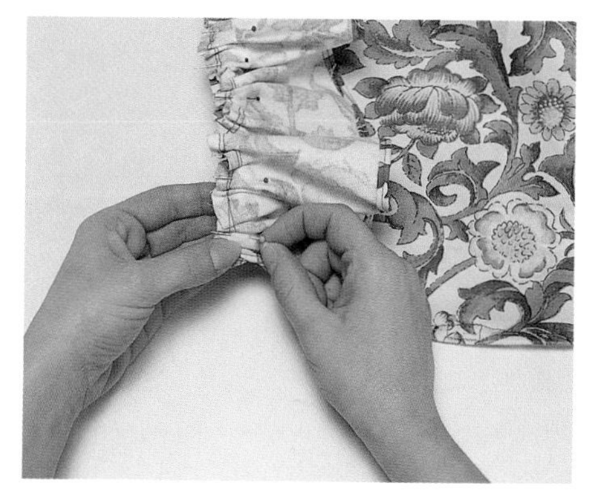

6 Pull up the gathers on the ruffle to the required length. Pin and baste it along the three raw edges of one piece with right sides together and the ruffle facing in. Pin and baste two ties in each back corner.

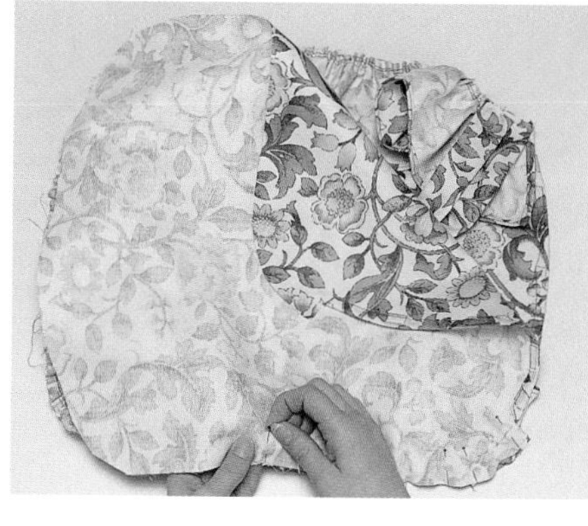

7 Pin the seat pieces with right sides together. Make sure the ruffle and ties are tucked inside the cover, out of the way of the needle.

8 Baste and stitch the cover along the sides and front. Turn it right side out through the back opening. Insert a pad (see page 270) and close the back. Tie the cushion in place.

9 The ruffle softens the hard-edged contours of the seat.

Bound tie-on chair cushion

1 Make a pattern for the chair seat as in step 1 on page 274. Cut two seat pieces from fabric. Cut binding strips to make two ties, two lengths for the back edge, and one length to go around the entire cover plus 24 in (60 cm). Mark seamlines and the tie position on one seat piece.

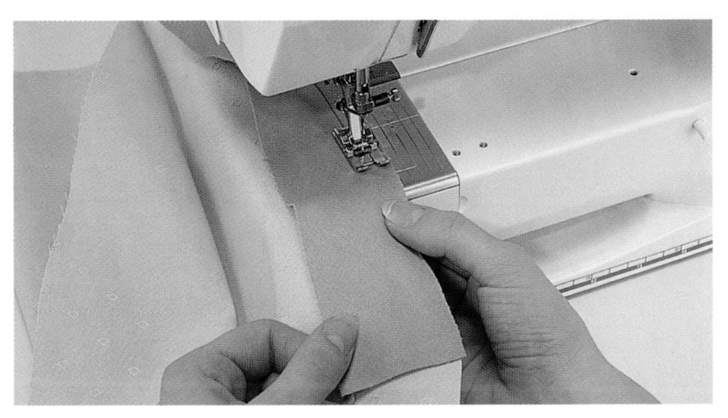

2 Pin and stitch a binding strip, right sides together, to the raw back edge of a seat piece between the points where the ties will be positioned.

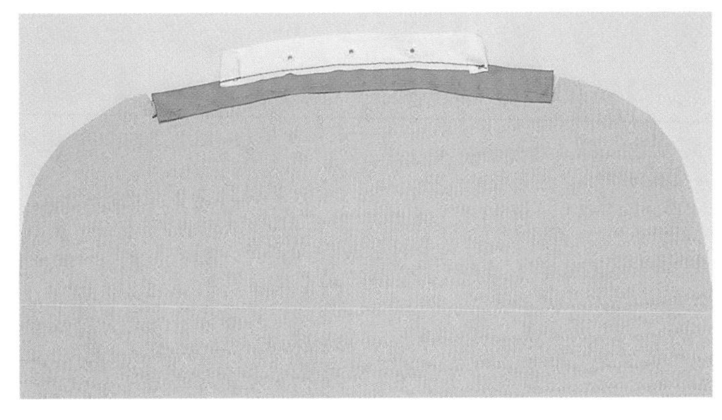

3 Turn the binding to the wrong side. Fold under the raw edges and baste in place. Stitch one edge of a length of fastener tape, right side facing the wrong side of the cushion, to the folded edge of the binding.

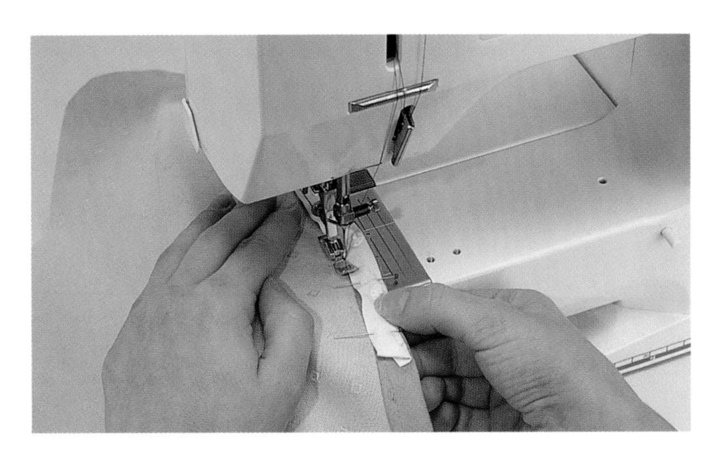

4 Fold back the fastener tape. Pin and stitch along the basting on the binding. Repeat steps 2, 3, and 4 on the second seat piece.

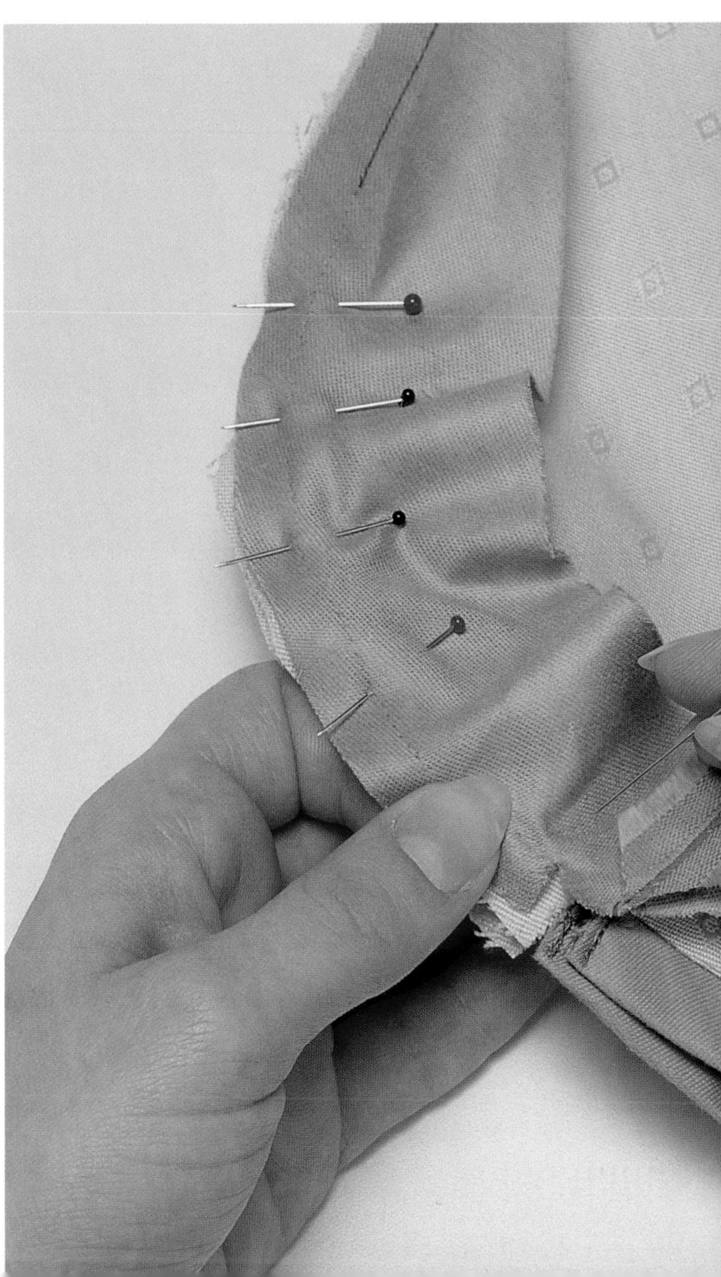

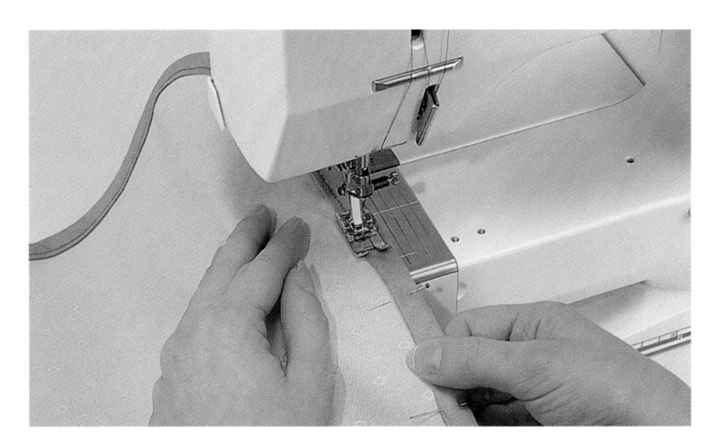

5 Place the seat pieces right sides together. Pin the long binding strip along the raw edges, leaving 12 in (30 cm) at each end to form ties. Clip the seam allowance at the back opening. Stitch the binding in place.

6 Press the binding to the other side. Fold under and pin the raw edges, making sure the raw edge where the binding meets the cushion is enclosed. Pin the binding around the seat and stitch from end to end.

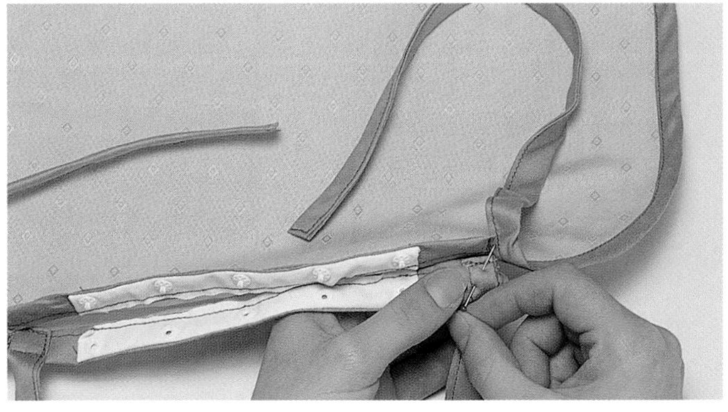

7 Make two separate ties, as in step 3 of tmaking a heart-shaped cover (page 271). Pin and stitch these ties to the binding. Insert a pad, close the back opening, and then finally tie the cushion in place on the chair.

8 This simple cushion is a neat way to pad a hard chair seat.

Box cushions

Box cushions are generally used as seat cushions. They are characterized by the separate strip of matching fabric, known as a box strip, that joins the top and bottom seat pieces.The box strip covers the depth of the cushion pad, which is usually made from thick foam.

Square box cushion with zipper

For this cushion, you will need a zipper 2 in (5 cm) shorter than one side of the cushion and corded piping twice the length of all four sides plus seam allowances.

1 Cut two seat pieces, one long box strip the length of three sides of the cushion times the depth of the pad plus seam allowances, and two narrower box strips, each the length of one side times half the depth of the pad plus seam allowances. Mark seamlines and corners on the wrong side of all pieces.

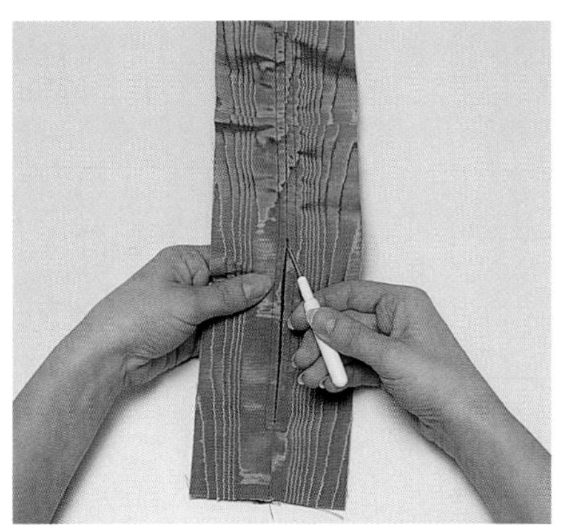

2 Place the narrow strips right sides together and mark the seamline to position the zipper in the center of the length. Stitch each end up to the zipper position and baste the rest of the seam closed. Pin, baste, and stitch the zipper in the seam on the wrong side. Remove the basting.

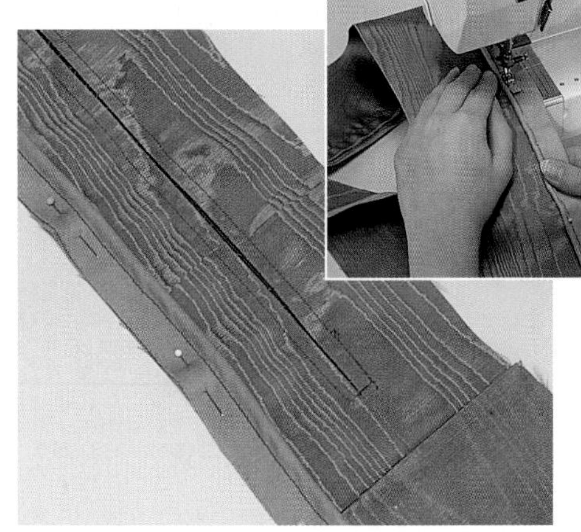

3 Stitch one short end of the long box strip to a short end of the zipper strip with right sides together. Press the seams open. Pin and stitch piping along one long edge (inset).

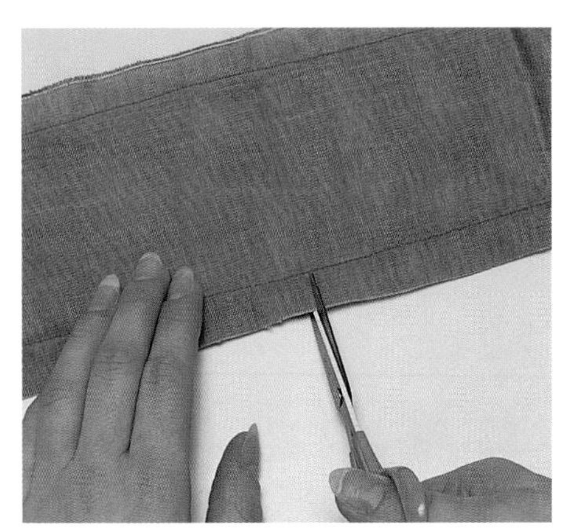

4 Pin and stitch piping to the other side of the strip. Clip into the seam allowance on both sides at each marked corner. Stitch the remaining two short ends, press the seam open, and clip the corner.

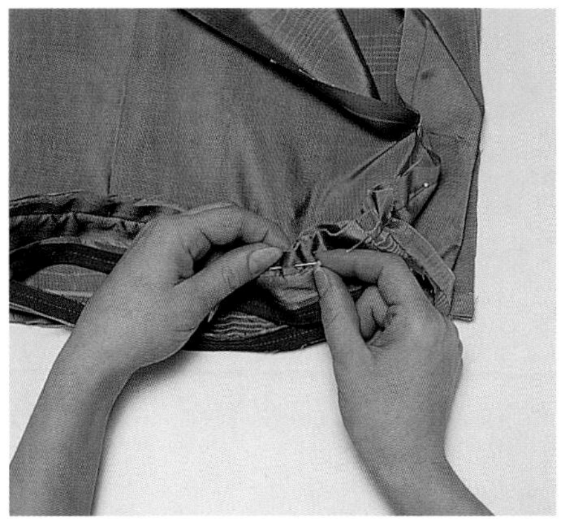

5 With right sides together, pin and stitch a seat piece to the piped strip along the seamline. Open the zipper. Pin and stitch second seat piece to the other side of the strip.

6 Trim the seam allowances and zigzag-stitch the raw edges. Turn the cover right side out through the open zipper and insert the pad.

Bench cushion

1 Cut two seat pieces, one long box strip the length of one long and two short sides of the cushion, and two narrow box strips (see step 1 opposite). Use fastener tape the length of one long side to close the cushion.

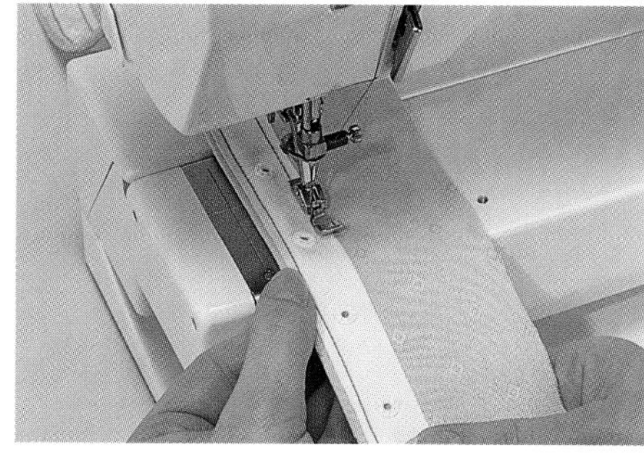

2 Fold a double hem to the right side of one long edge of a narrow box strip. Separate the tape and pin one half along the hem, turning under the short ends. Stitch the top and bottom edges of the tape to the right side of the fabric.

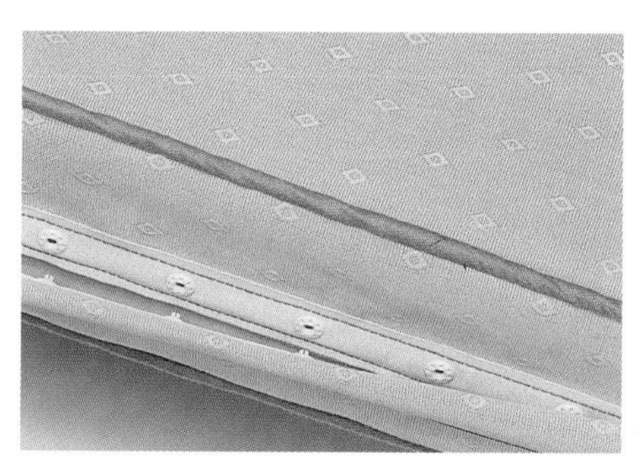

3 Stitch one long edge of the other half of the tape to a long raw edge of the other narrow box strip with right sides together. Fold the tape to the wrong side and pin. Stitch the other edge of the tape.

4 Join the fastener tapes and treat the strip as one piece. Follow steps 3 to 6 opposite to assemble the cover. Open the fasteners and turn the cover right side out through the opening. Insert the cushion pad.

A bench cushion makes a softer, more comfortable seating option. Zippers and various fasteners can be used interchangeably in box cushions.

Easy square cushion

1 Cut two pieces the same size as the pad plus half the depth of the pad plus seam allowances all around. With right sides together, pin and baste one side seam. Insert a zipper.

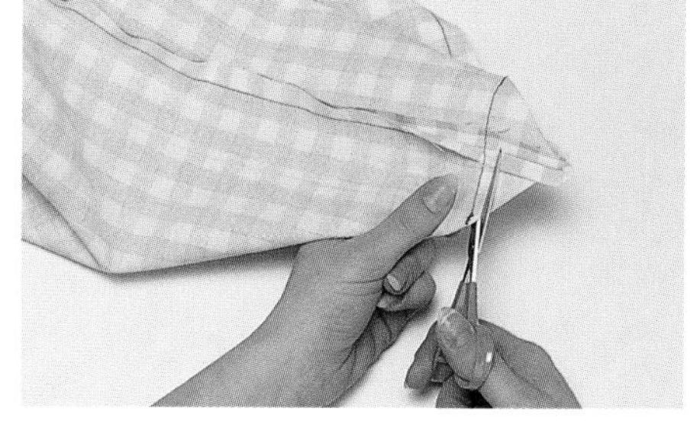

2 Remove the basting and open the zipper. With right sides together, stitch the other three sides. Press the seams open. Stitch across each corner to the depth of the pad with the seamline centered on each corner seam. Trim the corner seams.

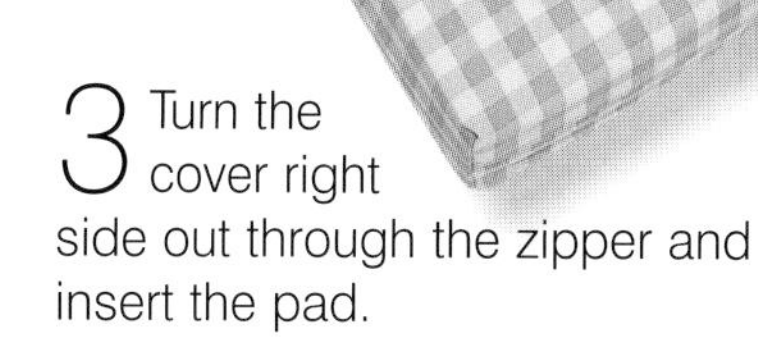

3 Turn the cover right side out through the zipper and insert the pad.

Piped circular box cushion

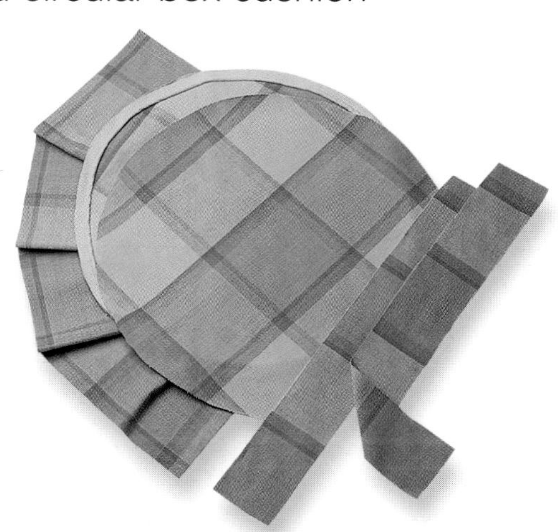

1 Cut two seat pieces, one box strip, and two narrow box strips. The narrow strips should be no more than one-third of the circumference of the pad, and half the depth plus seam allowances. The longer strip should be as long as the rest of the circumference plus seam allowances. You need a zipper 2 in (5 cm) shorter than the narrow strips and corded piping twice the circumference.

2 Pin and stitch a length of piping around each seat piece. Insert a zipper in the narrow strips and make the box strip as in steps 4 and 5 of the zipped box cushion (page 278). Staystitch ½ in (1.25 cm) from each long raw edge, then clip into the seam allowance at intervals of 1 in (2.5 cm).

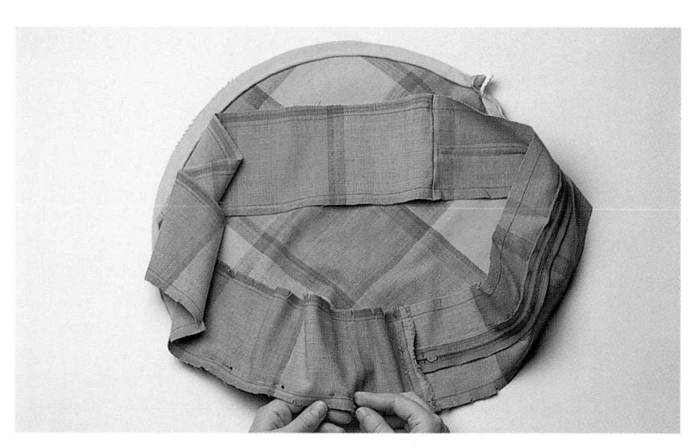

3 With right sides together, pin the box strip to the piped edge of one seat piece, keeping the piping just inside the seam. Stitch in place.

4 Open the zipper and join the other seat piece to the box strip. Trim and zigzag the seams. Turn the cover right side out through the zipper and insert the pad.

This cushion is perfect for any round-seated chair or stool.

Tufted box cushion

1 Cut three strips as long as the circumference of the pad plus seam allowances. The width of one should be the depth plus allowances. The other two should match the radius plus allowances. You need corded piping twice the circumference and two buttons or tassels.

2 Fold one of the wide strips in half with right sides together and stitch the short ends to make a tube. Repeat for the other wide strip. Press the seams open and run a double row of gathering along one raw edge on each strip of fabric.

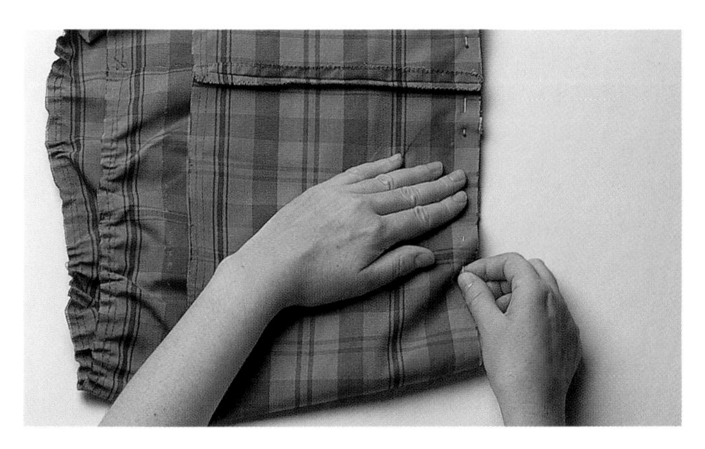

3 Apply piping to the long edges of the narrow strip. With right sides together and aligning the seams, pin and stitch the ungathered edge of one wide strip to one side of the narrow strip. Repeat for the other wide strip.

4 Trim and zigzag the seam allowances and press the seams toward the gathered edges. Pull up the gathers on one side and knot the thread firmly to secure.

5 Insert the pad and align the edges with those of the center strip. Pull up the gathers on the other side and knot them securely. If necessary, stitch to close the gaps.

6 Sew a button or other trim on each side to conceal the gathering. This cover has a period feel that will enhance many styles.

Bolsters

Bolsters are generally round, cylindrical cushions or long, narrow rectangles, which are used to transform a studio bed into a sofa by day. Bolster pads can be purchased or you can make your own.

Gathered bolster

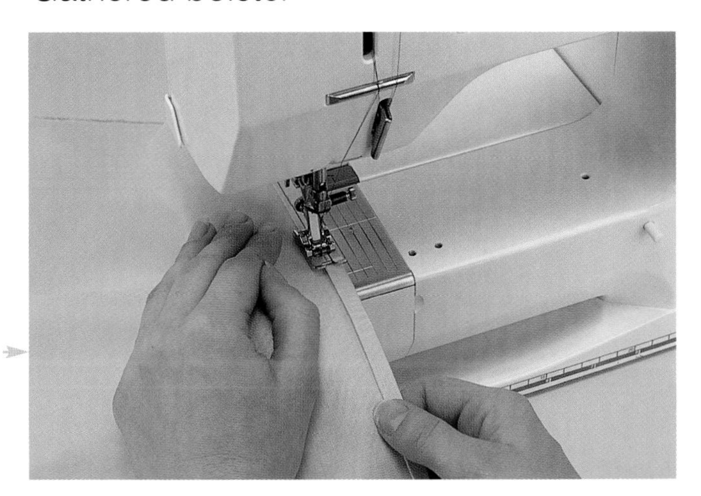

1 Cut a length of fabric. The width is the circumference of the pad plus seam allowances. The length is the length of the pad plus extra for the ruffle, facing, and casing at each end. Stitch a narrow double hem on both short ends.

2 Fold the fabric lengthwise with right sides together. Pin and stitch the long edge to make a tube and press the seam open.

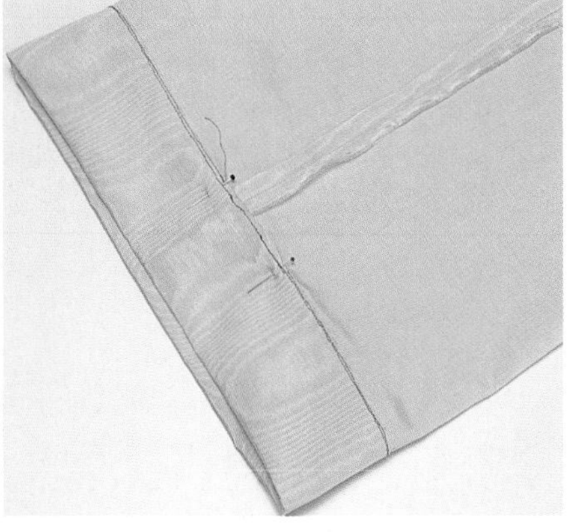

3 Turn under one end to make a deep facing. Matching the seam, pin and stitch along the fold of the hem, leaving a gap in the seam.

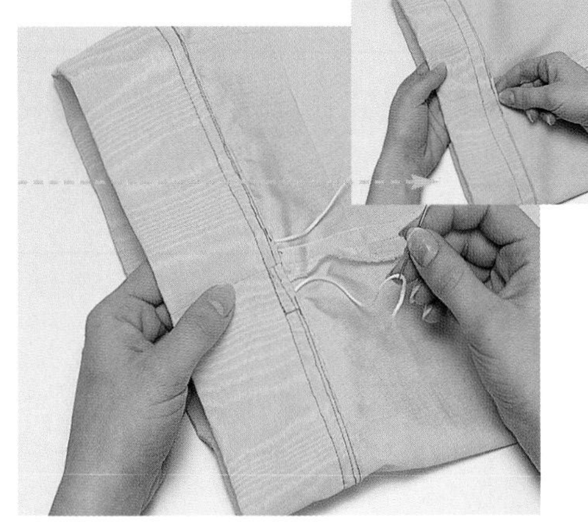

4 Stitch a parallel seam ⅝ in (1.25 cm) away to make a narrow casing. Stitch across the seam without leaving a gap. Repeat at other end of the tube. Pull a cord through one casing, and knot the ends (inset).

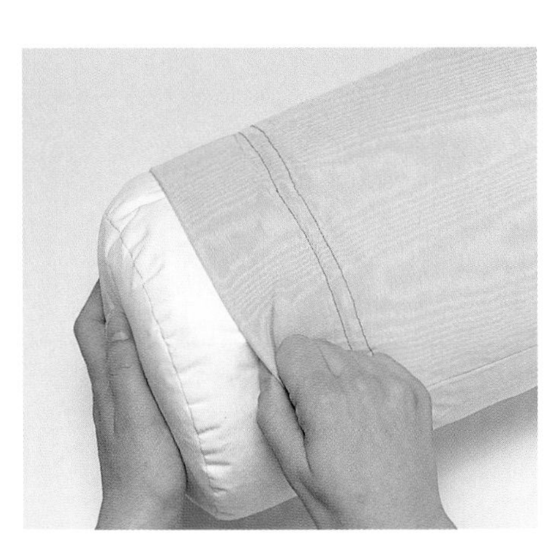

5 Thread a cord through the other casing, but do not pull it up. Turn the cover right side out and insert the pad. Pull up the ungathered cord and make a slip knot to secure.

6 The gathered ends can be left short or long, or you can face them with a contrasting fabric (see page 283).

Piped bolster with zipper

1 Cut one piece of fabric measuring the length and circumference of the pad plus a generous seam allowance all around. Cut two circles the diameter of the pad plus seam allowances. You will need a zipper measuring two-thirds as long as the pad, and corded piping twice the circumference plus seam allowances. Mark the seamlines on all pieces.

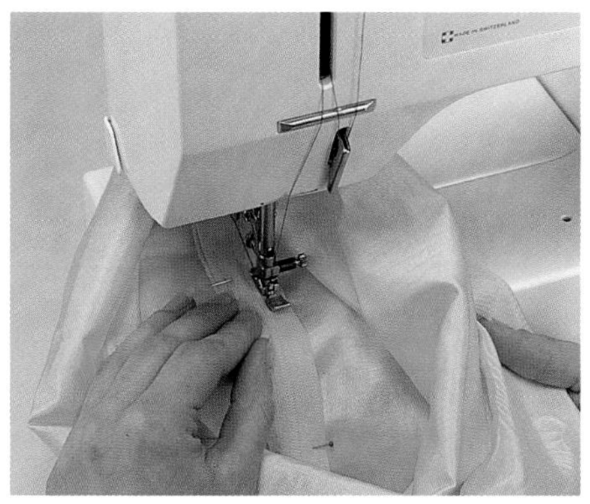

2 Fold the main piece of fabric in half lengthwise with right sides together. The zipper will be centered in the seam. Mark its position and stitch from each end up to the zipper position. Close the seam with basting, then insert the zipper in the seam on the wrong side of the piece. Remove the basting.

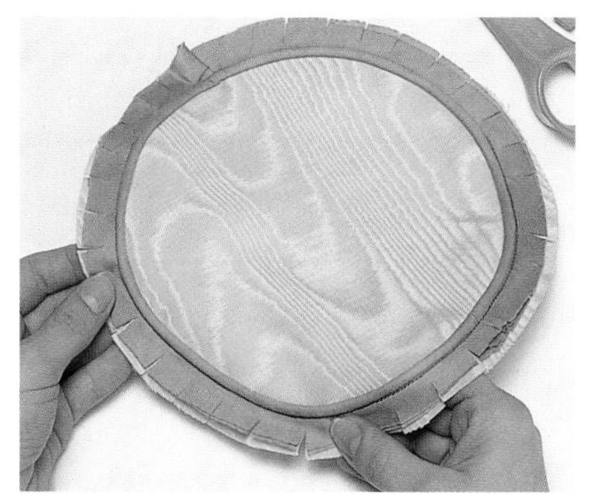

3 Apply piping around the edges of the end pieces. Clip the seam allowance all around to help ease the ends onto the main piece.

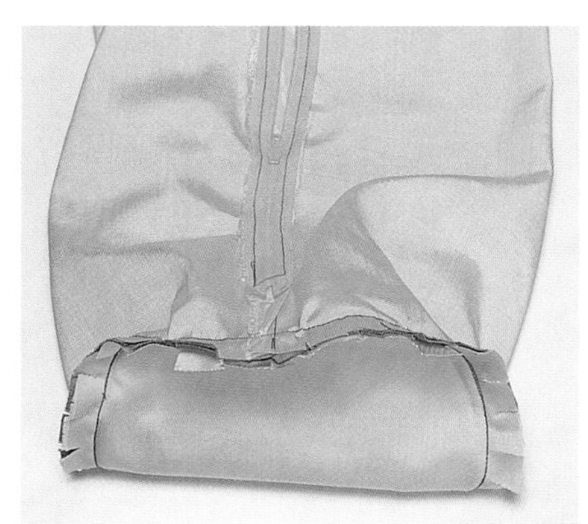

4 Clip into the seam allowances at the ends of the main piece. Open the zipper, and with right sides together, pin, baste, and stitch the end pieces to the main piece. Turn the cover right side out through the zipper and insert the pad.

DECORATIVE IDEAS

Faced gathered bolster
Facings in contrasting fabric have been sewn in as separate pieces at the ends. A length of ribbon with a decorated border has been tied around the end to make the gathers.

Pleated ruffle bolster
A ruffled trim has been applied at each end of the tube. Straight pieces have been added to the ends, then gathered on one edge, and trimmed with self-covered buttons to conceal the gathering.

Project: Colonial cushions

Scatter cushions are a great way to introduce an accent color, a new texture, or a cozy feeling into a room. A grouping of different but coordinated cushions piled on a wicker basket chair are definitely country style, but the same techniques executed in more formal fabrics could just as easily grace the most elegant living room sofa. Choosing fabrics in just two colors—here red and cream—but each a different pattern adds versatility and warmth within a coherent color scheme *(see also page 150).*

YOU WILL NEED

For a 16-in (41-cm) square cushion:

- *½ yd (50 cm) of 45-in (115-cm) wide cream linen fabric*
- *½ yd (50 cm) of 45-in (115-cm) wide red cotton fabric*
- *1⅜ yd (1.25 m) of 2¼-in (5.5-cm) cotton insertion lace*
- *16-in (40-cm) square cushion pad*

Making the cushion

1 Measure and cut out the following elements for the cushion cover: one 7½-in (19-cm) linen square; one 16¾-in (43-cm) linen square with an 8¾-in (22-cm) square cut out of its center to leave a 4-in (10-cm) border all around; two linen rectangles, one 10½ in (27 cm) x 16¾ in (43 cm) and one 13 in (33 cm) x 16¾ in (43 cm); one cotton rectangle 16¾ in (43 cm) x 36¾ in (94 cm); 1⅜ yd (1.25 m) of 2¼-in (5.5-cm) insertion lace.

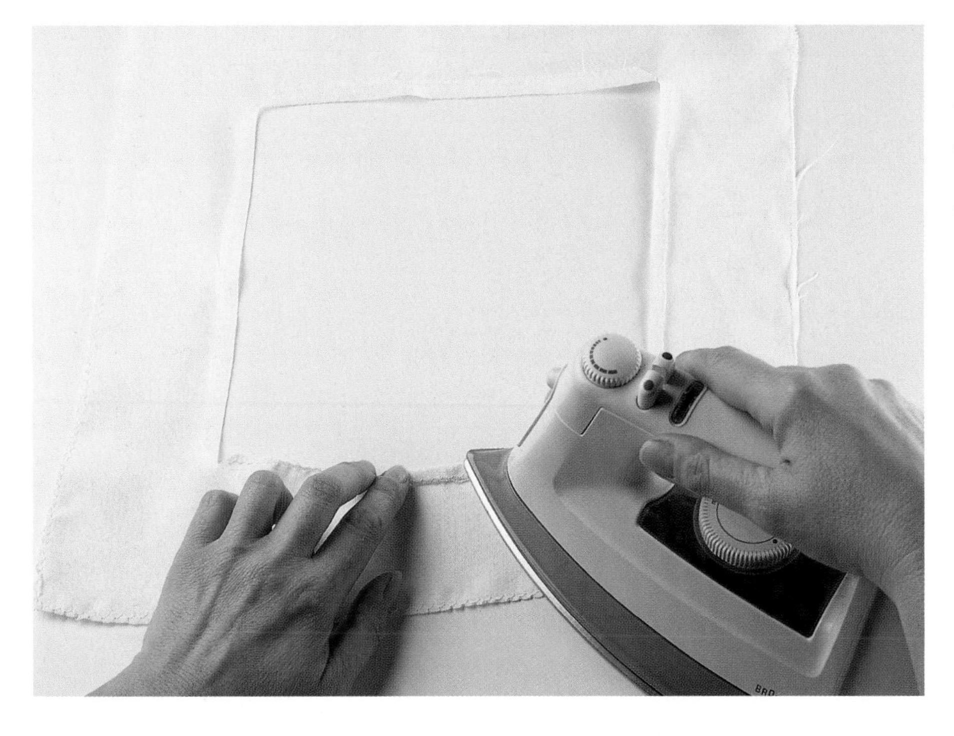

2 Zigzag-stitch around all raw edges to prevent the pieces from fraying. Press a ¼-in (5-mm) seam allowance around all edges of the border pieces, cutting into the corners of the frame to make it lie flat.

3 Turn the border piece to the right side and pin the lace around the inside of the frame. Start in one corner and fold the lace at a right angle to the back of the work at each corner. Stitch from the wrong side, making sure you catch in the edge of the lace and the seam allowance, but not the folded corners, as you work.

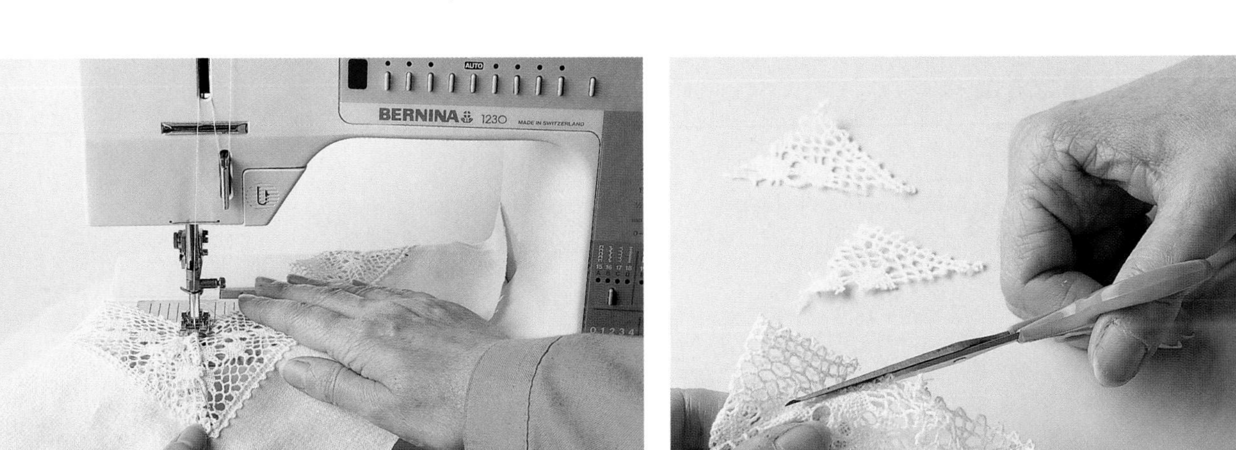

4 Turn the border to the right side and zigzag a double seam diagonally across the folded lace. Pull the threads to the back and knot them securely.

5 Using small, sharp scissors, carefully trim away the folded corner of lace on the back of the piece, making sure that you do not cut through any of the stitching.

6 Trim the center square to fit the inside edge of the lace, allowing a ¼-in (5-mm) seam. Press the raw edge of the center square under by ¼ in (5 mm) and pin the inside edge of the lace to overlap it slightly. Stitch the lace to the center square.

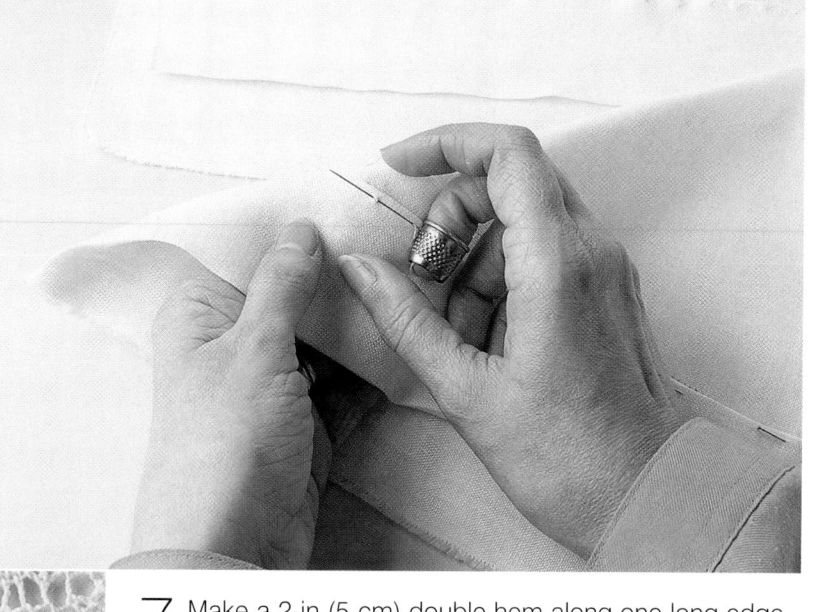

7 Make a 2-in (5-cm) double hem along one long edge of each back piece of fabric. For this part of the job you can stitch either by hand or by machine.

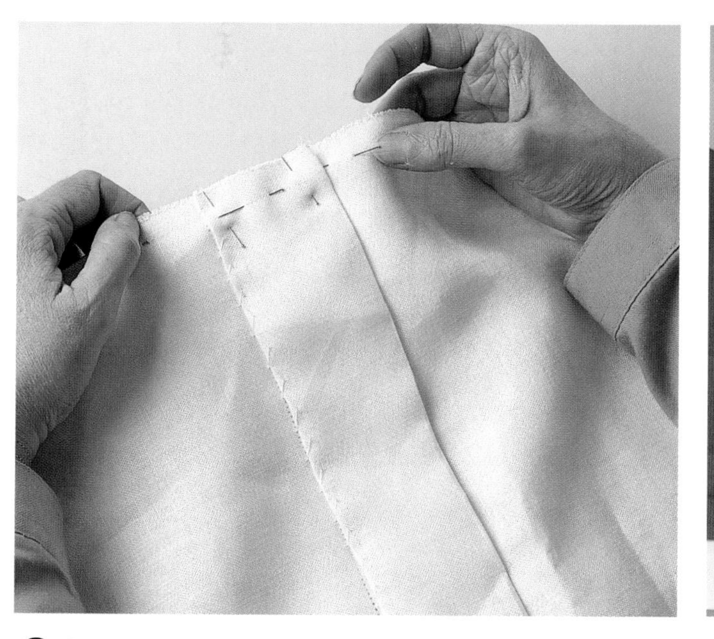

8 Pin the two back pieces, right sides up, with the hems overlapping to measure 16¾ in (43 cm) square. Pin the cover front to the back with right sides together and stitch them along all four edges. Turn the piece right side out through the opening and gently press.

9 Stitch a ⅜-in (1-cm) hem at each end of the cotton lining fabric. Fold one end over by 4 in (10 cm) and stitch the sides of the fold to make a flap. Fold the fabric in half with right sides together; then pin and stitch each side. Turn right side out and insert the pad. Fold over the flap to enclose the pad and put on the linen and lace cover.

Red mitered cushion

Cut out the fabric following the measurements given. Miter the corners of the border strip (see page 44). Turn under a ¼-in (5-mm) seam allowance along the raw edges of the center square and pin and stitch it to the inside of the border with right sides together.

Fold the loop strips lengthwise in to the wrong side with the raw edges inside, and press the fabric. Topstitch along the edge. Make a narrow double hem along one long side of each back piece and stitch the evenly spaced loops to one of the hems. Overlap the back pieces by 3⅛ in (8 cm) and pin, right sides together, to the front.

Stitch around all four edges of the fabric and then turn it right side out. Now sew buttons onto the cover to match the loops and insert the cushion pad.

MATERIALS

- *12-in (30-cm) square of cotton gingham*
- *½ yd (50 cm) of 45-in (115-cm) wide striped cotton fabric*
- *2 buttons*
- *15-in (40-cm) square cushion pad*

Front panel: 12 in (30 cm) square

Front border: four 4¾ x 18-in (12 x 46-cm) strips

Back: two 10½ x 18-in (26.5 x 46-cm) strips

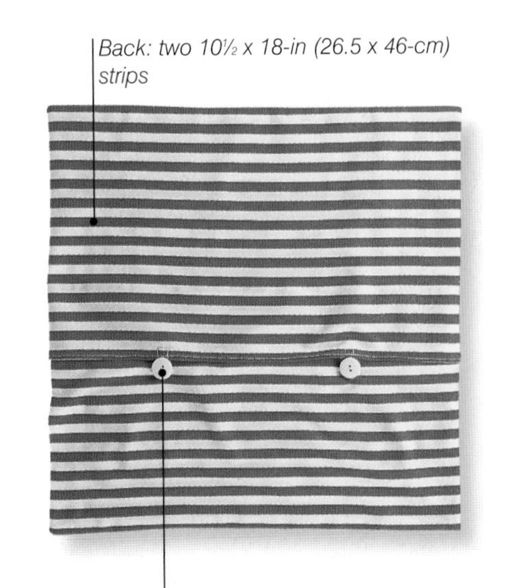

Loops: two 1 x 3⅛-in (2.5 x 8-cm) strips

Bow-tied gingham and striped cushion

Cut out the fabric following the measurements given. Fold all the ties in half to the wrong side lengthwise with the raw edges inside and press. Turn in one short end. Topstitch along the edge.

Make a ⅜-in (1-cm) hem along one short side of the front and sew the front ties equally spaced to the outside of the hem. Turn the hemmed edge under 2¾ in (7 cm) and stitch the sides to make a facing. Attach the back ties to the back piece in matching positions to the front along the selvage.

Pin front to back with right sides together and stitch around the three untied edges. Turn right side out and press. Insert the pad and tie the ties.

MATERIALS

- *½ yd (50 cm) of 45-in (115-cm) wide striped fabric*
- *½ yd (50 cm) of 45-in (115-cm) wide check fabric*
- *15-in (38-cm) square cushion pad*

Front: one piece 17 in (43 cm) x 19¾ in (50 cm)

Front ties: two 1¼ x 14-in (3 x 36-cm) strips

Back ties: two 1¼ x 14-in (3 x 36-cm) strips

Back: one piece 17 in (43 cm) square with one selvaged edge

Embroidered good morning cushion

Cut out the fabric following the measurements given. Transfer the embroidery design on below (or choose one of your own) to the center of the front piece and stitch the design, here done in stem stitch. Make a 2-in (5-cm) double hem in one long side of each back piece. Add a button and matching buttonhole in the center of the hems if desired. Pin the backs together, one right side to one wrong side with the hemmed edges in the middle and overlapping by 3 or 4 in (7.5 to 10 cm), to make a 16½-in (42-cm) square.

Pin the front to the back with right sides together and stitch. Trim the corners, turn right side out, and press. Topstitch 1 in (2.5 cm) in from the edge all around the cover and insert the pad.

MATERIALS

- ½ yd (50 cm) of 45-in (115-cm) wide "homespun" cotton fabric
- Stranded embroidery thread
- Button, if desired
- 13-in (34-cm) square cushion pad

Back: one piece 12½ x 16½ in (31 x 42 cm) and one piece 11¼ x 16½ in (28.5 x 42 cm)

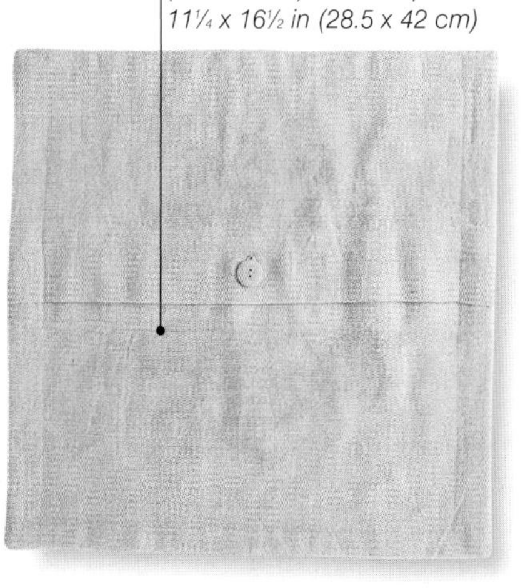

Front: 16½-in (42-cm) square

Project: Velvet pillow

Velvet has a warm, opulent look that is particularly appealing in the winter months. A few scatter cushions will transform your room to reflect the changing seasons. Look for remnants of velvet that you can combine with taffeta or damask ribbon. Velvet frays easily, so always use very sharp scissors for cutting and leave a generous seam allowance. Press with a cool iron to avoid scorch marks.

YOU WILL NEED

For each pillow:

- *⅔ yd (60 cm) velvet, 56 in (140 cm) wide*
- *2 yd (2 m) ribbon, 1¼ in (3 cm) wide*
- *Three 1-in (2.5-cm) easy-cover buttons*
- *16-in (40-cm) square pillow pad*

1 Cut a piece of velvet to measure 22 x 48 in (54 x 120 cm). Pin a hem along both short ends of the piece turning ⅝ in (1.5 cm), then 2 in (5 cm) to the wrong side. Stitch both hems in place.

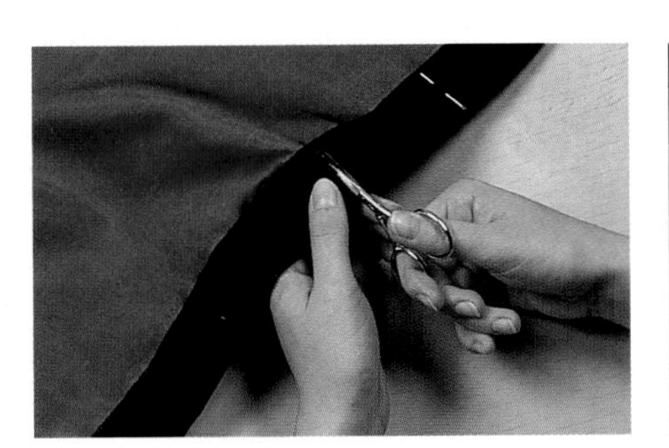

2 Make three buttonholes placed centrally along one hemmed edge, with the first buttonhole in the middle of the hem and a buttonhole 4 in (10 cm) on each side of the first.

3 Mark the front of the pillow using pairs of pins along both edges to indicate the fold lines, placing pins 9 in (23 cm) from the buttonhole hem edge and 13 in (33 cm) from the hemmed edge. Cut the ribbon to make a square frame with inside edges of 15 in (38 cm), mitering the corners. Pin the ribbon to the front so the side edges are 1⅜ (3.5 cm) from the fold lines and 2 in (5 cm) from the raw side edges. Stitch in place close to both sides of the ribbon.

4 With right sides together, fold the cover, folding the buttonband section first, then the buttonhole band, so the hemmed edges overlap by 2 in (5 cm). Pin and stitch along both raw edges. Trim the seams and corners.

5 Cut out circles of velvet from scraps and cover three buttons following the manufacturer's directions. Stitch the buttons in position to match the buttonholes.

Slipcovers

Making a loose slipcover for a sofa can appear to be a daunting task. While some basic sewing skills and a reasonable-sized working area are needed, if you follow the steps here, re-covering a sofa or a large armchair should be a straightforward project that can save money. The secret is to make an under-cover from inexpensive plain cotton fabric, which can be cut, marked, and stitched together to check the fit, and then used as a pattern for cutting out the cover itself. Choose a slipcover fabric that can be cleaned if the furniture will be heavily used.

Making a fabric pattern

1 Measure the sofa, allowing for a center-back opening. Roughly, but generously, cut one outside arm section from muslin (calico).

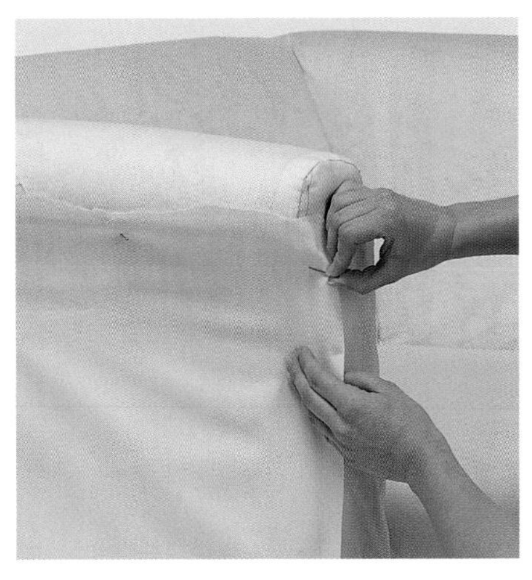

2 Using large dressmaker's pins, pin the cut piece all around in position as close as possible on the outside arm of the sofa.

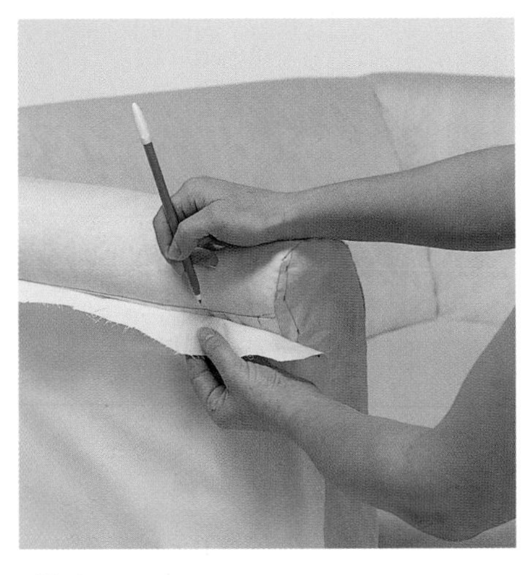

3 Mark the seamline all around the pinned piece. The marks can be rough but must be clear. Cut, pin, and mark another identical piece for the other outside arm section.

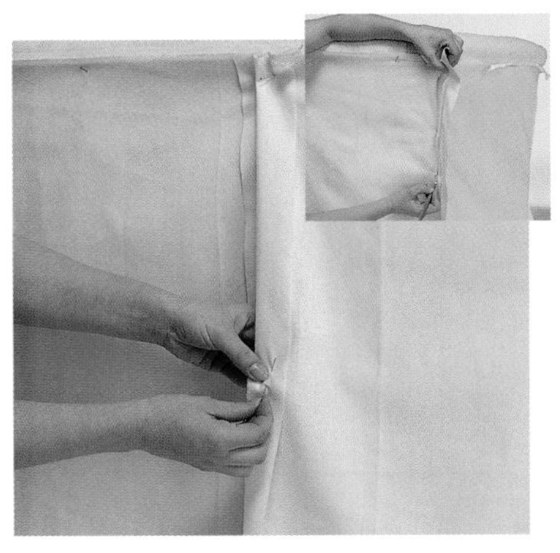

4 Roughly cut out the back section in two pieces, allowing for an overlap. Pin the first back piece in place. Turn back and pin the center fold. Repeat for the other back piece. (Inset): Mark all back seamlines on both pieces.

5 Roughly cut out one inside arm section generously to allow for tuck-ins and shaping at the corners. Pin in place and cut a dart as necessary to make the corners fit. Repin until the corner and outside arm piece fit together snugly.

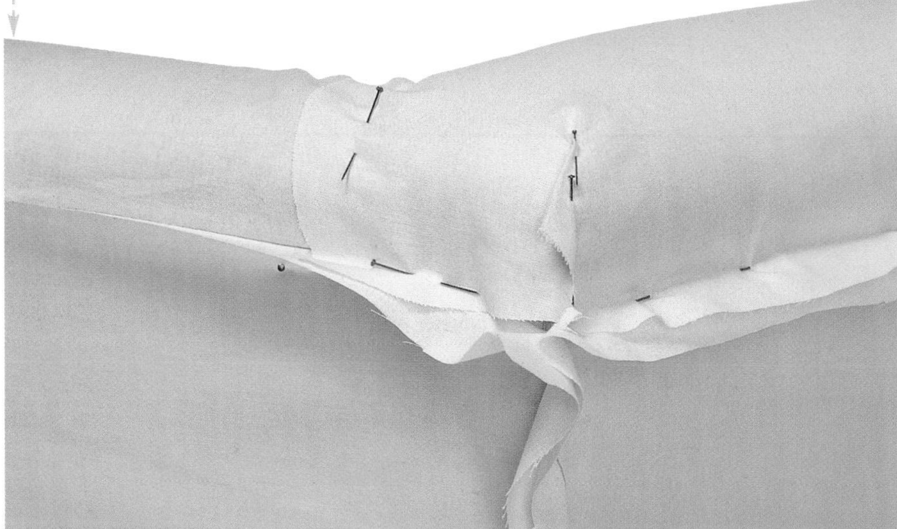

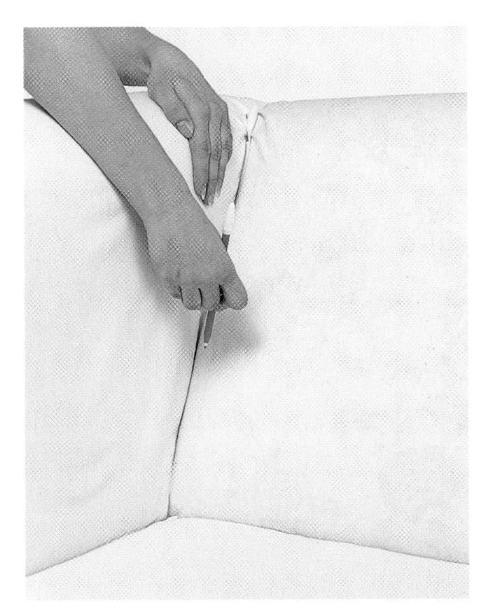

6 Smooth the inside arm and tuck it into the corners. Mark the seamlines clearly, especially inside the tuck-in. Slash into the seam allowance at the top inside corner to ease the tension and mark the corner. Repeat steps 5 and 6 to make the other inside arm.

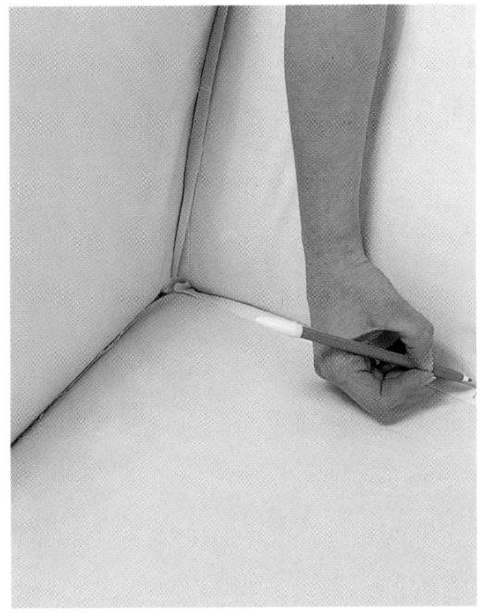

7 Cut out the inside back piece and pin it in place. Smooth and tuck in the fabric where the piece meets the seat. Mark the seamlines, pushing the pen into the tight corners.

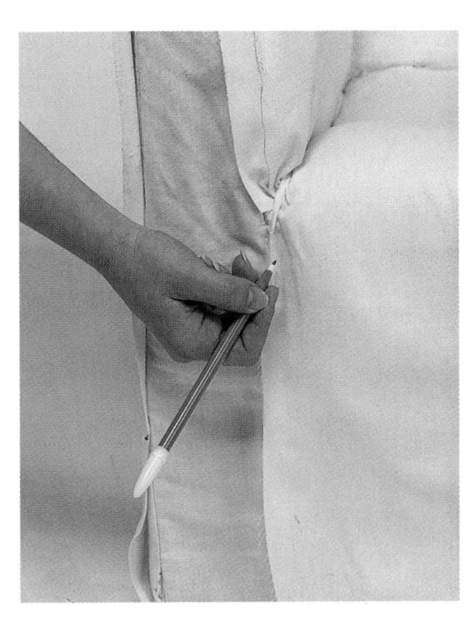

8 Cut the seat and front skirt as one section. Starting where the seat meets the inside back, smooth it toward the front, tucking it into the corners on all three sides.

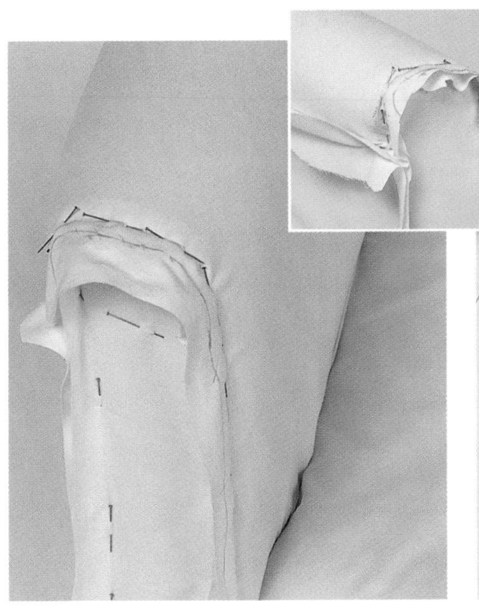

9 Roughly cut a narrow front arm gusset. Pin it to join the inside and outside arm sections, starting at the top of the curve. (Inset): Pin along the long edges so the front arm is pinned to the outside and inside arms and the skirt. Repeat for the other front arm.

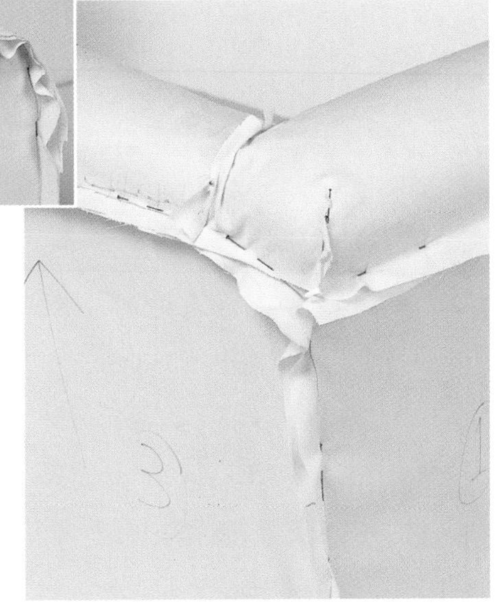

10 Mark each section with numbers or letters to identify them. For example, mark both outside arm pieces as 1, both inside arms as 2, etc. Draw arrows to indicate the top of each piece.

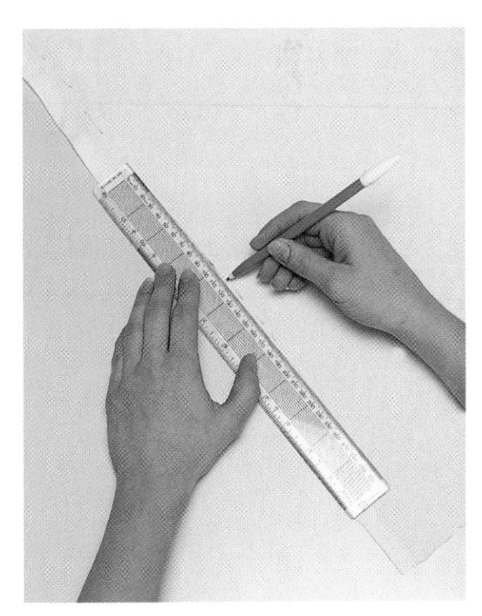

11 Unpin all the sections. Lay each one flat and straighten the seamline markings using a ruler.

Checking the fit

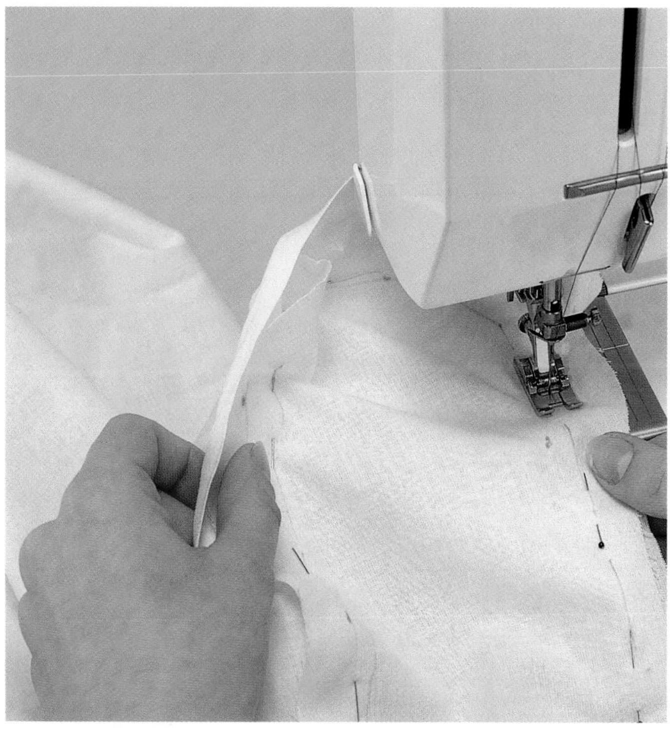

1 Work in the same order as making the pattern. Using a loose basting stitch that can be unpicked easily, stitch the cover together along the marked seamlines.

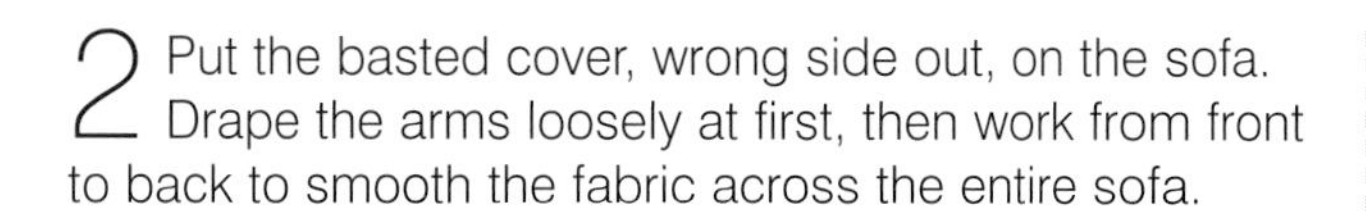

2 Put the basted cover, wrong side out, on the sofa. Drape the arms loosely at first, then work from front to back to smooth the fabric across the entire sofa.

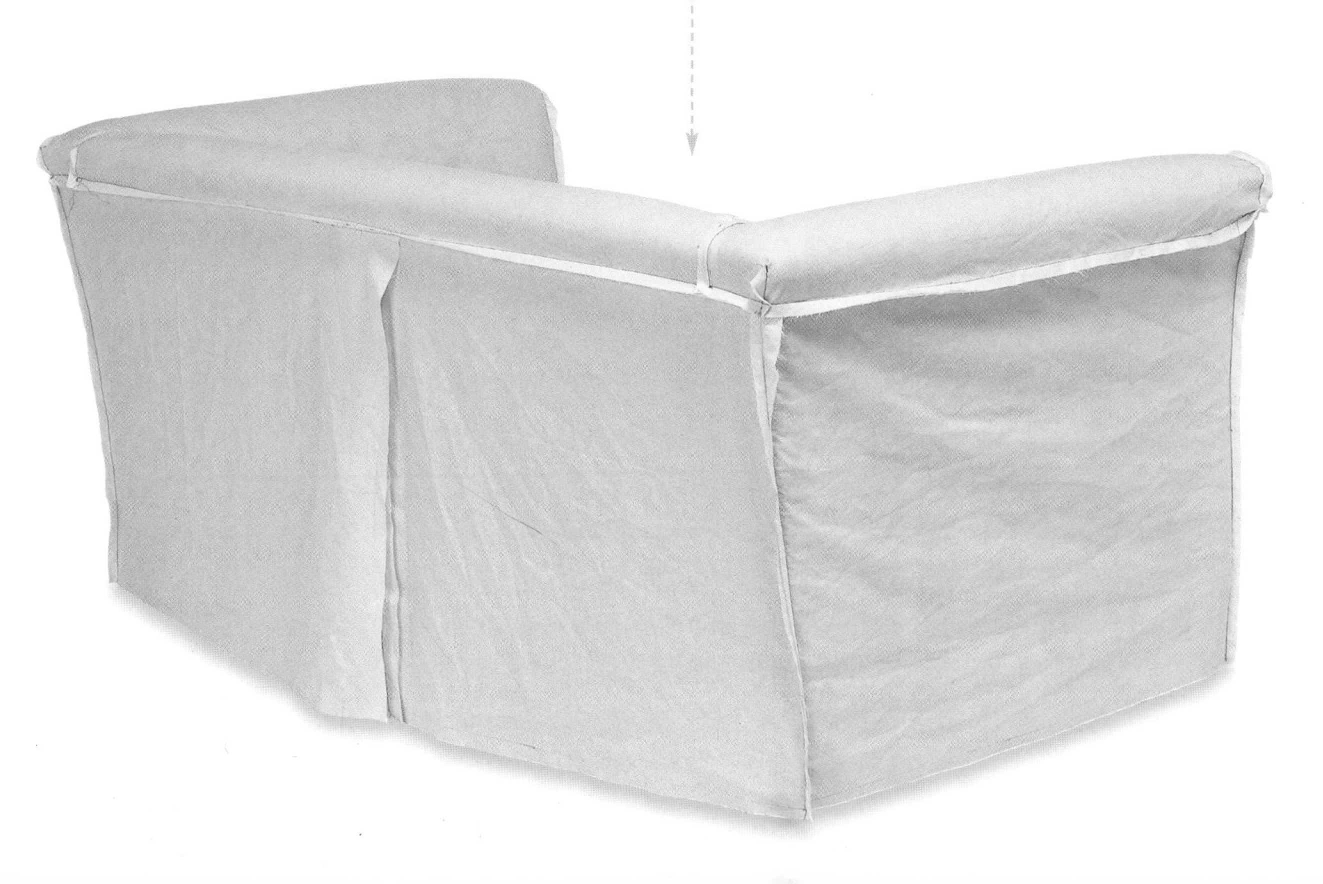

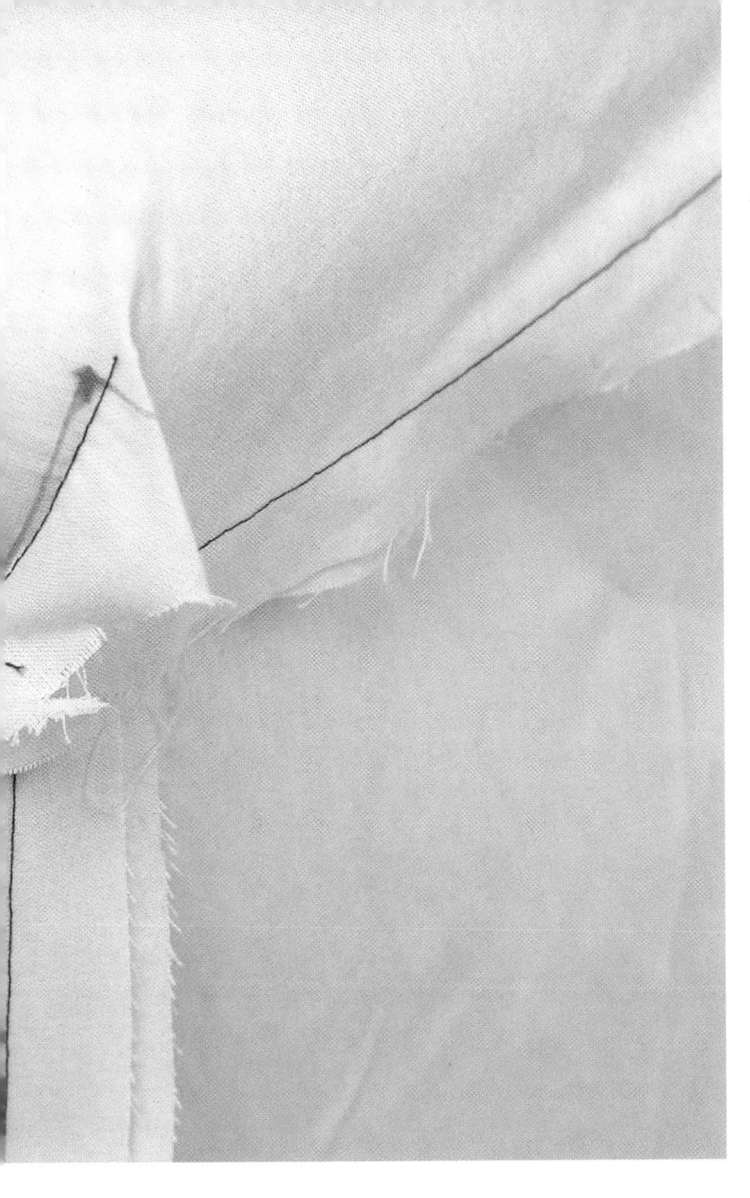

3 If the fit is not perfect, re-mark the seams, drawing dashes through old marks as shown. Repin along the new seamline. Remove the cover and unpick where necessary, then machine-baste along the new seamlines.

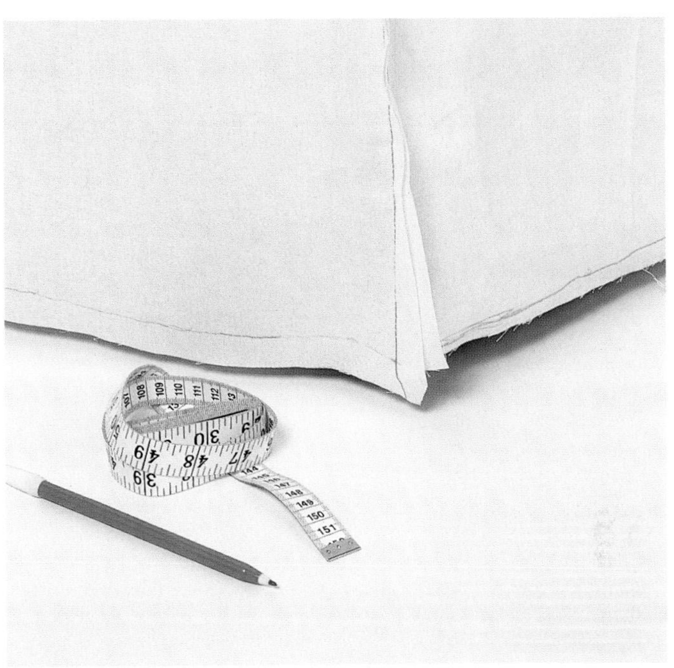

4 Repeat step 2 to try on the restitched cover and, if necessary, repeat step 3. When you are satisfied with the fit, measure and mark the bottom hemline all around.

5 Making sure that all the identifying marks are still fully visible, unpick the basting for the entire cover. Press each section flat using a dry iron.

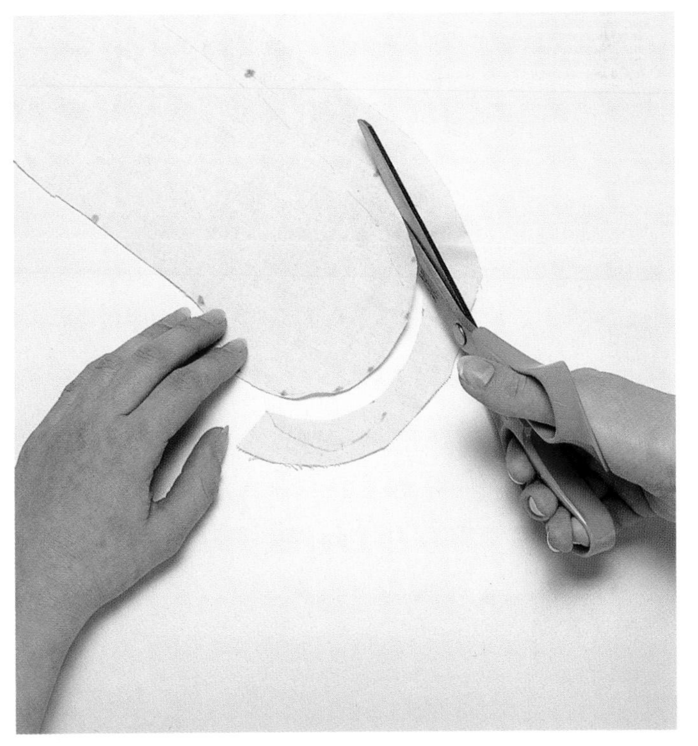

6 Trim each section carefully along the seamline, but remember to add a generous seam allowance for each piece when cutting out the main fabric.

Finishing the slipcover

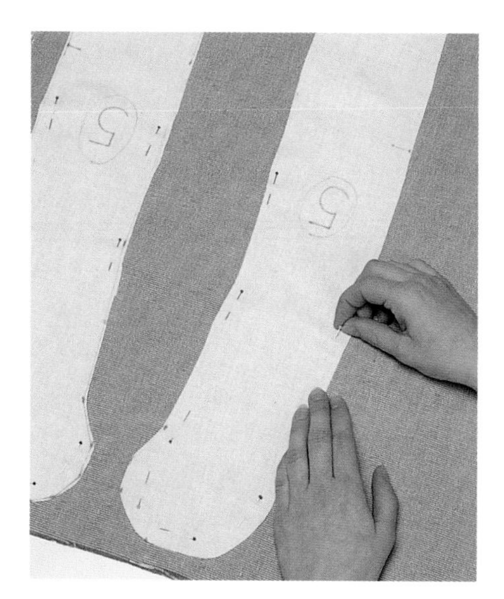

1 Using the trimmed sections as the pattern, pin them on the wrong side of the main fabric, allowing for generous seam allowances all around each piece. Check that they are the right way up and that you have positioned for left- and right-hand pieces where needed. Match fabric patterns carefully if necessary.

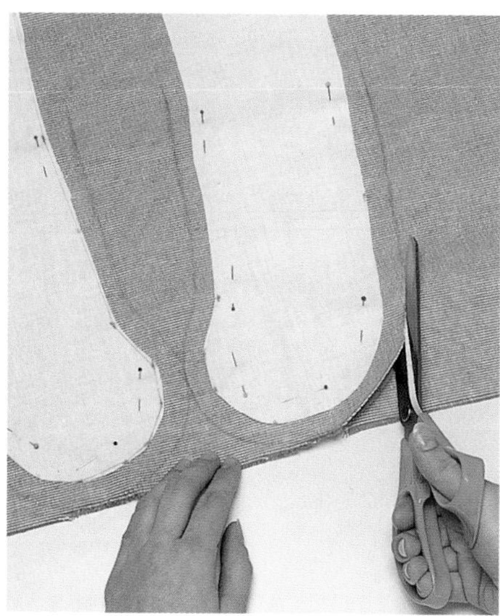

2 Mark around each piece allowing a ½-in (1.25-cm) seam all around, and transfer all the identifying marks. Cut out and stitch the pieces together in the same order as for making a fabric pattern (see pages 293–295).

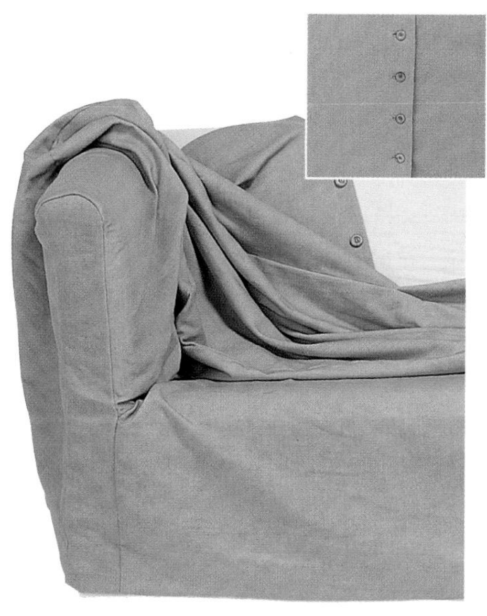

3 Put the finished cover on the sofa from front to back. Check the fit, then mark and hand-sew the bottom hem all around. Mark and work buttonholes on the overlap at the center back and sew corresponding buttons on the underlap (inset). Put the cover back on the sofa.

Making armcovers

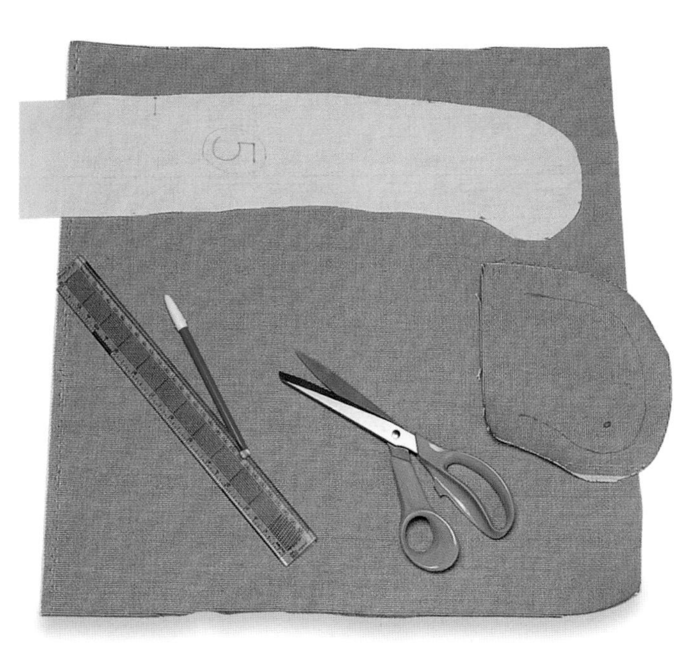

1 Cut two rectangles of main fabric each measuring the same as the inside arm of the sofa. Cut out two pieces from the main fabric using the top of the front arm pattern piece. Add hems and seam allowances.

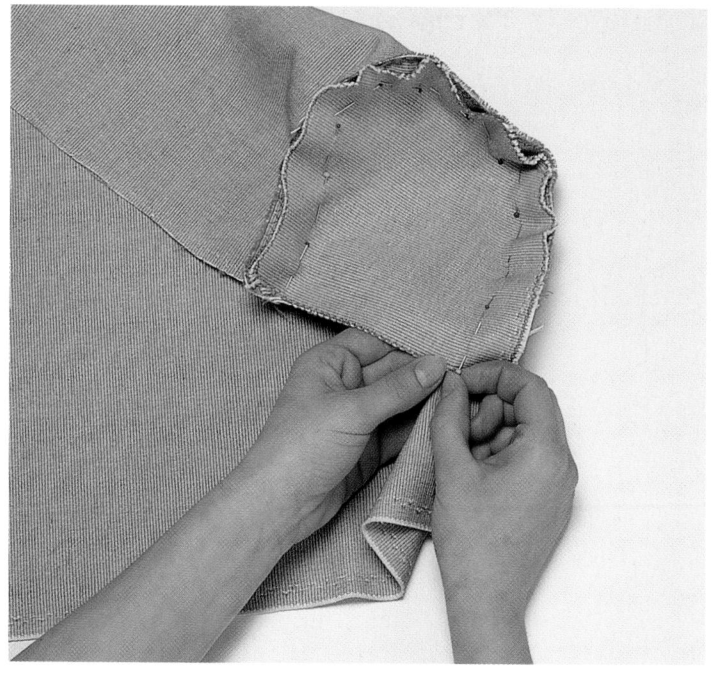

2 Zigzag-stitch along the raw edges of the front arm pieces. Pin and baste one front arm piece to one rectangle, starting at a straight edge of the rectangle. Repeat the step to make a mirror-image piece.

3 Zigzag-stitch along the raw edges of the rectangle. Turn the piece and pin a hem along all the edges. Pin the seam on each short edge. Open and fold out the seam on each long side as shown.

4 Starting at the long front corner on one armcover, stitch a single hem all around, turning the corners neatly. Repeat for the other armcover.

The finished sofa cover with its matching armcovers looks inviting and stylish. Instructions for making and covering seat cushions and for making scatter cushions are given on pages 268–291.

Chair cover

This upright Victorian chair could be covered in the same way as the sofa on pages 292–297, but it would be a shame to hide the pretty detailing on the wooden arms, so the original cover was removed and used as a pattern instead of cutting a new fabric pattern.

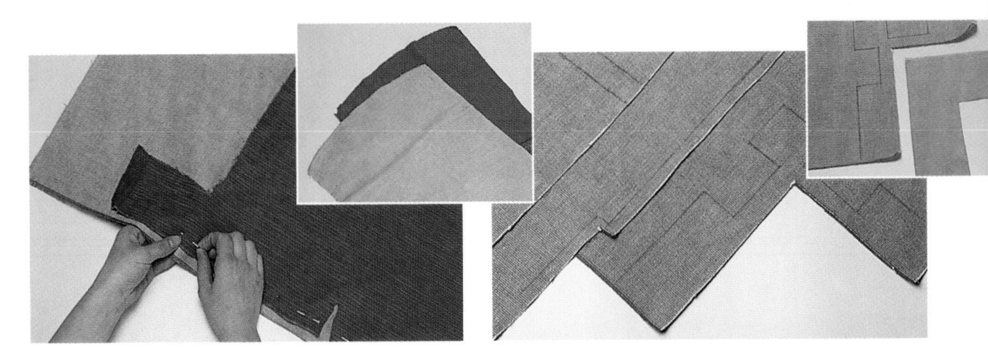

1 Remove the old cover and unpick the seams. Press the pieces and use them to cut out a new piece for each old one. Transfer all darts, flaps, and other marks. (Inset): Using the old pieces for guidance, mark seamlines on each new piece.

2 Mark the tabs, positions for armholes and back uprights, and all other features. (Inset): Make facings for the tabs by cutting a generous piece from a matching medium-weight dress fabric to fit the particular position (see Facings, opposite).

3 Pin the facing to the right side of the fabric and stitch along the marked seamline. Cut away up to the seam allowance and clip the corners. Turn the facing to the wrong side and stitch it in place.

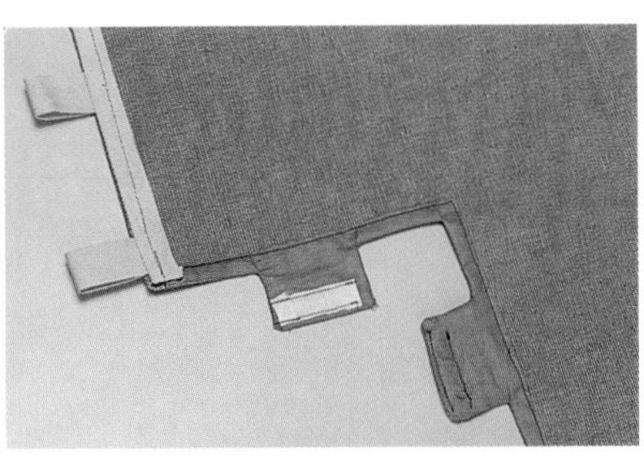

4 At each corner, sew popper-snap tape to the wrong (faced) side and a corresponding length to the right side of the tab. Pin and stitch a length of woven loop tape to the front and side edges.

5 Face the corners of the lower section of the back piece by pinning the facing to the back. Cut a triangular piece of main fabric below the armhole. (Inset): Fold each facing, trim, and snip the seam.

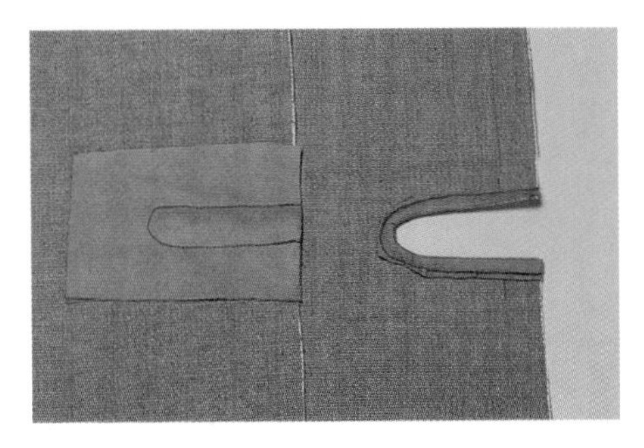

6 Face the backrest armholes by cutting two rectangles at least 2 in (5 cm) bigger than the armhole. Pin and stitch to cover the armhole positions on each side; hem the edges.

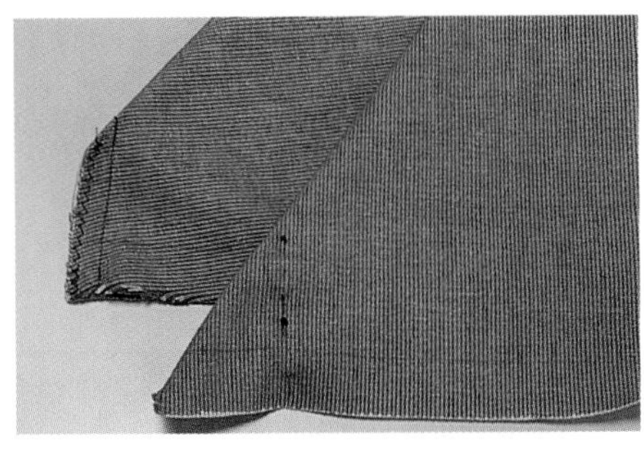

7 Make a dart by folding each corner to the required depth and pin it in place. Stitch the seam, trim the corner, and zigzag the edges together. Pin and stitch the back and backrest pieces together along the armholes.

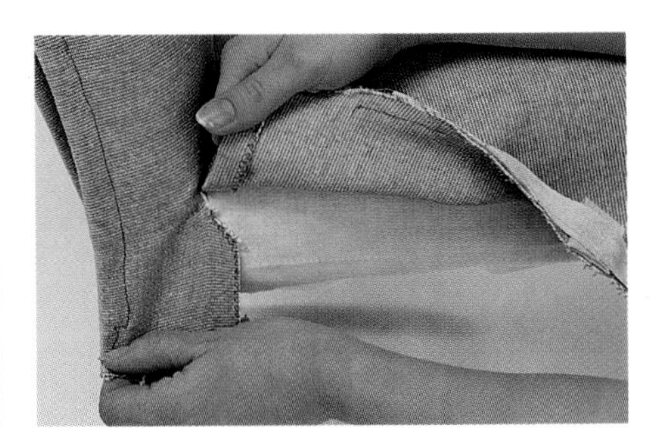

8 Try on the assembled back with the seat piece in place. Adjust the pieces to fit along the back seat seam and clip corners as necessary. Remove the pieces and zigzag all edges.

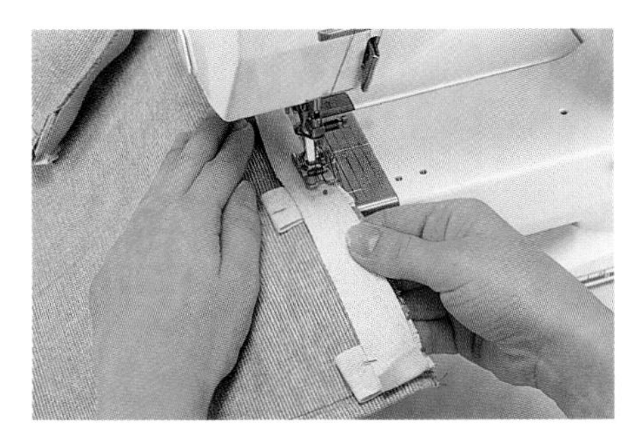

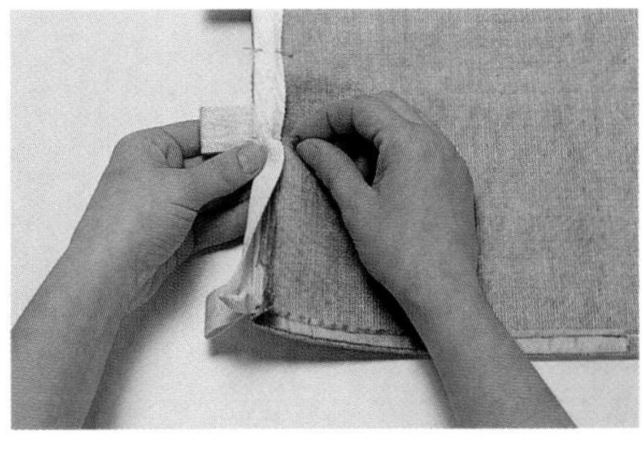

9 Cut a piece of plain cotton tape the length of each edge of the seat plus 1 in (2.5 cm). Cut 2-in (5-cm) pieces of tape to make loops that can be applied to the edges and pulled tight. Fold the tape pieces in half and pin at regular intervals. Pin and stitch the tape over the loops along the four raw edges of the cover.

10 Turn the lengths of tape to the wrong side with the loops along the edge. Pin and stitch the unsewn edges of tape along the length to secure them to the seat piece.

11 Pin and stitch the seat piece to the backrest piece. When it fits well, remove and pin popper-snap tape onto each single hem below the armholes on the backrest. Stitch corresponding tape to each facing on the back piece Zigzag seams.

12 Put the cover back on the chair and fasten the snaps. Turn the chair over and lace string through the loops to pull the cover tightly into place.

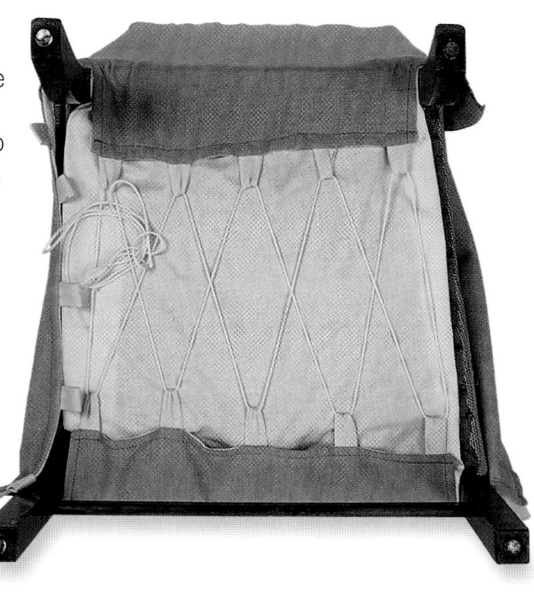

The finished cover should fit snugly and smoothly over the chair.

FACINGS

Facings on slipcovers finish edges and carry ties or fasteners securely.

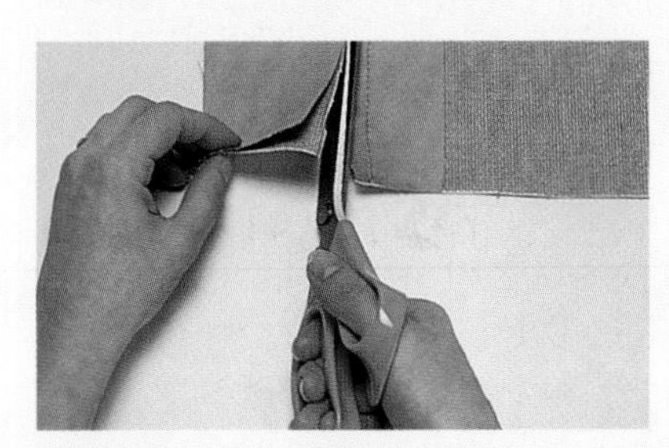

1 Mark the seamline on the main fabric. Cut a piece of lining fabric larger than the area to cut away. Pin and stitch along the seamlines, right sides together. Clip away the excess and clip corners.

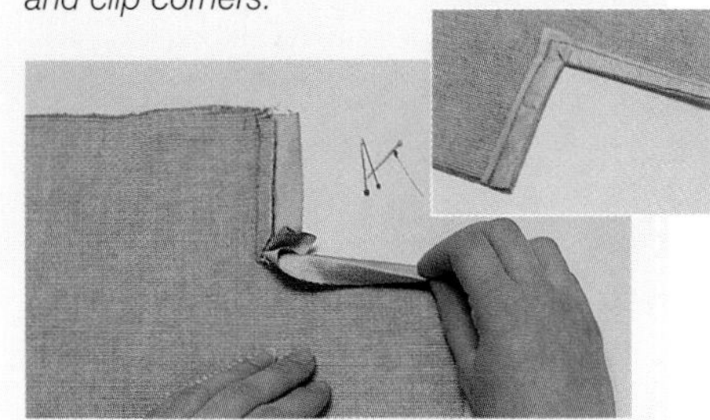

2 Turn the facing to the wrong side of the fabric to enclose the raw edges. Pin and topstitch (inset). The stitching appears on the right side, the facing on the wrong side.

Project: Chair cover

A set of loose chair covers is a simple and inexpensive way to transform and update your decor without you having to replace your kitchen or dining room chairs. Matching chair covers are also a clever way to turn several similar but not identical chairs into a set. If you want to cover the legs with a skirt, simply extend the side and front flaps to the floor.

YOU WILL NEED

- *Sturdy fabric cut to the width of the chair back and seat including flaps, and the length from the front edge all along the seat and seat back to the back edge, plus ⅝in (1.5-cm) seam allowance all around.*
- *8 strips of 1-in (2.5-cm) wide cotton webbing, each 14 in (35 cm) long.*

Making the cover

Take measurements and draw a plan. Cut the fabric as shown using your own measurements. The position of the ties is marked by asterisks * on the plan.

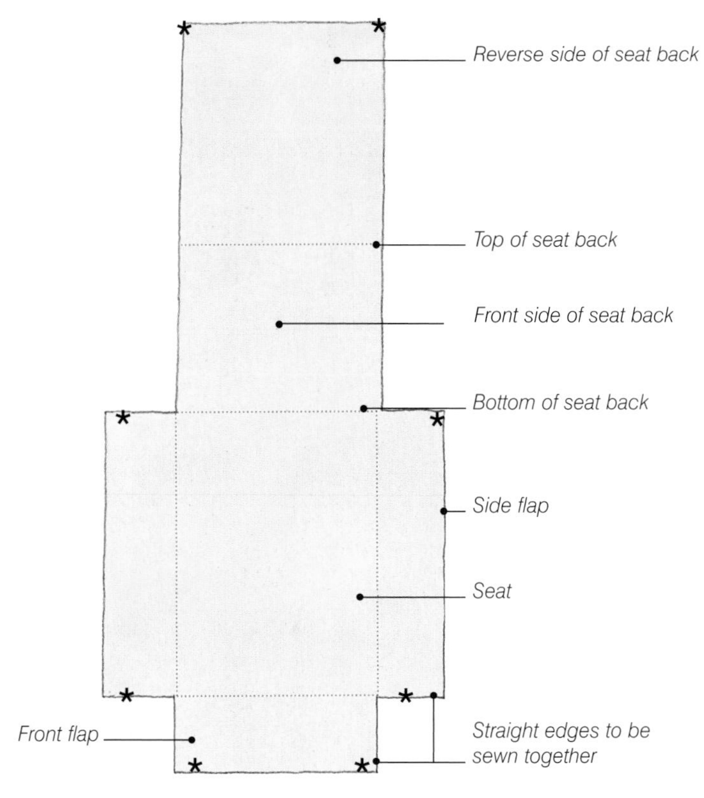

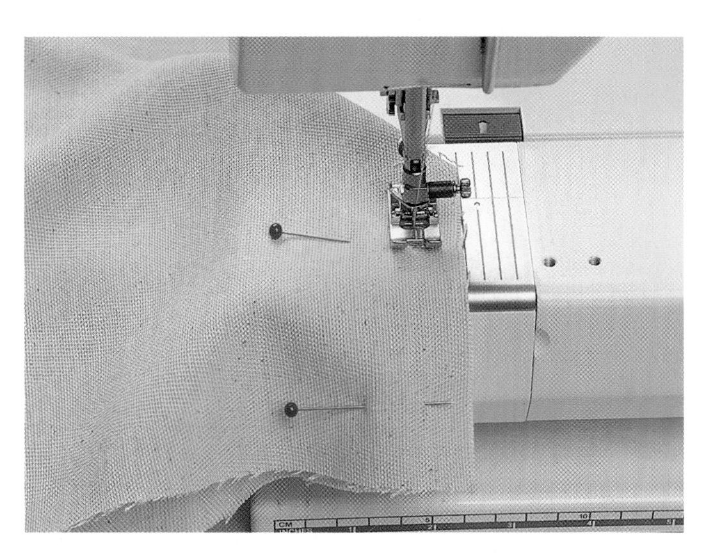

1 Place the straight edge of one side flap, right sides together, with the corresponding edge of the front flap. Pin together and stitch in position. Make a ⅝-in (1.5-cm) seam allowance and backstitch at both ends to secure. Repeat for the other side flap.

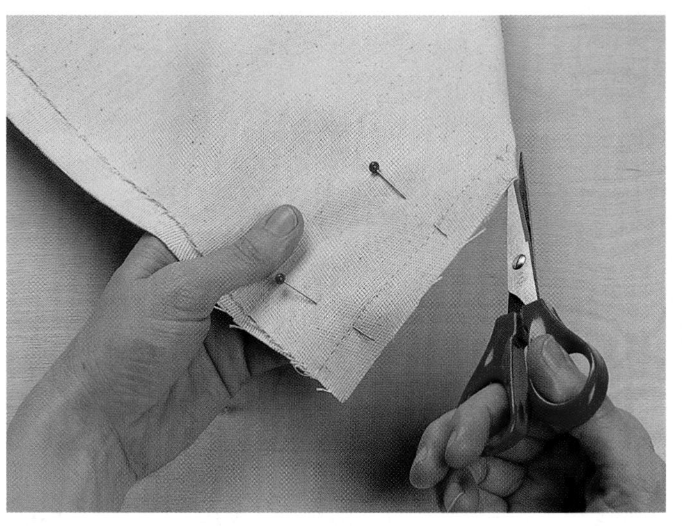

2 Clip the top (diagonal) corner of each seam and gently press the seams open.

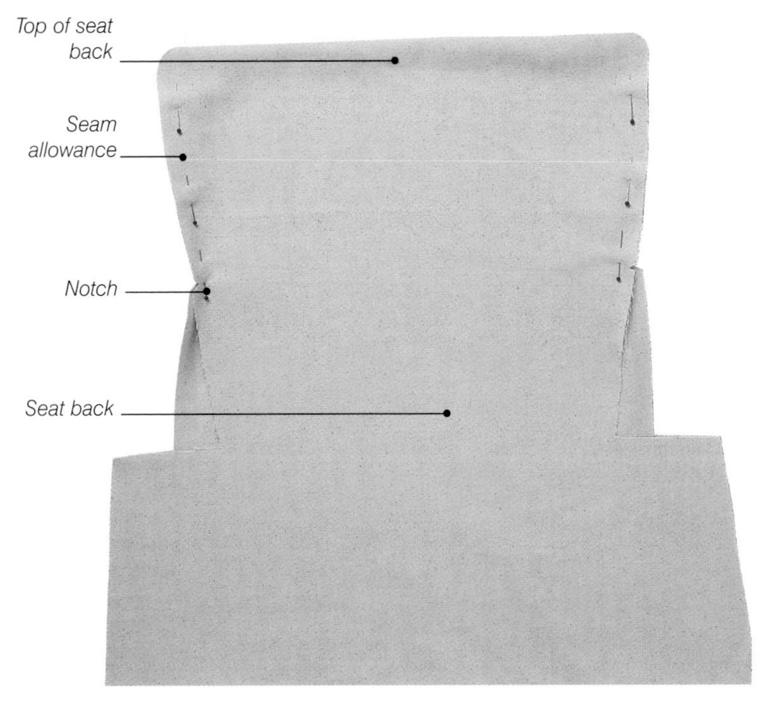

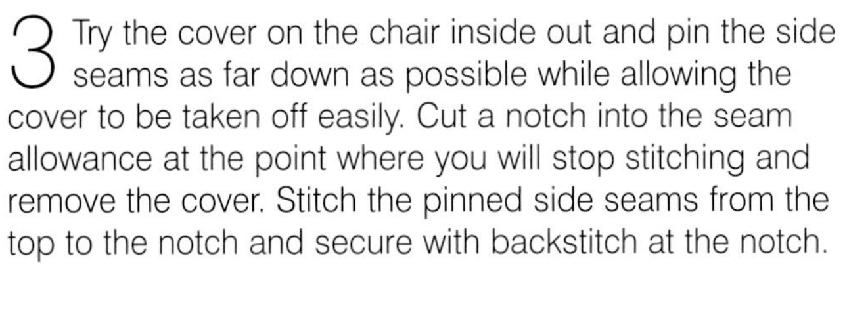

3 Try the cover on the chair inside out and pin the side seams as far down as possible while allowing the cover to be taken off easily. Cut a notch into the seam allowance at the point where you will stop stitching and remove the cover. Stitch the pinned side seams from the top to the notch and secure with backstitch at the notch.

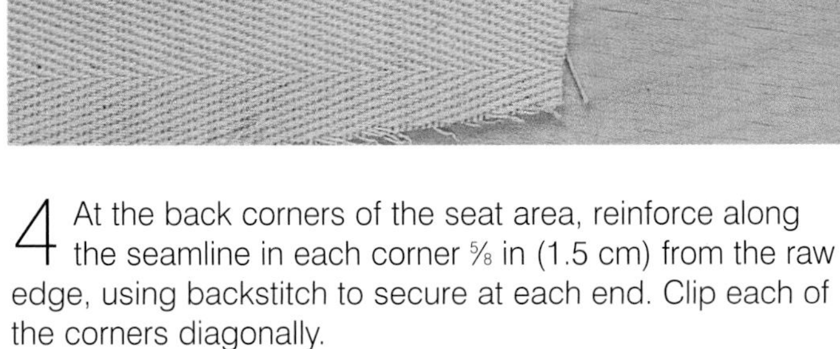

4 At the back corners of the seat area, reinforce along the seamline in each corner ⅝ in (1.5 cm) from the raw edge, using backstitch to secure at each end. Clip each of the corners diagonally.

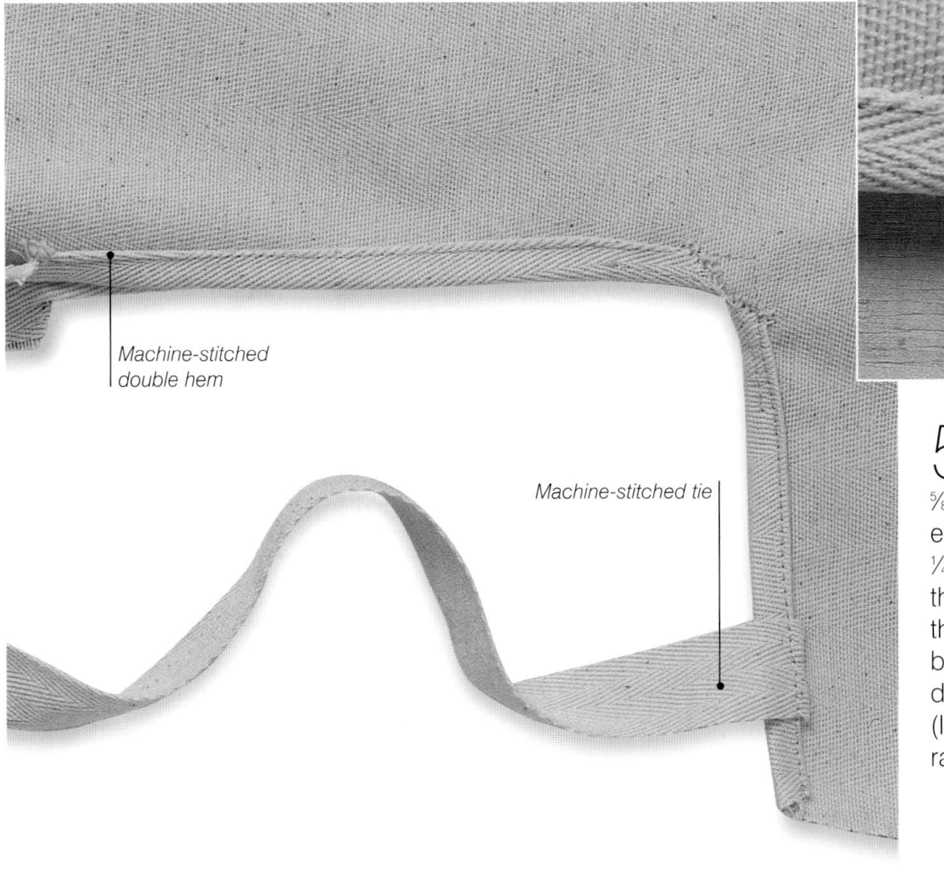

5 Pin a tie onto each short edge of the side flaps at the seat back, ⅝ in (1.5 cm) away from the side edge. Press a double hem, folding ¼ in (5 mm), then ⅜ in (1 cm) along the raw edges of the corners up to the side seam notches on the chair back. Stitch the hem from the notch down, turning the corner neatly. (Inset): Zigzag-stitch over the clipped raw edges at each of the corners.

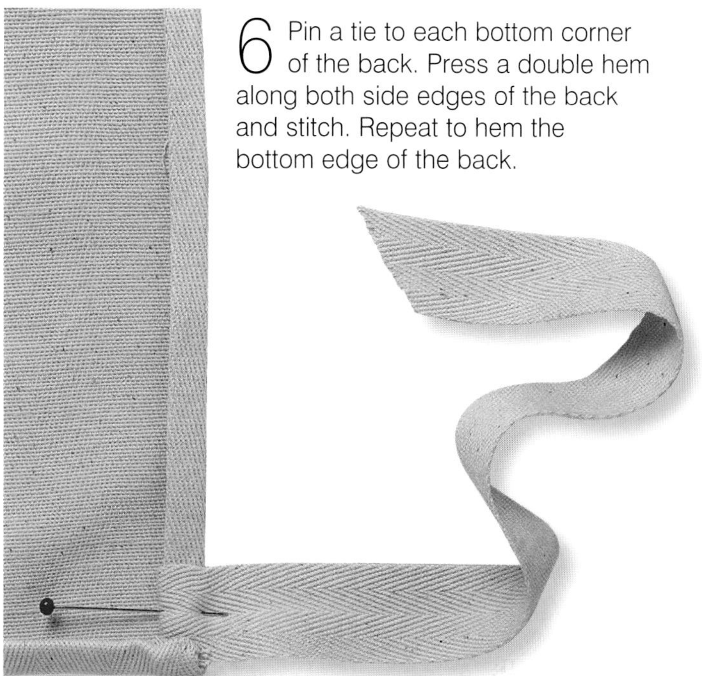

6 Pin a tie to each bottom corner of the back. Press a double hem along both side edges of the back and stitch. Repeat to hem the bottom edge of the back.

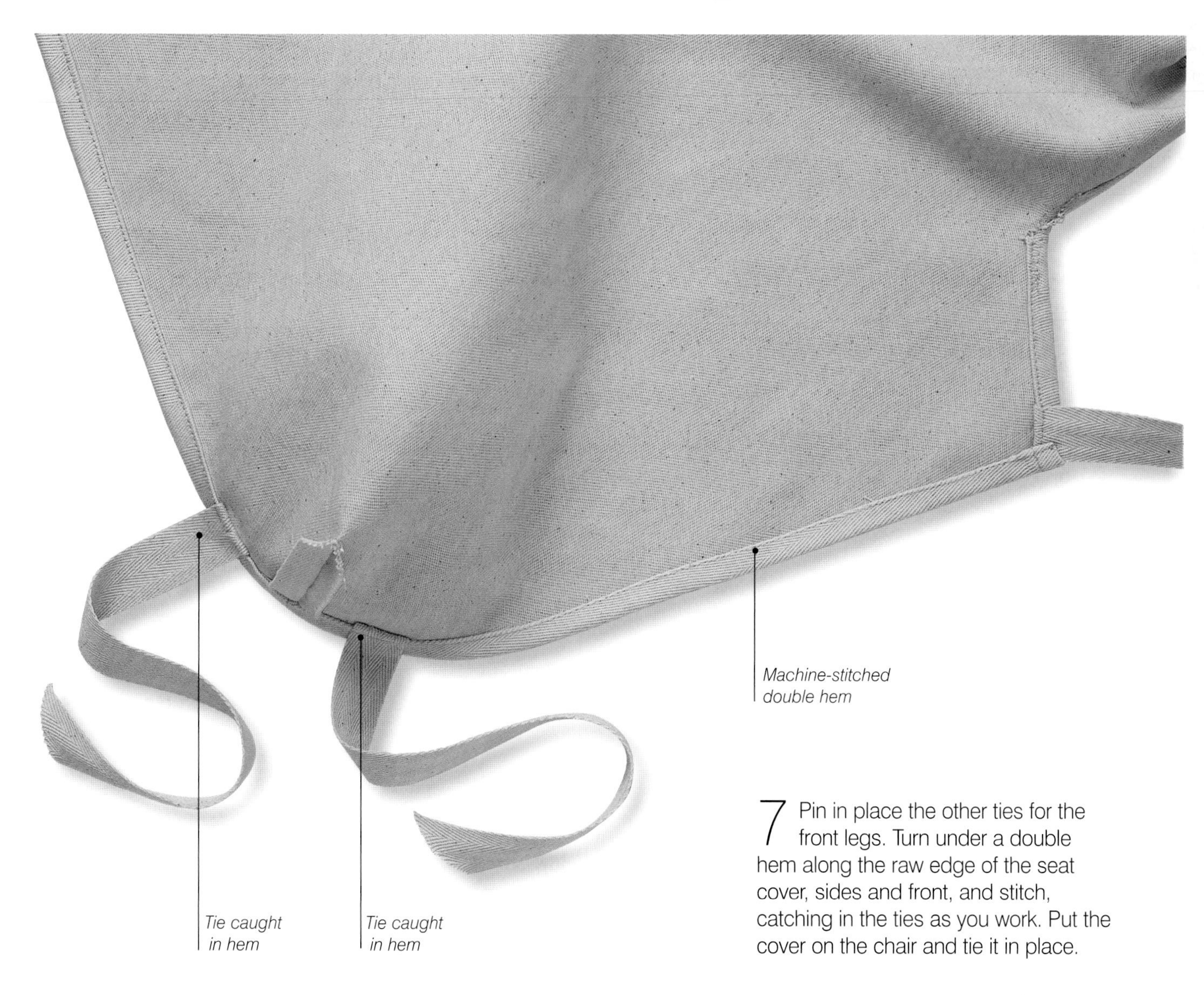

7 Pin in place the other ties for the front legs. Turn under a double hem along the raw edge of the seat cover, sides and front, and stitch, catching in the ties as you work. Put the cover on the chair and tie it in place.

Project: Sofa drape

This attractive floor-length drape is easier to make than a slipcover and will add an informal elegance to any room. Choose the fabric carefully: it must be sturdy and hardwearing, but it also needs to drape well. The bright-colored version shown here is made from heavy cotton chenille. The seat cushions are covered in the same fabric and trimmed with piping the same color as the braid trimming around the edge of the drape.

You can use a drape to transform an old sofa, to protect a good sofa from the wear and tear of family life, or to change the room in line with the seasons. Make sure that both the fabric and the braid are preshrunk and colorfast.

YOU WILL NEED

- *Two lengths of fabric that measure the full width of the sofa from floor across arms and seat to floor, plus 2-in (5-cm) seam allowances*
  NB: If the width of the fabric is less than half the depth of the sofa, you will need three lengths
- *Braid to go around the outside edge of the joined lengths*

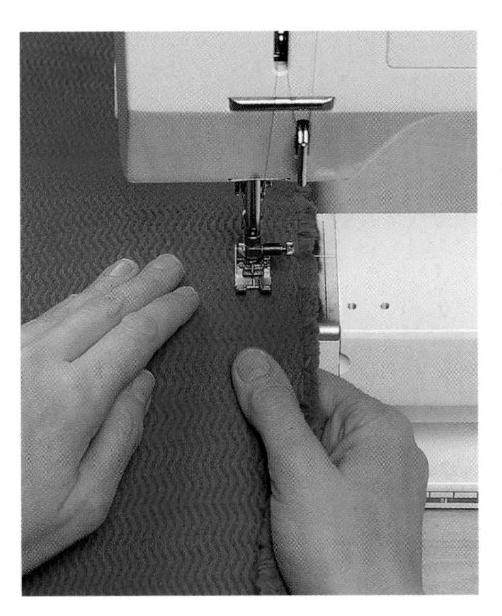

1 Stitch the two lengths of fabric, with right sides together, along one long edge. Strengthen the seam by working a second row of stitching along the seamline.

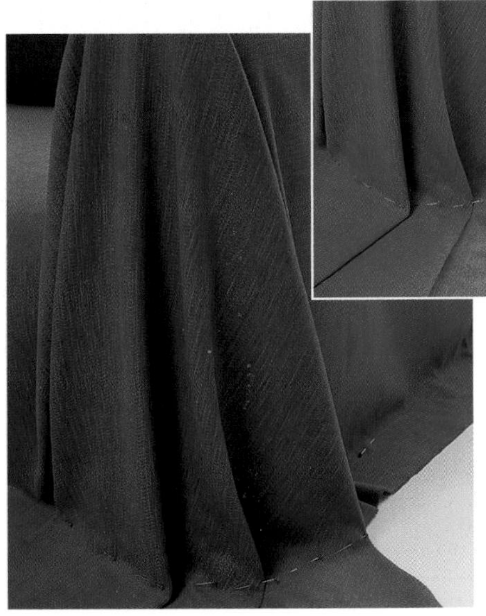

2 Drape the fabric over the sofa, making sure it is even at both ends and at the back and front. Tuck the seamline in at the back of the seat or cover it with seat cushions. Use pins to mark the line where the fabric meets the floor all around the sofa.

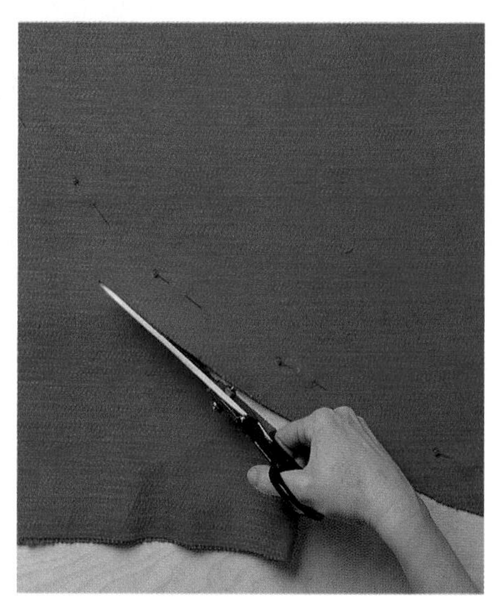

3 Lay the fabric on a flat surface and cut away the fabric below the pinned line, leaving a hem allowance of 1 in (2.5 cm).

4 Press a double hem all around and stitch it in place.

5 Pin the braid over the hem on the right side of the fabric. Stitch in position, working along the top and bottom edges of the braid all around the drape.

hand
fait à la

Care & Repair

While darning socks may not be practiced by many stitchers any longer, everyone has experienced a tear or stain in a favorite garment or furnishing that, if repaired or removed, would extend its life. This chapter provides imformation about simple mending, laundry and cleaning information, and stain removal to help you care for treasured items.

Care and repair

Taking care of home-sewn or purchased garments and fabric furnishings keeps the items looking good, while regular cleaning or laundering means that they stay fresh. Mending or darning a small tear in a favorite piece of clothing means it can continue to be worn, and many repairs can be done so that they are not noticeable. Removing stains before they spread or damage fabric also extends the life of clothes and furniture.

Darning a hole in wool

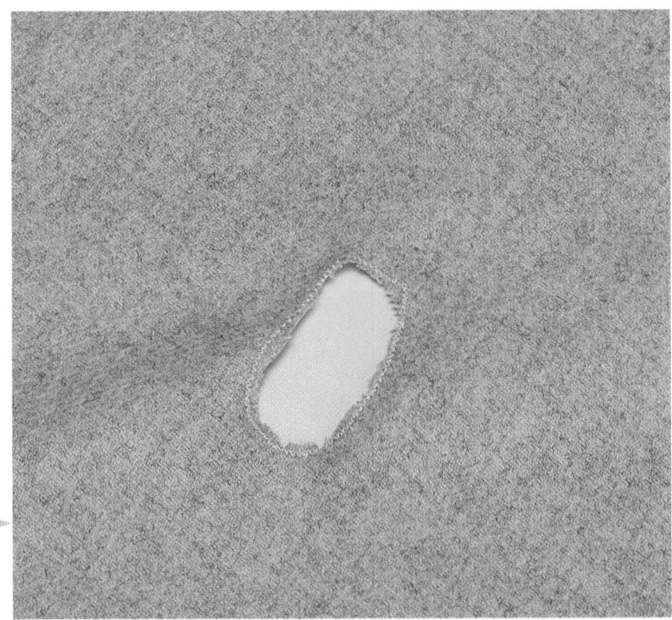

1 To darn a small hole in a piece of wool clothing, trim around the hole to neaten the edges. Zigzag-stitch all around the shape, working close to the edges.

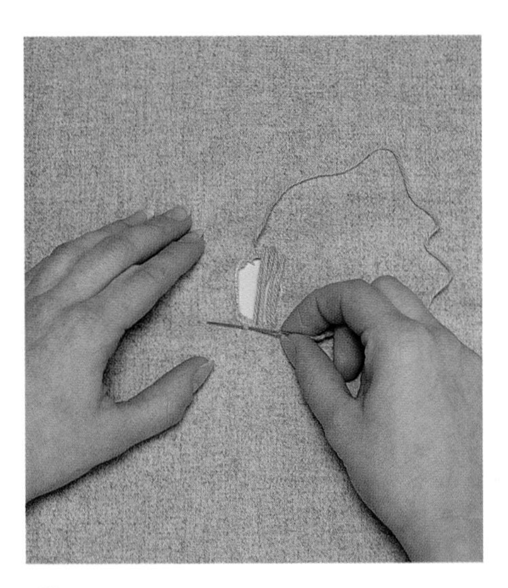

2 Work vertical threads side by side to cover the hole completely. Use a thread that matches the fabric in both color and weight.

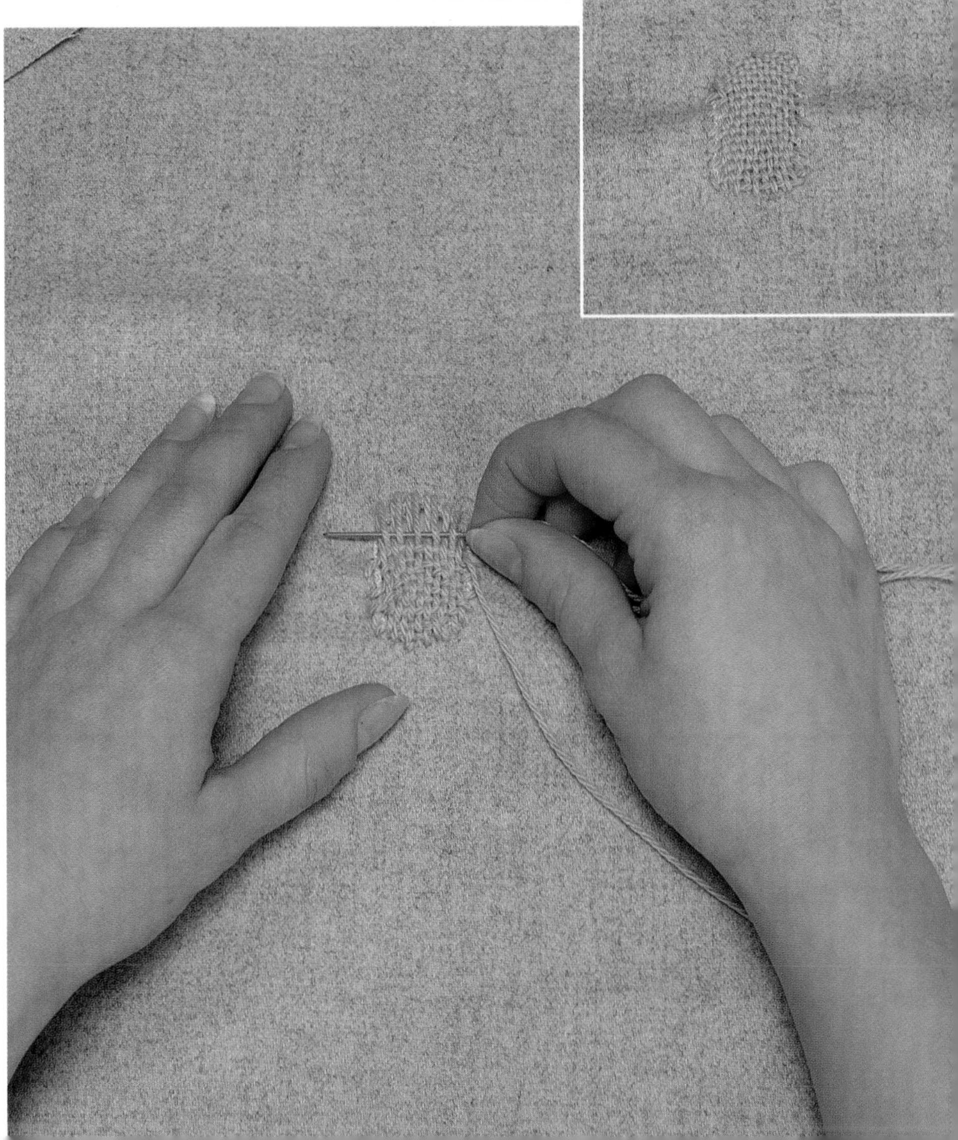

3 Weave crosswise threads in and out of the vertical threads, keeping each row as close to the previous one as possible. Stitch over the edge of the hole to begin each new row. The completed darn will be almost invisible (inset).

Patching a hole in plaid fabric

1 Cut away the tear to form a square that follows the pattern of the plaid. Cut out a new patch, making sure it is larger than the hole and that it matches the pattern.

2 Pin and stitch the right side of the patch to the wrong side of the garment using matching thread. On the right side, clip halfway to the stitching at all four corners.

3 Working on the right side, fold each raw edge under to the clipped corner and pin. Topstitch the folded edges in place using matching thread (NB: white thread has been used here to show the example clearly). The finished patch blends into the pattern (inset).

Repairing a torn seam

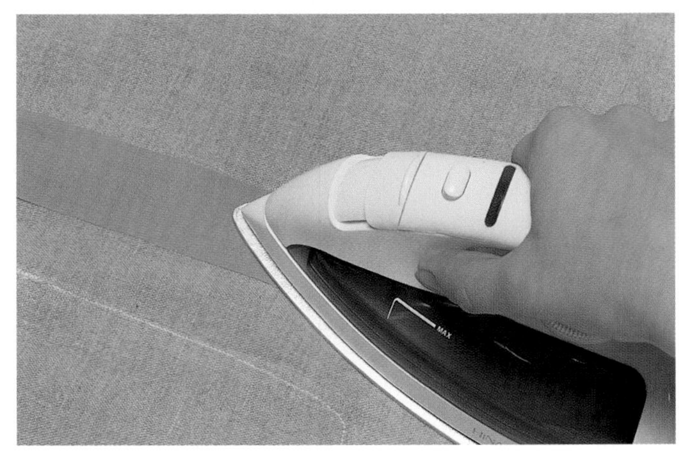

1 To mend a seam that is torn along the stitched seamline, cut a strip of iron-on mending tape slightly wider than the seam. Gently press the tape in position on the wrong side over the torn area.

2 Working from the right side of the garment, stitch along each side of the torn seam to secure the mending tape. The seam is shown from the wrong side.

READY-TO-USE PATCHES

Patches can be used to cover holes or worn areas to extend the life of a garment. They are also used to reinforce areas that are subjected to heavy wear and tear. Since they can only be used on the right side, they should be used as decorative repairs.

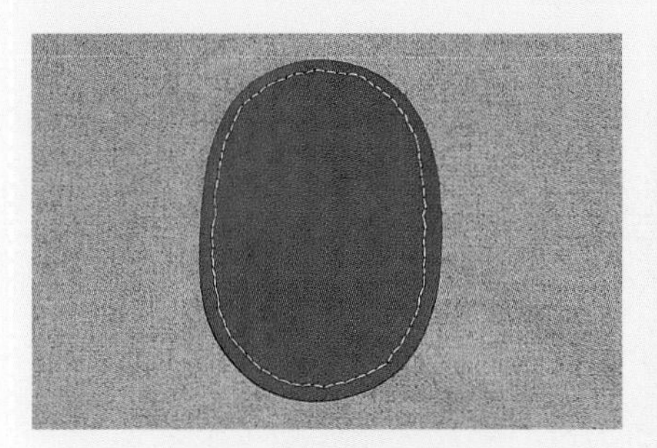

READY-MADE LEATHER PATCHES

These patches are available as shown or with prepunched holes. They can be sewn by hand or machine to cover elbows and knees. Thin suede or leather can be cut into shapes and used as well.

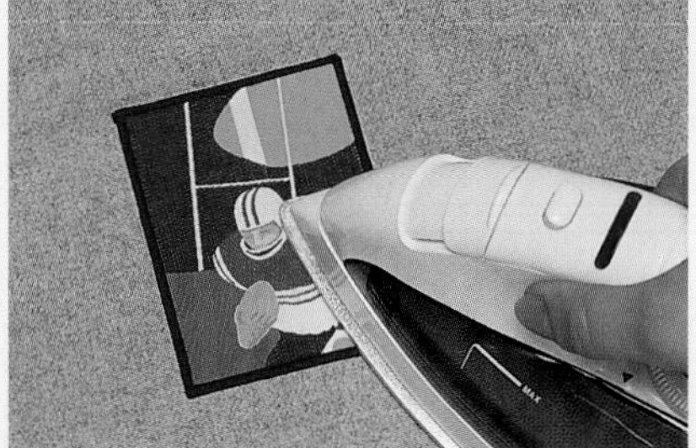

IRON-ON APPLIQUÉ PATCHES

These decorative patches are available in a wide choice of sizes, colors, and designs and are simple to apply following the manufacturer's instructions.

WOVEN PATCHES

These patches are available both with and without an adhesive backing, and need to be securely stitched to garments and furnishings.

Repairing worn buttonholes

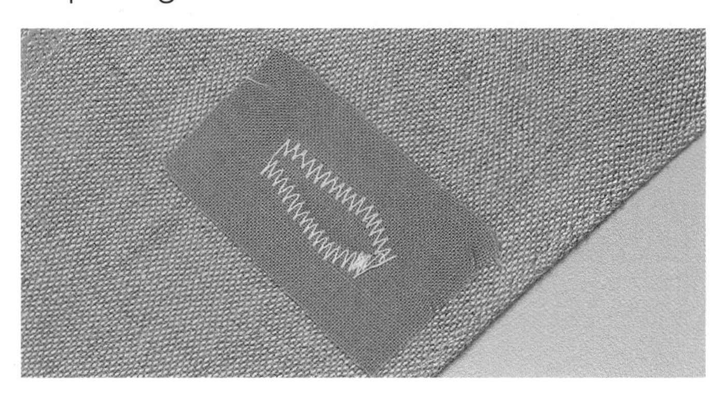

1 Cut out a patch of iron-on mending tape large enough to cover the torn area completely. Iron the patch to the wrong side of the garment over the tear. Zigzag-stitch around the buttonhole on the right side.

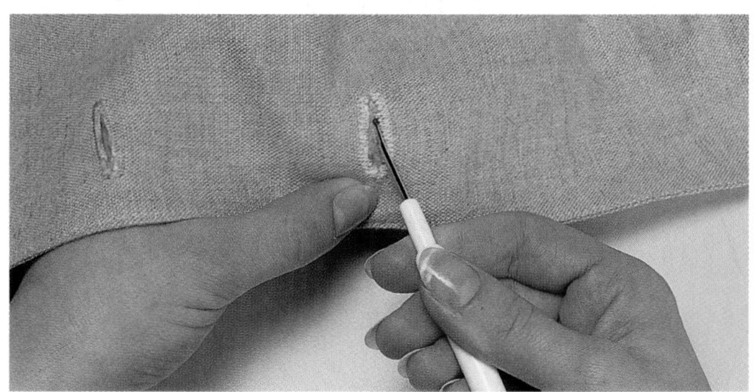

2 Carefully slit through the mending tape with a seam ripper or small, sharp scissors to open the buttonhole. Trim away any visible mending tape.

Repairing a torn button band

1 Cut out a generous patch of iron-on mending tape and iron it in position over the tear. Work a small circle of running stitches around the torn area.

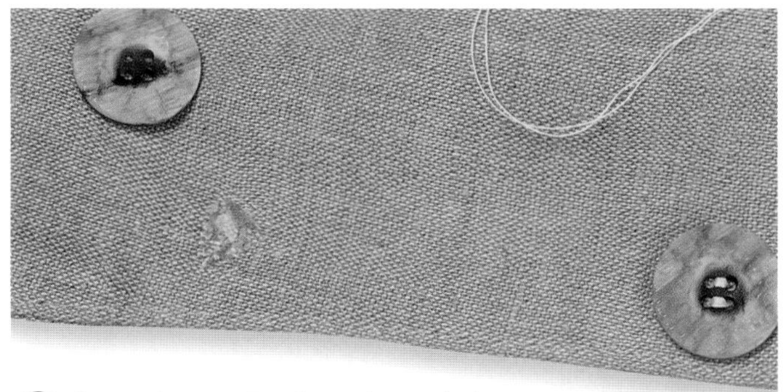

2 Sew a button in place through the mending tape. The button will hide the torn area, and the tape makes the area strong enough to stitch through.

Ripping seams

Most home sewers occasionally need to remove a row of stitching, to repair a torn seam, for example.

Using a seam ripper

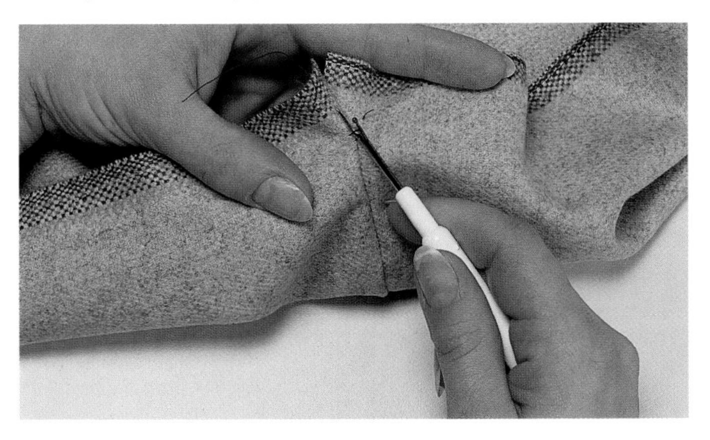

Hold the seam open at one end and insert the seam ripper carefully between the first stitches. With a quick upward action, slice through the stitch to cut the thread, then move on to the second stitch. Cutting one stitch often causes several more to unravel.

Using scissors

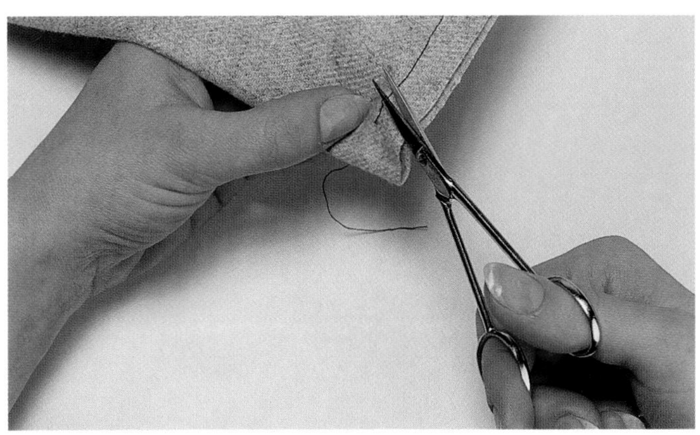

Lay the garment flat and insert the point of one blade (of small, sharp scissors) under a stitch carefully. Cut the thread, then repeat every three to four stitches. The seam then opens easily and the threads can be pulled out gently.

FABRIC CARE

Following the manufacturer's recommendations about the care and laundering of a fabric will help to keep your garments and furnishings in good shape.

A universal pictograph system of care symbols is used in most countries, with the exception of the United States, where most fabric care labels are printed in words.

Washing

Normal cycle at 140°F (60°C), normal spin

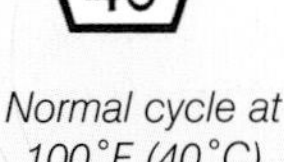

Normal cycle at 100°F (40°C), normal spin

Normal cycle at 85°F (30°C) or gentle cycle, normal rinse, normal spin

Handwash only

Dryclean only

Do not dryclean

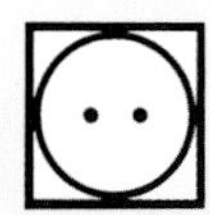

Tumble dry at high heat

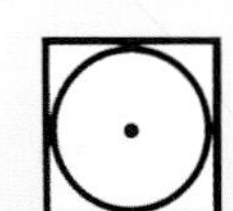

Tumble dry at low heat

Do not tumble dry

Bleaching

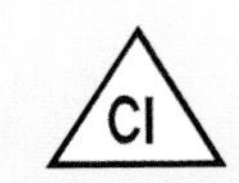

Diluted cold chlorine bleach may be used

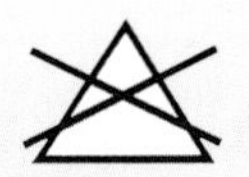

Do not use chlorine bleach

Any solvent except Trichlorethlene

Ironing

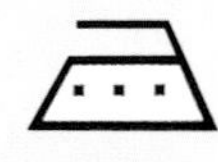

High cotton/linen , 400°F (200°C)

Warm polyester blends/wool 300°F (150°C)

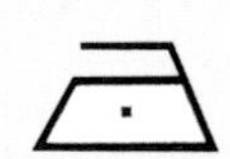

Low synthetics/silk 200°F (110°C)

Do not iron

STAIN REMOVAL CHART

These treatments apply to washable fabrics. Stains on non-washable and delicate fabrics should be handled by a professional drycleaner. Find the stain to be treated in the left-hand column. Follow the numbers in sequence. Where the numbers are repeated, use the most convenient method. Repeat the treatment if necessary. Set the temperature and washing cycle specified on the garment label.

Key

Cold water

Warm water

Hot water

	PROCEDURE											
STAIN	Soak	Rinse	Wash	Blot	Harden by rubbing with an ice cube	Scrape	Pretreat with appropriate chemical	Bleach (whites only)	Lemon	Salt	Press	Remarks
Adhesive and glue	4		4		1	2	3					
Alcohol			1									1 part white wine vinegar to 3 parts water if stain persists
Blood	1						2					
Chewing gum			4		1	2	3					
Chocolate		1					2					
Cosmetics							1					
Eggs							1					Treat basically as grease
Grass							1	2				Use enzyme (biological) washing powder
Grease and oil			2				1					
Ink			2				1					Washing may set the stain
Mildew			2					1	1	1		Mix lemon juice with salt and sun-dry
Milk			1									
Paint: water-based		1	2									
Paint: oil-based			3	1			2					
Perspiration	1		2									Soak affected area in water with a spoonful of borax added
Rust			3						1	2		Mix lemon juice and salt and hold over steaming water
Scorch marks			1						2	2		
Shoe polish						1	2					
Tea and coffee	1						2					
Wax			3		1						2	
Wine and fruit juice	1		4	2			3			1		

NB: If no temperature symbol is given, follow the washing instructions for the garment.

Index

a

b

c

d

e

S

t

U

V

W

Z

Credits and Acknowledgements

To Peggy Humphrey McCormick, who taught me to sew.

Thanks to all at Collins & Brown, especially Emma Baxter, Kate Kirby, and Niamh Hatton; the team at Axis who brought together all the elements; and David who supported behind the scenes.

Also thanks to the following authors whose work was included in this book: Wendy Baker, Linda Barker, Miranda Innes, Gail Lowther, Gina Moore, Gloria Nicol, Melanie Paine, Maureen Whitemore and Caroline Wrey.